SUMMARY OF THE CONTENTS

Writer's Guide

Good English

Meeting the reader's expectations

Qualities of writing

Writing a paper

alphabetical **Index to English**

Writer's Guide and Index to English

Third Edition

For this revision, Karl W. Dykema made extensive contributions to the arrangement and the content of both the chapters of the Guide *and the entries of the* Index. *William Coyle of Wittenberg College wrote the first version of Chapters 10, 11, 12 and revised Chapter 13. The exercises for Chapters 1 through 9 were prepared by Kenneth Bennett. Throughout, the manuscript received the careful attention of the publisher's editorial staff, especially of Mrs. Carol Pitts Oppenheimer. Since I have gone over all the copy and made extensive alterations in both the old and the new material, the responsibility for the final version is mine.*

P. G. P.

Writer's Guide and Index to English

Porter G. Perrin
University of Washington

Third edition

revised with the assistance of
KARL W. DYKEMA
Youngstown University

Scott, Foresman and Company
Chicago, Atlanta, Dallas, Palo Alto, Fair Lawn, N.J.

Printed in the United States of America.

L. C. Catalog Card #59-10793

Except in a few instances where the publishers
requested credit lines with the selections themselves,
the courtesy of author and publishers in granting permission
for quoting passages from their works
is specifically acknowledged on pages 771-778.

Preface

This third edition of *Writer's Guide and Index to English* continues the general plan of earlier editions and their general aim: to present a realistic description of current English in a framework of practice in composition.

The principal change from previous editions is the addition of three chapters (10 to 12) on writing personal experience, information, and opinion papers, three sorts of factual writing especially adapted to practice in a composition course. To allow for this added material, the old chapters have been somewhat condensed and some repetition between *Guide* chapters and *Index* entries eliminated. The addition of a General Index makes readily available the treatment of all topics.

The varieties of English have been changed (see table pp. 18-19) so that General English now refers to the most widely used variety and Informal English is limited to the sort of usage its name suggests. The aim of the distinction among varieties is to help students form their judgment of why one word or construction is better than another in a specific situation. In this way they can take much of the responsibility for their expression and for their growth in effective and confident speaking and writing of good English.

The chapters and their exercises are the basic instructional material for class discussion of general topics and their application in writing. A course could be organized to begin with Chapter 9, The Stages in Writing, and so stress the composition aspect, or with Chapter 1, Varieties of English, for an emphasis on the language. In either plan Chapter 1 should be taken up fairly early to establish the principles for discriminating between competing items of usage and between different styles.

The alphabetical entries in the *Index* are primarily for students' individual reference at the time of writing or revising papers. The *Index* also contains some sixty specific correction entries, identified by abbreviations in the margins and reached through the abbreviations listed inside the back cover and in the General Index. Scores of common lapses from Good English can be marked on papers by putting a ring around the word in question (*its, like, percent, to, who,* and so on) to show that there is a specific entry on the item. In addition to these entries, the *Index* also contains, for study or browsing, a grammar of English, some background information about the language, some definitions from linguistics, and some added optional material, as in *References in scientific papers and *Logic.

The essential thing to remember is that our language is not a taskmaster but an opportunity. It offers anyone with material he wishes to convey to others the means for presenting it to them. Curiosity about actual language processes and some feeling of freedom will in the long run produce better writing than rote learning and restrictions. Granted some information about actual usage, Good English is to a considerable degree a by-product of interested, purposeful communication.

I hope the book will continue to encourage students to an active observation of the language and will help them improve their judgment and increase their confidence in shaping their material and expressing it in readable papers.

P. G. P.

Table of contents

The two major parts of this book are shown below in broad outline. Details of the contents of Writer's Guide *are shown on pages viii-xii, and of* Index to English *on page xiii.*

Writer's Guide

Good English

Meeting the reader's expectations

Qualities of writing

Writing a paper

Chapter 12 | *pages* 323-348

Opinion papers

Chapter 13 | *pages* 349-400

Reference papers

Part two | *pages* 401-770

Index to English

This INDEX *contains entries in alphabetical arrangement that fall roughly into four categories:*

A Entries on particular words and constructions, such as *continual, continuous; *fiancé, fiancée; *get, got; *like–as; *route; *shall–will; *so...that; *very

B Entries for correction and revision of papers, indicated by abbreviations before the entry word

C Articles on English grammar giving definitions and examples of such matters as *Case, *Conjunctions, *Plurals, *Principal parts of verbs

D Articles on various facts of language, such as *American and British usage, *Foreign words in English, *Linguistics

---

Bibliography

The following works have been most useful in gathering the material for this book. They are frequently referred to (usually by author's name only) in the chapters of the *Guide* and in the alphabetical entries of the *Index*.

American Speech, New York, Columbia University Press. A periodical, founded in 1925, containing much direct observation of current American usage, especially vocabularies of particular regions and vocations.

Baugh, Albert C., *A History of the English Language,* New York, Appleton-Century-Crofts, 1935; revised 1957. A substantial and readable history of the language.

Bloomfield, Leonard, *Language,* New York, Holt, 1933. A basic work on the general principles of language study.

Carroll, John B., *The Study of Language,* Cambridge, Harvard University Press, 1953. Chapter 2 is a brief and clear introduction to linguistics.

Curme, George O., *Syntax,* Boston, Heath, 1931; and *Parts of Speech and Accidence,* Boston, Heath, 1935. A very full grammar of modern English, with much historical material. (Referred to as Curme, *Parts of Speech*)

Fowler, H. W., *A Dictionary of Modern English Usage,* Oxford University Press, 1926. Although based on British usage and now somewhat dated, still a readable and often illuminating book.

Fries, C. C., *American English Grammar,* New York, Appleton-Century-Crofts (NCTE Monograph No. 10), 1940. A number of points of grammar discussed with special reference to differences between levels of usage. (Referred to as Fries, *AEG*)

Fries, C. C., *The Structure of English,* New York, Harcourt, Brace and Company, 1952. Presents a realignment of the parts of speech and a program of sentence analysis based on this realignment. (Referred to as Fries, *Structure*)

Gleason, H. A., *An Introduction to Descriptive Linguistics,* New York, Henry Holt and Company, 1955. Exactly what its title implies.

Hall, J. Lesslie, *English Usage,* Chicago, Scott, Foresman and Company, 1917. Historical discussion of 141 locutions on which usage is divided or questioned.

Jespersen, Otto, *Essentials of English Grammar,* New York, Holt, 1933. An abridgment of Jespersen's seven volume *Modern English Grammar,* the most complete description of English available.

Kenyon, John S. and Thomas A. Knott, *A Pronouncing Dictionary of American English,* Springfield, G. & C. Merriam Co., 1944. The most reliable guide to American pronunciation of individual words.

Marckwardt, Albert H. and Fred G. Walcott, *Facts About Current English Usage.* New York, Appleton-Century-Crofts (NCTE Monograph No. 7), 1938. Includes the data of the Sterling A. Leonard study (1932) of debatable and divided usage, with additional information.

Mencken, H. L., *The American Language,* 4th Edition, New York, Knopf, 1936; *Supplement I* (1945); *Supplement II* (1948). A mass of material on various varieties of American English, with commentary and references to further sources.

Pooley, Robert C., *Teaching English Usage,* New York, Appleton-Century-Crofts (NCTE Monograph No. 16), 1946. Discussion of a number of debatable locutions, with evidence and recommendations for teaching.

Roberts, Paul, *Understanding Grammar,* New York, Harper, 1954. A good, brief systematic English Grammar.

Robertson, Stuart, *The Development of Modern English,* New York, Prentice-Hall, 1934; revised 1954 by Frederic G. Cassidy. Gives the background of many points of current syntax.

Skillin, Marjorie and Robert M. Gay, *Words into Type,* New York, Appleton-Century-Crofts, 1948. A detailed manual of publishers' style.

Summey, George, Jr., *American Punctuation,* New York, Ronald Press Co., 1949. The most thorough and authoritative treatment of punctuation.

United States Government Printing Office Style Manual, Washington, Government Printing Office, revised edition, 1953. Detailed directions for preparing government publications, most of which could be safely followed by any writer. (Referred to as *GPO Manual*)

The University of Chicago Press, *A Manual of Style,* 11th edition, Chicago, The University of Chicago Press, 1949. The stylebook of a distinguished conservative publishing house.

More specific works are cited in the various articles to which they are appropriate. A list of current dictionaries will be found on page 210.

Part one WRITER'S GUIDE

The circle of the English language has a well defined centre but no discernible circumference.

OXFORD ENGLISH DICTIONARY

Chapter 1

The varieties of English

Formal written English is not the language;

it is merely one type of English.

Its rules are pertinent only to people studying or writing

formal written English; other types of English have their own rules.

JAMES B. MACMILLAN

We began to learn our language by imitating what our parents said, and soon we picked up enough words to make our wants known and then to talk with others. At first our parents were so pleased to have us talk that they accepted some of our infantile contributions to the English vocabulary. Milk might be *nuck,* a hammer an *agboo,* an elephant an *umpy-dump.* We used our own forms of words and our own syntax: One youngster, struggling with irregular verbs, said, "Mother did gave me a lot of pants. She shouldn't have gaven me so much pants this summer." For a while the grown-ups thought this sort of language was cute, but by the time we were four or five, they began to expect us to talk about as they talked, and so far as we could talk that way, we did.

In school we added to our skill in using English by learning to read and write. We studied "grammar," which told us that "It is I" and other expressions were correct and "It is me" and a lot more were not. If a reason was offered, it was generally something like "The verb *to be* is followed by a predicate nominative." We may have tried to follow this grammar in the schoolroom, but outside we talked about the same way we always had. Some of us, though, began to realize that English, which we supposed we just talked naturally, was a pretty complex matter and that opinions about it differed, sometimes violently.

By the time we reach college and find that we are almost ready to take our places in public affairs we begin to have some concern for our language. We want to feel confident in our pronunciation and our choice of words. When we sit down to write something, we want to have control of the language, to be able to use it readily and presentably. And we want to be able to speak and write effectively in the more mature communication situations in which we find ourselves.

Confidence and effectiveness in the use of English come in part from a realistic knowledge of the possibilities of language. We need to know how to choose the forms of expression which are most effective for us, and we need to practice so that the sort of English we want to use comes easily and becomes a habit. The habit of using good English is formed not so much by memorizing rules and trying to apply them as by reading the work of good writers and listening to good speakers, occasionally noticing how they gain their effects. But to observe language profitably we need some conscious knowledge of how it works and some specific guidance; a composition course and a book like this can help.

We all use English with ease and with a good deal of effectiveness in the situations in which we feel at home. But when we meet new people, perhaps from a different social circle or a different part of the country, or when we have to give a talk or write an important letter, a paper for a college course, or something that will be printed, we may become acutely conscious of *how* we are speaking or writing. Fortunately the greater part of our language raises no questions; it can be used at any time, under any circumstances: the ordinary names of things *(dog, dresses, politics)* and of acts *(walking, swimming, voting)* and thousands of other words are in general usage; most of the forms of words are pretty well standardized *(theirs, people's, lived),* as well as the order of words in phrases and sentences. But some questions about usage do come up. Sometimes we have to make choices among words and forms and constructions, and because our choices contribute to the impression our talk or piece of writing makes, they are important.

These questions about English usage arise chiefly because there are different varieties of the language that cannot be used with equal effectiveness in every situation. The questions may be simple, like Is it all right to say "It's *me,*" "Go *slow,*" "It's *real* interesting," or "It's *laying* on the table"? Does *phony* fit in this sentence? Is *solon* better than *congressman* here? Or the questions may be more complicated, like Should this be one sentence or two? How can I show the connection between these ideas? Are these words specific enough? What is the best order for these ideas?

The answers to some of these questions are clear-cut and definite, but the answers to others vary with the circumstances. English, like every other widely used language, is not one single group of words and constructions, everywhere and always the same, but a variety of such groups that have much in common but are still far from uniform. There are two reasons for stressing these varieties in this book: one is to show the immense resources our language offers, and the other is to help form habits of easy and automatic choice in your actual usage —habits that will be appropriate to the varying situations you meet A mature use of English means speaking and writing the sort of English that is appropriate to the situation in which you find yourself, for *English is not just "good"; it is good under certain conditions.*

Sources of variation in English

The varieties of English that you find around you are all natural growths, and students of the language are able to describe and in part account for them. Understanding the principal sources of the differences will give you perspective on the language and will help guide you in making some choices.

Variations due to time

It is natural that a language used by millions of people over centuries of time should change. Occasionally changes are relatively sudden and far-reaching, as after an invasion by a nation with a different language, but ordinarily they are slow and barely noticeable—slightly different pronunciations, new shadings in the meaning of words, and gradual shifts in grammatical constructions. You know from reading older literature that English has changed a good deal in the centuries during which it has been written down.[1] A play by Shakespeare needs a good many notes to tell us what some of the words meant to the people who first heard the plays over three hundred fifty years ago. If we go back far enough, English seems like a foreign language, though we may recognize in the older forms the ancestors of some of our current words. Language changes as naturally and as steadily as other customs do—in clothes, food, literary fashions.

Words, forms, or constructions that are no longer in use are called *obsolete*. No one today refers to a *bottle* of hay, or uses *can* in the sense of *know,* or *coy* in the sense of *quiet*. Usages which are now dis-

---

[1] For further discussion, see *Index* entries *Change in language and *English language; histories of the English language, especially Baugh (Books cited by name of author only will be found in the Bibliography, pp. XIV-XV); Otto Jespersen, *Growth and Structure of the English Language* (various editions); George H. McKnight, *English Words and Their Backgrounds* (New York, 1923); *Oxford English Dictionary, Dictionary of American English.*

appearing from the language are called *archaic*. Fashion has just about driven out *betrothed* in favor of *fiancée*. Archaic expressions survive in some situations, such as the *thou* and *saith* of church services. A few archaic or even obsolete words are used in set phrases, such as "much *ado*," "in good *stead*," and many are preserved in uneducated or dialect speech after they have disappeared from other varieties of English. *Learn* in the sense of *teach, you was* in the singular, *he don't,* and the *double negative[1] were all once in general and reputable use. It is often hard to tell when a word or construction is sufficiently uncommon to be called archaic; a good many words not so labeled in dictionaries are really used very rarely (like *betimes, deem, doff*).

Because we learn our language chiefly by imitating what we hear and read, obsolete and archaic usage offers few problems, but occasionally in trying to "improve" his language a student will use an archaic expression, and sometimes a strained effort at humor produces words like *quoth* or *wight*.

We do not need to know the whole history of our language, but realizing that it has a history should help us adjust to reading older literature and will explain many of the peculiarities of the current language (in spelling and verb forms, for instance) that we will need to consider in this book.

Words, constructions, and styles are still changing. Recent years have seen the addition of many words (*baby sitter, bathyscaphe, astronautics, blip,* names for scores of new chemical compounds, and so on),[2] the dropping of some from general use, and a tendency toward more concise idioms and constructions.

People used to shy away from new words until they had "proved themselves a permanent part of the language." It is true that dictionary editors watch for new words in books and magazines and include them if they continue to be used. But users of the language don't need to be so hesitant. The use of a word should depend on its fitness rather than on its passing a probationary period; dictionary recording comes only as the result of use. Obviously the name of a new invention or of a new social situation is needed immediately and should be freely used. No apology is necessary for words like *televise, iron curtain, deep-freeze, fringe benefits, newscast*.

---

[1] Throughout this book, references to *Index* articles are indicated by asterisks (*).

[2] *American Speech* treats many new words as they appear, and the annual supplementary volumes to the principal encyclopedias have lists of such words.

While new words for new things are natural additions to our vocabulary, it is wise to hesitate before adopting new words for things that have already been named. This is especially true of the abstract words (such as *recreational facilities, urban area, causal factors*) that higher education and occupational specialization seem to be substituting for the common words for some activities and situations (see "Big Words," p. 228).

New words used to make their way into literary usage rather slowly, but most writers today use a new word whenever it is appropriate. (*Pecking order,* for instance, was used in fiction by Aldous Huxley and Ford Madox Ford almost as soon as zoologists had begun to use it.) It is important for a writer to make the fullest possible use of the current language. When you write naturally, from your observation of language, you usually write current English, and you should aim for no other kind.

Variations due to place

No language is spoken exactly the same way in all parts of the country or countries in which it is used. We can easily spot an Englishman because some of his pronunciations and some of his words and constructions are different from ours. (See *American and British usage.) We can also very often tell what part of the United States a person comes from by listening to him talk. Differences in words, pronunciations, stress, phrasing, and grammatical habits that are characteristic of fairly definite regions are called *regional dialects;* more accurately, a dialect is speech that does not attract attention to itself in the region where it is used. A pronunciation, a word or meaning of a word, or an idiom that for usually traceable historical reasons is current in one region and not in others is called a *provincialism* or a *localism.*

Dialects are not peculiar to backward regions, for the "Oxford accent" forms a minor dialect and the people of Boston and of New York speak differently from each other. Nor are dialects the result of lack of education or social standing. An educated Westerner will speak somewhat differently from a Southerner or New Englander of a similar degree and quality of education. A dialect may show traits of differing British dialects spoken by early settlers or of foreign languages spoken by large numbers of people in the region, as in German sections of Pennsylvania or in the Scandinavian sections of the Middle West. It may show traits of a neighboring language or of the language of an earlier settlement: the dialect of the Southwest contains Spanish elements; of New Orleans, French elements.

There are fewer differences among the dialects of the United States than would be expected in a country of such size, many fewer than exist among the dialects in much smaller Great Britain.[1] The relative freedom of movement of the American people, transportation facilities that have prevented even the Rocky Mountains from marking a linguistic boundary, the educational system, the circulation of books and national magazines, and more recently radio and television—all keep people who are thousands of miles apart speaking substantially the same language.

Three major speech areas of the United States have been traditionally recognized: *Eastern* (New England and a strip of eastern New York), *Southern* (south of Pennsylvania and the Ohio River, extending west of the Mississippi into Texas), and *Western* (extending from New Jersey on the Atlantic, through the Middle West and the whole of our Pacific coast), sometimes called *General American,* or *Northern.* As a result of the work being done on *The Linguistic Atlas of the United States and Canada,* the boundaries are being more exactly drawn, subdivisions indicated, and lines of influence between areas shown. The major speech divisions have been renamed *Northern, Midland,* and *Southern,* but their lines have not been carried far enough westward so that they can take the place of the traditional areas in amateur discussion. Regional varieties exist within each of the three main areas, as in the Ozarks or in New York City, but the differences between the speech of California and Illinois are fewer than the differences between either of these and, say, Georgia or Massachusetts. Roughly one twelfth of the population speaks Eastern, one sixth Southern, and three fourths Western or General American.

A professional student of American English observes many differences among these regions that the ordinary person might miss, but we are all aware of some of them. Some New Englanders use a broad *a* (äsk, gräss, päst) where most Americans have short *a;* they usually slight *r* (*bän* for *barn*). A Westerner has a distinct, perhaps even a

---

[1] See Baugh, Ch. 11, especially § 250; Bloomfield, Ch. 19; *Dictionary of American English;* Otto Jespersen, *Mankind, Nation and Individual from a Linguistic Point of View* (Oslo, 1925); G. P. Krapp, *The English Language in America* (New York, 1925), pp. 225-73; Mencken. Many articles in the magazine *American Speech* record facts of various American dialects. Linguaphone album L-19 has recordings of twenty-four American dialects. For some results of work on the *Linguistic Atlas,* see Hans Kurath, *Handbook of the Linguistic Geography of New England* (Providence, 1939), *A Word Geography of the Eastern United States* (Ann Arbor, 1949), and E. B. Atwood, *Survey of Verb Forms in the Eastern United States* (Ann Arbor, 1953).

prolonged, *r,* after vowels as well as before. Like most Americans he has *ä* for the *o* in *hot, lot, cot.* Like many Americans he rounds the *o* in *hog, frog, log.* Beginning in New York State, most speakers of the Western type do not distinguish *hoarse* and *horse, mourning* and *morning,* pronouncing *ōr* (like the word *ore*) in all. A Southerner from the lowlands (as distinguished from the hill country and the hillbillies) does not sound *r* after vowels (for example, *suh* for *sir, douh* or *doh* for *door*). The long *i* both in the lowlands and the hills may suggest *ä* as in the popular spelling *Ah* for *I.* Southerners from the hills usually pronounce *r* after vowels–as all fanciers of hillbilly music know. Each region–Eastern, Southern, and Western–also has its characteristic stress and speech rhythm.

In vocabulary, different words will be found for many common objects. Which of the following is used in your locality, or is some other word used?

bag–sack–poke
gumshoe–overshoe–rubber
piazza–porch–stoop–veranda
seesaw–teeter-totter–teeterboard
doughnut–fried cake–cruller–fat cake–nut cake–cookie

The accompanying map shows several words that are used within the relatively small limits of New England for the common earth-

Dialect Chart for "Earthworm"

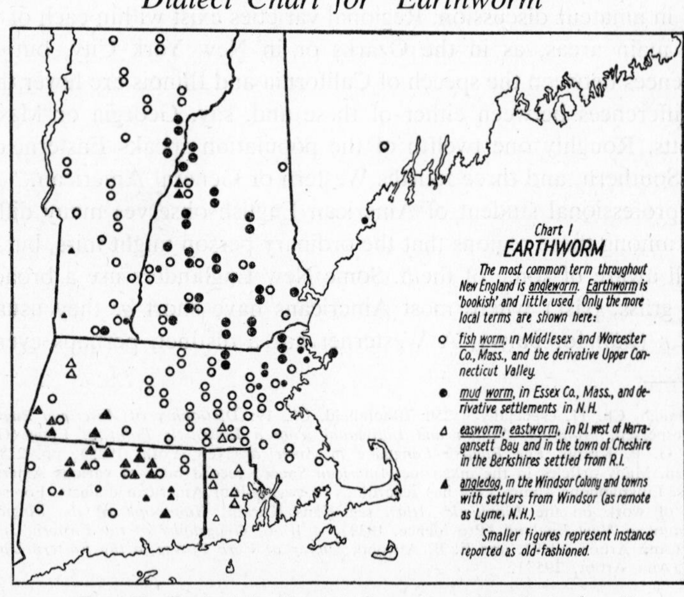

From *Handbook of the Linguistic Geography of New England,* p. 38

worm: *angleworm, angledog, easworm* (for *eastworm*), *fish worm.* In other regions it is known by some of these names and by others as well.

Besides these varying names for common objects, each region has special words for local features of the landscape or for occupations that are more or less local: *coulee, hogback, sierra, mesa; mesquite, piñon; mule skinner, vara* (a surveyor's measure in the Southwest). And there are local idioms like the Southern "I would *like for* you to do it," or like those for telling time—New Englanders generally say quarter *of* four, Southerners quarter *till* four, and Westerners quarter *to* four.

Increased travel, education, and reading are probably reducing the dialectal variety in the United States, just as they are blotting out the dialects of Great Britain. Words peculiar to a local terrain or to local occupations will probably survive, since they fill a real need and usually have no equivalents in other dialects. The frequent use of localisms on radio and television and in stories may help make one region more tolerant of the language of others, and it may very well introduce into general use words formerly characteristic of a particular locality.

People's attitudes toward the use of localisms vary greatly. Some believe that they should be weeded out; others believe that a person should retain as much as possible of the flavor of his native speech. It is a problem each person will have to settle for himself on the basis of appropriateness and effectiveness. An educated person will tend to shed the more conspicuous local pronunciations of his youth, and he may have little occasion to use purely local words. But conscious effort to change his speech to a different pattern will often result in an unhappy combination of elements from both. Natural, gradual, unconscious change is best.

Localisms are more appropriate in speech than in writing. Conspicuously formal writers tend to avoid them. Their words come characteristically from the general or specifically formal parts of the vocabulary; distinctive localisms would be used only for special effects and might be placed in quotation marks. In General and Informal English (defined in later sections of this chapter), localisms have more place. They are necessary to narrative, both in histories and accounts of personal experience and in stories and plays. Consider this description of a meal from a novel of Florida:

> There were poke-greens with bits of white bacon buried in them; sandbuggers made of potato and onion and the cooter he had found crawling yesterday; sour orange biscuits and at his mother's elbow the

sweet potato pone. He was torn between his desire for more biscuits and another sandbugger and the knowledge, born of painful experience, that if he ate them, he would suddenly have no room for pone. The choice was plain.—MARJORIE KINNAN RAWLINGS, *The Yearling,* p. 12

Many young people first become conscious of their native speech when they go away to school or college. They should study their speech if it attracts attention, but they need not abandon it just because classmates remark about it. They should try to find what in it is suitable and effective and what seems to defeat easy communication. We would hate to see everyone's speech smoothed to the colorless, placeless tones of a network radio announcer.

Differences between speaking and writing

Basically language is spoken; its written symbols develop long after speech is established. We learn to speak before we learn to write, and most of us throughout our lives will listen and speak more than we read and write. But listening and speaking, reading and writing (not to mention the even greater use of language in "thinking," about which we know so little) are related, overlapping skills, and a serious lack in one is likely to affect the others. In a language like English, with a voluminous amount of written and printed material, the relations between speaking and writing are complex and so far have not been sufficiently studied to let us discuss them very exactly.

First we should realize that writing is a greatly simplified representation of speech. We can represent words fairly well by spelling, at least well enough for a reader to recognize them, and we can indicate some major groupings of words by punctuation, especially sentences, clauses, and the longer phrases. But the stresses and slight pauses and various "tones of voice" that carry so much of our meaning in speech, qualifying, emphasizing, even sometimes reversing the meaning of the words themselves (as "Oh, I'm very fond of him" can be said so as to mean "I dislike him") cannot be directly represented on paper. This fact shows that writing is not simply a representation of speech, and it never has been. Representing speech fully on paper is a problem for linguists, who need to record it exactly for study, rather than for writers, who need to convey their meaning to readers.

There are several nonlinguistic reasons why writing has developed some characteristics of its own. Readers are often at a distance and may be strangers, with backgrounds different from the writer's. They will probably read silently, no doubt rapidly, and they will expect to find what they read in a form easy to follow. This is one reason for stressing clearness and precision in writing. Another reason is that writing lies on the page and can be examined closely, while speech goes by rapidly. This has led to establishing standards for the written language which, though they have a fairly wide range, are much more uniform than standards for speech. Most of the details of written form have been developed by printers and publishers, who naturally enough wish for consistency in what they publish, and they enforce the details through copy editors and proofreaders, who tidy up copy to meet the standards. This standardization allows for wide circulation of printed matter, one of its greatest assets. Any writer who presents his copy for others to read is expected to approach (though not to meet in every respect) these standards by writing clearly and following the most definitely established conventions of published writing.

Two of the more conspicuous differences between oral and written style are in vocabulary and sentences. The vocabulary of conversation is likely to be somewhat limited. We do not draw on our full stock of words, partly because we do not talk much about some of the subjects we write about, partly because we use phrases or clauses instead of single words (*practices that are not desirable* instead of *undesirable practices* or even *malpractices*), and partly because we can convey our meaning without very exact words. Instead of trying to find exact words in describing something or giving our opinions, we fall back on *good, bad, pleasant,* perhaps even on *nice,* and express the degree of our meaning by tone of voice, gesture, or facial expression. In writing we need more exact words to make up for lack of this support. It might be better if we used more exact words in conversation, but searching for words while we are talking is likely to take the life out of our speech and make it seem formal and aloof. Usually the added exactness of writing does not depend on rare words but just exact ones, as in this simple descriptive statement:

> At the top of the pole crouched a shivering gray kitten, mewing faintly and clinging desperately to the wood with her claws.—WILLA CATHER, *O Pioneers!* p. 5

The grammar of speech is more variable and less exact than that of writing, at least of edited, publishable writing. We use pronouns rather casually, omit prepositions (*a couple birds*), use only a few connectives, sometimes relying heavily on *and* and *so,* and yet we make ourselves clear. Many of the matters marked on student papers are simply such traits of spoken language transferred to paper. Spoken sentences are usually shorter than written, or if they are long it is because one statement is added to another rather than because clauses are built together with subordinating conjunctions. Written sentences need to show the relationship between their parts more carefully, to give the reader more guidance in following them through.

But written English is not a different language from spoken. All these differences are in relatively small matters of style that can be tended to in revising a paper. It is usually best to write nearly as you speak and then test what you have written by reading it as a stranger might, making sure that you are telling him what you mean so exactly that he can understand it without hearing you say it, and that you are in general following the conventions of printed English. The best basis for your writing is your better speech, reshaped a little so that it can stand scrutiny on paper. Some languages have entirely different forms for speech and writing, but in English, and especially in present-day English, the relationship is close. We sometimes say someone "talks like a book," meaning that his talk is uncomfortably elaborate or stiff; it is more often a compliment to say "he writes as he talks." Letters and accounts of personal experience are likely to be quite close to speech; term papers for courses and most academic work need to be in the more formal tradition of writing. It is best to be ready to use as wide a range as possible, drawing on both spoken and written English. The ideal has been put this way: "One would like to think that all of us will come to the stage of refusing to write what we would not, indeed could not, say, though that, of course, is not to limit our writing to what we actually do say."[1]

Differences due to use

Many words of similar meaning, though they are in current and general use, cannot be used interchangeably in all situations. Consider the following groups:

indigent, impecunious, underprivileged, in want, penniless, poverty-stricken, *poor,* hard up, broke, flat

spent, fatigued, weary, exhausted, *tired,* worn-out, played out, used up, dog tired, all in, pooped

stripling, youth, lad, *boy,* youngster, kid, punk

Similarly, many idioms and constructions represent the same idea but suggest different varieties of speech:

dare not, daren't, *do not dare,* don't dare, dassent

were it not for, if it were not for, *if it was not for,* if it wasn't for, if it wan't for

Poor, tired, and *boy, do not dare* and *if it was not for* certainly belong to the central part of the language and might be used by anyone

[1] Bonamy Dobrée, *Modern Prose Style* (Oxford, 1934), p. 229.

in any circumstance; the same is true of the words near them in these series. But as we move away from these central expressions, the words become somewhat more limited, until those at the ends would be found only in quite formal or quite informal situations. Probably most of us would not use *indigent, spent, stripling*—they suggest old-fashioned or rather bookish usage. We all might use *broke, all in, kid* in casual company but not when we were talking to someone on whom we wanted to make a good impression. These differences are due not to the meaning of the words but to the circumstances in which they have been generally used and which they suggest. That is, their quality depends on the social situations in which they have been and are predominantly used.

There is no well-established system of naming these varieties of English, though they have been often discussed.[1] In this book four principal varieties are presented, *General* English, *Formal* English, *Informal* English (the three together making up *Standard* English), and *Nonstandard* or *Vulgate* English.[2] These varieties are defined in the table on pages 18-19, and because they are so important in everyone's judgment of his own language, they are elaborated in the next four sections of this chapter.

Although differences are easily observable between these varieties, they must not be thought of as mutually exclusive but as relatively different, shading into each other. A passage may be considered Formal because it has a few conspicuous traits characteristic of that variety, and thus a Formal "feel" or "tone," even though the language of most of the passage is in General usage. Although people's judgment of the boundaries will differ somewhat, the principal characteristics of the varieties are pretty clear, and the illustrations in the following sections should make it possible to distinguish them.

General English—unlimited use

Most speaking and writing situations call for General English, the great central body of words and constructions of our language. In speech we find it in good conversations, in discussions, in most talks to general audiences; in writing we see it in letters, in newspapers and magazines, in plays and novels, and in books of all sorts for general circulation—in most of what we read.

---

[1] See, for instance: Bloomfield, p. 52, 149 ff.; Fries, *AEG*, in which usage is treated according to social varieties; John S. Kenyon, "Cultural Level and Functional Varieties of English," *College English*, 1948, 10:1-6; Marckwardt and Walcott; Pooley, Ch. 3.

[2] In earlier editions of this book General English was called Informal. Informal is now kept for a distinctly "informal" type of Standard English.

General written English lies close to good speech, but it is not speech exactly reproduced, partly because the resources of the written language are somewhat different. The words are likely to be from the central vocabulary, of wide currency in both speech and writing (*roomy* rather than *spacious, rainfall* rather than *precipitation*). They are likely to be concrete, close to experience, referring to things, people, actions, and events more than to abstractions, and familiar to a large number of readers. The constructions are likely to reflect those of speech (*look into, give up, take over*), and the sentences are relatively short, one or two clauses without interrupting phrases or involved movement.

General English is especially appropriate to narratives of personal experience and to presentation of people and action, whether in fiction or factual accounts. In the following paragraph about life on a Pacific island, the sentences are short, averaging twenty words, but not monotonous. With thirteen verbs and seven nouns or modifiers made from verbs (*cooking, cleaning, surging*), and with some phrases that suggest speech (*paddle off, right on the beach, when hungry*), the passage gives an active and immediately understandable picture.

> Life drifts along more or less becalmed in these native villages. There are no pressing duties to be done. The men paddle off to their fishing grounds when they feel like it, and when they return the catch is distributed and often eaten right on the beach without so much as cooking or cleaning the fish. The older men sit cross-legged on the sand, chipping away on logs with a kind of adz, out of which eventually they fashion their canoes. The children move around in little animated groups, surging back and forth like schools of minnows. When hungry, they tear their fish apart with fingers and teeth, or break open a coconut and gnaw the white meat out of the fragments.–DAVID BRADLEY, *No Place to Hide,* p. 161

Ideas, too, though they are by nature abstract and are often presented in Formal English for rather restricted groups of readers, may be expressed in General English. The following definition of the word *sign,* a term important in philosophical discussions of meaning, is presented concretely for general readers by a professor of philosophy. The early specific details lead to the generalization at the end. The constructions are based on verbs (*the way we will dress*), in simple, direct sentences, averaging twenty-two words. (The longest sentence, the third, is a series of clauses.)

> What do all these events have in common that causes us to lump them together as signs? One core similarity: *they all influence the way*

we tend to react toward something other than themselves. The alarm tells us the time, the sight of our face in the mirror informs us about our appearance, the newspaper tells us what has happened in the world, the pressure from the oranges or the odor of eggs determines which one we will select, the note to the milkman tells him how we wish him to act. The appearance of the sky or the words of the weather report influence the way we will dress, the way we will behave outdoors. We do not put on our raincoats indoors nor raise an umbrella between us and the newspaper. We eat not the menu but rather what its printed words stand for. Signs denote something other than themselves, other things or other aspects of the thing of which they are a part. The marks on the newspaper stand for happenings in China; the rate of our pulse beat stands for the condition of our heart. Signs influence our beliefs, our preferences, our feelings, our actions with respect to what they signify. They dispose us to react to something other than themselves in one way rather than another.—Reprinted with permission of Prentice-Hall, Inc. from *The Open Shelf* by Charles Morris. © 1958 by Prentice-Hall, Inc., Englewood Cliffs, New Jersey. Published by Prentice-Hall, Inc.

The most likely danger of General English is flatness, though this often comes from flat or obvious subject matter as much as from the language. In this passage from a short story the language is a compressed form of what we all might say (except perhaps *the world leaps into proportion*), but it has the quality of feeling that we associate with literature:

The man who expected to be shot lay with his eyes open, staring at the upper left-hand corner of his cell. He was fairly well over his last beating, and they might come for him any time now. There was a yellow stain in the cell corner near the ceiling; he had liked it at first, then disliked it; now he was coming back to liking it again.

He could see it more clearly with his glasses on, but he only put on his glasses for special occasions now—the first thing in the morning, and when they brought the food in, and for interviews with the General. The lenses of the glasses had been cracked in a beating some months before, and it strained his eyes to wear them too long. Fortunately, in his present life he had very few occasions demanding clear vision. But, nevertheless, the accident to his glasses worried him, as it worries all near-sighted people. You put your glasses on the first thing in the morning and the world leaps into proportion; if it does not do so, something is wrong with the world.—STEPHEN VINCENT BENÉT, "The Blood of Martyrs," *Thirteen O'Clock,* p. 23

General English is hard to describe by itself, partly because its characteristics are so familiar to us, but it will become clearer by comparison with the other varieties that follow. Obviously it has a wide range, shading off into Formal English in one direction and Informal in the other. It is the most useful variety, without the limitations of the

Summary of the Principal

Nonstandard English (Limited use)	Informal English (Limited use)
Chiefly spoken	*More often spoken than written*
Language not much touched by school instruction; often conspicuously local; not appropriate for public affairs or for use by educated people	Speaking and writing of educated people in informal situations; often includes shoptalk or slang and some localisms
Typical uses:	*Typical uses:*
Conversations of many people at home, with friends, on the job Representations of this speech in stories, plays, movies, comic strips, on radio and television (See pages 24-26)	Casual conversation Letters between intimates; diaries, personal writing; writing close to popular speech, as in fiction and some newspaper columns (See pages 22-24)

Comments:

1. Informal, General, and Formal English together make up Standard English.
2. The varieties are to be thought of as shading into each other–not as sharply defined and mutually exclusive. A passage might be regarded as Informal, for instance, if it had several conspicuous traits characteristic of that variety even though the greater part of the passage was in General English.
3. Usage is said to be *divided* when choices exist between two usages in General English, both of which are in good standing (for example, the spellings *catalog* or *catalogue,* or a comma or no comma before the *and* of the last item in a series).
4. *Slovenly* (impoverished speech, often including obscenity and pro-

Varieties of English

General English (Unlimited use)	Formal English (Limited use)
Both spoken and written	*More often written than spoken*
Speaking and writing of educated people in their private or public affairs	Speaking and writing for somewhat restricted groups in formal situations
Typical uses:	*Typical uses:*
Conversation; talks to general audiences	Addresses and lectures to special audiences
Most business letters and advertising	Some editorials and business writing
News and feature stories, newspaper columns	Literature of somewhat limited circulation: essays and criticisms, much poetry, some fiction
Magazine articles and books on subjects of general interest	Academic writing: reference works, dissertations, term papers, some textbooks
Most fiction and other literature for general circulation	Scientific and technical reports
(See pages 15-20)	Books and articles dealing with special subjects for professional groups and experts
	(See pages 20-22)

fanity) may be regarded as the extreme of Nonstandard and *Stilted* (pretentious and unnecessarily heavy speech or writing—"gobbledygook") may be regarded as the extreme of Standard English.

5. The varieties are characterized by some differences in word forms, in pronunciation, in vocabulary, in grammatical constructions, and by the avoidance of certain locutions (as Standard English avoids double negatives). The chief differences, and the easiest to discuss, are in vocabulary.

6. Labeling a usage as belonging to any one of the varieties is meant to indicate that it is characteristically used as the description of that variety suggests, that its connotation comes from this use, and that it is not characteristic of another variety. Such labeling is not intended to prevent a word's use under other conditions but does suggest that it may be conspicuous in another variety and that its connotation should be intended.

others, and since it has such wide currency and in fact can reach practically all readers, it is the most necessary to master, and is the proper goal of instruction.

Formal English—limited use

Formal English is typically found in books and articles of mature interest, intended for circulation among a somewhat restricted group, among teachers, ministers, doctors, lawyers, and others of general or specialized intellectual interests. It is found also in addresses and other formal talks and often colors the conversation of people who do a good deal of reading, but it is more characteristic of writing than of speaking.

Although Formal English will contain a good many traits of General English, it will show enough of the Formal vocabulary and constructions to give it a definite tone. The vocabulary has many words little used in ordinary speech, specialized words from various scientific and scholarly fields and words of more general meaning associated with the literary tradition (like *desultory, ubiquitous, redoubtable*). It uses a good many abstract nouns, which summarize rather than present experience directly (*comfort, distinction, research*). For people familiar with the words, they often carry a good deal of suggestiveness (*bosky, ominous, paradox, transcend*) and often have some appeal of sound or rhythm (*quintessence, immemorial, memorable*).

In Formal English the constructions are usually filled out; short cuts characteristic of General and Informal English are not taken. Contractions are avoided, relative pronouns are not omitted, prepositions and conjunctions are likely to be repeated in parallel constructions, and so on. Sentences tend to be somewhat longer than in General writing, binding more ideas together. They may be elaborately constructed with parallel and balanced clauses, the word order may be different from the usual English pattern, and modifiers may come between the main elements of subject, verb, and object. Allusions to literature and to events of the past are as common as to current affairs.[1]

This does not mean that Formal writing is stiff or dull, though there is danger that it may be; but the nature of the language of Formal writing makes its appeal somewhat limited. It often demands considerable concentration and presupposes in the reader an interest

[1] For further discussion of the traits of Formal sentences, see Ch. 7, *Sentences*.

in specialized subject matter or in general ideas and some awareness of our cultural tradition. The special audience for which it is written will not only follow the material but, if it is really well expressed, will appreciate the style as well. To some readers, one appeal of Formal English is its very difference from everyday language.

Two examples will show some of the traits of Formal English. In the first, from an impersonal, scientific book on some psychological aspects of painting, the sentences average twenty-four words in length, but though they combine several facts, they move directly. The chief Formal trait is the vocabulary. Some of the words are essential to the subject (*expressive appearance, perceptual classification*), and others are not likely to be used by the average person, although he understands them (*spontaneously, animate, inanimate, dynamics, manifest*). *Linnean classification* is an allusion to a system of botanical classification.

> Some objects and events resemble each other with regard to the underlying patterns of forces; others do not. Therefore on the basis of their expressive appearance, our eye spontaneously creates a kind of Linnean classification of all things existing. This perceptual classification cuts across the order suggested by other kinds of categories. Particularly in our modern Western civilization we are accustomed to distinguishing between animate and inanimate things, human and nonhuman creatures, the mental and the physical. But in terms of expressive qualities, the character of a given person may resemble that of a particular tree more closely than that of another person. The state of affairs in a human society may be similar to the tension in the skies just before the outbreak of a thunderstorm. Further, our kind of scientific and economic thinking makes us define things by measurements rather than by the dynamics of appearance. Our criteria for what is useful or useless, friendly or hostile, have tended to sever the connections with outer expression, which they possess in the minds of children or primitives. If a house or a chair suits our practical purposes, we may not stop to find out whether its appearance expresses our style of living. In business relations we define a man by his census data, his income, age, position, nationality, or race—that is, by categories that ignore the inner nature of the man as it is manifest in his outer expression.—RUDOLPH ARNHEIM, *Art and Visual Perception,* pp. 368-9

In a somewhat more personal way, the second passage presents an important idea of social development. The words carry a good deal of force and suggestiveness (*high* in a special sense, *guardians of culture, time-honored, outrage*), and some are of rather restricted currency (*occupational disease, disparate, diverse*). Most of the meaning is carried by nouns and adjectives. The sentences are longer, averaging thirty-seven words, but their parts are closely and naturally related.

> All such perversions of high traditions are intensified by traditionalism, the occupational disease of guardians of culture. The guardians

tend to forget that tradition has always been the great enemy of the founders of great traditions: that Socrates was a radical who did corrupt the youth of Athens by impiously urging them to question the time-honored ways; or that the teachings of Christ were an outrage to precisely the most cultivated, respectable, God-fearing people of his time; or that the American Revolution was strictly a revolution, illegal, violent, and bloody. In particular, the traditionalists abuse our Western heritage by singling out some one school of thought as the 'essential' or 'true' tradition; whereas diversity and nonconformity are the very soul of this heritage. It is the richest tradition that man has ever known simply because it includes so many disparate elements from diverse sources, and has never been at rest.—HERBERT J. MULLER, *The Uses of the Past,* p. 58

There are some conspicuously formal types within Formal English. Some highly individual styles in literature require detailed study to be understood because of the unusual use of words and the uniquely personal associations of words as well as various departures from the typical patterns of current English. In the quite different styles characteristic of scholarly and scientific writing at its best, a precise and specialized vocabulary is employed in a compact, impersonal statement. And beyond these are abuses of Formal English: the cumbersome, archaic, and highly repetitious language of most legal documents, and the pretentious, abstract, and equally repetitious style of some bad academic writing and of much of the official writing of government and business, popularly and appropriately known as gobbledygook.

But as the two paragraphs just quoted show, Formal English often presents important and illuminating ideas worth thinking about. The ability to read Formal English is a requirement for educated people and one of the abilities to be cultivated in college. Although a good deal of writing is more Formal, or at least more difficult, than it needs to be, we have to face the fact that our intellectual growth demands its mastery. In some college writing, as in term papers for advanced courses, the writing is appropriately Formal, though it should not be excessively so, never to the extent of seeming affected. A development toward somewhat more Formal expression will naturally come with increased experience in reading college-level material.

Informal English—limited use

Informal English is at the other side of General English and grades off into Nonstandard English. When we write for our own convenience or amusement or when we talk or write to members of our family or to friends, we use English with more freedom than when addressing strangers or people with whom we are only slightly acquainted. When Informal English is used publicly, it presupposes a regular relationship of some sort between user and receiver; it may be used in a recurring radio program or newspaper column, or for a distinctly informal situation or subject: amusing little experiences, comment on social foibles, sports, humor.

Informal English has considerable range, sometimes including distinctly Formal traits for contrast or Nonstandard forms for accuracy or novelty. Most conspicuously it uses words and phrases characteristic of familiar conversation, words often marked *Colloquial* in dictionaries or not recorded at all (*comeuppance, in-laws, digger-upper, arty, doohickey*); or words of special currency at the moment (*do-it-yourself, egghead, gung ho, run-around* as a noun); informal coinages for common things or situations (*emcee, boy friend, dog sit* on the analogy of *baby sit*); clipped words (*decal, hi-fi, prefab*). It may include more localisms than General English ordinarily would, *shoptalk (words from occupations, like *mike, hypo, close-up*), and *slang, words continually being formed and given a temporary currency in offhand or flashy speech: *date bait, draft bait, blooper, bobble, boo-boo, fluff*. Since writer and reader usually have a good deal in common, much can be taken for granted—in material, in allusion to common experiences, and in the special current connotation of words.

The carelessness we sometimes permit ourselves in writing letters is not a legitimate characteristic of Informal English, which has its chief use in lively conversation and in some writing where the subject and situation warrant a light touch, as in this columnist's comment on the prevalence of candle heating devices for the table:

> Gone are the days when a man got his coffee all saucered and blowed and at the right temperature, only to have the latter drop so rapidly that the beverage was stone cold by the time he got his handle-bar mustache parted and ready. . . . Now a man saucers and blows the stuff and puts it on a little iron cradle over a lighted candle, where the brew starts boiling once more in nothing flat. Then he has to begin all over again. It's going to be hard on commuters until they get the hang of the new gimmick. . . . The ironmonger is jubilant and the fire insurance companies will be as soon as they get hep to this situation and jack up the rates. It makes for a nice, lively business cycle, with the boys at the firehouse scarce able to get through a checker game before the siren sounds again.—INEZ ROBB, "Candle Is Remarkable Invention," *Seattle Post-Intelligencer,* Feb. 6, 1954, p. 11

General, Formal, and Informal English together make up what is known as *Standard English.* Standard English presents, then, a wide range of usage, offering a writer many choices of words and constructions—choices which in any given paper will set its tone and define its possible audience. Some principles to guide these choices will be discussed in the last section of this chapter.

The basis of Standard English is social, the "differences due to use" described on pages 14-15. Its basis has been well described by Professor Fries:

> On the whole, however, if we ignore the special differences that separate the speech of New England, the South, and the Middle West, we do have in the United States a set of language habits, broadly conceived, in which the major matters of the political, social, economic, educational, religious life of this country are carried on. To these language habits is attached a certain social prestige, for the use of them suggests that one has constant relations with those who are responsible for the important affairs of our communities. It is this set of language habits, derived originally from an older London English, but differentiated from it somewhat by its independent development in this country, which is the "standard" English of the United States. Enough has been said to enforce the point that it is "standard" not because it is any more correct or more beautiful or more capable than other varieties of English; it is "standard" solely because it is the particular type of English which is used in the conduct of the important affairs of our people. It is also the type of English used by the *socially acceptable* of most of our communities and insofar as that is true it has become a social or class dialect in the United States.—C. C. FRIES, *American English Grammar,* p. 13

The attention given to encouraging the use of Standard English in schools and colleges is intended to help young people prepare themselves to take their part in public affairs, to speak and write for educated people, and so to continue or broaden their range of possible social contacts. Writing in composition courses is practice for later work in college and after college.

Nonstandard English—limited use

The everyday speech of many people, relatively untouched by school instruction or by the tradition of printed English, makes up Nonstandard or Vulgate English, the name popularized by H. L. Mencken in *The American Language* and given in *Webster's International Dictionary* as the third sense of *vulgate.*[1] This speech variety is a very real and important part of the English language and is studied by linguists with the same seriousness with which they study

[1] See Leonard Bloomfield, "Literate and Illiterate Speech," *American Speech,* 1927, 2:432-9; Fries, *AEG;* Mencken.

other varieties. It is not made up of lapses from any brand of reputable or Standard English but is a different development from the same language stock, representing a selection of sounds, words, forms, and constructions made under different social conditions. It works very well in carrying on the private affairs and occupations of millions of people and is consequently worthy of study and respect. Its avoidance in business, government, or literature is due to social rather than to linguistic causes. It is not ordinarily printed, since, for various historical and social reasons, the printed language is a selection of words, forms, and constructions considered appropriate to public affairs and so to Standard English.

Nonstandard English is most conspicuously different from the other chief varieties of English in the use of pronoun and verb forms and in the freer use of localisms. Many of its words have a longer history in English than the more genteel words that have replaced them in "society." Many of the forms and constructions have a continuous history back to a time when they were reputable: Chaucer could use a double negative occasionally; *ant* (*are not*) and *he don't* were reputable until less than a century ago; what is popularly referred to as "dropping the *g*" in verb forms spelled with *-ing* is a continuation of an original participle ending. Many other features of Nonstandard English are equally natural developments of the language that by some accident of dialect or other circumstance did not become adopted in Standard English.

Nonstandard English is primarily spoken. Its forms (like *ain't, dassent, scairt, you was*) are not particularly conspicuous when we hear them spoken rapidly and with appropriate, not exaggerated, emphasis. They appear in many radio and television programs, in plays, and in the conversation of stories. You will find them, often intensified, in many comic strips. Occasionally a Nonstandard form is used in humor or for special effect, as in Josh Billings' epigram: "It isn't so much the ignorance of mankind that makes them ridiculous as knowing so many things that ain't so."

The monolog of the barber in Ring Lardner's story "Haircut" is a fairly accurate representation of Nonstandard. A few traits of pronunciation are shown (though the *of* in "she'd of divorced him" has no relation to the preposition *of* but is the spelling of the normal contraction of *have*—"she'd've divorced him"), adverbs without the *-ly* ending, *seen* for *saw, beat her to it,* and so on.

> Jim didn't work very steady after he lost his position with the Carterville people. What he did earn, doin' odd jobs round town, why he spent pretty near all of it on gin, and his family might of starved if the stores

hadn't of carried them along. Jim's wife tried her hand at dressmakin', but they ain't nobody goin' to get rich makin' dresses in this town.

As I say, she'd of divorced Jim, only she seen that she couldn't support herself and the kids and she was always hopin' that some day Jim would cut out his habits and give her more than two or three dollars a week.

They was a time when she would go to whoever he was workin' for and ask them to give her his wages, but after she done this once or twice, he beat her to it by borrowin' most of his pay in advance. He told it all round town, how he had outfoxed his Missus. He certainly was a caution.—RING LARDNER, "Haircut," *Roundup,* p. 25

Schools carry on their work in the language of the upper social classes, Standard English. Students who go into the professions, into many branches of business, and into most white-collar jobs continue to use Standard English more or less consistently. Those who go into manual labor and the less well-paid and less socially elevated jobs often return to the use of Nonstandard English. Naturally and necessarily, though, speech is gradually losing many of its Nonstandard traits because of the increased number of white-collar jobs, the greater number of contacts between white-collar and other workers, and the increasing effects of education.

In the lower schools, where pupils are likely to be in daily contact with Nonstandard speech, it forms a serious problem. This is seldom true at the college level, though the speech of many college students is cruder than their social standing would warrant and is consequently a poor background for their writing.

The objection to this variety is not that its grammar is "bad," but that Nonstandard words and constructions are not appropriate to the readers for whom college students and college graduates write or to the subjects they are handling. Complex ideas and dignified subjects cannot be discussed adequately in the vocabulary of Nonstandard English. Nonstandard is necessary in writing the conversation of many characters in stories, or at least it should be approximated, and it should be used occasionally to give a note of realism to portraits of real people who naturally speak it. But most other uses are inappropriate in college writing. When an expression in this book is marked "Nonstandard," it should not be used except for good reason. Many Nonstandard practices are discussed in the next two chapters.

What is Good English?

To a student of language, all varieties of English are equally a part of the language, and one variety is to be observed and studied as much as another. But to a *user* of English the varieties are by no means equal. They differ in the impression they make on people and in the sort of ideas they can communicate.

Every educated person naturally wants to speak and write what may be called "Good English," just as he wants to "make a good personal appearance" and to "be intelligent." But the great range and diversity of the English language raises numerous questions about usage. The problem of English usage is much like the problems which face us in almost everything we do that comes under the eyes of others, in our manners, in the jokes we tell, in our food, in our living quarters, in our political ideas. In dress, to take the most convenient parallel, we gradually develop something we call taste or judgment, in part by imitating others, consciously or unconsciously, in part by consulting people who are supposed to know what is good form, in part by following our own preferences in design and color and fabric. Our usual dress lies between the extremes of work, sport, and formal clothes. It is comfortable; it reflects something of the taste of the wearer; it is appropriate to going about personal affairs, to work in stores and offices, to college classes, to informal social affairs. But a person needs to have and to be able to wear several kinds of clothes, and he needs to know for what occasion each is appropriate. In the same way, anyone who is going to take his place in public, business, or social affairs needs to know the resources of the various sorts of English and when they can profitably be drawn on. For answers to questions about English usage, you can often consult books, especially dictionaries and handbooks. You can ask people who write well; you can ask teachers who have made the study of the language part of their professional training. And you can always be watching what effective writers do—how the language is handled in the better books and magazines. This observation is especially important, because, as in dress and in manners, more or less conscious imitation of those you approve of or wish to be associated with will bulk large in forming your own habits. Few will ever write with real ease unless they listen and read a good deal and so unconsciously absorb the ways of their language by direct experience.

Basis of Good English set by the purpose of communication

Of course, anyone may talk to himself or write for his own amusement, relief, or "self-expression"; or he may wish to deceive or puzzle, and then his usage is his own affair. And a writer may experiment as much as he wishes, as James Joyce and Gertrude Stein and others have done, creating for themselves a limited audience willing to study out their meaning in spite of handicaps. But the ordinary and principal function of language is effective communication, making someone understand or feel something, or getting him to do something that we want him to do.

This fundamental purpose in speaking and writing prevents usage, complicated as it is, from falling into chaos, and sets the broad limits of Good English. We use words in the meanings they have acquired from their past use, and we try to make our statements in understandable patterns. From this point of view, Professor Fries defines the basis of Good English:

> ... language is a means to an end and that end is specifically to grasp, to possess, to communicate experience. Accordingly, that is good language, good English, which, on the one hand, most fully realizes one's own impressions, and, on the other, is most completely adapted to the purposes of any particular communication.–C. C. FRIES, *What Is Good English?* p. 120

In other words, so far as the writer's language furthers his intended effect, it is good; so far as it fails to further that effect, it is bad, no matter how "correct" it may be.[1]

Since Good English is English that serves the definite intention of a person to communicate something to another person or group, the answer to most questions of usage can be found by considering the appropriateness of the word or expression to the immediate purpose. This appropriateness is threefold: to the subject and situation, to the expected listeners or readers, and to the writer or speaker himself. Considering these will yield *principles,* rather than *rules,* to guide actual usage.

Appropriateness to subject and situation

In conversation we automatically adjust our language as well as our topics to the situation in which we find ourselves. Similarly, our talks and papers, whether they are assigned or voluntary, should have a suitable tone. The language of an informational paper for a popular audience will be somewhat different from that of the discussion of an idea or from that of a plea for action or even from a talk for a general audience. (See Chs. 10-13 on types of writing.) The tone of the language depends chiefly on the variety of English used.

---

[1] Fries, *AEG,* Ch. 1 (an unusually good statement); Fries, *The Teaching of English* (Ann Arbor, 1949), Ch. 5; Otto Jespersen, *Mankind, Nation and Individual from a Linguistic Point of View* (Oslo, 1925), Ch. 5; Pooley, Part I.

Good judgment in choosing the variety of English is one of the signs of a practiced and mature writer. Slang may fit in a letter or in a popular newspaper column; it is usually out of place in discussing a serious or elevated subject. Most fiction is General or Informal. Writing on a technical or professional subject is more likely to be Formal. The language of a church service and of religious and philosophical discussion is Formal.

Students—all writers, for that matter, who try for language appropriate to subject and situation—come at last to the same resolve: *to treat simple subjects simply,* or, in terms of our varieties of English, to treat them in General English. Most subjects are relatively simple, or at least the writer is going to give only a simplified version of them. Much of their interest is lost when the language is Formal. Amateur writers are often not content to be themselves but assume a dialect that is really foreign to them, too Formal to be appropriate to their subjects. A boy with a few shrewd remarks to make on modern suicides began this way:

> Through the ages, people have been accustomed to making a premature departure from this "vale of tears" by manifold means. Some favored hanging or a certain type of strangulation; others have been partial to poison, gunshot, or any of a variety of other methods.
>
> However, during recent years a radical change has occurred in the gentle art of self-elimination. This has been due in a large part to the advent of tall buildings. They are seemingly attracted by a strange fascination for the height in combination with a desire to put a spectacular end to their relations with this world.

He may seriously have believed that this kind of writing was better than saying in some simple way that hanging, poisoning, and shooting have given way to jumping off tall buildings, and then going directly into his subject. He might even object to being told that his sentences were bad English, worse perhaps than if they had contained actual Nonstandard expressions. Such errors could be quite easily corrected, but his inflated and pompous paragraphs must be completely rewritten to be acceptable.

Students should also avoid writing too Informally in papers which discuss serious subjects. But the better students in a composition course often err in the direction of overly Formal writing, probably because of the emphasis on Formal correctness throughout their school careers.

Teachers and students will not always agree in their judgments of particular passages, though they will agree on a surprising number of them. But once students understand the principle of appropriateness they will never again return either to unnecessary pomposity or to unsuitable lightness. They will soon come to appreciate the simple appropriateness of this account of an interview with a dean:

"I guess you're next, son," he said, motioning me into his office. Walking to a chair he had pointed out beside his desk, I sat down. "Well," he said, leaning way back in his swivel chair with his hands folded across his waist, "what seems to be your trouble?" "The trouble, sir, is that I have a couple of F's as you already know." He didn't smile so I was sorry I said that. Pulling out my deficiency report from a pile on his desk he read it with frowning eye-brows. Looking up at me he said, "How much studying have you been doing?" "Practically none, sir," I said in a weak cracking voice. Laying down the report he started in on a long speech on studying. He looked me straight in the eye and I tried to glare back at him but couldn't. I shook my head every once in a while and said, "That's right," to show him that I was listening. He went on to explain how I should make out a time schedule and stick to it, how I should write out notes on little cards and carry them around with me so that I could review them at spare moments, outline this and outline that. Go to your professors and ask them for suggestions–they'll tell you how and what to study, get your tutor to help you. After he had finished, he got up, slapped me on the back and said, "So, son, get down to work and you'll pull through all right." "Thank you, sir, and good-day," I said as I rushed out of the office. Back to my room I slowly plodded, hands shoved deep in my pockets, chin on my chest, feeling very guilty indeed. Slumping into my chair I lit my pipe and began to think. "Gotta get down to work," I thought. "Guess I'll start–next week."

The tone of a passage should be consistent unless the writer has special reason for departing from it. The lines between the varieties of English cannot be drawn precisely, but a conspicuous lapse from Formal to Informal or from Informal to Formal should ordinarily be avoided. These examples show obvious and awkward lapses:

Formal to Informal: If our Concert and Lecture program this year is not superior to that of any other college in the country, *I'll eat every freshman lid on the campus.*

Informal to Formal: *I was bowled over* by the speed with which the workmen assembled the parts.

Some writing–in *The New Yorker,* for example, and in many newspaper columns–fuses distinctly Informal words with quite Formal ones. The expressions are unified by the vigor and smoothness with which they are brought together and are not lapses from appropriateness. Consistency is not so important as the fundamental appropriateness to the situation. But, in general, one variety of English should be kept throughout a piece of writing.

Both in a composition course and out of one, keep a Formal style for complex or scholarly subjects and an Informal style for light or humorous ones; write in General English on most matters. If you know the variety of English that is appropriate for the piece of writing you are doing, this advice is relatively easy to follow. You can settle for yourself most problems of appropriateness to subject and situation simply by considering what the usual tone is in such articles.

Appropriateness to listener or reader

If you are trying to reach a particular type of reader, you will adjust both your subject matter and your expression to him. To reach him, to really get your points across, you have to be more than merely intelligible: you have to meet him pretty much on his own ground. You already do this automatically in your letters, writing in somewhat different ways to different persons. You no doubt adjust your expression to the expectations of different teachers. Certainly in many other situations you pay some attention to the language you believe is expected of you.

Some types of writing are in theory completely adjusted to their readers, notably directions to be followed, newspaper writing, and advertising. Although we realize that they often fail, either from cheapness or from dullness and unintended Formality, in a general way they do meet their readers' expectations.

Themes are sometimes difficult to write because you lose the sense of having a reader. It is better to try to visualize some particular audience, to direct your paper to some magazine, or, more commonly, to write for the class of which you are a member. Directing your paper to the members of your class will help you select material that will interest and inform them or at least will appeal to a certain part of the group, and it will help you judge what words and what kinds of sentences are appropriate. Remember that you are not writing for everyone but for a selected audience. Novels are for readers of differing tastes, and even the audiences of best sellers like *The Robe* and *The Wall* were not identical. For practice work in which you can choose your style, a firm General one is probably best, for many people prefer it and anyone can be reached through it.

Clearness. Since your aim is to convey some fact or opinion or fancy or feeling to a person or a group, appropriateness to a reader means clear expression. This means exact words and, for the most part, words that lie within the knowledge of the person you are addressing. If the subject requires words that may not be familiar to him, their meaning can usually be made clear from the way they are used. If not, you can throw in a tactful explanation or in extreme instances resort to formal definition.

Clarity also requires careful sentence construction. Experienced readers can take more elaborate sentences than those who read little or who read hurriedly. But anyone will be pleased with direct, straightforward sentences. Matters of clarity should be carefully checked in revision.

Correctness. A large part of a beginning writer's adaptation to a reader is avoiding errors that might attract unfavorable attention. People tend to judge us by superficial traits, in language as in other matters. Spelling, for example, bulks larger in most people's judgment of writing than it reasonably should. Certainly many people take delight in finding what are (or what they consider to be) errors in language, especially in the writing or speech of those supposed to be educated or of anyone soliciting their favor. Courtesy demands that a writer should do his best in anything he is submitting to another: soiled manuscript, many interlineations, confusion of common forms like *its* and *it's,* misspelling of common words (*similiar* for *similar*) are ordinarily the result of carelessness or thoughtlessness. The chief reason for mastering the "minimum essentials" of English forms (the sort of things discussed in the next two chapters) is to meet the expectations of educated readers. You should not worry about these matters as you write, but you should reserve some time for revision to bring the paper to the best state you are capable of.

Liveliness. There is so much unavoidable dullness in the world that any reader will appreciate some liveliness in writing, in the expression as well as in the material. Striving for novelty is dangerous, and its results are often self-defeating. But students frequently hide behind a flat sort of language, squeezing all the life out of their writing until it sounds as though it was written by someone three times their age. Your words need not be out of the ordinary, just those that might be used in an active conversation. Your sentences should not be formless or dragged out; they should suggest an alert interest. Refer to things people do and say, use plenty of lively detail to demonstrate ideas and to keep up interest, and pay special attention to the beginnings and endings of your papers.

Some professional writers have set themselves the rule "Don't write anything you couldn't read yourself." Following this principle means that you will choose your best available material, write it as interestingly as you can, and make it genuinely readable. If you promise yourself that you won't turn in a paper that you couldn't read yourself with interest and perhaps profit, you will be accepting responsibility for your work, doing composition of actual college grade—and you will be permanently improving your control of expression, laying a sure foundation for continued growth in Good English.

In general, satisfy your reader's expectations insofar as you believe they are worthy of respect. One warning is needed: Don't aim at your reader's worst, compromising yourself and insulting him. Visualize him in his better moments and write for him as he is then.

Appropriateness to speaker or writer

In the speaker-listener or writer-reader relationship, the speaker or writer actually dominates. He makes the choices; his judgment or unconscious sense of fitness finally controls. Your language in the long run represents your personality, and you are finally responsible for the language you use. To take this responsibility you first need to make every effort to inform yourself of the possibilities of the English language by observing what is actually spoken and written, by using dictionaries and other reference works, and by consulting people who have studied English as a language. Then you can apply this information in your own work according to your best judgment. There is nothing mysterious about the matter; it is just a natural process of learning and applying what is learned.

The most important step in beginning to improve your language habits is to watch your own speech and writing to see what their good qualities are and what shortcomings they may have. Can you confidently pronounce the words you need in conversation or recitation? Does your language tend to be Formal, or is it predominantly Informal or General? Do you rely too much on slang or on trite words, or do you lapse into Nonstandard expressions? When you talk or write to someone older than yourself or when you write a paper for a college course, do you choose the best part of your natural language, or do you assume an entirely different sort of English?

And, finally, is the language you use consistent with the rest of your conduct? If you are a rather casual person, informal in dress and manner, we should expect your English also to be somewhat Informal; if you are conventional in dress and manner, we should expect your English to be more Formal. It is necessary for you also to realize the direction in which you are moving, for young people, especially in college, are changing, becoming more flexible in their ideas and manners or more positive and conventional, or making some other change. Their language should be moving similarly. In your first papers in a composition course you should write as naturally as you can, so that both you and your instructor can see the present state of your language and so that you can decide together on the direction your growth should take. Such growth will in part be in the direction of increased sincerity, of greater appropriateness to yourself.

As a result of this approach to Good English you should have confidence in writing. The greatest handicap in writing is fear—fear of pencil and paper, fear of making a mistake, fear of offending the reader's (teacher's) taste. The opposite attitude, cockiness, is a nuisance and is equally at odds with good writing, but not so many students suffer from that as from inhibitions about their language. As yet psychologists can't tell us much about the mental activity involved in thinking or writing, but some of them believe that the fundamental condition for effectiveness is a positive feeling of readiness—which amounts really to a sort of faith that when you prepare to write, language appropriate to the occasion will come. A wide knowledge of the possibilities of current English, backed up by sufficient practice in writing for definite readers and sufficient care in revision, should increase your confidence. Only with such confidence can you write your best and give that extra something that places your writing above mere competence, that makes it really Good English.

It is obvious that the three sorts of appropriateness here suggested for arriving at Good English (appropriateness to the subject and situation, to the listener or reader, and to the writer or speaker) will not always be in harmony. When they conflict, the solution will have to come through the writer's judgment. The subject may seem to demand words that are not appropriate to the reader. The writer can usually solve such a problem either by finding simpler words or by explaining the necessary but unfamiliar ones. The reader's expectation and the writer's natural manner of expression may be different. Such a conflict can be solved by the writer—deciding how essential to his purpose his own turns of expression are, whether he can honorably yield to the reader's expectation or whether his usage is so necessary to his sense of the subject that compromise is impossible. In the long run the writer's sense of fitness, his pride in his work, will resolve most such conflicts.

Good English, then, is not primarily a matter of rules but of judgment. You are not struggling under a series of prohibitions; you are trying to discover among the magnificent resources of modern English what best suits your purposes. Your desire to communicate something is fundamental; it sets the limits beyond which you will not ordinarily go. This general limitation is made more specific by considering whether the variety of usage and the particular expressions are appropriate to the subject and the situation, to your expected readers, and, finally and most important, to yourself.

Chapter 1

SUGGESTED STUDY AND WRITING

1. Study the language in the following passages and decide what variety of English (see table, pp. 18-19) is used in each. Be prepared to cite particular words and expressions that support your decision. Comment on the appropriateness of the language to the subject and to the people who would probably read it.

A) Greenwich Village in New York is one place where a man can see a white horse looking out of a third-story window and believe his eyes. The horse is Muzzle, a 20-year-old gelding who spends most of his time pulling a bakery cart and lives in a four-story stable that is just below Washington Square. The floors are joined by a gently inclined ramp. Muzzle's master, who rents horsedrawn carts to peddlers, has put the carts on the top and bottom floors. The horses are kept on the floors between. Muzzle, who has been working for his master for about six years, is a privileged tenant. He occupies a stall with a view.–*Life,* Dec. 9, 1957, p. 172. Courtesy *Life* Magazine. Copr. 1957 Time Inc.

B) I'll put a stop to this once and for all! Next time I see her we'll have this thing out. Won't pull any punches either–give it to her straight from the shoulder–instead of freezing into a polite smile and nodding my head as if I agree with everything she says. After all, why should I take it? Bet a dollar if I took her precious second graders into the art room and taught them to say "ain't" or convinced them that two and two are five, she'd blow her stack. She'd be right of course–but that's exactly the point. She's the expert in her field, and I have to respect her judgment. If I did something contrary to what she thought was in the best interests of the kids, she'd let me know in nothing flat that my actions would not be tolerated.

Well, by gosh, I'm an expert too! And teaching 'em to say "ain't" is no more detrimental to their development than those darned color-book-type hectograph drawings she passes out for busywork every day.–JOHN C. BIGHAM, "Time to Get Tough with Busywork Art," *School Arts,* Nov. 1957, p. 18

C) In research centers, individual wishes for recognition are implemented by administrative imperatives, so that the intensity of competition and the large number of competitors multiply enormously the real and alleged contributions to the advancement of learning. That a strong emphasis upon scholarly productivity results in tremendous positive values from leading universities is generally known. That it also interferes with the performance of other functions and in marginal cases produces flamboyancy, exhibitionism, quantitativeness without regard for quality, and other results indirectly inimical to knowledge itself is not so generally acknowledged.

The patterning of higher education is such that even for those (the majority) who will engage primarily in teaching, graduate training means research training. When the social structures, functions, and evaluative methods of leading universities are indiscriminately copied in all sorts of institutions, chaotic consequences are inevitable. Equally productive of personal and institutional disorganization are the unstudied procedures imposed by administrative whim or faculty sentiment. To offset the wasteful division of labor and haphazard evaluative methods found in the present anarchic state of affairs, it is unquestionably high time that faculty committees as well as administrative officers should base their proposals and actions upon a more objective knowledge of social organization.—LOGAN WILSON, "The Functional Bases of Appraising Academic Performance," American Association of University Professors *Bulletin,* Oct. 1941, p. 449

D) That Flem Snopes. I be dog if he ain't a case, now. One morning about ten years ago, the boys was just getting settled down on Varner's porch for a little talk and tobacco, when here come Flem out from behind the counter, with his coat off and his hair all parted, like he might have been clerking for Varner for ten years already. Folks all knowed him; it was a big family of them about five miles down the bottom. That year, at least. Share-cropping. They never stayed on any place over a year. Then they would move on to another place, with the chap or maybe the twins of that year's litter. It was a regular nest of them. But Flem. The rest of them stayed tenant farmers, moving every year, but here come Flem one day, walking out from behind Jody Varner's counter like he owned it. And he wasn't there but a year or two before folks knowed that, if him and Jody was both still in that store in ten years more, it would be Jody clerking for Flem Snopes. Why, that fellow could make a nickel where it wasn't but four cents to begin with. He skun me in two trades, myself, and the fellow that can do that, I just hope he'll get rich before I do; that's all.—WILLIAM FAULKNER, "Spotted Horses," from *Scribner's Magazine,* June 1931, pp. 585-6

E) Magazine reading and reading in general have both been hard hit by television and still are—though there's been some improvement. Newspaper reading was never affected much and still isn't by TV. Newspaper circulation has steadily risen (probably proportionate to population rises) and the amount of time the individual spends reading his paper remains steady within a matter of a few minutes over the years. Radio listening, of course, was devastated in the early years, the percentage of evening listeners dropping from 60 per cent to 5 per cent, but it has bounced back to 16 per cent.

All these slight increases in visiting, movie-going, reading, and radio listening had to be matched by some decrease in average viewing time—and they were. But it was slight. New Brunswick people (and theoretically all of us) still spend an awful lot of evening hours looking at television—7½ hours weekly for children, 9½ for teen-agers, 13 hours for husbands, 14 for wives.—JOHN CROSBY, *New York Herald Tribune,* Jan. 12, 1958

F) The most thumbed items in Burrows' sanctum are the thirteen volumes of the Oxford English Dictionary and Skeat's authoritative etymological work, which Burrows has in two editions, concise and diffuse. If it weren't that the Oxford set weighs ninety pounds, he would carry it with him wherever he goes. "A good comedy writer has to be word-oriented," he says. Burrows' attitude toward words is both ardent and ambivalent. While he deliberately salts his own speech with arrant solecisms, because he knows people find his grammatical sloppiness amusing, he is a purist when it comes to anybody else's use of words, and nothing pains him more than to have an associate not only condone but actually favor slovenly grammar. He still winces at the recollection of hearing an actor at one of the rehearsals of "Can-Can," for which he wrote the book, say "between you and I." Burrows gently remonstrated with the fellow, pointing out that the script read otherwise. "I know I didn't say the line the way you had it, Abe," the actor replied patiently, "and I know that my way probably sounds strange to you, but I wanted to get it right."—E. J. KAHN, JR., "The Easygoing Method" (A profile of Abe Burrows), originally published in *The New Yorker,* May 18, 1957, p. 41

2. Group the following words according to the varieties of English in which they would be typically used. Refer to the table on pp. 18-19 and consult a dictionary if necessary—it won't distinguish the four varieties but it will give you some hints. For those words which are not typical of General English, give the equivalent General word or expression.

abrogate	give up	rend
alto	hark	rev (verb)
aperture	hiccup	ruffled
blat	hungry	sidekick
blurt	jitters	smog
boughten	juggle	snide
can't hardly	mire	spunky
clomb	nope	therein
conniption	often	this-here
domicile	OK (verb)	thrombosis
drownded	passim	victuals
edit	perfectest	viewpoint
ere	pucker	wacky
feller	redd up	whence

3. With the help of the *Index* articles on the starred expressions, rewrite the following sentences in General English. Note that some expressions do not need to be changed.

1. They were a fine **appearing* couple, and seemed fond of **one another.*
2. The major **wants for* you to **try and* find his garrison cap.
3. He **need* not come to the meeting; **however,* he would be welcome.
4. **Between you and me,* the **heighth* of that tree, as George has measured it, can't be right.
5. He **most* always went into the subject **farther* than he really needed to.
6. A little **ways* over the hill, we **had better* pull off the road to **fix* the motor.
7. Even the second satellite didn't **faze* him.
8. After all that has **past* between them, how can you say that everything will be **alright?*
9. Maggie and **myself* can always **leave* our homework go till the last minute.
10. **Prior to* enrolling at Harvard, he was **graduated* from Groton with honors.

4. Look up in the *Index* three matters of usage that have already attracted your attention, either in your own speech or writing or in something you have heard or read. (If you don't find a separate entry for the item, it may be included under a general heading, such as *Plurals or *Principal parts of verbs.) Make notes of what you find and be prepared to contribute to a class discussion on how to use this book to answer questions about English usage.

5. Read the following passages from student writing. In each case, decide what variety of English seems appropriate to each subject and then revise the language of each example to make it more consistent.

1. "Look, Dad," cried the excited boy. The disconcerted adult turned from his conversation with a peanut vendor in time to see the object of his son's delight. Down on the floor of the arena, two fast-breaking guards were bearing down on the basket. All that stood between them and the goal was a single defensive man. Again the youngster's voice broke the air, "They're going to score. It's two points for us!"
2. A new word, unfamiliar to the reader, can also cause great difficulty in spelling. This word should be looked up previous to its use. It should, moreover, be written and learned to facilitate its correct spelling henceforth.
3. Just then I heard the bell–the last bell signifying that class was to convene. I dashed into the classroom and tried desperately to relax and make myself think that he probably wouldn't call on me anyway. Even if he did, he couldn't flunk me for answering one little question wrong. But it was to no avail; the second question he asked was pointed right at me.
4. Alfred was waiting for me in the hotel lounge, and as he walked toward me, I noticed how handsome he looked in his sharp black suit.

5. Oftentimes, when I was a junior in high school, my dad picked me up after classes to go fishing. Those many afternoons spent on a sun-warmed bank drew us close together in a kindly father-son relationship. It mattered not that we caught no fish. His stories and presence made those outings profitable to my maturing young mind.
6. Then I remembered Jerry's accident and what can happen to a young person when he starts messing around on a public highway that wasn't meant for racing.
7. Cress didn't want to come home to see her grandfather when he was real sick because she didn't want any unmerited invasion of her privacy.
8. It has been affirmed that student government is a democratic organization and all democratic organizations institute effective employment of parliamentary procedure. Parliamentary procedure is necessary to hold down confusion in meetings and discussions.

6. Answer these questions, indicating the influence your environment and reading habits may have had on your present use of English:

1. Where did you grow up?
2. What places have you lived in long enough to have some impression of the language used in them?
3. Are you conscious of any specific influences on your speaking and writing–particular people, teachers, books, English courses, work?
4. Characterize your typical speech and writing in terms of the varieties of usage. If your speech deviates from General usage, give examples of words, pronunciations, and constructions which you habitually use.
5. Are there any localisms current in your region that might not be appropriate in General English?
6. What foreign languages, ancient or modern, do you know something of (and about how much)?
7. What kind of books and what writers do you read by preference? What periodicals?
8. Do you regularly read a newspaper? What sections (including comic strips)?

7. Prepare one of the following assignments:

A) Copy from a book or magazine, giving full reference to its source, a good paragraph showing either Formal or General usage. In the margin comment briefly on any distinctive words or constructions.

B) Analyze a sample of the writing of a well-known columnist. Characterize the level of usage and the style of writing, the columnist's attitude toward his readers, and the appropriateness of the language to the subjects discussed. What are your impressions of the columnist's personality as it is reflected in his writing?

C) Make a study of the way one of your textbooks is written. Does the author seem to be writing for students of your educational level, or does the approach seem too advanced or too elementary? Select a passage you find hard to understand; try to decide whether the difficulty is due to the style of writing, to the language used, or to the complexity or unfamiliarity of the ideas. Choose a passage which seems to illustrate the variety of English used throughout the book; what words and constructions led you to your choice?

8. Keep a speech notebook and write down characteristic campus expressions, slang, phrases, pronunciations. When you have gathered sufficient material, write a paper on the student speech at your college. Comment on differences you have observed between the levels of speech used by college students inside the classroom and outside.

Words and sentences are subjects of revision;

paragraphs and whole compositions are subjects of prevision.

BARRETT WENDELL

Chapter **2**

Writing and revising sentences

Sentences, not words, are the essence of speech,

just as equations and functions, and not bare numbers,

are the real meat of mathematics. . . .

As we shall see, the patterns of sentence structure that guide words

are more important than the words.

BENJAMIN LEE WHORF

One aim of a composition course is to help you develop the habit of preparing acceptable manuscript copy, copy that will represent your best efforts and that will receive favorable attention from anyone who reads it. This chapter and the next one deal with some elementary but important matters in written English.

It is useful to begin with sentences—they are clearly marked, conspicuous units that include the other, smaller units, and you need to be competent in handling them. The steps which will help you improve your sentences (as well as other elements of your writing) are definite and simple.

1. *Know what is appropriate to General English—the form or phrase or sentence pattern that is most commonly used by educated people.* You learn what is good spoken English by listening to good conversation, talks, and lectures; you learn what is good written English by reading it in books and magazines and by looking up words in a dictionary or studying the descriptions of usage in a reference book such as this. To analyze sentences and their parts and understand the criticisms made of your writing, you will need a few of the most useful terms of grammar (*subject, verb, complement,* and so on). Be sure that you can identify the mistakes named in the margins of your papers: fragmentary sentence, comma fault, dangling modifier, or whatever. You won't need the whole vocabulary of English grammar to discuss the most important points, but you will need a selection of it, as it is used in these chapters. (Further discussion of these terms and additional examples will be found in *Index* articles.)

2. *Train yourself to proofread your papers carefully enough to find your mistakes, in the final copy as well as in the early draft.* Proof-

reading your papers requires primarily a habit of attention to the written marks on the paper. Ordinarily we read for subject matter, and as writers we are naturally so familiar with what we have written that we often read it over too rapidly to see the details of spelling or punctuation or phrasing. You may for a time have to do something special to slow your reading and fix your attention on details, like holding a pencil point or a card just below the line to help you concentrate on every mark. If you are not sure of some particular point–spelling, pronouns, comma faults, for example–go over your paper once looking for that point alone. Proofread your papers for other courses, too–it will help them as well as your work in English. Finding and correcting mistakes in all your written work is your responsibility.

3. *Revise the faulty sentences you find in proofreading so that they will meet the readers' expectations.* Leave plenty of space in your first draft for making revisions. If you find something in the final copy that needs changing, make the change neatly between the lines. Care in revising will pay dividends, both in improved grades and in personal satisfaction, and it will eventually help you form habits of writing more correctly in the first draft.

Fortunately the greater part of our language raises no questions, but the problems that do arise can cause mistakes that are conspicuous and easily spotted by others. This chapter reviews the most important grammatical characteristics of English sentences in order to give some guidance in discussing and writing sentences. (Other aspects of sentences are taken up in Ch. 7.)

The favorite English sentence

We use sentences so continually and so unconsciously that studying them may seem artificial and perhaps even irritating. But sentences can be studied profitably, and in order to revise them and to discuss our own or anybody else's sentences, we have to examine them and sometimes identify their parts.

In speech, sentences are marked by various sorts of stress, pitch, and pause that we use and understand automatically. *This is mine,* for example, can be said quietly, with a falling voice, so that it could be written with a period; or more intensely, so that an exclamation point would be appropriate; or with a rising inflection, making it a question; or it can be said as part of a sentence, as in "This is mine, I think." *Yes* can be said so that it will mean to a listener anything from "You are absolutely right" to "I don't really believe what you are saying."

In written sentences these qualities of voice are necessarily lost, and to make his sentences clear a writer must often revise them in the light of his intention and according to the conventions of form and punctuation found in published material. About all we can say is that a written sentence is what a person with some experience in the language intentionally punctuates as a sentence—that is, what he begins with a capital letter and ends with a period, question mark, or exclamation mark. This means that sentences are to a certain extent a matter of judgment, certainly of choice among a variety of possibilities. In fact they are so individual that sometimes a writer cannot see why someone else objects to a particular one he has written. But the more we know about the typical sentence forms, the easier it is to describe our specific sentences and come to an agreement about them.

The pattern most commonly used ("the favorite English sentence," as Jespersen has called it) is centered on a subject and a verb. But it may have other words in various relations to these and more than one subject-verb construction in a single sentence, so that these simple elements can be used to build a large variety of sentences. For convenience in describing the parts of sentences, we can indicate the elements by letters and mark three levels of relation—main, secondary, and third.

Main elements

The typical English sentence is composed of a *subject* (S), the starting point of the statement, and a *verb* (V) or a *linking verb* (LV), sometimes called "copula" (*be, become, feel, seem*). This subject-verb construction may be continued by an *object* (O) or by an object and an *indirect object* (IO); the subject-linking verb construction is continued by a *complement* (C), which may be either a noun or an adjective.

These examples show the main elements in ordinary patterns:

S	V
Alex	laughed.

S	V	O
They	bought	a sailboat.

S	LV	C
Harold	felt	tired.

S	LV	C
The highest ranking student	becomes	valedictorian.

S	V	IO	O
Mrs. Pennoyer	bought	him	a dozen eggs.

S	V	O
He	said	that they ought to know better.

In the last sentence the object, *that they ought to know better,* is a clause with a subject and a verb of its own, but it serves the same grammatical function as a single word. In English, word groups often function as single words do.

Sentences with *anticipatory subjects* (AS), as in *there is, it is,* have the actual subject after the verb:

AS	LV	C	S
It	is	hard	to know who is right.

AS	LV	S	C
There	are	five	in bloom.

Each part of a divided phrasal verb may be labeled V:

S	V		V
They	had	already	parked.

Secondary elements

Words, phrases, and clauses that are not one of these main elements may be related to the sentence as modifiers of one of the main elements (The *highest ranking* student becomes valedictorian). These secondary elements, modifiers, may be indicated by M: adjective elements modifying the subject (MS), the object (MO), or the complement (MC); adverbial elements modifying the verb (MV) or the whole sentence (MS).

MS	S	V	O	MV
Coming into the open,	he	could see	the tracks	plainly.

MS	S	MS	V	MO	O	MV
The high school	orchestra,	which was directed by Mr. Appley,	played	two	numbers	between each act.

MS	S	V	O
Certainly,	he	knew	it.

(This differs from "He certainly knew it," in which *certainly* modifies *knew.*)

MS	S	LV	MV	LV	MC	C
If we take motive into account,	the crime	does	not	seem	so	serious.

Third elements

Other words may be related to the pattern of the sentence by modifying the secondary elements (The *local* high school orchestra, *more* plainly). Since their relationship to the secondary elements is like that of secondary elements to the main, there is no need for a separate symbol for them, but if it is necessary to indicate the relationship, another M (MMS for *modifier of modifier of subject,* for example) can be used:

MMS	MS	S	V	MMV	MV
The local	high school	orchestra	played	unusually	well.

There may be further degrees of modification (An almost | completely | accurate | description), but since the fundamental relationship is the same, it is rarely worth while regarding them as a separate rank in describing the movement of the sentence.

Completing the sentence analysis

A pattern for analyzing sentences completely would be extremely complicated. Fortunately, in discussing our writing we do not often need more items than those which have been presented. Some less common constructions, such as *appositives or *direct address, are described in articles in the *Index* part of this book.[1] In an analysis they may be labeled by their full names or by convenient abbreviations (AP, DA).

For discussing the general qualities of sentences it is not necessary to name the individual words of phrases and clauses that function grammatically as single words. The prepositions that introduce phrases and the conjunctions or relative pronouns that introduce clauses are not elements of the whole sentence but belong to the word groups in which they occur.

	MV	S	V	MV
Phrase:	Between the acts,	they	went out	for a smoke.

	MS	AS	LV	MV	S	MV
Clause:	When the party broke up,	there	were	still	six couples	there.

If a conjunction relates a sentence to the one before, it is an element of the sentence and can be indicated as a *sentence connective* (SCON).

A few other details of analysis will be brought out in later sections of this chapter.

Order of sentence elements

The effect of a sentence depends in part on the order in which its elements stand. The more elaborate the sentence is, the more important is the way it is built up.

The typical order of the main sentence elements is: subject–verb–object or complement.

S	V	O
Sixty students	got	permission to leave early.

[1] Throughout this book asterisks (*) indicate references to articles in the *Index*.

S	LV	C
Ash Wednesday	is	the first day of Lent.

No matter how many modifiers may be in the sentence, its basic pattern will usually be S–V–O. This typical order of sentence elements is such a fundamental part of English grammar that we ordinarily identify subjects and objects by their position before or after the verb respectively (Jim [s] beat Frank [o]).

One standard departure from this typical S–V–O order is *inversion,* in which the complement or an emphatic modifier of the verb stands first, followed by the verb and then the subject (C–V–S). Or the object or complement may precede the subject and verb (O–S–V).

C	S	LV	(appositive)
Foolish	he	was,	just plain foolish.

O	S	V	MV	V	MV
This book	he	was	now	reading	for the third time.

MS	V	S	V	O
Only then	did	he	realize	what he had done.

Inversion of subject and verb is the usual order in questions:

V	S	MO	O
Have	you	a few	minutes?

MS	V	S	V	O
Where	did	you	get	it?

V	S	V	O
Does	he	think	he can fool us?

The English habit of placing modifiers close to the words they modify is another important part of grammatical word order. Secondary elements should clearly refer to the words they modify; otherwise the reader may be momentarily confused.

Confusing order	*Clearer order*
But the principal disapproved of the petition and enforced the law which he had made *with the aid of the hall squad.*	But the principal disapproved of the petition and *with the aid of the hall squad* enforced the law which he had made.
The jury convicted the defendant of assault and battery *after deliberating two hours.*	*After deliberating two hours* the jury convicted the defendant of assault and battery.

These basic facts of word order are grammatical, because they are relatively fixed in English. Elements whose position can be varied are matters of style and are discussed in Chapter 7.

Kinds of sentences

It is conventional to classify sentences as simple, complex, compound, and compound-complex, according to the number and kind of subject-verb constructions they contain. Being able to recognize these types will prepare you for some of the particular topics in later sections of this chapter.

Simple sentences

A simple sentence contains one grammatically independent statement—that is, one independent subject-verb construction. About a third of published sentences are simple, but because of four kinds of possible elaboration they are not necessarily short.

Prepositional phrase modifiers. Almost every English sentence has one or more phrases introduced by prepositions:

> *From my experience in the Navy* I would divide the men into two groups.
>
> *After a few days of penicillin treatment* she was out of danger.
>
> A lathe operator must be highly skilled, *with years of experience.*

Verbid phrases. Phrases made with infinitives (the base form of a verb with *to*), participles (the *-ing*, or *-ed* form used as a modifier), and gerunds (the *-ing* form used as a subject or object)—all parts of a verb that do not make independent sentences—are common elements of simple sentences.

Infinitive phrases as subjects or objects or modifiers:

> As subject: *To review the whole course in three hours* wasn't easy.
>
> As object: He tried *to avoid work.*
>
> As modifier [of *efforts*]: His first efforts *to get a job* failed.

Participles as modifiers of subject or object:

> He watched them *going by in little groups.* (Modifies *them*)
>
> *Locked up like that,* he wasn't going to hurt anyone. (Modifies *he*)

Gerund phrases as subject or object:

> As subject [of *requires*]: *Proofreading your papers* requires a habit of attention to the written marks on the paper.
>
> As object [of *from*]: He got confidence from *knowing so much* about the subject.

Compound subjects. Two or more words may be the subject of a single verb:

> Finally *the husband* [s1], *wife* [s2], and *the two children* [s3] moved to the city.

Compound predicates. Two or more verbs may have the same subject:

> The husband *has aged* [v1] ten years in the last two and *looks* [v2] tired and unhappy most of the time.

Although these sentences contain several constructions, they have only one main clause and so are classified as simple sentences.

Compound sentences

A rather small proportion of sentences in printed material are compound—that is, made up of two or more clauses that might stand as independent sentences but that are joined together in equal grammatical rank.

With connectives. The majority of clauses in compound sentences are joined by one of three kinds of connectives: Coordinating conjunctions—*and, but, for, nor, or, yet;* Correlative conjunctions—*both ... and, either ... or, neither ... nor, so ... as, not only ... but (but also), whether ... or;* Conjunctive adverbs—*accordingly, also, besides, consequently, hence, however, indeed, namely, nevertheless, so,* and some others.

The first type is by far the most common:

> We had expected to get there by noon, *but* the radiator delayed us.

The chief danger is an overuse of *and* when some other connective, especially a subordinating conjunction, would be more exact (see p. 51).

Correlative conjunctions are not very much used in speaking or General writing, except for *either...or:*

> *Either* the postman hasn't come *or* there isn't any mail for us today.

Conjunctive adverbs are usually Formal words, out of place in short sentences—ordinarily *but* is better than *however*. In current writing they are more likely to connect two separate sentences than two parts of the same sentence:

> There is a growing body of evidence that no significant growth in personality is brought about by such education. *Indeed,* there is some good evidence that the contrary often occurs, and that the prolongation of formal education results in a deterioration of personality.—HENRY C. LINK, *The Return to Religion,* p. 145

Their connecting force is so weak that when used within a sentence the clauses are usually punctuated with a semicolon:

> Such contradictions provide us with no guide to action; *hence* they leave us with the tensions of indecision and bewilderment.—S. I. HAYAKAWA, *Language in Thought and Action,* p. 153

Without connectives. When there is no conjunction between the clauses of a compound sentence, the individual clauses are called *contact clauses.* The conventional punctuation between the clauses is a semicolon:

> In American sports, especially in baseball, the umpire is not respected; he is frequently challenged, and occasionally threatened by the players, and most frequently insulted by the partisan spectators. Nevertheless, it is the "umpire" aspect of the American government which meets with the least suspicion and contempt; the Supreme Court and its members are seldom suspected of improper attempts to increase its or their authority.—GEOFFREY GORER, *The American People,* p. 36

The two parts of these sentences are loosely related and in some styles would stand as separate sentences, but the writer wished to hold the ideas together and made them compound sentences. Professor Summey (see Bibliography) found that one fourth (102 out of 400) of the compound sentences in his materials had no connective. Of these, 75 were punctuated with a semicolon, 13 with a colon, and 5 with a dash. These marks all indicate a break almost as great as that between two sentences.

Complex sentences

Nearly half the sentences in current writing are complex, having one main clause and one or more subordinate clauses. (Professor Summey reports 44.5% complex sentences and 5.95% compound sentences in his passages.) We identify complex sentences by the words used to introduce and connect the subordinate clauses to the main clauses. These are either *relative pronouns* or *subordinating conjunctions.*

With relative pronouns. Many subordinate clauses are connected to the main clause by the relative pronouns *who, whose, whom, which, that, whoever,* and so on. These clauses either modify a noun in the main clause and are called *adjective clauses,* or they are subjects or objects or complements and are called *noun clauses.*

> Then there are the people *who are very unhappy* and *who do nothing at all to cover up their feelings.* (Two adjective clauses modifying *people*)
>
> He had no sense of *what was appropriate.* (Noun clause, object of the preposition *of*)
>
> The man *whom I met by accident* became a firm friend. (Clause modifying *man*)

This last type of clause is often made without the relative pronoun (The man *I met by accident* became a firm friend), but the construction is the same.

With subordinating conjunctions. Subordinate adverbial clauses are connected to the main clause by subordinating conjunctions, of which the most common are:

after	because	since	unless
although	before	so that	when
as	how	that	where
as if	if	though	while
as long as	in order that	till	why

Some men are sportsmen *because they have a lot of energy.*

When people watch a football game they try to keep their eyes on the man with the ball.

The subordinating conjunction *that* introduces noun clauses, usually as objects:

They didn't know *that the bell had rung.* (Object of *know*)

This type of clause is often made without the *that*: They didn't know *the bell had rung.*

Uses of complex sentences. Complex sentences are common in writing because they are more flexible than compound sentences, more varied, and–most important–more exact, because the subordinating conjunctions have more specialized meanings than the coordinating conjunctions listed on page 121. The following inexact sentences, with possible revised forms, will illustrate how careful subordination can make statements more accurate.

Inexact connection	*Revised*
Illustrations were given in every case *and* the plan was easily understood, which made it all the more interesting.	Illustrations were given in every case *so that* the plan was easily understood and all the more interesting.
The Stanley Steamer looked like one of those cars of the nineties in every way except its wheels, *and* they were changed so as to use pneumatic tires.	The Stanley Steamer looked in every way like one of those cars of the nineties except for its wheels, *which* were changed so as to use pneumatic tires.
Often a grave will contain no burial goods. Others might contain a few tools or beads. The latter is the more usual.	*Although* sometimes the graves will contain no burial goods, usually they will have a few tools or beads.
He may have attended both of the preceding classes, *and* by chapel time he begins to feel the desire for a respite from mental work.	*If* he has attended both of the preceding classes, by chapel time he begins to feel the desire for a respite from mental work.

Compound-complex sentences

A rather small number of sentences have two or more main clauses and one or more subordinate clauses. This student sentence has three subordinate clauses (introduced by *if, who,* and *if*) and two main clauses:

> If the reckless pilots who break these safety rules can be weeded out, and if the public can be educated to understand the light plane and the private pilot, [First main clause:] the fear of the small plane will disappear, [Second main clause:] and private flying may know the boom now enjoyed by the automobile.

Minor sentence types

The great majority of written English sentences belong to the "favorite" type, centered on a subject and a verb. But enough good sentences without one or both of these elements occur so that the definition "A sentence is a group of words having a subject and predicate" is not quite accurate, even for writing, and a realistic grammar must take account of the sentences without these elements. These minor sentence types are not to be confused with sentence fragments, discussed in the next section. Nothing is omitted from these sentences, and no words should be "understood" in analyzing them. They are natural forms of expression to be taken just as they are. When they appear in print, they are used deliberately and for a special purpose (for dialog, for emphasis, or to avoid colorless and repetitious verbs).

Subjectless sentences

Sentences without subjects are much less common than sentences without verbs. There are a few of a traditional pattern like *No sooner said than done,* and commands and requests (imperative sentences): *Don't let me ever hear you say that again. Please try.* Other subjectless sentences are confined almost entirely to narrative, in which the subject is easily carried over from the context, or to definitely Informal writing. This type of sentence is most appropriate in representing dialog in stories or in informal sketches of people:

> "Guess I can live on the town if I've a mind to. Been paying taxes for thirty years and more."—ERSKINE CALDWELL, *We Are the Living,* p. 219

They took no interest in civilized ways. Hadn't heard of them, probably.—CLARENCE DAY, *Life with Father,* p. 30

Verbless sentences

Several types of sentences without a main verb are common and in good if rather limited use in all varieties of speaking and writing. The verbs are not "left out"; they are not thought, spoken, or written. The statements are complete and independent without them.

Exclamations. One kind of verbless sentence is the exclamation, from *Ouch!* and other monosyllables to *What a mess!* and on to more intricately phrased statements of feeling.

Answers to questions. Another type is the answer, from *Yes* and *No* and *Not if I know it* to longer and more specific statements:

And what was the philosophy behind the Sherman Act and the Clayton Act? *Individualism, pure and undefiled. "The New Freedom" as President Wilson phrased it in literary language.*—C. A. BEARD, *The Myth of Rugged American Individualism,* p. 14

Descriptive details, added modifiers. Often in passages that are chiefly descriptive, especially if the details are given as impressions, the only verb possible would be a colorless *is* or *are* or *has* or *have.* Without a verb there is no loss of meaning and an actual gain in economy and sharpness.

And after all the weather was ideal. They could not have had a more perfect day for a garden-party if they had ordered it. *Windless, warm, the sky without a cloud.*—KATHERINE MANSFIELD, *The Garden Party,* p. 59

Often in passages portraying a character's thought the speed and naturalness of movement are increased when there are no verbs:

Principles—he mused—*au fond* were pocket; and he wished the deuce people wouldn't pretend they weren't! *Pocket, in the deep sense of that word, of course, self-interest as members of a definite community.* And how the devil was this definite community, the English nation, to exist, . . .—JOHN GALSWORTHY, *The White Monkey,* p. 3

Appositional sentences. The sentence in which an adjective or other modifier is set beside its noun without a verb is fairly common:

An understatement, this.—S. E. MORISON, *Harvard College in the Seventeenth Century,* p. 320

No verb no predication.—P. B. BALLARD, *Thought and Language,* p. 83

Appositional sentences sometimes serve as transitions:

So much for the proviso "English." Now for a more important proviso, that of "period or periods."—E. M. FORSTER, *Aspects of the Novel,* p. 21

Clauses and phrases. Occasionally expressions in the form of phrases or subordinate clauses stand alone as sentences. These are usually light in tone (*Which is another story*), or almost formulas (*Not that it matters*), or *because* or *which* clauses set off for emphasis:

There we are; now let us classify them. *Which he does.*—E. M. FORSTER, *Aspects of the Novel,* p. 27

Marks! Your marks had to be up to a certain standard. You had to get good marks to get promoted. *Into the next grade. Into high school. Into college.* Marks counted.—JOHN R. TUNIS, *Ladies' Home Journal,* Sept. 1938

The minor sentence types discussed in this section are entirely acceptable and appropriate in their contexts, but inexperienced writers should ordinarily avoid punctuating added modifiers or subordinate clauses and phrases as sentences.

Revising sentence fragments

Most sentences in published writing, especially in factual writing, are of the "favorite" type, with at least one main clause. Most subordinate sentence elements punctuated as sentences are sentence fragments (usually marked *Frag* in theme correction). While a phrase or subordinate clause is sometimes used as a sentence in certain contexts (see the preceding section), writers should avoid such constructions until they are certain of the difference between minor sentence types and sentence fragments.

Sentence fragments show by their form as well as by their incomplete meaning that they are parts of other constructions and are not meant to stand alone. Because readers rightly expect the form of statements to represent the actual relation of their parts, editors and teachers expect most sentences to fall into the typical S—V—O pattern.

There are three common types of sentence fragments, each to be spotted by a different test.

Explanatory phrases

Sentence fragments that are simply explanatory phrases are often introduced by *like* or *such as.* The test for these is to look for the verb

–there isn't any–and the remedy usually is to join the phrases to the preceding sentence.

Sentence fragment	*Revised*
After these cards have been run through, the firm knows what volume of business has been done during the week in each of the departments. *Such as tobaccos, candies, canned fruits, fresh produce.*	After these cards have been run through, the firm knows what volume of business has been done during the week in each of the departments, such as tobaccos, candies, canned fruits, fresh produce.
When I first arrived all was quiet, but soon men began to gather with their dinner pails. *Some on foot, others in wagons, and the higher class in Model T Fords.*	When I first arrived all was quiet, but soon men began to gather with their dinner pails, on foot, in wagons, and the higher class in Model T Fords.
Although air embolism is often mistaken for the bends, it is far more dangerous. *Not so much to the deep sea diver as it is to the shallow water and sport diver.*	Although air embolism is often mistaken for the bends, it is far more dangerous, especially to the shallow water and sport diver.

Participle phrases

In identifying participle phrases as sentence fragments, remember that the *-ing* form of the verb by itself does not make an independent verb. (Combined with some form of *be* it can make a sentence, as in "The plane *was running* on three engines.") The test here is to look at the verb form, and the remedy is either to join the phrase to the preceding sentence or to complete the verb.

Sentence fragment	*Revised*
Looking carefully through his water glass he finds a liner deep in the quicksand, lying on her side. *The nearest porthole being twelve feet down.* He dives down to the porthole and tries to break it.	Looking carefully through his water glass he finds a liner deep in the quicksand, lying on her side, her nearest porthole twelve feet down. He dives down to the porthole and tries to break it.
At the end of each reporting period each subject was marked numerically, on the basis of one hundred. *The Deportment column covering the behavior of the child.*	At the end of each reporting period each subject was marked numerically, on the basis of one hundred. The Deportment column covered the behavior of the child.
The jobs the machinist does in this shop vary considerably. *Anything from making a bolt to*	The jobs the machinist does in this shop vary considerably, from making a bolt to cutting a

cutting a gear twenty feet in diameter.	gear twenty feet in diameter.

Subordinate clauses

In subordinate clauses punctuated as sentences there is a subject and verb, but the construction is introduced by a subordinating connective. The test is to look for a relative pronoun (p. 50) or one of the subordinating conjunctions listed on page 51. If the "sentence" consists only of such a clause, it should be joined to the preceding or following sentence or made into an independent sentence.

Sentence fragment	*Revised*
At the time my old rowboat with its three horsepower motor seemed to be a high-speed job to me. *Although it only attained a speed of about twelve miles an hour.*	At the time my old rowboat with its three horsepower motor seemed to be a high-speed job to me, although it only attained a speed of about twelve miles an hour.
Leather-Stocking was first drawn as an old man and his youth described last of all. *While the other periods of his life were filled in in a very erratic order.* Yet he is the same character from beginning to the end.	Although Leather-Stocking was drawn first as an old man and the other periods of his life were filled in in a very erratic order, his youth the last of all, he is the same character from beginning to end.

In the following examples, contrast the two *because* clauses, the first of which seems stable because it is in direct answer to a question, the second not stable because it directly explains the preceding statement and should be joined to that statement:

> Why? Because service and ethics are service and ethics, and the business of business is business.
>
> This had been a more happy season for me. Because I now had my own boat and I thought I was on my way to bigger and better outfits.

Revising comma faults

The terms "comma fault," "comma blunder," or "comma splice" are applied to written sentences made up of two main clauses separated by a comma that is felt to be too weak to show the actual degree of separation. (If there is not even a comma between the clauses, the mistake is sometimes called a "fused sentence." This is not really a different mistake but simply a grosser carelessness on the part of the writer.) Comma faults are relatively easy to identify. You look first to see how many main subject-verb constructions you have in a group of words punctuated as a single sentence. If there are two main clauses, you look to see if you have a connective between them.

In the following "sentence" three constructions with a subject and complete verb (and so capable of standing as separate sentences) are run together without any connective and with only commas separating them:

> Their future looked pitifully black, they were working and getting nowhere, instead of profiting by their labors they were losing.

In reading this aloud, your voice might not pause much at the first comma, but the second demands a full stop; in reading silently we can get by the first comma, but the second is pretty jarring. Punctuated as three sentences it becomes readable, though not very smooth:

> Their future looked pitifully black. They were working and getting nowhere. Instead of profiting by their labors they were losing.

There are four principal ways to revise comma faults: subordinating one or more clauses, rephrasing to make a single main clause, adding a connective, or repunctuating.

Subordinating one or more clauses

Probably most of the comma faults in student writing occur because the writer has written two main clauses for what should have been a main and a subordinate statement with the relationship between them clearly indicated.

One of the commonest types of comma faults uses a noun or a personal or demonstrative pronoun (*he, it, they, this, that*) instead of a relative pronoun (*who, which*):

Comma fault	*Revised*
The *Ranger's* crew is made up of 26 professional sailors, *most of them* are of Scandinavian ancestry.	The *Ranger's* crew is made up of 26 professional sailors, *most of whom* are of [*or:* most of them of] Scandinavian ancestry.
While a boy lives at home he is dependent on others, *they* help him out of his difficulties and provide at least for his necessities.	While a boy lives at home, he is dependent on others *who* help him out of his difficulties and provide at least for his necessities.

Making one statement

Many comma faults are due simply to separating ideas that should be written as one statement:

Comma fault	*Revised*
One part receives the stimulus from outside and transmits the impulse to the cell, *this is known as the dendrite.*	One part, *known as the dendrite,* receives the stimulus from outside and transmits the impulse to the cell.
The pressmen were a good-natured bunch *who seldom complained about their conditions, instead they usually joked about them.*	The pressmen were a good-natured bunch *who usually joked rather than complained* about their conditions.

Another common type of comma fault is one in which a second verb is used in a construction that does not require it:

Then came the speeches, some of them *were* very amusing while others *were* very serious.	Then came the speeches, some of them very amusing, others very serious.

In each of these examples the thought seems to be single and rightly put in one sentence, but the connection between parts of the thought was not made close enough. Very often such sentences profit from more drastic revision than is shown in these examples.

Adding a connective

Sometimes inserting a conjunction in a comma fault sentence will make the sentence conventionally compound or complex:

Comma fault	*Revised*
I think it would do a lot of Americans good to read this book, they would get a background on which to form a more exact knowledge of the English people.	I think it would do a lot of Americans good to read this book *because* they would get a background on which to form a more exact knowledge of the English people.
This last piece of work was very difficult, the hacksaw blades grew hot and broke.	This last piece of work was so difficult *that* the hacksaw blades grew hot and broke.

Repunctuating

Only once in a while can a comma fault sentence be improved by the easiest (laziest) change, repunctuating with a period or a semicolon. Unless there is a connective, a semicolon ordinarily should not be used to correct a comma fault. It would not materially have helped any of the sentences given above.

In the first sentence below, and possibly the third, a semicolon would be useful. The second comma fault sentence might be helped by a period:

The vigilantes did not bother with courts, which might cause a wait of six months for satisfaction, [; better here] instead they hung their men as close to the scene of the crime as possible and left the body there as an example.

The long days of Front and Market streets were a thing of the past, [probably new sentence here] the store now opened for business at eight in the morning and closed at six-thirty, including Saturdays.

Business today does not wait for a young fellow to learn, [; or . depending on emphasis desired] if the new employee does not seem fitted for the job, another is found to take his place.

In reading all of these "sentences" aloud you would pause and "drop your voice" appreciably at the comma, which indicates that the clauses have the form and value of two separate sentences. To decide whether a semicolon or a period would be better, first consider whether the ideas are closely enough related to stand properly in a single sentence, and then whether the relationship has been shown.

Contact clauses

In books and articles by writers of high standing we occasionally find run-on sentences which have been passed by editorial copyreaders. Here are a few:

Men are said to be partial judges of themselves. Young men may be, I doubt if old men are.—T. H. HUXLEY, *Autobiography*

She loved Marise, nobody had a nicer little girl, nor a prettier.—DOROTHY CANFIELD, *Rough-Hewn,* p. 135

This is to be our vision of them—an imperfect vision, but it is suited to our powers, it will preserve us from a serious danger, the danger of pseudoscholarship. . . . They are gateways to employment, they have power to ban and bless. . . .—E. M. FORSTER, *Aspects of the Novel,* pp. 22, 24

Main clauses joined without pause or change in pitch are common in speech ("Hurry up, we'll be late"), and recently, with the increasing Informality of written style, they have become more common in writing. (Nine of Professor Summey's 102 contact clauses were separated only by commas.) One of the best ways to test such a run-on sentence is to speak it aloud in a natural tone. If at the end of the first clause your voice pauses and falls as it does at the end of a sentence, the comma is wrong, and the clauses should be written as two sentences or revised in some other way. If your voice does not drop ("They had to take him out finally, he was crying so loud") and if the two clauses read naturally with no more pause than ordinarily stands between two clauses of the same sentence, it may be a good sentence.

In addition to using this oral test, you should consider the closeness of the relation between the ideas of the two clauses. The punctuation between two contact clauses should represent the writer's intention. A period marks the greatest degree of separation. A semicolon between clauses means that the relation between them is closer than that between either of them and the statement preceding or following. A comma should mean that they are very closely related and that they can be spoken as one genuine sentence.

You should also consider the appropriateness of contact clauses to other features of your writing, and you should remember that there is a widespread prejudice against such contact clauses—editors do not often let them stand in matter they publish. They are almost always inappropriate in Formal English, which usually avoids definitely Informal constructions. Two contact clauses in the middle of a rather fully and formally developed passage will ordinarily seem a letdown, a bit of carelessness. They are rare, too, in discussions of ideas, even when the discussions are not very Formally written, because the writer intends to show relationships between statements, and that usually means linking them by specific connectives.

Contact clauses are most useful in easy, rapid narrative (factual or imaginative), in which the clauses are relatively short, approaching the short turns of speech, and in which relationships can be rapidly grasped without connectives. In fact connectives would often bring an unneeded note of Formality into such narrative.

These principles can usually help a writer decide in revising his manuscript whether he should let contact clauses stand or should rewrite them. To guard against carelessly run-on sentences (comma faults) in themes, some teachers ask students to mark contact clauses they wish to leave by a star or the word *intentional* in the margin.

Agreement of subject and verb

The verb is the key word in the typical English sentence, with the subject and object or complement the words most closely related to it. The relation between these three elements is most commonly shown by their position, by word order. In the typical sentence the subject precedes the verb and is the starting point of the statement (not necessarily the "doer"; see *Passive verbs). The object ordinarily follows the verb. If both subject and object precede, the first noun is the object (This *book* [object] *he* [subject] had written first). In some constructions the order is inverted:

In questions: *Have you* any kerosene? *Does he expect* us to read all that?

In some conditions [a Formal construction]: *Had he known* then what he knew now, he would have hesitated.

After emphatic adverbs: Never *have I seen* such a mess.

All these basic matters we pick up early and without conscious effort. The few trouble spots come from slight complications in a few particular constructions and from the fact that in several of these we tend to choose our verb forms because of the meaning, rather than the form, of the subject.

Compound subjects

Two or more words, usually connected by a conjunction, are frequently subjects of one verb.

1. Usually the verb with a compound subject is plural:

Pat and *Stan have* eyes of the same color.

Both the *grammar* and the *style* of advertising *vary* considerably from Formal English.

2. When the two words of a compound subject refer to the same person or thing or otherwise form a unit, the verb is usually singular:

The *philosopher and scientist was* in unusually good spirits that day. (But the verb is plural if the idea is not single: The *philosopher and the scientist* in Professor Werner's make-up *were* at odds on this question.)

New York City and vicinity was suffering from a strike of delivery truckmen.

Silver cuts like wood when the proper *tool and the proper technique is used.*

3. Singular subjects connected with *or* or *either . . . or* have a singular verb when the idea is clearly singular:

Either a dentist or a doctor is to treat such cases.

Frequently the idea is felt to be plural (especially in questions, where the verb precedes):

If *you or anyone else* want to come, there is plenty of room.

With negatives (*neither . . . nor*) the situation is similar, with the plural the more common:

Since *neither chemistry nor physics were required* [more Formal: *was required*], most students had no basic physical science.

4. When a singular subject is joined to a related noun by a preposition (*with, together with, as well as, in addition to*), the verb in Formal English and usually in General is singular:

That *decision,* as well as other precedents, *was* the deciding factor in the trial.

In General English, when the sense is obviously plural, the verb is sometimes plural:

The captain with these three teammates were given the credit.

And is usually the more natural connective, and simpler to handle, making a typical compound subject that would take the plural.

5. When the two elements of the subject are pronouns in different persons, the verb is usually plural:

You and I are sure to go, anyway.
Either you or he are likely to go. (*Is* is possible here to emphasize the singleness of the choice.)
Neither you nor I are fit for that job.

Collective subjects

Collective nouns are singular in form but refer to a group of objects or persons or acts: *army, athletics, committee, jury, public, team.* When the group is meant as a unit, the verb is singular; when the individuals are meant, the verb is plural:

The jury [as a group] *has been out* five hours.
The jury [the individual members] *have been arguing* for hours.

A number of terms of amount and measure have collective agreement, with the singular the more common:

Sixteen and a half feet makes a rod. (Or: *make* a rod)
Six tons was all we used to get.

Blind agreement

When a construction with a plural noun comes between a singular subject and its verb, there is a temptation to make the verb plural. Keep it singular.

1. Long intervening phrases or clauses containing plural nouns often conceal the real subject:

The state has hired men to see that *everything* that has the least contact with the milk, from the milker to the caps on the bottles, *is* spotless.

Here and there a *man* such as Columbus, Galileo, and others *has* ventured into the unknown physical and intellectual worlds.

Occasionally a *blitzkrieg* of apples and pillows, followed by water fights, *disturbs* our floor until early morning.

2. A short dependent phrase, especially an *of* phrase closely related to the singular subject, frequently causes trouble:

I decided to see exactly how *one* of these present-day cars *is* put together.

Memory of summer heat and summer friends soon *fades* in the first exciting days of the college year.

Words like **type, part, series, *kind, *number,* likely to be followed by a plural phrase, are particularly troublesome:

The greater *part* of their inventions *has* no economic importance.
A *series* of articles *was* planned, written, and published.

In spoken usage and in a good deal of General writing a plural verb is found after these closely knit phrases because their sense is plural. Appropriateness to your writing is important in such constructions, though in college writing it is perhaps best to play safe and follow Formal usage.

3. Relative clauses introduced by *who* or *that* or *which* have verbs agreeing with the pronoun's antecedent:

A skunk *that has been captured* young makes a good pet.
Skunks *that have been captured* young make good pets.

In sentences containing the construction **one of those who,* Formal usage has a plural verb for *who* because its antecedent (*those*) is plural; General usage more often has a singular because the main idea is singular:

Formal: Dad is one of those men *who see through* people at the first meeting.

General: Dad is one of those men *who sees through* people at the first meeting.

Subject–complement

When the subject and the complement are of different numbers, the verb should agree with the subject:

Our chief *trouble was* [not: *were*] the black flies that swarmed around us all during the trip.
The *material* for a good story *is* the experiences of the early settlers.
The territory comprised what *is* [not: *are*] now Texas and Oklahoma.

Subject of gerunds

The subject of a gerund (an *-ing* verb form used as a noun) is either in the genitive or the objective form. The genitive is more common with pronouns. With nouns the genitive form is sometimes used, but the common form is more usual:

They had never heard of *his asking* for such a privilege.

They had never heard of a person [less common: *a person's*] asking for such a privilege.

Ordinarily use whichever seems the more natural. (See *Gerunds for further distinctions.)

Revising dangling modifiers

The verbid constructions made with participles, infinitives, and gerunds are usually modifiers, either of individual words or of whole statements:

Infinitive: The easiest way *to loosen a screw top on a jar* is to thump it a few times on the floor. (Modifies *way*)

Participle: *Coming suddenly to a dead end street,* we had to start all over again. (Modifies *we*)

Gerund: *In painting four of these pictures,* he used his wife as model. (Modifies *he*)

Dangling verbid phrases

In the examples just given, the phrases are closely related to the rest of the sentence, because the verbid directly relates to a word in the main construction. When the relationship is faulty, the phrase is misrelated or *dangling.* In the following sentences the italicized phrases seem to modify words that they cannot sensibly modify:

By darting through clouds and keeping themselves well hidden, the enemy battleships are taken by complete surprise. (The phrase actually refers to the airplanes mentioned in a preceding sentence.)

Hit in the neck by a squashy snowball, memories of those distant winters in Wisconsin came crowding back to him.

He knew what to do when the first frost set in *to prevent the walls from cracking.*

The difficulty may come from the position of the phrase, as in the last sentence; or it may be that a different construction, such as a clause, would be more natural, as in the second example (When he was hit in the neck by a squashy snowball); or the trouble may arise from an unfortunate choice of subject for the main clause, since the second sentence would be all right if the main clause was "he remembered those distant winters in Wisconsin."

The verbid phrases that distract the reader, puzzle him even briefly, or obviously break a sentence into two parts instead of making it a unit are dangling and should be rewritten.

"Absolute" verbid phrases

Many verbid modifiers, though objected to by those following strict "rules" of agreement, are actually clear and not misleading. Such verbid phrases really rank as subordinate clauses. A number of verbs for mental activity are generally so used, especially when the main statement is impersonal:

> *Considering that they were handmade,* the price was reasonable enough.

The most common use of the absolute phrase is for a detail added after the main sentence:

> The two men strolled unconcernedly down the street, *their outlandish costumes making everyone turn his head to look at them.*

These constructions require judgment. Some writers will find that following strict agreement is the easiest way, but most will prefer using the natural expressions when they are not misleading or awkward. (See *Dangling modifiers and *Absolute phrases for further examples.)

Making constructions consistent

A number of matters of tidiness can be grouped under the head of consistency. In general, notions of the same value in a statement should be in grammatical constructions of the same sort and the same value; that is, they should be in "parallel constructions." A beginning writer is sometimes not sensitive to little shifts in construction, but with practice he can cultivate a sensitiveness to his words as words. Formal writing is more insistent on parallelism than is conversation or General writing; but similar expressions for similar notions help hold any sentence together and make for clear and easy understanding.

Several matters of consistency have been treated in earlier sections of this chapter. Here two general sorts are brought together.

Shift in approach to the statement

Although it is not always necessary for the two clauses of a compound or a complex sentence to be of the same pattern, shifts frequently keep them from being a neat unit.

Not consistent	*Consistent*
1. SHIFT IN SUBJECTS	
Perhaps *one* should not com-	Perhaps I should not com-

plain, but I would like a little more recognition.	plain, but I would like a little more recognition.
Tires should be checked for pressure at least once a week, and *you* should move them to different wheels every few months.	Tires should be checked . . . and moved . . .; or: You should check tires . . . and move them . . . .
2. ACTIVE–PASSIVE VERBS	
Therefore the group does not work together [active] and a minimum of accomplishment is expected [passive].	Therefore the group does not work together or expect to accomplish anything.
3. PERSONAL–IMPERSONAL	
He immediately told his companions of the vast amount of water power these falls represented, and since they were a thrifty lot, it was decided to import a herd of sheep and manufacture woolen blankets.	. . . and since they were a thrifty lot, they decided to import a herd of sheep and manufacture woolen blankets.

Shift in grammatical rank

In longer pairs or series of constructions having the same relation in a sentence, the grammatical value and usually the individual components of the construction should be similar.

Shifted constructions	*Consistent (parallel)*
Dad took us aside and gave us a pep talk on sportsmanship [noun] and to remember [infinitive] that even on opposing teams we were still brothers.	. . . and told us to remember . . . Or: . . . a pep talk on sportsmanship and on remembering [verbal noun] . . . .
I noticed that I was sweating very freely, not because of the climate, but because of being nervous.	. . . but because of nervousness.
By employing these various methods–combination, predatory competition, rebates from railroads, and having influential friends where they were needed –John D. Rockefeller in 1878 came to control 95% of the petroleum industry of the country.	. . . and the use of influential friends where they were needed . . . .
An illustration of politics in the service is in the experience of two brothers from my home town, one with no education	

after high school and the other has a doctor's degree.

... and the other with a doctor's degree.

Any young man who likes a little adventure and to save money at the same time will find working on an ore freighter ideal.

... who likes a little adventure and who wants to save money ....

Making statements meaningful

Youngsters and people without much feeling for their language use sentences in a rather random way; their sentences are likely to be "choppy" or else to "run on and on." More mature writers develop a sense of the sentence as a unit and succeed in holding together the small phrases of their thought so that a reader sees not only *what* the writer had in mind but *how* his thoughts are related to one another. This section offers some ways to make *what you write* express more directly *what you mean.*

Too little meaning

Length of sentence is primarily a matter of style: a writer has a wide choice among short, average, and relatively long statements. (See "Range in sentence length," p. 179.) But regardless of length, each sentence should further the meaning of the composition. Amateur writers sometimes let sentences stand that say little or nothing, that don't give the reader his money's worth, as in these examples:

> My first course in math was taken at Riverside High School in Milwaukee. This was first-year or elementary algebra.

The reader feels that he is not getting full value from the individual sentences. It might go: I took my first course in math, elementary algebra ....

> Now what business does need is some good, sound supervision. Many laws have been passed. The Sherman Anti-trust forbade monopolies.

Of course "Many laws have been passed." Perhaps the writer meant "Among the many laws passed attempting to regulate business, the Sherman Anti-trust Act. . . ."

> There were also several groups which were campaigning for the Senator in this election. These groups in the election of 1952 were for the most part unheard of.

Of course there were several groups campaigning; the first sentence has not advanced the idea at all. Perhaps the writer meant "Several groups that campaigned for the Senator were almost unheard of in 1952."

Some useful but commonly overlooked methods of packing more into a single sentence are:

Series. Two or three details instead of one give more meaning per sentence:

> It is not *newspapers, radio scripts, and movies* that spoil our tongue so much as *textbooks, official documents, commencement speeches, and learned works.*—JACQUES BARZUN, *Teacher in America,* p. 55
>
> Oxford men are *no more brilliant, no better looking, no more cultured and possessed of no greater inherent ability* than countless undergraduates of American universities; but they think they are.—KENNETH ROBERTS, *For Authors Only,* p. 350

Compound predicates. Using two or more verbs for a single subject often makes it unnecessary to have several short sentences of little meaning:

> Under the foregoing circumstances, how may the playwright *do his work, maintain his integrity,* and *manage to survive* economically?—WILLIAM SAROYAN, "Confessions of a Playwright," *Tomorrow,* Feb. 1949, p. 19

Modifiers. The most common way of making sentences mean more, and the one most neglected by amateur writers, is a greater use of phrases and clauses that make particular words or whole statements more exact:

> As we passed swiftly, the natives rushed out on the shaky, board-and-log bridges, staring in wonder, the women with babies astride of their hips, the copper-skinned children now and then tumbling into the water in their excitement.—WILLIAM BEEBE, *Jungle Peace,* p. 85
>
> This nation embraces an increasing number of middle-sized cities, large enough to make metropolitan gestures and to entertain metropolitan pretensions, yet small enough to become infuriated over the same neighborhood matters which stirred the passions of the ancestral Four Corners settlement.—DUNCAN AIKMAN, *Harper's Magazine,* April 1925, p. 513

When you revise your papers, combine statements of little meaning into more complete ones or add informative details to statements that seem flat, so that each sentence is effective in its own right.

Interfering with advance of meaning

Three types of statement definitely interfere with the advance of thought:

Two statements for one. Amateur writers frequently say in two statements what could be said more effectively in one, so that a reader has to do more rearranging of the thought than he should.

Two statements	*One statement*
It was three or four miles to the nearest village and these people used to walk it at least once a day.	These people used to walk the three or four miles to the nearest village at least once a day.
This is only a typical example; the author has more examples.	This is typical of the author's many examples.
When one is in the fresh air most of the time, as a hunter is, it tends to keep a person healthy and to develop his body.	Being in the fresh air most of the time, as a hunter is, tends to keep a person healthy and to develop his body.

Incongruous statements. A writer may put together details that do not seem to belong together, producing a sentence which may raise a question in the reader's mind or even confuse him.

As Byron is the poet of youth, it is appropriate that we should publish on March 1 the new and completely reset edition of his *Poems.*

Presumably *youth* and *March 1* are to be related in some way, but the association seems pretty far-fetched.

Lady Beaconsfield affectionately called him "Dizzy" and she did everything in her power to make him the success he was.

Combining a nickname and a wife's help in building a statesman's career can only make a reader smile. He cannot make the leap between the ideas thus presented, and the writer shouldn't ask him to.

He has a nervous habit of toying with the last two buttons on his vest when thinking and uses his deep voice to the best advantage when excited or angry.

Perhaps these two characteristics could be put together as signs of nervousness, but certainly they are too different to be connected simply by *and.* Two sentences would be easier to grasp.

Statements that cancel out. Amateurs write a surprising number of sentences in which one part cancels the other. These sentences come sometimes from an effort to put in a fact that doesn't quite belong, as in the first two examples, and sometimes from a clumsy attempt at qualifying a statement, as in the third:

Her marriage to another writer, who teaches at Harvard, may have some influence upon her style; *however there is no evidence to support this.*

To do Sicily, one might start in at Taormina and end up at Palermo, but father and I determined on doing it in the opposite direction, probably because it is convenient to take the overnight boat from Naples to Palermo.

The next day we visited the ancient mosques, where we tried to walk in sandals which fitted—*or rather refused to fit*—over our shoes.

In revising the sentences of a paper, see that the individual sentence and its various parts really advance the thought.

Fuzzy phrasing

Exact expression is partly a matter of direct phrasing. A general fuzziness in statements annoys and confuses readers:

Fuzzy phrasing	*Direct phrasing*
My own outlook on the subject of whether I gained or lost in my first semester is more inclined to be on the loss side of the argument.	I am afraid [or some such qualifying expression] that in my first semester I lost more than I gained.
Several of my family have died of cancer and I didn't know whether it was hereditary so I decided to find out.	I decided to find out whether cancer was hereditary, because several of my family had died from the disease.

Sometimes well-meant sentiment that might pass in conversation seems nonsensical when it is stated in writing:

When both the team and the student body are in there fighting and cheering till the final whistle, they really cannot be beaten, no matter what the score.

He has made mistakes, yes, but who hasn't; we must never criticize too severely a man who tries.

An elementary sort of fuzziness comes from subordinating the actual subject of the sentence.

Subject subordinated	*Subject clarified*
As for forwarding, it deals with the mail of persons who have moved out of the city.	*Forwarding* deals with the mail of persons who have moved out of the city.
I believe that *by adding fluorine to the water* it would be a great help to the younger children.	I believe that *adding fluorine to the water* would be a great help to the younger children.

Though the history of grammar shows that the satisfactory description of sentences is difficult, describing them is nevertheless much easier than providing rules for writing them effectively. One reason is that we are not conscious of individual sentences in speaking—and shouldn't very often be in writing. We can figure out the plan of a paper before writing, and we can see the general form of a paragraph in our mind before putting it on paper. But sentences are usually best written without too much conscious attention—*and then revised.*

The points that have been made in this chapter should be applied in revision, when you read over what you have written and can consider matters of form without interrupting the process of writing. Some analysis of sentences may be necessary to show how they are put together. One method of analysis is shown on pages 44-47: dividing a sentence into its smaller elements and then seeing how they are related.

Practice on the points that you have not mastered as you would practice a play in a sport or the use of a tool that you want to become skillful with. The exercises in this book will help you. More important is revising your papers according to the corrections and criticisms made on them. Most important of all is revising your papers for all courses before they are handed in. Read them aloud to see how they sound. Careful proofreading will cut down the number of mistakes surprisingly, for most college students know (or at least suspect) what good usage calls for. Taking the responsibility for your own usage in this way is the quickest way to improve your papers and to get full credit for your progress.

Chapter 2

SUGGESTED STUDY AND WRITING

1 *The favorite English sentence*

A) Make up a sentence using each of the patterns listed below. (Add as many secondary elements as you wish, but keep the *main* elements in the order specified.)

1. s-v
2. s-v-o
3. s-lv-c
4. s-v-io-o
5. as-lv-s
6. v-s-v-o
7. o-s-v
8. c-v-s
9. v-s-o
10. mS-v-s-v

B) Identify the *main* elements in the following sentences, for example:

s	v	o
The storm waves	reached	an enormous size.

1. Her ship leaves on the sixteenth.
2. They gave Bill their old television set.
3. It is impolite to chew with your mouth open.
4. I knew that this would happen.
5. Blue is your best color.
6. A pattern for completely analyzing sentences would be extremely complicated.

7. Would you support this foolish, impractical plan?
8. Knowing better is no excuse.
9. The rest of the story you can imagine.
10. Was Amelia Earhart an American?

C) Copy the following sentences, leaving space between the lines, and label the *main* and *secondary* elements described on pages 44-45.

Example:

SCON	MS	S	MS	v1
Then	the gray	ice	that had seemed so firm	broke

MV	v2	MV
with a crack	and surged	toward the shore.

1. The Soylake Company maintains a resort for the use of its employees.
2. The road seemed grayer and grayer as it stretched into the distance.
3. There were in every cottage three large, empty cans.
4. Seven or eight of the traitors have been tried at one time.
5. After they had paid their bills they gave the welfare society six dollars.
6. In each bed that she inspected were the forbidden slingshots.
7. Raised to the level of the sea, the ships would very soon be released from the locks.
8. Could he, though, give them so much time?
9. Moreover, it is never right to accept money from strangers.
10. Very old rockers, which are almost impossible to find now, can be refinished by enterprising collectors quite easily.

2 *Kinds of sentences*

A) Number the sentences in the last three paragraphs of this chapter, and then on a separate piece of paper label each one simple, compound, complex, or compound-complex.

B) This chapter has stated that nearly half the sentences in current writing are complex, about a third are simple, a smaller number are compound, and even fewer are compound-complex. Make a brief study of the sentences in six paragraphs of a current magazine or book, tabulating the relative frequency of the four kinds of sentences; then compare your findings with this estimate.

3 *Phrases and clauses*

A) In this passage identify the italicized phrases and clauses, point out which phrases are verbid (gerund, participle, or infinitive) and which are prepositional, and tell what each one modifies:

Advertisements are all like tacks (1) *placed in the road,* and the mind (2) *of the American consumer* is somewhat like an automobile tire. The outer layers (3) *of the tire,* (4) *made of black, smoke-cured apathy,* are resilient and hard (5) *to pierce.* But a good sharp tack can do it, and a superior tack can go on and puncture the inner tube. (6) *When that happens,* the consumer comes (7) *to a shuddering halt* and the man (8) *who put the tack in the road, or hired somebody else* (9) *to do it for him,* steps (10) *out of the bushes* and sells the consumer an icebox. There is nothing wrong (11) *with this*—most of the time the consumer needs the icebox anyway, and (12) *in buying it* he performs a function vital (13) *to the operation* (14) *of the economy.*—ROBERT GRAHAM, "Adman's Nightmare: Is the Prune a Witch?" *The Reporter,* Oct. 13, 1953

B) In this passage identify the italicized groups of words as prepositional phrases, verbid phrases (gerund, participle, or infinitive), or subordinate clauses (adjective, adverb, or noun). Tell what each modifies or how it is used.

(1) *For the better part* of a Sunday morning he crouched dangerously at the open cellar door, (2) *waiting for the rat to show his whiskers* (3) *which the rat was kind enough not to do.* Our two excellent cats were also staying inside, (4) *sitting complacently* and (5) *with some professional interest* directly behind my husband. The rat hunt was broken up (6) *when the kitchen door banged open* and Laurie crashed in with three friends to see (7) *how his father shot the rat.* Eventually, I suppose, the rat wandered off, (8) *although I do not see how he could conceivably have been frightened by the prospect* (9) *of being shot.* Probably he had never realized until then (10) *that he had strayed into a house with cats* and *children.* At any rate, my husband and the cats, (11) *hunting in a pack,* managed (12) *to bring down even better game;* it must have been about the Tuesday (13) *after the rat hunt* that our female cat, Ninki, (14) *who is something of a hunter,* caught a chipmunk. She has done this before and will do it again, although I am sure she will never again ask (15) *my husband to sit in with her.* —SHIRLEY JACKSON, *Life Among the Savages,* p. 31

4 *Sentence fragments*

Study the groups of sentences that follow; revise those which contain sentence fragments. Be careful to discriminate between fragments and minor sentence types (see pp. 52-56). Be prepared to justify your decisions and to describe the fragments as explanatory prepositional phrases, participle phrases, subordinate clauses, and so on.

1. He gave me the feeling that he didn't mind my slow steps with his larger, quicker ones. Even though he would sometimes have to wait for me.
2. The street is lined with open booths, some inside of huts but most set up on the open ground. Everything they need in order to live is sold there. Rice candy and other candies, which, no matter how long you eat them, can never compare with candy here.
3. The best theme from each group was then read to the class. This seemed to be very popular. I suppose, because we liked to hear what our friends had written and because it exposed us to a continuous flow of new ideas.
4. And when will the supply lines be re-established? Whenever the high command gives the signal to go ahead. But that may not be until May.

5. When Mary had closed the door she gave her verdict in no uncertain terms. "Nice shirt. Nice tie. But that horrible suit!"
6. If he continually makes mistakes and in general runs the job into the ground. He will make his superiors unhappy and in return he will be unhappy because he will have to look for a different job.
7. Grit and grime everywhere. All the tables, chairs, books were drenched in nine weeks' dust. Hadn't been cleaned since Frances left, probably.
8. Her argument that if fraternities and sororities were abolished, the cliques and clubs that were formed would be more natural. At first this would be true, but after a few years changes would take place.
9. I limit my reading chiefly to four types of books. Those dealing with hunting and trapping of animals, plays, historical novels, and fiction.
10. At that moment the visiting team had two men on base. The only out coming when Fox stabbed Williams' liner. Then the fans began to clap and stamp their feet.

5 *Comma faults*

Decide whether the clauses in the following sentences are punctuated correctly or not. Revise those sentences with comma faults and be able to give reasons for leaving the contact clauses punctuated as they are.

1. Some individuals proclaim that there is no room in college for daydreamers. These people are usually right, a person can't expect to pass his courses if he never studies.
2. When this happens the water pressure tends to compress the diving suit, this in turn pushes the diver into the helmet.
3. That's what my father always used to say about money: It's hard to come by, it's easy to lose, and it doesn't go very far in between.
4. My writing inadequacies therefore do not enable me to write exactly what comes from my heart; constant practice, patience, and perseverance are bearing fruit however, thereby my writing fulfillments appear closer.
5. The twentieth century is the mechanical age—the atomic age, with these ages must come people who have the knowledge to do the jobs conceived by research, offered by new discoveries.
6. Every once in a while, however, a wonderful transition comes over our room, beds are made, the dirty clothes are hidden, and the mess on the desk is scraped into a handy drawer.
7. After waiting six days, she was overjoyed at the response. Everyone began to call, no one failed to reply.
8. Over in one corner of the bright room was the old Victorian sofa edged in red, the sofa on which Dad used to put his feet. All of the other furniture in the room had been sold to neighbors or relatives, most of them didn't appreciate it.
9. He said that he was directly responsible for his squadron's safety, therefore any error due to mechanical carelessness would not be tolerated.

10. Mrs. Adams was having breakfast in a lovely blue robe with stars all over it, this she called a camisole.

6 *Agreement of subject and verb*

Rewrite the following sentences, making the indicated changes and any others that are necessary. Be able to justify your choice of verb forms.

1. Change *its* to *their* and add *type of* before *gears.*
   The research crew has used practically all its resources to find out which gears are going to be most efficient.
2. Change *some* to *either one* and substitute *is one of those jobs that* for *job.*
   Do some of those men have adequate equipment? This job requires an accurate micrometer.
3. Change *husband* to *lord and master.*
   These days her aging husband sits on the broad veranda and peers into the white distance.
4. Change *Six brief* to *A short series of.*
   Six brief lessons hardly make her an accomplished musician.
5. Change *One* to *Three.*
   One yard of gravel is almost enough to resurface the driveway.
6. Change *both . . . and* to *either . . . or.*
   Please give us a ring if both your father and mother are coming.
7. Change *together with* to *and* and *aide* to *staff.*
   The general, together with his aide who was always poking his head into our barracks, was unhappy about the state of morale.
8. Add *in all literary endeavors* after *success.*
   I realize that success is obtained by constant vigilance and perseverance.
9. Change *many short art songs* to *one continuous bore.*
   The second and third portions of the concert were many short art songs.
10. Add *one* before *of.*
    Are any of these engravings to be auctioned today? If so, their future owners are probably planning right now how to rearrange their living rooms to show them off to the best advantage.

7 *Dangling modifiers*

Read the directions for each sentence carefully and write the revised sentence, making the change asked for and any others necessary.

1. Add *to marry a plumber's daughter.*
   His ancestral pride was much too strong.
2. Begin *To judge the situation correctly.*
   Surveys and opinion polls must be conducted this month.
3. Begin *After dreaming all night of his own death and resurrection.*
   The only sensation he could recall was that of gently floating through space.
4. Begin *Breaking the sound barrier.*
   The vibrations he felt were not quite so violent as he expected.

5. End with *entering the factory gate.*
   Each day the guards checked the workers' identification badges.
6. Begin *Earlier than usual.*
   The desk still seemed to be piling up with work for her.
7. Add *even assuming that all the facts are known.*
   The verdict seems rather harsh.
8. Begin *Suddenly turning the corner in our Ford.*
   Two trailer trucks were hurtling down the highway.
9. Add *because of finally giving in to David.*
   The effectiveness of Will's eloquence began to be doubted.
10. Add *to water-ski safely.*
    Mary Ann's skill is not yet great enough.

8 *Consistent constructions*

Recast the following sentences to avoid shifted constructions and to make elements which are parallel in idea parallel in form.

1. You would think that all the early birds would be out catching worms, but one shouldn't be surprised to find a few still slumbering in their nests.
2. After he removes the wool he inspects the skin, keeping in mind its size, thickness, and if it is damaged or cut in any place that may ruin it for future use.
3. The contractor got all sorts of complaints about the shingles being loose and that the concrete walks were not allowed to ripen properly.
4. In Jamaica we found the people really exciting, full of fun, and had an atmosphere of warmth and friendliness.
5. One shouldn't buy too many of these cheap books he sees, and they are sold at all the newsstands and drug stores.
6. We had our choice either of writing three short themes on personal experiences or we could write one long paper using library resources.
7. This theme is fascinating and a cleverly phrased piece of writing.
8. All I knew about deep water was what I saw in the movies, and most of the swimmers had narrow escapes as broken eardrums or were attacked by sharks.
9. The Navy has a system so that a good sailor never has a chance to get his roots down too deep, by never letting him stay in one place more than two years.
10. On my own car I have a filter, which would be classed as moderately expensive, that by changing the filter every 5000 miles I am able to keep the oil almost as clean as it was when it came out of the can.

9 *Meaning and phrasing*

A) Study the following sentences in the light of the discussion on pages 67-70 and then revise them. Be prepared to describe briefly why each is faulty.

1. The bicycle is the most popular transportation but there are a few cars, but these are usually owned by government personnel.

2. The restaurants are centered in one section of the city, which has acquired the reputation for being such an area.
3. In giving away all his change to the beggar it resulted in his having nothing smaller than a five dollar bill for bus fare.
4. Although my first impression was not very good, I should say that the time was not very appropriate to receive a good impression.
5. The transit numbers were designed for easier, faster sorting and greater efficiency by banks so that they can sort checks in a surer way and make the collection period of checks shorter.
6. She was much more affectionate toward her cats than she was to me, and they ate fish only on Friday.
7. Talking is done by almost everyone in our society at one time or another. Conversations are held about numerous subjects, but are these conversations useful or interesting to the participants and listeners?
8. Most of the major league teams made trades along toward the midnight deadline; at least a few of them did so.
9. There would be a startling improvement in attendance at ten o'clock classes by serving coffee.
10. This is an example to show how lazy he is: he never gets up to get an ashtray for his ashes and he always taps the ashes into his trouser cuffs.

B) Condense the following student paragraphs into one good one, eliminating and combining sentences without enough meaning and revising those that are contradictory, confusing, or too complex.

Everyone gets that certain excitement and enthusiasm about every four years. Why do people get so excited, and what about? Well, every four years the sports world has a ball. This is the time all the people all over the globe select the best athletes to represent them in the Olympic games. In choosing these stars it is necessary to hold numerous meets all over the world, and these are considered as preliminaries.

The Olympic games are divided into two parts or fields. In the winter, the winter sports are run off in a cold or northern part of the world. In the summer the outdoor or summer sports are run off. This is usually in a place of a warm climate.

Many athletes are involved. There are so many sports and so many fields of sports. These people have trained for many years for the experience, glory, and fun of an Olympic game. There are so many memories and lifelong friends made at these games.

Review exercise

This student theme contains many of the errors discussed in this chapter. Find these and revise the sentences in which they occur. (The sentences are numbered for convenience.)

Emergency Room

(1) It's a cold December night about three o'clock in the morning. (2) The wind is blowing so hard outside that the windows are rattling. (3) Their erratic noises sounding like the knock of an anxious visitor.

(4) You're sitting at the nurses' desk, trying to keep awake. (5) But you're so tired that you can't keep your eyes open, when all of a sudden the telephone rings, you jump to your feet, not sure of what's happening. (6) You reach over, pick up the phone, and a voice is heard on the other end that says, "A police ambulance with six seriously injured crash victims are coming in in about five min–"

(7) You drop the phone and run. (8) Yes, run because you are nervous, you run all the way to the emergency room door, walk in and hurriedly set up for the worst. (9) Just finishing your work, the wail of a siren can be faintly heard. (10) Then the ambulance is standing right outside there, its red light flashing savagely in the dark. (11) The stretcher carriers begin to bring in the patients, at a glance one can tell just about how bad they are. (12) You pick up the phone and notify the doctor on call. (13) After making the call, you hang up. (14) Then you set to work sterilizing the surgical instruments, one of those things that has to be done thoroughly in spite of the emergency. (15) Too rushed to worry about the next step, the work goes fast.

(16) Soon it will all be over and everything will be back to normal, although nothing is normal in a hospital this size, really. (17) There is always something going on in a city hospital. (18) This is only one of the many sleepless nights there is when you work in the emergency room of a hospital.

. . . standard English is an ever-changing and never-fully-attained ideal toward which the entire English-speaking race is steadily striving, but good English—or may we change the term to better English—is the aim and goal of every intelligent speaker of the language, just as better thinking is always the desire of such a person.

ARTHUR G. KENNEDY

Chapter 3

Revising words and phrases

It is, methinks, a very melancholy consideration

that a little negligence can spoil us,

but great industry is necessary to improve us.

SIR RICHARD STEELE

The mistakes treated in this chapter are small and some of them superficial from the point of view of language, but they are practices avoided by writers of General English. They are important from a social point of view because educated readers do not expect to find them in what they read. While amateur writers cannot expect to achieve the exactness of printed material that has been worked over by editors, compositors, and proofreaders, they can aim for it and take pride in seeing how close they can come to producing completely accurate copy.

As a college student you are already in general control of the English language, both spoken and written. But if you are like other college students, you are often careless in speech, and sometimes your written copy does not represent your best work. There are various reasons for this. Sometimes it is from lack of knowledge of what is expected by readers or from not having paid enough attention to the English of your reading or to previous English teaching; or it may be from carelessness at the time of writing; or it may come from using Nonstandard forms or constructions, either because of social background or because of a sort of laziness.

To overcome these small mistakes the three-point program suggested at the beginning of Chapter 2 is helpful: gaining accurate information about the usage of General English, making a habit of carefully proofreading your papers, and revising the mistakes you have made so that gradually they will disappear altogether from your writing. If you make the sort of elementary mistakes treated in this chapter, you should immediately take steps to eliminate them so that you can get full credit for your papers and can take pride in them.

Spotting careless mistakes

Because the most obvious and elementary mistakes are usually the result of carelessness, not ignorance, they can easily be eliminated by attentive proofreading.

In hasty writing it is easy to leave out an occasional letter–the *n* in *an,* a final *-y* or *-ed*. Watch especially *used to,* because even though we *say* "use to," we should write "used to": He had a hard time getting *used to* college; We *used to* do it the other way. (See *-ed.[1])

Be sure to put in end punctuation marks, especially the question mark (not a period) at the end of a question and the closing quotation mark after something quoted.

Do not run small words together. Watch out especially for those that frequently seem to form units: *a / lot, in / turn, any / more, on the other / hand, in a / while.*

Sometimes small words, usually connectives, are carelessly repeated:

> I hardly felt *that* in the one day (no *that*) much could be lost. (The first *that* introduces the clause *in the one day much could be lost;* there should be no second *that.*)
>
> *On* this one point I have already commented *on.* (Either *on* could be kept; probably the first *on* is preferable in writing.)

Some words are commonly confused, and it may take a moment's thought to see which one fits:

a–an. A stands before words beginning with a consonant sound: *a box, a fight, a hotel, a European hotel. An* stands before words beginning with a vowel sound: *an orange, an M, an icebox, an hour.*

to–too. To is a preposition introducing phrases (*to* the top, *to* bed) or infinitives (*to* walk). *Too* is an adverb meaning either "also" (He is going *too*) or "more than is desirable" (*too* much). Keep them straight by making a sentence using both (He was *too* tired *to* want *to* go *to* the dance *too*).

than–then. Than is used in comparisons (He is older *than* I am. He came earlier *than* we expected). *Then* is a word of time (*Then* we tried once more. He couldn't come just *then*).

In addition to these three common confusions, the following word pairs often cause trouble: *affect–effect, whether–weather* (or *wether*), *quite–quiet, principal–principle.* You can probably add to the list. Some of these are discussed in the *Index;* see also Chapter 4 and *Homonyms.

---

[1] Throughout this book, references to *Index* articles are indicated by asterisks (*).

The remedy for mistakes of this sort is a sharp eye and perhaps some special little trick for remembering the distinction between the words.

Using apostrophes

Faulty use or omission of an apostrophe may result from carelessness, since the uses are well established, or it may be the result of some uncertainty about the ways this mark of spelling is used in English.

An apostrophe should be used:

In the possessive (genitive) of nouns. In a singular noun the apostrophe ordinarily comes before the *-s: the secretary's report, today's lesson, my driver's license, the company's retirement plan.* In a plural noun the apostrophe ordinarily comes after the *-s: the doctors' offices, the secretaries' records, the companies' retirement plan.* See *Genitive case for exceptions.

In the possessive of the indefinite pronouns. An apostrophe before the *-s* is used in *anybody's, anyone's, everybody's, somebody's, somebody else's, one's.*

In contractions. An apostrophe is used to show that a sound is omitted in speaking an unstressed syllable, especially when *not* is reduced to *n't: aren't, can't, doesn't, isn't, I'll, it's* (as the contraction of *it is:* It's late). Only one apostrophe is used in *shan't, won't.*

An apostrophe should not be used:

In the possessive of personal pronouns. No apostrophe is used in *his, hers, its* (*its* end, *its* cause), *ours, yours, theirs, whose.*

In clipped words. There is no apostrophe in conventionally clipped (shortened) words: *ad, phone, varsity.*

For further details see *Apostrophe, *Contractions, *Genitive case.

Checking verb forms

A few verb forms are a source of elementary mistakes and need to be checked. The forms of our verbs are so limited in number (*ask, asks, asking, asked*) that they raise very few questions, and not many problems occur with verb phrases (*have gone, may go, did see*) that have replaced old special forms. Even the irregular forms for **be* and **go* are so common that we easily get control of them.

Most English verbs make their past tense and past participle by adding a *d* or *t* sound to the simple (infinitive) form. This sound is ordinarily spelled *-ed* (*asked, hunted, beautified*), but in a few verbs it is *-t* (*kept, slept, wept*); and with some verbs both forms are used (*dreamed–dreamt, kneeled–knelt, spelled–spelt*). In these last examples the *-ed* forms are now the more common.

Some "strong verbs" continue to make the past tense and the past participle by an older method, changing the vowel sound (*throw, threw, thrown–write, wrote, written*). Some of these have two forms, either because they are changing to the typical past in *-ed* or because two vowel changes are current: infinitive, *dive;* past tense, *dove* or *dived;* past participle, *dived* or *dove;* infinitive, *sing;* past tense, *sang* or *sung;* past participle, *sung.*

Standard and Nonstandard forms

A few verbs have forms in Nonstandard English that should be avoided in General English, such as:

Infinitive	*Past tense*	*Past participle*
begin	began (NS: begun)	begun
burst	burst (NS: busted)	burst
drink	drank (NS: drunk)	drunk
fall	fell	fallen (NS: fell)
see	saw (NS: seen)	seen

In some others, spelling has to be watched and associated with the spoken forms: choose (chōōz), chose (chōz), chosen (chō′zn); lead (lēd), led (led), led (led). And for a few there are some regional differences. The General English forms for *eat* are *eat* (ēt), *ate* (āt), *eaten* (ē′tn), but in some regions the two past forms are *eat* (pronounced et). The General forms should be used in writing.

A list of irregular verbs will be found in *Principal parts of verbs.

Three particular verbs

Three common verbs deserve particular attention because of differences between Standard and Nonstandard usage.

Lie–lay. These verbs illustrate the tendency of educated or at least written usage to hinder or deny a natural language change. The verb *lie,* to "recline," is going out of use–even in the conversation of educated people–and the verb *lay* is taking over its work, so that, like so many other English verbs, it is being used both with an object (*Lay* it on the table) and without one (He let it *lay* there). But since this usage is regarded as conspicuously Nonstandard in written English, students should keep the following distinctions:

Intransitive (without an object): *lie, lay, lain*
He let it *lie* there. She *lay* down for a nap.
The boards *had lain* in the sun for months.
Transitive (with an object): *lay, laid, laid*
You can *lay it* on the table. They *laid the linoleum* yesterday.
She *had laid it away* for some future use.

Sit–set. The General English distinction in the commonest meanings of *sit* and *set* is:

Intransitive (without an object): *sit, sat, sat*
Let's *sit* down. They *sat* for over an hour without moving.
They have *sat* that way every Sunday morning for years.
Transitive (with an object): *set, set, set*
Set the box in the corner. He *set out a dozen tomato plants.*
They *had set one too many places* at the table.

Let–leave. These two verbs are quite distinct:

let, let, let, meaning "allow"
You can *let* him go. He *let* the baby play with it.
They *had let* it happen again.
leave, left, left, "go away from" or "let remain"
I must *leave* it here. I *left* him a book.
I *had left* the house.

In some regions *leave* is used in the sense of *let* in such expressions as *leave it go*. This is Nonstandard in written English, although the particular idiom *leave . . . alone* (*leave it alone, leave him alone*) is established. (See *lay–lie, *set–sit, *let–leave.)

Further details on verb forms may be found in the following *Index* articles: *Auxiliary verbs, *Linking verbs, *Split infinitives, *Tenses of verbs, *Transitive and intransitive verbs, *Verbs, *Voice.

Checking pronouns

The chief reason pronouns are a problem in written English is that greater exactness is expected in writing than in speaking. In conversation pronouns are inconspicuous words, casually serving various grammatical functions. But in writing they can be looked at, and schools and publishers have traditionally given them considerable emphasis, perhaps more than they deserve. The fairly careful use of pronouns is then not so much a matter of exact meaning–they are usually not ambiguous–as of tidiness and conforming to the expectations of educated readers. Checking the use of pronouns is one of the jobs of revising a paper.

Object and subject forms

Six of the eight commonly used personal and relative pronouns have special object forms, though nouns and the indefinite pronouns (*anyone, everybody, someone,* and so on) do not. We know the subject-object pairs (*I–me, we–us, he–him, she–her, they–them, who–whom*) but sometimes neglect to make the distinction between them, mainly because in English we rely more on word order than on word form to tell us the function of words in a construction. Pay special attention to the following uses:

1) After prepositions the object form should be regularly used: *with him and her, *between you and me, To whom was this sent?*

2) When a pronoun (usually the first person plural, *we*) is directly joined with a noun, the appropriate case form should be used (*Subject: We children* used to make a wide circle around the cemeteries. *Object:* They used to terrify *us children*).

3) After forms of the verb *be,* Formal English usually has the subject form, General English frequently the object form (*Formal:* I was hoping it would be *she*. *General:* I was hoping it would be *her*). Much fuss has been made over the *It's I–It's me* construction. All responsible grammars now present *It's me* as the usual form, and since it can scarcely occur except in a conversational setting, there is no point in trying for the subject form. (See *it's me.)

4) Usage is divided on *who* or *whom* as the object form when it precedes a verb or preposition. *Whom* has practically disappeared from the spoken language, so that we naturally and regularly say, "*Who* were you with?" In writing, most editors and teachers try to keep the object form, "*Whom* were you with?" In Informal writing the subject form is proper in this kind of construction; in Formal and General writing the object form is preferred. (See *who, whom.) This is one of several small matters of usage that make it important to know what variety of English you are writing. (See *Pronouns, types and forms.)

Misleading or vague reference

Sometimes an amateur writer's pronouns seem to just happen, as in this:

We pulled out our spare, which was under the seat, and put *it* on. *It* sort of dampened our spirits but we decided to try *it* again.

The first *it* refers to the spare tire, the second to the operation of changing tires, and the third to the road or trip. A sentence like this needs to be rewritten. Usually the situation is simpler:

Students and teachers are working at the same job but sometimes they don't seem to realize it and seem to be competing with *them.*

The *they* seems to refer to both students and teachers but by the end of the sentence we see it should refer to students only. The sentence could be revised:

Students are working at the same job as the teachers, but sometimes *they* don't seem to realize this and seem rather to be competing with *the teachers.*

But readers should not be perverse and pretend there is misunderstanding when none is necessary. In this sentence the context keeps the meaning of *he* and *him* straight, even though two people are intended:

He hoped *his* grandfather wasn't in because *he* always scolded *him.*

Sometimes a statement including pronouns referring to different nouns can be made clear by making one of the nouns (and its pronoun) plural:

One way to approach criticism is to compare *an inferior work* with *good ones* to see what *it* [the inferior one] lacks that *the others* [the good ones] have.

The most common reference fault in amateur writing is using a pronoun to refer to a noun that is only implied in the statement:

The actual sport of sailing has changed very little from the time when only the wealthiest had the pleasure of owning *one.* (Better: of owning a sailboat.)

The other fellow enlisted about two years ago and had spent a year of *it* in Persia. (Better: The other fellow, who had enlisted about two years ago, had spent a year of his service in Persia.)

Agreement in number

Frequently we forget whether we are using a singular or plural notion, as this student did:

The value that *a person* can receive from understanding *these* give-and-take methods will stand *them* in good stead for the rest of *their* lives.

 This sentence could be tidied up by making the reference consistently singular: will stand *him* in good stead for the rest of *his life*. But the notion seems actually plural–a statement of general application–so that a slightly better revision might be to change *a person* to *people.* It is not always the pronoun that needs to be changed.

Collective pronouns

A collective noun may be taken as singular or plural. (See p. 62.) When we have a collective noun as subject in conversation, we frequently make its verb singular and make a later pronoun referring to it plural. This shift in number is frequently found in writing too, especially when the meaning is clearly plural, but it is better avoided.

> If the University *wants* to play big time football, why *don't they* go out and get big time teams? (More accurate: why *doesn't it go out*. . . ?)
>
> Sometimes there is a lot to do and the *crew is* not allowed to run things to please *themselves.* (More accurate: and the *crew are* not allowed. . . .)

A shift in number is especially likely to occur in references to the collective pronouns: *anyone, each, everybody, everyone.* In speech these are almost universally referred to by plural pronouns; usually in writing, the singular is used or the subject is changed to a plural:

> *Anyone* who has spent part of *their* [better: *his*] time abroad can see *their own* [better: *his own*] country in a different light. (Or, the *anyone* could be changed to *people: People* who *have* spent part of *their* . . . .)
>
> It is a rule that before entering an operating room everyone must scrub *their* hands thoroughly. (Change *their* to *his* or change *everyone* to something like *all doctors and nurses.*)

(See *Collective nouns and *every and its compounds.)

Reference to an idea

This, that, and *which* are regularly used to refer to the idea of a preceding statement:

> The mud was eight inches deep, *which* made the road to Edward's Bay impassable.

The addition of *condition* after *which,* insisted on by some purists, adds nothing to the clarity of the sentence, and makes it heavier; but care should be taken in such a construction not to use a pronoun that may seem to refer to a particular noun:

> I proceeded to go to the phone, *which* decided my fate for the rest of the summer. (Better: Answering that phone decided my fate for the rest of the summer.)

Indefinite reference

English lacks a comfortable pronoun like German *man* or French *on* to refer to people in general. Since *one* is definitely stiff and formal, we use *they* or *we* or *you.* The indefinite use of these pronouns should not be confused with their definite use. In speech the distinction is clear because there is less stress on the indefinite pronoun. (Compare *They say* meaning "People in general say" with the same words meaning "The people over there say.") The only problem in the use of indefinite pronouns is consistency. Use whichever pronoun seems most natural in a passage, but avoid shifting from one to another unless there is a genuine shift in point of view. (Compare *he or she.)

Because of these small problems with pronouns, some students (and some journalists) tend to avoid them; but they are necessary for easy and clear writing. If you keep an eye on them in revising a paper and occasionally recast a sentence, you will bring them out all right. Remember that it is not always the pronoun that needs to be changed but sometimes another part of the sentence. (For other examples, see *Reference of pronouns.)

Revising modifiers

Next to the subject-verb-object relation, the most important grammatical relationship is of *modifier* to a principal word or construction, called the *headword.* We distinguish between modifiers of nouns and pronouns (*adjectives*), and of verbs, adverbs, and other modifiers, and complete statements (*adverbs*).

Adverb forms

There are few problems of form in adjectives and adverbs, though some adverbs without the usual *-ly* ending are worth noting. The typical English adverb is made by adding the suffix *-ly* to an adjective: *dim, dimly; hurried, hurriedly.* Some common adverbs, however, have the same form as the adjective, and have had for centuries. We can say either "Go slow" or "Go slowly"; "Don't talk so loud" or "Don't talk so loudly." In General English the shorter form is usually preferable, though the *-ly* form is often used when the adverb comes in the middle of a construction: They drove *slowly* back and forth in front of the school.

In Nonstandard and Informal English the adverbs without suffixes tend to be more numerous, and such words as *easy* and *real* are used where written English has *easily* and *really*. *Special* and *considerable* are found for *specially* and *considerably*. In writing use the *-ly* form of these and other adverbs that do not have accepted short forms. A list of the more common ones will be found in *Adverbs, types and forms, §1. See also *bad, badly.

Comparison of adjectives and adverbs

There are two standard ways of comparing adjectives and adverbs to show a greater degree of the quality named: adding *-er* and *-est* to the simple adjective or adverb, or preceding it with *more* or *most*. Either way can be used with short words.

Positive	*Comparative*	*Superlative*
crisp	crisper	crispest
	more crisp	most crisp
even	evener	evenest
	more even	most even

Words of three syllables and many of two ordinarily use only *more* and *most: more beautiful, most beautiful; more easily, most easily; more childish, most childish.* When both forms are possible for a word, the choice will ordinarily depend upon sound, though there is a slight difference in emphasis. In the *-er* and *-est* forms the stress tends to be on the quality: *kind*er, *dull*est; with *more* and *most* the emphasis falls more on the degree: *more* kind, *most* dull. (See *Comparison of adjectives, §5.)

Position of adjectives and adverbs

Since adjectives do not have distinctive forms, except in comparisons, their relation is shown by position; single word modifiers usually precede the headword (the *tallest* buildings) and longer modifiers usually follow it (the buildings *of the new plant,* the buildings *that are tallest*). The position of adverbial modifiers is somewhat less definite. Those modifying specific words are usually near those words (He drove *fast;* an *almost* imperceptible breeze), and those modifying the whole statement tend to stand first or last in the sentence (*Certainly* you know who did it; *Since the trolleys had given way to buses,* most of the tracks had been torn up; It was impossible to keep up with them *because the traffic was so heavy*).

Many times there is a choice of position for an adverb, allowing for variety and a little different emphasis. (He turned the dial *slowly.*

He *slowly* turned the dial. *Slowly* he turned the dial.) A good deal of useless effort has been spent on the placement of **only*. Formal usage tends to put it directly before the element it modifies (There have been *only* four presidents people in general admire). General usage tends to place it next to the verb (There have *only* been four presidents people in general admire). But adverbs should not be carelessly placed so that they are misleading or seem to belong to words they are not intended to modify: Using several pen names, the two editors had *almost* written every article in the magazine. Since the *almost* belongs with *every,* this should be: Using several pen names, the two editors had written *almost* every article in the magazine.

Predicate adjectives

Be and a number of other verbs (*become, feel, grow, taste*) are used as linking verbs (or copulas). Since a modifier following one of these relates to the subject, it is an adjective rather than an adverb (He became *silent*. The tree grew *straight*. This tastes *flat*. She looked *sad*). Such predicate adjectives should be distinguished from the adverbs that modify these same verbs or other verbs (He felt the edge *carefully*. She looked *sadly* out of the window). See *Linking verbs.

Revising unidiomatic expressions

The grammar of English, and our own daily usage, involves many constructions that occur less frequently than most of those we have been discussing.

Particular idioms

Every language has a number of expressions that do not fit easily into its general grammatical patterns and yet are in good use. You can use thousands of words as subjects or verbs of sentences, but you cannot substitute any other adjective in the phrase *in good stead,* and the number of sentences you can make on the pattern of *you had better* is distinctly limited. These single or very limited patterns are called *idioms*. Some idioms are survivals of early patterns of expression: *many is the time, come fall, good-bye, a dollar a pound*. Others are made for convenience or to fill some need: *let's don't, to make good, easy does it*.

Proponents of Formal English have sometimes discouraged such idioms, even some in widespread use, like "*I don't think* so and so is" instead of "*I think that* so and so *is not*." Another idiom of long standing is *try and* do something, *go and* get something, instead of the more conventionally formed *try to, go to*. Not all unconventional phrasing works, but writing is impossible without some widely used idioms, and straining to avoid them results in stilted style.

Since these idioms are really formulas, they should ordinarily be used whole and in their standard form: *on the whole* (not *on a whole*); *if the worst comes to the worst* or *if worst comes to worst* (not *if the worse comes to the worst*).

Idiomatic prepositions

A number of words are conventionally related to other words by a specific preposition:

belief *in* technocracy
conform *to* public opinion (but: in conformity *with* public opinion)
conscious *of* his position
interest *in* mathematics

Since the prepositions in these expressions are not used in their original specific meanings, they have to be learned in phrases, with the words to which they belong. We pick up these idioms by hearing and reading them, and in learning new words we should see them in use, see how they fit into sentences, not learn them as isolated "vocabulary." Dictionaries generally show the conventional preposition used with particular words.

A word may occur in idioms with different prepositions, like *agree on* a plan, *agree with* a person, *agree in* principle; for some of these idioms (for example **different*) usage is divided.

When two words which conventionally call for different prepositions are used with a single object, both prepositions should be given:

> We know for a fact that most of our players lost a great deal of respect *for* and confidence *in* the coach.

Probably most mistakes in the use of prepositions come from the confusion of two constructions of similar meaning: "I was *informed to* report to the branch office in the morning" might be a confused blending of "I was *informed that* I should report" and "I was *asked to (ordered to) report*."

Infinitive or gerund

Some words are followed conventionally by an infinitive and some by a gerund, as illustrated by the following examples:

Infinitives	*Gerunds*
able *to work*	capable *of working*
take pains *to tell*	the idea *of writing*
the way *to cut*	this method *of cutting*
neglect *to say*	ignore *saying*

With a number of words either is used:

no reason *to express* them–no reason *for expressing* them
a chance *to learn*–a chance *for learning*

Gerunds may be used so that their noun aspect is emphasized (The *trusting* of women is a mark of a gentleman) or their verb aspect (*Trusting* women is the mark of a gentleman). The latter construction is the more active and is increasingly used in General writing. (See *Gerunds.)

Idioms for comparisons

The idioms for simple comparisons are not troublesome: He is *younger than* I thought; It was the *hardest* fight of his career. But when other elements are involved, there are some questions of idiom.

Most people say "The summer was *as* dry if not *drier than the last*." Formal and General English would complete both constructions: "The summer was *as* dry *as* if not *drier than* the last" or "The summer was *as* dry *as* the last, if not *drier*." (See *as . . . as.)

Other is used in a comparison between things of the same sort but not between things of different sorts:

This picture is a better likeness than the other portraits.
This portrait is a better likeness than the bust.
There is not a more enjoyable light novel by any writer.
(Not: by any other writer.)

The two things compared should be actually comparable. This means using a possessive if the name of the first thing is not repeated:

His muscles were firm, like an athlete's. (Not: like an athlete.)
The president's recommendations were more practical than the committee's. (Not: than the committee.)

See *Comparison of adjectives and adverbs.

The aim of work in a composition course is improvement in writing, in presenting information and ideas to others. The principal emphasis is on the activity of writing, gathering and selecting and organizing material for readers. The language of these papers should be Standard English, General or Formal, the sort expected by educated readers. Studying the word forms and constructions by themselves is, then, a means to an end, to help you use English with confidence. No matter what your present usage may be, this study will bring about improvement and will set up habits of continuing value.

Chapter 3

SUGGESTED STUDY AND WRITING

These exercises follow the order of the chapter sections, with special attention given to problems most frequently encountered in student writing. Wherever varieties of usage are involved you should be ready to discuss the reasons for your choice of one word form rather than another. For practice in recognizing and correcting errors as they occur in writing, two themes are included, one at the beginning of the exercises and one at the end as a review.

1 *Proofreading*

A) The following theme was written at the beginning of a freshman composition course and contains a variety of errors ranging from misspelling to faulty sentence construction and wording. Find as many of these as you can, suggest revisions, and point out which errors might have been due to carelessness.

My Training in English

1 My experiences with the English language has been a very hard
2 road for me. The writing which I was required to do was at a mini-
3 mum standard. We were required to submit twelve themes thru out
4 the school year. In my writing thru out my four years of high school
5 I have only been required to write two term papers. I believe this was
6 vary far below the amount which I should have been required to
7 submit. But the writing was not limited to themes alone. We were
8 required to write a summary of twelve books, which consisted of
9 approximately two hundred words apiece. This is the extent of my
10 writing of manuscripts thru high school.
11 My grammar training, I believe, was to a much higher state than
12 was the writing. In my four years I have covered four grammar books
13 from cover to cover. The emphasis in grammar being the basal parts
14 in my first two years and the stressing of vocabulary in the later two.
15 My senior year was made up of a great striving toward vocabulary so
16 as to better prepare us for the forth coming of college. I do not be-
17 lieve the vocabulary was stressed enough in my last year, as I did not
18 have any vocabulary at all untill my junior year and that was very
19 limited.
20 The amount of training which I have had in speech and reading
21 aloud can be put into a nut shell. I have never taken a speech course
22 and we were not required to do any in our classes. The only oppor-

23 tunity I had for speech activities has been very well limited. The
24 stressing of poetry and plays was on a little broader basis than speech.
25 We read some of Shakespeares' plays and a few plays of the more
26 well known playwrights.

27 We did not even make an attempt toward the learning of com-
28 munication in any means. We completely forgot about the writing of
29 applications, ect., which were found in the grammar books so we
30 could stress more so on other things.

31 I may as well be very frank with you, but I just dispised English
32 to the utmost thru out high school. One thing I enjoyed doing very
33 much was the writing of research papers but which were much to
34 limited. I believe the vocabulary was of great help, but we only hit
35 on a very small portion of what we should have.

B) Make a study of your recent themes and calculate roughly the proportion of mistakes caused by carelessness. Tabulate the errors to see which ones occur most frequently, and keep the list handy when you are writing papers. Try to find ways to increase your accuracy; you might type rather than write in longhand, let the paper "cool off" before recopying and again before proofreading, read the paper backward to catch typographical errors, and so on.

2 *Apostrophes*

Before beginning this exercise study the *Index* article on *Genitive case. Rewrite any of the following sentences that contain errors in the use of the apostrophe. If more than one form is possible, indicate the variety of English in which each would be appropriate. If the sentence is accurate as it stands, write C by its number.

1. Is'nt there a stock question about the King of England's death—something like "But what's to be done with King Charles head?"
2. No doubt Martha and Henry's share of the estate is smallest, but whose to blame for that?
3. She's only asking for whats rightfully her's and her husband's.
4. Thats' the sort of private idea that one doesnt tell even to ones best friends.
5. Dont you think its time that everyone stopped frothing about womens' rights?
6. Those hoodlums aren't friends of mine; they're friends of my cousin's.
7. Certainly Keats' letters show that he was something more than a ladies' man and a poet's poet.
8. What I'm going to do with the Mortons' dog is hardly anyone elses business, least of all the Barnes'.
9. Though I cant vouch for anyone's actions but my own, their's seem less selfish than most people's.
10. Carolyn's worried about her petition: it's fate is in the hands of the board of trustee's.

3 *Verb forms*

A) Rewrite the following sentences, changing the verb forms in the present tense to past and those in the past to past perfect. Consult the *Index* for irregular *Principal parts of verbs and give alternative forms where possible.

1. I know that she swam the channel regularly in this weather.
2. Although Jerry goes to school on a bus, his ears freeze while he stands waiting for it.
3. Then they lighted a roaring fire, drank a toast to the queen and forgot all their troubles.
4. When I ask him what he got for his birthday, he flies into a rage.
5. Occasionally I dream that I almost dive into an empty pool.
6. Suddenly I spring from the board and swim through the air.
7. Then I wring out my dripping suit and hang it up to dry.
8. In the next act the child leads his blind nurse away just as the boat sinks.
9. The demons shrink back in fear as the maiden sings her prayer.
10. The early shoots grow from seed he sowed last summer.

B) In each of the following sentences, supply the past tense or the past participle of the verb in parentheses. If more than one form is acceptable, explain in what variety of English each would be used.

1. The children (slide) down the ravine in an old dishpan.
2. A study of the election returns has (prove) most informative.
3. They crowded around to see what she had (catch).
4. Before I (choose) the ring, I had (get) a price list from Peacock's.
5. If Martin hadn't (drown), he certainly would have been (hang).
6. Sarah, did you know the pipes had (freeze)?
7. Roland (blow) his horn until his ears (burst).
8. Tell me what you (weave) last year.
9. The casings had (tear) loose from their bearings.
10. You must know how much you (lend) him!

C) Choose the forms of the verb in parentheses appropriate to Formal usage, remembering that *lie, sit,* and *rise* are intransitive, *lay, set,* and *raise,* transitive. If you are in doubt about certain idiomatic usages of these verbs, consult the *Index* or a dictionary.

1. The tomb of the pharaoh had (laid, lain) buried in the desert for centuries.
2. As soon as the dough (raises, rises), (set, sit) it in a warm place and (leave, let) it stay there for half an hour.
3. (Sitting, Setting) on the lake were eight decoys, but the ducks (left, let) them alone.
4. There in the basket (lay, laid) three blue eggs.
5. The slaves worked all night (raising, rising) a monument in spite of the (raising, rising) tide of the river.
6. After lunch she had (laid, lain) down for a nap.

7. Their summer cabin (lays, lies) on the island just above the tidal falls.
8. Not till the eighth did the pitcher (leave, let) them have anything to swing at.
9. No self-respecting hen would (set, sit) on those eggs.
10. Please (leave, let) the napkins (laying, lying) on the table.

4 *Pronouns*

A) Rewrite the following sentences, changing any pronoun forms inappropriate to General English. If more than one form is possible, indicate under what circumstances each might be used. If the sentence is all right as it stands, write C by the number.

1. If you look closely, you can see the slight resemblance between her and I.
2. Does Mildred know who the package has been sent to?
3. They can't say that we children have been difficult today.
4. No wonder they object to you singing first; you sing so much better than them.
5. Gladys has arranged for him and me to attend the convention.
6. The minute I opened the door I knew that it was her.
7. You know we boys are eager to help, but we don't know who to ask.
8. Only the Nortons and us are going to the party.
9. The whole camp was aroused by his shouting, not to mention her screaming.
10. Please let Ned and myself do the job alone.
11. We heard many rumors about who the thief really was.
12. There's no love lost at all between we and the Garrisons, especially since us Burtons stole their chickens.
13. Who'd you give it to?
14. George and Dick and me were still stalking across the snowy fields looking for our first pheasant.
15. The king will bestow the medal on whoever shows the greatest bravery in combat.

B) Revise any of the following sentences in which the pronoun reference is unsatisfactory or in which there is a shift in number or person.

1. When Louise was little and went shopping with her aunt, she could hardly keep up with her, and sometimes she even lost sight of her when she lingered too long to look at an attractive toy.
2. Procrastination is the thief of time, but I often do it anyway.
3. She talked a good deal about the technique of horsemanship, although as a matter of fact she had never ridden one in her life.
4. The tide of war has turned in our favor, but it's far from over.
5. He didn't feel like writing a letter–he never did–but he liked to receive them and so he forced words onto paper.
6. I seriously advise a beginner to watch someone caulk and overhaul their boat before thinking of repairing your own craft.

7. How much aid are the professors to the student if he never comes in contact with them except in the lecture hall?
8. The carpenter is happy because he enjoys seeing things constructed while knowing that he has had a hand in constructing it.
9. He was brought up by good parents, which his manners plainly show.
10. Some people claim that a good gun dog should never be kept in a house but always in a kennel because it spoils them.
11. When one starts out on this expedition they may hear and see things that will tend to make you believe it is not really worth it.
12. I enjoyed skating very much, but I didn't enjoy having to sharpen them by hand.
13. In order for the average person to understand the situation they would first have to know a few things about atmospheric pressure.
14. Each of them may leave their job in an hour, but only if his or her tools are put away properly.
15. The government ought to give him a pension; they really owe it to employees of twenty years' service.

5 *Adjectives and adverbs*

Choose the adjective or adverb form that seems appropriate to General English. If the other form is also used, indicate in what variety it would occur. Use the *Index* articles for specific words and constructions.

1. Always treat the customer (fair, fairly) was his motto.
2. Under the leaves, the children found a caterpillar rolled up (tight, tightly).
3. Under the same circumstances, the twins never acted very (different, differently).
4. Of the last three days this one is by far the (hottest, most hot).
5. His eyes looked (dark, darkly) at her from under his knitted brows.
6. Of the two, the rat in the left-hand cage was given the (more fatal, most fatal, more nearly fatal, most nearly fatal) dose.
7. Long after the campers left, the stones (nearest, most near) the fire were still warm.
8. Later on she won't feel so (bad, badly) about it.
9. This cheese has (the most unique, the most nearly unique) taste of any.
10. The eyes of that hound are the (soulfulest, most soulful) that I have ever seen.
11. Even with a catcher's mitt, Johnny played second base fairly (good, well).
12. Take three or four steps before you deliver the ball, whichever is (easier, easiest).
13. With new Rocco gasoline your motor will start (easier, more easily) and run (smoother, more smoothly).
14. His remarkable stamina enables him to finish (more strongly, stronger) than the other members of the team.

15. Lindeman's speeches always sound (convincing, convincingly) when he gives them in class, but they don't hold up so (good, well) when you study them on paper.

6 *Idioms*

Revise the unidiomatic expressions in the following sentences. Be ready to give your reasons if you think any of the expressions you have revised might be appropriate in certain varieties of usage.

1. Joe was made still more unhappy by watching the people on the sidewalk, who looked as if they were either coming or going back to a soft office job.
2. Lois says she plans on driving downtown Wednesday rather than Thursday.
3. Whenever Adrian wrote a criticism about a book, he seldom or ever suppressed his personal prejudices.
4. The coddling method should be substituted by a more mature system in college.
5. The exercises are found on the page opposite of the rules.
6. Perhaps college has made me more conscious to the opportunities around me.
7. Every teacher has a different method to teach poetry.
8. What is to prevent these "citizens of the world" to stage a gigantic revolution?
9. Camping tests your ability of roughing it in the open.
10. Many states have laws that prohibit out-of-state architects to plan homes built in the state.
11. Mary had no sooner hung her clothes on the line when two skunks ran across the yard.
12. But it seems to me that my parents' gift has been more to their own advantage than to either my brother or me.
13. We seem to be the most patriotic of all the other schools.
14. Amazingly enough, this mayor is as competent if not more so than the previous one.
15. Minneapolis happens to be the largest of any city in Minnesota.

7 *Review*

In the following student theme you will find examples of many of the trouble spots taken up in the preceding exercises. Revise any mistakes that you find, including unidiomatic expressions, unnecessary shifts in tense or subject, and errors in spelling, punctuation, and usage.

True Progress

1 In the beginning, I remember, we all met first on dry land; but this
2 was the last time, for the next meeting would be in the sea-green
3 water of the swimming pool. We found our swimming instructor to
4 be a young woman a few years older than ourselves. In commencing
5 to describe the course we were told that this particular swimming

6 class was strictly for beginners, with each girl getting a grade based on
7 how much they learned and not how much they already knew. Some
8 of us were scared, others glad, and still others relieved to hear this.
9 She went on to tell us the rules; rules that were definitely hard to
10 follow. No jewelery would be worn in the pool, no late comers,
11 shower before entering the pool, no bobby pins worn under our
12 caps (the hardest of the rules to follow), there would be exercises
13 (or limbering up, as she called it) before entering the pool, and so
14 forth. By the time she finished with these rules, most of us were
15 scared, a few glad, and none relieved.

16 Those first days were spent in getting acquainted with the water
17 and our neighboring blunderers. One of the most difficult feats to
18 conquer was the courage to jump, or even climb, into the water and
19 submerge for a second of two in order to get thoroughly wet. It
20 was'nt that the water was so frightening–just cold. It was during
21 these first days that we learned who was at ease in water and who
22 wasn't. One girl, who was always the first one in the pool because
23 she went in before the exercises rather than afterwards as every-
24 one else did, had lived for a short time in a place where she went
25 swimming (used in a broad term) practically every day in a deep
26 water pool; she made the rest of us look like scared rabbits.

27 One of our initiating tasks to learn was floating on our stomaches.
28 At first we would line up along the edge of the pool, grab hold, and
29 try to raise our feet. We all felt pretty important when we accom-
30 plished this feat, but this feeling quickly deserted us when our
31 instructor told us to let go. To let go would surely mean sinking, at
32 least thats what we thought. A few brave ones tried it, then the
33 remainders of us followed suit. It wasn't so hard after all . . . espe-
34 cially when we had a partner standing nearby. But it wasn't long
35 till we learned, once more, who were the really frightened and who
36 were the brave; some just couldn't do it alone. We all felt terribly
37 sorry for one particular woman because whe was quite a bit older
38 than the rest of us and had never learned the first things about
39 swimming, so she had alot more fear to conquer than we did.

40 Our next step was learning some strokes, starting with the feet.
41 As before, we lined up along the pool's side, grabbed the edge, and
42 kicked. It was such fun and we all got terribly carried away with
43 ourselves. I think we visualized ourselves as little mermaids, or
44 something. In a short time we let go of the edge, however, and
45 pushed out a way from the side, then propelled ourselves back again.
46 This was a tremendous accomplishment because now we were ac-
47 tually moving (if, be chance, we were ever lost in the deep blue sea,
48 we could at least move a few feet!). Then came the day we were to
49 float across, kicking, the width of the pool . . . via solo. True, none
50 of us were Esther Williams, but we made it across that pool. We got
51 used to that, too, and were soon doing it like small motor boats.

52 Now, we were ready for some new strokes, using our hands. We
53 stood in the middle of the pool, bent over, each ear alternately
54 touching the water's edge, and stroking our arms in a pinwheel

55 fashion. Then we added our breathing exercises. This was hard be-
56 cause we had to get our breathing in just right or...we missed our
57 chance to breath. We learned to walk across the pool width stroking
58 our arms and breathing, until we were finally told to combine our
59 arm, feet, and breathing actions. We were mighty proud when we
60 were told to do this because we realized this was the basic swimming
61 stroke. But our egos deflated quickly when we tried to do it. It takes
62 real concentration to tell your lungs, arms, and legs what to do
63 spontaniously while counting to a rhythem: 1 2 3 . . . 4 5 6, 1 2 3
64 . . . 4 5 6, Breathing on 1 and 4. It was something like a waltz, but
65 not quite.

66 After awhile most of us achieved something that resembled a cross
67 between the crawl and a dog paddle. Perhaps it wasn't real swim-
68 ming, but at least you could move through the water without touch-
69 ing bottom. Then the day finally came when we could "swim" the
70 length of the pool without stopping and without taking in more
71 water than air. I know that for the other mermaids and I this was
72 the big splash forward. And I think the instructor must have been
73 releived.

I hold that a word is something more than the noise it makes;
it is also the way it looks on the page.

T. S. ELIOT

Chapter 4

Spelling

The man who writes with no misspelled words

has prevented a first suspicion of the limits of his scholarship

or, in the social world, of his general education and culture.

JULIA NORTON MC CORKLE

Probably no one is a complete master of English spelling. Everyone sometimes comes to his limit—some sooner than others—and reaches for a dictionary. But everyone can learn to spell well enough to meet the expectations of educated readers. First he needs to understand something of the social pressure for uniform spelling and accept the responsibility for meeting it, and then he needs to discover the sources of his own difficulties, some of which may be faults of the language. The rest is work.

The social demand for uniform spelling

Students of language regard spelling as an incidental and superficial aspect of language, almost as a necessary evil in getting the spoken language on paper. But a reasonably consistent spelling is a genuine convenience to a reader because he has become accustomed to the conventional visual form of whole words or phrases. Unusual spellings distract him, make him look twice or even guess at the word, and so interfere with easy communication. Standard spelling makes it easier to list and to find items given in alphabetical order. And it is necessary in some occupations: for secretaries (since many employers need to buy their spelling); for editors, proofreaders, and compositors, who prepare material for printing; and, in general, for people whose writing goes to others without passing through the hands of someone professionally trained in bringing it up to public standards.

Actually our spelling has been largely standardized by printers and editors, who naturally wish for consistency in what they print and so

usually revise manuscripts according to the dictionaries or according to their own stylebook lists, which are based on the spellings of the dictionaries. Dickens and other celebrated writers were "poor spellers" whose copy was corrected by editors. Our spelling is the most conspicuous example of the influence of editorial standards.

The spellings established by publishers have gradually been adopted by the educated class. In the eighteenth century there was a special drive for uniformity in various matters of language. After the appearance of Samuel Johnson's dictionary in 1755 and later of Noah Webster's, spelling received special emphasis. In the United States, Webster's blue-back speller—over 60,000,000 copies of which were sold in the nineteenth century—helped make spelling one of the main jobs in school. The spelling lesson was something definite; the goal was well defined in the dictionary and spelling book; progress toward it could be marked. There is now over a century of this school pressure behind the desire for uniformity in spelling.[1]

Back of the schools and the editors there is a more general social demand for uniformity. Mistakes in spelling are easily noticed, even by people who would have difficulty with some of the more complex matters of language. Consequently, spelling is a convenient test of literacy and even of respectability. The main reason for "learning to spell" is that educated readers expect to see words in the standard forms and are likely to undervalue a person who does not use them. Employers of college graduates frequently complain that "they can't spell," implying that they do not meet a minimum requirement of education. Good spelling is an important—if superficial—trait of Good English.

Reasons for difficulties in spelling

English is admittedly a badly spelled language, compared for instance with Italian. We represent the forty-odd sounds of our speech with an alphabet of twenty-six letters, three of which—*c* (or *k*), *q*, and *x*—merely duplicate the work of other letters. The twenty-three active letters singly and in combinations like *th, ea, sh* have to represent all the sounds. The difficulty is greatest in the vowels: *a*, for instance, spells the vowel sounds of *lay, lap, far, fare, was,* not to mention untypical words like *many* and the sound of the second *a* in *comparative*.

[1] Allen Walker Read, "The Spelling Bee: A Linguistic Institution of the American Folk," *PMLA*, 1941, 56:495-512.

Besides the limitation of the alphabet there is also difficulty because English spelling has failed to keep pace with the gradually but steadily changing pronunciation. Our spelling tradition was established by the thirteenth century and was stabilized chiefly by the printers of the sixteenth and seventeenth centuries. Since then the pronunciation of many words has changed, but the spelling has not. This fact accounts for many of the curious English spellings: *meat* and *meet* once represented different sounds; *colonel* was a word of three syllables, spelled with an *r* between the *o*'s and pronounced ko-ro-nel; the *gh* in *night, though,* and other words was sounded, as it still often is in Scotland. The curious group including *bough, cough, though,* and *through* is largely explained by different pronunciations in different English dialects–the pronunciation of one word comes from one dialect, of another from a different dialect, but the original spelling is kept.

The English habit of borrowing words generously from other languages is responsible for such groups as *cite, sight, site,* and for hundreds of words that do not follow conventions of English spelling—*bureau, croquet, hors d'oeuvre, khaki, onomatopoeia*. An even greater problem comes from our perpetuating spellings that were significant in another language, like the pairs of Latin endings *-ance -ence* and *-able -ible*. Each pair is now pronounced the same and has the same meaning so that it is very difficult to remember which one is expected in a particular word. Such inconsistencies cause many mistakes in spelling.

These facts suggest that though English spelling cannot be defended, both its general confusion and the form of a particular word can be explained by reference to the history of the language.[1] This does not help us spell a given word, but it does help us understand why the difficulties exist, why our spelling can be made the butt of so many jokes and can furnish curiously spelled rhymes for limericks.

Choice in spelling

A writer now has a choice of simpler spellings in some hundreds of words. The choice he makes between forms will depend upon his feeling of appropriateness. Formal writers are consistently conserva-

[1] Henry Bradley, *Spoken and Written Language* (Oxford, 1919); W. A. Craigie, *English Spelling* (New York, 1927); Thomas R. Lounsbury, *English Spelling and Spelling Reform* (New York, 1909); Robertson-Cassidy, Ch. 11, pp. 330-5, 353-73; (Books cited by name of author only will be found in the Bibliography, pp. XIV-XV.) K. W. Dykema, "Spelling" in *Encyclopedia Americana,* 1950 and later printings; Donald W. Emery, *Variant Spelling in Modern English Dictionaries* (Champaign, 1958). The section "Orthography" at the front of the Webster dictionaries, especially the International size, contains a great deal of information about English spelling.

tive in spelling. General writers make use of the shorter forms more readily. At present, scientific and business English are most open to changes in spelling. In the Informal writing of personal correspondence many people are more adventurous than in writing intended for strangers.

The essential point is to realize how generally the shorter form is used and then decide whether or not to use it. *Altho, tho,* and *thru* are in general use in advertising and in familiar correspondence and have been adopted by enough periodicals so that these words are included in recent dictionaries as alternate forms. *Nite* and *naborhood,* on the other hand, are not found outside advertising and familiar writing, and *brot* or *thot* have hardly reached the advertising columns. For many words (*catalog–catalogue, program–programme, esthetic–aesthetic*) usage is divided, and the shorter forms are becoming the more usual.

In general, when usage is divided in spelling a given word, choose the simpler or more natural form. Most people writing today, and certainly anyone who has difficulty with spelling, will ordinarily prefer:

1) The more modern of two equally reputable spellings of common words: *catchup, mold, sirup,* rather than *catsup* (or *ketchup*), *mould, syrup.*

2) The simpler form of a less common word if it has attained currency among people who use it most: *anesthetic, medieval, sulfur* rather than *anaesthetic, mediaeval, sulphur.*

3) American rather than British spellings (though both spellings are usually current to some extent on both sides of the Atlantic): *center, color, labor, pajama, story* (of a building), *traveler,* rather than *centre, colour, labour, pyjama, storey, traveller.* Of course in spelling British proper names or in direct quotation, British spelling should be kept, as in "the Labour party."

Suggestions for improving spelling

In spite of its admitted difficulty, fairly correct spelling is possible for anyone, though if you have reached college age without having acquired the knack, it will mean work. The goal for a "poor speller" is not to spell perfectly but to spell well enough so that his copy will not attract unfavorable attention–and to know how to check possible errors. The fatal mistake is to give up, to enjoy poor spelling as a hypochondriac enjoys poor health. (Some people even seem to enjoy the attention bad spelling brings them.)

The first step, if you are really a poor speller, is to recognize that the demand for standard spelling is a social fact: in stressing spelling, your English course is merely representing the community. The next step is to take the responsibility for your own improvement, to want to improve, and to do something about it. It is your problem, and you will have to find ways that work for *you*. The old suggestion of keeping a notebook page of your commoner mistakes is sound. Keeping lists of your own spelling problems and working on them is more important than using lists made up by others. Copying short passages that contain words you need to use helps fix them in mind, and writing them down from dictation is even better. This lets you write the word in its context and so helps you get accustomed to putting it in a natural setting. The following suggestions should also prove useful.

Visualize words in reading

In reading you do not look at each individual letter of a word but at the word as a unit, and then usually as part of a phrase. In recent years great efforts have been made in the schools to increase the speed of silent reading, with real gain for students. But as a result they probably have less clear images of individual words. In rapid reading the vowels especially are not seen—and the majority of spelling mistakes are in vowels. People vary greatly in the accuracy with which they remember visual images. If your visual memory is weak, you may have to make a special effort to look at some words as you read—particularly common words like *physicist, quiet, quite, pamphlet, separate, similar.*

Watch the pronunciation of certain words

Curiously enough, the discrepancy between pronunciation and spelling is not such a common cause of misspelling as might be expected. We usually remember words that seem furthest from their sound, like the *-ough* words and those with silent letters (de*b*tor, *p*sychology, sa*l*mon). The trouble comes in words like *arctic* (or *Arctic*), since few people pronounce a *k* sound in it, and *sophomore,* in which the second *o* is almost never spoken, and in words like *accidentally* and *occasionally,* in which the *-al* is either not spoken or very much cut down in speech. Some words spelled with vowels for which the word's sound is no clue (*Neutral vowels) can be remembered by associating them with derivatives in which the vowel is clearly sounded:

comp*a*rable—com p*a*re′	comp*e*tition—com p*e*te′
hypocr*i*sy—hyp o cr*i*t′ i cal	priv*a*te—pri v*a*′ tion

Some words are misspelled because in speech we do not clearly distinguish certain consonants like *c* and *g* or *v* and *f;* as a result we may write *signifigance* for *significance,* or *enfironment* for *environment.*

Only a few nonstandard pronunciations appear in spelling, the commonest of which is *athalete* for *athlete.* In some words an unstressed syllable leads to a substitution (*undoubtably* for *undoubtedly*) or to the omission of a letter: *ever* or *evry* for *every, tenative* for *tentative, quanity* for *quantity, continous* for *continuous.*

Although spelling is primarily a visual matter, so that the sound of words is a treacherous guide, in a few words like these accurate pronunciation may lead to accurate spelling.

Use a dictionary

A college-size dictionary will have all the words you need, and more, and is the best help in checking spelling. If you are quite unsure of a word, you may have to look in more than one place: it may begin with a *g* or a *j,* or the first vowel may be an *e* or an *i.* Don't rely on a roommate or someone else who happens to be around—his guess may be no better than yours. Get the dictionary habit.

Learn new words accurately

With new words, learn both the spoken and written forms at the same time. Making a word your own is chiefly a matter of attention to its sound and its appearance. Pronounce a new word distinctly, perhaps visualizing it in syllables (*Han-se-at-ic, he-mo-glo-bin, u-ni-cel-lu-lar*) as well as visualizing it as a unit (*Hanseatic, hemoglobin, unicellular*). If you have any doubts about its meaning or pronunciation, consult a dictionary. If the word is at all difficult, study it carefully and then say it without looking at it; next write it down, and compare what you have written with its printed form. Continue saying and writing it a few times until you are sure of it. Focus on the word's appearance by holding a pencil point under it. Underline new words, if they are going to be important to you, so that they will stand out on the page and thus help you remember their exact form. At times it is necessary to counteract the habit of rapid reading in order to really *see* and fix in mind the individual words and even the letters of the words.

Work on confusing forms

Two closely related words sometimes show differences in spelling that are hard to keep separate: f*ou*r–f*o*rty, compar*a*tive–compar*i*son, curi*ou*s–curi*o*sity, pron*ou*nce–pron*u*nciation. A vowel may be dropped or changed when an ending is added to a word: ent*e*r–ent[ ]rance, disast*e*r–disast[ ]rous, maint*ai*n–maint*e*nance. Or the vowel may be retained: temp*e*r–temp*e*rament, mount*ai*n–mount*ai*nous. Because such words usually don't show any difference in sound, they have to be remembered.

One of the greatest nuisances in our language is a group of prefixes and suffixes with two different forms: **en- in-;* **in- un-;* **-able -ible;* **-ance -ence;* **-er -or.*[1] The following samples show how common and necessary these groups of words are:

en-(or em-): embark, enable, encourage, enforce
in-: inclose (or enclose), infuse, inquire, insure (or ensure), instruct
in-(not): inactive, incompatible, infrequent, impractical
un-: unacceptable, uncontrollable, unrecognizable
-able: advisable, changeable, desirable, laughable, usable
-ible: audible, credible, eligible, flexible, irresistible, legible
-ance (noun) -ant (adj.): attendance–attendant, intolerance–intolerant, resistance–resistant
-ence (noun) -ent (adj.): confidence–confident, independence–independent, persistence-persistent
-er: advertiser, consumer, manufacturer, subscriber
-or: administrator, conqueror, editor, proprietor, ventilator

Similar as a spelling problem is the group: *precede, proceed* (but *procedure*), *recede, supersede.*

English is rich in *homonyms, pairs of words pronounced alike but often spelled differently: *pair–pare, piece–peace, plain–plane, coarse –course, stationary–stationery*. The context keeps their meaning clear. Since most of them are in common use, confusing them in writing is usually the result of carelessness. If you have trouble with any of them, try writing them in phrases or sentences that will show their meaning:

The *capital* of California is Sacramento.
The *capitol* has a gilded dome.
the city *council–counsel* for the defense–good *counsel*
the *principal* of the school–4% on the *principal*–a man of *principle*

Affect–effect, weather–whether, which are homonyms in most people's speech, also belong in this group.

Proofread carefully

Students usually know how to spell most of the common words they miss on papers. In conference they will frequently spell a word right that had to be marked wrong on a theme. To close the gap be-

---

[1] Throughout this book, references to *Index* articles are indicated by asterisks (*).

tween knowledge and performance, careful proofreading of the final copy is necessary.

Spelling has to be checked in revision. This is the most important general advice to remember. Don't stop when you are writing to look up a word or even to worry about it. You will almost certainly lose something more important if you do—the trend of your thought, the movement of your sentence at least. If you are suspicious of a word, you may mark it in some way (with a ? or √), and then check up on all dubious spellings when working over what you have written. Always scrutinize the final copy for careless spellings. Careful reading of a paper just for the spelling is the best advice for anyone who is likely to make mistakes. To make your eye slow down, if you need to, read with a pencil point just below the line so that you will see every syllable.

For continued improvement, see your spelling words in three groups. First be sure of the common everyday words (*companies, definite, professor,* and so on). Then learn the words for subjects that interest you and especially those needed in your college courses. Beyond these you can go as far as you wish in the vast wordstore of English.

Much sheer memory work is necessary to become a good speller, but there are a few rules and word groups that will simplify the task. Because you've heard them since the early school grades, they are not repeated here, but for your convenience they are given in detail in the *Index,* often with word lists.

In addition to the entries already mentioned in this chapter, see especially the following:

*-al ly
*-ce, -ge
*Doubling final consonants
*E §5
*-ed
*-ei-, -ie-
*-er, -re
*-ize, -ise
*-le words
*-or, -our
*Silent letters

The article *Spelling and the suggested study for this chapter have lists of words that may be useful, but they cannot take the place of a dictionary.

Chapter 4

SUGGESTED STUDY AND WRITING

1. The following student theme exhibits more than the usual spelling difficulties. Find all the misspelled words and spell them correctly. Make a list of other errors that you find and evaluate briefly the organization, the paragraphing, the sentence structure, and any other important matters.

By Their Shoes Shall Ye Know Them

1 The most interesting thing about a person is his shoes for a persons
2 shoes tell more about him than any other idem or trait. Watch the
3 shoes go strolling by and with each clip clap of heel and toe, listen
4 to the story of the person above the shoe. Children are not usually
5 included in this fasinating study, for what child really controls his
6 own appearence?
7 First of all there are the workmans' shoes. Always coated with
8 a thin film of plaster dust and spotted with white paint, these shoes
9 *never* hurry. They clomp. Morning, noon, and night–they clomp.
10 It is not to difficult to picture the man above the shoes. He is un-
11 shaven and his pants bag. He carries a lunch pail and a crushed
12 package of Camels. All you really need to see, however, is his shoes.
13 In complete contrast, there are the shoes of the frustrated career
14 girl. This girl has always wished for a glammor job, but somehow
15 the opportunity never was there. She wears black patent leather heels
16 –spike heels. Because she wears such a slim sheeth skirt, she can't
17 really stride so she has to "mince" along the street. Yes, her shoes
18 tell all.
19 Crepe-souled shoes under a well-pressed crease shows up a hidden
20 personality. Here is a man who would rather be walking a fence than
21 walking to the 6:30 train. He is typical, average–yes, even conven-
22 tional. Only his shoes tell of the desire to be kicking a football rather
23 than stumbling over a fileing cabinet.
24 The good sturdy walking shoe is, without a doubt, the backbone
25 of America. For herein resides the level-headed homemaker. She is
26 no doubt shopping for Johnny's new blue jeans. The way she walks
27 is determined and even a little hurried, although undoubtedly tired.
28 In these "good, sensable shoes" walks the woman who preverbially
29 keeps the home fires burning.
30 It would surely be possible to continue indefinately, for every
31 shoe tells a story. Why don't you sit here on the curb awhile and
32 watch the shoes go by? I'd stay, but I have to go and polish my
33 white bucks.

2. The following words are very commonly misspelled in student papers. Errors resulting from a confusion of forms like *there, their, they're* and *weather, whether* are not included. Each word is divided into syllables so that you may visualize how it is put together. Before studying the words, have someone dictate the list to you and score your paper. Then study the words you miss, reviewing them as often as possible. At the end of the term take this test again.

1. academic (ac a dem ic)
2. accommodate (ac com mo date)
3. acquainted (ac quaint ed)
4. across (a cross)
5. adolescence (ad o les cence)
6. analysis (a nal y sis)
7. argument (ar gu ment)
8. article (ar ti cle)
9. athlete (ath lete)
10. attendance (at tend ance)
11. beginning (be gin ning)
12. believe (be lieve)
13. benefited (ben e fit ed)
14. Britain (Brit ain)
15. business (busi ness)
16. candidate (can di date)

17. changeable (change a ble)
18. college (col lege)
19. continuous (con tin u ous)
20. curiosity (cu ri os i ty)
21. definite (def i nite)
22. developing (de vel op ing)
23. disappearance (dis ap pear ance)
24. disappoint (dis ap point)
25. disastrous (dis as trous)
26. embarrassed (em bar rassed)
27. environment (en vi ron ment)
28. exaggerate (ex ag ger ate)
29. existence (ex ist ence)
30. experience (ex pe ri ence)
31. familiar (fa mil iar)
32. fascinate (fas ci nate)
33. foreign (for eign)
34. forty (for ty)
35. fraternity (fra ter ni ty)
36. government (gov ern ment)
37. grammar (gram mar)
38. hindrance (hin drance)
39. humorous (hu mor ous)
40. hygiene (hy giene)
41. immediately (im me di ate ly)
42. incidentally (in ci den tal ly)
43. independent (in de pend ent)
44. instructor (in struc tor)
45. interest (in ter est)
46. irrelevant (ir rel e vant)
47. laboratory (lab o ra to ry)
48. leisure (lei sure)
49. library (li brar y)
50. maintenance (main te nance)
51. medicine (med i cine)
52. misspelled (mis spelled)
53. monotonous (mo not o nous)
54. niece (niece)
55. ninety (nine ty)
56. noticeable (no tice a ble)
57. nuisance (nui sance)
58. occasionally (oc ca sion al ly)
59. occurrence (oc cur rence)
60. omitted (o mit ted)
61. opportunity (op por tu ni ty)
62. optimistic (op ti mis tic)
63. parallel (par al lel)
64. particularly (par tic u lar ly)
65. perform (per form)
66. possess (pos sess)
67. practically (prac ti cal ly)
68. prejudiced (prej u diced)
69. privilege (priv i lege)
70. procedure (pro ce dure)
71. professor (pro fes sor)
72. pronunciation (pro nun ci a tion)
73. psychology (psy chol o gy)
74. quantity (quan ti ty)
75. receive (re ceive)
76. recommend (rec om mend)
77. referring (re fer ring)
78. religious (re li gious)
79. resemblance (re sem blance)
80. roommate (room mate)
81. sacrifice (sac ri fice)
82. sensible (sen si ble)
83. seize (seize)
84. separate (sep a rate)
85. similar (sim i lar)
86. sophomore (soph o more)
87. studying (stud y ing)
88. succeed (suc ceed)
89. successful (suc cess ful)
90. surprise (sur prise)
91. temperament (tem per a ment)
92. tendency (tend en cy)
93. thoroughly (thor ough ly)
94. tragedy (trag e dy)
95. transferring (trans fer ring)
96. truly (tru ly)
97. unnecessary (un nec es sar y)
98. until (un til)
99. wholly (whol ly)
100. writing (writ ing)

3. Add the suffixes indicated to the following words and give alternate forms if they exist. Study *Doubling final consonants, *E §5 and *-ce, -ge, before you work out this exercise.

1. drop + ed
2. kidnap + er
3. courage + ous
4. control + ed
5. dine + ing
6. acknowledge + ment
7. travel + ed
8. desire + ous

9. service + able
10. like + able
11. bias + ed
12. endure + ing
13. confer + ed
14. grieve + ous
15. quarrel + er
16. mile + age
17. prove + able
18. singe + ing
19. worship + er
20. repay + ed
21. refer + al
22. deter + ent
23. tie + ing
24. clot +ed
25. ridicule + ous
26. profit + able
27. equip + age
28. parallel + ed
29. infer + ence
30. shoe + ing

4. Troublesome words can often be more easily remembered by using them in sentences. For each group of these frequently confused words, make up a sentence showing their correct use. Example: After running *awhile* together, they separated for *a while.*

accept–except
affect–effect
already–all ready
breath–breathe
capital–capitol
choose–chose
complement–compliment
conscience–conscious–conscientious
council–counsel–consul
formerly–formally
its–it's
lead–led
loose–lose
moral–morale
principal–principle
quiet–quite
site–cite–sight
stationery–stationary
there–their–they're
whether–weather
whose–who's

5. In your spelling notebook keep a list of words encountered in your reading that you will have to use in various courses. Also list words you have misspelled and new words you will want to use in general writing. To fix the spelling more definitely in your mind, divide the words into syllables as you enter them; consult your dictionary for this purpose. Use the names of your subjects for headings, for example:

History	*Psychology*	*Zoology*	*General*
me di e val	ap per cep tion	car ti lag i nous	dor mi to ry
Med i ter ra ne an	cor re la tion	ap o neu ro sis	soph o more
Ren ais sance	ho me o sta sis	Eu sta chi an	sched ule

An experienced writer means a point as definitely as he means a word.

ARLO BATES

Chapter **5**

Punctuation

Good punctuation is possible only in good writing.

If sentence structure is lame or stiff, punctuation is only patchwork,

helping after a fashion but also showing how bad the word pattern is.

GEORGE SUMMEY, JR.

Punctuation marks do more than indicate such obvious facts of language as "This is a sentence," "This is a question." They help us separate both words and thoughts and so present them distinctly to a reader; they help group and keep together related words and related ideas; they set off certain words for emphasis. Their use affects the tempo of writing—too many marks may slow the reader to the point of exasperation, and too few may make him go over a passage two or three times to get its meaning. The writer who wishes his work to appear to the best advantage will give close attention to its punctuation.[1]

Most marks come easily enough. Even in a hastily written first draft a writer will feel the natural grouping of his ideas sufficiently to mark the sentences and most of the subordinate elements in a fairly reasonable way. But punctuation is not completely automatic, even with practiced writers. The boy who put at the end of a class theme "Not time to punctuate" was partly right, for punctuation needs careful checking in revision. By far the largest number of slips in punctuation in student papers are caused by carelessness—end quote marks omitted, periods put after questions, commas or apostrophes forgotten. Most of the suggestions about the use of particular marks made in this chapter and in the alphabetical articles in the *Index* are to be applied in revising papers rather than in writing the first draft.

The practices of punctuation are set by the editors of books and periodicals, who draw up statements of their usage in stylebooks and

[1] See Summey for the most thorough study of current punctuation practices (Books cited by name of author only will be found in the Bibliography, pp. XIV-XV); see also Harold Whitehall, *Structural Essentials of English* (New York, 1954), Ch. 10. The stylebooks of publishing houses treat punctuation.

change the manuscripts they print to conform to these rules. Though the practices vary somewhat among publications, they agree on most points. English teachers try to encourage students to follow the more important and commonly accepted usages. Since readers have come to understand punctuation marks as signals in interpreting what they read, it is to a writer's interest to know and to follow the usual conventions and also to know where he has a choice.

Appropriate punctuation

Effective punctuation depends on a knowledge of the meaning and function of the various marks and on a knowledge of their actual use in current writing. Some functions are so fixed in typical writing and printing that the marks serve as definite signals to readers, and because the conventions are so widespread and definite, they are no problem for a writer. The marks at the ends of sentences, for example, are well standardized; the uses of some other marks, such as the period after abbreviations, the colon, and quotation marks, are also quite definite.

But in a number of situations within a sentence ("internal punctuation") you have a choice among several punctuation marks and will need to use your judgment. Your aim is to make your statements easily grasped by your readers–remembering that strangers coming cold to your sentences may need a little more guidance than you, who are already familiar with them. In addition you should consider the appropriateness of the punctuation to the other traits of your writing.

Two groups of marks that are similar in function can illustrate the choices often possible. The first series–the comma, semicolon, and period–may be used to separate elements or statements. These marks differ in the degree of separation indicated. A comma makes a slight separation, a period a complete separation, and a semicolon a separation that is between the other two but much nearer the period than the comma. Look at these versions of the same statement:

1. The person, the time, the place, the purpose, the preliminary assumptions–these enter into all discussions of human affairs; it seems impossible to conceive of any discussion without these features.
2. The person; the time; the place; the purpose; the preliminary assumptions: these enter into all discussions of human affairs. It seems impossible to conceive of any discussion without these features.
3. The person. The time. The place. The purpose. The preliminary assumptions. These enter into all discussions of human affairs. It seems impossible to conceive of any discussion without these features.

The first is obviously the most rapid, holding the elements most closely together; the second is more emphatic and slower; the third gives still more emphasis to each element but moves more rapidly than the second. Professor C. A. Beard actually wrote the third way (*The Discussion of Human Affairs,* p. 14), giving the statements still more emphasis by having them stand as a complete paragraph. The second seems unnecessarily Formal and not likely to be used. The first would be appropriate to a more General style.

A second series of marks that have much the same meaning but different tone consists of two commas, two dashes, or parentheses used to "set off" part of a statement. Consider the emphasis on *but actually turns out to be a help* in these four versions of the same sentence:

1. One thing which at first seems to be an obstacle for an athlete but actually turns out to be a help is the fact that he usually has less spare time than a nonathlete.
2. One thing which at first seems to be an obstacle for an athlete, but actually turns out to be a help, is the fact that he usually has less spare time than a nonathlete.
3. One thing which at first seems to be an obstacle for an athlete—but actually turns out to be a help—is the fact that he usually has less spare time than a nonathlete.
4. One thing which at first seems to be an obstacle for an athlete (but actually turns out to be a help) is the fact that he usually has less spare time than a nonathlete.

The first version could go in a General style using as few marks as possible. The second, with commas, throws more emphasis on *but actually turns out to be a help,* the idea that is to be developed in the rest of the paper; the dashes emphasize it still more, while the parentheses subordinate it, make it less essential than the writer would want it to be. Whether he chose the second or third would depend on whether he wished to be more or less emphatic.

More complex (not necessarily longer) sentences need more and heavier points (semicolons rather than commas, perhaps) to guide the readers; shorter and more direct sentences need fewer. Many of the "rules" ordinarily given for punctuation are based on nineteenth-century style, in which the sentences were longer, averaging about forty words, and contained more constructions; sentences in current writing average nearer twenty words, have fewer constructions, are more direct, and so need fewer marks.

The preference in General English today is for rather "open" punctuation, using the marks conventionally expected and only as many more as may be required for clarity. Formal writers tend to use more

The Principal Punctuation Marks

1. SENTENCE MARKS. Used principally to mark the end of sentences:

.	*Period,* at the end of statements (and after abbreviations, in decimals, dollars and cents, and so on)
?	*Question mark* (interrogation point), at the end of questions: He said, "Do you want to come?"; not used after indirect questions: He asked if we wanted to come.
!	*Exclamation mark* (exclamation point), at the end of an exclamation or vigorously stressed sentence
——	*Long dash,* after a statement that is interrupted
. . .	*Ellipsis,* after a statement that is left uncompleted, or a speech that is allowed to die away

2. INTERNAL MARKS. Used to separate or to indicate the relation between elements within a sentence:

,	*Comma,* the most common mark, basically a mark of slight separation between words, phrases, or clauses. It has a number of routine uses, as in *dates.
;	*Semicolon,* indicating a degree of separation greater than that marked by a comma and slightly less than that marked by a period
:	*Colon,* a mark of anticipation, pointing to what follows. It is used after the salutation of a business letter and to introduce formal quotations, explanatory statements, or series too long or too heavy to be prefaced by commas.
–	*Dash,* a mark of separation more intense than a comma. It is used when the construction of a sentence is abruptly broken and when a note of surprise or feeling is indicated. Two dashes may set off a parenthetical expression.
( )	*Parentheses,* or curves, used to inclose an explanatory statement not built into the construction of a sentence
[ ]	*Brackets,* used to inclose matter that has been inserted in quotations and as parentheses within parentheses

3. QUOTATION MARKS " " used to inclose speeches in real or imagined conversation and any short quoted words or statements

marks, often because they need them in their rather elaborate sentences but often also because they follow a tradition of "close" punctuation. The following passage, given with Formal or "close" punctuation and with General or "open," illustrates some of the differences between the two styles:

Formal (close) punctuation

Now, the chief literary and dramatic vice of the scientists and philosophers, is that they seldom begin at the point of the reader's or hearer's interest. Here, for example, is a book on botany. It begins with a long account of the history of botany, and continues with an even longer account of the general principles of the science. But what do you, or what do I, want to know about the feeble beginnings of botany? We want to know—provided, of course, that we want to be something more than the ladylike botanists who know only the names of flowers—we want to know what the problems of botany are; in what direction botanical research is tending; what differences all this botanical research makes anyway; why it is worth studying.

General (open) punctuation

Now the chief literary and dramatic vice of the scientists and philosophers is that they seldom begin at the point of the reader's or hearer's interest. Here for example is a book on botany. It begins with a long account of the history of botany and continues with an even longer account of the general principles of the science. But what do you or what do I want to know about the feeble beginnings of botany? We want to know, provided of course that we want to be something more than the ladylike botanists who know only the names of flowers, we want to know what the problems of botany are, in what direction botanical research is tending, what differences all this botanical research makes anyway, why it is worth studying.

Since most writers today, and certainly most student writers, write in rather short and direct sentences, they usually are encouraged to follow the General custom. The movement of this thirty-six word sentence from a brief review of a novel in the London *Times Literary Supplement* shows how directness removes the need for internal marks.

> Cardiac failure has been so often used as a device that the reader's own heart sinks slightly on learning in the first chapter that John Raymond was given six months to live by a Harley-street specialist.

To answer questions about punctuation you need to know current practices from observing good writing and from studying textbook summaries, and you need to be able to sense what is appropriate to your writing. College students tend to use too many punctuation marks, especially too many commas. The boy who wrote this sentence was taking no chances:

Naturally, the first thing he does, after his interest is aroused, is to attempt to build a small receiving set of his own.

None of the commas is wrong but no one of them is necessary either, and without them the sentence moves more easily, and more appropriately to a simple account of experiences in amateur radio:

Naturally the first thing he does after his interest is aroused is to attempt to build a small receiving set of his own.

Partly because punctuation depends on the other qualities of your language, it is better not to pause in writing the first draft to decide on a problematical mark but to go on and to pay some special attention to the punctuation in revising your paper.

The remaining sections of this chapter review the principal punctuation situations, with special attention to those in which usage is divided or a choice of marks is possible. (Articles on the individual marks will be found in the *Index.*)

At ends of sentences

In the great majority of sentences no question arises about end punctuation. Most sentences are statements and are marked by a period.

A question mark is used after a clear-cut question: *Did you know that he had been to Alaska?* It stands immediately after a question that is included within a sentence: *What do all these facts prove? you may ask.* (A comma might be used here, giving a good deal less emphasis to the question: *What do all these facts prove, you may ask.*) A question mark is not generally used after a request phrased as a question (*Will you please give this your immediate attention.*), though it might be used in rather Formal style. A question mark is not used after an indirect question: *He asked if we wanted to play tennis. He asked his mother why he could not leave the house on Saturday.* (The direct question would be: *He asked his mother, "Why can't I leave the house on Saturday?"*)

Whether or not a word or statement is regarded as an exclamation depends on the stress it receives. (In this respect, writing is largely a representation of speech.) The one-word exclamations range from strong ones like *Ouch!* which would almost always carry an exclamation mark to mild ones like *Oh* that might warrant one or might deserve only a comma. In general, exclamations (*You! You there with the glasses!*), vigorous commands (*Don't you dare say that again!*), and occasional emphatic statements (*This was a markup of 300%!*)

have exclamation marks. But they are less used than formerly except in advertising and in some excited personal writing.

Between subjects, verbs, objects

Commas should *not* be used between the main elements of a clause or sentence, between its subject and verb or between its verb and object or complement, or between a preposition and its object. The temptation to punctuate these elements is strongest when they are long or are themselves clauses. There should be no mark where the brackets stand in the following sentences:

Subject and verb: Boys who are supposedly wild [ ] should not be sent to a strict preparatory school.

My friend estimated that the average news program that is fit to be put on the air [ ] takes one man approximately five hours to prepare.

Verb and object: We all know [ ] that the person who is hardworking and willing has a good deal put over on him.

The manager frequently said [ ] if he had his way the project would be abandoned. (The clause is a direct object, not a quotation formally introduced by a construction like *He said*. See p. 128.)

Verb and complement: Another way in which the schedule should be arranged is [ ] so that the games in the last week can be at home.

Preposition and object: He would not have done it except [ ] that everyone was daring him to.

Formal and somewhat old-fashioned writing occasionally uses a comma between a long subject and its verb; for example, it might add a comma to the sentence above beginning "My friend estimated," but this practice is not advisable in student writing.

The verbs in a compound predicate (two verbs having the same subject) should not be separated by a comma unless they are long or some confusion might result or the comma is needed for contrast.

Compound predicate: Thus in fifteen years rabbit raising has ceased to be a hobby [ ] and has taken a definite place among the industries of the world.

Pop could talk himself out of trouble [ ] and also talk himself into a lot of trouble. (Comma might be used in this sentence to emphasize the contrast.)

Sometimes several subjects of the same verb (compound subject) are summarized by a word like *all*. This summarizing word is usually preceded by a dash: The characters, the plot, the theme, the scene—all are trite in this play.

Between coordinate clauses

A comma between the clauses of a compound sentence connected by *and, nor, or, yet* emphasizes their distinctness and gives the writing a slightly slower pace. Formal writing ordinarily has a comma; General writing is likely not to have one unless the clauses are long or have different subjects. The use of a comma really depends on the tone the writer wishes.

> They read novels by the dozen and they write a report on every one. (Closely related clauses; comma unnecessary)
>
> Most textbooks have tended to encourage close punctuation, and students sometimes seem to see how many commas they can put in. (Clauses have different subjects; comma optional but convenient)
>
> These increased orders meant a demand for labor, and workers began to stream in from all parts of the state. (Clauses have different subjects; comma better)

Commas are ordinarily used between clauses connected by *but* or *for:*

> There are recognizable dialects in the United States, but they show fewer differences than would be expected in a country of such size.
>
> Yet this is not a characteristic test, for the same reaction is given by several other aromatic compounds.

When there is no connective between the clauses, or when they are connected by a conjunctive adverb (*however, therefore . . .*), a semicolon is used:

> No connective: In rather formal papers for college courses and in theses, Formal usage should be followed; in formal papers, like many themes, either General or Formal may be used, as the instructor prefers.
>
> Conjunctive adverb: Medical schools keep requesting the colleges not to teach "medical subjects"; however they still give the advantage in admissions to students with a good deal of chemistry and zoology.

The latter sentence is rather heavy, and General usage would have a comma and *but* rather than a semicolon and *however.*

When the second clause of a compound sentence repeats the idea or makes specific the meaning of the first, a colon is used:

> There is one thing that I am sure of now: at this stage of his experience he should have followed my advice.

When the writer shifts his construction abruptly or wishes to emphasize the separateness of the clauses, a dash may be used:

> How many times she must have said this before–I shuddered at the simple thought.

Clauses of the type *the more . . . the more* ordinarily have no mark:

The more education a man has the more likely he is to be independent in his views and obstinate in sticking to them.—JOYCE CARY, "The Mass Mind: Our Favorite Folly," *Harper's Magazine*, March 1952, p. 26

After preceding subordinate elements

A comma is used after a subordinate clause or long phrase that precedes the main clause, especially in Formal style. A comma is not used in General writing if the preceding element is short and closely related to what follows, especially if the two clauses have the same subject.

Comma not necessary: As soon as they register they must pay their fees.

Comma optional: When we lost the fourth of the six games, [or no mark] we just about gave up.

Comma needed: Because so much of the land has been taken for farms, regions where birds and wild animals can live have been greatly reduced. (Clauses have different subjects.)

Comma with long phrase: In a society without hereditary social standing, a person's job is the chief sign of his status.

Short preceding modifiers should not be punctuated unless a comma is necessary to give special emphasis or to prevent misreading:

Soon [ ] we were at the gym and in less time than usual were in our uniforms.

In my opinion [ ] these youthful marriages are absolutely justifiable.

Several times in recent years [ ] one of the heavy tractors has sunk out of sight in the thick winter mud.

When you do separate a subordinate element from the rest of the sentence, be sure to use a comma, not a semicolon:

Because learning to live together is so much harder than learning to fight each other, [not ;] the nations of the world make little progress toward peace.

Before subordinate elements

The punctuation of words, phrases, and clauses coming after the words they modify depends on the closeness of the relationship between the modifier and its headword.

Close or restrictive modifiers—no commas

A modifier that closely limits or restricts the meaning of its headword is not set off by commas. The principal type is the restrictive adjective clause:

Boys *who are supposedly wild* should not be sent to a strict preparatory school. (Not all boys are supposedly wild.)

The man *who had the aisle seat* had to get up four times.

The house *that burned* was pretty well gone to pieces anyway. (Most adjective clauses beginning with *that* are restrictive.)

The first three cars *we saw* were going the wrong way. (See "Long and short constructions," p. 188.)

Other close modifiers are epithets and occupations that are treated as part of a name (Charles the Good, Lang the baker) or that obviously limit a noun (His friends Jock and Harry were the first to arrive) and adverbial clauses that would be spoken without a pause:

He must have left *because he had another appointment.*

A freshman has a chance to see all that is going on at a fraternity *when he receives an invitation to dinner.*

Loose or nonrestrictive modifiers—commas

A modifier that does not limit the headword but adds descriptive details is marked by a comma, or by two commas if it does not come at the end of the sentence.

Another time Frank spent an unforgettable week with his father, *who had broken a leg and was unable to go to the office.*

A. T. Fowler, *assistant professor of zoology,* teaches the course.

His best friend, *Jock,* was the first to come.

Old Nat, *who had been a great fisherman in his day,* wouldn't believe our story.

He must have left, *because his coat and hat are gone.*

In saying or reading sentences like these there is a slight drop in tone and a very brief pause before the modifier. Contrast the sound of these sentences:

The man *who was standing at the head of the line* had been there since five o'clock. (No pause or tone change—restrictive—no comma)

Bill, *who was standing at the head of the line,* had been there since five o'clock. (Slight pause and drop in tone on Bill—nonrestrictive—commas)

He must have left *because he had another appointment.* (No pause or tone change—close modifier—no comma)

He must have left, *because his coat and hat are gone.* (Slight pause and tone change—loose modifier—comma)

Frequently a writer has a choice of using or not using commas with a following modifier, using them if he wants to emphasize a slight relation, not using them if he wishes the sentence elements to seem more closely related. There is often little difference in meaning but some difference in tone and movement. In sentences like the following, commas might or might not be used around the italicized expressions, depending on the tone and emphasis desired:

The man *who had previously glanced at us* now really stared.

We must *of course* face the facts.

This atmosphere is completed when you are greeted by the doorman *dressed up like a vaudeville admiral.*

The best test is reading the passage aloud, using commas if you change your voice and pause slightly before the modifier, not using them if you read without change.

A phrase modifying the whole clause is set off by a comma:

The time per sample varies, *depending on the nature of the sample being run.*

"How'd you like to go to the game tomorrow?" he asked, *much to my surprise.*

(See " 'Absolute' verbid phrases," p. 65.)

Do not use a semicolon to set off modifiers of the sort described in this section:

It takes quite a bit of courage to start *War and Peace,* [not ;] because it is not only long but has a lot of characters with curious Russian names.

Around interrupting elements

A phrase or clause that interrupts the direct movement of the sentence should be set off by commas, *two* commas:

This last semester, *if it has done nothing else,* has given me confidence in myself.

Over in the corner, *beside the dark and broken window where a newspaper was stuffed to keep out the rain,* sat Verona.

Did intelligent people, *he asked himself,* do things like that?

Usage is divided over setting off short parenthetical words and phrases like *incidentally, of course*. Setting them off with commas is more characteristic of Formal than of General writing, though there is often a difference in emphasis according to whether or not commas are used:

These early attempts, of course, brought no results.

These early attempts of course brought no results.

The famous artist, oddly enough, preferred the company of common laborers to that of his own kind.

The famous artist oddly enough preferred the company of common laborers to that of his own kind.

Adverbs that modify the verb or the statement closely should not be set off by commas when they are in their natural position:

Perhaps [ ] they had never intended to come.

They had never intended to come, perhaps.

When a *conjunctive adverb[1] stands after the first phrase in its clause, as it often does, it is set off by commas, and often it is set off when it stands first in the clause:

The next morning, however, they all set out as though nothing had happened.

The second plan, therefore, was the one determined upon for the holiday.

However, [or no comma] they all set out the next morning as though nothing had happened.

But and other lighter conjunctions are a part of the clauses in which they appear and should not be set off:

I was positive that if someone would just give me some guidance I could do much better, but [ ] the semester continued the same as before.

Dashes are occasionally used to emphasize a parenthetical expression:

They think that they are the last radicals–and the greatest–and that their ideas and their works will live forever.

Parentheses are used to inclose added details or illustrations not built into the construction of a sentence or to subordinate an aside or an obvious fact. They are more appropriate for Formal exposition and should be used sparingly in more General sorts of writing.

The few verb endings that English now retains (*-s, -ed, -ing*) are being still further reduced in ordinary speech.

The largest additions to the territory of the United States (the Louisiana Purchase and Alaska) were gained by purchase.

A punctuation mark belonging to a part of a sentence that includes a parenthesis comes *after* the second curve:

---

[1] Throughout this book, references to *Index* articles are indicated by asterisks (*).

There are several words of foreign origin that keep their original plural forms (like *alumnae, alumni, analyses*), and many that have two forms (like appendix, cactus, formula).

Square brackets [ ] are used chiefly as parentheses within parentheses or to mark words inserted in a direct quotation:

Each pronunciation of *process* (pros' es and [much less commonly] prō' ses) has a history.

According to Dr. Roberts, "It [the institution of private property] is in our time under attack in many parts of the world."

(See *Parentheses and *Brackets.)

In lists and series

Commas separate the items of a series of three or more short elements:

The typical freshman's program includes English, social studies, a language, and some sort of science.

When to get up, when to eat, when to work, when to have fun, when to go to bed were all laid down in the regulations.

Commas usually are not used when the items are joined by connectives:

Fire insurance and life insurance and accident insurance and car insurance and all other forms of insurance are bets placed on odds more or less scientifically determined.

Formal usage regularly retains a comma before the last member of a series when it has a connective (literature, painting, sculpture, music, and drama); General usage is divided, but often does not (literature, painting, sculpture, music and drama) unless some misinterpretation would result, as when the last item itself contains a connective (tired, dirty, and black and blue). A writer should be consistent in this use or non-use of the final comma, but he has the option of choosing whichever practice is more appropriate to the other traits of his style. (See *Series.)

Two items connected by *and* are not usually punctuated:

In high school the student is paid ten dollars a month for helping the teachers in their work [ ] and for doing odd jobs about the school building.

A construction formally introducing a series is followed by a colon (a mark that looks ahead, as the salutation of a letter [*Gentlemen:*] looks ahead to the text of the letter):

Then come the employees in charge of the various departments: the soda fountain, the ice cream, the grill, and the clams.

When several adjectives modify a single noun, commas are used between them:

When the long, cold, lonesome evenings came, we would gather about the old wood stove and eat the chestnuts.

In this sentence there are commas between *long–cold–lonesome* because each stands in the same relation to the noun *evenings*. But there is no comma between *old* and *wood* because *old* modifies *wood stove* rather than just *stove*. A comma following *old* would throw more emphasis upon *wood* and might sometimes be wanted. Compare these two versions:

The room presents a colonial effect with its old-fashioned, cross-beamed ceiling and gray, brick fireplace.

The room presents a colonial effect with its old-fashioned cross-beamed ceiling and gray brick fireplace.

Either version is correct, but in the first *cross-beamed* and *brick* stand out as separate modifiers of their nouns.

For emphasis and clearness

A comma tends to keep distinct the constructions it separates and to emphasize slightly the construction that follows the mark:

Temporarily the wine industry was all but ruined, and farmers turned to dairying, and to cooperation to give them a market.

This is especially true when a connective is omitted:

And afterwards I told her how I felt, how I kept feeling about her.

Often a comma can guide a reader in interpreting a sentence and make it unnecessary for him to go back over it for meaning because he has mistaken the grouping of the words. *For* or *but* may be either a conjunction or a preposition, and confusion may be avoided by using a comma before either when it is used as a conjunction:

He talked about Germany but he never went, for money was too scarce to spend on voyages. (To avoid reading "went for money")

The surgeon's face showed no emotion, but anxiety and a little nervousness must be seething behind that impassive mask. (To avoid reading "no emotion but anxiety")

It is not necessary to have a session like this very often, but when you do, get everything off your mind that is disturbing you. (Not: but when you do get everything off your mind. . . .)

After all, the students had gone quietly. (Not: After all the students. . . .)

The only way that you can develop honestly is to discover how you write now, and then write naturally in everything you hand in. (Not: how you write now and then. . . .)

When the same word occurs consecutively a comma may be used, though usage is divided on this:

What the trouble really is, is of no interest to him.

Around quotations

Quotation marks are used to inclose real or imagined speeches, conversation and short excerpts from printed matter. Either double quotation marks (" ") or single quotation marks (' ') may be used for a quotation, though the double marks are much more common. If there is a quotation within a quotation, the marks are alternated:

"The first eight I called on answered, 'Not prepared,' " Miss Stoddard complained.

Or: 'The first eight I called on answered, "Not prepared," ' Miss Stoddard complained.

When a speech is introduced by a formula like *he said,* it is preceded by a comma. If it is built into the construction of the sentence, there is no preceding comma:

I rode with him two hours and his only remark was "Do you think it's going to rain?"

The following passage shows the typical uses of quotation marks and paragraphing for conversation:

A man and a woman stood on the observation platform of a large eastern airport. In the distance a light plane roared down the runway and took off toward the far horizon.

The man said, "That's the way to travel. No waiting around. When you feel like going, you go."

"Well!" The woman seemed shocked. "You'd never get me into one of those things!"

"What? But you've flown before."

"In an airliner, yes," the woman said, "but that's different. Why, I'd no more trust my life in one of those–those kites than. . . ."

Most American publishers put a comma or a period inside the closing quotation mark, regardless of whether it belongs to the quotation or to the sentence as a whole:

"In the beginning," he said–probably meaning "two years ago."

Exclamation points and question marks stand inside the quotation marks if the quotation is an exclamation or a question, outside if the including sentence is the exclamation or question:

> Then suddenly he shouted, "Get out of here, all of you!"
> You don't mean that he actually said "You're another"!
> She asked, "Won't you please try to do it for me?"
> Did she say, "Please try to do it"?

In expository matter quotations of more than one sentence are often indented and printed in smaller type without quotation marks—as is frequently done in this book. In longhand manuscript simply indent such quotations about half an inch; in typed copy, indent and single space. (For further details see *Quotation marks.)

In conventional positions

Besides indicating parts of sentences, periods and commas have several conventional uses; some of the more common ones are listed here. Uses of the period:

1) *Abbreviations:* Dec. N.C. e.g. vol. When the letters of the abbreviation are frequently spoken instead of the words they stand for, the period often is not used: CIO, TVA, USSR (see *Abbreviations §3).

2) *Dollars and cents:* $14.28 $0.87 (but not in 87 cents, 87¢). See *Money.

3) *Decimals:* .4 .04 14.33 (but 4%, 4 percent).

Some conventional uses of the comma are:

1) *In dates,* between the day of the month and the year: May 20, 1958. When only the month and year are given, a comma is not necessary (May 1958), though it is frequently found (May, 1958). See *Dates.

2) *In addresses,* between town and state or city and country when they stand on the same line: Waco, Texas; Seattle, King County, Washington; Casablanca, Morocco.

3) *After the salutation of personal letters:* Dear Fred, Dear Aunt Dorothy,

4) *In figures,* grouping digits by threes: 6,471,063

5) *After names followed by titles or degrees:* A. H. Hazen, Ph.D.; Arthur Garfield Hays, Esq.; J. F. Forsythe, Jr.; Annie T. Bowditch, Secretary.

6) *After exclamations* like *well, oh, why* when they are not emphatic.

Using capital letters

The principal uses of capital letters in English are well standardized and give very little trouble. These are: first words of sentences, names of people and places, proper adjectives derived from these names, days of the week, months, the important words in *titles, ordinarily the first word of a line of verse, the pronoun **I*, the exclamation *O,* nouns and pronouns referring to Deity, names of companies and organizations.

Some items formerly capitalized no longer are: the seasons, points of the compass (except when they refer to a region, *the Southwest*), common nouns derived from proper names when they have lost the suggestion of the name (*paris green, jersey, macadam, volt, fedora, shrapnel*).

Many class nouns are capitalized when they refer to an individual thing or person: I dislike all professors–I dislike Professor Weems; He was taking geography–He was taking Geography 106. A title standing for a particular person may be capitalized: *the Senator, the Principal.* Names of members of a family are not capitalized when used as common nouns (*my father, his brother*), but when used specifically, like a proper name, they usually are: We told *Mother* what we had done. Similarly, either *He was in the army* or *He was in the Army* might be used, the first indicating that he was in *an* army, the latter that he was in the United States (or Canadian or French or British) Army.

In the title of a book, article, play, or movie, the first and last words and all other words except articles and the short prepositions and conjunctions are capitalized: *The Brothers Karamazov; Yesterday, Today and Tomorrow; No Place to Hide;* "The Garden Party" (a short story).

Most magazines and books use capitals on words like *street, river, church, hotel, park* when they are parts of proper names, although newspapers do not. Most General writers follow book conventions (*Bond Street, Potomac River, First Methodist Church, Drake Hotel, Lincoln Park*).

Capitals may be used for stylistic reasons, as for emphasis, especially in Formal writing. (Her precious Intuition, I suppose). This practice is rare now and is not recommended unless other traits of style make it appropriate.

Typically, students use more capital letters than are necessary and should limit them to the standard situations. (See *Capital letters.)

Underlining for italics

Words or statements that would be printed in italics are underlined once in manuscript. Formal, especially academic, writing follows the conventions of book publishing, using italics in a number of standardized places; General writing is more likely to follow newspaper usage, which has largely given them up. The principal uses are:

1) To indicate the titles of books, plays, motion pictures, and other complete works. Newspapers and many magazines put such titles in quotation marks. (Titles of articles, short stories, and short poems are put in quotation marks.)

2) To indicate the titles of periodicals and newspapers: *Harper's Magazine, The New York Times* (or The New York *Times*). See *Titles of articles, books, etc.

3) To mark words and expressions considered as words rather than for their meaning: There is a shade of difference between *because* and *for* used as conjunctions.

4) To mark words from foreign languages that are not regarded as English: *persona non grata, coup d'état, Götterdämmerung;* but not "chassis," "coup," "blitzkrieg." (For a list see *Foreign words in English.)

5) To emphasize words or statements, especially in factual writing. Spoken emphasis may be represented, though this device is best used sparingly: It was *his* night, all right.

Underlining, as well as the other matters of punctuation, should be checked when you proofread your papers.

An appropriate use of punctuation marks will help make your meaning clear to readers, even to strangers, and often will show the exact emphasis you intend. The following *Index* articles deal with particular problems of punctuation:

*Abbreviations
*Apostrophe
*Brackets
*Capital letters
*Caret
*Colon
*Comma
*Dash
*Division of words
*Ellipsis
*End-stop
*Exclamation mark
*Hyphen
*Leaders
*Letters
*Numbers
*Parentheses
*Period
*Question mark
*Quotation marks

*Restrictive and nonrestrictive
*Semicolon
*Series
*Titles of articles, books, etc.
*Underlining

Chapter 5

SUGGESTED STUDY AND WRITING

1. Read the following passage and then write down what mark, if any, should be used in each of the lettered spaces. Be prepared to give reasons for each mark you use, to explain possible optional marks, or to justify the omission of a mark.

> The horrors of war are all *a* that they are supposed to be. They are even worse *b* for the worst horror can never be written about *c* or communicated. It is the frightful monotony and boredom *d* which is the lot of the private with nothing to think about. Since my education had given me nothing to think about *e* I devoted myself *f* as the alternative to suicide *g* to the mastery of all the arts implied in the verb *h* "to soldier." I learned to protract the performance of any task *i* so that I would not be asked to do another. By the end of the war *j* I could give the impression that I was busy digging a ditch *k* without putting my pick into the ground all day. I have found this training very useful in my present capacity. But *l* on the whole *m* aside from the physiological benefits conferred upon me by a regular *n* outdoor life *o* I write off my years in the Army *p* as a complete blank. The arts of soldiering *q* at least at the buck-private level *r* are not liberal arts. The manual of arms is not a great book.—ROBERT M. HUTCHINS, "The Autobiography of an Uneducated Man," *Education for Freedom,* p. 5

2. Supply appropriate punctuation for the following passages, from which the punctuation marks have been removed. First, glance through a passage to get an idea of its content and general movement. Decide whether Formal or General punctuation is appropriate to it, taking into consideration what you may know about the author and source. Then copy the passage and insert punctuation marks, capital letters, and paragraph symbols, but make no other changes. Be prepared to tell why you used each mark.

A) picasso is ranked as the wittiest artist and best conversationalist since whistler if very different he has become famous for his talk and what could be called his carnivorous wit since it usually eats other people alive even his friends speak with almost helpless appreciation of how his malicious eyes scintillate as he like his listeners enjoys his malefic tongue he does not converse but talks solo creatively decisively and fascinatingly with wit ideas and odd images his ever present spanish accent seasoning his phrases which emerge in bursts the only attention he pays to anything that may be said in comment or reply is to change it so much on dealing with it as to make it unrecognizable to whoever has just said it moreover picasso then holds the speaker responsible for what he has not said as a woman friend of his once remarked if he has been in the wrong about something he always forgives you—JANET FLANNER, "The Surprise of the Century," Originally published in *The New Yorker,* March 9, 1957, p. 58

B) there seems to be no chilly distance existing between the german students and the professor but on the contrary a companionable intercourse the opposite of chilliness and reserve when the professor enters a beer hall in the evening where students are gathered together these rise up and take off their caps and invite the old gentleman to sit with them and partake he accepts and the pleasant talk and the beer flow for an hour or two and by and by the professor properly charged and comfortable gives a cordial good night while the students stand bowing and uncovered and then he moves on his happy way homeward with all his vast cargo of learning afloat in his hold nobody finds fault or feels outraged no harm has been done—MARK TWAIN, *A Tramp Abroad,* p. 27

C) there is another and good reason for making a will a person who dies without one leaves his property to be distributed according to an official formula that may work hardship on his family for example if a widow and children survive the widow receives only one third of the estate and the children two thirds if a childless widow and parent brother or sister or descendant of a deceased brother or sister survive the widow gets all personal property but only half the real estate the other half going to the other heirs if there are no kin all personal property goes to the state and all real estate to the county a lawyers fee for writing a simple will isnt much and its worth it—"If You Die Without a Will," Chicago *Sun-Times,* June 25, 1957, p. 29

D) the brilliant young renaissance prince had grown old and wrathful the pain from his leg made henry ill tempered he suffered fools and those who crossed him with equal lack of patience suspicion dominated his mind and ruthlessness marked his actions at the time of his marriage with catherine parr he was engaged in preparing the last of his wars the roots of the conflict lay in scotland hostility between the two peoples still smouldered ever and again flickering into flame along the wild border reviving the obsolete claim to suzerainty henry denounced the scots as rebels and pressed them to relinquish their alliance with france the scots successfully defeated an english raid at halidon rig then in the autumn of 1542 an expedition under norfolk had to turn back at kelso principally through the failure of the commissariat which besides its other shortcomings left the english army without its beer and the scots proceeded to carry the war into the enemys country their decision proved disastrous badly led and imperfectly organized they lost more than half their army of ten thousand men in solway moss and were utterly routed the news of this second flodden killed james v who died leaving the kingdom to an infant of one week mary the famous queen of scots—WINSTON CHURCHILL, *The New World,* pp. 81-2

3. Study the punctuation in these passages from student themes and prepare answers to the following questions about them: What marks of punc-

tuation should be added or omitted? What other changes seem necessary? desirable? Is the punctuation appropriate to the variety of English and to the subject matter? Are there any inconsistencies within the individual passages?

1 A) In many ways our Dalmatian is a typical member of the family.
2 He prefers dessert to dinner, he thoroughly enjoys chewing gum—
3 although he is somewhat impolite about his chewing habits. His eating
4 habits, too, are somewhat rude; but, then, he is only a baby. There are
5 of course the obvious tasks which he does quite well. Things such as
6 shaking hands when the occasion arises, walking in a straight line on
7 two legs, opening the garbage can by stepping on the pedal and eating
8 snacks in the living room while the television set is going. During the
9 spring, he is quite a help when it comes time to dig up the garden and
10 if hes not helping with that, he's out somewhere playing ball.
11 Needless to say, he is spoiled and selfish. If he, by some chance,
12 gets hold of something he shouldn't have–especially matches, he re-
13 fuses to give them up at any cost, even if you threaten his life. Yet
14 when he comes up to you and licks your hand it is hard not to love him
15 and give him all the affection he wants and needs.

1 B) My first job, as an elevator operator, was the most thrilling job,
2 as it is with most people. To me it was almost as if I was an actor,
3 waiting my cue to speak and move! My audience responded! (How
4 could they help it? They had to get off!!) But I thought myself a per-
5 son of great authority and recognition–however false that feeling turned
6 out to be!

1 C) One thing that every girl scout learns before leaving camp is
2 how to build a fire and cook a one pot stew. This seems like a very
3 safe and sane project, but believe me, last summer it wasn't! The first
4 step (also the most nerve-wracking) was to calm down and organize
5 twenty-four excited little ten-year olds. After this step was fairly well
6 accomplished, we started gathering wood for the fire: We sent some of
7 the girls out to see who could collect the most dead tinder. This
8 resulted in little girls continually running to us and asking, "Is this
9 dead enough?", "Is this small enough?" or "Does this one snap?".
10 After the wood was gathered and the fire laid in a basic A, we elected
11 a camper to light the fire. (The reason for this was that we didn't want
12 the campers to know that the counselors couldn't light it with just
13 one match!) Several matches and one head of singed hair later the fire
14 was blazing.
15 Meanwhile, the rest of the girls were kept busy with their jackknives
16 peeling potatoes, carrots, and onions in the sink. We finally got every-
17 thing including the bugs and dirt that go along with a cook-out in the
18 pot and on the fire.

1 D) Freedom of religion may be defined as the ability of a citizen to
2 decide whether he would like to go to church or not and if he chooses
3 to, which church he will attend. For people attend a church or syna-

4 gogue out of devotion for a higher being, from whom they gain guid-
5 ance, love, and a reason for life. But the freedom of religion may be
6 lost in many ways, two of these are a persons social standing and his
7 immaturity. Due to the complexity of our civilization some people are
8 "forced" to go to church against their personal feelings in order that
9 they may retain prominent social positions within a community.
10 Children in such families are born into an atmosphere missing the
11 quality of freedom of religion; for if the parents go to church the
12 children will be taken along, and conversely if the parents do not at-
13 tend church the children will not. But when the child becomes of age,
14 he may however, forsake all of his knowledge gained at home, and in
15 this way gain freedom of religion.

4. The following sentences are punctuated in a close style. Repunctuate them in an open style, but do not remove any necessary punctuation. Be ready to explain your changes in class and to tell whether the original or the repunctuated version seems more appropriate.

A) For instance, the highest occupation, according to Plato, is the study of philosophy; but this would not be possible for man if he had to be continually feeding, like a grazing animal, with its nose to the ground. Now, to obviate the necessity of eating all the time, long intestines are useful; therefore the cause of long intestines is the study of philosophy. —GEORGE SANTAYANA, *Three Philosophical Poets,* p. 73

B) Yet, it is to this white-collar world (a fragmented world, to be sure), that one must look for the typical twentieth-century mode of living.

C) Books, therefore, do not suggest an idea coextensive and interchangeable with the idea of literature; since much literature, scenic, forensic, or didactic (as from lecturers and public orators), may never come into books, and much that does come into books may connect itself with no literary interest.—THOMAS DE QUINCEY, "The Literature of Knowledge and the Literature of Power"

D) The arrival of Northey and Luckner at the crossroads is a very trifling, and somewhat irrelevant, incident; but we could read a dozen other boisterous tales from beginning to end, and not receive so fresh and stirring an impression.

E) After Calmus had finished his oration, the Republicans applauded wildly, and the Democrats looked glum; no one, on either side, slumped into bored indifference.

5. After studying a variety of contemporary sources, prepare a report on some particular problem of punctuation. Write down on cards all the examples that you find, citing the source of each. Don't forget to cite the instances in which no punctuation occurs. Suggested topics: punctuation after introductory expressions, the use of commas and semicolons to separate main clauses, the various uses of the colon, the frequency of the comma before *and* in a series.

6. Characterize your punctuation after you have examined several of your recent papers. Is it consistently open or close, or a mixture of both? Is it appropriate to other qualities of your style of writing?

7. What comments have been made about the punctuation in your written work? Study the corrections you have been asked to make on your papers to see if you have any recurring problems in punctuation. Before revising your next paper refer to appropriate articles in the *Index* to see how far you can go toward solving these problems. (*Index* articles concerning punctuation are listed on pp. 131-132.)

Remove a good sentence from a good paragraph and you leave behind,

not a gap with clean-cut edges,

but an ugly rent with broken threads at both ends.

P. B. BALLARD

Chapter 6

Paragraphs

But the first thing to remember is that the division (into paragraphs)

is for the benefit of the reader or hearer.

It is a device for making the whole clear to someone else.

This does not in the least make the process less valuable to the writer;

it merely forces upon him the right point of view.

A division is good in proportion as it helps a hearer or reader to follow.

CHARLES SEARS BALDWIN

There is an old saying that anyone who can write a good paragraph can write a good paper. There is a good deal of truth in this, because the kinds of movement found in paragraphs are also found in articles, stories, and books, and the qualities of a piece of writing can be seen in its component parts. A study of paragraphs is almost a study of composition.

A paragraph is a group of related statements that a writer presents as a unit in the development of his subject.[1] To the eye it appears as a unit because its first word is usually indented, its last line is sometimes short, and occasionally space above and below set it off from surrounding paragraphs. More essentially, a paragraph strikes the mind as a unit because of the relation that exists between the statements it contains. These related statements represent a stage in the flow of the writer's thought. By the mechanical device of indention and by the connection between his statements, he indicates these stages in his material to his reader and tries to impart the movement of his thought as nearly as possible as he sees it himself.

Paragraphs separate as well as join. In a single paragraph the continuity of material is the most important feature, but in a series of paragraphs, although each one relates to the subject of the paper, each develops a somewhat different phase of it. Indention is a sign to the reader that the thought is going to shift slightly, and he adjusts his attention automatically. Without paragraphing, the reader would be forced to puzzle out for himself the writer's intended organization. (Imagine trying to read a book not divided into paragraphs!)

---

[1]E. H. Lewis, *The History of the English Paragraph* (Chicago, 1894); Herbert Read, *English Prose Style* (rev. ed., New York, 1952), Ch. 5; Summey, Ch. 2. (Books cited by name of author only will be found in the Bibliography, pp. XV-XVI.) All rhetorics and handbooks have discussions of paragraphs.

Paragraph development

A paragraph is a series of statements representing the material we have in mind or on notes when we begin to write. These statements can be classified in various ways, but for the purposes of reading or writing, one of the most useful classifications is according to their content–details and generalizations. Statements range from the very specific to the very general.

Details and generalizations

We have in our minds a continuous succession of images–traces of sights, sounds, smells, and so on that we have experienced–and of words, some of them names for the images and experiences, some more general, for "ideas." We all realize that the statements we make in speech or writing are more or less specific or more or less general. These two main categories could be subdivided into an indefinite number of types, not mutually exclusive but grading into each other.

Details, the more or less specific statements, can be divided into at least three types: (1) *Images,* statements of particular sights, sounds, and so on that describe what we have seen or sensed and that convey this to the reader; (2) *Summarized images,* statements, usually plural, concerning a number of images; (3) *Facts,* particular statements of occurrences that can usually be verified or tested by other observers.

Details

Image: We passed a policeman standing knee-deep in swirling flood water.

Summarized image: Dozens of abandoned cars lined the highway.

Fact: The area received over six inches of rainfall in one hour.

Generalizations move away from such details, becoming more and more inclusive: (1) *Interpretations,* comments on the meaning of some particular observation, closely related to details; (2) *Opinions,* our judgments of some particular thing or occurrence (good, bad, better than, useful for); (3) *Generalizations proper,* ideas, statements of considerable inclusiveness.

Generalizations

Interpretation: The downpour came too fast to be absorbed by the soil or drained off.

Opinion: The flood was the worst one in over twenty years.

Generalization proper: Man still has not succeeded in controlling nature.

Details are chiefly a matter of careful observation (our own or someone else's) and of exact statement of this observation. Generalizations are usually based on a large number of observations. Most of our generalizations we acquire from other people or from reading, but some we make for ourselves by putting two and two together. They are more difficult to handle accurately because they may be influenced by other ideas or even by prejudices. But it is possible to be scrupulous in using generalizations, and necessary, too, since we can't carry in our minds all the details of experience, much less put them on paper.

All of these types of statements can be found in nearly any kind of writing except the most specific or the most abstract and theoretical. Here are six statements taken from *Under the Sea Wind* by Rachel L. Carson:

Details

An insect with a body like a fragment of twig supported by six jointed legs was walking over the floating leaves and skating on the surface of the water, on which it moved as on strong silk. p. 218 (image)

All day flights of broad-winged hawks passed down along the ridges of the hills, going south. p. 220 (summarized image)

The nest was six feet across at its base and more than half as wide at the top. p. 84 (fact)

Generalizations

Fish pursed in a seine usually tried to drive the net down, to sink it by sounding. But these fish were terrorized by something in the water—something they feared more than the great boat monster in the water alongside. p. 206 (interpretation)

The boats were squat and ungraceful of line and they pitched and rolled in the winter sea. p. 252 (opinion)

For in the sea, nothing is lost. One dies, another lives, as the precious elements of life are passed on and on in endless chains. p. 101 (generalization proper)

Here, for a passage from a naturalist's notes, the kind of statement and the type to which it belongs (D for detail, G for generalization) are indicated in the margin:

Kind of statement	
G Interpretation D Summary D Image D Summary	These were old tumbleweeds, the product of other seasons. Only a few of the new crop had broken free. We saw them anchored in place, like unreleased balloons—millions of them—all across Wyoming. Their seeds were ripening, their tiny leaves drying, and in some storm of the latter days of autumn or in winter their stems would break in a ragged fracture just

	above the ground and their travels would commence.
G Interpretation	For these plants "a time to keep" would end and "a time to cast away" would begin.
D Fact	The rolling tumbleweed, almost in the manner of a pepper shaker, scatters its seeds across the land.
D Fact	A botanist once counted 180,220 minute, glossy black, lens-shaped seeds on a single plant of the common tumbleweed, *Amaranthus albus*.
G Generalization	For man, autumn is a time of harvest, of gathering together.
G Generalization	For nature, it is a time of sowing, of scattering abroad.
D Summary	Seeds are shot away as though from tiny cannons.
D Summary	They are transported by running water.
D Summary	They ride long distances in mud adhering to the feet of birds.
D Fact	Travelers on the prairie in early days were mystified by great circles of plants like giant pixie rings.
D Summary	It developed that buffalo cows bedded down for the night in a circle, enclosing the calves, and in this position shook free from their shaggy manes seeds that had collected there during the day.
D Fact	William T. Davis, the Staten Island naturalist, one autumn examined two small turkey feathers that were being blown along the ground by the wind.
D Fact	Attached to both, ten to one and fourteen to the other, were the seeds of bidens or beggar-ticks.
G Opinion	Among the many devices employed in the seed-scattering of autumn—the bur that adheres, the nut that rolls downhill, the fluff that takes wing—one of the simplest and most effective of all is the wandering of the tumbleweed. . . .

—EDWIN WAY TEALE, *Autumn Across America*, pp. 150-1

In order to discuss the qualities of paragraphs it is necessary to be aware at least of the broad categories of details and generalizations.[1]

Paragraphs of details

The bulk of most writing consists of details—statements of images and particular facts. Details make up the principal content of descriptions, of narrative scenes, both factual—as in news stories—and fictional, and of explanations of objects, processes, situations; and they are the evidence, the foundation of general ideas. Often the details are massed, forming the whole paragraph, as in this one from an account of New York's great blizzard of 1888:

[1] In addition to the following sections, see "The meaning of words," pp. 216-220, and Chs. 10, 11, and 12.

The actual fall in 53½ hours was 20.9 inches, or more than twice as much snow as had fallen all that winter, but this figure gives no conception of the difficulties travelers met. For the wind continued high, and the soberest observers reported drifts of fifteen and twenty feet. It was almost impossible to walk. A few hacks took to the streets, the drivers charging anything they could get and in some cases forcing whiskey down the throats of their horses in order to keep them alive. Surface cars struggled for a little while, and then stopped; many of them were literally buried. The Third Avenue Elevated Railway, not then electrified, ran a few trains downtown—one car each, with two or even three dinkey engines pushing it—but these too were stalled. In one of them, helpless between stations, were thirty men; but though they could not get down, they were so fortunate as to be in front of a saloon, and hot toddies were hoisted to them by means of a pail and a length of cord, so that the men remained tolerably happy for the fifteen hours of their captivity, and even were heard to sing. Sturdy little boys with ladders went from place to place letting people down out of second-story windows; generally they charged (this being in the days before Boy Scouts) fifty cents for the descent.—DONALD B. CHIDSEY, *The Gentleman from New York: A Life of Roscoe Conkling,* pp. 381-2

Details, especially particular facts, often are the chief content of technical and scientific writing:

When a volume of air saturated with water vapor is cooled, it condenses in either the liquid or solid form, depending upon whether the temperature is above or below 0° C. This condensation does not occur throughout the entire mass of humid air, but around small condensation nuclei, chiefly sea salts, which are constantly present in the atmosphere. A cloud then is composed of a great number of small water droplets, ice crystals, or both, which are separated from each other but yet limit the visibility. The diameter of the water droplets is very small, ranging from 1 to 70 microns with the most frequent diameter being 12 microns. There are about 50 to 500 of these particles in a cubic centimeter of cloudy air. The rate of fall of these droplets is so small, a few millimeters per second, that the slightest ascending air current is sufficient to hold them aloft. Rain drops, on the contrary, which are composed of an accumulation of small droplets, are comparatively large and fall with appreciable velocities.—*Weather Manual for Pilots* (War Department, TM 1-230), p. 69

Details in relation to generalizations

More commonly, details and generalizations are used together. Selected details make a generalization clearer or more interesting or more convincing than it would be by itself.

The most typical development is for the details to illustrate a generalization or to make clear an object or general situation indicated in the opening statement. In the following paragraph the opening generalization is illustrated by seven groups of facts, which are tied together at the end by another generalization.

> [Generalization] The busy spades of archaeologists are further complicating matters by digging up not only objects but whole cultures unknown even a few years ago. (1) In 1900 the Hittites were hardly more than a name in the Bible. Today Yale is publishing a bulky Hittite dictionary. (2) The jungles of Cambodia have been torn aside to reveal the astonishing remains of Ankor Vat and the vanished Khmer civilization. (3) [Negative] Moslem fanatics still prevent excavation of the South Arabian ruins of Saba whose queen may have visited Solomon nearly three thousand years ago, (4) but in the Indus valley a cluster of cities perhaps as old as Babylonia or Egypt has come to light. (5) On Crete and in the Aegean the Minoans are emerging from the mists. In 1953 a British architect who had worked on Nazi spy codes during World War II cracked the most common form of Minoan writing. (6) Studies of the early Germans and Celts are fast changing our notions of what the Romans found when they marched north of the Alps. (7) And in the Americas, Aztec and pre-Aztec, Inca and pre-Inca cultures, always curious and sometimes magnificent, are turning up in most embarrassing profusion. [Generalization] We really don't know what to do with all the history we now have.—LYNN WHITE, JR., "The Changing Past," *Frontiers of Knowledge in the Study of Man,* pp. 68-9

Sometimes a single emphatic illustration, though by no means proving the point, is enough to suggest the accuracy of a generalization:

> The more education a man has the more likely he is to be independent in his views and obstinate in sticking to them. A committee of professors, I can assure you, is much harder to manage than a council of African chiefs.—JOYCE CARY, "The Mass Mind: Our Favorite Folly," *Harper's Magazine,* March 1952, p. 26

Several similar or contrasting details may be used to support or contradict a generalization. The comparisons or contrasts may be between things in the same general field or in quite different ones. This paragraph takes its details from two periods of surgery, the contrasts supporting the opinion of the first sentence:

> I have interpolated the preceding in order to show that kitchen surgery had many advantages. Even the modest, intelligent, well meaning assistant can make himself a nuisance. Only one person can work at a time and while an assistant is doing something the operator is idle—that is his hands are, but his mind is thinking horrible thoughts. On the other hand if one operates alone in a kitchen his instruments are just where he placed them. One kept the instruments in the dishpan, took them out when needed, and put them back in again when he had finished with their use. They were always to be found in an area of a foot and a half, the diameter of the dishpan. There was no nurse to grab

them, rub off real or imaginary blood and then place them somewhere else.—ARTHUR E. HERTZLER, *The Horse and Buggy Doctor,* pp. 221-2

Sometimes an unusual comparison both clarifies and fixes an idea in mind, as in this likening of the ways of a political liberal to some characteristics of a dog on a walk:

The liberal holds that he is true to the republic when he is true to himself. (It may not be as cozy an attitude as it sounds.) He greets with enthusiasm the fact of the journey, as a dog greets a man's invitation to take a walk. And he acts in the dog's way, too, swinging wide, racing ahead, doubling back, covering many miles of territory that the man never traverses, all in the spirit of inquiry and the zest for truth. He leaves a crazy trail, but he ranges far beyond the genteel old party he walks with and he is usually in a better position to discover a skunk. The dog often influences the course the man takes, on his long walk; for sometimes a dog runs into something in nature so arresting that not even a man can quite ignore it, and the man deviates—a clear victim of the liberal intent in his dumb companion. When the two of them get home and flop down, it is the liberal—the wide-ranging dog—who is covered with burdocks and with information of a special sort on out-of-the-way places. Often ineffective in direct political action, he is the opposite of the professional revolutionary, for, unlike the latter, he never feels he knows where the truth lies, but is full of rich memories of places he has glimpsed it in. He is, on the whole, more optimistic than the revolutionary, or even than the Republican in a good year.—*The New Yorker,* Jan. 17, 1948. Reprinted by permission. Copr. 1948, The New Yorker Magazine, Inc.

Since generalizations run a risk of being somewhat vague and of meaning different things to different people, details can be used to pin them down and make them more precise. This may take the form of a simple definition, in which the writer sets the limits and gives the essential characteristics of the thing or situation he is talking about, rather than just the word that stands for it.

The terms *preface, foreword,* and *introduction* are often used interchangeably. It is, however, desirable to differentiate them. A preface or foreword deals with the genesis, purpose, limitations, and scope of the book and may include acknowledgments of indebtedness; an introduction deals with the subject of the book, supplementing the text, introducing the text, and indicating a point of view to be adopted by the reader. The introduction usually forms a part of the text; the preface does not.—MARJORIE E. SKILLIN and ROBERT M. GAY, *Words into Type,* p. 41

To make a generalization more precise you may need only to add a word, like *sometimes* or *generally,* or to say *some* instead of *all,* or to drop *only* or *nothing but*. But usually it is better to develop the idea by details, as in this paragraph:

> In seeking to improve our political life we must be careful not to expect too much, and not to rest our democratic faith on assumptions which cannot be supported. If we say that the common man is infallible, or that the voice of the people is infallible, we are talking nonsense and inviting the disappointments which must ensue. But if we say that the opinions of the common man, when he is given a fair chance to form opinions, tend to show good sense and to be the best basis for the decisions of government, we are saying what can be proved both from the record of the past and from the experience of the present. On this unboastful statement we can build a politics consonant with man's dignity, and we may even hope in time to unite the world in the name of that dignity.—HERBERT AGAR, *A Time for Greatness,* p. 79

Frequently the relation between the details and a generalization is one of cause and effect. In this paragraph about flying over the North Pole, the effect is given in the first sentence ("it's hard to find your way") and is repeated in specific terms at the end, with details of several causes making up the bulk of the paragraph.

> The special thing about the Pole is this: it's hard to find your way. The compass goes crazy near the Pole, and the mind, too, suffers a strange kind of dizzy spell. As for the compass, it is a dislikable instrument anywhere: the slightest turn or bump of the airplane makes it swing so that it's hard to get a good reading. It doesn't really point at the North Pole but at the Magnetic Pole, a place in Northern Canada, a thousand miles away from the true Pole and it doesn't even do that reliably, but has an error in its error! All this gets worse as you go north. There are places in the Arctic where the compass says South when it means North. And when you get within a thousand miles or so of the Magnetic Pole, the compass thinks it is already there, and quits pointing altogether. It turns aimlessly round and round, or it points at the nearest chunk of iron—the airplane's engine. On one SAS [Scandinavian Airlines System] survey flight, they had four different compasses point in four different directions.—WOLFGANG LANGEWIESCHE, "The Polar Path: Where Every Direction Is South," *Harper's Magazine,* Nov. 1956, p. 72

Very often the details give reasons for the writer's belief or conclusion. In the following three examples, the first gives reasons from the writer's experience, the second uses summarized images to lead to a final generalization, and the third supports a generalization from zoology with facts from that science.

In this one, Mr. Fadiman sketches his reasons for believing that "the trash of my generation was superior to the trash of today":

> I say trash. Actually such books are "trash" only by standards which should not be applied to children's reading. They have the incalculable value that listening to perfectly inane, adult conversation holds for chil-

dren: they increase the child's general awareness. They provide admittedly rough paradigms of character, motivation, life experiences. That is why it seems to me that the trash of my generation was superior to the trash of today. I submit that *The Rover Boys in the Everglades* and *Frank on a Gunboat* are preferable to Superman and his kind on two counts: they were cleanly and clearly written, and their characters were credible and not entirely unrelated to the child's experience. When I was nine I could learn something interesting about life from even such highly colored affairs as the Frank Merriwell series but I know that my son can learn nothing whatsoever of genuine interest (that is, which he can check against the expanding universe within himself) from the comics. I believe firmly that the current juvenile literature of the impossible is meretricious compared with the honest hackwork my own generation enjoyed. I also think that the kids are about ready to kick over this thriller fare in favor of something saner and more natural.—CLIFTON FADIMAN, *Reading I've Liked,* Preface, p. xvi

Without explicitly labeling the relation between his statements, Professor Barzun gives reasons for passing examinations:

Examinations are not things that happen in school. They are a recurring feature of life, whether in the form of decisive interviews to pass, of important letters to write, or life-and-death diagnosis to make, or meetings to address, or girls to propose to. In most of these crises, you cannot bring your notes with you and must not leave your wits behind. The habit of passing examinations is therefore one to acquire early and to keep exercising even when there is a possibility of getting around it.—JACQUES BARZUN, *Teacher in America,* p. 215

The third paragraph develops with examples the reasons why certain evolutionary developments in animals have prevented their further improvement:

Another type of restriction is the long-term limitation imposed by certain types of construction. Animal types which exploit the possibilities of a radial construction, like starfish or medusae, are thereby debarred from developing a true head, for this can only evolve in a bilaterally symmetrical creature: and only animals with heads have the possibility of evolving elaborate brains and eyes. But the most illuminating example is that of the insects. By adopting tracheal respiration, in which oxygen and carbon dioxide are carried directly to and from the tissues by microscopic air-tubes instead of in the blood-stream, they were able to colonize the land extremely successfully. However, for physical and physiological reasons into which it is not possible to enter here, tracheal respiration becomes inefficient with increased size. An insect the size of a rat would be a biological impossibility, and, in point of fact, no insects exist over the size of a mouse. This limitation of absolute size of course limits the size of the brain, and the small size of the brain in turn limits the power of learning and the degree of intelligence, since these demand a much larger number of nerve-cells and nerve-paths than do even the most elaborate of fixed instincts. Thus the adoption of tracheal respiration by insects imposed a drastic limitation both on their size and on their intelligence, and so made possible the evolution of higher vertebrates and the emergence of man.—"Evolutionary Principles," *The Times Literary Supplement,* Aug. 31, 1951, p. 542

It is true, as many people insist, that our opinions and generalizations are often unreliable, but it is also true that we can train ourselves to be relatively accurate in them. One aid is to assume that our readers think differently than we do: we will then avoid extreme views and mere prejudice and try to give the best evidence we can find for thinking as we do. In writing of ideas one of the best safeguards is to refer our generalizations as much as we can to the particular observations and facts from which we derive them or to which they may apply. The interrelation of generalizations and details not only makes for good paragraphs but for responsible and effective writing.

Adequate development

The length of paragraphs is partly determined by the kind of publication in which they appear. Short paragraphs can be read more quickly and easily than long ones. Because of the usually simple narratives of news stories and the narrow columns which make long, unbroken stretches of type forbidding, and because they are intended for hasty reading, paragraphs in newspapers run distinctly short, the great majority of them being under 75 words, 20 to 40 words being typical. Paragraphs in magazines of restricted circulation approach book paragraphs in length, but in popular magazines the paragraphs would rarely be 200 words long and would typically run from 100 to 150 words. Books show great variety, but as a rule paragraphs of less than 125 words would be short and paragraphs of over 250 rather long except in books intended for a somewhat limited audience. (Fiction shows considerable variety in paragraph length, approximating periodical length.) In any given article, of course, the paragraphs will vary considerably, because subordinate points will be of differing importance, some deserving fuller and others shorter treatment.

This does not mean that you should stop to count the words in your paragraphs, but you should be able to visualize their length as they would stand in typical magazine and book form. Most writers get about 200 words of longhand on a page and about 300 in double-spaced typing. It is obvious that you should look closely at any page of your manuscript that shows more than two paragraph breaks—not because they are necessarily wrong, but because you should be sure they represent actual stages of your material and are appropriate to the subject, to the reader, and to the emphasis you intend. Conspicuously short paragraphs are likely to be symptoms that you are not developing your material sufficiently, not putting in enough details or building enough small ideas together; or they may show that you are dividing your subject into units too small to guide your reader to an understanding of the relationships between points.

Similarly, you should look closely at paragraphs that run over a manuscript page, to see if they are actually unified or if perhaps they should be broken for emphasis or for the reader's convenience. Paragraphs are likely to be longer than average when the thought emphasizes relationships between facts or ideas. In works of criticism, in philosophy and science, the paragraphs are rightly longer than in pictures of the life around us. Length is a symptom of other qualities of paragraphs; it should be considered in the light of subject matter and purpose and should be a sign of adequate and appropriate development. At the beginning of a composition course paragraphs are likely to be conspicuously short, sometimes averaging under 75 words; often the attention given to them in a single term will double their average length.

Sometimes conscientious students feel that developing an idea fully, building out a statement into a paragraph, is "just padding." There are two chief reasons why a bare statement is insufficient: First, it does not really represent the fullness of the writer's thought and often gives such a small sample that he does not seem to know his subject or at least does not seem to be thinking about it at the time of writing. Second, it cannot convey to a reader, who may know nothing about the subject, enough to let him see it as the writer sees it. To make an impression on the reader, it is necessary not just to mention the subject but to present it, develop it, lead him to think about it.

Actually developing paragraphs by full use of the appropriate materials also removes a frequent worry of student writers, "getting the required length." Most writing is planned for a fairly definite length (a page of a typed letter, an article for a particular magazine) so that specified length for compositions is natural. "About 600 words" means that you are to take a subject and select from your thinking about it what can be conveyed in about that number of words. The bulk of the actual space in most papers will be taken up with specific details, but all pertinent material should be used. A final test question for a paper is "Have I put in enough of what I know and believe about this subject to lead a reader to see it as I do?"

Paragraph movement

Obviously the thought of a paragraph should move: the reader should be better informed at the end than he was at the beginning. The statements advance in a sequence that leads him to an understanding of a unit of the whole subject. There are numerous kinds of movement, but most of them fall into four general types: movement in time, *narrative;* movement of sense impression, especially of things seen, *descriptive;* and two sorts of movement of facts and ideas, *expository* movement of *support* or of *climax.*

Narrative paragraphs

Probably the easiest movement in speaking and writing is chronological, the time movement of narratives of real or imagined events. In conversation we give accounts of what I did, what we did, what they did; and we write accounts of personal experiences, autobiographies, biographies, explanations of how things are done, and so on; or we may write fiction–short stories and novels.

Narrative paragraphs, in terms of the first section of this chapter, are made up principally of details (images or summarized images), with generalizations rarely introduced and used chiefly to furnish background or interpret the meaning of an occasional detail or scene. The principal types of narrative vary according to how close the reader is brought to the event. If there are many details, images of action, conversation, and so on, he is brought close to it and may even feel he is observing it. Such direct presentation of scenes is called *dramatic* narrative. Summaries of details (*summarized* narrative) may condense a good deal of action into a short space. (A particular type of summary is *generalized* narrative, which tells what was usually or repeatedly done.) Typically in both fact and fiction, summarized action prepares for dramatic action or bridges between two events by briefly telling what occurred between them. There is nothing difficult or curious about these types, as a patch of very simple narrative will show:

Kind of narrative	
Generalized	On Fridays there were the regulars who dropped in at the *Gazette* office to buy their papers because it was more convenient than to call at the postoffice or paper store.
Summarized	One was Miss Mariana Pickering, a congenial, pink-cheeked old lady who had seldom missed a Friday for years.

Summarized	Once, to our surprise, she said she had made
Generalized	up her mind to subscribe. We wanted subscriptions more than almost anything, because
Interpretation	subscriptions were what you could count on and bank on.
Dramatic (Scene)	"Oh," said some of us, "but we'll miss seeing you every Friday."
Dramatic	"That's so," she said, "I'll miss seeing you."
Summarized	So she didn't subscribe after all.—HENRY BEETLE HOUGH, *Once More the Thunderer,* pp. 27-8

The following account is much more detailed but still summarizes in a single paragraph the actions of perhaps a couple of hours:

> In the morning Karl and his outfit started for the salt-lick and Garrick, Abdullah, M'Cola and I crossed the road, angled behind the village up a dry watercourse and started climbing the mountains in a mist. We headed up a pebbly, boulder-filled, dry stream bed overgrown with vines and brush so that, climbing, you walked, stooping, in a steep tunnel of vines and foliage. I sweated so that I was soaked through my shirt and undergarments and when we came out on the shoulder of the mountain and stood, looking down at the bank of clouds quilting over the entire valley below us, the morning breeze chilled me and I had to put on my raincoat while we glassed the country. I was too wet with sweat to sit down and I signed Garrick to keep on going. We went around one side of the mountain, doubled back on a higher grade and crossed over, out of the sun that was drying my wet shirt and along the top of a series of grassy valleys, stopping to search each one thoroughly with the field glasses. Finally we came to a sort of amphitheatre, a bowl-like valley of very green grass with a small stream down the middle and timber along the far side and all the lower edge. We sat in the shadow against some rocks, out of any breeze, watching with the glasses as the sun rose and lighted the opposite slopes, seeing two kudu cows and a calf feed out from the timber, moving with the quickly browsing, then head lifted, long staring vigilance of all browsing animals in a forest. Animals on a plain can see so far that they have confidence and feed very differently from animals in the woods. We could see the vertical white stripes on their gray flanks and it was very satisfying to watch them and to be high in the mountain that early in the morning. Then, while we watched, there was a boom, like a rockslide. I thought at first it was a boulder falling, but M'Cola whispered.—ERNEST HEMINGWAY, *Green Hills of Africa,* pp. 170-2

Few amateur writers would be able to condense so much detail into a single paragraph as Hemingway did in this one. But lack of detail is fatal, because it is only by means of the small particular actions that a reader can see what is going on. A boy who had told elaborately of preparations for a particular baseball game ended his paper with this paragraph, which gives a reader no clue at all to what really happened:

> The game itself did not prove to be an exceptional one. I know that I, for one, played in better games that summer and I might add I also played better games as an individual. Even so, it will be a very long time before I forget this great experience.

The reader wonders why the game will be so hard to forget.

As a rule the narrative should run continuously without being interrupted by comment or interpretation. If the comment is unavoidable it should be kept brief and so far as possible be made in terms of the narrative. In the Hemingway paragraph just quoted, the single sentence interpretation "Animals on a plain can see so far that they have confidence and feed very differently from animals in the woods" is closely related to the scene being described.

Change in point of view—that is, change of the person from whose view the action is being presented—is generally unconvincing and distracting. Usually a paragraph of narrative should keep the same point of view, not shift from one actor or group of actors to another, as the following paragraph does:

> The four of us went in, laughing and pushing each other around. We sat in a booth in the back corner and noisily ordered our drinks. [Shift:] The bartender thought that he would be in for some trouble before long. He began to be very busy but kept throwing an eye in our direction. [Return to original point of view:] We kept up our racket and arranged for Eppie and Lew to stage a friendly little scrap.

The shifted sentence might be brought in line: We could see that the bartender thought he would be in for some trouble, because he began to be very busy but kept throwing an eye in our direction.

The connection between statements in a narrative paragraph is usually simple. One detail appears after another as they happened in time or as they are imagined to have happened. The verbs usually carry this movement, and the continuity is made stronger by the continuation of the same subject from one sentence to another. The time may be emphasized and made more obvious by adverbs—*after this, before, soon, when, in a few days*—or by adverbial clauses—*when he got to the corner, after the last dance ended.*

Indicating the verbs and adverbs of time in this opening paragraph of a short story shows how large a part time and action play in narrative:

> Elizabeth Montgomery *woke up in the morning* wondering whether or not she *was engaged*. She *had been out* with Bob McEwen *the night*

before and *at the end* there *had been* some spontaneous and apparently serious love-making. That is, she *knew* she *must have felt* pretty serious about it because *this morning* she *couldn't remember* where she *had put* her gloves. And *now* he *had left* for Chicago *for a few days* and he *had promised to write.*—SALLY BENSON, *People Are Fascinating,* p. 27

Since narrative is usually of events that have happened or are imagined to have happened, it is typically written in the past tense. Occasionally for liveliness, especially when the passage records vivid feelings or vivid sense impressions, the present tense is used. This "historical present" is used by D. H. Lawrence in describing the bustle (note the verbs) and the sensations of his leaving Palermo:

Our ship is hooting for all she's worth. An important last-minuter comes surging up. The rope hawsers are being wound clankily in. Seagulls—they are never very many in the Mediterranean—seagulls whirl like a few flakes of snow in the upper chill air. Clouds spin. And without knowing it we are evaporating away from the shore, from our mooring, between the great *City of Trieste* and another big black steamer that lies like a wall. . . .—D. H. LAWRENCE, *Sea and Sardinia,* p. 41

As a rule the past tense should be used unless there is some definite reason for using the present, and meaningless changes in tense should be avoided.

Since a narrative is usually continuous, breaking it into paragraphs is somewhat arbitrary. A new paragraph represents a new emphasis, a new focus of attention in the action, a change in time, or movements of a different person (the real reason for paragraphing the speeches in a conversation). The purpose of narrative paragraphs is to show the reader the small stages of the action that the writer wishes to mark off, to emphasize. They tend, consequently, to run somewhat shorter than the other types of paragraph and to vary considerably within a single piece of writing. (For a discussion of narrative paragraphs in a paper, see pages 278-292.)

Descriptive paragraphs

Descriptive paragraphs are harder to write than narrative, partly because we are ordinarily not very close observers and partly because there is no necessary order to the details (and summaries of details and facts and interpretations) of which they are principally made up. They are rarely the dominant sort of movement in a whole piece of writing but are included where they can give support.

In some factual writing, especially in manuals and other specialized works, a detailed picture of some object or place is called for. A pretty complete presentation is given, with accuracy and compactness the chief qualities. Often the content is more facts than images, as in this beginning of a description of one of the Egyptian pyramids (which was accompanied by a diagram to help the reader visualize the details):

> Internally, Chephren's Pyramid bears little resemblance to the Great Pyramid. It has two entrances, one in the north face, at a height of nearly 50 feet, and the other directly below, hewn in the rock foundation of the surrounding pavement (fig. 16, 4 and 1). Both entrances are situated at a distance of about 41 feet to the east of the Pyramid's main north-south axis. From the upper entrance, a low and narrow corridor descends at an angle of 25°55′ through the core of the Pyramid until it enters the rock; here it becomes horizontal and continues on a level plane to the tomb-chamber (fig. 6, 3).—I. E. S. EDWARDS, *The Pyramids of Egypt,* pp. 117-9

Occasionally in rather Formal description the details are given in a spatial order. This description of the United Nations General Assembly chamber moves from outside the building to a selection of images of the chamber as seen from a definite position. (Previously the writer had spoken of the chamber as covered "by a huge inverted tub.")

> The chamber is on the second floor of the Assembly Building, that strangely curved northernmost of the U.N. cluster. (The flattish gray dome projecting from its roof is the exterior of the tub's bottom.) From the galleries, the audience looks out over the seated delegates toward the dais—a pyramid of green-carpeted steps leading up to two landings. On the lower landing is the lectern, sheathed in slabs of greenish-black marble, at which the delegates stand when speaking. Above and behind this, on the second landing, is the President's desk, shaped like a judge's bench and finished in oyster-white marble. Still higher, on a shaftlike gilt panel rising behind the President's desk, is fixed a big bronze disc bearing the U.N. emblem—a global map of the world, in white. At the President's desk are places, each with its microphone and glass of water, for three men.—CHRISTOPHER RAND, "A Pageant in Sack Suits," originally published in *The New Yorker,* Jan. 19, 1957, p. 63

For writing of general appeal, the task is to focus the reader's attention first on what would strike an actual observer most strongly and then to fill out the picture as far as seems rewarding. This means that conspicuous and suggestive details or those that focus the impression will stand out and that others will be subordinated. The scene will be bounded in space; that is, it will be limited by the area to which the observer is directing his attention. But the relation between the details is not only spatial. It depends on the senses, attention, and associations of the writer. To show how much a description depends on these qualities of observation, simply ask two people to describe the same scene. Both of them may mention the conspicuous details, but they will almost certainly put them in a different order, and they will choose and arrange differently the less obvious ones. The selection and order depend on the interests and past associations of the writer, and it is these that make the paragraph a unit instead of a mere enumeration of separate details.

The details of a descriptive paragraph are typically held together by adverbs of place (*next, beyond this*) and especially by their relation to an opinion or to a general impression, or by a narrative thread, either of the observer in the act of seeing or of some activity in the scene itself.

Descriptions of people especially are more successful if they are less like posed studio portraits and more like candid camera shots. This excerpt from a short story gives a small but revealing handful of details about a woman in a definite time and place, with a slight bit of action:

> Snow fell softly and the sidewalks were wet but Mrs. Rose Carey had on her galoshes and enjoyed feeling thick snow crunching underfoot. She walked slowly, big flakes falling on her lamb coat and clinging to hair over her ears, the lazily falling snow giving her, in her thick warm coat, a fine feeling of self-indulgence. She stood on the corner of Bloor and Yonge, an impressive build of a woman, tall, stout, good-looking for forty-two, and watched the traffic signal.—MORLEY CALLAGHAN, "An Escapade," *A Native Argosy,* p. 135

The descriptive details in the following paragraph from a review of La Guardia Airport, written just after its opening, are given as reasons to support the opinion stated at the beginning and end:

> The hangars are pretty good. The roof of each of the hangars—there are three in each group—forms a shallow arch, and on one side the brick wall is shortened to accommodate a panel of green glass between it and the roof to let overhead light into the interior. The window units run in horizontal lines, accentuated by the bands of brown brick that frame them and connect the separate bays. The entrance in the centre of each building breaks this horizontal line, and, like the windows, it is framed in brown brick. These buildings are not conspicuously handsome, but they reach a very decent standard.—LEWIS MUMFORD, "Millions for Mausoleums," originally published in *The New Yorker,* Feb. 30, 1939, p. 45

To give a reader a picture of something you have seen, imagine as you are writing that you are actually facing the scene once more and put down what you "see in your mind's eye." (You may find that you need some specific words that you don't ordinarily use to represent the images definitely.) Everyday writing offers many opportunities for descriptive movement. Putting a little more actual picture and scene in your personal letters, for instance, will help you form a habit of using images that will make your other writing more interesting.

Expository paragraphs: order of support

Most college writing, and perhaps most writing, is expository; that is, it presents facts, gives directions, interprets facts, presents opinions. There are, consequently, various expository paragraph movements, but most of them can be grouped as paragraphs of support, discussed in this subsection, or of climax, discussed in the next one. (They are similar to the two sorts of plans for whole papers described in Ch. 9, pp. 252-253.)

In the support paragraph a generalization comes first or at least early and is followed by details or by less general statements that elaborate or support it. This type of movement is often spoken of as "from general to particular" or as "deductive movement." The more specific statements stand in some obvious relation to the generalization:

The main generalization (topic sentence)	The first triumph of radio was that it learned to live with itself, within its limitations, and that the good men in the profession never lamented the absence of the visual.
A comparison	Their position was that of King Vidor and of Charlie Chaplin when sound came to the movies: they would use sound, but they had not missed it because they had learned to tell their stories with the materials the silent film afforded them.
A summary and opinion	This getting the most out of the conditions imposed on you, getting a positive advantage where others see only a loss, has always been recognized as the true signature of a master craftsman.
A fact	The good professionals in radio never said or implied, "If you could *see* this, you would understand. . . ."
A specific example	Without a picture to illustrate the genes and the chromosomes, they could strike a chord on the piano two or three times to establish one combination of genes and then, altering only the top note of the chord, illustrate how the slightest variation creates an entirely new entity.
A fact	They learned to use evocative words, they worked the pictorial and inevitably fell into the merely picturesque—but one thing stood always to their credit: in the days of the motion picture and later in the days of the movie with sound,
An opinion	no one actually found radio lacking in power to stir the imagination, to deliver what it had to deliver fully and well.—GILBERT SELDES, *The Public Arts*, p. 69

The general statement is often called a *topic sentence*. Some topic sentences summarize the idea of the paragraph, as in the Seldes paragraph just quoted. Sometimes they do little more than announce the subject, as in this example (which for convenience of reading and for emphasis was divided into two closely related paragraphs):

> There are several ways of taking notes. One is to copy the exact words of the author. This is the lazy man's way of historical writing, unless you are planning to edit selected documents or excerpts from the materials you use and do not intend to do any interpretative writing of your own at all. Another and better way is to read the paragraph or page at least twice (once for general sense and a second time for detailed analysis), and then to try to put the idea expressed by the author into your own words, copying verbatim only such words, phrases, or sentences as are so expressive or colorful that you want them exactly as the author said them. This second method will insure your understanding what the author is trying to say, for unless you understand his statement you will not be able to paraphrase it in your own words.
>
> A third way is to "boil down" the author's statement to as brief a form as possible, that is, giving a summary. In taking notes it is not advisable to do much summarizing, unless you are certain that the subject summarized is one which you will not need to discuss in great detail later on. It is better to paraphrase at the note-taking stage and then to summarize when you begin to write. Rather have too much than too little when taking notes.—DONALD DEAN PARKER, *Local History*, p. 95

Often the general subject is announced first, as in the following paragraph, but the full statement of the idea comes later (The sentence beginning "The basis of formal design" is the topic sentence, followed by more details):

> Let us analyze the two types of garden treatment and see what makes a successful example of each. Step first, in imagination, into a formal garden and look at its design. You immediately become conscious of a strong central axis or imaginary line running down the middle of the garden. The design on one side of this dividing line is a duplicate of the other side. This is symmetrical balance. Straight lines, geometric patterns and forms, and pairs of specimens at all important points of interest make up the design. The basis of formal design is a completely symmetrical balance of geometrically shaped beds and architectural objects with the boundaries of the area very strongly marked and defined. In such a design the plant material is subordinated to geometrical pattern. Clipped hedges and clipped specimens of trees or shrubs are used to form and accentuate the structure of the design.—JOHN A. and CAROL L. GRANT, *Garden Design*, p. 8

A paragraph may begin with a generalization (topic sentence) whose idea is repeated at the end, usually somewhat elaborated. The effect of the paragraph is one of support, with a clincher at the end.

> National security has ceased to exist in any absolute sense. Our awakening tomorrow to participate in the life of a happy and healthy nation is subject to the whim of a foreign totalitarian regime—a regime armed with H-bombs and presumably with the means to deliver them almost unhindered. That whim is fortunately kept in check by our ability to retaliate, giving us a perhaps illusory feeling of confidence that we will work and enjoy many tomorrows. But national security has been reduced to a question of probability, instead of certainty, that we will survive any year without being blown to bits.—DAVID INGLIS, "National Security with the Arms Race Limited," *Bulletin of the Atomic Scientists,* June 1956, p. 196

Though practiced writers are not usually conscious of their topic sentences, occasionally it is useful for a beginner to concentrate on these focal statements by writing a topic sentence or a series of them and then developing the ideas into paragraphs. A series of topic sentences from a paper should reveal not only the content of each paragraph but also the relation between paragraphs.

Paragraphs of support, partly because of the focus provided by topic sentences, are probably the safest type for a writer who feels uncertain of the movement he is giving to his material. With the generalization stated first it is easier to see how the details are related to it.

Expository paragraphs: order of climax

Paragraphs of climax begin with a particular detail and follow with others that usually move toward some point the writer wishes to make, a "particular to general" or "inductive" order. *Climax* may be too strong a name for this natural and common pattern, but it emphasizes an actual movement frequently found in writing. It allows the writer to pick up the reader's attention quickly and lead him to the end, which is often a generalization, as in this comment:

> We stopped for half an hour the other afternoon in bright sunshine to watch the digging where the Murray Hill Hotel used to be. There were about forty of us kibitzers, every one a male. A huge Diesel shovel named Lorain was hacking the last few tons of dirt and rubble from the hole and dropping them deftly onto trucks. This was a large-scale operation—big, ten-wheel Mack trucks, plenty of mud and noise and movement. The shovel operator was conscious of his audience and played to it. Bathed in sunlight and virtuosity, he allowed his cigarette to drip lazily from his lips while he plucked his levers as cunningly as a chimesmaster. We men in the audience were frozen in admiration,

in respect, in wonder. We studied and digested every trick of the intricate operation—the thrust, the hoist, the swing, the release—conscious of the power and the glory. To a man, we felt instructed, elevated, stimulated. To a man, we were at the controls, each one of us, learning the levers, nudging the rocks, checking the swing, clicking the jaws to coax the last dribble. The sun warmed us in our studies. Not a woman, of the many who passed, paused to watch and to absorb. Not one single female. There can be no question but that ninety-five percent of all the miracles in the world (as well as ninety-five percent of all the hell) are directly traceable to the male sex.—*The New Yorker,* Feb. 19, 1949. Reprinted by permission. Copr. 1949, The New Yorker Magazine, Inc.

Often the subject is announced at the beginning but the full idea comes as a climax at the end, as in this series of particular opinions that lead to a final broader generalization:

These observations give a sort of base-line for estimating the effect of pocket-size books on the general cultural level. At their very worst they are immensely better than the comics. Still at their worst, they are a little better than the pulps; often they are written by the same authors, but with somewhat more care and consecutive effort. At their best they are better than any of the mass-circulation magazines—and the statement remains true even if we set aside the pocket-book series that have achieved some literary or scholarly distinction, like Mentor Books, Anchor Books, and Penguins imported from England. Except for a few of the Mentors, these seldom appear at newsstands in shabby neighborhoods, but even there the assortment is likely to include some admirable works that were never before available at low prices. Pocket-size books as a class are making possible a considerable improvement in the reading habits of the American public.—MALCOLM COWLEY, *The Literary Situation,* pp. 105-6

The final statement need not be a generalization but simply a more impressive detail that seems to round out the subject of the paragraph:

The God Makemake was associated with the sooty tern, a sea bird whose eggs and young were an important article of food. The terns nested on a rocky islet offshore and one of the most elaborate native ceremonies was associated with getting the first egg each nesting season. The man who obtained this egg became for a year the incarnation of the God Makemake. He lived in a special stone house and was subject to numerous taboos, some of which were far from pleasant. However, he could demand offerings of food from everyone and acquired a social prestige which lasted for life. The year of his incarnation was ever after known by his name and at death he was buried with other "bird men" in a special sacred place.—RALPH LINTON and PAUL S. WINGERT, *Arts of the South Seas,* p. 43

Most paragraphs belong to one of these four kinds—narrative and descriptive paragraphs and expository paragraphs of support or climax. Each kind of development is appropriate to certain materials and fits into the mental habits of both writers and readers. Revising your paragraphs with these movements in mind may help you make your papers more consistent and more effective to a reader. The real value of this knowledge is not in classifying paragraphs after they have been written but in organizing and writing material; using more than one of the movements in a paper makes possible a welcome variety.

Continuity in paragraphs

Whether a paragraph makes its full point depends largely on the way the reader is led from one statement to the next. The relation between the statements should be obvious not only to the writer but also to the reader for whom it is intended. To make sure of this, the writer usually needs to check his paragraphs in revision, taking a reader's point of view as far as he can. If a sentence sounds as though the paragraph was beginning again, it probably needs attention. If it is difficult to pass from one statement to the next, the reader may be thrown off the track. If the statements can be firmly tied together, they will probably compose a satisfactory paragraph and embody a consistent chain of thought. The connection must first exist in the ideas and then be shown in the writing.

The second sentence of the following paragraph does not follow from the first; it seems to make a new start. The whole paragraph needs to be rewritten from a single point of view (either of the player trying to find a good polo pony or of the men trying to produce one) and the relation between the statements needs to be clarified:

> For many years men have been breeding, raising, and schooling different types and breeds of horses in an effort to produce the ideal polo mount. When a player wishes to purchase a high-type pony, he looks for four things–quickness, speed, stamina, and ability to stop easily. A combination of these four essentials is difficult to find in one animal. Several have two or three of the qualifications, but very seldom do you find a pony with all four.

Fortunately there are a number of ways to show the connection between statements naturally and simply. Relationship may be shown by:

1) continuing the same subject from sentence to sentence, using the same words, synonyms, or pronouns

2) using some words of the first sentence, perhaps the object, at the beginning of the second, perhaps as the subject

3) using a pronoun referring to a word in the preceding sentence

4) using a conjunction or adverb (*however, but, and*) to show thought relationship (cause or effect, reason, illustration)

5) making sentences parallel in structure

The following paragraph shows the most common of these signs of continuity (indicated by the italicized words):

(1) Critics have not been lacking, *of course,* who pointed out what a hash democracy was making of its pretensions to government. (2) *These critics* have seen that the important decisions were taken by individuals, and that public opinion was uninformed, irrelevant and meddlesome. (3) *They* have usually concluded that there was a congenital difference between the masterful few and the ignorant many. (4) *They* are the victims of a superficial analysis of the evils they see so clearly. (5) The *fundamental difference* which matters is that between insiders and outsiders. (6) *Their* relations to a problem are radically different. (7) Only the *insider* can make decisions, not because he is inherently a better man but because he is so placed that he can understand and can act. (8) The *outsider* is necessarily ignorant, usually irrelevant and often meddlesome, because he is trying to navigate the ship from dry land. (9) *That* is why excellent automobile manufacturers, literary critics and scientists often talk such nonsense about politics. (10) *Their* congenital excellence, if it exists, reveals itself only in their own activity. (11) The *aristocratic theorists* work from the fallacy of supposing that a sufficiently excellent square peg will also fit a round hole. (12) *In short,* like the democratic theorists, *they* miss the essence of the matter, which is, that competence exists only in relation to function; that men are not good, but good for

Suggests continuation from a preceding paragraph

Subject of 1 repeated

Pronoun, referring to *critics,* subject of 1 and 2

Pronoun, as in 3

Fundamental contrasts with *superficial* of 4; *difference* repeated from 3

Pronoun *Their* refers to *insiders and outsiders*

Insider repeated

Outsider repeated from 5, contrasting with *insider* in 7

Pronoun *That,* summarizing idea of 8

Pronoun *Their,* referring to the subjects of talk in 9

Aristocratic theorists echoes *critics* of first sentences; *excellent* echoes *excellent* of 9 and *excellence* of 10

In short, a connective

Pronoun *they,* referring to *theorists* of 11; *democratic theorists* contrasting with *aristocratic*

A firm, emphatic final sentence, topic sentence and goal of the

something; that men cannot be educated, but only educated for something.—WALTER LIPPMANN, *The Phantom Public,* pp. 149-50	preceding statements (climax movement)

It would be impossible to begin reading this paragraph at any sentence without feeling that something had gone before, something needed to get the full meaning of the sentence. Even at the spots where the connection is least close (sentences 5, 7, 11), the sentences mean more because of what has preceded.

The principal characteristics of a paragraph can be seen by analyzing it for its development of material (the relations between details and generalizations as described on pp. 139-147) and for the signs of continuity between the statements. Accompanying the two passages that follow, some points are made at the left about development of material and at the right about signs of continuity.

The first passage is from an advanced textbook in psychology, the opening paragraphs of a chapter on *canalization.* This introduction to the subject is not technical, though much of the treatment that follows is. The paragraphs are conspicuously close-knit, since the generalizations and details are tied closely together.

Material		*Continuity*
Topic sentence (generalization)	(1) Needs tend to become more specific in consequence of being satisfied in specific ways.	(Starts a new unit)
Example (and evidence)	(2) Children all over the world are hungry;	Relation obvious
Details	their hunger may be satisfied by bread, by ice cream, by peanuts, by raw eggs, by rice, or by whale blubber.	Repetition of *satisfied* from 1
General idea repeated in less general terms	(3) Eventually they develop, when hungry, not a demand for food in general, but a demand for what they are used to;	*they* refers to *children* of 2; *hungry* repeated from 2
Repeated in details	in one part of the world peanuts are good food, whale blubber disgusting, and vice versa.	
Another example	(4) So, too, over the face of the earth, children enjoy rhythms; the need is satisfied by different kinds	*So, too,* connective; *children* repeated as subject

Made more specific	of rhythms, different games, different types of music.	
Part of general idea restated	(5) Soon they find the ones which they are "used to" natural and satisfying; others seem awkward, difficult, unsatisfying.	*Soon* suggests continuity, *they* referring to *children*
Idea repeated with two examples	(6) If a person is hungry, oriented toward food in general, he may nevertheless be more hungry for bread than for corn, for beef than for mutton.	*hungry* echoes preceding paragraph
Idea progressively refined and limited	(7) Attitude toward food is general, the valuation of absent food is general; but specific attitudes are defined within the general, and within the specific there are some still more specific,	*Attitude* translates *oriented toward; food* and *general* repeated; *specific* repeated from preceding paragraph
Illustration	so that one wants not only currant buns but the one with the darkest crust.	
Compact restatement of general idea	(8) Tastes have become specific.—GARDNER MURPHY, *Personality,* p. 161	*Tastes* echoes *attitudes* and *needs; specific* repeated

The first paragraph is of the support type, beginning with the general statement that is developed in more specific terms; the second is of the climax type, beginning with particulars and ending on a strong general statement. A conspicuous trait is the repetition of the key words of the first sentence: in the two paragraphs *specific* occurs six times (and, contrasting with it, *general* four times), *satisfied* and *satisfying* four times, and *needs* and its equivalents (*demand, attitude, wants, taste*) eight times. Since the words represent the core of the idea, their repetition is not bothersome but keeps us aware of the general idea: "Needs tend to become more specific in consequence of being satisfied in specific ways." The last forceful sentence, "Tastes have become specific," is the final source of emphasis.

The second passage, from a book for general readers, is not quite so compact. It gives reasons for moving from the opinion of the first sentence to the opposite opinion in the last. The words that continue the thought are less exactly equivalent than in the preceding example but they still carry on the general theme unmistakably.

Material		*Continuity*
The topic (but not a topic sentence)	(1) Public opinion polls contrive to give the impression that as a nation we are in a constant state of agitation over all sorts of domestic and foreign problems	
Restatement in more specific terms	(2) Eighty or ninety or sometimes ninety-nine per cent of the people interviewed are able to say that they are for or against a particular man or a particular measure, and that is what the investigators want.	*people interviewed* connects with *polls* in 1
An objection or qualification	(3) Some experts, however, have begun to admit that people often have opinions on subjects about which they are less than adequately informed.	*however,* connective
Specific instance	(4) The man in the street, they confess, may strongly support or bitterly oppose a bill that is before Congress without being able to describe one of its provisions.	*they,* referring to *some*
Writer's opinion of 3-4	(5) This admission is healthy, but the experts need to take another step.	*This admission* refers to idea of 3-4; *experts* repeated from 3
Writer's point Topic sentence	(6) A man may turn up an opinion on demand, and yet have only the slightest interest in the subject about which he is being interviewed.	
Restated in specific questions	(7) How much does the individual in question think about the subject?	Restatement of *another step; individual* refers to *man* in 6
	(8) Does he feel that it has any real relevance	*he* and

	to his own life? (9) How do his thoughts and emotions on this subject compare with his thoughts and emotions on other subjects?	*his* refer to *individual* Roughly parallel question form, 7-9
General point restated	(10) The problem that I wish the experts would investigate is not what people think about this or that but what they think about.	*the experts, what people think* carried over
Made more specific	(11) Both psychologists and novelists suggest that people think mostly about themselves.	*people think* repeated
Details	(12) The stream of ideas—call it interior monologue or what you will—that passes through the average human mind is concerned with *me:* my health, my state of mind, what people think about me and what I think about them, my problems, my children, my job, what I said to Joe and what he said to me, mostly what I said to him.	*stream of ideas* equals *what people think* *concerned with me* equals *about themselves* of 11
Concluding generalization, directly contrary to that in 1	(13) Even the most public-minded citizen, I suspect, devotes only a fraction of his attention to the affairs of city, state, and nation, and any conception of democracy that postulates the constant and alert interest of the citizenry is purely romantic.—GRANVILLE HICKS, *Small Town,* pp. 100-1	*Even* has connecting force; *public-minded citizen* contrasts with *average human mind* of 12

Both of these paragraphs are of the climax type (showing that the label "climax" does not demand intensity) since in each the writer is moving *toward* his important point. The first is in three stages (sentences 1-2, 3-5, 6-9), of which the third carries the main point. The thought proceeds easily, but each paragraph ends with a direct and forceful phrasing.

Paragraphs in a paper

Paragraphs seldom occur singly except in practice writing. In the series of paragraphs that makes up a paper or article there are special considerations for the opening and closing parts and for the relationship between the various paragraphs in sequence.

Opening paragraphs

The first few sentences of a paper have a double function: they must get the subject under way, or at least get definitely started toward it, and they should interest the reader enough to make him want to read on. Herbert Read summarizes their qualities: "the first words should be either familiar or arresting, and the last should be emphatic."

Regard for the reader is particularly important in beginnings. Amateur writers are often tempted to concoct an elaborate "introduction" and so postpone the real matter of the paper, or to begin routinely ("It is the purpose of this paper to show how to select vacation work"), or even to open with an apology. They frequently begin with a large generalization. "On the banks of the great St. Lawrence waterway are many towns and settlements, some on the American side, and some on the Canadian" is so obviously true that it does not need saying. And the following sentence, so general in its application that it might begin a paper on almost any social topic, actually began one on sharecroppers: "All men are endowed by their Creator with certain inalienable rights, among which are life, liberty and the pursuit of happiness."

Of course when you are writing the first draft the important thing is to get started, and it is unwise to wait until a perfect beginning occurs to you. A formalized opening will let you get under way, but one of the chief points of revision should be to look at the first sentences to see if they really attract the reader. It is the experience of many writers that their beginning paragraphs are their worst and should simply be discarded. Often the paper can be started with the second or third paragraph, but sometimes a new opening must be written.

The reader's attention can be picked up by putting first the part of the subject that is nearest his concern or by beginning with details that have definite human interest. Perhaps the writer can dramatize some point by having people say or do something.

Of the seven factual articles in an issue of *Harper's Magazine,*[1] four open with some kind of narrative, each having an obvious relation to the subject of the article as it is shown by the title:

> A whimsical old professor of mine at college in South Carolina stopped in the hall one day and demanded to know my grandmother's name on my father's side. Given the fact, he mused upon it a long moment, and declared, "Your grandfather, my boy, came from better people."—WILLIAM FRANCIS GUESS, "South Carolina's Incurable Aristocrats," p. 44
>
> My large, motherly, Intourist guide was firmly negative that first morning as we stood talking in the lobby of the Hotel Astoria in Leningrad last May.—STERLING A. CALLISEN, "Inside Russia's Treasure House," p. 66
>
> In September 1925 I landed for the first time at New York on my way to Harvard. Now I have just completed a year in which I have spent more than two-thirds of my time in the United States, in every section of the country. I have had an opportunity to reflect on the changes in American life that I have noted in over a score of visits in thirty-two years and on the present role of the United States in the world, contrasted with that which I gave it—naïvely but not, I think, wrongly—in 1925.—D. W. BROGAN, "Unnoticed Changes in America," p. 27

One of the narrative openings is impersonal, reporting a recent event pertinent to the subject of the article:

> On the evening of April 27, 1952, several thousand citizens of Philadelphia crowded onto the main platform of the Pennsylvania Railroad's old Broad Street Station, on the northwest corner of the great square which surrounds the City Hall—the organic as well as the political heart of the city. None of them would ever be there again, for next morning the demolition of this landmark would begin. The railroad, after thirty years of leisurely consideration, had at last decided to level the station and the "Chinese Wall" which carried its tracks to the Schuylkill River and the company's newer station at Thirtieth Street. The resulting cleared area—probably the largest single space to become available at the center of an American city in the twentieth century—had already been given a name: Penn Center.—JAMES REICHLEY, "Philadelphia Does It: The Battle for Penn Center," p. 49

One of the openings is a paragraph of details supporting a brief generalization:

> American women have been maneuvered back into the kitchen. The evidence is unmistakable: a flurry of specialized cookbooks every

[1] *Harper's Magazine,* Feb. 1957.

month; a kaleidoscope of luscious food pages in the magazines; and, even in the most ordinary family kitchen, mingled orders of wine and garlic, sesame and coriander, *shoyu* and dried bonito fish.—MARILYN MERCER, "The Gourmets Get out of Hand," p. 34

The two non-narrative openings are generalizations, but they make an effort to capture the reader's attention, the first by catchy phrasing and the second by appealing to the reader's natural concern about a grave political situation:

> Horsepower, rather than horse-sense, still dominates American automobiles in 1957; and in step with greater power is greater length, to make thousands more home garages and city parking-meter systems obsolete. Some very exotic things have been done with the tail lights, too. But except for improved stability from a lower center of gravity there are no startling additions to the auto safety features which caused such a stir in 1956.—PAUL W. KEARNEY, "How Safe Are the New Cars?" p. 38
>
> The outbreak of fighting in the Middle East made it painfully clear that the order we had tried to maintain in that area is hopelessly unstable. Sources of the instability include pathological nationalism, racial and religious hatreds, embittered reactions to Western contempt, and inexperience in responsible government. But Poverty is its basis, the poverty that everywhere underlies these specific miseries—and not only the fact of poverty, but also the frustrating hopelessness of being so mired in want that no way out is visible. It was no accident that the recent tragic round of events was touched off by the abrupt and humiliating withdrawal of American support for the Aswan Dam project, one of the few symbols of escape from the economic morass.—DAN LACY, "Foreign Aid: Is It Still Necessary?" p. 72

The openings of these articles suggest that it is effective to begin directly with some part of the material that is to be presented and that instead of leading up to the subject it should be started at once, and started as interestingly as possible. The reader who finds himself in the very first sentence in a definite time and place very often will be led to read on. Considering your prospective audience is as important when you begin a theme as when you start an article, and paying attention to the opening sentences will help remove the impression that so many themes give of being written in a void.

Not all writing, of course, needs to appeal to the audience in the manner just illustrated. Articles in technical and professional journals seldom begin in such an attractive way. But the audiences that read such journals turn to them because they are determined to work their way through the articles no matter how forbidding and difficult the material and the style may be. Your task is to make your style and material as attractive as possible without sacrificing accuracy and honesty.

Concluding paragraphs

The last paragraph of a paper, like the opening paragraph, has a double function: It rounds out the subject and gives the final emphasis. If rightly done it will leave the reader with exactly the impression the writer intended. It should also sound like a last paragraph; that is, by its subject matter and its style it should satisfy a reader's sense of having reached the end.

There are two types of ending that are usually unsatisfactory: (1) endings made up of minor details and (2) apologies.

A concluding paragraph is usually unemphatic when it is made up of *minor details* or references to other matters that could be but are not discussed in this particular paper. Instead of concentrating the reader's mind on what has been said, it sends it off in other directions. For example, this ending, at the close of a paper on pitching, suddenly turns to a generalization about the other members of a baseball team:

> Baseball is one of America's favorite sports, and to spend an afternoon at the Yankee Stadium, watching two great pitchers battling for a victory, attracts thousands of fans. What I have said about pitching gives you an idea as to what a pitcher must keep in his mind while out there on the mound, or as a substitute on the bench. There are eight other players on the team besides the pitcher and the same can be written about each individual player and his position.

It is true that every subject suggests others and is in some way related to others, and sometimes this relation should be indicated. But if it is, or if incidental matters are referred to, they should be thrown in earlier in the paper, not allowed to blur the final emphasis.

An *apology* as a conclusion also weakens the effect, and attempted cuteness may let a paper die away when it should end strongly:

> I guess old Mike was not really an unusual character. Just a plain citizen who had had more than his share of bad luck. Today is the first time I've thought of him. I don't know why he should have been recalled to my memory now. Maybe it's spring, weather, or something else. I really don't know.

Often a writer feels quite properly that his subject needs a better treatment than he can give it; sometimes he needs to explain why the treatment is limited in some way. But the place for such qualifications is early in the paper (though not at the beginning, because there it would make a weak start). If such explanations are made early and briefly, the ending can then represent the best the writer is capable of and form a vigorous conclusion.

In a short, informal paper a mechanical summary of content is rarely needed, and such bald statements as "In this paper I have shown that" are inappropriate. Summaries are more appropriate in formal academic papers, where they may be necessary if the material is complex or in some way difficult to follow. Whenever a summary is used, it should be arranged carefully so that it ends with the particular emphasis the writer intends.

The important thing is that the conclusion should leave the reader with the idea that the writer wants to get across. It is likely to be a generalization, though it may be stated in terms of details. The endings of two of the articles from *Harper's Magazine* (used to illustrate beginnings on pp. 166-167) show good final emphases, the first rounding out, informally summarizing the writer's opinion, the second recommending a partial solution to a problem:

> The hopes, beliefs, enthusiasms that I brought to America in 1925 have not been deceived. [A reference to the first paragraph of the article.] America, today, is a more interesting, civilized, promising society than it was in that year, and the pursuit of happiness is still less of a waste effort there than in any other country known to me. It is not a race that many people win, but Americans, I think, enjoy the race more than we do. It is the fashion in Europe (and even in America) to sneer at the simple optimism of nineteenth-century America, but if it is not "the last, best hope of earth," where is that happier and more hopeful land?–D. W. BROGAN, "Unnoticed Changes in America," p. 34
>
> Nobody has ever questioned the fact that the engineers know as much or more about safe car design than any of their critics. But they will never be allowed to put that knowledge fully to work until the sales executives are banned from the drafting rooms, just as they've been banned in the field of washing machines, electric blankets, gas furnaces, oil burners, and a score of other devices with high accident potentials.
>
> The cue for Detroit is clear. Human nature being what it is, the survivable accident will always be with us. The function of applied crash research is to curb needless injury and death.–PAUL W. KEARNEY, "How Safe Are the New Cars?" p. 43

As these examples have shown, the style of the final paragraph is of special importance because it contributes conspicuously to the tone, whether it is humor, simple directness, encouragement, impressiveness, or some other. This means that the last paragraph should be especially scrutinized in revision so that empty phrases, false emphases, and anything else that might detract from the intended effect can be taken out. It means also that the phrasing may need to be intensified slightly to make the words more meaningful and, when possible, suggestive. In short, the ending should be as well expressed as you can make it, and your phrasing of the last sentence should if possible be both exact and happy.

Transitions between paragraphs

Between the opening and concluding paragraphs the material stands as the writer has planned it and probably laid it out in an outline. The outline is roughly related to the paragraphs, but a main head in an outline may be represented by one paragraph in a short paper or several paragraphs in a fuller treatment of the subject. The outline is a guide to the order of material and to the scale of treatment, but the number of divisions does not usually represent the number of actual paragraphs.

However the material is divided, the paragraphs should show continuity from one to the next, much as the sentences within a paragraph do. The connection between the parts of the subject, the words that lead the reader from one thought to another, are called *transitions*.

One of the most common weaknesses of amateur writing is beginning a later paragraph as though nothing had yet been said, instead of building on what has gone before. The two following paragraphs could have been linked by some expression like "The principal advantage I found in the prep school is that every student gets individual attention."

> I think that a preparatory school education is better than a high school education. During the last four years I went to prep school. Many times my friends would tell me that it was just a waste of time. They'd say, "Gosh, but you're missing a lot of fun" or "Don't be a sucker and spend the best four years of your life in prep school."
>
> Individual attention is the main objective of prep schools. Classes are limited to ten or twenty students. We never had to study in a room where another class was reciting. The work is not entirely left to the pupil, as regular study halls are held. If one is low in a subject the prof will find time to tutor him. Tests are corrected and recorrected until every mistake is cleared. Most fellows coming to college from a prep school know how to study. This does not mean that they are smarter than anyone else but that they have been taught to budget their time.

The transition should show a connection both with the topic of the whole paper and with the topic of the preceding paragraph. If it can be done naturally, it is sometimes a good idea to name or allude to the topic of the article, or at least to that of a subdivision of the article, in the first sentence of each paragraph. In this excerpt about

Buffalo, the city is named near the beginning of each of the six paragraphs:

> Buffalo is a place of contrasts—of big and distinctly different communities bound together into a huge blustery city beside the tossing waters of Erie, stormiest of the Great Lakes....
>
> And the people in those depths are equally indifferent to the lake shore. To thousands of its people Buffalo means the golden glow and desperate drudgery of a steel furnace, the stuffy interior of a flour mill, ...
>
> The casual wanderer through Buffalo's residential streets will not walk far without coming upon a corner redolent with the smell of beer and sauerkraut, cheese and apple dumplings....
>
> Last and more powerful of the groups that make up Buffalo are the rich old families living in heavy elegance behind the respectable excesses of the scroll saw....
>
> The four chief streams of Buffalo's population become aware of each other only at City Hall and in the downtown business section....
>
> The Irish, the Germans, and the rich old families have kept Buffalo on the conservative side politically through most of its later history....
> —CARL CARMER, *Listen for a Lonesome Drum,* pp. 43-6

Showing the connection with the paragraph immediately preceding is easier and perhaps more important than showing the connection with the general topic. The purpose is to indicate that the subject is being continued. When paragraphs are short, the signs of continuity may not differ essentially from those used between sentences. There are transitional words and phrases like *this* or *that* or other words that refer directly to a word or idea at the end of the preceding paragraph, and transitional expressions like *on the contrary, another reason, in the second place, besides this,* and other indications of thought relationship. Such genuine connectives are more essential than the flabby *then too* or mechanical expressions like *Now let us turn to* or *It is interesting to note,* which are symptoms that the writer has not sensed the actual relationship between the points he is making.

The sign of transition between two paragraphs usually appears at the beginning of the second one rather than at the end of the first. Often it is enough to carry over only an essential word or two or an idea expressed in slightly different words from the end of the preceding paragraph, using the devices of continuity between the sentences of a paragraph discussed on pages 159-165.

Of course, while you are writing a paper you are considering what you want to say rather than how to say it. You are not interested then in describing the kinds of sentences or paragraphs you are putting on paper. But it is useful once in a while to analyze your papers to see if there are some ways in which you can improve or if there are desirable traits which you can intensify. Some conscious application of the variety of methods available will make your writing grow in effectiveness. And paragraphs are an especially fruitful field for experimenting and practice.

Chapter 6

SUGGESTED STUDY AND WRITING

1. After studying the illustrative paragraphs in this chapter, answer these questions:

A) List each type of detail which Hertzler (pp. 143-144) uses to support his opening statement.

B) Which sentence or sentences most clearly state the basic opinion in the paragraphs from *The New Yorker* (p. 144), Agar (p. 145), and Barzun (p. 146)?

C) In the passage by Langewiesche (p. 145), which sentence states the cause? In the passage by Fadiman (pp. 145-146), which states the superiority of one kind of trash over another?

2. Study the following passages in relation to what has been said in this chapter. Then prepare answers to these questions: What type of movement does each selection have? Which statements are generalizations and which are details? Which of the expository paragraphs contain topic sentences—what are they? If the paragraph does not have a topic sentence, formulate a general statement that will cover the content.

A) (1) Depression? They [young people] don't even think about it. (2) If they are pressed into giving an opinion on the matter, their explanations would suggest that America has at last found something very close to the secret of perpetual motion. (3) And the gears, they believe, can no longer be reversed. (4) "They can't dispossess everybody," goes a frequent observation, and equally frequent is the even more optimistic thought that the government not only wants to keep prosperity from slipping even slightly, but that it knows exactly how to do it. (5) "The depression would be a political issue," explains a twenty-six-year-old junior executive. (6) "The government would certainly see to it that a depression would not take place." (7) In the unlikely event one did take place, some add, it wouldn't hurt them personally. (8) Whatever their occupation, almost all organization people feel their particular job is depression-proof. (9) ("People always need electricity"; "The food business couldn't go down much," etc.) (10) Furthermore, it would all be relative. (11) "If my salary goes down," as one puts it, "prices would be going down too, so in the end I would be just about as well off as I was before."—WILLIAM H. WHYTE, JR., *The Organization Man*, p. 353

B) (1) At that time Hilda was twenty-four. (2) She was a small, slim, rather timid girl, with dark hair, beautiful movements and—because of having very large eyes—a distinct resemblance to a hare. (3) She was one of those people who never say much, but remain on the edge of any conversation that's going on, and give the impression that they're listening. (4) If she said anything at all, it was usually "Oh, yes, *I* think so too," agreeing with whoever had spoken last. (5) At tennis she hopped about very gracefully, and didn't play badly, but somehow had a helpless, childish air. (6) Her surname was Vincent.—GEORGE ORWELL, "Hilda," *Coming Up for Air*, p. 155

c) **(1)** This legend purported to offer a terrible and edifying example, a warning to all Christians to avoid the snares of science, of pleasure, and of ambition. (2) These things had sent Doctor Faustus into hell-fire; his corpse, found face downward, could not be turned over upon its back. (3) Nevertheless, we may suspect that even at the beginning people recognized in Doctor Faustus a braver brother, a somewhat enviable reprobate who had dared to relish the good things of this life above the sad joys vaguely promised for the other. (4) All that the Renaissance valued was here represented as in the devil's gift; and the man in the street might well doubt whether it was religion or worldly life that was thereby made the more unlovely. (5) Doubtless the Lutheran authors of the first chapbook felt, and felt rightly, that those fine things which tempted Faustus were unevangelical, pagan, and popish; yet they could not cease altogether to admire and even to covet them, especially when the first ardours of the Old-Christian revival had had time to cool.—GEORGE SANTAYANA, *Three Philosophical Poets*, p. 133

D) (1) Mrs. Cadman sat down by the fire and, gratefully, kicked off her tight shoes. (2) In the warmth her plump feet uncurled, relaxed, expanded like sea-anemones. (3) She stretched her legs out, propped her heels on the fender and wiggled her toes voluptuously. (4) They went on wiggling of their own accord; they seemed to have an independent existence. (5) Here, in her home, where she felt so "put wrong" and chilly, they were like ten stout confidential friends. (6) She said, out loud: "Well, *I* don't know what I've done."

(7) The fact was: Lucille and Rosa resented her. (8) (She'd feel better when she had had her tea.) (9) She should *not* have talked as she had about the vicar. (10) But it seemed so silly, Lucille having just him. (11) She did wish Lucille had a better time. (12) No young man so much as paused at the gate. (13) Lucille's aunt had wrapped her own dank virginity round her, like someone sharing a mackintosh. —ELIZABETH BOWEN, "A Queer Heart," *Look At All Those Roses*, p. 210

E) (1) One indication of the revolution in manners which her headlong pursuit of freedom brought about was her rapid acceptance of the cigarette. (2) Within a very few years millions of American women of all ages followed the lead of the flappers of 1920 and took up smoking. (3) Custom still generally frowned upon their doing it on the street or in the office, and in the evangelical hinterlands the old taboo died hard; but in restaurants, at dinner parties and dances, in theater lobbies, and in a hundred other places they made the air blue. (4) Here again the trend in advertising measured the trend in public opinion. (5) At the beginning of the decade advertisers realized that it would have been suicidal to portray a woman smoking; within a few years, however, they ventured pictures of pretty girls imploring men to blow some of the smoke their way; and by the end of the decade billboards boldly displayed a smart-looking woman cigarette in hand, and in some of the magazines, despite floods of protests from rural readers, tobacco manufacturers were announcing that "now women may enjoy a companionable smoke with their husbands and brothers." (6) In the ten years between 1918 and 1928 the total production of cigarettes in the United States *more than doubled.* (7) Part of this increase was doubtless due to the death of the one-time masculine prejudice against the cigarette as unmanly, for it was accompanied by somewhat of a decrease in the production of cigars and smoking tobacco, as well as—mercifully—of chewing tobacco. (8) Part of it was attributable to the fact that the convenience of the cigarette made the masculine smoker consume more tobacco than in the days when he preferred a cigar or a pipe. (9) But the increase could never have been so large had it not been for the women who now strewed the dinner table with their ashes, snatched a puff between the acts, invaded the masculine sanctity of the club car, and forced department stores to place ornamental ash-trays between the chairs in their women's shoe departments. (10) A formidable barrier between the sexes had broken down. (11) The custom of separating them after formal dinners, for example, still lingered, but as an empty rite. (12) Hosts who laid in a stock of cigars for their male guests often found them untouched; the men in the dining-room were smoking the very same brands of cigarettes that the ladies consumed in the living-room.—FREDERICK LEWIS ALLEN, *Only Yesterday,* p. 109

3. Study the above paragraph by Mr. Allen and answer the following questions:

A) This passage concerns the American woman's acceptance of smoking. List words throughout the paragraph that repeat the idea of *American woman;* list words and phrases that repeat the idea of *smoking.*

B) Since this paragraph discusses a trend, time relationships are important. List the words and phrases other than verbs used to indicate time. How do they add to the continuity of the paragraph?

C) How is repetition used to relate sentences 6, 7, 8, and 9?

D) What do the following pronouns refer to? How do they add to the continuity of the paragraph? (3) *their, they* (3) *it* (8) *it* (11) *them*

4. Each of the following paragraphs or groups of paragraphs from student papers is unsatisfactory in one or more ways: interrupted movement, poor transition, change of direction, lack of focus, unemphatic beginning, weak ending, or failure to group separate ideas together (overparagraphing). Be ready to discuss in class the flaws in the organization of each paragraph and to give your suggestions for improvement.

A) (1) Watching a high school football game is an exciting two hours of enjoyment for most people, but as for me, I like to watch the spectators. (2) All the small girls and boys ranging from ages 6 to 10 are running around the bleachers having a wonderful time, and their faces look so happy that it makes a person feel good to see them at play.

(3) Meanwhile, the parents of the children are trying to watch the game and their children too. (4) Because of the confusion which results, this is the most interesting time to watch the parents' faces. (5) While the game is quiet, the children are quiet; then the game gets exciting and the children get out of hand. (6) At the end of the game the parents look as if they had gone through a wrestling match. (7) Their hair is a mess, their clothes are askew, and they are beginning to look somewhat worn out.

(8) When all the students are smiling, if the game ended well for them, their faces show that they are happy over the outcome.

(9) Next time you go to a game, watch the people instead of the game because it's more interesting even though it isn't being very loyal to the school.

B) (1) Like her husband, Georgia didn't help the marriage become successful. (2) She wanted to be loved and understood; therefore, when the opportunity presented itself she married. (3) Coming from a penniless family, she had learned to be very thrifty. (4) She was forever telling her husband that there were too many bills and not enough money. (5) She had the feeling that she ought to be perpetually working herself into a stew about the lack of money. (6) She never stopped worrying. (7) By constantly nagging, she drove her husband to hate the sight of her. (8) She always lived in a depressed state, never interested in things for their own sake. (9) For Georgia, life had no feeling or joy. (10) It is best that young couples get to understand each other before they marry.

C) (1) Jane had short, curly, red hair. (2) She had clear, white skin which was a perfect setting for her eyes, which were large and blue and shining with friendliness. (3) They seemed to smile, even though her mouth did not. (4) Her nose was slightly turned up, just enough to fit her sparkling personality. (5) Her average figure was always enhanced by nice clothes. (6) She chose the colors that complemented a redhead.

(7) She was an only child and a doctor's daughter. (8) Her family had one of the nicest homes in town, which included a private swimming pool. (9) The recreation room in the basement provided a place to play pool, watch television, dance, and, of course, eat. (10) She had almost anything she wanted, but all this didn't spoil her. (11) Their home was a favorite place to go after the basketball and football games.

D) (1) Can an inferior student help himself by adopting certain study habits which a superior student uses? (2) Usually the main fault in the study habits of an inferior student is that he has no actual desire to learn. (3) This desire must be developed before he can begin to adopt good study habits. (4) These improved study habits will be formed easily if his attitude toward his work is a determined one. (5) As an example of a firm attitude, the superior student is determined to get an A on that test. (6) He is also determined to make every free moment useful for study. (7) When one of his friends comes around while he is studying, the superior student does not jump up and crack jokes or dash out of the room; he simply converses for a while and then directs his attention back to his lessons. (8) The inferior student could simply adopt this routine and never stray from it. (9) Another important point which an inferior student should adopt is that when he is confronted with a problem, he should not say, "Well, I'll leave it for a while." (10) He should immediately try to solve it. (11) Probably the most important point besides having a firm attitude toward study, is that the student should be happy in school. (12) The inferior student is confronted with several worries and problems, usually connected with his studies. (13) All he would have to do is to complete his studies when he knows they should be completed and never to procrastinate. (14) If an inferior student were to adopt many of these habits, he would be well on his way to developing a successful academic record.

5. Make a study of the material and the paragraph structure of your recent papers, using the following questions as a guide. Summarize your evaluation in a paragraph or two.

A) What types of paragraph movement predominate in your writing? Which do you do best?

B) To what extent does the material consist of details (images, summaries, facts) in contrast to generalizations (interpretations, opinions, generalizations proper)? What possibilities can you see for the use of more specific details?

C) Are your paragraphs adequately developed? Count the number of words in each paragraph and the number of paragraphs in each paper, finding the longest, the shortest, and the average. Then compare the results with those tabulated on page 147.

D) How do your opening and closing paragraphs relate to the rest of the paper? What types of opening and closing do you most commonly employ?

E) What devices for continuity within the paragraph do you use most frequently? What ones might you add effectively to your writing?

6. Take an issue of *The Atlantic, Harper's, The Saturday Evening Post,* or some other magazine suggested by your instructor and study the opening and closing paragraphs in three expository articles. Pick the best set, copy it, and make a brief report describing the material used, the reasons for the effectiveness of the paragraphs, and their relation to the rest of the article.

Literature maintains an endless quarrel with idle sentences.

ROBERT LYND

Chapter **7**

Sentences

Composicion . . . is an apte joyning together of wordes in suche order,

that neither the eere shall espie any jerre,

nor yet any man shalbe dulled with overlong drawing out of a sentence.

THOMAS WILSON (1553)

Chapter 2 discussed chiefly grammatical points, matters of fundamental form that are to be considered in nearly all sentences. The subject and object must be clear, for example, and the modifiers rightly placed. The form of a sentence should seem stable and intentional to the reader and lead him to a direct understanding of its meaning. But there are a number of more variable qualities of sentences in which a writer has more leeway, more freedom for personal choice.

English sentences offer various ways of expressing substantially the same basic idea, even a very simple one like this:

> That book bored me. I found that book boring.
> I was bored by that book. That is a boring book.
> That book is boring. That book seemed boring to me.
> My impression is that that book is boring.

It is easy to imagine different neighboring sentences that would make one of these seem more appropriate than some of the others, though all of them are good English sentences. The sentences you write may be long or short, direct or involved, emphatic, rhythmical—you may or may not use many of the facilities of the language. These are not matters of grammar but of style.

Styles of writing can be described but not prescribed. You have to develop a sense of when and where and how they can be used effectively. Experience in both reading and writing will help. How others have written good sentences is your best guide; it pays occasionally to reread and analyze a passage that appeals to you, observing the sentences closely. In your own papers, don't stop to notice sentences as you write them; wait until the first draft is done, and then try to see them as a reader will, changing them so that they will convey your meaning accurately and with sufficient variety to make them pleasing.

With a little attention your skill in writing sentences will improve greatly.

This chapter describes several traits of sentences and offers some principles to help you see how other writers produce their effects and how you can develop an effective style in your own writing.

Range in sentence length

The most obvious sentence characteristic is relative length. Some writers tend to give a detail or two in each sentence; others build several together into longer sentences. The shorter sentence is characteristic of most newspaper writing, of much business writing and advertising, of familiar writing, as in diaries and letters, of most fiction today, and of many discussions of ideas in both books and magazines–in brief, it is characteristic of Informal and much General English. At worst, short sentences become choppy and jerky, breaking the ideas into units too small for a reader to follow conveniently; or they become unemphatic and monotonous, tiring a reader if they occur in long sequences. At best, they allow the ideas to come directly, to follow each other naturally as they were thought, or at least as they might be spoken. Shorter sentences can be taken in more rapidly in silent reading, but this probably is more a consequence of their necessarily rather direct movement than of the length alone. In this paragraph from a diary-like book about the atom bomb tests at Bikini, the sentences range from 5 to 17 words in length, averaging 12:

> Sadeyes soon wired back to both of us to discontinue our surveys. We were thankful for that. It is not that we were in any immediate danger. But with radiation so intense at such an altitude, that at water level would certainly be lethal. And this wasn't just a point source, it was spread out over an area miles square.–DAVID BRADLEY, *No Place to Hide,* pp. 96-7

Longer sentences, in which several contributing details or generalizations are combined, characterize Formal styles, especially discussions of ideas; they are also fairly common in fiction, especially in descriptive passages, and in newspaper leads, where the most important information of a news item is summarized in a sentence or two. This sentence of 60 words specifies several parts of what the writer sees as "the role of the American college":

> To increase the number of men and women who can live with themselves in some self-assurance and confidence in the meaningfulness and influence of their own lives and can live with their neighbors in a widening arc of friendly, informed, and democratic competence in the social

scene—this is, indeed, one way of characterizing the role of the American college.—ORDWAY TEAD, "Higher Education for the Days Ahead," *School and Society*, July 12, 1952, p. 17

Writers should be concerned, not with the length of single sentences, but with the variety of sentence lengths in a passage. Most factual prose today will average sentences of about 20 words, but this is an average, a summary figure that represents a range of lengths, usually from 5 words or so to above 50. (The fifteen sentences of the first four paragraphs of this chapter, omitting the specimen sentences in the second paragraph, range from 8 to 48 words and average about 21.) The six sentences of the following paragraph discussing the effects of the first battle of Bull Run average 22 words, with the shortest 9 and the longest 49:

(19) Nobody listened, the victory was not followed up, and the whole thing would have to be done over later. (9) Indeed, this battle had some unexpected results all around. (14) For the North, which lost it so shamefully, it was a blessing in disguise. (26) It ended the wild "On to Richmond" talk and compelled government and people alike to understand that this was going to be a long, hard war. (49) Within a week the Lincoln government had called in young Gen. George B. McClellan—a poor man for campaigning and hard fighting, but as good an organizer and drillmaster as the United States Army ever had—and told him to make an army out of the new volunteer levies. (15) The rose-colored glasses were gone, and the land was buckling down to the long job.—BRUCE CATTON, "The Incredible Battles of Bull Run," *Holiday*, July 1956, p. 137

It is the range in length that makes possible variety in the more important sentence traits, such as the number and arrangement of clauses and long phrases.

Children begin writing short sentences and gradually increase their length and complexity until, by the time they are college students, their sentences approximate those of professional writers, as shown in the following table:

Average number of words to the sentence

4th grade	11.1 words	High school freshmen	17.3
6th grade	12	sophomores	17.8
7th grade	13.5	juniors	18.
8th grade	15.2	seniors	19.8

University freshmen 19.9
upperclassmen 21.5
Professional writers 20.9

M. J. STORMZAND and M. V. O'SHEA, *How Much English Grammar?* p. 19

The sentence averages of a student whose sentences were growing in maturity would show a rough correspondence with these figures, though those given for university upperclassmen and certainly for professional writers may be a little lower than is really typical.

Although occasionally a student, by running a long series of clauses together, makes a "stringy" sentence, a more typical fault in college writing is "choppy" sentences—sentences that are too short. The longest sentence in the following paragraph from a theme is 21 words, and the eight together average slightly over 12, the figure given in the table above for sixth-grade writers:

> Probably the hardest job is the handling and treating of grain. The treating consists of running the grain through a machine called a "Fanning Mill." This machine thoroughly cleans the grain and adds a chemical which protects it against winterkill, smut and other common diseases. The most common kind of storage bin for grain is the tank type. It is a round tank with straight sides and peaked roof. These bins have flat bottoms. Grain will not run out by gravity. Someone has invented a simple elevator that can be pushed into the grain to elevate it out.

With some rephrasing, sentences 2 and 3, 4 and 5 and 6, and 7 and 8 might be made into three sentences (try it), showing closer relations between the statements as well as giving variety and an impression of more mature writing.

You should know whether in general you tend to build your material into long sentences or to present it in short ones. Then in revising a particular paper you can be on guard to see that your sentences represent your material in sufficiently varied units, the units in which you see it and hope the reader will see it. There is no special virtue in long sentences or in short ones, but they may be an indication of other qualities. If your sentences in an expository paper average less than 18 or 20 words or more than 30, you should look at them to make sure, if the figure is low, that you are building your details together into mature sentences or, if the figure is high, that the sentences are clear and appropriate to the material.

Variety in sentence movement

Series of sentences of about the same length and general pattern become monotonous. Varying the length helps avoid such monotony, but even more important is changing the order of elements in the sentences. In speech the basis of variety lies in stress and rhythm, the emphasis on individual words, intonation of the various sentence elements, and the pauses between them. Some sense of these qualities carries over even into silent reading, but the chief way to vary written sentences is to change the order of their parts.

Varying position of modifiers

In a paragraph the arrangement of sentences is governed by the writer. But in a sentence the writer has to follow standard grammatical patterns in the arrangement of words. Since the s-v-o order probably occurs in nine tenths of English sentences, the chief source of variety is in the positions for modifiers.

Because the subject is usually conspicuous and emphatic, a series of sentences beginning with unmodified subjects tends to become monotonous. If modifiers of the subject or of the whole sentence occasionally stand first, the monotony is broken. Notice the different movement of these openings:

> The attempts were failures.
> The first serious attempts were failures.
> In spite of their seriousness, the first attempts were failures.
> Although he worked with great seriousness, his first attempts were failures.

An occasional sentence beginning with a long phrase or with a subordinate clause takes the stress away from the subject and makes for variety.[1] With six similar facts to state in this passage, the author begins half the sentences with the subject and half with modifiers that vary the sentence opening:

> [Subject:] *The theoretical type* seeks to grasp the nature of things. [Adverbial modifier of sentence:] *When the reality sought is not local and temporary but cosmic,* we have the religious type. [Adverbial modifier of sentence:] *When not the abstract relations but the persons about one are valued,* we have the social type. [Adverbial phrase:] *In the person for whom individuals are significant not for themselves but as pawns in a game for power,* we have the political type. [Subject:] *The economic type* finds value in the relations of gain and loss. [Subject:] *The esthetic type* values the relations between sensory objects that are directly and immediately satisfying.—GARDNER MURPHY, *Personality,* pp. 283-4

Similarly the sentence may end either with the object or with a modifier of the object, as in the last two sentences in the paragraph above.

Inverted movement

A less common means of varying the sentence pattern is *inversion,* in which the order of the main elements departs from the usual s-v-o.

---

[1] Professor Summey found (*American Punctuation,* p. 241) that about half of the sentences he studied began with the subject (often with an adjective modifier) and over a quarter began with adverbial modifiers, ranging from connectives like *however* and sentence adverbs like *certainly* to long phrases and *when, if, although* clauses.

Some inversions are purely grammatical, but in most sentences they are stylistic. A complement or an emphatic modifier of the verb may stand first, followed by the verb and then the subject (C-V-S, MV-V-S); or a complement or object may precede the subject and verb (O-S-V).

MV	V	S	MS
Then	came	the greatest treat	of all.

O	S	V	MV
This job	he	kept	six years.

C	S	LV	MS
A bargain	it	was,	at that price.

Inversion is not very common and ordinarily is not used unless the words put first really deserve special emphasis. It has been a mannerism of *Time* magazine ("Singular was the U.S. attitude in one respect"), which *The New Yorker* critically parodied, "Backward ran the sentences until reeled the mind."

Questions

Since the grammatical order in questions is inverted (Can you come tomorrow? How could you say that?), they give variety to the sentences in a paragraph. In addition they are helpful, if sparingly used, to focus the reader's attention, either to introduce a change in subject or to emphasize an important point, as in this passage:

> We are beginning to see that the ideal of a liberal education is too large to be put into four years of a college course. It is the growth of a lifetime spent in contact with the actual world. But it is not too much to ask that in a university the student should be brought into contact with different types of the intellectual life, and that each type should be kept distinct. He should learn that the human mind is a marvelous instrument and that it may be used in more than one way.
>
> Variety in courses of study is less important than variety and individuality of mental action. How does a man of science use his mind? How does an artist feel? What makes a man a jurist, a man of business, a politician, a teacher? How does ethical passion manifest itself? What is the historical sense?
>
> These are not questions to be answered on examination papers. But it is a reasonable hope that a young man in the formative period of his life may learn the answers through personal contacts.—SAMUEL MCCHORD CROTHERS, *The Pleasures of an Absentee Landlord,* pp. 48-9

Occasionally a question makes an effective opening for a paper, but it should be a genuine question, leading to the subject, and not a general one concocted just "to get attention."

Interrupted movement

As a rule we do not put words between the major elements of a sentence unless they are short modifiers closely related to one of the main elements (as in "He does *not always* pay his bills promptly"). If the modifiers are long or not very closely related to the main elements, the movement of the sentence is sufficiently interrupted to attract attention:

> This background of crusades and crimes, *with imaginary castles and gallows in the distance,* shed a kind of glamour on the lives of these mild Quakers, who, *in spite of the Quaker ban on worldly fiction,* must, *it appears,* have been reading *Waverley Novels* on the sly. And was it not for them all perfectly authentic? Had not one of them crossed the Atlantic and made a special pilgrimage to Scotland, and there *on the spot, when visiting the estate of this family,* been overcome by a profound conviction of its truth?...What genealogist could demand, *what documents, the family felt, could provide,* more convincing evidence than that?—LOGAN PEARSALL SMITH, *Unforgotten Years,* pp. 6-7

Such interruptions give variety to sentences, but they also make slower and sometimes even difficult reading. They are more characteristic of conspicuously Formal than of General style, in which such modifiers are likely to precede or follow the main sentence elements. Usually it is better to allow only very short modifiers to come between the main sentence elements. The following sentences show how awkward interruption may be in ordinary writing.

Interrupted	*Revised*
During the summer of 1955, I, as did so many others, found the draft board casting a significant eye in my direction.	Like so many others in the summer of 1955, I found the draft board casting a significant eye in my direction.
Ski trails down the sides of the biggest mountains in New England were cleared.	Ski trails were cleared down the sides of the biggest mountains in New England.
Then he impresses on the freshman the fact that he is getting the pictures practically at the price the materials on which they are printed cost.	Then he impresses on the freshman the fact that he is getting pictures practically at the cost of the material they are printed on.

Loose and periodic sentences

Another classification of sentences shows the relation of arrangement to meaningful effect. The sentence you are now reading is so constructed that the completion of its meaning and effect depend on reading it to the very last word. Such a sentence is called *periodic,* as contrasted with the other type, *loose,* of which this is an example—a sentence that might be stopped at several points (in this sentence, after *periodic, type, loose, example,* or *points*).

> [Periodic] Yet to this day in England, as in Australia and the United States, the tradition survives that boys who are good at killing animals, or propelling balls, or leaping obstacles, or running very rapidly, are healthier-minded, and therefore more attractive, than boys who devote their attention to art or literature. [Periodic] This seems in many ways an admirable tradition. [Loose] It renders English intellectuals unassuming, and provides the state and the commercial community with a constant supply of apprentices who lack imagination and are therefore obedient. [Periodic] The disadvantage is that the athlete, after short years of glory, may have to endure an unhappy middle age. [Periodic] Even as the mediaeval knight, who once his hawking days were over found his afternoons lonely and his evenings dull, so also may those who have rejoiced only in the transient marvel of their physical strength discover in later life that their range has become restricted and their interests few. [Periodic] It is thus recommendable that Olympic champions should acquire the reading habit while still young.—HAROLD NICOLSON, *Good Behaviour / Being a Study of Certain Types of Civility,* p. 141

Loose sentences are characteristic of conversation, in which we typically add subordinate statements after the main statement. Periodic sentences are somewhat more Formal. The reader's or listener's attention is suspended until the end; he has to hold the complete sentence in mind rather than let later elements modify the earlier parts. The danger of periodic sentences is that they may seem unnatural; the danger of loose sentences is that they may be unemphatic. While there is no reason to strive for either type, especially in a General style, loose sentences are so much more common that an occasional periodic sentence contributes not only suspense but variety.

Parallelism and balance

In Chapter 2 (pp. 65-67) we learned that putting sentence elements of equal value into parallel constructions was one way of making the sentence a unit. More elaborate parallel movement becomes an element of style and stands out sufficiently among the more casually constructed sentences to give a note of variety. It is more characteristic of Formal than of General style.

The first two of the following examples of parallelism are natural and simple; the third is rather Formal, but still the parallel locutions are sufficiently varied in length and form so that they do not seem monotonous:

She walked slowly, big flakes ‖ falling on her lamb coat and
‖ clinging to hair over her ears...
MORLEY CALLAGHAN, *A Native Argosy*, p. 155

The most serious criticism leveled against American civilization is
‖ not that its work is standardized and its business engulfing,
‖ but that its pleasures are mechanical and its leisure slavish.
IRWIN EDMAN, *An Irwin Edman Reader*, edited by CHARLES FRANKEL, p. 117

‖ Although some were shouting,
‖ like the men and women on the pier,
although some were hysterical,
‖ like the men and women crowding around the plank,
‖ although some were dazed,
there was a difference between them and the persons who awaited them.
LEANE ZUGSMITH, *Home Is Where You Hang Your Childhood*, p. 65

When the parallel constructions, especially clauses, of a compound sentence are noticeably equal in length and similar in movement, the sentence is called *balanced*. Even in a plain style, balanced sentences are fairly common for emphatic statements and especially for comparisons and contrasts:

> They have been educated to achieve success; few of them have been educated to exercise power.—WALTER LIPPMANN, *A Preface to Morals*, p. 66

Economy in sentences

Economy in writing means leading a reader to your exact meaning without unnecessary handicaps to understanding. Few, simple, exact words are its basis, but the pattern in which the words stand has a good deal to do with it. The fewest words and simplest constructions are not always the most economical, for they may oversimplify the message, or they may limit its readers to those who are practiced in following a compact style. But *unnecessary* words and *needlessly* complicated expressions cannot be economical. For amateur writers the chief way to achieve economical expression is to remove wordy expressions in revision until after a while they fail to appear even in the first draft.

Removing deadwood

Deadwood is a convenient label for a lazy word or phrase that adds nothing to the sense of a sentence. A bit of deadwood can be omitted with no loss at all in meaning and with positive gain in economy. Note the bracketed phrases here:

Every thinking person these days seems inclined to agree [with the conception] that the world has gone mad.

Anyone acquainted with violin construction knows that the better the wood is seasoned, the better [the result will be as far as] the tone of the instrument [is concerned].

To my surprise the damage was not so bad as I had expected [it to be].

[It was] during this time [that] the greatest number of cases came down.

[There is] only one excuse [that] is acceptable, [and that is] "I have a class this hour."

It was the first time [in my life] I had seen Niagara Falls.

At the end of an hour and a half we arrived at [the spot where] the red flag [was situated].

The following statistics [serve to] give a good idea of the effects of tobacco.

He kept things moving at breakneck speed throughout [the entirety of] the performance.

A common type of dead phrase is the addition of *color* to a word that can mean only color ("green color"), *number* to a number ("nine in number"), *shape* to a definite form ("rectangular in shape"), or locutions like the following:

The architecture [of the houses] and the landscaping [of the grounds] whisper a word of town pride to the passers-by.

A few words are particularly common—and doubly bad in that they not only add useless weight but often take the emphasis from more important words:

case: While this probably would be true in some cases, I do not think it would be true of the average case. (Revised: While this might sometimes be true, I do not think it would be typical.)

Many of them have been put to death in individual cases. (Revised: Many individuals have been put to death.)

character: The second was quite different [in character].

These things, though [of a] useful [character], were not what he wanted.

exception: Most young actors experience numerous difficulties in their early appearances. I was no exception. (Revised: Like most young actors I experienced many difficulties in my early appearances.)

fact (the fact that): He was quite conscious [of the fact] that his visitor had some other reason for coming.

happen: [It happened that] we were exactly the same age.

line: He had always thought he would do something along agricultural lines. (...in agriculture.)

nature: He was never popular because he was awkward [by nature].

variety: I bought two kinds of rolls for the dinner–two dozen plain and one dozen [of the] pecan [variety].

Elimination of deadwood is one of the easiest ways to begin the attack on fuzzy writing: simply draw a line through the word or phrase.

Direct phrasing

A writer should also avoid *circumlocution,* expressions that use too many words in conveying a single notion. A conspicuous number of roundabout expressions result in flabbiness, make the writing seem immature, and tire the reader.

Wordy	*Revised*
During the time that she was in Los Angeles she had at least six different jobs.	While she was in Los Angeles, she had at least six different jobs.
The way psychologists measure ability is by tests.	Psychologists measure ability by tests.
It has some of the best ski trails in the country and as far as the other cold weather sports are concerned, they have them too, along with one of the most fashionable hotels in the country.	They have a very fashionable hotel, all the cold weather sports, and some of the best ski trails in the country.

Here are some typical examples of circumlocution:

destroyed by fire means *burned*
come in contact with usually means *meet* or *know*
the necessary funds usually means no more than *the money*
in this day and age means *today*

In speaking we often use more words than are necessary, but in writing circumlocution is conspicuous.

Long and short constructions

English offers a choice between a longer and a shorter way of expressing certain relationships. Relative clauses may or may not use the relative pronoun: "the professor *I saw*" is as good as "the professor *whom I saw.*" Not all clauses have verbs: *"If possible,* come a little early" or *"If it is possible."* The conjunction *that* may or may not be used: "We like to think *that* our scholarship standards are higher than yours" or "We like to think [ ] our scholarship standards are higher than yours."

The choice between these forms is a matter of style, to be determined by appropriateness. Formal English tends to fill out most constructions; General English uses the shorter forms more freely. In revising a paper you can usually tell from the movement of the passage whether or not you should make your constructions fuller. In ordinary writing a fairly frequent use of the short forms makes for economy.

Reducing predication

An "idea"–a small part of our meaning–may be expressed in one of four grammatical units: in a word, a phrase, a subordinate clause, or a full sentence:

Word: The snow *blanketed* the countryside.
Phrase: The snow covered the countryside *like a blanket.*
Clause: The snow, *which lay like a blanket,* covered the countryside.
Sentence: *The snow lay like a blanket.* It covered the countryside.

Obviously the chief difference is between the first two, containing one verb, and the last two, containing two predications. Which expression would be more appropriate would depend on the writer's intention and on other traits of his style. But from the point of view of economy alone, the first two are better.

Modern style tends to use fewer predications, fewer clauses, than were used a century ago. One mark of inexperienced writing is the use of a predication for an idea that a more practiced writer would reduce to a phrase or a single word.

Amateur	*More economical*
Labor was quick to realize the advantages of this new form of passive resistance, and *before another year rolled around,* no less than two hundred sit-down strikes had been reported.	Labor was quick to realize the advantages of this new form of passive resistance, and *within a year* no less than two hundred sit-down strikes had been reported.
A few of the fellows *who were less serious* would go to a bar *where they would have a steak dinner and a few glasses of beer.*	A few of the *less serious* fellows would go to a bar *for a steak dinner and a few glasses of beer.*
We taxied back and forth in front of the starting line, waiting impatiently for the sound of the gun *which would mean that the race was started.*	We taxied back and forth in front of the starting line, waiting impatiently for the sound of the *starting* gun.

Of course as you write, you can't always be stopping to ask "How much is this idea worth?" But in revising papers, especially in the early stages of your writing experience, you will occasionally find it worth while to see if you have made the expressions longer than necessary to express your complete meaning. Writing can be made so compact that it is hard to follow, but most beginning writers need to be encouraged to use a more economical style. Length in a paper should not come from piling up *words* but from piling up *material*—ideas and especially details of observation that convey meaning. Proper economy comes from trying to say more in a given number of words.

Emphasis in sentences

The emphasis in a piece of writing comes principally from the use of strong and distinctive words and from a progressive arrangement of statements in paragraphs and of the paragraphs in the whole, but sentences contribute to this general impression. Economy is an important factor, for wordiness buries the meaning, but there are also some specific means to sentence emphasis.

Mechanical devices

Writing and printing have various mechanical means—underlining (italics), capitals, emphatic punctuation—for stressing words and passages. These devices are often used by inexperienced writers in an attempt to make up for deficiencies in style or content and usually result in the "forcible-feeble," as in this speech, a crucial one in the novel from which it is taken:

> *"I go on through!"* he repeated earnestly. "I have suffered—but I know that I am Destiny's darling! . . . *You* have suffered but *you, too, can carry on through!* . . . Take it from me! I know! In spite of all the little detainments, disappointments, disillusionments—*I get the lucky breaks! I get the signal to go forward!* I have been delayed—long—long—long—but—at length—*I get the* GREEN LIGHT!"

This speech might be effective if spoken as the writer has marked it, but the italics, capitals, and punctuation marks are being called on to do more than they really can. With increased skill in writing, a person relies less and less on these mechanical devices. He depends more on distinctiveness of expression, position, and other rhetorical means of showing that one statement is more important than another.

Intensives

There are several ways of emphasizing meaning by the use of special words, particularly in speech. A speaker can stress *too* or *very* or *much* so that it will have a good deal of force (and the activity of the stress gives him a certain physical satisfaction). On paper these intensives are less convincing, in part because the tone of voice is lacking and in part because written style is likely to use words more accurately than oral.

A number of adjectives and adverbs are primarily intensives: *much, *very,*[1] *such, *too, highly, certainly, extremely, tremendously.* They may be used for an accurate emphasis, but they usually suggest an oral stress and are often out of place in writing. An overuse of them suggests a lazy style. Most small profanity belongs in this category, the words allowing a satisfying stress and bite but not contributing otherwise to meaning.

In writing, quite often a statement would actually be stronger if the intensive was omitted:

> We had [such] a lovely time at your party.
> Everybody was [so] tired after the holiday round of parties.
> In pushing the product the slogan has [surely] been [unquestionably] of paramount importance.

The colloquial superlative, used to indicate a considerable degree of a quality instead of the greatest, is a typical intensive in conversation, but it is not often appropriate to writing:

> She had the nicest manners [for *nice* or some more exact adjective].
> He is a most important figure in the book [an important figure].

The pronouns with *-self* are idiomatic intensives both in speaking and writing:

> He picked the flowers himself.
> I must see Catherine herself.

There are scores of words of rather intense meaning—*thrill, intriguing, devastating, passion*—all of which have their necessary and legitimate uses and all of which are likely to be abused when applied to some feeling that does not really deserve such a vigorous word.

The use of intensives should be a matter of appropriateness, especially of appropriateness to the subject. But often, particularly in speech, their appropriateness to the person who is using them is more important. At their best they may represent a vigorous and emphatic personality; at their worst they show insensitiveness to the values of words. If they are used much in writing, they are sure to result in weakened statements.

Repetition

Repetition of words and phrases can be an excellent means of emphasizing or relating ideas. On the other hand, repetition that serves no function is unpleasant and should be avoided if possible.

Unhappy repetition. Meaningless repetition of words or phrases may be the result of small vocabulary, but most of it is due to plain

[1] Throughout this book, references to *Index* articles are indicated by asterisks (*).

inattention to writing—certainly to a lack of revision. Both small vocabulary and carelessness are back of the five *beautiful*'s (not to mention one *beauty*) in this passage:

The landscape is *beautiful.* There are myriads of *beautiful,* stately trees, which contribute greatly to the *beauty* of the place in every season of the year. There are also many *beautiful* wild flowers and other pretty forms of undergrowth. The climate and the absence of smoke and dust of the city makes it very easy to cultivate a *beautiful* lawn, with flowers and shrubs. The lake is a wonderful part of the landscape. There are many *beautiful* views in different times of the day and season.

More typical of careless repetition are such sentences as these:

This dam was without doubt going to be the largest [dam] in the world.

[The problem of] feeding her ever increasing population is one of Japan's most acute problems.

Repetition of whole phrases is likely to be more objectionable, because a group of words naturally attracts more attention than a single word:

The next morning we noticed the river had risen considerably and was flowing *at a very fast pace.* We decided to resume our journey immediately, and soon we were once more traveling downstream, but this time *at a much faster pace* [better: even faster].

Especially to be watched is repetition of the same word in two different senses, easy to do in English because of the number of meanings many words can carry:

My *marks* showed a *marked* improvement.

No President in time of war has dared to fight the powerful financial *interests* of this country who have *interests* in the belligerent countries.

A slightly different form of careless repetition is doubling the meaning of a word unnecessarily. We write *continue on* when *continue* is enough, *repeat again* when we mean merely *repeat.*

The modern college student [of today]. . . .

In this modern melting pot, I found people [there] who were unacquainted with the English language.

I believe that colleges should offer scholarships but they should not offer only athletic scholarships [alone].

the [resultant] effect

Dams have been built with [about] four or five sluices in them. (*Four or five* is indefinite enough without the *about.*)

I know many officers who try to give you any *possible* assistance [that they *can*].

The remedy for all this loose, careless repetition is the same: careful revision. Reading a paper aloud is perhaps the surest way to catch such expressions, since our ears will sense more than our eyes.

Successful repetition. Repetition of words and repetition of ideas in other words are useful stylistic devices. Repetition may help hold a passage together, it may emphasize ideas, and it may suggest emotion.

A controlled repeating of key words is useful in keeping the reader's attention focused on the subject, and it is especially helpful in binding sentences together. Writing of the Supreme Court, you will have to mention the Supreme Court frequently and it is often better to say *Supreme Court* than to hunt for synonyms (like *the highest tribunal*). Simply see that the sentences are economically constructed to avoid *unnecessary* repetition and that pronouns are used where they can be.

The repetition of *power, imperative,* and *coalition* binds together the thought of this paragraph and emphasizes its meaning:

> Intolerant power respects power, not weakness. It is imperative therefore to build and better the balance of power. Conspiracy and incitement prosper in disunion and discontent. It is imperative therefore to build and better the unity and well-being of the free world. We cannot do it alone. It is imperative therefore to build and better the coalition. And here we encounter our greatest danger and our final task. A coalition built on expedient reaction to the common danger will not stand, because the Sino-Soviet alliance has the power to blow hot and cold, like Boreas and Phoebus in the fable; it has the power to relax or increase the tension as it sees fit. But our coalition cannot live by fits and starts; it must rest on an enduring community of interest. And successful communal relations mean give and take, cooperation, consultation, accommodation–a decent respect for the opinion of others. Our coalition is a partnership, not a dictatorship.–ADLAI E. STEVENSON, *Call to Greatness,* pp. 107-8

No writer needs to fear repeating the key words of his subject, and rightly used, their repetition will add emphasis.

Separating elements

In speaking, one of the most used and most effective means of emphasis is a pause. It allows what has just been said to sink in, or if the voice is suspended, it throws emphasis on what is to follow. It is difficult to transfer this effect to the written page, but something of its value can be had by keeping constructions separate.

The most emphatic separation, of course, is into individual sentences:

> You do not revise dogmas. You smash them.–RANDOLPH BOURNE, "What Is Opinion?" *The New Republic,* Aug. 18, 1915

Internal punctuation, commas and especially semicolons, keeps statements separate and tends to force a pause even in rapid eye reading:

> One remembers the old stories of invisible kingdoms where princes lived with ladies and dragons for company; and the more modern fairy-tales in which heroes drift in and out of dimensions more complex than the original three.—JOHN STEINBECK and EDWARD F. RICKETTS, *Sea of Cortez,* p. 80
>
> There are three ways of seeing animals: dead and preserved; in their own habitats for the short time of a low tide; and for long periods in an aquarium.—*Ibid.,* p. 189

(Commas could have been used instead of semicolons in those two sentences, but the separation would have been less emphatic.)

In a series of parallel words or constructions, repeating the conjunctions or prepositions may add emphasis to the individual elements. Contrast the movement of the two versions of these sentences:

The collecting buckets *and* tubes *and* jars were very full of specimens—so full that we had constantly to change the water to keep the animals alive.—*Ibid.,* p. 78	The collecting buckets, tubes, and jars were so full of specimens that we had constantly to change the water to keep the animals alive.
In the course of a lifetime of voyaging he went *to* China, *to* India, *to* all parts of Africa, and even *to* the Arctic.	In the course of a lifetime of voyaging he went to China, India, all parts of Africa, and even the Arctic.

An abrupt break in the direction of the thought movement may make for sharp emphasis:

> A hardness about this technicolor epic makes it difficult to enjoy all the way through—the eventual hardness of the theater seat.

Position

An important means of emphasis is *position,* ordering the words and parts of the statement so that attention is directed unmistakably to the words you want to stress. The end of a sentence, interrupting the flow of thought, and the beginning of the sentence, starting it, are both emphatic positions.

The subject of a sentence is usually important enough to deserve the emphasis of initial position. "Anticipatory subjects" (*there* is, *there* were, *it* is, *it* was) waste this emphasis unless they permit a rearrangement of elements not otherwise possible.

Unnecessary anticipatory subjects	*More emphatic*
There are many people who read history to raise their self-esteem.	Many people read history to raise their self-esteem.

There is some evidence pointing to the gradual disappearance of hazing in our colleges.	Some evidence points to the gradual disappearance of hazing in our colleges.
Useful anticipatory subject	*Less emphatic*
It is silly to quarrel about words.	To quarrel about words is silly.
There are in the world a number of interfering, fanatical, greedy, reckless people who, given the chance, will behave in such a way as to make life intolerable and civilization impossible.—CLIVE BELL, *Civilization,* p. 149	A number of interfering, fanatical, greedy, reckless, brutal people, who, given the chance, will behave in such a way as to make life intolerable and civilization impossible, are in the world.

Departures from the normal word order, as described on pages 181-183, are usually made to emphasize the words put first:

Charles he had beaten twice, but never his brother.
Who they should have in jail is that brute over there.
Last of all came the man they had expected would be first.

The ends of sentences deserve special attention. In speech we can seldom foresee the ends of our sentences. We are likely to add various unemphatic elements and in general let them run downhill. In writing we can revise our sentences to give them more definite form:

Unemphatic	*Revised: more emphatic*
In regard to hedging, we had a hard time trying to understand its complexity.	We had a hard time trying to understand the complexities of hedging.
This is nobody's fault but their own with few exceptions.	With few exceptions, this is nobody's fault but their own.
Be sure that your sentences end with words that deserve the distinction you give them.—BARRETT WENDELL, *English Composition,* p. 103	End with words that deserve distinction. WENDELL, p. 103

With a little practice such lapses from firm expression can be avoided. This often means putting elements in an order of *climax*—that is, arranging words, phrases, clauses, or sentences in an order of increasing value. The increase may be in mere physical length, for usually in a series of phrases or clauses the longest is put last. The increase may be in force of sound or distinction of phrasing. Or the increase may be in complexity of meaning or of emotional or ideal value. The scale of value of course is the speaker's or writer's; it is his sense of the importance of the various bits of his idea represented by the climax.

Here is a conventional climax pattern, with the last of the three parallel phrases the fullest in expression and the most important for the writer's purpose at the moment:

> They come from an intellectual level where conformity seems the highest of goods, and so they lack the primary requisite of the imaginative author: the capacity to see the human comedy afresh, to discover new relations between things, to discover new significances in man's eternal struggle with his fate.—H. L. MENCKEN, *Prejudices, Fifth Series,* p. 177

Climax is the natural order for arranging the items of a series unless there is some necessary reason for another order. Failing to use a climactic order results in a weak sentence or, if the last member of the series is conspicuously less important than the preceding, in definite anticlimax:

> It spoiled the rest of the summer for the boys and disappointed them terrifically.
>
> No degree will be conferred unless the applicant shall have sustained a good moral character, completed the necessary study, and paid all fines to the library.

Intentional use of anticlimax is one of the sources of humor:

> "Because Luxembourg is divine," he said, his eyes lighting. "I spent a most wonderful vacation there a year or two ago. It is a cameo, a miniature. It is a little country and everything in it is little: the inns, the mountains, the waiters, the people, the prices [anticlimax]."—IRWIN EDMAN, *Philosopher's Holiday,* p. 65

Emphasis, like most sentence qualities, is to be tested in revision, when a writer takes the role of reader and tries to make his words represent to someone else his own view of his subject. Finding ways of making this emphasis is one of the most challenging parts of writing.

Sound and rhythm of sentences

Although much prose is not written to appeal to the ear and is generally read silently, what it would sound like still has a bearing on its readability. Though we have been taught "silent reading" from our early years, there is still some echo of the sound as our eye goes over the sentences, for we stumble when we come to a word we can't pronounce. It doesn't stop us, as it would if we were reading aloud, but it shows that there is an oral image for the visual one. In hasty, casual reading, the echo is faint indeed. The average news story, planned for eye reading, becomes a form of punishment when read aloud, as does much other writing. But the echo becomes an important factor in more distinctive prose.

Qualities of sound

Some combinations of sounds are more pleasant ("The silken, sad, uncertain rustling") than others ("propelled by the repeated and seemingly needlessly brutal remarks and jabs of the detectives"). What makes them so is a matter of dispute–and people will differ in their judgment of particular combinations. Words that are difficult to say, like *particularly, statistics, hospitable, femininity, unanimity*, may even seem annoying. So is the repetition of unstressed syllables, especially similar ones (seeming*ly* needless*ly* sil*ly*). Your best guide is your ear, which will usually warn you when you read your sentences aloud. But it may be useful to be reminded of two devices of sound that are factors in binding words and phrases together:

**Alliteration*, the same sound at the beginning of words or of stressed syllables within words, is not uncommon in prose, as in the quotation from Adlai Stevenson on page 193: "It is imperative therefore to *b*uild and *b*etter the *b*alance of power."

**Assonance*, similar vowel sounds in syllables that have different consonant sounds, is quite common in prose: a perfume esc*a*ped on the g*a*le.

Rhythm

We do not need to go into an elaborate study to realize that prose has a noticeable if varied rhythm, that stresses differ in intensity and in number and in combination. Two basic kinds of prose rhythm can be distinguished: the simple movement that suggests the rather casual rhythm of conversation, and the more elaborate and varied rhythm that suggests Formal or "literary" prose. By reading aloud the contrasting passages in the *Index* entry *Style, you can hear the difference. Read aloud other passages that appeal to you to see what kind of rhythm they have. This will help you realize the possibilities of the language and of your own use of it, not only in the qualities of sound but in other qualities of sentences as well.

Writing good sentences

Talking about the qualities of sentences one by one makes writing seem much more complicated and artificial than it really is. Our discussion has been intended to show some (by no means all) of the possibilities of sentence style, and to suggest that good sentences are more a matter of judgment than of rule. Effective composition comes from experience and practice–experience in reading the effective writing of others and practice in developing your own. Along with experience and practice, you will find that good sentences come easily when you are familiar with what you intend to say and confident that you can make it interesting to your readers. This will let you write rapidly, so that the ideas will really move and will seem to follow each other naturally.

If for some reason you have not had much practice in purposeful writing, you can profit by studying the points in this chapter, by reading good prose, and by consciously experimenting with sentences, revising those that come haphazardly. Gradually—sometimes rapidly—the general texture of your sentences will improve. The aim is not any one pattern but a varied and pleasing style that not only will convey your meaning but will be appropriate to it, to your hoped-for readers, and to yourself.

Chapter 7

SUGGESTED STUDY AND WRITING

1. Make a close study of the sentences in one of your recent papers, answering these questions:

A) How many words are in the longest sentence? In the shortest? What is the average number of words per sentence? Compare the results with those in the table on page 180.

B) How many sentences begin with a modifying phrase or clause? How many sentences have some order other than s-v-o?

C) Are there any sentences or parts of sentences that could be omitted or condensed to achieve more direct phrasing?

D) Do you find evidence of the conscious use of repetition, separation, or position to emphasize an idea in your paper? Do you find examples of parallelism, balance, assonance, alliteration?

On the basis of this study, write a short report telling what you have discovered about your sentences. Point out their good features and describe specifically what you can do to strengthen your sentences.

2. In the following passages look for some of the devices (interrupted movement, parallelism, repetition, and so on) that give variety and emphasis to sentences. What variety of English uses these devices extensively? Be prepared to comment on the appropriateness and effectiveness of the sentence structure.

A) (1) The atomic bomb is real. (2) The war we are engaged in, whether or not we call it war, is real. (3) Terrible possibilities are real: that we may be led into a world-wide war, whose duration or even whose outcome we cannot foretell. (4) It is true and real that, if the big war does not come, at best the United States must expect an indefinite period of armament for war, constant vigilance, and a national effort that will forever change and harden the way we live. (5) Fear of these dangers in an age as desperate and precarious as any the world has ever seen is sane, logical, and justified. (6) Fear of real danger is always intelligent and always a valuable weapon with which to combat danger.—BERNARD DEVOTO, "Homily for a Troubled Time," *Woman's Day*, Jan. 1951

B) (1) Certainly, style is not affectation. (2) Conscious though it may be, when self-conscious it is an obstruction. (3) Its purpose, to my way of thinking, is to give the reader pleasure by sparing him the work which the writer is duty-bound to have done for him. (4) Writers, notwithstanding their hopes or ambitions, may or may not be artists. (5) But there is no excuse for their not being artisans. (6) The style is the man, we are told. (7) True in the final and spiritual sense as this is, style is more than that. (8) It is the writing man *in print*. (9) It is, so to speak, his written voice and, if it is truly his voice, even in print it should be his and his alone. (10) The closer it comes to the illusion of speech, perhaps the better. (11) Yet the closeness of the written word to the spoken can, and in fact should, never be more than an illusion. (12) For the point of the written word is planning, as surely as the charm of the spoken one is its lack of it.—JOHN MASON BROWN, "Pleasant Agony," *Still Seeing Things*, pp. 314-5

C) (1) Once more she slept, and once more the bus stopped and she woke frightened, and Jim brought her again to a restaurant and more coffee. (2) Her tooth came alive then, and with one hand pressing her cheek she searched through the pockets of her coat and then through her pocketbook until she found the little bottle of codeine pills and she took two while Jim watched her. (3) She was finishing her coffee when she heard the sound of the bus motor and she started up suddenly, hurrying, and with Jim holding her arm she fled back into the dark shelter of her seat. (4) The bus was moving forward when she realized that she had left her bottle of codeine pills sitting on the table in the restaurant and now she was at the mercy of her tooth. (5) For a minute she stared back at the lights of the restaurant through the bus window and then she put her head on Jim's shoulder and he was saying as she fell asleep, "The sand is so white it looks like snow, but it's hot, even at night it's hot under your feet."—SHIRLEY JACKSON, "The Tooth," *The Lottery*, p. 213

3. Study the sentences in the following student paragraphs to determine the major weaknesses. What specific changes would you suggest to gain variety, emphasis, economy, and rhythm? Write an improved version of each.

A) Mr. Mayo had a way of thinking about how students felt about him that was very different from any other instructor I have ever met. One day he told me that his favorite teachers who he remembers now as liking the most were the ones he disliked the most when he was in school.

B) Mrs. Gray is a music instructor. She taught in my high school my senior year. She has a very wide knowledge of music. Besides teaching music at the high school she had classes at a college. Too well I remember when she would compare our class work with her class in college. When she taught the two classes, it gave us competition.

c) Many things are done at a charivari. It usually takes place after a wedding ceremony and reception, before the couple leave on their honeymoon. A variety of noisemakers is used. Horns, dishpans, kettles, bells, Halloween noisemakers, and any piece of stray metal that makes a noise are brought along. The newlyweds are sometimes taken for a ride on an old truck, wagon, hayrack, or tractor. The bride and groom may be separated and taken in different directions. In one case the groom pushed the bride up the main street of a small town in a wheelbarrow. There is always the car to take care of too. Decorations of all kinds are used. Crepe-paper streamers are strung from one end to the other, the windows are soaped, and straw bales are put on the seats. Liquid shoe polish is smeared over the car, gravel stones placed in the hubcaps, and the air let out of the tires.

d) Reading was highlighted by literature which was taught in all four years. Furthermore, the reading of outstanding books in all courses of study was encouraged. Moreover, the required term papers of the junior and senior years required much research and specifically reading. This was true in other courses, as well as English. As a result the libraries were used necessitating the use of their reference books, encyclopedias, and dictionaries. Using these, I believe, helped me to appreciate their value and helped teach me to make better, more satisfactory, use of them.

e) Most people would think that the Northwest portion of the United States is rather poor for a hard-working person. That certainly is a wrong idea. There is quite a variety of jobs. In Northern Idaho, for example, the most important way of living is working for lead and silver mines. There is always a call for mining engineers, geologists, and other types of jobs connected with mining. Another type of job has to do with the lumber that is produced from the vast forests of this area. One could get a very worth-while job as a lumber distributor or as a manager or even owner of a lumber company. There are also several jobs open in the field of forestry and wildlife conservation. These are excellent jobs for a lover of nature and the outdoors. For the merchant, the towns in the Northwest are always growing; therefore, there is a great call for new stores and new merchandise. There are certainly many opportunities for an opportunity seeking person.

4. The following passages from student papers contain many words and phrases that add nothing to the meaning. Revise each passage by removing the deadwood and subordinating wherever possible to achieve greater economy of expression.

1. There are two different medical plans that could be used in order to be of some benefit to those people who have on occasion incurred serious injury.
2. We are not born with poise any more than we are born with knowledge. Both come to us after a long time of practice and study. We

do not know at birth that two and two equal four. It is the same with poise. Poise must be taught to us through the medium of education and training.

3. People today should, by all means, find some way to forget the problems of living life to gain the feeling of complete satisfaction of knowing that life is worth living.
4. To me, intelligence means that a person is smart enough to do things for himself without someone telling him what to do, is able to figure things out for himself, and is able to understand people to enable him to get along in the world with very little trouble to others.
5. Frankie is only nine years old, is of average height, and weighs about sixty-five pounds. In these respects he is just a normal nine-year-old boy, but he has an excessive amount of energy. From his appearance, he looks like a shy little boy, but in his case looks are deceiving.
6. College class schedules are fairly confusing, and in some cases a good deal of confusion may arise from them. This particular plague usually strikes the green students, namely the freshmen. Let me relate to you one such experience which I had. Classes had been in session for a full week, and I thought that after such a long period I had mastered my class schedule.
7. After a few days had passed my dad mentioned the fact that one of his men at the factory had just bought at a reasonable price a new car which was really nice looking. It was a Mercury which was solid yellow in color with a black and white leather interior.
8. Those of you who know of the intricate system of keys and springs that a saxophone has will know the reason why I was worried.
9. When my brother wanted a new tennis racquet, he bought it, even though he didn't really play much. In many phases of his life he has reacted the same way. Another example of my brother's way of doing things is the time he went deer hunting for the first time. He left the first morning of the season and was back at eight o'clock the same morning with his eight-point, 125-pound deer.
10. In the Bible there is a scripture which relates a parable which concerns doing more than your share of work.

5. Recast the following sentences, revising shifted constructions and putting related elements in parallel form.

1. I am glad I had this course because it gives you self-confidence when speaking in front of a group or when I tried to talk to an employer.
2. Working conditions in the country are much different from those of a city worker.
3. Each pupil had to give five speeches in front of the class. After each speech there would be time for criticism and class discussion on good and bad points of your presentation. By watching others we could see some of our own faults and thus be able to try to rectify them.
4. We pick out the man we are going to follow as he starts up the

steep hill to the left of the flag. As he reached the top of the hill the overhanging branches cut smartly at his rhythmically swinging arms.

5. Cora is one of the most interesting personalities I have ever known. Since I had associated with her from second grade through high school, I felt as if I had known her fairly well.
6. If we were all as broad-minded as we should be, we would realize that our failures are due to our own weaknesses, such as lack of self-discipline, lack of faith, lack of principle, or our own human smallness.
7. Without a word he proceeded to pass out small slips of paper which for some of us would be good news, but for others only failure.
8. Sea grasses are collected for fertilizer and to stuff seats, as in automobiles.
9. Our coach would not hesitate a moment to lend some money, his car, or even give stag parties for his boys.
10. To increase my vocabulary and because I enjoyed my history courses in high school, I signed up for a year's history course at one of the state university extensions.

6. Using the discussion on pages 181-186 as a start, make a list of the possible ways in which to begin a sentence, and construct one or two good examples of each.

7. Rewrite the following sentence in at least six different ways, keeping the same basic idea but using different orders and constructions. Which versions seem to have good sound and rhythm? Which would be appropriate chiefly in a Formal context?

This simple exercise gave even the experienced gymnasts aches and pains.

8. In your reading of books, magazines, or newspapers, look for examples of (a) the dullest and flattest sentences you can find, and (b) the best sentences of several different types. Comment on the reasons for the effectiveness of each example.

9. Before submitting your next paper (or any other paper), read it aloud, or if possible, have someone read it to you. Examine any passage that needs to be reread for its meaning or that fails to convey the emphasis you intended. Revise all repetitious and awkward constructions and any sections that need more variety or better movement. Although you may not be writing your papers to be read aloud, this practice will frequently reveal grammatical errors and ineffectual phrasing that might otherwise escape your attention.

I have been leading up—or down, if you like—
to an extremely simple and obvious but fundamental remark:
that no word can be judged as to whether it is
good or bad, correct or incorrect, beautiful or ugly,
or anything else that matters to a writer, in isolation.

I. A. RICHARDS

Chapter **8**

Words

In other words "meaning" is a property

of the mutually relevant people, things, events, in the situation.

Some of the events are the noises made by the speakers.

But it is important to realize that "meaning" is just as much

a property of the people, their "sets," their specific behaviour,

the things and events of the situation as of the noises made.

J. R. FIRTH

Anyone who is at all concerned with his speaking and writing gets interested in words. He gets curious about their meaning and the ways in which they are used; he becomes conscious of some words that he lacks but really needs, and of some that he only partially knows. This book might have begun with a discussion of words, since we feel that they are the smallest meaningful elements of speech and writing.[1] But if our purpose is communication, we are first aware of ideas expressed consecutively, of words as they stand in statements (sentences) and in groups of statements (paragraphs). After considering first the larger units, we are ready now to look more closely at the qualities of the single words of which they are composed. This chapter discusses a selection of points about the meaning of words and their use, about what words can and cannot do for us in our attempts to tell others something or to understand what they are trying to tell us.

Learning new words

The exact number of English words is not known and cannot be known. The "unabridged" dictionaries have over half a million entries, but many of these are compound words (*lamplight, combat fatigue*) or different derivatives of the same word (*rare–rarely, rarefy, rarity*), and a good many are obsolete words to help us read older literature. Dictionaries do not attempt to cover completely many

[1] Students of language are not agreed on what they will regard as "a word," preferring to analyze language into smaller elements (*Phoneme, *Morpheme), but as amateurs we can use the rule of thumb that what an educated person would separate in writing or print is a word. In this text we are more interested in the use of words–how they are combined to "say something"–than in theories about them.

large groups of words that we can draw on: the Informal vocabulary, especially slang, localisms, the terms of various occupations and professions; words used only occasionally by scientists and specialists in many fields; foreign words borrowed for use in English; or many of the three thousand or more new words or new senses of words that come into use every year and that may or may not be used long enough to warrant inclusion. It would be conservative to say that there are over a million English words that any of us might meet in our listening and reading and that we may draw on in our speaking and writing.

The individual's vocabulary

How many words an individual uses cannot be exactly measured either, but there are numerous estimates. Professor Seashore concluded that first-graders enter school with at least 24,000 words and add 5000 each year so that they leave high school with at least 80,000. The average for college students he puts at twice this number.[1] These figures are for *recognition* vocabulary, the words we understand when we read or hear them. Our *active* vocabulary, the words we use in speaking and writing, is considerably smaller.

In the following paragraph of academic prose some of the words illustrate possible distinctions between a recognition and an active vocabulary. They are italicized for later discussion.

> Two sorts of experience are recognized as having *worth,* or as capable of having it, an *active* and a *passive;* one is *creation* or control, and the other *appreciation.* These are not strictly separate experiences, but rather *"aspects"* of experience, yet they are practically *separable* to a large degree. The worth of active creation or control is a kind of appreciation; usually the worth of the experience of activity depends more or less upon a feeling of worth toward or appreciation of some "result" brought about. But though the two things are usually more or less associated and overlapping, we are all familiar with extreme cases in which on the one hand the feeling of worth is nearly or quite purely passive and on the other the worth of an activity is nearly or quite independent of the character of the result. The literature of *value,* like that of science, shows a *bias* for *monism,* so there is a tendency to reduce all value to *"contemplation"* or to the "joy of being a cause," according to the *temperamental predilections* of the particular writer, but a *candid* observer must accept both, and all sorts of mixtures of the two.—FRANK H. KNIGHT, "Scientific Method in Economics," *The Trend of Economics,* edited by R. G. TUGWELL, p. 230

---

[1] Robert H. Seashore, "The Importance of Vocabulary in Learning Language Skills," *Elementary English,* 1948, 25:137-52; "How Large Are Children's Vocabularies?" *Elementary English,* 1949, 26:181-94.

Probably most college students would recognize and understand more or less accurately every word in this passage, except perhaps *monism,* though some would have trouble defining *predilections.* A good many would recognize but would not ordinarily use *aspects, separable, bias* (though they would use *biased*), *contemplation,* and perhaps *temperamental. Passive, creation,* and *appreciation* they might use in writing but ordinarily would not use in their conversation. The words *worth* and *value* are common enough, but not in the senses in which they appear here: *worth* is here a noun instead of, as more commonly, an adjective ("worth so much"), and *value* is used in a philosophical sense. Probably most students would not use *candid* outside the phrase *candid camera.* It is quite proper that many of these words remain in the average person's recognition vocabulary; it would be for the individual to decide whether he could conveniently use *bias* or *predilections* or *monism* or any of the others. But it is important to recognize that there are different areas in everyone's vocabulary, no matter what its size.

You cannot always produce a word exactly when you want it, as you probably know from the exasperating experience of fishing for the name of a casual acquaintance. But consciously using the words you recognize in reading will help get them into your active vocabulary. Occasionally in your reading pay particular attention to these words, especially when the subject is one that you might well write or talk about. Underline or make a list of words that you feel a need for and look up the less familiar ones in a dictionary. And then before very long make it a point to use some of them. Once you know how they are pronounced and what they stand for, you can safely use them.

Increasing vocabulary by learning new subjects

"But my vocabulary is so small!" is a common complaint of students in composition courses and of other people who have some intention of writing. Or they say, "I know what I mean but I can't put it into words." They seem to think that some sort of injection of new words will magically transform them into good writers, as though having an inadequate vocabulary was an affliction like myopia or hay fever, to be remedied by glasses or by an antihistamine.

If your vocabulary is small, that is only the symptom and not the disease, for words cannot be considered apart from their meaning and usefulness. If you have a good grasp of what you want to say, you won't have much trouble finding the words to express it. There are sense impressions, moods, and feelings—a variety of subjective sensations–for which you may have no specific words, but in most of your writing you are not discussing these. Not being able to "find the words" usually means not being able to think out very clearly what you want to say.

The words you already have are in the areas of your knowledge and your interest. Consequently, the most natural way to increase your stock of words is by learning something more, something new, perhaps from observation or conversation or from reading a magazine or a college textbook. You can't take facts and ideas away with you unless they are in verbal form. The easiest way to extend your vocabulary is by acquiring groups of words from new experience. In learning to drive a car you picked up a number of new words; you will learn several in visiting a printing plant or a radio station or some other new place for the first time. New words come from every experience, from every job, every sport, every art, every book, from every field of thought and study. Consider the words that would be added to a person's vocabulary from a newly acquired interest in electronics, cooking, sailing, music, poetry, or astronomy.

To make these new words your own, you must know what they stand for. Explain to someone what you have just learned, talk it over with somebody else who is interested in it, try to teach it to someone who knows nothing about it, or write about it.

In college your stock of facts and ideas increases enormously, with a corresponding increase in vocabulary. As you come to understand what *registrar, curriculum, honors course, schedule, conflict,* stand for you will find yourself using them easily and naturally, as well as the colloquial and slang vocabulary of the campus (*dorm, poly sci, home ec, pan hell*); you may take up a new sport or some other activity and acquire more words; and a course in a new field will probably add three or four hundred new words to your vocabulary, some of them technical and of restricted use, many of them of more general application. Acquiring the vocabularies of biology or sociology or history is an essential part of the respective courses; certainly you can't go far without the names of the facts and ideas taken up.

You should learn these words accurately *the first time you meet them:* look at their spelling, pronounce them as you hear them in class or as a dictionary specifies, and study their exact meaning. Probably a good deal of students' trouble in courses comes from only partly understanding the specialized words when they are first met. Once these words are understood, they should be used. Many of them will be called for in recitations or examinations or term papers, but using them in talking over the course work or using them casually in conversation, even humorously if they can be made to carry a joke, will help impress what they stand for on your mind and therefore make the words themselves come more easily. In this way you will acquire those thousands of words with which the statistics on vocabulary credit a college graduate.

Other ways of increasing vocabulary

You can add individual words to your vocabulary in various ways. Frequently you may learn a word simply because it appeals to you. The typical process is seen in picking up slang: you hear the word, you like it, and you use it, perhaps for its own sake. The same holds true for more serious words. Conversation and casual reading will provide a good many, perhaps most of them fitting into general situations rather than special fields of study. They may be words a little off the beaten track but accurate and expressive—*livid, echelon, prink, eupeptic*—the language is full of such words that can make your speaking and writing more exact and more vivid.

Some people actually "read" a dictionary and perhaps pick up some words that way, or at least increase their recognition vocabulary. Games like crossword puzzles and Scrabble give practice in playing with words—though the more unusual ones in such games are pretty hard to work into conversation.

More useful is some knowledge of compounding elements, most of them Greek and Latin words used in making English words, especially in the sciences:

bi-	(two)	*hemo-*	(blood)	*photo-*	(light)
bio-	(life)	*-lith-*	(stone)	*poly-*	(many)
-graph-	(writing, written)	*mono-*	(one)	*tele-*	(at a distance)

A knowledge of these is most helpful when there are contrasting pairs of words (*binomial—monomial, atrophy—hypertrophy*) or when you learn a number of related words in a special field. But since the sum of the meanings of the parts usually only approximates the meaning of the whole word, it is about as easy—and often safer—to learn such words as you learn other English words.

However you go about increasing your vocabulary, a desire to learn—to learn both subject matter and words—is basic; you need an inquiring and receptive attitude, almost recapturing the youngster's open curiosity and continual "What's that?" by which we all acquired our first few thousand words. The essential point is that you are not merely "increasing your vocabulary." You are acquiring more meaningful and useful ideas, increasing your powers of understanding, and extending your range of interests, as well as adding to your command of the enormous supply of English words in order to think, speak, and write in the manner of educated people.

The use of dictionaries

The most useful tool for a writer, in or out of a composition course, is a good dictionary. Nowhere else can you find so much information about words and their use. You will use your dictionary most in revision and should get the habit of turning to it frequently while revising a paper and preparing the final copy.

Evaluating dictionaries

There is no such thing as *the* dictionary, one which can be quoted to settle any question about words. There are a number of dictionaries, all (except the scholarly specialized dictionaries) commercial ventures—that is, the editors compile the best book they can with the money and conditions provided by the publisher. Dictionaries obviously vary in three fundamental respects (as well as in minor matters like typography and arrangement of entries): in *date,* in *size,* and in *responsibility of editing.*

An up-to-date dictionary is necessary because words are continually being added to the general stock of the English language, other words are used in new senses, some drop out of use, spellings and pronunciations change. Although some alterations are made between printings, the date of compilation—not of printing—is the important one. Bookstores handle only recent editions, but if you are buying a second-hand dictionary, look at the copyright statement on the back of the title page.

For specialized reading and detailed work with words it is necessary to go to a recent "unabridged" dictionary. For everyday work, the smaller "college" size, costing usually from five dollars up, according to binding, is more convenient and is generally adequate. Still smaller dictionaries, down to pocket size, may be handy for checking spelling, but they are not sufficient for college work.

The date and size of a dictionary are easily determined, but it is more difficult to judge the editing. Responsible editing is what makes the dictionary really useful and gives it whatever "authority" it may have. It should be a compilation from a vast accumulation of actual recorded uses of words, not a patchwork from existing word books. This raw material should be worked over by specialists in various subjects and by trained editors, who digest the evidence and compose the dictionary's brief entries. Since it is difficult to determine how well dictionaries have been edited, most people have to rely on reviews or on the advice of someone who has studied them.[1]

The following dictionaries, listed alphabetically, are currently available; composition courses usually recommend certain ones for students to buy:

American College Dictionary (1947). Simplified pronunciation key and pronunciations based on current usage; comprehensive treatment of technical words; good synonym studies; all words (general words, proper names, abbreviations) in one alphabetical list; common meanings of each word come first in entry; frequently revised.

New College Standard Dictionary (Emphatype edition, 1947). Intelligent handling of technical definitions; greatly simplified pronunciation key with few diacritical marks; no synonyms; common meanings first.

Thorndike-Barnhart Comprehensive Desk Dictionary (1951). Contains 90,000 entries as contrasted with the 120,000 to 140,000 in the "college" dictionaries listed here; synonym studies; simplified etymologies; simplified pronunciation key and especially accurate record of current American pronunciation; usage notes; common meanings first in entry; one alphabetical list of all words; frequently revised.

Webster's New Collegiate Dictionary (Merriam-Webster, 1949). Long established; careful treatment of usage problems and general vocabulary; four alphabetical lists of words: (1) common and technical words and foreign words and phrases, (2) biographical names, (3) geographical names, (4) abbreviations; synonym studies; earliest meaning of a word stands first in each entry; frequently revised; preliminary supplement of new words.

Webster's New World Dictionary of the American Language (1953). Emphasizes simplified definitions even for technical terms; includes many Informal words and phrases; common meanings first in entry; etymologies unusually full; all words in one alphabetical list; new words added annually.

Since dictionaries differ in these and other features, you should know your own thoroughly to make maximum use of it. Look through

---

[1] See, for example, Karl W. Dykema, "Webster's New World Dictionary, College Edition," *American Speech,* 1954, 29:59-65. Dictionaries are listed, with critical notes, in Constance M. Winchell, *Guide to Reference Books* (7th ed.; Chicago, 1951, and supplements), pp. 217-20, and dictionaries of special subjects, pp. 220-6.

the table of contents to see what units of material there are besides the main alphabetical list of words. You may find a grammar of English, a discussion of punctuation, a guide to letter writing, a table of signs and symbols, or perhaps a list of the colleges and universities in the United States.

Uses of a general dictionary

To get really acquainted with your dictionary, read a page or two consecutively; look up a few words that you know and a few that are new to you to see how they are handled. Try pronouncing some words, familiar and unfamiliar ones, to see how the pronunciation key works. The next sections describe in some detail the main features of a typical dictionary and their uses.

Spelling. A word is entered in a dictionary under its usual spelling. As a rule you can come close enough to this to find a word you are in doubt about, but sometimes you have to keep in mind other common spellings of a sound–so that if you fail to find *gibe* you will look under *jibe*. When more than one spelling is given, both are in good use: *esthetic, aesthetic; although, altho*. Ordinarily take the first of two forms unless the second for some reason is more appropriate to other traits of your writing. The entries in a dictionary show where a word should be hyphenated at the end of a line, as in *mor ti fi ca tion, dis-par ag ing ly*. They also show whether the editors have found compound words most often as two words, as one word, or with a hyphen. (Most dictionaries suggest the use of more hyphens than are necessary for General writing.) The introductions to most dictionaries contain general discussions of English spelling.

Pronunciation. Dictionaries respell words in specially marked letters to show their pronunciation, as you will notice in these examples. The exact sounds represented by the symbols are usually shown at the bottom of the page and are further explained in a discussion of pronunciation in the preface.

ac·cli·mate (ə klī′mĭt, ăk′lə māt′). *v.t., v.i.,* **-mated, -mating.** *Chiefly U.S.* to habituate or become habituated to a new climate or environment. [t. F: m.s. *acclimater*, der. *à* to + *climat* climate] **—ac·cli·mat·a·ble** (ə-klī′mĭt ə bəl), *adj.* **—ac·cli·ma·tion** (ăk′lə mā′shən), *n.*

cer·ti·o·ra·ri (sûr′shĭ ə râr′ĭ), *n.* *Law.* a writ issuing from a superior court calling up the record of a proceeding in an inferior court for review. [t. L: to be informed (lit., made more certain)]

ac·cli′mate (ă·klī′mĭt; ăk′lĭ·māt), *v. t. & i.* [F. *acclimater*, fr. *à* to + *climat* climate.] To habituate, or become habituated, to a climate not native; to acclimatize. — **Syn.** Inure, season, harden. — **ac·cli′mat·a·ble** (ă·klī′mĭt·ȧ·b'l), *adj.* — **ac′cli·ma′tion** (ăk′lĭ·mā′shŭn; ăk′·lī-), *n.*

cer′ti·o·ra′ri (sûr′shĭ·ō·rā′rī; -râr′ī), *n.* [From *certiorari* to be certified; — a term in the Latin form of the writ.] *Law.* A writ from a superior court to call up for review the records of an inferior court or a body acting in a quasi-judicial capacity.

By permission. From *Webster's New Collegiate Dictionary*, copyright 1949, by G. & C. Merriam Co.

Dictionaries are somewhat imperfect guides to pronunciation.[1] Their chief source of material, published books and articles, naturally contains very little evidence about pronunciation. Pronunciation must be studied from actual speech, and an adequate record of the actual speech of a large country like ours is hard to make. Sometimes a dictionary gives full or "platform" pronunciation, which if followed exactly would give a person's speech a slow and somewhat stilted sound. Ordinary speech uses less distinct vowels than the usual dictionary symbols suggest, and stress may vary with the position of a word in a phrase. Furthermore, our dictionaries do not recognize sufficiently the regional variations in American pronunciation. But people can usually rely on dictionaries for the pronunciation of unusual words, and the sound of common words they are likely to learn from hearing them.

Dictionaries show divided usage in the pronunciation of many words, as in the Webster examples of *acclimate* shown above. If more than one pronunciation is given without qualification, each is acceptable. As a rule a person should use the pronunciation most common among the educated people of his community.

Definition. The definitions of words take up the bulk of space in a dictionary. Definitions of unusual words help you get the full sense of a passage that treats new material. But often you will need more information than a dictionary has room for, and will need to go to an encyclopedia or other work.

It is not so much the meanings of uncommon words, like *hackbut, pyrognostics,* or *zymurgy,* that you need, as the meanings of those that are almost but not quite in your active vocabulary. Nearly any series of dictionary entries will illustrate these words, and also the scope and method of dictionary definition:

---

[1] The most authoritative guide to American pronunciation is Kenyon and Knott, *A Pronouncing Dictionary of American English* (1944), published by the makers of the Merriam-Webster dictionaries but more discriminating than the dictionaries.

check·row (chĕk′rō′), *Agric.* —*n.* **1.** one of a number of rows of trees or plants, esp. corn, in which the distance between adjacent trees or plants is equal to that between adjacent rows. —*v.t.* **2.** to plant in checkrows.
check·up (chĕk′ŭp′), *n.* **1.** an examination or close scrutiny for purposes of verification as to accuracy, comparison, etc. **2.** a comprehensive physical examination.
Ched·dar cheese (chĕd′ər), American cheese. Also, **ched′dar.**
chedd·ite (chĕd′īt, shĕd′īt), *n.* an explosive used for blasting made up of a chlorate or perchlorate mixture with a fatty substance, such as castor oil. [t. F: f. *Chedde* place name (of Savoy) + *-ite* -ITE[1]]
cheek (chēk), *n.* **1.** either side of the face below eye level. **2.** the side wall of the mouth between the upper and lower jaws. **3.** something resembling the human cheek in form or position, as either of two parts forming corresponding sides of a thing. **4.** *Colloq.* impudence or effrontery. —*v.t.* **5.** *Brit. Colloq.* to address or confront with impudence or effrontery. [ME *cheke,* OE *cēce,* c. D *kaak*]
cheek·bone (chēk′bōn′), *n.* the bone or bony prominence below the outer angle of the eye.
cheek by jowl, side by side; in close intimacy.
cheek pouch, a bag in the cheek of certain animals, as squirrels, for carrying food.
cheek·y (chē′kĭ), *adj.*, **cheekier, cheekiest.** *Colloq.* impudent; insolent: *a cheeky fellow, cheeky behavior.* —**cheek′i·ly,** *adv.* —**cheek′i·ness,** *n.*

There are three points to remember in using dictionary definitions. (*a*) A dictionary does not *require* or *forbid* a particular sense of a word but *records* the uses that have been found for it. Now and then a word is in the process of acquiring a new meaning or somewhat altering its usual sense. (*b*) The dictionary definition is for the most part a record of the denotation of a word and often cannot give its connotation. For this reason it is safest not to use a word unless you have heard or read it and so know it in part from experience, at least what suggestion it carries if it is not a simple factual word. (*c*) Finally and most important, the words of the definition are not the *meaning* of the word; they, along with the examples or illustrations, are to help you understand what, in the world of objects or ideas, the word refers to. (See pp. 216-220.)

Labels of usage. Words that are unlabeled in a dictionary are supposed to belong to the general vocabulary; other words are labeled *dialectal, obsolete, archaic, foreign, colloquial, slang, British, United States,* or are referred to some field of activity—*medicine, law, astronomy, baseball, printing, electricity, philosophy*. These labels are rough guides to usage, but a writer should bring his own observation and judgment to bear on individual words. Many that carry no label are rarely used (*impavid, ustulate*) and would mar most writing. Usually the dictionary editors' point of view is rather conservative, and many words marked *Dial.* or *Colloq.* would fit perfectly well into General writing. It must be clearly understood that these labels are descriptive terms and are not intended to prohibit or even to discourage the use of the words so labeled. *Colloq.* in a dictionary, for example, usually means that the word is characteristic of the ordinary conversation of educated people and of General rather than Formal writing.

Synonyms. Most dictionaries gather words of similar meanings into a group and show in what ways they are alike and in what ways different, as in the following entries which appear after the word *discuss* in *Webster's New World Dictionary:*

> ***SYN.*—discuss** implies a talking about something in a deliberative fashion, with varying opinions offered constructively and, usually, amicably, so as to settle an issue, decide on a course of action, etc.; **argue** implies the citing of reasons or evidence to support or refute an assertion, belief, proposition, etc.; **debate** implies a formal argument, usually on public questions, in contests between opposing groups; **dispute** implies argument in which there is a clash of opposing opinions, often presented in an angry or heated manner.

The discrimination of synonyms is often a helpful addition to the definition in selecting the right word to use. (See pp. 230-231.)

Linguistic information. A dictionary entry indicates the part or parts of speech in which a word is generally used, the transitive or intransitive use of verbs, the principal parts of irregular verbs, plurals of irregular nouns, and any other distinctive form a word may assume. (It is useful to remember, however, that this information, based on printed material, does not always accurately reflect general practice.) The history of the word–its etymology–is usually given. Sometimes this is merely a statement of the language from which the word came into English; sometimes it is a more complicated chain of source and change of form, as in this *Webster Collegiate* statement on *course,* tracing it from Latin, through Italian and French, to English:

> **course** (kōrs; 70), *n.* [From F. *cours* (OF. *cors, curs*), fr. L. *cursus,* and fr. F. *course,* fr. It. *corsa,* fr. *correre* to run; both fr. L. *currere, cursum,* to run.]

Etymologies are often interesting, but since they are history, they may have little bearing on the present meaning of a word.

The introductions to dictionaries contain principally linguistic information. The discussions of word forms, pronunciation, spelling, and grammar deserve careful reading because they make the individual entries more meaningful.

Miscellaneous information. Most dictionaries contain some reference material, such as lists of places and prominent historical figures, abbreviations, foreign words and phrases. Formerly these items were run in lists in the back of the volume, but in recent dictionaries the tendency has been to put them in the main alphabetical listing.

Special dictionaries

Dictionary making (lexicography) is a highly specialized art, or applied science. The general dictionaries are supplemented by a considerable number of special word books and several more are now being compiled.[1]

Historical dictionaries. The *Oxford English Dictionary,* published in ten large volumes, is the great storehouse of information about English words. It traces the various forms of each word and its various meanings, with dates of their first recorded appearance and quotations from writers illustrating each. There is a *Supplement* giving material on new words and evidence on earlier words not found in the original work. An abridgment, the *Shorter Oxford English Dictionary,* in two volumes, is also very useful for interpreting past literature.

The *Dictionary of American English* (4 volumes, 1938-1944), on the same plan as the *Oxford,* gives the histories of words as they have been used in the United States. An entry begins with the first use of the word by an American writer and continues, with quotations, to 1900. In this way it is especially useful in reading American writers. The more recent *Dictionary of Americanisms* (1951) selects from, interprets, and supplements this work.

Besides these there are dictionaries for Old English and for Middle English, and other period dictionaries are being compiled, like the *Dictionary of Early Modern English* (1500-1700).

Dialect dictionaries. Besides Joseph Wright's *English Dialect Dictionary* (6 volumes), giving words in the various dialects of England, there are a number of special word lists from different regions, which appear in books and in periodicals like *Dialect Notes* and *American Speech.* (See Ch. 1, pp. 8-12.) Eric Partridge's *Dictionary of Slang and Unconventional English* is a historical dictionary of English slang.

---

[1] *A Survey of English Dictionaries* (New York, 1933) by M. M. Mathews is a history of English dictionaries. *Dictionaries British and American* (New York, 1955) by J. R. Hulburt and *Dr. Johnson's Dictionary* (Chicago, 1955) by J. H. Sledd and G. J. Kolb are more recent surveys.

Dictionaries in special subjects. Because the general dictionaries cannot give the complete vocabulary in specialized fields of work, they are supplemented by a growing group of dictionaries in special subjects, like the following:

Alsager, C. M., *Dictionary of Business Terms*
Ballentine, J. A., *Law Dictionary*
Dorland, W. A. N., *American Illustrated Medical Dictionary*
English, H. B., *A Student's Dictionary of Psychological Terms*
Good, C. V., *Dictionary of Education*
Hackh's Chemical Dictionary
Henderson, I. F. and W. D., *Dictionary of Scientific Terms* (biological sciences)
Rice, C. M., *Dictionary of Geological Terms*

The meaning of words

One of our commonest and most important questions in listening or reading is "What does he mean by that?" And in our own speaking or writing we often wonder "Will they see what I mean by this?" In speech we may repeat a remark in different words if we are not understood; in revising a paper we can change words or phrases to make our intention more nearly unmistakable. In speech our tone of voice does much of the work of indicating what we mean, but in writing our words need to be picked more carefully, because there is nothing else to carry the meaning.

The nature of meaning

The meaning of words is studied in the division of linguistics called *semantics*. A complete study of meaning involves other fields too, especially psychology and philosophy. In spite of a great deal of study by specialists in recent years, we do not have a generally satisfactory theory of meaning, but there are a number of particular ideas widely agreed upon.[1] In this short account we can only suggest some of the points of semantics that are obviously useful to a writer.

Strictly speaking, words have "meaning" only as they are used in particular statements. They can be studied individually, but as they are recorded in a dictionary, for instance, they have only typical or possible meaning. One way to show that meaning is *not in the word*

[1] Three elementary books lead to the more difficult original works: S. I. Hayakawa, *Language in Thought and Action* (New York, 1949) to the "general semantics" of Alfred Korzybski (Books cited by name of author only will be found in the Bibliography, pp. XIV-XV); Hugh Walpole, *Semantics* (New York, 1941) to I. A. Richards' contribution; and Stephen Ullmann, *Words and Their Use* (New York, 1951) to his own more elaborate work. Bloomfield, Chs. 9 and 24, and Eugene A. Nida, *Morphology, The Descriptive Analysis of Words* (Ann Arbor, 1946) are more specifically linguistic. Max Black, *Language and Philosophy* (Ithaca, 1949) evaluates the principal writers on semantics.

is to consider some words that are used in several senses: What is a *knot? a cut? a seal? a play?* What do you do when you *play,* or *strike,* or *fly,* or *fall?* A *knot* may be a tie of some sort in a rope, a group of people, a spot in a board, a tough problem, the measure of a ship's speed. Which sense was intended is usually clear from the sentence in which it is used—that is, from the *context.* It is so hard to tell how much we understand from a given word and how much from its context that it is not very profitable to consider the meaning of isolated words.

The meaning of a statement, then, is in a situation; it is the consequence of the statement and is the result of several factors, of which the most important are: (1) the speaker's intention and attitude, his past association with the words, his knowledge of or experience with the thing or idea the statement is about; (2) the typical use of the words by people who speak the language, the associations the words are likely to arouse; (3) the listener's attitude and his associations with both the words and the subject; (4) the object or situation or idea to which they are referring. For convenience in a brief discussion of meaning we will begin with this last factor, taking as the core of a word's meaning in a particular statement *what it stands for to the speaker or writer, listener or reader*—what in their experience or imagination or feeling it refers to.

The object (or class of objects), act, situation, quality, idea, or fancy to which a word refers is called its *referent,* and by representing this referent for many users a word gets a core of meaning, its *denotation.*

The dictionary definition of chair—"a seat for one person, usually with four legs and a back"—is not the meaning of the word but an attempt to get the reader to picture a chair in his mind. This is fairly easy when the referent is a chair, or another *thing,* especially some thing the reader has already seen. But when the referent is intangible, like *light,* or abstract, like *beauty,* not only does the definition become more difficult, but the variability of meaning among all speakers and listeners, writers and readers, increases. The following three classes of words will show this varying definiteness. Other groups could be made according to some trait of their meaning, but these are enough to suggest that the problem of using words exactly is more complex than it might seem at first.

Concrete words

Concrete words have meanings established by more or less regular reference to actual objects. *Chair,* for example, has a definite core of meaning because it is used to apply to a kind of seat. Even though people might disagree over a particular untypical chair—one might be called *stool* or another might be called *sofa*—almost always the meaning of *chair* would be definite enough for one's purposes. *Morris chair, rocking chair, ladder-back chair* are more definite in their reference. The specific image that a word raises in the minds of different people will vary somewhat: at a given moment *robin* may be pictured by one person as *robin-pulling-at-a-worm;* by another, as *robin-on-a-nest;* by another, as *robin-crying-rain;* but in each there is a core of meaning for *robin*. A word with which a person has had no experience (perhaps *spandrel, tenon, farthingale, rickrack,* or *tachistoscope*) will have no meaning for him.

A speaker or writer would not as a rule use these concrete words without a fairly definite knowledge of their core of meaning; a reader or listener will either know this meaning, be able to approach it through a dictionary definition or through other reading, ask someone who knows, or learn it by observation. It is lucky for all of us that such a large part of our vocabulary consists of these fairly exact words and that we can be pretty sure that other speakers of English understand them as we do.

Relative words

Words for qualities have not so much a definite meaning as a *direction* of meaning, and their reference in a given instance depends a good deal on the experience and intention of the user. *Red,* for instance, runs from orange to violet and for a reasonably definite meaning needs to be qualified by another word, *light, dark, orange*. To a person in "the upper brackets," a family with $4000 a year might be *poor,* but to someone out of work that family might be *well off*. Similarly, *warm, heavy, thick, rough, pretty, honest, tall* are relative in meaning. Although attempts have been made to provide an exact or standard sense for some of these words, as in the scale for exact naming of colors in art, or in the standardized weights and measures of physics, or in definitions by law of words like *drunk* and *speeding,* these arbitrary definitions are useful only in certain situations.

In using these descriptive words, especially those that record our attitudes and judgments, it is important to distinguish various degrees, to provide as exact shading as possible. In ordinary conversation we don't make many distinctions. A person is a *jerk* or a *good egg* (or whatever the equivalent slang is this year), a movie is *terrific* or *lousy*. Members of our own group are *honest, generous, loyal,* and so on;

people we don't like are——? Actually we know—and when we are trying to talk accurately we say—that they fall somewhere between the extremes. We and our acquaintances are neither saints nor double-dyed villains but somewhere between. Can we say just about where? To try is a challenge and a step toward civilized living—as well as a triumph in the disciplining of thought, and therefore in the use of words.

The general method for attaining approximate accuracy in relative or evaluative statements, when accuracy is desirable, is to consider a series (known as a *graded series*) of possible terms between the extremes, from *good* to *bad, light* to *dark,* and to remember that the terms and the statements in which they occur can be made more exact by qualifiers: *more, less, rather, extremely,* and so on.

Abstract words

Also difficult to use accurately are *abstract words,* which do not have specific observable referents against which their meaning can be checked. The most definite abstract words refer to acts or relationships or directions: *trading, murder, cost, citizenship, nation, height.* They have definite meaning because English-speaking people generally agree in the way they are used. Other abstract words are collective; that is, they stand for a number of individual items—*college, jazz, the administration* (of a college or of the United States). They summarize one or more common traits belonging to a number of particular people or things or situations. Although they have a pretty definite core of meaning, they may be used with very different values. The danger in such words is that when we use them we often lose sight of the particular individuals or things for which they stand. *Personnel,* for instance, is a much used word today that may conceal the notion of living people and let us or lead us to make statements that we never would make if we visualized clearly even a dozen of them. *Capital* usually means employers and investors collectively, and *labor* stands for workmen. But as the words are often used, there is little suggestion of actual people; they are more likely to suggest vast, impersonal forces.

Many other words do not have referents even as commonly agreed on as these. The meaning of such words as *beauty, art, the good life, culture, evil, education, Americanism* is a complex of reasoning and feeling that varies from person to person. An adequate definition of any such word would be an essay, and its meaning would depend on the past experience, the emotions, and the general outlook of the person writing it. Obviously, understanding is difficult here, because the reader may have a different experience from the writer, a difference increased by dissimilar feeling and philosophy.

We cannot expect that more or less haphazard people, as we all are, will always use these words carefully, but we should strive to be as exact as possible. One way to do this is to translate our meaning into other terms and by giving two or three versions reach something approaching exactness. As speakers or writers our intention is not to lead a listener or reader just to words but to make him aware of objects or ideas in a real or imagined world. To do this we should give wherever possible specific, concrete examples of what we mean.

Another way is to realize the range of meaning that relative and abstract words have and make clear where in this range our immediate intention falls. The word *poetry,* for example, ranges through at least three general senses. It may mean no more than composition in verse; it may be used collectively to mean a large body of particular poems; or it may mean an idealized form of writing–that is, poems having certain characteristics that we respect or are fond of. (The *Oxford English Dictionary* and the *Century Dictionary* are particularly useful in pointing out such ranges of meaning.) Obviously, for exact and reasonable communication it is highly important that you know where in the range of possible meaning your immediate meaning falls, and that you make this clear to your listeners or readers. The attempt to attain fairly exact communication is one reason for the concreteness of much modern style. (Compare pp. 139-141 on details and generalizations.)

The suggestion of words

The denotation of a word, its more or less factual and informative reference discussed in the preceding section, is what we ordinarily think of as its meaning. But this may be considerably modified by the circumstances in which the word has been generally used and by the particular context in which it occurs. This suggested quality is called its *connotation.* It is an essential part of the meaning of many words, separated from their denotation only in more or less arbitrary analysis.

The connotations of words

The words in each of the following groups have substantially the same denotation, but their connotations vary, so that their total meanings are often quite different:

average (factual); *mediocre* (derogatory)

childlike (approving); *childish* (derogatory)

saliva (factual, slightly Formal, with scientific suggestion); *spit* (the usual word but to many people "an ugly word")

antique (generally approving); *old-fashioned* (factual, though often suggesting disapproval); *antiquated* (derogatory); *passé* (lightly derogatory)

drunk (in General use); *intoxicated* (more polite); *under the influence* (euphemistic–minimizing); *pie-eyed, soused, loaded* (Informal speech)

reporter (factual); *journalist* (slightly pretentious); *newshawk* (usually with slight derogatory or humorous note); *legman* (shoptalk)

slender (factual, tending to approval); *thin* (factual, tending to disapproval); *skinny* (disapproving); *scrawny* (derogatory); *sylphlike* (Formal); *svelte* (fashionable)

The connotations of these words suggest an attitude or a feeling of the person using them and would arouse a similar (or perhaps an opposite) attitude or feeling in most readers or listeners. The context in which the word has been generally used, the variety of usage it comes from, and the general social attitude toward its referent and toward the people who generally use it (politicians, advertising men, teachers, children, seamen) all contribute to the connotation. The force of slang and of much profanity comes mainly from the connotation of the words. The connotation may change as the words or their referents move up or down in social esteem. *Methodist* and *Quaker* started as words of dispraise but are now simply factual, often words of esteem. *Propaganda* only a few years ago meant a means of spreading a truth or a faith, but it now implies spreading falsehood or at least presenting information unfairly.

Besides connotations that are more or less permanent characteristics of words and may therefore be given some attention in a dictionary definition, there are more immediate connotations that come from context or from the way words are used at a specific time. In speaking we can alter or even invert the usual meaning of a word by the tone of voice or facial expression or gesture. We can call a person a liar in such a way that he will know he is being flattered. In writing, the tone is set by the general style and by the tenor of ideas expressed. *Democracy, communism, monarchy* are primarily words for types of social organization, but they may also carry suggestions of loyalty or suspicion or hate. The full possibility of meaning of many words cannot be indicated by a dictionary; consider what would be omitted in a standard definition of such words as *fascism, income tax, ball game, quintessence, the founding fathers, scab, the forgotten man, horse and buggy era.*

The use of connotative words

Connotative words give writing a quality that is called *suggestion.* They are often referred to as emotive, evaluational, intensional, loaded, or slanted words. As most of these names themselves suggest, connotative words tend to be regarded with suspicion. It is true that their use is often an abuse of statement. It is easy to find slanting—in newspaper headlines, columns by news "analysts," advertisements, political and social discussions—that may range from inconsequential to deceptive and malicious. Reducing such material to neutral statements is good sport, and it is necessary for right thinking. We need more straightforward, denotative writing, especially about problematical social situations. But outside of strictly scholarly and scientific writing, nonconnotative statement is rare. In everyday life and in literature, suggestion—the connotative force of words—is essential. As human beings we have feelings, attitudes, opinions, desires which we need to express, and we have the right to express them.

But we live among people and have a responsibility to them. If we wish to deceive, language offers us the means; by intentional misuse of words or by an irresponsible manipulation of the emotional suggestion in words, a "propagandist" (or anyone else) can distort truth and make error prevail, at least for a time. The difficulty is not so much in the words as in the intentions of the person using them. But an honest attempt at communication can be made to succeed. Although we sometimes fail because we make a careless or unhappy choice of words or because we don't make full use of the facilities of our language, a sincere effort to convey material with which we are really familiar can be successful.

Absolute exactness is not always desirable. A person who in conversation is overexact or overcareful is likely to become a bore, sacrificing immediate appeal to precision. Often in a poem so much depends on the connotation of the words that several "meanings" are possible, and properly enough, so long as a reader does not insist that his interpretation is necessarily the one the writer intended. In attempts to persuade and in any sort of emotional speech, the connotation counts for much. Our aim should be to fit our use of words to a reasonable view of the particular situation and to a reasonable purpose.

For self-protection in our reading, a useful device is to think of other ways the statement might be made. We probably won't be able to judge its accuracy but we can judge the way the words are used. Without being captious we can translate the idea, especially if it represents an opinion or attitude, into other words which are neutral or have a different connotation. Various people, for example, might state what they think (and feel) is the central reason for rising prices:

Slanted phrasing	*Neutral*
Continued wage grabs by big labor.	Higher wages secured principally by labor unions.
Inflated corporation profits given away as dividends.	High corporation profits paid out in dividends to investors.
Outrageous bonuses paid to company big shots.	Large bonuses to top executives.
Lazy and fussy consumers' demands for daily services, fancy packages—for everything they should do for themselves.	Consumers' increasing desire for labor-saving products, convenient packaging, servicing.

This device of translating will not necessarily produce "the truth," but it may give us something new to think about and at least keep us from being too easily taken in by irresponsibly slanted statements—even when they fit with our own views.

For the protection of our readers, the first step is to examine our own views and to see that they are based on the best evidence available to us and that they represent our whole and better selves. It may be helpful to state directly or at least imply clearly what our general approach or bias is. The remedy for irresponsible statement is first in attitude and only secondarily in words.

The second step is to be aware of other people's attitudes and feelings, especially of those differing from our own. On most important questions, opinions may legitimately differ—otherwise they would be facts rather than opinions. The serious opinions of others should be met squarely and in their best expression, not their shoddiest. A decent regard for the feelings of others will also reduce the thoughtless, loose, insensitive, or even hostile use of words. Such a concern will reduce the offensive epithets for races, nationalities, occupations, social groups of all sorts and the oversimplification of complex situations—perhaps even some of the unanalyzed terms of virtue we wish to apply to ourselves—*rights, liberty, free enterprise, peace, the Free World*. Within the limits of reasonable attitudes and of understanding, we still have the right to express ourselves strongly.

Since most of the writing in a composition course is neither completely objective nor entirely personal, it offers a good field for practice and conscious experiment in the responsible use of words. Conscientious students tend to rely too much on impersonal denotations and to squeeze out of their writing the personal, suggestive quality. (The thoughtless ones may well go too far in the other direction.) This practice in the honest expression of ideas cannot alone produce effective writing, but it can result in a responsible and perhaps impressive use of words.

Choice of appropriate words

The principles of appropriateness given as the basis of Good English (pp. 28-34) apply to all phases of our use of language but are easiest to demonstrate in discussing words. Obviously, many words come primarily from the subject written about and must be used. But others are not specifically demanded by the subject–one writer might use them, another might not. In choosing these words, some balance is to be struck between the reader's expectation, his knowledge and taste, and the writer's usual habits of expression. This section is concerned with some hindrances to communication between reader and writer and with some traits of words that can add not only to a reader's understanding but to his pleasure.

Mistaken words

The most elementary fault is simply not using the word the writer intends, using a word for a meaning that it has not acquired in its previous history:

> How are the coaches outwitting their *prototypes* [*competitors?*]?
> An educated man seems to have an expression signifying shrewdness, *comprehensibility* [*understanding?*], and originality.

Usually, as in the last sentence (note the *signifying*), such errors occur when a writer is attempting to use a vocabulary in which he is not at home or when he confuses two words of similar sound (*temerity–timidity, mystification–mysticism, moral–morale*). Confusion is especially likely to occur between words of opposite meaning (*concave–convex*). Confusions in the use of words that are pronounced alike (homonyms) are a matter of spelling rather than of meaning (*meat–meet*). Even if the context makes the meaning clear, such inaccuracies are a mark of carelessness. They are usually marked on themes by D (for *diction,* choice of words), or WW (wrong word).

Vague words

Some words are too general to convey an exact meaning. They are more characteristic of conversation than of writing. Words like *fine, bad, good* should usually be replaced in writing by more definite adjectives, and even words like *interesting* or *important* frequently stand for some particular sort of interest or importance that could better be named, so that the reader's thought is brought nearer to the writer's intention. (See *Counter words.[1]) Many phrases could be replaced by single exact words with a gain in economy and sometimes in definiteness:

> The men with axes would then trim off the branches, while the men with crosscut saws cut the *large part of the tree* [*trunk*] into ten-foot length.
>
> Last year in a nearby city an *occupant* [*prisoner*] in the county jail escaped.
>
> *The other thing that I have in mind* [*My other intention–hope–plan?*] is to go to France.

Such words are usually marked D on themes.

Trite words

A *trite expression* (or a *cliché* or a *hackneyed term*) is a phrase that has been overused. Obviously, certain necessary function words –*a, the,* the prepositions, the conjunctions–do not wear out; the actual names of things and acts and qualities do not wear out; and formulas like *How do you do* and *Yours truly* may be used over and over without attracting any real attention at all. Expressions that are direct and exact do not deserve to be called trite. We can call for *bread* as often as we need to–but *staff of life* is quite a different matter, stylistically. It is a figure of speech, once bright and perhaps startling, now threadbare and hardly serving even a weak attempt at humor.

We should not be too severe about triteness in ordinary conversation, where the common expressions have their place and prevent awkward hesitation. But the use of many trite expressions in writing is a symptom that the writer isn't taking care or showing interest, or else that he is inexperienced with words.

Most trite expressions will be found to be outworn figures of speech, frayed quotations, or phrases that are repeated intact more often than is pleasing.

---

[1]Throughout this book, references to *Index* articles are indicated by asterisks (*).

Worn-out figures of speech. We are all familiar with figures of speech that have been overused:

Father Time	tide of battle	flowing with milk and honey
history tells us	irony of fate	
darkness overtook us	commune with nature	trees like sentinels
better half [wife]	crack of dawn	run like a flash
Mother Nature	bolt from the blue	a watery grave

Make your own list. A good deal of slang that is wearing out also belongs in this category.

Frayed quotations. Shakespeare has so many magnificently quotable lines that a writer who confines himself to the most used (All the world's a stage—Uneasy lies the head—To be or not to be—Not wisely but too well) makes his readers suspect that he has never actually read Shakespeare or he could make fresher choices. The Bible is similarly sinned against, though so many of its phrases have passed into the General language that it is not always fair to label them trite. If you want to illustrate a point by quotation, however, it is safer to take one from your own reading than to rely on these overused expressions.

Stock phrases. The commonest sort of triteness comes from set phrases—adjectives that are too often found with the same nouns, adverbs that come with the same verbs. In this passage from one of Frank Sullivan's "Cliché Expert" series you will recognize many words and phrases overused in political campaigns:

> Q—Mr. Arbuthnot, I can't figure out *where* you stand. Let's get back to your campaign-oratory clichés. What kind of questions have you been discussing?
>
> A—Burning questions. Great, underlying problems.
>
> Q—What have you arrayed yourself against?
>
> A—The forces of reaction. There must be no compromise with the forces of reaction.
>
> Q—And now, Mr. Arbuthnot, may I ask you to characterize these times?
>
> A—These are troubled times, sir. We are met here today in an hour of grave national crisis.
>
> Q—What do you, as a campaign orator, propose to do in this grave hour?
>
> A—I shall demand, and denounce, and dedicate. I shall take stock. I shall challenge, pledge, stress, fulfill, indict, exercise, accuse, call upon, affirm, and reaffirm.
>
> Q—Reaffirm what?
>
> A—My undying faith in the principles laid down by the Founding Fathers. And I shall exercise eternal vigilance that our priceless heritage may be safeguarded.

Q–Admirable, Mr. Arbuthnot. And that reminds me: What is it you campaign orators rise above?

A–Narrow partisanship. We must place the welfare of our country above all other considerations, including our desire to win.

Q–Mr. Arbuthnot, how do you campaign orators dedicate yourselves?

A–We dedicate ourselves anew to the task that lies before us.

Q–How does your party approach this task?

A–With a solemn realization of the awful responsibility that rests upon us in this hour of unprecedented national stress.

Q–When our country is——

A–Sore beset by economic ills.

Q–How else do you approach the task?

A–With supreme confidence that our ga-rate party will prove worthy of its ga-lorious tradition.

Q–And if your party failed to approach the task in that spirit, Mr. Arbuthnot, would you say that——

A–It would indeed be recreant to its sacred trust.–FRANK SULLIVAN, "The Cliché Expert Testifies on Politics," *A Rock in Every Snowball,* pp. 115-6

You can make a similar collection from any "field of endeavor."

Your instructor, as a professional reader with a longer exposure to clichés, may find more trite expressions in your writing than you realize are there. Of course you should not slow up your first writing by stopping to find original phrases, but you should become sensitive enough to triteness to remove it from your copy in revision. The remedy is nearly always the same: look squarely at what you are talking about and present it as simply and concretely as possible.

Euphemisms

A *euphemism* is a pale or comfortable word or phrase used instead of the more explicit or abrupt name for some discomfort or suffering, or for something presumed to be offensive to delicate ears. The substitute is often more vague, less harsh in sound or connotation, than the more exact and literal term it displaces; and it is often an abstract word or one derived from Latin rather than a native English word.

The most excusable euphemisms are those intended to soften the misfortunes of life: *pass on* or *pass away* for *die, laid to rest* for *buried.* In intimate human relationships, in letters and in conversation with bereaved people, these are a sign of human sympathy; but their use in impersonal situations, in journalism or literature, makes for weakness.

The largest group of euphemisms has a somewhat prudish origin, for it consists of substitutes for the vigorous monosyllabic names of certain physical functions and social unpleasantness. For years *sweat* was taboo among "the upper classes" as both verb and noun and was replaced by *perspire* and *perspiration.* Spit became *expectorate; drunk* was *intoxicated;* both *stink* and *smell* gave way to *odor, belly* to *abdomen,* and so on.

Euphemisms show one side of the relation between language and social attitudes. They sometimes indicate timidity, but more often they are a conscious seeking for "respectability." People who would never say *damn* could say *P.D.Q.* without qualms. At a more serious level, newspaper euphemisms like *companionate marriage, love child, social diseases* once allowed virtuous people to talk about matters they would never have mentioned by their more common names. Some of these euphemisms are now being dropped. The recognition of the seriousness of venereal diseases, for example, has led to persistent campaigning by doctors for more direct discussion, so that most papers have taken *syphilis* from their black lists.

At present there is a conspicuous group of euphemisms found in the treatment of social situations. The *aged* or *old people* are *senior citizens. Dull* children become *retarded* or even *exceptional.* What in 1893 was known as *hard times* is now called a *depression;* a slighter falling off of business a *recession.* Those *out of work* or *jobless* are the *unemployed,* perhaps the victims of *technological unemployment* (an accurate but distant noun); and the *poor* are the *underprivileged.* Some of these terms have so nearly displaced the older ones that a writer can hardly avoid using them, but he should keep clearly in mind the specific unhappiness and suffering they name.

Except for some journalistic and commercial terms and some taboos of radio and television networks, movies, and newspapers, the temper of the times is now against euphemisms in writing; and unless circumstances actually demand a substitute for the ordinary names of things and situations, a writer should call a spade a spade–simply and without unnecessary emphasis. Fowler's comment is true: "Euphemism is more demoralizing than coarseness."

Big words

The term *big words* covers several common faults of writing that come from an unhappy use of words. The words may not be long or uncommon (*deem, doff, dwell* are big words in the sense of this discussion), but they are big in that they are *too heavy for their place.*

There is little objection to long words when they are called for by the subject, come naturally to the writer, and are appropriate to the reader. Long words are the only and necessary names for many ideas and for many things, and they must be used in much technical, scientific, and professional writing–though they may be overused even in the writing of specialists. *Sphygmograph, schizophrenia, Pleistocene* all have their place, though it is a restricted one. (If one of these words is needed in ordinary speech, a shorter form or a substitute usually arises, like *DDT* for *dichloro-diphenyl-trichloro-ethane.*) Some longer words may be needed, especially in Formal writing, for their rhythm or connotation: *immemorial, multifarious, provocative, infinitesimal, anticipation.*

Big words are words that do not fit, that are too heavy or too pretentious for the subject. The writer may use them because he is writing carelessly or trying to show off, but he may also use them in a serious attempt to "improve" his expression. He fails to realize that he will improve his writing not by translating his thought into pretentious words but by expressing it in more exact and suggestive words. As Fowler puts it in his article on "Long variants": " 'The better the writer, the shorter his words' would be a statement needing many exceptions for individual persons & particular subjects; but for all that it would, & especially about English writers, be broadly true. Those who run to long words are mainly the unskilful & tasteless; they confuse pomposity with dignity, flaccidity with ease & bulk with force."

It is perhaps natural for a person to feel that his own speech is not good enough to use in public appearances and in writing. It may not be–but the remedy lies in improving and extending its best features, not in attempting an unnatural language. The goal of much English teaching used to be the development of a Formal style, and conscientious students dutifully translated their material into such passages as this, in which a girl introduces us to a fat man oiling a lawn mower at some historic shrine that she does not bother to name or place:

> As we approached one of the beautiful historic buildings of western New York as yet unscarred by time's relentless talons and having about it an intangible aura of antiquity, we observed a man of over ample proportions kneeling beside a lawn mower to lubricate its creaking wheels. The act lent a jarring and anachronistic note to the peaceful scene.

This sins against Good English on three counts: first, the material, a simple picture, is obscured by such phrases (both "big" and "trite") as *time's relentless talons, intangible aura of antiquity, a jarring and anachronistic note*—not to mention the *man of over ample proportions lubricating the creaking wheels of the lawn mower*. Second, the writer did not visualize her readers. Ordinary people are bored by such formality and few readers are fooled by the affectation. Third, and most important, the language is not appropriate to the writer, an alert and intelligent girl.

Big words are a special curse today in much government writing ("gobbledygook"), in the more pretentious journalism, and in some academic writing, especially, it seems, in the social studies. Try putting into your own words the following (quite true) statement:

> Out of the interstimulation of conversation there emerges an interweaving of understanding and purpose leading to co-individual behavior. Of course the conversation may be divisive, as well as integrating. But even these divisions may be regarded as mere differentiations within the general synthesis of human behavior. Thus in conversation is found that mutual understanding and common purpose essential to effective and continuous cooperation.

The continued use of big words not only alienates readers, but it may let you write without feeling or even without really knowing what you are saying. Some of the commonest big words that occur in student writing are:

advent	domicile	peruse
behold	dwell	reside
congregate	metropolis	stated (for said)
deem	nuptials	termed
doff, don	participate	transpire

The remedy for big words is simple: Read aloud what you have written; then, if you find it conspicuously different from the way you would *tell* the same thing to a friend, consider the words carefully and see if you can't use simpler words that are natural to you. Let no others stand in your copy, except for very good reason.

Synonyms

To choose exact and appropriate words you need to consider synonyms. A *synonym* is a word of nearly the same meaning as another. Often the real difference is in their connotations. There are very few pairs of completely interchangeable words. Even names of specific things, like *rhubarb—pieplant, bucket—pail, flicker—yellowhammer,* differ; although they refer to the same objects, their connotations are not the same because one of the pair is used in a definite part of the country, or by a specific group of people, or under certain circumstances, and so it cannot be regularly substituted for the other. English is especially rich in words of slightly different shades of meaning: *joke–jest; obedient–dutiful–yielding–compliant–obsequious; multitude–throng–crowd–mob*. Because of these differences in connotation, merely trying to escape repetition of a word is not a sufficient motive for using a synonym. It is better to avoid unpleasant repetition by using pronouns or by recasting the sentence.

When a writer looks for a "synonym," what he usually wants is a word that can give his meaning in the particular sentence more exactly than the word he has on hand. The important point, then, in looking at two or more words of similar meaning is to know how they *differ*.

As a rule, testing the exactness of words is a matter of revision. Only when they stand in a context can they be tested for exactness of meaning and for appropriateness to the subject and to the readers. Sometimes a single word can take the place of a long phrase; sometimes a word of specific meaning can replace a general or ambiguous one: *funny* might be *amusing, laughable, odd, queer, different, peculiar,* or *walk* might be replaced by a more descriptive word–*stroll, trip, saunter, stride, pace, tiptoe, amble, march*. Sometimes the change is to bring a word in line with the variety of usage of the rest of the paper, choosing one either more or less Formal: *want–wish–desire; roomy–spacious; fast–rapidly*.

There are various tools at hand. Dictionaries group words of similar meaning and indicate the general distinctions between them. There are also several books of synonyms: *Webster's Dictionary of Synonyms* (Springfield, 1942), Fernald's *Standard Handbook of Synonyms, Antonyms, and Prepositions* (New York, 1947), Soule's *A Dictionary of English Synonyms* (Boston, 1938), and Roget's *International Thesaurus* (rev. ed., 1946). The *Thesaurus* is probably the most used book of synonyms. It lists words by topics, giving words of opposite meaning in parallel columns, and offers a wide range from slang to Formal and even obsolete words. Since it does not give definitions, its chief use is to remind a person of those words he recognizes but does not use readily. In this way it helps the writer to bridge the gap between his recognition and active vocabulary and is often useful in revising a paper.

But the prime source of synonyms, as of other words, is conversation and reading. Paying close attention to the use and meaning of new words you meet is the best background for making the choice of exact words easy.

Figurative use of words

Although we may not be aware of it, we use figurative language in our conversation all the time. Practically all writing, even reference works and scientific or scholarly papers, makes some use of it. Since it is one way to make our meaning more exact, more complete, more interesting, or more impressive, it is a valuable resource in writing.

Many words which originally had narrowly restricted senses have come to be used figuratively and have extended their meaning. *Head* has its original, literal meaning as a part of the body but is applied to the highest or foremost or principal part of a wide variety of things—of a screw, nail, pin, army, the force of a stream of water, bay, news story, stalk of grain, hammer, bed, golf club, beer, boil, barrel—not to mention parts of a number of machines and the leaders of all sorts of institutions and governments and movements. Ordinary speech is full of these figures: we *play ball* when we work with others; we may *chime in* by adding our voice to others.

Such figurative uses become new "senses" of words, as *head* of a pin or nail has—there is no other word for it and it is listed as one of the regular meanings of *head* in dictionaries. These are no longer real figures but ex- or dead figures. We are here concerned with more or less fresh adaptations of words to different meanings that will add interest to our writing.

The following sections describe some of the commonest and most useful figures, grouped according to the contribution they make to meaning.

Comparison: metaphor, simile, analogy

Metaphors and similes and analogies all make comparisons, but the three figures differ in form and in fullness. A *metaphor* is the shortest, most compact; in it the likeness is implied rather than stated explicitly. Typically, the writer asserts that one thing *is* another (in some respect) or suggests that it acts like or has some of the qualities of something else, as in the examples below:

> But meaning is an *arrow* that reaches its *mark* when least encumbered with *feathers*.—HERBERT READ, *English Prose Style*, p. 16
>
> Yet Tchaikovsky succeeded because he was a *lyric poet* with a *pipeline* to the simplest and strongest emotions.—EDWARD SACKVILLE-WEST *et al., The Record Guide*, p. 765

. . . the tracks of field mice were *stitched* across its [the snow's] surface in the morning.—JOSEPHINE JOHNSON, *Winter Orchard,* p. 307

. . . for *the waves* cast by a *pebble of thought* spread until they reach even the nitwits on *the shores* of action.—IRWIN EDMAN, *Four Ways of Philosophy,* p. 100

Where the metaphor implies the likeness, a *simile* says specifically that one is like the other, using the words *like* or *as*. A literal statement of similarity is not a simile—"the Congress is like a state legislature" is plain statement of fact. A simile is a comparison in which two objects differ in most respects but still may be strikingly alike in some one that is important to the writer's immediate purpose:

. . . woods *like Persian rugs* where Autumn was commencing.—WILBUR DANIEL STEELE, "Bubbles"

What seems to be lacking in the older prose is the sense of the uninterrupted flow of the mind: Bagehot, for example, appears to cut off this continuum, shall we call it, into arbitrary lengths, *as we slice chunks off a cucumber.*—BONAMY DOBRÉE, *Modern Prose Style,* p. 225

And yet if the new generation were fed exclusively upon the best of scientific writing it is doubtful whether they would be conditioned against war. For such great impulses as the dangerous, competitive life are, of course, emotional and spring from ancestral regions into which the logic of facts penetrates *like a bullet which shoots through the trunk of a tree leaving only a hole which the living tissues quickly close.*—H. S. CANBY, "War or Peace in Literature," *Designed for Reading,* p. 89

An *analogy,* unlike the metaphor and simile, ordinarily notes several points of similarity instead of just one. Suggestive analogies often bring home or emphasize an idea, as in the second sentence of this:

By what process of reasoning can a man who is quite conversant with the separate meanings of *put,* of *up,* and of *with* ever infer that *to put up with* means *to endure?* We might as reasonably expect the person who has discovered the several properties of carbon, hydrogen, and oxygen to infer from them the amazing properties of alcohol. In neither case do the elements afford a clue to the nature of the compound.—P. B. BALLARD, *Thought and Language,* p. 168

Relationship: metonymy, synecdoche

Metonymy and synecdoche are two figures of speech which substitute for the exact name of something the name of something closely associated with it. Strictly, *synecdoche* gives the name of a part when the whole is meant (so many *mouths* to feed, a *sail* in the offing, plant employing sixty *hands*), or of a whole for a part (*Minnesota* [the team] won, the *army* adopts a policy). *Metonymy* is the use of one word for another that it suggests: (a) the material for the object made of it: *rubber* for footgear made of rubber; (b) the maker or source for the thing made: *Shakespeare* for Shakespeare's plays; *Java* for Javanese coffee; (c) any word or phrase closely associated with the object: *grandstand* for the audience.

Metonymy, a common figure of speech (common in both Formal and General usage) illustrates one way in which the meanings of words change. Long use of *crown* for *king, heart* for *courage* or *sympathy* and similar use of hundreds of other words have given these words definite secondary meanings.

Degree of statement: exaggeration, understatement, irony

Exaggeration (also called *hyperbole*) is a figure of speech when it is used not to deceive but to emphasize a statement or situation, to intensify its impression. Exaggeration may involve simply choosing a word of broader or more intense meaning than literal accuracy would call for (like *perfect* for *excellent, mob* for *people, starved* for *hungry, rout* for *retreat*), or it may involve developing a more complex statement, as in the following passages:

> But the feelings that Beethoven put into his music were the feelings of a god. There was something olympian in his snarls and rages, and there was a touch of hell-fire in his mirth.–H. L. MENCKEN, "Beethoven," *Prejudices: Fifth Series,* p. 89

> These little self-contained flats were convenient; to be sure, she had no light and no air, but she could shut it up whenever she liked and go away.–JOHN GALSWORTHY, *The Man of Property,* p. 224

A too free use of superlatives or of intense adjectives is weakening and should be avoided:

> Within the limits of Colorado, New Mexico, Arizona, and Southern California there are four centers of sublime and unparalleled scenic sublimity which stand alone and unrivalled in the world.

Exaggeration is a frequent source of humor, both literary and popular. Many American anecdotes and tall tales hinge on it–as does the yarn told of Kit Carson (and probably of others) that in the Valley of Echoes in Jackson County, Wyoming, it took eight hours for an echo to return, so that he would shout "It's time to get up" as he went to bed and the echo would wake him up in the morning. The Paul Bunyan stories make a cycle of popular exaggeration.

Exaggeration is just as much a part of more sophisticated humor and satire:

> Englishwomen's shoes look as if they had been made by someone who had often heard shoes described, but had never seen any, and the problem of buying shoes in London is almost insoluble–unless you pay a staggering tariff on American ones. What provokes this outburst is that I have just bought a pair of English bedroom slippers and I not only cannot tell the left foot from the right, but it is only after profound deliberation that I am able to distinguish between the front and the back.–MARGARET HALSEY, *With Malice Toward Some,* pp. 99-100

Understatement is the opposite of exaggeration. It may mean stating an idea in negative terms (litotes) or in less strong words than would be expected: "Joe Louis was not a bad fighter." It is often used in unfavorable criticism; for example, the *Times Literary Supplement* followed a quotation of some very bad verses with the comment: "This is absolutely representative of the whole work, which is about as long as *Paradise Lost* but not so good."

Irony implies something markedly different, occasionally even the opposite, from what is actually said. Light irony is a form of humor, severe irony usually a form of sarcasm or satire–though exact definition in such matters is difficult and rarely fruitful.

> "We made two dollars," Merle told her, "off nineteen steers. The cattle business is very good. Next year we might try twenty and buy a big dishmop in the fall."–JOSEPHINE JOHNSON, *Now in November,* p. 222

The broadest form of irony is an inversion of the intended meaning, as in the following passage from William Saroyan. Saroyan means exactly the reverse of the advice he seems to be giving about the use of unessential adjectives:

> But rules without a system are, as every good writer will tell you, utterly inadequate. You can leave out "utterly" and the sentence will mean the same thing, but it is always nicer to throw in an "utterly" whenever possible. All successful writers believe that one word by itself hasn't enough meaning and that it is best to emphasize the meaning of one word with the help of another. Some writers will go so far as to help an innocent word with as many as four and five other words, and at times they will kill an innocent word by charity and it will take years and years for some ignorant writer who doesn't know adjectives at all to resurrect the word that was killed by kindness.–WILLIAM SAROYAN, Preface to *The Daring Young Man on the Flying Trapeze*

Word play

Occasionally we try experiments in words, either by making old words do new tricks or by inventing new ones. The results are often disastrous–in fact usually so–but now and then the effect comes off.

Clipped words of recent creation seem slangy or familiar (*natch, psych, ex-pug*), though older ones are thoroughly respectable (*cab, bus, varsity*). The same is true for blends: *Time's cinemadolescent* looks like a word that wouldn't be in a dictionary–it isn't–but *cinematography* gets in. The commonest experiment with words is the pun: More trouble is made by in-laws than by outlaws; Don't learn traffic laws by accident; or Belloc's "When I am dead, I hope it may be said: 'His sins were scarlet, but his books were read.' "

Word play is risky because the failures are conspicuous, but a full use of language calls for some freedom. If you try it, review carefully what you have done to make sure it comes off.

Allusion

Sometimes a writer includes incidental matter in his paper to add interest or to explain more clearly or to emphasize what he is saying. This may be an *allusion,* a brief reference to literature, to history, to things, to people and what they do. Since it is a voluntary addition of the writer, its effect is stylistic–a way of saying something that could have been put differently–and may properly be included in a study of the choice of words.

Many people who write have read widely and have been so interested in what they read that allusion to it naturally appears in their explanation of other matters. (They may use quotations, too, but we are talking of less specific reference to their reading.) Speeches from two Shakespearean plays are referred to in the following passage:

> There is nothing new in heaven or earth not dreamt of [Hamlet] in our laboratories; and we should be amazed indeed if tomorrow and tomorrow and tomorrow [Macbeth] failed to offer us something new to challenge our capacity for readjustment.–CARL L. BECKER, *The Heavenly City of the Eighteenth Century Philosophers,* p. 23

William Beebe refers to a Poe story in describing the life cycle of a tiny animal:

> Poe wrote a memorable tale of a prison cell which day by day grew smaller, and Opalina goes through much the same adventure.–WILLIAM BEEBE, *Jungle Days,* p. 22

Allusion to written literature is more characteristic of Formal than of General English, which is apt to borrow from proverbs, current phrases, advertising, and the great stock of colloquial phrases (more fun than a barrel of monkeys). Homely, everyday phrases can be used to advantage in any Informal discussion:

The thing for the faculty of the University to do is to *take it easy*. Don't get excited. *Walk, don't run to the nearest exit* and *enjoy life in the open*. In a few months the sun will shine, *water will run down hill, and smoke will go up the chimneys* just the same.—WILLIAM ALLEN WHITE, *The Emporia Gazette*

We often allude to outstanding events in the past: to Waterloo, ettysburg, D-Day, and to the lives and characters of important ersons:

The voice of duty speaks differently to Savonarola, to Cromwell, to Calvin, to Kant and to the contemporary communist or fascist.—IRWIN EDMAN, *Four Ways of Philosophy*, p. 292

etailed historical reference is rather characteristic of Formal writing; rief reference to better known events characterizes General writing.

More typical of current writing is allusion to current events, perons in the public eye, immediate affairs. But one difficulty with such asual allusions is that in time they become hard to identify—a reason hy Shakespeare's plays and other older literature need explanatory otes. This was written in 1921:

Suppose a young man, just out of college and returned to his moderate-sized home town in Ohio (*why not Marion?*), honestly tries to make those contacts with the national culture which Mr. Sherman so vigorously urges him to make.—HAROLD STEARNS, *The Bookman*, March 1921

Why not Marion?" is meaningless to young people today, and many f their elders will have forgotten that it was President Harding's ome town, often referred to in 1921. But missing the allusion does ot interfere with the point of the passage. As with other such refernces, if a reader does recognize the allusion, he has an added pleasre. Such topical allusions are best for immediate consumption, and nce most of us are not writing for the ages, they are quite fit. They elp make a piece sound as though it is written in the present and s though its writer is awake to what is going on.

One of the most fertile kinds of allusion, and one that is open to verybody, is to the things that people do, the things around us, our ork, our sports, our hobbies. It was natural for Carlo Levi, an M.D., write "The sky was a mixture of rose, green, and violet, the enhanting colors of malaria country" (*Christ Stopped at Eboli*, p. 63). he directness of modern style encourages such allusions to the life round us, as in this bit from a discussion of teachers' oaths:

But, it is said, teachers have great influence on the young; and we must be sure that the young are under proper care. Very well. If we are to insure the patriotism of those who have influence over the young, let us do so. Let us begin with parents and have them take an oath to support the Constitution. Let us include newspaper men, and especially the designers of comic supplements. Let us line up all the movie stars. Let us insist on an oath of allegiance from radio performers. If the teachers are to be required to take an oath, Amos and Andy should be required to salute the flag and sing the "Star Spangled Banner" twice a day.—ROBERT MAYNARD HUTCHINS, *No Friendly Voice,* pp. 122-3

Since allusions come from the writer's experience they reveal his personality. If he is interested in sailing or jazz or dramatics, bringing in a bit from one of these interests may point up the subject on which he is writing. Many papers seem depersonalized and distant because students avoid allusions. If they don't fit, they are easily taken out in revision. If they do, the words will have greater force and the paper will be livelier and more meaningful.

Use of figures of speech

Since figures of speech are likely to be a little conspicuous, they need to be used with care. It is better to do the best possible with literal words unless a happy and accurate figure comes to mind.

Effective figures are natural, consistent, and appropriate. Figures should seem to come from the way the writer sees his subject, to be the sort that he might use in his conversation. They should not be tacked on or used just to be different or "to make an impression"—they should bring the reader closer to the writer's actual sense of his subject. In speech there are many figures, especially comparisons *(tired as a dog, lap of luxury),* which are pretty threadbare but which still work when we're not too fussy about the effect we are making on our listener. In writing we should be more careful. "Trees that stand like sentinels" is an example of the lazy, trite, and really useless figure. Trees of course do stand like sentinels sometimes—but it would not occur to most of us to say so if we hadn't heard the phrase before. Stock or forced figures keep readers from seeing the picture clearly and tend to make them doubt the writer's sincerity. Struggling for freshness usually brings on either these trite figures or strained ones. The figures to use are the ones that come easily to your mind when you are trying to give an exact account of the subject. They do not need to be unusual, but should fit in their context, sound as though you were actually thinking them, and—most important—add something to the sense.

If a figure is continued through more than one phrase, sometimes it becomes "mixed"—inconsistent in some way (called the *mixed metaphor*). The sophomore who wrote "My father is a limb in a chain of the business cycle" couldn't have been thinking either about his father or about his writing.

Mixed figures are often used intentionally as a sort of easy but sometimes effective humor–like those attributed to Samuel Goldwyn ("They're always biting the hand that lays the golden egg") or this from *Jurgen:*

> "Indeed, it is a sad thing, Sylvia, to be murdered by the hand which, so to speak, is sworn to keep an eye on your welfare, and which rightfully should serve you on its knees."–JAMES BRANCH CABELL, *Jurgen,* p. 124

Since figures are used to make a passage in some way more effective, they should be accurate enough to contribute to the meaning and they should be in tone with the subject and style. This is out of key:

> In learning more about him I found that he was just about the kindest man I have ever met. He had the heart of an elephant and the mind of a genius.

And these figures seem much too violent to suggest even voracious reading:

> He sank his teeth into the throat of the book, shook it fiercely until it was subdued, then lapped up its blood, devoured its flesh and crunched its bones. . . .

Range and liveliness

The qualities of words that we have been discussing contribute not only to communicating information and ideas but also to the life and force of writing, to its readability. Colorless and impersonal writing may at times be adequate and even appropriate, as in some scholarly papers, but it makes a less deep impression and limits the readers to those already having a concern for the subject.

The following paragraph is quite accurate but quite colorless–very few people could read through the fifteen-page pamphlet from which it comes.

> Our way of life is menaced today and we are concerned about its defense. The first step in the defense of democracy (as we realize more readily in times of crisis, though it was just as true in easier days of security) is to ensure an understanding and appreciation of its essential values and of the obligations it entails. So many young people have grown up thinking of the advantages of democracy in terms of their personal liberty to do what they like, and so devoid of any sense of the claims of democracy upon their service, that we are now able to see clearly how seriously our educational institutions have been failing to

transmit our ideals and to play their part in developing the attitudes and loyalties on which our free society depends for its very survival.

One of the outstanding traits of modern writing is the range and vigor and suggestiveness of the words used. We do not need to go to works that make primarily a literary appeal to find these qualities. Here are paragraphs from two factual discussions that show range and a generally lively style. One is from an article on intelligence tests, the other is a survey of recent American painting. The writer's attention in each is firmly centered on his immediate subject, but he has not switched off the rest of his mind. He takes words and instances as he finds them, puts them to work, and conveys not only his ideas but a sense of life. An outstanding trait of each is the *range* of the vocabulary, from Informal to rather technical words.

> Half the ability in this country goes down the drain because of the failure of intelligence tests to measure the real mental ability of the children from the lower socio-economic groups, and because of the failure of the schools to recognize and train this ability. This country cannot survive as the leading world power unless we learn how to discover, recruit, and train more of the brains in the lower-income groups.—ALLISON DAVIS, "Poor People Have Brains, Too," *The Phi Delta Kappan,* April 1949, p. 294

> Another irritant contributing to the drift of the American artist into his present state of forthright nationalism was his old grievance against the European portraitist, usually a third-rate member of the pretty-pretty school of eyelash affixers, who crosses the Atlantic to batten on portrait commissions from the culturally illiterate. These "artists" are merely commercial limners, skillful in surface flashiness and clever masters of the technique of publicity and social flattery. Americans who try to click heels with them usually end up on an elbow. The news and society reporters (not the art critics) give them yards of publicity with photographs dramatizing their records among European royalty. A visit to Washington would produce sittings from Congressmen, a member of the Cabinet or even the President—every American ruler since 1912, except F. D. R., patiently sat to some foreign painter, for "reasons of state." After a year among our dollar aristocrats, the "artist" would carry back across the Atlantic with him as much as $50,000—his departure attended by the futile curses of better but less suave American portraitists. It is a condition that obtains even today. American taste in the upper brackets being what it is, our lords and ladies of breeding and position like to feel that the same brush that painted Duchess Thisque or Countess Thatque can be hired by Mrs. Smith to outshine Mrs. Jones.—PEYTON BOSWELL, JR., *Modern American Painting,* p. 73

You can aim to express your ideas with similar life. Through observant listening and reading, plenty of good talk, and practice in using the full range of your vocabulary, you will come to write with increasing effectiveness. Sometimes in revising your papers, test them with questions like these: Do these words present my subject accurately, without distortion? Will these words say to my readers what I wish them to say? Are these words varied and lively?

Chapter 8

SUGGESTED STUDY AND WRITING

1. Select one of the columns in the following list and classify the words in it by number; mark them (1) words you now use in speaking or writing, (2) words you understand but do not use, (3) words you feel you have seen before and might understand in context, (4) words totally unfamiliar to you. Look up the words you have numbered 4. Which ones might be useful to you?

allegory
antiphony
appliqué
backlog
bereave
bruit
campanile
captious
cataclysm
centrifugal
coalition
colander
cubism
cursory
decathlon
deciduous
denigrate
dormant
ebony
élan

engross
façade
fallow
febrile
filament
ghoul
glower
gusto
hedonist
histology
homily
iconoclast
infest
inscrutable
insipid
jackanapes
jargon
juxtaposition
kibitz
lurid

lyre
macabre
meretricious
morbid
mulch
myopia
narwhal
ominous
ozone
pagan
paradox
penchant
pithy
polyglot
prone
quintessence
quorum
rapport
recalcitrant
rigorous

sauté
scrupulous
scull
seismic
servility
snide
stymie
suave
surreptitious
synthesis
tacit
tête-à-tête
thermostat
tiara
torpid
tyro
ukase
uncanny
voracious
vulnerable

2. Make a list of at least ten new words you have come to know in your college courses and arrange them according to course. To refresh your memory, consult your notes and papers and check the indexes of your textbooks. Write out a statement summarizing the different ways in which you learned these words.

3. Collect new words from newspapers, conversations, and television and radio programs. List those which seem too recent to be included in any dictionary; then look them up in the most up-to-date dictionary available. How many do you find? Write a paragraph telling the results of your study.

4. Write out the following information about your dictionary: (1) Title (2) Publisher (3) Date of original copyright (on the back of the title

page) (4) Date of the latest copyright (5) Approximate number of words listed (6) Does it have a supplement of new words? (7) Where are the biographical and geographical names listed? (8) What supplementary sections are included at the beginning and the end? (9) Does it show who was responsible for the editing?

5. Look up the following words and copy them with the symbols used in your dictionary to indicate their pronunciation. If more than one pronunciation is given, list them in order and then underline the one you most frequently hear and use.

absolutely	dahlia	interest	room
adult	*economics	oblique	*route
alternate	*either	*often	short-lived
amateur	February	pecan	strata
and	garage	*pianist	suggest
*clothes	*government	pumpkin	surprise
creek	harass	research	which

6. Look up the following words in your dictionary to see what usage labels (*Colloq., Slang, Dial., Obs.*, and so on) are applied to them. If different dictionaries are used by the members of your class, compare the various findings. Do you agree with the labeling?

ballyhoo	daffodilly	hush puppy
bobby	dogie	mammy
bogus	enthuse	oomph
clepe	facer	pencel
clime	hombre	slubber
complected	honky-tonk	tizzy

7. Look up the following words in the *Oxford English Dictionary* or the *Century Dictionary and Cyclopedia* and determine from the etymologies what the earliest recorded meaning of the word was. How close is the present meaning to the oldest known meaning?

academy	fraternity	lyceum	travel
alcohol	hussy	maternal	viper
deer	idiot	museum	wan

8. Make up four or five sentences for each of the following words to show a variety of contexts they may have. Be able to describe the differences that you are illustrating. Are the differences primarily in denotation or connotation?

alone	fair	trouble	quiet	early	distant

9. Substitute specific words for some of the general ones in the following sentences, making the statements as lively and vivid as you can. This will often mean limiting the meaning. (For example, "A man sat in the park" might become "Old Mr. Mensen sat propped against an elm tree in Lincoln Park.")

1. The police drove up to the scene of the accident just as if they had been waiting for it to happen.

2. "Say," said the woman, "what are you going to do with all that furniture?"
3. Going under the long bridge bothered him almost as much as going through the tunnel had.
4. Through the heavy rain came a number of foreign vehicles.
5. Higher education offers a student a great opportunity to obtain the finer things in life.

10. Collect a list of euphemisms from your reading. Ads and business pages in your newspaper make good sources. Carefully vague statements by leaders of business, labor, and government are also good. Be prepared to translate the euphemisms into matter-of-fact words.

11. Class exercise: Take four or five minutes to write down all the connotations and associations which a given word (suggested by your instructor) may have for you. Then on the blackboard put the core of meaning (denotation), the connotations common to the rest of the members of the class in the order of their frequency, and the personal connotations peculiar to individual members of the class.

12. In your reading look for a passage illustrating irresponsible or slanted use of words. When you have found a good example, copy it and prepare to discuss in class the individual words in the passage.

13. Point out any words misused in these sentences from student themes. Give the accurate wording, and make other changes as necessary.

1. The daughter of the family is away at college and is desperately trying to rid herself of some of these homing ties.
2. If these graphs were not important, they would not have been included; in fact, a whole test could be placed upon them.
3. Release from anxiety may be obtained by training the mind to see things in a balanced and calm light.
4. The snow covers the dead foliage and dormant ground, and transposes the world into a sparkling fairyland.
5. Their parents were too dominant and showed little or no affection for them.
6. Students should not be regulated to a fixed position because of their parents' social status or wealth.
7. It is ironic that this country has been diffident to jazz, something we ourselves created.
8. Many of her actions are synonymous of a seventeen-year-old girl. Perhaps this is because she has a very romantic personality.
9. Because I have been to Niagara Falls a number of times I have learned a numerous amount of facts about this phenomena.
10. So with no other alternation before me, I hitchhiked home, bought a chain, and the next day returned to the town where I had left my bike.
11. The distances that followed were characterized by hundreds of miles on the speedometer and inches on the map.

12. Although grammar succumbed to literature and writing later on, it never lost its importance, especially in our written assignments.

14. Fill in the blanks in the following phrases with the expected word or words. Then try to express the same ideas more freshly, changing the word order if necessary.

1. smooth as ________
2. busy as a ________
3. innocent as a ________
4. tried and ________
5. cold and ________
6. slow but ________
7. runs like ________
8. naughty but ________
9. selling like ________
10. it's raining ________
11. higher than ________
12. madder than a ________
13. bright-eyed and ________
14. calm, cool, and ________
15. fast and ________
16. few and ________
17. gone but not________
18. stubborn as a ________

15. Collect from your reading one or two examples each of good use of metaphor, simile, analogy, understatement, and exaggeration. Look for these examples in all kinds of reading matter, from classical literature to the sports page. Be prepared to discuss the reasons for your choice.

While we may cheerfully concede that the great writer,

like the poet, is born and not made,

we need not hesitate to say that

the ordinary writer is made and not born.

B. A. HINSDALE

Chapter 9

The stages in writing

Thinking means shuffling, relating, selecting

the contents of one's mind

so as to assimilate novelty, digest it, and create order.

JACQUES BARZUN

Writing a paper is work, and it should be gone about in a workmanlike manner. There is no mystery about it (unless you find yourself doing much better than you expected) and, like any other job, it should be done in a definite series of steps. Each step has its characteristic problems and makes its characteristic contribution to the finished paper. Most people who have not written much try to see the finished paper at the very start, sometimes even before the topic is definite in their minds, usually before the material has been got together and lined up. Actually, at this point they cannot even worry intelligently about the paper, much less imagine what the finished paper will be like.

Writing a paper can be divided for convenience of discussion into eight steps or stages, shown in the table on page 247. Of course any such analysis is somewhat arbitrary because of the variable conditions involved in a particular paper—the writer's habits and background, his purpose, the complexity of the material, the proposed length, and the time at his disposal. In writing a letter to a friend the stages are telescoped and can hardly be distinguished, but in writing a letter applying for a job each stage may be painfully distinct. Any intelligent student with a grasp of his subject should be able to write a 200- or 300-word essay answer or a class paper of similar length without much conscious effort at organization; but writing a long, complex paper will require careful attention to each stage. Making due allowance, then, for the telescoping of some of the steps and for the varying weight given to each because of differences between writers and between specific writing projects, we may take them (or all of them except the last) as typical of most writing.

Stages in Writing a Paper with the Contribution of Each

1. *Focusing on a subject*—Definition of topic, sensing of problems involved and of possible sources of information
2. *Gathering material*—Notes (in mind or on paper) from memory, observation, interviews, reading, speculation
3. *Evaluating and selecting the material*—A tested and selected body of information to be presented in the paper
4. *Planning the paper*—A synopsis or outline of the paper
5. *Writing the first draft*—Tentative copy of the paper
6. *Revising*—Necessary changes in material, corrections and improvements in words, sentences, paragraphs
7. *Preparing the manuscript*—The completed paper, ready for reading or for printing
8. *Seeing the manuscript into print*—The printed copy

It may be useful for you to look at your writing habits in order to find which stages you do best and enjoy most and which ones give you difficulty. Realizing the stages you have trouble with (and something of the feelings that accompany them) will show you where to work for improvement. One student in a composition course diagnosed her case this way:

1. General interest in some subject.
2. Collecting and reading material or concentrated thinking—expansion.
3. Rest.
4. Deducing some idea.
5. Attacking it any way, some way—to get a start.
6. First draft. Bad, very bad. All sorts of irrelevant ideas crop up. No sense to anything. Despair absolute.
7. Dutifully hanging on to some thread.
8. A sudden inspiration. New viewpoint of the whole thing.
9. Shaping an outline.
10. With outline in mind and in *sight* beginning fresh copy.
11. Gradual and painful progress. Matter of discrimination. Pulling in all relevant material. Arranging material so that it will bear upon a POINT. Translating into language my deductions.
12. Finally an end.

> Am in habit of thinking slow (perhaps chaotically)—writing slow—and usually get stuck at points 5 and 6—and very often cut the whole process off right there—result: all sorts of blasphemous statements.

Before considering the steps in detail, you should remember that your background is one of your fundamental resources. Certainly your general attitudes and ways of thinking, as well as the words and habits of expression that you have accumulated, will be put to use. Out of this background comes the entire material for some papers. (See Ch. 10, "Personal experience papers," p. 274.) Also from it ought to come your point of view—the way you look at your subject—without which the paper is likely to be impersonal and dull. Finally, from this source should spring some individual words and personal phrases, illuminating comparisons and illustrations, incidents, information, bits of color and life that can contribute to the main subject in small but important ways.

Your background is steadily growing. The value of new experiences and ideas can be increased if, combing your memory, you bring to light half-forgotten experiences and enthusiasms, consider past and present together, and bring your whole mind to bear on the ideas you are trying to express. If you do this, your papers will sound as though they were written by a living person, not by an automaton; and they will sound as though they were written by you, not by somebody else. Both your knowledge of English and your total experience are different from those of any other person, because no two people develop in exactly the same way. It is these differences that give you your individuality, that make you see things differently from others. Although too much insistence on your point of view will strike your reader as prejudice, some modest indication of the person behind your writing will increase his interest.

The early stages in writing

Because the early stages of writing a paper—selecting a specific subject, gathering material for it, and selecting material for presentation—differ a good deal for different kinds of papers, they are discussed in detail in later chapters (10 to 13); only a few general points are made here.

Focusing on a subject

The first stage in producing a particular piece of writing is to focus your attention on some field of knowledge or experience or on some definite topic. Often the subject is determined by circumstances (a letter or a report for some specific purpose) or by assignment (to a reporter on a newspaper or to a student in an examination). But usually you have some choice, especially in a composition course in which your subject is limited only by the type of paper you are asked to write.

Often it will be possible to take a subject completely familiar to you. Your experience, no matter how limited it may seem to you, will have many elements that are not common to everyone; at any rate the parts that really interest you are most likely to be interesting to others, in writing as in conversation. Your family, the people you have known either as individuals or as groups or types, your school experiences, your jobs, hobbies, sports, the places you have lived in or visited, your opinions and ideas, all offer material. It might prove useful early in a composition course to think over your more interesting experiences and make notes of those that are promising for future use in papers.

Often, too, your subject can grow out of your desire to extend your experience, to know more than you do about something in history, literature, economics, biology, or whatever else has aroused your interest. Except in course papers that call for routine summaries of material, choose a subject in which you will not be merely rehashing some stereotyped material or rewriting something you have read. Take one to which you can make some contribution, no matter how small, even though it may be no more than your attitude or opinion, or illustrations or applications drawn from your experience.

Sometimes circumstances will force you to write in a field that is unfamiliar or even on a subject that is unattractive to you. In some courses you may have to train yourself to do this competently–and remember that at least you are extending your stock of information. But ordinarily you will have some freedom in selecting a subject. When the paper is to be based on reading or other investigation of unfamiliar material, try to choose a subject that you have some curiosity about, so that you will feel you are learning something worth while as well as preparing a paper. Everyone would like to know more about scores of subjects that come up in conversation (What is NATO? Mercator's projection? Univac?) or that have been touched on briefly in a college course. There are the whole fields of history, science, literature, or social organization to choose from.

The aim is not only to get a good subject but to find one that is good for *you,* if possible one that you do or could or would like to *talk* about. An interest in your topic makes the rest of the work easier and will ordinarily lead to a good paper.

Obviously, the earlier you decide on a subject the more time you will have for the later stages. It is too late to decide what you will write about when you sit down to put words on paper; waiting until then for a subject to come to you wastes valuable time and may be completely discouraging.

Limiting a subject

A writer sometimes chooses a subject that is too small for a paper of the length he is attempting, so that he has to build it out by going into trivial detail or by touching on closely related matters. But students ordinarily choose subjects that are much too large. Most college papers are short; even one of 1000 words would make up only a single newspaper column, or a quarter of a typical magazine article, or a little over two pages in this book. The purpose of a paper is to enlighten a reader, to give him some special information or ideas, not just to remind him that the subject exists or to rehash familiar information on a general subject. Limit your subject to one that can be handled adequately in the length expected. Unless you were writing a very condensed article for a reference work, there would not be much point in writing 1000 words–or even 5000 words–on Benjamin Franklin, but something could be done in a short paper with some phase of Franklin's career, his work as postmaster general, his part in the founding of the University of Pennsylvania, his relations with other statesmen, or his life in Paris. Similarly, "education" or "labor unions" or "Sinclair Lewis" or "dress designing" are not subjects but fields, within which a great many possible subjects lie. The aim is to get a subject that can be adequately treated in the length of paper you are to write.

One way to narrow a subject is to consider the backgrounds and interests of your readers. This is especially important in treating well-known or commonplace subjects. A general topic like "Learning to Drive a Car" would probably be unsuccessful, because today almost everyone knows something about driving. If the writer considered what might be of use or interest to his readers, he would probably choose a narrowed and more specific subject, such as "School Driver Training Programs" or "Compulsory Inspection of Automobiles."

Another way to limit your subject is to work out a sentence statement. If you are not sure exactly what the aim of the paper is, try to define it in a sentence or two or in a question that will be answered by the paper. Suppose you are a ham radio operator and are going to "write about it." Several different papers could be written in this general field. You could tell about various types of equipment, building your own equipment, the legal regulations and procedure of getting a license, the abbreviations and language of ham operators, transmitting as a hobby, and so on. You might be tempted to say a little something about all of these, and as a result write so generally that you would tell your readers nothing new. But a sentence statement would record your choice among possibilities. It might be: "Government regulation of amateur radio protects both the public and the ham operator." Besides giving you a limited and workable topic, such a statement will prevent you from wandering off the subject in later stages of writing.

Sometimes the subject cannot be definitely limited until after some material has been gathered. This is especially true in writing long papers for which a working bibliography of books and articles must be assembled as part of this preliminary analysis. (See Ch. 13, "Reference papers," p. 363.)

Once you have selected and limited your topic, the first stage in writing is over. You should know pretty definitely what the paper is to be about and how and where you will get the material for it.

Gathering material

The material for letters and short papers about personal experiences may come spontaneously, but often even for these kinds of writing a little time given to jogging your memory may be well spent. For more elaborate papers, by far the largest part of your time will be taken in assembling material. This material-gathering stage is the most likely to be neglected by a hurried writer, but he should not wonder why he has trouble in writing a paper when the simple reason is that he hasn't enough to put down.

Your material comes from memory, from observation and experiment, from interviews with people, from reading and study, from reasoning and speculating on what you have learned in all these ways, and, for stories, from imagining scenes and actions. While it is hard to direct your memory, thinking about some past experience for a time and then recalling it at intervals can often bring back details that at first were forgotten.

Sources of material outside your own mind can be more consciously worked, and skill in handling them can be cultivated. In particular, your command of the direct sources of original material—observation, experiment, interviews—can be greatly improved by attention and practice. The habit of noticing details can help you in your writing, for a writer's chief distinction often comes from small bits of information which he has picked up from his own observation, and the interest and value of many papers rest on the amount of first-hand detail they carry. For some papers you may also need to know some of the methods of research used by scientists and scholars. (See Ch. 13, "Reference papers," p. 366.)

Very little of importance can be written without some interpretation or opinion concerning the "facts" assembled, and for critical papers in any field these reflections become the central material. (See Ch. 12, "Opinion papers," p. 324.) Opinions are by definition less certain than facts, but they can be well grounded in specific information. Common sense and practice in making interpretations and judgments, as well as training in logic and in critical techniques, can improve the reliability of your evaluations and conclusions. At any rate, reasoning and speculation supply an important part of the material of writing.

The material for short papers on simple and familiar subjects can usually be carried in your head, though often scratch notations are a help–they keep ideas from slipping away. More complex material requires a body of written notes.

Evaluating and selecting material

Since your assembled material will vary in its reliability and its importance for the particular paper to be written, you should go over, sort, and evaluate it. This is a stage for questions. If your paper is based on personal experience, you may ask whether the incidents selected are striking and meaningful. If your paper is based on reading or research, you will need to ask a number of questions: Is this statement accurate? Is this book reliable–in its facts, in its reasoning? Have I enough material for the paper proposed? Have I tried all the best sources? Can I get more material by talking with someone? Have the important phases been covered? Which are the most important facts and conclusions for my paper? Which are of secondary importance? What is of most interest and possible importance for my readers?

After the material has been gathered and thought through, check the relevance of your material in view of the purpose statement you made when limiting the subject. (With your material before you, you may want to revise your statement of the subject or make it more exact.) You will find it helpful to sort out essential points–those that must be included–and contributing points that may or may not be used, depending on circumstances in the actual writing.

The product of the third stage in writing should be a sifted body of material–material you are thoroughly familiar with, brought in line with the purpose of the paper, and selected after considering its accuracy, importance, and interest for your purpose.

Planning the paper

While you are evaluating and selecting the material for your paper you will also be thinking about the order in which the various points should stand. The plan—whether in your mind or on some scribbled notes or in a formally prepared outline—is a record of the order in which you expect to arrange the material.

Developing the plan

Your plan grows primarily out of your material, and you may make one or perhaps several outlines while you are selecting and evaluating content. A narrative paper can be planned early, since all that is required is to visualize the climaxes or incidents that will divide it into stages. But drawing up the actual working outline of an expository paper or revising a tentative outline into a final one must come at a relatively late point in the writing process.

The outline should arrange related material in a series of blocks or stages. It may be easier to see your main divisions if you list the important points, putting related ones together in columns or on separate slips of paper, or if you draw squares and jot down related matters in different squares. The labels for these groups of material will probably form the main heads of your plan or outline. Usually there will be three to five main heads. A paper with only two, unless it is very short, is likely to break in the middle. On the other hand, a fairly short paper with five or more heads is probably overdivided. In a paper of 1500 words or so, five points would average only 300 words apiece—and 300 words does not say very much. Even magazine articles of 6000 words rarely have more than five or six main divisions. Any outline of more than five main heads should be examined carefully to see if the material has really been put together properly or if perhaps too much is being attempted for a short space.

Next, the small special points can be arranged under the main heads to which they belong. Sometimes these points will in turn form several groups, which will stand under subheads in the outline.

After the main blocks are decided on, their order can be determined. There are two principal general plans for expository papers. One, which may be called the *order of support* (sometimes called *deductive*), begins with a general statement of the subject or idea, which is then developed in a series of specific supporting blocks. (See

Theme #3, p. 268.) The other, the *order of climax* (sometimes called *inductive*), begins with a specific fact or situation and then goes on unfolding the subject until at the end it stands complete. (See Theme #4, p. 268.) The first is more common in developing scientific and

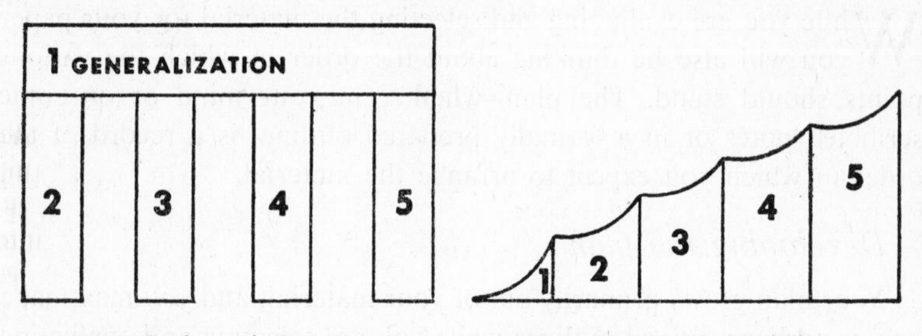

The Order of Support *The Order of Climax*

technical subjects and opinions that are methodically substantiated; the second is more common in popular and Informal papers. Whichever plan you follow, the last part of the paper should be the most important, meaningful, intense, or interesting part—it should emphasize the point or points that you most want the reader to get. Try to see your paper as a series of waves of increasing height (that is, of increasing value, not necessarily of increasing length). The beginning has the double duty of attracting the reader's interest and getting him into the subject. The last point is the one he is to carry with him. (See "Opening paragraphs," p. 165 and "Concluding paragraphs," p. 168.) In between, the topics can be arranged according to any reasonable plan that will advance the subject.

Types of outlines

An outline is a schematic statement of the material in a paper, showing the order of topics and the general relationship between them. While an outline can test the organization of a completed paper, the chief purpose of outlines is to facilitate writing. Once you have organized the material, writing is relatively easy. You can focus on one stage at a time. You can see how the whole will shape and don't have to worry whether to put a particular point *here* or wait until later—in other words, you can write with confidence. Scratch notes may be all you need for short, simple papers. But the longer the paper and the more complicated the material, the more important a plan, represented by some sort of outline, becomes.

Scratch outline. Most writing is done from very casual notes, jotted down with due attention to meaning but without regard to form. The points are grouped according to some system of the writer's own devising. Since the scratch outline is an entirely personal document, not to be shown to anyone else, there is no point in making suggestions for its form. Every writer should work out some method by which he can help himself sort out and organize his material to make it easier for him to write an orderly paper.

Topic outline. The most common type of formal outline is the topic outline. The subjects are noted in brief phrases or single words, numbered consistently as they are in the following example:

I Have Learned to Work [Title]

Learning to work in my early years has given me money for clothes and for my college education and has established habits that have been useful in many ways. [Sentence statement]

I. Early formation of work habits [Main head]
  A. Parents' warning against the evils of idling [Subhead]
  B. Required chores for all children in my family
  C. A newspaper route for fun and profit
II. Summer vacation work during my high school years
  A. Necessity of earning money
    1. For various school activities
    2. For my future college expenses
  B. Ways and means
    1. Selling popcorn and candy at baseball games
    2. Selling magazines and subscriptions
    3. Acting as lifeguard at seashore resort
III. Beneficial results of this work
  A. Practical results
    1. Many additional clothes and social activities
    2. A bank account for my college expenses
    3. Skills and contacts valuable for getting jobs during college vacations
  B. More permanent results
    1. Strengthening of character
      a. Avoiding mischief
      b. Habit of industry
    2. Realization of value of money
    3. Carry-over of work habits into academic life
    4. Development of self-reliance

Sentence outline. A sentence outline differs from a topic outline only in that each head and subhead is a complete sentence. It is more formal and requires more effort to draw up. Its chief advantage is that it forces the outliner to think through his ideas thoroughly in order to give them complete statement. The following outline is for a paper based on Stephen Crane's *The Red Badge of Courage.*

The Transformation of Henry Fleming

Henry Fleming's romantic ideas of war were destroyed in his first battle, but after running away he returned to his regiment and by overcoming his fear regained his confidence and became a man.

I. Henry's boyish idea of war underwent a change on the eve of battle.
    A. He had enlisted because he thought of war romantically and pictured himself performing heroic feats.
    B. A few days before his regiment was to have its first engagement, his idea of the glory of war was modified.
        1. He observed his fellow soldiers, listened to their boastful remarks.
        2. He began to doubt his own courage, feared he might run from danger.

II. He failed in the first test.
    A. As the regiment went into the firing line, he wished he had never enlisted.
    B. For a time he remained in the line and did his duty.
        1. He was bewildered.
        2. Feeling himself to be in a "moving box," he did as the others did about him.
    C. Overcome by fear, he finally turned and ran to the rear.
    D. As a skulker, he had a miserable experience.
        1. Discovering that his regiment had unexpectedly held its ground, he felt cheated.
        2. Joining a column of the wounded, he was shamed when asked about his own wound.

III. He regained his self-confidence.
    A. Dealt a blow on the head by a deserter, Henry rejoined his regiment, expecting to be ridiculed.
    B. When his fellow soldiers assumed that he had been wounded in action, Henry saw that his cowardice had passed unnoticed.
    C. In the next day's battle he acted creditably.
        1. Enraged at the enemy, he fought furiously and desperately.
        2. Praised by his lieutenant, he saw himself in a new light.
        3. He became color bearer and urged his fellows on to the charge.

IV. After this engagement, Henry was no longer his old self.
    A. He had had a chance to see himself in a new perspective.
    B. For a time he was tortured by thoughts of his cowardly conduct of the first day.
    C. Then he rejoiced at having become a man and overcome fear.

Paragraph summaries. It is sometimes helpful to prepare for writing a short paper by jotting down in advance the topic of each paragraph. But this method doesn't work well for long papers because it fails to distinguish subheads. This is the only type of outline in which the entries correspond exactly to the paragraphs of the paper.

Outline form

Most of the conventions of outline form are shown in the examples just given, but they are worth isolating for comment.

The title. The title of the paper should stand over the outline, but it is not a part of the outline and should not be numbered. The heads should carry their full meaning and not refer back to the title by pronouns.

Sentence statement. It is a good idea to put between the title and the first main head a sentence stating the subject and scope of the whole paper. If this is done it should be a full, meaningful sentence, not a mere announcement of the topic.

Numbering systems. The most widely used numbering system alternates letters and figures, as shown in the examples on the previous pages. Avoid intricate or confusing schemes of numbering.

Indention. Write the main heads flush with the left margin and indent subheads two or three spaces from the left–enough to make them clearly in a different column. Heads that run over a single line should be further indented, as in the sentence outline on page 256.

Punctuation and capitalizing. No punctuation is needed at the end of lines in a topic outline. In a sentence outline the punctuation should follow regular sentence practice. Only the first word of a head and proper names are capitalized; an outline head is not a title.

Meaningful heads. Each head should be meaningful, understandable by itself. This outline is useless:

My Vocation
- I. The work I am interested in
- II. Why I prefer this type of work
- III. What my responsibilities would be
- IV. The chances for success

Subheads should carry full meaning. General labels like "Causes" or "Results" are useless, as are these from an outline for a paper on "The House of Morgan":

- A. Started by Junius Spencer Morgan
  - 1. What he did
- B. Succeeded by J. P. Morgan I
  - 1. What he did
- C. Succeeded by J. P. Morgan II
  - 1. What he did

Meaningful heads are especially important in outlines which are to be shown to someone for criticism.

Heads of equal importance. The main heads of an outline, those usually marked by Roman numerals, should be of equal importance to the subject: they show the several main divisions of the material. Similarly, the immediate subdivisions of these heads, those usually marked by capital letters, should designate logical and equally important divisions of one phase of the subject. The same principle applies to further divisions under any subhead.

Unequal headings:	*Equal headings:*
Books I Have Enjoyed	Books I Have Enjoyed
I. Adventure stories	I. Adventure Stories
II. Historical novels	II. Historical novels
III. *Treasure Island*	III. Character studies
IV. Autobiographies	IV. Autobiographies
V. What I like most	V. Books on ethics and religion

Headings in parallel form. Parallel heads or subheads are expressed in parallel grammatical form. A sentence outline should use complete sentences throughout; a topic outline should use topic heads only. Topic heads or subheads should use parallel phrasing for all heads of the same rank; that is, the heads in one series should be all nouns or all adjectives or all phrases, or whatever is the most appropriate form.

Heads not parallel:	*Parallel heads:*
The Art of Putting	The Art of Putting
I. The stance is fundamental	I. The stance
II. The grip	II. The grip
III. Importance of the backswing	III. The backswing
IV. Stroking the ball	IV. The contact with the ball
V. Follow through with care	V. The follow-through

Division of topics. Since a topic is not "divided" unless there are at least two parts, an outline should have at least two subheads under any main head. For every heading marked *I* there should be at least a *II,* for every *A* there should be a *B,* and so on.

Illogical single heads	*Proper subdivision*
The Tripartite System of Government	The Tripartite System of Government
I. The executive branch	I. The executive branch
A. President and Cabinet	A. President
	B. Cabinet
II. The legislative branch	II. The legislative branch

A. The House	A. The House of Representatives
B. The Senate	B. The Senate
1. Functions	1. Special functions
	2. Special privileges
III. The judicial branch	III. The judicial branch
A. The Supreme Court	A. The Supreme Court
	B. Lower courts

If there is a single detail, it may be included in the heading. For example, for an organization in which the whole executive power lay in the president the head might be:

I. The executive branch (The President)

Sometimes an exception is made for an outstanding illustrative example, which may be put in an outline as a single subhead:

B. Injustice of grades in figures
  1. Example: My almost-Phi Bete roommate

Introductions and conclusions. Dividing a paper into "I. Introduction, II. Body, III. Conclusion" is bad practice. The introduction and conclusion to a paper are usually too short to need a special heading–the paper is all body. The first and last topics are from the main body of material, chosen with a special view to their fitness for meeting and for leaving a reader.

Position of outlines

If the outline is to be part of the final manuscript, it should be revised to represent the actual development of the finished paper. An outline of less than half a page may stand on the first page of a paper with the text beginning below it. A fuller outline should stand on a page by itself and be placed before the first page of text.

Writing the first draft

Of course some writing has been going on in the last three steps, but actual consecutive composition usually takes place as the fifth step in developing a paper. If the preliminary stages have been well done, this writing should be free from worry, perhaps even enjoyable. The feeling of being ready to write is the prime result of careful work in the early steps and the best guarantee of a good paper.

People's habits of writing differ greatly, but it seems safe to say that if you have thought over your subject you will be able to write several sentences without stopping (much), and that in time you should be able to write at least a whole paragraph at a time. Efficiency demands that you keep your attention fixed as much as possible on your writing; if you do pause, try to pause between paragraphs or between the larger stages of your paper.

If you are writing from a good outline it is easy to see the stages in the material and so concentrate on one stage at a time. A long paper should be broken up into sections (corresponding to the main heads of the outline) and each section should be written more or less by itself. Writing a paper of 3000 words may appear a dismaying task, but if it is thought of–and written–as a series of three or four discussions of different, although related, aspects of the subject, it will seem much more manageable. Another advantage of this method of composition is that if you bog down in one section, you may go to work on another. Then, having successfully finished the latter, you can return with renewed confidence to the section you found difficult. (If the writing of the various sections is done at different times, however, it is well to reread what you have already written before continuing.)

Try to make the first draft rather full. You may even include some material that at first may seem trivial or minor, because the inclusion of all the detail will help you later on to see what is relevant and important and what is not. It is always easier to take out unwanted matter than to fill in topics that have been done too sketchily.

Don't worry at the outset about getting an ideal opening–this is really a sort of procrastination. The paper must be started somehow, and it is better to make a tentative start, the best that suggests itself at the moment, and change it later if necessary. After a few pages you will find that you are writing better, and often you will find you have a good opening simply by crossing out the first paragraph or two.

Your paper will have more life and will represent your feeling for the material more closely if you write it rapidly than if you pause to perfect each sentence before going on to the next. Don't stop to look up spellings or to check mechanics as you write the first draft; these small but important matters can be better attended to in one operation after you have written the whole paper.

Since the first draft shows you for the first time your ideas expressed in words, you will expect to rework it. To make this revision easy, give the first draft plenty of space on the paper. Don't crowd the copy to the margins or let the lines stand so close together that you can't write new words between them. Some writers put only one paragraph on a page or use only the upper half of the sheet in the first writing, so that they have plenty of room for additions and alterations of all sorts. Work out some scheme of physical arrangement on paper so that your writing can be carried on conveniently.

Revising the paper

Few people work so exactly that their first draft represents the best they can do. In general, good writing is rewritten writing. With most of the task of actual composition completed, you can go over your work and improve it, sometimes in its larger arrangements, almost always in the details. This criticism and reworking should make the paper a more accurate and effective presentation of the subject you have chosen.

In revising, you take the point of view of a reader or critic as far as you can and look at your work to see how it will read. This means testing it for material, for plan, for style, and finally for the mechanics of writing.

Material

A check of material is necessary to make sure that enough has been put in the paper to achieve its intended purpose. Occasionally too much will be included, but not often. Usually the writer has become so familiar with the topic that he forgets to put in enough details to inform or interest his readers. The first questions then are: Is the material complete enough for my purpose? Do I need more examples or details? Do the facts given need more interpretation?

The accuracy of the statements should be checked; if you are uncertain about anything, the uncertainty should be acknowledged by words like *perhaps* or *probably*. The interpretations and opinions should be examined once more for their reasonableness and convincingness. A writer should always think: Would I like to read this paper? Could I profit from reading it?

Plan

Reading the almost completed paper will test its plan. Is space wasted at the beginning? Will the first few sentences appeal to a reader and make him want to continue? Do the opening sentences make clear what the paper is about? Is the subject advanced by clear-cut stages? Is the relation between one stage and the next shown? A paragraph which sounds like a new start, as if nothing has already been said, obviously needs attention. Does the conclusion leave the reader with the point you want him to carry away? Often irrelevant matters are brought in at the last, or the writing goes flabby or shows signs of haste. The beginning and ending of any paper need special attention in revision.

Style

You should look at the language of your draft, at the qualities of the paragraphs, sentences, and words that together make up its style. (The qualities are discussed in Chs. 6, 7, and 8.) This is not a question of correctness but of effectiveness. The English language gives you many choices in words and constructions and sentence movement, all in good standing but not all equally effective. You have read many passages that impressed you as vigorous and direct, accurate and clear, satisfying in their movement and their rhythm. And you have read others that somehow seemed shapeless and clumsy. With this experience to aid you, you can ask such questions as these: Does this word say just what I mean, or do I need to search for a more accurate one? Are there words which should be taken out because they add nothing to the sense? Is this long sentence confusing, or does it carry the reader easily to its end? Does each sentence seem to follow naturally from the preceding one, or do successive sentences appear disconnected? Is the style reasonably consistent? Have I used words from another variety of English which seem out of place here?

Many questions of this sort can best be answered by reading the paper aloud. The ear catches qualities which the eye may not see. For example, a shapeless sentence may be recognized even by a person unable to analyze its structure–he may find it difficult to read without stumbling.

Mechanics

Finally in revising, you should see to the spelling and capitalization of words you are unsure of and check punctuation and elementary grammatical matters. At this point, a good dictionary and the *Index* of this book are especially useful, since they answer many particular questions, and Chapters 2 to 5 give a background for checking these matters. This is the process of *proofreading* described on pages 42-43. The final copy of the paper should be proofread too.

Preparing the manuscript

The final step in writing a paper is preparing the manuscript for another person to read. This may be simply making a fair copy of a first draft, or, as in research papers, it may also involve preparing footnotes and a bibliography. Whether it is a letter, a class paper, or an article or book for publication, the aim is the same–to make a manuscript that reads easily and represents your best work.

Materials

The materials for copy have now been pretty well standardized. Paper 8½ by 11 inches is almost universally used, except in legal documents. For longhand copy conventional "theme paper" having lines about half an inch apart is best. Odd sizes do not handle or file well, and narrow-lined notebook paper makes hard reading. For typewritten copy use a fair grade of bond paper. Lined paper should not be used if copy is typed, and paper torn out of notebooks with spiral binders is not acceptable. Flimsy paper such as onionskin should not be used because it is difficult to handle and mark. Handwritten manuscripts should be in ink, although some instructors will permit pencil for themes written in class. Pale ink is often illegible, and colored inks are regarded by many as in bad taste; black or blue black is the best. For typewritten manuscripts a good black typewriter ribbon and clean type make a readable page.

The page

Leave comfortable margins at the ends of lines. A good right margin will not only improve the looks of a page but will reduce the number of words that have to be divided at the end of lines. An inch and a half at the left, an inch at the right, an inch and a half at the top, and an inch at the bottom are typical margins. Very short papers should be centered on the page.

Typewritten copy should be double spaced. An extra space can be left between paragraphs but is not necessary. More useful is an extra line left between the main stages of the paper.

In longhand copy the ascenders and descenders of letters like *b, l, f, g* should not be allowed to cut across letters on the line above or below, and letters easily confused (*a-o, n-u*) should be made clearly. The letters of a word should be connected so that the reader's eye can grasp the word at a glance.

Paragraphs are indented about an inch in longhand and from five to eight spaces in typescript. In typewritten manuscript it is better to start a new page than to allow the first line of a paragraph to stand alone at the bottom of a page, and it is better to avoid starting a new page with the last line of a paragraph.

Only one side of the sheet should be used.

Pages should be arranged in their proper order (it is surprising how many times they are not), and pages after the first should be numbered, preferably in the upper right hand corner and in Arabic numerals (2, 3, 4).

The title should be centered on the top line in longhand manuscript or about two inches from the top on unlined paper; the text should begin about an inch below. On lined paper leave the line below the title blank. A title should not be underlined or set in quotation marks unless it is an actual quotation. No end punctuation is necessary unless the title is a question or exclamation. Since the title is not a part of the body of the paper but is rather a label put upon it, the first sentence of the text should usually be complete in itself and not refer back to the title by a pronoun.

In long papers the use of subheads, centered in the line and spaced above and below, may be a helpful guide for readers.

Common practices that should be avoided are: (a) indenting the first line on a page when it is not the beginning of a paragraph; (b) leaving blank part of the last line on a page when the paragraph is continued on the following page; (c) putting punctuation marks, other than quotation marks or a dash, at the beginning of a line. A mark belongs with the word that it follows, not at the beginning of the next construction.

Endorsing the manuscript

Most course papers in college are folded vertically and endorsed near the top of the outside front fold, as the instructor may direct. Most teachers want to have available:

Student's name
Topic, title, or assignment of paper
Date submitted

Other facts, such as the number of the paper, the name and section of the course, or the instructor's name, may be put below these three lines. Clear and uniform endorsement is a real convenience to the teacher who must handle the papers.

If the papers are to be handed in flat, this endorsement should be on the back of the last sheet or on a special title page as the teacher directs. Sheets should be held together by paper clips that can be slipped off, not by fasteners that pierce the paper or by pins, hairpins, or string.

Corrections in copy

The final copy should be made as accurate as possible, but later corrections are sometimes necessary. If there are many, or if they are complicated, the page should be done over. If they are relatively minor, for instance adding a letter to a word or substituting or deleting a single word, they can usually be done neatly without damaging the page.

Words that are to be eliminated should be struck out by having a line drawn through them. (Do not use parentheses for this purpose.) Words to be added can be written in the margin or between the lines, and a caret (∧) inserted at the place where they belong. In correcting mistypings while the paper is still in the machine, erase completely and retype; do not merely strike over the wrong letters.

If you want to indicate the beginning of a paragraph in copy that you have written solid, put the paragraph symbol in the left margin and draw an angle before the first word of the new paragraph, like this:

> ¶ If you have formed either of these habits, you should break it. ⌊If you want to indicate the beginning of a paragraph in copy that you have written solid, put the paragraph symbol in the left margin and draw an angle

If you want to indicate that what you have written as two paragraphs should be joined as one, write *No ¶* in the left margin and if possible draw a line from the end of the preceding to the beginning of the following paragraph.

The goal is a clean, legible copy that can be read easily by someone else. Reading this final copy aloud rather slowly will be a good last check to make sure that mistakes have not slipped in during the copying.

From manuscript into print

The manuscript form is the final state of most college writing, but some of the papers in composition courses find their way into campus periodicals. Anyway, since the goal of much writing is publication and since a college graduate is almost certain to write something that will see publication of some sort, he should know something of this last stage. It may be merely a final check preparatory to mimeographing, or it may be an elaborate process of editing, revising at the suggestion of an editor, and proofreading, before the words are finally published. A number of books are available which deal minutely with such matters. A few of the more important details are treated in the *Index* articles *Proofreading and *Submitting manuscripts.

Perhaps this sketch of the writing process doesn't seem to pay much attention to the gliding of pencil on paper or to the click of typewriter keys. It stresses that putting words on paper is a result of other effort and that its success depends chiefly on the early steps. If you approach any job of writing with a sense of these stages, you will develop steadily in your actual and effective use of written English.

Chapter 9

SUGGESTED STUDY AND WRITING

1. The following themes were written at the beginning of the second semester of a composition course. Students were asked to diagnose their major writing problem and to suggest some sort of specific solution in a paper 300 to 500 words long.

Read these papers through once as a group; then study them individually to answer the following questions:

A) Which theme gives the most vivid and convincing description of the writer's problem?

B) Which one offers the most satisfactory solution?

C) What errors in usage, sentence structure, spelling, and punctuation do you find? Which paper is the most accurate?

1. My Writing Problem: Inaccuracy

1 Often in high school, and now in college, I recieved a C on a
2 theme that would ordinarilly have recieved an A or B. This grade was
3 because of my lack of accuracy in spelling, punctuation, and phras-
4 ing. Spelling has always been my major downfall in writing. I spend
5 too much time when writing a theme in looking up words in a dic-
6 tionary. Usually I know how to spell these words, but I am unsure
7 of myself and for safety's sake look the word up. The words that I
8 have trouble with are everyday words that any freshman in high
9 school should know how to spell, but I, a freshman in college, trip
10 up on them.

11 My punctuation trouble is minor, yet still annoying enough to
12 warrant corrective measures. In one theme I will continually avoid
13 using much punctuation. When I recieve the paper back, I am in-
14 formed that I have omitted necessary punctuation. In the next theme
15 I go wild and use so many comas and other marks that my paper
16 looks as if it were blasted with birdshot. This abundance of punctua-
17 tion makes my sentences choppy and tireing to the reader. I never
18 seem to find a desireable compromise.

19 Lack of subject-verb agreement has been my most outstanding
20 phrasing problem. When using long sentences, I often forget my sub-
21 jects number by the time I have used two or three verbs, or I find
22 that my verbs don't agree in tense.

23 These are my writing problems. I have had to find a solution to
24 each of them. Correcting my poor spelling is an almost impossible
25 task, so I must take measures to keep spelling mistakes out of my
26 written work. My only solution to this problem previously had been
27 to look up every word that I wasn't sure of. Now, however, I have
28 found that typing my themes corrects many spelling errors. In typing
29 you are forced to spell out almost every word as you type it. This
30 weeds out words that are misspelled from habit. The only defence I
31 have found against punctuation and phrasing errors is proofreading
32 and more proofreading. Each punctuation mark is tested for its
33 proper use, and punctuation omissions are looked for. Phrasing errors
34 are routed by isolating, and pairing subjects and verbs to see if they
35 are in agreement. Usually after all of this effort some errors sneak
36 through, but these are not bad errors. Eventually these precautions
37 will cure me of my carelessness.

2. A Big Problem

1 The greatest trouble that I have when writing a theme is restricting
2 the subject. No problem can be found that is more discouraging to
3 me than this problem. No one can fully realize what anxiety the re-
4 peated failure to restrict the subject properly in the eyes of the pro-
5 fessor can do to a person.

6 For an example, take the last theme I wrote. I have realized all
7 along that restriction is very fundamental to a good theme; therefore
8 with each new theme assignment I tried harder and harder to make
9 effective restrictions, but each time when I had finished and then had
10 reread my rough draft, I found that my topic went off in six different
11 directions at once. My last theme was my worst in this respect. My
12 rough draft showed all the evidence of confusion. Besides lack of di-
13 rection, it was too general; there was too much material to be
14 handled in a short theme; there were too many irrelevant details. I
15 was determined to restrict this theme. When I finally finished chop-
16 ping away at it. I had absolutely nothing left. I was right back where
17 I started from. What a waste of time and energy that was, and such
18 a strain on the nerves to work for hours and hours and then end up
19 with nothing! This time I vowed to find a solution to the problem.

20 With previous themes I had tried to solve my problem of restric-
21 tion after I had written my rough draft. I would strip down and pick
22 away at my draft until there was only a skeleton left. Examination
23 of the problem showed that it was best to do a good deal of thinking
24 and restriction before even attempting to write. The first thing to do
25 is to make a positive definition of your purpose for writing the
26 theme. This automatically restricts the topic somewhat. In addition
27 further restriction can be made by developing one particular point
28 of view. This narrows the subject even more. Finally, I decided that
29 to make an outline was invaluable. It not only helps determine your
30 purpose, it also acts as a check and as a result helps to restrict the
31 topic before the theme has gone as far as the rough draft. These solu-
32 tions are more easily stated than followed, but I hope that future
33 themes of mine will benefit from them.

3. To Gain Your Interest

1 Many times when our assignment calls for a theme, some students
2 are immediately confronted with the question of what to write
3 about. Others have no trouble choosing a topic but find that ac-
4 curate grammar and punctuation come hard. When it is my duty to
5 write a theme, I am bothered by having to try to write interesting
6 and pertinent details which will bring reality to my purpose. Often-
7 times I feel that either anyone who reads my theme might find it
8 uninteresting or he might not understand my purpose.

9 All too often it is easy to use dull, flat statements which have
10 meaning but do not add to the mental vision which a reader forms. I
11 think anyone would be more interested in reading something that
12 gives a clear picture and if my writing does not stir up some imagina-
13 tion it isn't very good. If I write about an old man driving a car the
14 reader might think well, so what? However if I mention that the car
15 has badly worn tires and a broken connection in the steering column
16 he would likely wonder about what might happen and read further
17 on without hesitation. Along this line another problem shows up. For
18 example, I could also say that the car is two-tone blue with rusted
19 chrome strips. Such a statement would not add anything to the idea
20 that the car is unsafe. It would only add extra, unimportant words
21 that might distract from the meaning.

22 It is not hard to see that using specific, useful details is one step
23 toward solving the problem of creating interest and expressing pur-
24 pose. I think that if, when I write a theme, I pay special attention to
25 each paragraph and each sentence, I can write better because I can
26 add things which give more lifelike visions, and I can omitt things
27 which serve only to add words and distract from the intended mean-
28 ing. I imagine the problem will always be present but these things
29 compose a helpful approach to it.

4. Grand Central

1 "Set aside a suitable place for your work and begin promptly.
2 Concentrate until you have finished the task." So Samuel Smith be-
3 gins his Successful Writing chapter of his book *Best Methods of*
4 *Study*. Mr. Smith evidently has never lived in a college dorm, or he
5 would not so matter-of-factly assume that a "suitable place" (which
6 he later defines as "one isolated and quiet") is something one just
7 naturally finds in college life. For a person whose biggest problems
8 in theme writing are inspiration and concentration, Mr. Smith's ad-
9 vice is rather quixotic.

10 The natural place to do my work would seem to be at my own
11 desk in my own private room during the quiet of evening study
12 hours. Not so. The room is *not* private and the study hours are *not*
13 quiet. Take tonight, for example. I have been going through my usual
14 frenzied process of trying to find a topic. This involves much leafing
15 through newspapers and magazines, and a careful inspection of sur-
16 roundings in search of some idea stretchable to three hundred words.
17 After sharpening my pencil, finding paper, cleaning my desk drawer,

18 and turning off the radio, I finally settled down to the desk thinking
19 that the worst was over. I waited for ideas to flood my ready mind.
20 The doorknob rattled, and in walked one of the girls carrying
21 her Spanish book. "Say, pal, I'm having a little trouble with this
22 translation. . . ." Half an hour later she was animatedly describing
23 the "doll" who sits next to her in psychology class. As soon as I
24 could, I explained that I just had to get a theme written, so I'd have
25 to get down to work.
26 I started a tentative first sentence, chewed thoughtfully on my
27 Venus Velvet #2, and sat. Somewhere down the hall Lawrence Welk
28 was bubbling away. Next door Darlene energetically practiced her
29 cheerleading. After a while a new steady was thrown into the
30 shower, kindness of hordes of shouting friends. The shower is right
31 across from my room, so I got all the sound effects. I decided that
32 the quickest way to end the noise was to help get her wet and finish
33 the thing. So I did. Then I put on dry clothes and sat down again.
34 The doorknob rattled, and Vinnie came in and plopped dejectedly
35 on my bed, staring into space. "Hi," I ventured. "I didn't get a
36 letter," she bravely began, and then snuffled loudly into my stuffed
37 tiger. An hour later she smiled wanly as she left and said, "Thanks
38 a lot for listening to all my troubles."
39 After another friend had come in to borrow my new black crew
40 neck for that quick run over to Old Main for late coffee with HIM
41 (She probably wouldn't even take her coat off!), and another one
42 came to try out her new "Sammy Davis Swings," I was close to
43 despair.
44 Quiet reigned once more, but not for long. In bounded my room-
45 mate, returning from one of her myriads of committee meetings.
46 "My gosh!" she shouted, "I've simply been starving all night. Let's
47 go down to the kitchen and pop some corn. Quick, before lights out!
48 Or should you be doing something instead?"
49 Do you blame me for jumping up and shouting, "Okay, I haven't
50 got a thing to do!"?

2. Analyze your own writing experiences to determine what your strengths and weaknesses are. Answering the following questions will help get at some of the more important problems:

A) What kinds of writing (themes, term papers, letters, newspaper articles) have you done and how often? Which do you like most? Least?

B) What subjects do you prefer? Personal experiences (vacations, sports, family affairs)? Argumentative topics (current problems in school, national politics)? Informative subjects (history, new scientific discoveries, how-to-do-it papers)?

C) Which do you prefer, writing in class or at home? What are the special problems of each?

D) How do you go about writing? What preliminary steps do you take? Do you use an outline or notes?

E) What steps in the writing process give you the most difficulty? Picking a topic? Getting enough material? Writing the opening or closing paragraph?

F) How do you revise your writing, and what portion of your time do you spend in revision? What weaknesses do you have to watch for most closely (paragraphing, sentence structure, spelling, punctuation)?

G) What demands will your future college courses and your probable vocation place upon your writing skill?

3. For future reference in selecting topics to write on, draw up two lists of possibilities: (a) From your past experience make an inventory of interesting places you have been, people you have known, movies and plays you have seen, sports events, hobbies, jobs, problems—anything that you think might make for interesting writing and good reading. (b) Prepare a list of subjects for investigation. These may range from the production of prefabricated houses to the authorship of the Homeric epics.

4. Arrange each of the following groups of topics so that the most specific is at the bottom, the most general at the top. Then decide which topics would be best for papers of 500 words and 1000-1200 words.

A) George Washington Bridge
toll collection on George Washington Bridge
bridges of the twentieth century
modern suspension bridges
traffic control on George Washington Bridge

B) how much power should student governments have?
how a student body president should conduct meetings
principal duties of a student body president
student government
electing student officers

C) Dior's contributions to dressmaking
creations by Dior
twentieth-century fashions
Dior's "new look"
modern French dress design

D) choral music of Bach
Bach's B Minor Mass
choral music since Bach
choral requirements for Bach's B Minor Mass
history of religious music

5. Take a very general subject like government or nursing or sports and make a list of gradually narrowing topics, ending with three or four that would be suitable for a 500-word paper. Be prepared to write on any of these that your instructor chooses.

6. Criticize the form and content of the following outline and suggest specific improvements wherever possible.

American Opera: The First Hundred Years

Though opera in America was limited at first by circumstances, its gradual but sure development revealed the strong need for this art form among the American people.

I. The New Setting for Opera
  A. Limited by struggle to live
  B. Opera didn't fit present life
II. First Performances

A. *Flora*
   1. February 18, 1735
   2. Charleston, South Carolina
   3. Quality of performance
      a. Singing
   4. Attendance

B. *The Beggar's Opera*

C. Audience
   1. Fashions
   2. Divided by classes

III. Types of Early Operas
   A. Ballad operas
      1. Plots concerned with daily life
      2. Used popular tunes for music
   B. Folk operas
      1. Plots based on folklore
      2. Music derived from traditional tunes

IV. How Presented
   A. Traveling stock companies
      1. Limited wardrobe and settings
      2. Limited number of artists

V. Expansion of American Opera
   A. French influence
      1. French popularity after Revolution
      2. French operas in New Orleans
   B. Italian influence
      1. Steamboat
      2. Visits by Italian touring companies
      3. Erection of first permanent opera house in New York by Lorenzo da Ponte

VI. Conclusion

7. Take the following sentences and arrange them in a three-level outline to support the following central statement:

Problems in the social adjustment of a gifted child arise partly from his heredity and partly from his environment.

1. In play, the talented child will prefer older companions, but they may ignore him.
2. Mary K., for example, was capable of becoming an accomplished painter, writer, and even a mathematician.
3. More often the gifted child comes into conflict with his environment.
4. Frequently one person will have remarkable ability in both music and mathematics and cannot decide which should be vocation, which avocation.
5. Occasionally problems are created for the gifted child by certain combinations of hereditary traits.
6. Very often the gifted child will be superior in many areas, making vocational guidance difficult.
7. Parents may not realize a child's superior intelligence and unintentionally retard his development.

8. The gifted child may inherit remarkable musical abilities but may be rather poor in verbal skills.
9. Teachers may have difficulty providing him with enough work and he may become a nuisance.

8. Fill in the blanks in the skeleton outline with topics from the list below.

How to Buy a Used Car

In buying a used car, the customer should pay little attention to the salesman's blandishments and the shiny exterior and concentrate on what is under the hood.

I. Salesmen's appeals to the customers' weaknesses
  A. ______________________________
    1. Low price
    2. ______________________________
      a. ______________________________
      b. Many long years to pay
    3. ______________________________
      a. Automatic shift
      b. ______________
      c. Power steering
      d. Horn that plays a tune
  B. Appeals to pride
    1. ______________________________
    2. The prestige of a later model
II. ______________________________
  A. Finish almost like new
  B. ______________
  C. Wrap-around windshield
III. ______________________________
  A. Performance of motor at high speeds
  B. Condition of rings and valves
  C. ______________
  D. Condition of minor parts
    1. Filters
    2. Spark plugs
    3. __________

Topics: (1) Radio and heater
(2) Miles of well-polished chrome
(3) State of the transmission system
(4) Keeping up with the Joneses
(5) Appeals to the pocketbook
(6) Extras for less
(7) The lure of the lovely exterior
(8) Fan belt
(9) Easy credit terms
(10) The hard facts under the hood
(11) Low down payment

It takes a great deal of experience to become natural.

WILLA CATHER

Chapter 10

Personal experience papers

Any man's available speech material is a complete record of his conscious experience as far as he remembers it. . . . The words and phrases that he has at his disposal, if they could be collected, would serve as an index to his life, his reading, and what he has been told.

E. H. STURTEVANT

This chapter and the next three describe various types of papers. Some of them resemble papers written in other college courses, and most are also similar to articles published in newspapers and magazines. All of them involve skills discussed in previous chapters and require competence in developing paragraphs, writing effective sentences, and using appropriate words.

The least complicated in material and arrangement is the personal experience paper. The material for this comes from your own life; no research is needed other than jogging your memory to bring back the details of some past incident. The plan more or less takes care of itself because it is based on time, the simplest order in which a paper can be arranged. And if your topic is interesting to you and well expressed, it is very likely to be interesting to your readers. You may find the personal experience paper your most enjoyable and satisfying type of writing.

Topics suitable for a paper

Personal experience papers are a type of *narrative;* that is, events are described in the order of their happening, with little analysis or comment. In a narrative you don't attempt to explain or prove an idea; your purpose is to re-create an experience so vividly that the reader shares it.

The first step is to choose an interesting experience to tell. Students often feel that their own lives are too humdrum to be interesting to a reader. They write about the possibilities of space travel or the eating customs of Trobriand Islanders instead of a hike to Bear Mountain or a summer job as a carpenter's assistant. The remote topic often seems attractive, but its attraction is usually deceptive. When the writing actually begins, no material is available except vague generalities and second-hand information recalled from reading.

Sometimes a student looks only for spectacular events—narrow escapes and last-minute rescues. But ordinary events can make good topics, and they are certainly more plentiful. "Doing" is the basis of narrative; since no one lives without doing things, anyone's life is filled with incidents suitable for papers. You may not be interested in writing about the events of your life, but you must be interested in the events themselves. A football rally, a country fair, a surfboard ride —topics like these can be made interesting if they held your interest when they occurred.

Events that happened some time ago often make the most effective narratives. Memories of childhood—either pleasant or unpleasant—are vivid and sharply focused. The reminiscence can be viewed more objectively than an episode that took place yesterday afternoon. Also, some of the difficult task of selection has been done without effort—the memory has filtered out irrelevant and colorless details. Whatever its origin, the topic should be one that arouses your interest. An incident that affected you in some way can be developed more effectively than one that left you indifferent.

Single episodes

The simplest topic is a single episode—one action with definite time limits. The following list merely suggests the wide range of possible topics for papers of this kind:

A visit to Walden Pond
Digging for clams
The worst day in basic training
My first formal dance
Entertaining my father's boss
The first thing I remember
The great May blizzard
The locker room between halves
Trimming our Christmas tree
My first boat trip
Painting the garage
The day the governor came to town

Because each of these topics involves a single event, a paper written on any of them would be unified in time and place. They are intended as examples rather than specific topics and each of them might be adapted to fit your own experiences (for example, *A visit to* a television station, a planetarium, the dean's office). You will find it helpful to make a list of topics that you could develop as simple narratives.

The simplicity of a one-action paper can be seen in a student's notes for a paper on an evening spent baby sitting:

Central idea: A baby sitter has all of the exasperating difficulties that a mother does and none of the rewards except for her fifty cents an hour.

1. Agreeing to stay with neighbor's children
2. Meeting the children
3. Trying to entertain them
4. Putting them to bed
5. Drinks of water and one more story
6. Peace at last

Some of the topics in this list would take up several paragraphs in the paper, others only a sentence or two. All together, they would describe the events of a single evening. (See pages 292-294 and 295-296 for examples of single-episode papers.)

Several related incidents

A paper covering several related incidents is usually fairly long. The individual events are somewhat separated in time and are selected from a larger series of events. You pick the most interesting and most revealing ones and usually show the relation between them or their relation to the central idea. A week or a month at a summer camp might be covered in one paper, if only a few vivid incidents were selected as samples to represent the whole experience. An account of learning some skill like playing bridge or swan-diving or developing pictures would probably require this kind of treatment. The chief advantages of a paper like this are the wider range in time and place, the full development of an attitude or a situation, and the possibilities for effective use of contrast. The chief dangers are confusing time shifts, vague, generalized development, and failure to tie the various episodes together.

The narrative paper covering several incidents can be illustrated by notes for a 750-word paper on near-sightedness:

Central idea: Ever since I can remember, being near-sighted has caused me embarrassment and inconvenience.

1. When I was a meek little freshman in high school, a senior invited me to a dance. I was so thrilled that I ignored my mother's advice and didn't wear my glasses. (Narrative)

2. Although dances have caused me much embarrassment, learning to drive a car was more frightening. (Narrative of the first lesson)

3. After I had learned to drive, parking was my chief worry. (Two incidents—scraping the fender and backing into Alumni Hall)

4. Besides dancing with a partner I don't recognize and trying to drive along a whitish blur, I am plagued by several minor difficulties.

(Three incidents–not recognizing hostess at a party, trying to study in the library, and picking out clothes)

The seven incidents to be combined in this paper all took place at different times. Obviously, more transitional material would be needed than in the paper on baby sitting.

Narratives of development

A somewhat more complex type of narrative is one dealing with a person, showing his development over a period of time or illustrating his characteristics through sample episodes. The episodes may reveal some of his character traits–ways in which he differs from other people–or they may show experiences that have influenced him. A person who stirs your curiosity and interest is a suitable subject for this kind of paper. Anyone you know well–a roommate, a football coach, a relative, an Army sergeant, an employer–is a potential subject.

Strangely enough, a person may be too familiar to be a good subject. If you try to write about someone you see every day–a traffic policeman, a drug store counterman, or a janitor–you may discover that you have been seeing him as part of the landscape and not as an individual. It is also sometimes difficult to individualize someone to whom you feel a strong emotional tie; a paper about your mother, your sweetheart, or your best friend can easily become sentimental. The best subject is a person you see objectively and understand as an individual.

In a paper about her favorite uncle, a student followed this general plan:

Central idea: Uncle Max usually seemed too busy taking orders from Aunt Ruth to notice me, but I felt a deep affection for him and I still do.

1. Taking me to the zoo when I was seven (streetcar ride, visit to monkey house, seeing giraffes, eating hot dogs, explaining to Aunt Ruth why we were late)
2. At Christmas (incidents when I was eight, eleven, and thirteen)
3. At my high school graduation

Although the notes are simpler, this narrative would be somewhat more complex than the near-sightedness essay because it not only tells of separate happenings but also analyzes the writer's attitude toward her uncle.

A similar selection of specific scenes would be followed in showing the development of a family, a club, a business, or even a community that you have seen change and have taken part in. And it could easily be applied in writing a section of your autobiography. Instead of just following the calendar, you could select interesting and revealing incidents and present them in clear scenes, so that a reader might see the events that have had some influence on you or that illustrate some of your characteristics.

Tactical decisions

You cannot just pick a topic and start to write a narrative paper. You need to think through the material and decide how it can be made interesting to the reader. If the incident you choose is so familiar that you take its details for granted, it is helpful to back away mentally and imagine how it would have appeared to an observer. Thinking about some past experience for a time and recalling it at regular intervals helps stir up forgotten bits of information. One image will suggest another—the memory of a picnic table covered with a checkered tablecloth may set up a chain of associations that bring back a dozen other details.

In your preliminary survey of the material you must make some important decisions: the overall impression or effect—the "meaning"—of the experience, the point of view most suitable to the material, the kinds of narrative to be used, and the time pattern of the incidents. These decisions are not made in any set order; at least one is usually made for you by the nature of the material. But all are important and should be considered before actual writing begins.

General effect

A narrative of personal experience is not expected to develop an abstract idea, but it should have some central meaning and a unified effect. As the action begins to shape itself in your mind, you should ask what it means. What will be the dominant purpose of the paper, the center of the reader's interest? Your purpose gives direction to the planning, to the selection of details, and to the actual writing.

Stating the central purpose in one sentence is a good test of a topic. The sentence itself may be expressed in the paper, or it may be only implied. But if you cannot formulate your general purpose in one sentence, you probably need to narrow your topic to bring it more sharply into focus. Such general interpretations are made naturally in conversation, and imagining how you might introduce your narrative in telling it to a friend may suggest a usable purpose statement.

The statement of your purpose should be simple and narrow. No one expects a profound philosophical message in a paper on "My First Date." "The services of the medical profession are of inestimable benefit to mankind" is pretentious in breadth and in style for an account of an appendectomy; much better would be the simple statement, "While I was in the hospital for an appendectomy I began to appreciate the work of doctors and nurses." A few words (for example, *interesting, impressive, important, exciting*) are overworked in the purpose statement. If you use one of them, be sure that it is justified by your material.

Point of view

Before starting a rough draft, you should decide what point of view is best suited to your material and your purpose. Defined most simply, point of view means the pronoun by which the writer refers to himself. Some novelists (Henry James, Joseph Conrad, and William Faulkner, for example) have experimented with various points of view, and these subtle variations are a complex feature of their techniques. In factual narrative, however, point of view is relatively simple; a paper can be written in first, second, or third person. The chief necessity is to select the one that is most appropriate and to maintain it consistently throughout your paper.

The *I* (or *we*) paper is by far the most common in narrations of experience. The first person lends itself naturally to autobiographical narrative or to any account in which the writer plays a leading role. Sometimes a student feels that too many *I*'s are offensive, but they are usually less conspicuous than they seem. The "I was there" account has the credibility of personal testimony, the vivid directness of firsthand observation. If you substitute *she* for *I* in the following excerpt from an account of a German prison at the moment of its liberation, much of the tension and excitement is lost:

> Stepping over my cellmates, I got the stool that was our one piece of furniture, put it under the window, climbed onto it, rested one knee in a dent in the wall that we had made for just that purpose, and raised myself into a position from which I could grip the bars and look out. There was only a shimmer of daylight left; the stars were visible, and so was the moon. My eyes were already accustomed enough to the dark to see quite well. Below was our exercise yard, and beyond it the prison wall, and then the roofs of some buildings outside the wall and, a bit farther away, the few yards of sloping street that provided our only glimpse of normal life. I now concentrated on that fragment of street, and could just make out the whitish streak of pavement between the dark walls

of houses on either side. But there was nothing to see. My hands hurt from clinging to the bars, my knee from scraping against the rough cement of its support. I was almost ready to drop to the floor, defeated, when a lighted bus lurched down my little section of the street. Not only were its headlights on but its interior lights as well, enabling me to discern a few vague human shapes inside before it disappeared. One has to have lived through five years of blackout to imagine the utter incongruity of a bus with lights on, both inside and out. I dropped back down in such excitement that I kicked over the stool and landed on top of Mickey. "They're here!" I shouted. "They're here! I just saw them! There was a big bus with all its lights on!"—HENRIETTE ROOSENBURG, "The Journey Home," *The New Yorker,* Nov. 24, 1956, p. 70

Once you have limited yourself to a first-person point of view you should be consistent. The reader may be confused if he is told not only what you are thinking, but what everyone else in your story thinks. It is natural to describe what you—the teller—think and feel; but other characters can only be known by their appearance, conversation, and actions. You can say that Uncle Bill *seemed* to be thinking about getting back to the office, but if you say "Uncle Bill was thinking that he should get back to the office," you violate credibility, for in life you never really know what goes on in anyone's mind but your own. Here is an example of shifted point of view:

I pulled over and stopped the car, wondering what the policeman wanted and what I'd tell my father if I got a ticket. [Shift] The policeman thought to himself that kids who can't remember to turn on the headlights shouldn't be given licenses. But he softened up when he saw how scared I was.

[Revised:] I pulled over and stopped the car, wondering what the policeman wanted and what I'd tell my father if I got a ticket. Just as the officer came up to the window I noticed I'd forgotten the headlights. *I suspected* he was thinking that kids who can't remember to turn on the headlights shouldn't ge given licenses. But he *seemed to* soften up when he saw how scared I was.

The second person is seldom used throughout a paper, but it may be effective in a generalized or typical bit of narrative, especially if you are giving directions the reader might follow. Though less intimate than the first person, *you* may have a similar suggestion of participation. It invites the reader to share the experience or the mood. The following paragraph takes the reader directly into the scene:

When you awake in the morning the air is clean and cold in the mouth as water from a hill stream. You listen—and hear the silence. With the odd feeling of having been transported magically into some boyhood memory, you turn your head on the pillow and through the window see the ancient Caledonian pines on the lower slopes and, beyond them, the mountaintops. This is the deer forest and you are here.

—From "Deer Stalking in the Highlands" by Neil M. Gunn. First published in *Holiday*. Copyright © 1957 by The Curtis Publishing Company.

Used impersonally, *you* is evasive and ineffective. It is employed more or less as a substitute for "one" or "a person." Sometimes, when an incident takes an embarrassing turn, the writer shifts temporarily to *you*. To a statement like the last sentence of the following paragraph, a reader is likely to retort mentally, "Who, me?"

> During the freshman reception I stood in line for an hour to get a cup of punch. No one spoke to me except a gray-haired lady, who asked me if I had seen the dean. "Not since I registered last spring," I answered. She looked at me suspiciously, and I realized my mistake. You often make silly remarks like that in a strange situation where you feel embarrassed and out of place.

Occasionally in student papers the writer refers to himself in the third person, especially when writing about a typical or representative experience of "a new camper" or "the average freshman." More common and more effective is the "observer's point of view," in which the writer refers to himself as *I* and to his subject as *he, she,* or *they*. This point of view is especially effective in a narrative sketch written to characterize a person. In the following paragraph the writer (I) recalls his high school English teacher (he):

> Very different was dapper Mr. Groce, our teacher of English composition and literature, a little plump man, with a keen, dry, cheerful, yet irritable disposition, a sparkling bird-like eye, and a little black mustache and diminutive chin-beard. I suspect that he was too intelligent to put up patiently with all the conventions. Had he not been a public-school teacher, dependent on the democratic hypocrisies of a government committee, he might have said unconventional things. This inner rebellion kept him from being sentimental, moralistic, or religious in respect to poetry; yet he *understood* perfectly the penumbra of emotion that good and bad poetry alike may drag after them in an untrained mind. He knew how to rescue the structural and rational beauties of a poem from that bog of private feeling.—GEORGE SANTAYANA, *Persons and Places,* p. 157

The level of language and the tone of a paper are closely related to point of view. A recollection of a third-grade Christmas party might be written in a child's language or in adult language, but the two should not be awkwardly intermingled. The language must be accurate and appropriate. A falseness sometimes creeps into personal writing, even though the student writes naturally and simply in other kinds of papers. Because he feels self-conscious in writing about himself or because his subject has strong emotional connotation for him, he slips into an artificial style—flowery, trite, sentimental language.

The tone of a paper depends on the distance from which a writer views his subject matter; it may be formal or informal, light or serious, subjective or objective. Tone is an intangible quality which can be sensed but cannot be analyzed. In the following selection the point of view, the language, and the tone are all inconsistent:

> The game that would terminate the Little League play-offs was about to commence. I strolled nonchalantly to the second base bag and gave it a kick, as I had seen professional players do. My dad was sitting in the first row. He was sure that I would bobble the first grounder that came my way. I was confident that nothing so ignominious would occur. My buddy, who was pitching, took his last practice pitch. He desperately hoped that the first batter would not succeed in reaching base. I spotted the catcher heaving the ball down to second and hastened over to take the throw.

Such writing is as distracting as a singer who is off key. The point of view should suit the material, and the language should suit the point of view. With the heavy words (*terminate, commence, nonchalantly, ignominious, hastened*) taken out and the point of view controlled, the passage might read like this:

> The last game of the Little League play-offs was just starting. From the field I spotted my father sitting in the first row. He looked as if he thought I'd bobble the first grounder that came my way, but I was feeling pretty sure of myself. I walked over to the second base bag and gave it a kick the way professional players do. Then I saw my buddy taking his last practice pitch, and when the catcher tossed to second, I ran over to take the throw.

Kinds of narrative movement

Narratives can be classified in three broad types–generalized, summarized, and dramatized–depending on how much time is covered and how close the reader is brought to the action.

The least common is *generalized* narrative–repeated or representative actions used to describe typical events, to characterize a person in his habitual actions, or to show a way of life by telling of usual or customary actions. The verbs are often formed with *used to* or *would.* Adverbs like *always* or *frequently* also generalize the action, as in this account of a father's automobile driving:

> Dad always blamed the clutch for these bucking starts, and in fact carried a face-saving can of Neatsfoot Oil in the tool kit, so that he could annoint the clutch after particularly embarrassing takeoffs which ended in stalls.
>
> To drive with Dad through Nantucket's alley-sized streets was a spine-chilling, as well as a neck-cracking, experience. And it didn't add to our peace-of-mind to know that scores of Nantucketers, including

some of the old surrey-driving cap'ns were just learning how to operate cars.

There weren't any stop-streets in those days, but I doubt if Dad would have stopped anyway. He usually chose to ignore warning signs, on the grounds that compliance would only encourage the city fathers to new dictatorial extremes, such as cluttering up the beautiful landscape with even more signs. He also insisted that the Nantucket speed limit, plainly marked at twenty-five miles an hour, was probably meant to apply only to horses.—FRANK B. GILBRETH, JR., *Of Whales and Women,* p. 224

Summarized narrative gives a condensed account of actions and events. The reader does not "see" the action taking place but is told what happened. This is the characteristic method of historical and biographical writing and of personal narratives that cover a fairly broad time span. The following excerpt from a short story condenses what might be an hour's conversation into one paragraph:

I don't believe we were so much as nodding acquaintances until our third year. I thought of him, when I did, primarily as the owner of a red Chrysler convertible. The first talk we ever had was in the wrestling room. Don had come down there with the notion of scaring up material for a column about one of the obscure teams. His idea, a strange one for the man about to take over as football manager, was that too much attention had been lavished on the major sports. He found me alone, the others having taken off to the showers. I was trying to make weight, in one of those putrid rubber shirts. Don squatted on the edge of the big mat, and we talked for an hour or more. I showed him how to apply a windmill hip lock. He told me he was worried about how to keep Telford, our best halfback, in college for senior year. Telford's family had run out of money. "I may have to put the arm on some alumnus," he said. And that is just what he did, as it turned out.—EDWARD NEWHOUSE, "The Bromley Touch," originally published in *The New Yorker,* May 18, 1957, p. 34

Summarized narrative is not usually so vivid as an actual scene, but it is economical in that it covers a good deal of time in a short space. When it is well written it gives a sense of rapid movement. It is most often found in the narration of events less important or less interesting than those of the scenes, in episodes learned at second hand rather than from observation, and especially in the preparation for scenes. Summarized narrative used before a scene usually tells briefly what happened between it and the preceding scene or gives the setting and present situation so that the action can move rapidly without explanatory interruption.

A *dramatized* narrative presents an action more fully, in direct scenes. As a rule, it includes conversation and details that give a relatively complete picture of a happening. It usually is more vivid than the other two types because it *shows* the reader an action instead of merely telling him what it was:

"But," I said to Bob as we were looking over our first issue and groaning over the forty-two typographical errors, "my name isn't on the masthead."

Bob raised an eyebrow. "Well," he said, "what do you know about being an editor? You can't expect to have your name on the masthead until you can do everything, from make-up to the final fold."

"That's a fine thing," I retorted. "Here I thought this was a partnership, that we would be co-editors."

"You've got to prove yourself." Bob had a maddening gleam in his eye. "You never get anything for nothing in this world."

I clenched my fists and went back to rewriting the Upandatit Bible Class meeting for the fourth time. Working for your husband, I decided, wasn't quite the lark I had imagined it to be.—JANE S. MCILVAINE, *It Happens Every Thursday*, p. 45

The methods of generalized, summarized, and dramatized narrative are used in various combinations. Much of your success in writing about your own experiences will depend on your ability to judge which method is best suited to a particular episode. Your narrative paper will be made up mostly of interlocking summaries and scenes—and should contain some good scenes. An example of how the three types of movement work together is in this incident in the life of a national park ranger and his wife:

[Generalized:] It seems Bill is always on duty. If we are making a social call, driving into the city—inside the park or out—he never passes up anything that looks suspicious, or a person who might be in need of help. [Summarized, the immediate situation:] We were on our way to church one Sunday when he spied a car parked on a deserted stretch of road, and he stopped to look it over. The car was unoccupied, and nothing about it appeared unusual—I would have guessed that it belonged to a fisherman who was down at the river teasing the trout. But before continuing, Bill paused for a quick survey of the surrounding area—and stopped. [Dramatized, direct action:] Barely visible through the dense shrubbery was the deathly white face of a woman staring directly at us.

"You all right?" Bill called.

The woman's lips moved spasmodically, but she made no reply.

"Don't move!" he yelled, seizing his gun from the seat beside me.

He disappeared into the brush, and a moment later I heard a shot. Then he was making his way back to the road with the woman, unconscious, in his arms.

"Fainted," he said, laying her on the pine needles while he treated her for shock.

"What happened?"

[Summarized, past events learned from conversation:] It seemed the woman had been attracted by the profusion of wild flowers growing off the road and while preoccupied had stepped on a rattlesnake. Luckily her foot rested so near the snake's head that it couldn't strike, but she knew the second she raised her foot to make her escape it would instantly sink its fangs into her ankle. She had stood there with the snake rattling and curling about her legs for what must have seemed hours before we happened along. When Bill shot off its head, her relief was so intense she fainted in his arms. When Bill asked her afterwards why she didn't jump when she stepped on the snake, she said she had been too frightened to move.—MARGARET MERRILL, *Bears in My Kitchen,* pp. 145-6

Time sequence

A narrative follows a time order. One action follows another as it happened in the original experience. Of all the ways to develop a paper, a plan based on time is the easiest to keep clear. Since we live chronologically from second to second, hour to hour, and day to day, we frequently think or remember in a time order.

The time span of narrative may vary greatly, from a few minutes to several weeks or even years. Generally speaking, the shorter the time span the fewer problems you will have. If a long period of time is covered by several episodes, clear-cut transitions are needed. If the action is short and continuous, most or all of the narrative can be dramatized. If several events are covered, more of the action must be generalized and summarized.

Occasionally you may want to shift temporarily to an earlier time —the "cutback" or "flashback" used so often in movies and television plays. Such an interruption of the time order is often effective in compressing the time span and in avoiding long preliminary explanations. A cutback is usually summarized narrative, but it may be dramatic. The shift in time should be unmistakably clear and should seem a natural part of the paper. It is often signaled by an expression like "I remember" or "that was when." The following selection is from an account of a man's visit aboard a carrier on which he served twelve years before. The cutback is obviously well suited to such a subject.

> The end of the gangway, where I was standing, rested on the hangar deck. The deck looked narrower than I remembered it. There was a bulkhead that hadn't been on the old Randolph. I told this to the petty officer, and he said that there were spaces on the other side of the bulkhead, and that the flight deck above was wider than it used to be, with a greater overhang. I noticed that a couple of whaleboats and motor launches and the captain's gig were stored aft. There were no planes, of course; they were now probably at some naval airfield.
>
> Perhaps it was the absence of planes—anyway, I suddenly remembered the night off Okinawa when I left the after deckhouse and, not

realizing how dark it was (the ship, of course, was blacked out), started forward on the hangar deck and soon found myself bumping into parked aircraft. I got down on my hands and knees and tried to crawl between the planes, but, in the intense darkness, I still collided with wheels and propeller blades. Finally, when I was in real desperation, unable to find my way either forward or aft, I spied a tiny dot of light on the starboard bulkhead, and managed to make my way to a ladder and then, feeling very sheepish, to a passageway leading forward.—MONTGOMERY NEWMAN, "Return to the Randolph," originally published in *The New Yorker,* May 11, 1957, p. 130

Occasionally, too, you may want to use the present tense rather than the past to describe vivid impressions. (See p. 152 for a discussion of the historical present.)

Important in keeping the time pattern clear are adverbs and adverbial elements like the following:

Words: then, later, next, soon, afterwards, instantly

Phrases: after dinner, a week later, an hour having passed

Clauses: when he had finished, before the bus arrived

These time indicators ordinarily occur near the beginnings of sentences. Their position should be varied, however, and the same elements should not be used too often. (See Ch. 6, p. 151.)

Writing a narrative

Most of the "tactical decisions" discussed in the preceding section —the purpose, point of view, kinds of narrative movement, time arrangement—can be at least tentatively made by thinking about your material before you actually begin to write. In thinking about it you will be refreshing your memory of the actual experience, and that is the best preparation for writing narrative that makes an experience come alive.

A narrative, even one of a continuous event, moves by stages. They are easier to see in a longer narrative, where a person's moving to a new place may be one stage, his starting a job another, and so on. But even in a short paper the stages, which grow out of actual events, can be recognized. They are likely to be represented in the outline. If you note them down before you begin writing, you will find it easier to develop each one fully and move from one to the next.

The opening

The opening paragraph of a narrative should capture the reader's attention. There is often a tendency to flounder about for several sentences at the outset, probably because the writer has not determined the true limits of his material; but unnecessary discussions of preliminaries or vague generalities may leave the reader indifferent or hostile to the rest of the paper. The family's debate about a vacation spot, the task of packing the car, and the values of relaxation would not combine into a good opening for a paper on "Fishing at Rice Lake." Ponderous generalities about the necessity of education in the modern world would alienate the reader of a paper on "A Freshman's First Day."

Personal narratives open less formally than most types of papers, using description of place or person, action, dialog, or a brief general statement of the central idea. The main requirement is that the opening sentences should set the tone of a paper and engage the reader's interest. The following openings illustrate some possibilities:

> My Uncle Russell had always said that when he retired from the Royal Navy, he intended to settle inland—that if one lived on the coast, one had only three directions in which to take walks. His relatives had assumed from this that he was thinking of walks in the country, so we were all surprised when, on his retirement, he took a small apartment in a South Kensington hotel. He explained that there were several perfectly good parks handy to go walking in and that by living in London he would see something of his nieces; three of my cousins and I were students there at the time.—JOYCE WARREN, "Uncle Russell's Weekends," originally published in *The New Yorker,* May 25, 1957, p. 97

> I was shivering in a vacant lot one evening recently while my son "swept the skies" with his four-inch reflecting telescope, when a man accosted us.
>
> "See anything *interesting?*" he asked suggestively, pointing to the lighted windows of nearby houses.—ANITRA FREEMAN, "Star Light, Star Bright," *Atlantic Monthly,* Nov. 1956, p. 117

> Every year since I've lived in Arkansas I've had the urge to pick cotton. Everyone I know picked cotton in his or her youth and speaks with nostalgia of the good times and the fun. "You never picked cotton?" is asked in a "You poor thing. What kind of childhood did you have?" voice. My miserable, deprived childhood barely even hinted that cotton grew anywhere except in the medicine chest.—DOROTHY OTIS WYRE, "Cotton Picker," *Atlantic Monthly,* Aug. 1957, p. 88

Other opening paragraphs are illustrated in Chapter 6, pages 166-167.

Movement of paragraphs

Paragraphs in a narrative paper tend to be shorter and to move more rapidly than in other forms of writing. The length and the tempo of the paragraphs will depend on your topic and your purpose. An account of an exciting hockey match would probably be in short, fast-moving paragraphs. A recollection of a walk through a country meadow on a hot summer afternoon when you were a child might follow a more leisurely pace.

In a fully developed narrative a new paragraph usually shows a change to a different movement or to a different sort of material: a change from summarized to dramatized action, a shift to a later time, a flashback to the past, a change of scene, and especially a change of the principal actor. (This last is the real reason for paragraphing the successive speeches of a conversation.) But if the various sorts of material are very short, only a sentence or two, they can probably be combined, as in the first paragraph of the rattlesnake incident on page 284.

The important thing is to keep the narrative moving. To accomplish this, verbs are most important. Specific verbs that describe an action instead of just naming it will add vigor to your writing. The general verb *walk,* for example, names a movement characteristic of billions of creatures, including human beings. A specific verb like *limped* or *scampered* describes the movement. The forms of *be* are indispensable, but they lack movement. Passive verbs are also indispensable but often distant and nondramatic. Active verbs make things happen. The following excerpt from an account of a bullfight is kept in motion by vigorous verbs:

> As though crazed, the bull loped into the center of the ring, snorting, flinging his body to toss away those splinters of steel that bit ever deeper into his muscles and the red streaks of blood turned to broad, gleaming patches of scarlet that matted the black, bristling hair of his back.
>
> Then, to his right, another man appeared. The bull turned to face his adversary, settling solidly on his four hoofs, then advanced. The man advanced, holding two more red and green and white sticks tipped with steel. Pained, the bull pawed the sand, lowered his horns, sighting his target, and moved forward with quicker momentum, and the two steel tips tore and widened the gash in his neck. On he came and on came the man, and, at the point of meeting, when the horns of the bull seemed about to gore the intestines and you could hear the bull's vast lungs expelling a mighty breath, the man rose into the air, shooting the steel-tipped darts downward and into the gaping, bloody wound. The man was in the air when the sticks left his hands, and, upon landing lightly upon the sand, he leaped aside, veering from the searching horns, escaping to safety.
>
> The bull now stood and lifted his head and bellowed, raging, looking about for the vanished target, heaving his vast black shoulders and feeling the steel slashing his flesh and the streaks of blood now turned to rivulets. The peak of muscle back of his neck gushed blood.—RICHARD WRIGHT, *Pagan Spain,* pp. 101-2

Concrete details

Papers about personal experience require a high proportion of concrete details. (See Ch. 6, pp. 141-147.) During an actual visit to the dentist or a struggle to land a rainbow trout, sense impressions predominate. Abstractions, if they come at all, come after the experience is over. In narrating the experience, then, you need to convey your sense impressions, not your afterthoughts. Abstractly, *pain* is "a distressing sensation in a part of the body"; concretely, it is the throbbing of an abscessed molar or the high whirring of a dentist's drill. Which type of presentation is more likely to communicate the effect of an actual experience?

Another advantage of concreteness is that it individualizes an experience. One experience differs from another chiefly in its details. Abstractly, one automobile race is similar to all other automobile races; concretely, each race is unique. The special flavor of an experience can be caught only in its concrete picture and its specific actions.

Concrete details *show* the reader an action instead of merely *telling* him that it happened. The reader can visualize a statement like "Frankie tapped his toe and took quick puffs of his cigarette" and from it deduce that Frankie was nervous or angry. But given a general, abstract statement like "Frankie exhibited signs of nervousness," he cannot convert it into the image that was in the writer's mind. He probably will not visualize anything at all, but any image the abstraction suggests is likely to be fuzzy and is sure to be different from what was in the writer's mind. To re-create the essence of an experience, concrete sights, sounds, and smells are most effective.

Conversation

A narrative is likely to contain conversation. In a portrait of a person, what he says and the way he says it are an effective way of suggesting the kind of person he is. And dialog is dramatic—it holds the reader's attention. Notice how much easier it is to read the speeches in a novel than to read long descriptive or explanatory paragraphs.

Many student writers make conversation sound just like their other writing; in fact, they merely put quotation marks around their own words. A little observation of how people really talk will show what's wrong with this. Effective conversation uses the words and constructions of spoken English and is suitable to the person represented. It uses contractions and clipped expressions, the casual grammar of everyday speech. The first step in learning to write good conversation is to observe how you yourself talk and how others talk.

Yet a transcript of actual speech will not sound real. We depend so much on facial expression, gesture, and tone of voice that our language put down exactly as we speak it sounds jumbled and unnatural. Credible dialog is a *selection* from actual speech; the writer gives it clarity and consistency.

Speech peculiarities should be suggested, not reproduced literally. Even the most realistic novelists do not give all of their lustier characters' profanity and vulgarity. To represent the grammar of Nonstandard English exactly is not necessary; it can be suggested by avoiding obvious literary and Formal constructions, by inserting an occasional Vulgate form, and by using the sentence movement of spoken English. Pronunciation also should be suggested, not reproduced. After all, if anyone's talk was spelled phonetically, most of the words would look strange. Localisms, if appropriate to the speaker and if used sparingly, are more effective in suggesting regional speech than respelling every third word. A few dropped *g*'s and a few vowel sounds spelled as the speaker pronounces them (*idee* for *idea,* for example) will do a great deal to show the regional or social quality of a person's pronunciation. But only a few are necessary; a whole page speckled with apostrophes and phonetic spellings only distracts the reader.

The speech tags or stage directions (*he said* and *she replied*) should be chosen with care. Specific verbs like "whispered" or "blurted" are more effective than a monotonous sequence of *said*'s. On the other hand, it is possible to go too far in searching out unusual ones. Once the give and take of a conversation has been established, tags can be omitted. When they are used, they can be varied in position; the identification of a speaker may introduce, interrupt, or conclude a quotation. (Frank asked, "But what is he doing here?" "But what," Frank asked, "is he doing here?" "But what is he doing here?" Frank asked.) Above all, they should not be made conspicuous, either by monotonously repeating the same ones or by straining too hard for novelty with verbs like *affirmed* or *expostulated.*

To introduce or conclude a quotation, verbs referring to the act of speaking should be used, not verbs referring to facial expressions or gestures. Sentences like the following are incongruous:

> "I wonder where she put the dishes," he *grinned* [...he asked, grinning].
>
> Mac *pointed,* [.] "In the cupboard, I imagine."

Details can often be blended with the speech tags. Notice the narration and description mixed into the following dialog:

> That gentleman, when I questioned him, leaped to his feet, pointed straight ahead of us in the direction in which we were already set–Sophy reminds me of this–and asked, "You Americans?"
>
> I was the one who answered; the others moved ahead rapidly. "Yes," I said, "we are."
>
> The man joined me at once and was with me when I caught up with my friends.
>
> "I American, too," he told us all.
>
> Sophy groaned and said to her companions, "You see what I mean?"
>
> Their response was to close in with her and gang up against me. I felt it instantly.
>
> The newcomer continued, "I from Chicago. Anybody know Chicago?"
>
> I still think it would have been rude not to answer, though pressure has been brought to bear on me to admit this was where I made my greatest mistake.
>
> "Yes," I said, "I know Chicago. I grew up there."
>
> I thought for a moment the man would throw his arms around me and kiss me. He came perilously close, but stopped, his face pushed into mine, his arms wide. "Why I ever leave Chicago?" he demanded. "Tell me that. Chicago the most wonderful city in the world. You know the Loop?"
>
> "Yes," I said, backing away a little. "I know it."
>
> "You know wonderful store of Marshall Field?"
>
> "Yes," I said, "I do. I worked there once."
>
> With a deep sigh he lowered his arms, took my right hand in both his, causing my guidebook, notebook and sweater I was carrying under that arm, to fall to the ground. "Chicago is most beautiful city in whole world," he declared, while we both endeavored to pick up the objects that had fallen, not an easy process since he continued to hold my hand in one of his. "Why am I such fool to leave most beautiful city in world?"–EMILY KIMBROUGH, *Forty Plus and Fancy Free,* pp. 143-4

The close

Like the opening of a paper, the close should be straightforward and to the point. It should not be a series of generalities or a weak apology. Personal narratives usually don't need an elaborate summarizing close. The most effective ending may be a brief restatement of the central idea, a descriptive detail, or a bit of dialog–whatever will suggest the overall unity of the experience and give a note of finality.

Here are the conclusions of the three narratives whose beginnings are given on page 287:

Uncle Russell died suddenly, of a heart attack, in the fall of 1944. His brothers were already dead and his sisters too old to get about, so there were few people at the funeral, though several of his friends from the reformatory ship came, and a couple of godsons who were still too young to be away in the Navy. After the service, a middle-aged pleasant-looking man walked up to me and introduced himself. He was, he told me, the superintendent of the hospital where my uncle had for a long time spent the first weekend of every month, visiting the patients, reporting to them about their families, and, if they wished, helping them with their business affairs. The patients were going to miss him terribly, the superintendent said. All those he had visited were lepers.—JOYCE WARREN, "Uncle Russell's Weekends," originally published in *The New Yorker,* May 25, 1957, pp. 102-3

As long as his head is in the stars, his feet are on the ground, so to speak. At least until the arrival of the rocket age. And to give the boy his due, I suppose he could have picked a worse hobby. I know a woman whose young daughter is interested in natural science. *She* collects live snakes.—ANITRA FREEMAN, "Star Light, Star Bright," *Atlantic Monthly,* Nov. 1956, p. 118

I finally explained to the boss that I just didn't seem to have the knack for picking cotton, and I thought I'd quit. It seemed to me that he gladly, almost eagerly, paid me my earnings—$2.38. That was $0.12 less than the cotton sack had cost. I went home to bed. I was one cotton picker definitely on the decline. But at least in the future I too can speak with nostalgia, if not authority, about picking cotton.—DOROTHY OTIS WYRE, "Cotton Picker," *Atlantic Monthly,* Aug. 1957, p. 89

Other closing paragraphs are illustrated in Chapter 6, page 169.

A sample narrative of experience

Here is a complete student narrative of a personal experience, a single incident that lasted perhaps half an hour. Read it first to see what happened. Then go through it again to see what points made in this chapter it illustrates and form your opinion of its success.

A Visit to Madame Zena

One afternoon last October I climbed the steps of a dark stone house and nervously rang the bell. I had a four-o'clock appointment with Madame Zena, fortune teller. In my billfold I carried a list of questions to ask, some for my friends and some for myself. Of course I didn't *believe* in fortune tellers, I'd explained to my mother; but I was curious, and someone had told me it was really uncanny, the way this woman could name names and places and predict things that seemed to come true.

A middle-aged woman in an old cotton print opened the door. Her red hair was done up in bobby pins. I must have looked uncertain, because she explained, "I'm Madame Zena–come in. Do you have your list of questions?"

"Yes."

"Good. Then make yourself at home, honey; I'll be with you in about ten minutes."

She left me in the living room. It held a dusty grand piano, an oriental rug, various pieces of mahogany furniture, and a rather wispy portrait, evidently of some medium who had passed on. A table by the window offered dozens of pamphlets–"Your Horoscope," "Finding the Future," "Secrets of the Mind." I had just settled down with "Secrets of the Mind" when my fortune teller reappeared, this time with neatly combed hair and a black satin smock over her house dress.

"Follow me."

She left a trail of musky perfume. I followed her through the long hall to a shadowy study, where she sat down at her desk and told me to take the chair across from her. Then the phone rang.

"Yes, some potato salad. And, oh, I guess two pounds of coffee... About five-thirty? . . . Not now, I have a client. Thanks."

She hurriedly put down the phone and turned to me. "The list?"

"Here." I was beginning to feel a little foolish; I could remember my questions:

1. Will Jack ask Marj to the prom?
2. Will Bill ask Jan to the prom?
3. Will Dave ask me to the prom?
4. Will Don and Jo get back together again?

Madame Zena took the paper, folded it into a tiny wad, and closed her eyes. While she talked she folded and re-folded the paper slip.

"You are a bright girl," she murmured in a distant voice. "Things don't bother you too much. You are a happy girl...but sometimes you get depressed . . . Right now you are going through a period of indecision . . . Things will get better, things will clear up for you in a few months . . . You are a generous girl . . . You must be careful not to let friends take advantage of you . . . You get along well with your family ...You want very much to succeed..."

I looked modestly at the window shade. Not bad, I thought.

"Right now," Madame Zena droned, "you are wondering about a certain friend...several friends...You are interested in someone named Jack...Yes, you'll go out with him...But you won't like him as much as Bill . . . I see a party coming up . . . You want to know who will take you to the prom . . . I see another boy, a boy you don't know very well . . . You'll see a lot of him...Don...Don will take you to the prom..."

She opened her eyes long enough to see the puzzled look on my face. "Don't you know anyone named Don, honey?"

"He's my brother."

"Oh." Her face darkened. "Did you ask questions for other people?"

"A couple, yes."

"You shouldn't have done that. Your friends should come themselves. The psychic waves work *only* for the people I'm talking to."

"I didn't know." I could see she was really angry.

"I'm sorry, but I can't do any more with these questions. My powers have to be *concentrated*."

I fiddled with my billfold and felt uncomfortable. It seemed illogical to me that fortune tellers had these limitations.

"Is there anything else?" Madame Zena asked, relenting.

"Well, there's that other question—about Dave..."

"Yes." She was matter-of-fact. "He's a fine boy. He likes you, but he's shy."

This stopped me—Dave seemed anything but shy. "Thank you," I said, completely disillusioned with fortune tellers. "How much do I owe you?"

"Two dollars."

I paid her and started to leave. As I went down the front steps, Madame Zena called to me. "Remember what I told you, honey. You mustn't let your friends take advantage of you. If they want to know something, tell them about me."

"I will," I promised. "I will!"

Chapter 10

SUGGESTED STUDY AND WRITING

1. List three topics you could develop into a single-episode personal experience paper and three you might use for a paper covering several incidents. The topics listed on page 275 may give you some ideas.

2. Write a short narrative paper about a person you have met since coming to college. Include at least one dramatic incident.

3. In this student paragraph the point of view shifts. Decide on a point of view appropriate to the material and then revise the paragraph to make it consistent.

> In some ways high school was a disappointment. When I started as a trembling freshman, the juniors and seniors seemed impossibly talented and sophisticated, moving in a bright, sure world beyond mine. Then I became a sophomore, a little more at ease but still fascinated by upperclassmen, who drove cars and ran the school paper and seemed admirably blasé. When I started my junior year I thought I was entering their shining world at last. But I found that the shine was only distance—while it was fine to be in on running things, it wasn't as wonderful as I'd expected. Anyone who's ever gone through high school will know what I mean. By the time you're a senior you're tired of the system and think of nothing but getting out. I suspect college students go through the same disillusionment.

4. Look for an example of a flashback in a short story or novel. How is the reader prepared for a time shift? How smoothly is the transition made? Be prepared to discuss your example in class.

5. Choose one of the topics you listed in the first exercise. Write an opening paragraph for a possible paper, using conversation or action or some other method to interest readers immediately.

6. The indirect discourse below is colorless and prosaic. Replace the letters with names and convert the summarized speeches into dramatic dialog. Use vivid verbs as speech tags and add descriptive details. You may need to imagine the speakers in a particular setting–playing bridge in the student union, lounging on the library steps, or walking to a class.

A wonders when a test will be given in Psychology.
B hopes it will be after spring vacation.
A regrets missing class this morning.
B asks why A was absent.
A explains: I overslept.
B assures A that nothing important happened in class.
A asks what the new assignment is.
B says that it is the next chapter.
A suggests that they study it together.
B suggests meeting at the library at 3:30.
A must attend choir practice.
B suggests this evening.
A asks what time.
B suggests seven o'clock in the west reading room.
A reminds B not to be late.

7. For a period of several days pay close attention to the language of conversations around you. Carry a notebook with you so that you can write down statements you remember. Copy them as exactly as you can; pay special attention to word order, slang, shortened constructions, and so on. After collecting several pages of conversation fragments, review your material to determine some general characteristics of Informal conversation. Then write a paragraph on the results of your study, using some of the sentences in your collection to illustrate your conclusions.

8. Analyze the following student narrative. Consider the handling of time, the opening and closing paragraphs, the dialog, and the overall effect. How might it be improved?

My first voyage as a seaman got off to a discouraging start. I joined the ship by taking a launch from the foot of Wall Street. As we pushed out from the dock and slapped over the white caps, the skipper of the launch asked me where I was headed.

"The *Emma J. Quinn*," I told him.

"The *Emma J. Quinn*!" he bellowed, the ends of his drooping moustache springing up and his eyes widening.

"Yes," I repeated, "the *Emma J. Quinn*. Why?"

"Oh, nothing," he answered and leaned to port to spit out the end of his cigar which he had bitten off. I perched on my upturned sea bag, watched the waves bouncing by, and thought over the last three hours.

I had been sitting in the dispatching hall of the National Maritime Union for three straight days when I heard the dispatcher's bored voice: "Repeat...One A.B. wanted for the *Emma J. Quinn*...Collier bound for Galveston...." A group of high school students were being led through the hall by a prim looking lady who wrinkled up her nose at us. She was probably showing them what to avoid when they grew up. I had been so absorbed in trying to look carefree and adventurous that I had missed the dispatcher's first announcement. The fact that the hall was filled with A.B.'s who also needed a berth never occurred to me. I rushed to the dispatcher's desk and signed up.

So here I was. I watched the skipper out of the corner of my eye. I began to suspect that my opportunity was not as golden as I had thought. After a few minutes I noticed a battered rust-pot of a ship, a weary leftover from the Lakes trade. It was listing heavily to port, and thick smoke crawled from its stack.

"Look," I muttered to the skipper, "look at that hunk of junk."

"Yeah," said the skipper.

"Boy, nothing but rust from one end to the other."

"Yeah." Our eyes met for a minute, but he quickly looked away.

"I bet her top speed is about five knots," I said.

"Yeah."

"By the way," I said, "what ship is it?"

"That's the–" His voice failed him and he chewed on his cigar. "That's the *Emma J. Quinn,*" he said weakly.

"Well, here we are," he said as we pulled up alongside. He pointed to a pilot's ladder made of broomsticks and mop handles. "Goodbye," he said as I started up the ladder. It sounded awfully final. I looked back over my shoulder. He was chewing his cigar and shaking his head. As soon as I was on deck and had hauled up my sea bag, he hurried into the wheelhouse and got his launch away before the *Emma J.* tipped over on him.

Feeling low, I dragged my sea bag across the deck and dropped it into a black hole leading to the crew's quarters. I heard a splash and a few drops of water sprinkled my face. Dazed, I started down the ladder. Soon I was standing in water. What an unusual ship, I thought, as I reached for my sea bag. No bottom.

As my eyes grew accustomed to the darkness, I saw that there was a bottom but it was covered with rusty water on the port side. I stepped carefully off the ladder and started wading around. I saw a gray-haired seaman scooping up water and throwing it out a porthole.

"What's the matter, Pop," I asked wearily, "are we sinking?"

"Lord," he breathed, dropping his bucket, "are we?"

"Looks that way." I waved at the oily water.

"Oh, this," said the old timer, taking a deep breath and resuming his work. "This is just from the fresh water tanks. The barge that was pumping us up forgot to stop. It all overflowed and ran down here."

After a few hours he and I had bailed the water out of the hold. I put away my gear and braced myself for my first voyage as an A.B.

I learned a lot about the sea on the *Emma J.,* and I will always remember her as my first ship. I never regretted taking the job nobody else wanted, but maybe I was too young to know any better.

9. Write a personal experience paper covering several incidents and including both summarized and dramatized narrative. Before handing it in, check the opening and closing paragraphs, the use of concrete details and lively verbs, and the use of time indicators.

There should be two main objects in ordinary prose writing:
to convey a message, and to include in it nothing that will distract
the reader's attention or check his habitual pace of reading—
he should feel that he is seated at ease in a taxi,
not riding a temperamental horse through traffic.

ROBERT GRAVES & ALAN HODGE

Chapter **11**

Information papers

The best and only way to treat it [a fact] is to leave it alone

and be willing to follow where it leads,

rather than to press your own wishes upon it.

MARCHETTE CHUTE

Suppose you want to explain the rules of cribbage, the duties of a dental technician, the plan of a ranch house, or the organization and functioning of a suburban club. The paper you would write on any of these topics would be an information paper. The general method and the purpose are obvious: to gather a body of facts and present them to a particular group of readers so that they will be better informed about the subject than they were before. In an information paper, the thing seen is more important than the one who sees it; the emphasis is on the facts being conveyed, and the writer, in the role of reporter, ordinarily stays in the background.

Gathering material

Since accurate and adequate facts are the core of an information paper, the material-gathering stage is particularly important. Just how you will find your material depends on the subject you choose. A good subject should be a good one for *you,* which means that it should be something you know, or would like to know about, and should certainly be something that interests you, that you would like to share with others. Often the best way to pick a subject is to think of topics that you talk about, that you know a little more about than most of the people you talk with—your special interests, your hobbies, your sports, jobs you have had, places you have been, people you have known. Students too often make the mistake of passing up such familiar topics for more "original" ones about which they have little or no first-hand knowledge. While your paper may include information from something you have heard or read, its interest and often its chief value will be from its first-hand material, things you have actually done or seen.

From experience and observation

Your own past experiences can serve as the basis for either a personal experience paper or an information paper. For example, you might develop "Picking Apples" as a personal experience, describing an afternoon in an orchard with sense impressions (the fragrance of fallen apples, the heavy baskets) to show the effect the experience had on you. Or you might develop it as an information paper, explaining methods of picking, sorting, storing, and transporting apples. In the first paper you would be telling of your personal reactions; in the second you would be conveying facts, using details from your apple orchard experience as concrete examples. The first would be individualized, describing your experience for its own sake; the second would be generalized, in its application though not in its language, telling about the typical activity of picking apples.

By merely jogging your memory, you may recall enough detail from your past experience to provide material for your paper. But often you will want to check on your memory or add to your store of information by further observation. Suppose you are writing a paper on the organization of the Central Food Mart, a place you've been to dozens of times but never really "seen." You would probably go to it again to observe more purposefully. Before visiting it, you might make a list of questions: Where are the shopping carts? What route would a shopper follow? Are there special displays? Where are the staples? The frozen foods? The fresh produce? The meats? What reasons does the manager give for such an organization? Take these as genuine questions, not as preconceived notions of what you will find.

It would probably be a good idea to take some brief notes and perhaps make a diagram of the Mart. A diagram would be easier for your readers to understand than four pages of description. Notice also sizes and shapes, colors, textures, anything that will help make your paper concrete. And if your paper is to be rather Informal, watch for unusual, interesting side lights as well as the information you are after.

Observation is especially useful for papers about places, occupations, processes, and general human activities. The writer of an article on the grammar of soap operas tells how he gathered his material from observation and developed his central idea from it:

> In gathering examples for this paper I listened to radio and TV soap operas for a total of fourteen hours, spread over the two-week period from January 9 to January 20, 1955.

Somewhere along the line, in my reading or in my classwork, I had picked up the information that writers and editors of fiction designed for the edification and entertainment of American womanhood were scrupulous in their adherence to old-fashioned, grade-school-teacherish rules of grammar. In my listening, I found little evidence that this information was incorrect.

Generally speaking, all soap operas may be divided into two groups. There is Group I, concerned primarily with the domestic and occupational trials of the solid upper middle class. The doctors and lawyers involved in these melodramas violate only ethical principles, not grammatical ones. . . .

Group II deals with the affairs of the lower middle class: those people who own small businesses, or who work as minor bureaucrats, or who merely keep house. These people cultivate all the virtues, their neighbor's garden, and 'bad' grammar—'bad' in that it violates all the rules of prescriptive grammar. These melodramas are concerned with the affairs of 'just plain folks,' and the language of these people is slangier, more colloquial, and less consistent than that of the upper middle class.

[Quotations illustrating forms used by Group I characters are listed with identification by program and date. Contrasting quotations from Group II, similarly identified, follow. These are the fruits of the observation and the body of the article.]

As I have said, the grammar I noticed on the soap operas leads me to believe that the fiction aimed at the large audience of women in America adheres very closely to the rules most of us picked up in our early training in prescriptive grammar. A whole segment of soap operas, those in Group I, are exceedingly scrupulous in their observance of the rules. Those folksy soap operas which make up Group II are much more free in their constructions, but the writers (or actors), in dwelling on questionable usage, make it sound artificial. It is as if everyone concerned with the story were conscious of the grammar's incorrectness and were slightly embarrassed about using it, with the result that questionable usages are not slurred over, but accented. Group I observes the rules, and Group II, in its embarrassment, indicates that it thinks the rules are valid.—THEODORE WILLIAMS, "Soap Opera Grammar," *American Speech,* May 1957, pp. 151-4

From interview

Often you can get material for your paper by talking with someone: a member of your family, a fellow student, a jet pilot, a jeweler, a kindergarten teacher, a county welfare worker. The technique of interviewing is highly developed by newspaper reporters, who know how to ask revealing questions and to draw out the answers and who have trained themselves to remember what is said. You can do the same thing on an amateur scale.

Before beginning an interview you should know something of what you are to discuss and what you want to find out, and you should have some specific questions in mind. Listen carefully, mentally summarizing the less important points, fixing in mind the more important statements, as far as possible in the speaker's words, and perhaps making some notes. If he gives some figures, repeat them to be sure you have them right. If he qualifies a statement with "I think" or "perhaps" or "around," be sure you get the qualification in your notes.

In your paper you should name and identify the people who give you facts and specify what qualifies them as authorities. Don't write "Somebody told me. . ." or even "A local grocer said . . . ," but "Charles Anderson, manager of the Central Food Mart, said. . . ." If his personality is important to your paper, as it would be in a profile (see pp. 314-316), watch for details that may help indicate what he is like and use them in your paper—his gestures, appearance, likes and dislikes, even the room in which the interview took place.

You will probably want a few exact quotes for your paper. There are two reasons for direct quoting: either a statement summarizes a point in such a valuable way that it deserves exact quotation, or it is put in such an unusual way that it will add interest. A direct quote is often useful in beginning a paper. In this example a fragment of conversation introduces an article on the work of Scotland Yard:

> A year or two before the war I was lunching with Heinrich Himmler, chief of the German police, and quite naturally he asked me what crime was like in London.
>
> I replied that our main trouble was always housebreaking and shopbreaking. Himmler smiled in a rather superior way and said, "Ah, yes. We were worried about that in Berlin too. I mentioned it to the Führer, and he told me, 'The next burglars you catch, cut off their heads. That'll stop it.' So we cut off their heads, and it stopped it."
>
> I would not regard Herr Himmler as the most reliable of men, and I do not know whether any Berlin burglar really did have his head cut off, but this conversation has often set me thinking about my own country's attitude toward crime.—SIR RONALD HOWE, "My Scotland Yard Adventures," *The Saturday Evening Post,* Nov. 23, 1957, p. 23

From reading

You may need to do some background reading for your topic to find further details or additional facts. If you were explaining the rules of cribbage, for instance, you would probably write most of the paper from your present knowledge of the game, but you would check up on the points you couldn't remember or weren't sure of. If you know of a magazine article or book with useful information about your subject, it may be a real help.

Material for short papers will come chiefly from your own knowledge, but the content of longer, more comprehensive ones usually needs further support. A useful kind of project combines material from a college course with some first-hand information. A sociology course might provide you with some points about suburban developments that you could illustrate from your experience; a physics or a chemistry course might help you explain some new machine or a new medicine. In your paper you can combine two areas of your knowledge.

Your paper should make clear the sources of your material. People who have written articles or books like to have their material used, but they like, and deserve, credit for it. In an academic paper this is done formally by means of footnotes, but in a general paper the mention is made informally.

An article, "Families on Wheels," by Alvin L. Schorr in *Harper's Magazine* for January 1958, describes the attitudes and something of the life of "trailer families" in the United States. Most of the material comes from the writer's experience and observation ("My own contact with some of them began in February 1954. . ."), and several times he quotes people in the camps ("I talked to one man who had made the grand circuit for over a decade. . ."). He also uses several published works, referring to them specifically but not as completely as a college paper would:

> . . . William H. Whyte, Jr., author of *The Organization Man,* wrote in *Fortune:*. . .
>
> According to Dr. Jules V. Coleman, clinical professor of psychology at the Yale School of Medicine, . . .
>
> But, as Dr. Coleman sees it, . . .
>
> My colleague, Mrs. Martha Van Valen, made a study of a half-dozen of these families who turned up in Southern Ohio. Interesting enough, one of her conclusions, later published in a professional journal, was: . . .
>
> "The hope is," writes Dr. Paul Lemkau of the New York City Mental Hygiene Bureau, "that stronger relationships in the family will help to substitute for some of the ancient attachments to places and things."

Sources which have been drawn on extensively may be given in a note at the beginning or at the end of the paper:

> Much of the material for this paper was taken from Robert A. Lively, *Fiction Fights the Civil War* (Chapel Hill, N.C., 1957).

(Methods for more complete use of printed sources are given in Ch. 13, pp. 349-400.)

Writing an information paper

When you have enough information–enough for the length of your paper and for your purpose in writing it–you will follow the rest of the stages of writing: selecting the relevant facts, organizing them, writing them as interestingly, as economically, and as impartially as possible, and revising as much as necessary. For a short and relatively simple paper these stages are almost simultaneous, but longer papers require more thoughtful attention in each. This section emphasizes a few points especially important for information papers.

Selecting the material

For an information paper, as for any other paper, you will have some material that is so central to the subject that you must include it, and you will have other material that you may or may not decide to use. The decision will usually depend on the readers you intend to reach. You need to consider their interests and their probable knowledge of the subject. How much knowledge can you assume? There is often a fine line between insulting their intelligence with the obvious and puzzling them with insufficient detail. A paper on a scientific or technical subject for a general audience will need to explain special and unfamiliar terms, make comparisions with common experiences, and perhaps provide somewhat simplified drawings. For readers with some background in the field much of this would be unnecessary, and more technical details could be used. There is some danger of writing at too low a level, putting in things that almost everyone will know, but as a rule amateur writers do not explain fully enough or include enough details.

Your expected readers should also largely determine the variety of English you will use in your paper. A discussion of structural steel written for engineering students can be more technical and probably should be more Formal than a paper on the same subject for a group of liberal arts students.

Since most college papers are written for practice and not for publication, you may need to decide arbitrarily on some specific audience. You might address your paper to the readers of some campus publication, newspaper supplement, or magazine of special group appeal (to photographers, fishermen, teen-agers, travelers). If you have a particular one in mind, put its name on your paper. At least you can regard your classmates as the audience and consider what will interest and inform them. Having a particular audience in mind will help you focus your paper.

Planning and writing

The plan of an information paper grows out of its material. An account of a process or directions for doing something will probably be chronological. But most plans will be topical, some systematic grouping of the facts, as in the paper on soap opera grammar (p. 300). For many short papers the best plan will be unmistakable from the time you begin collecting material, but for others you may need to try various organizations before hitting on a suitable plan. Notes on plans for various information papers are given later in this chapter. You may find it helpful to review pages 253-259.

The beginning of an information paper may do several things: indicate the nature and subject of the paper, interest the reader in going on with it, and lead him from familiar to perhaps unfamiliar territory. To get the reader's attention, informal factual papers often open with a narrative incident or a stimulating question. To lead him into new territory, the writer may mention first something the reader already knows, using familiar vocabulary. Notice the devices used here:

Familiar examples	A man standing barefoot in a tub of ice water would not survive very long. But a wading bird may stand about in cold water all day, and the whale and the seal swim in the arctic with naked fins and flippers continually bathed in freezing water. These are warm-blooded animals, like man, and have to maintain a steady body temperature.
Question	How do they avoid losing their body heat through their thinly insulated extremities? The question brings to light a truly remarkable piece of biological engineering.
Topic of paper	It seems that such animals block the loss of heat by means of an elementary physical mechanism familiar enough to engineers, which nature puts to use in a most effective way. In fact, the same principle is employed for several very different purposes by many members of the animal kingdom from fishes to man.
Introduction of basic term	The principle is known as counter-current exchange. Consider two pipes lying side by side. . . .—P. F. SCHOLANDER, "The Wonderful Net," *Scientific American*, April 1957, p. 97

More Formal papers can begin more rapidly, since most of their readers are already interested in the subject and probably know something about it. The first paragraph may mention the scope and purpose of the paper and the sources of information and even give definitions of the more technical terms. This opening paragraph refers first to the general subject and then to the particular study which will be reported:

> In a recent investigation of the chemical constituents of fossil human bone conducted in our laboratory, it was observed that bones of great archeological age may contain appreciable quantities of organic nitrogen. The significance of these findings for dating prehistoric bone has been discussed elsewhere. It is highly probable that the source of this nitrogen is the original proteins, as suggested by Abelson. If so, a question of interest is: How many of the constituent amino acids are able to retain their chemical individuality under the conditions attending archeological preservation.
>
> [The body of the article follows the research procedure: each bone was hydrolyzed by hydrochloric acid, fresh human bones were examined as a control, fossil bones were examined, and the findings were compared with the control findings. The following is the concluding paragraph:]
>
> The preliminary results reported here therefore suggest the conclusion that decomposition of protein in buried bones proceeds extremely slowly over many thousands of years but tends to release in the process certain amino acids while retaining certain others with great tenacity.—HARRIETT C. EZRA and S. F. COOK, "Amino Acids in Human Bone," *Science,* July 12, 1957, p. 80

You should not begin or end a paper with an apology for the shortcomings of your investigation or with a complaint about the difficulties of finding information.

If you have a good outline and plenty of facts, the body of the paper won't be hard to write. Keep your readers in mind while you write, explaining any terms they may not know, giving known equivalents for sizes and shapes of unfamiliar objects, and including visual aids—diagrams, sketches, maps, graphs, photographs—if they are appropriate.

The conclusion of an Informal paper may be an anecdote, a bit of description, or a brief restatement of the central idea. A more Formal paper may close with a summary of the information given and the writer's interpretation of its meaning, as in the articles on soap opera grammar and on fossil proteins. But whatever the type of conclusion that is used, it should make the reader feel that he has come to the end of the paper.

Revising

In revising your paper you should always check the facts for accuracy. A figure omitted from a statistic or a "not" left out of a sentence may reverse your intended meaning. Since there are many possibilities for careless errors when material is copied several times, it is wise to compare the facts in your completed paper with their original sources.

You should also check your paper for completeness of information. Completeness, of course, is relative, but any paper should be "complete" as far as it goes. What your reader expects is sufficient data to make the subject clear, convincing, and interesting. A generality may remind you of your facts but it can't be expected to remind a reader of them. In an information paper, as in a narrative of experience, details are needed. For example, in an account of a tobacco auction you might add a lively touch by mentioning the raucous voice of the auctioneer, the heat of the tobacco sheds, and the appearance of the buyers. These details may be included so long as they don't detract from or crowd out material essential to the paper.

You should make a third check to be sure that your paper is objective. "Objectivity" is an attitude toward material rather than a special manner of writing; it implies avoidance, as far as possible, of bias and self-interest. (Which of the following statements is the most nearly objective? "The line held and threw the ball carrier back after he managed to pick up about three yards." "The visiting team gained three yards." "The fullback pounded through the line for a gain of at least three yards.") More positively, objectivity means treating the subject honestly and accurately. But your writing doesn't have to be as colorless and cold as a tabulation of statistics; you may use an occasional *I*, and your details may be as vivid as in a narrative. Nor should you completely exclude your own interpretations and opinions. There is no harm in their showing through, so long as they are incidental to the paper and are well supported by specific facts. Include enough facts to avoid distortions, and take care to be accurate in your use of words. Remember that your primary aim is to give information.

How well, in your opinion, does this student paper measure up to the qualities discussed in this section?

> Most people have seen an auto-trailer, but because they have never had a good look inside one, they think that trailers contain only a few things, and that only those who have little money ever travel in them. These people are mistaken. Let's take for an example a trailer around twenty feet long, a little over six feet wide, and a good six feet high,

selling for about three thousand dollars. What is jammed into this small space?

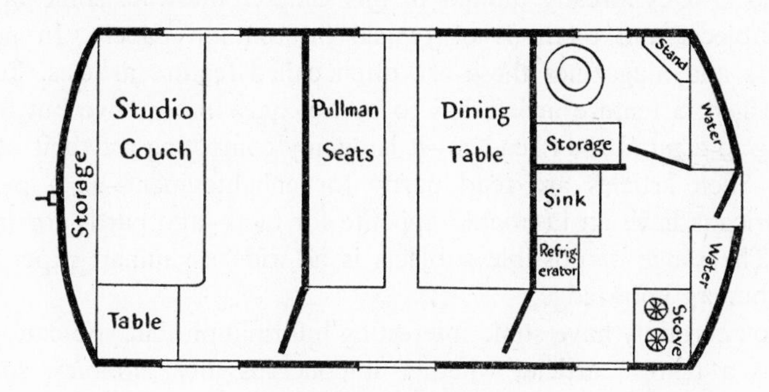

Trailer Diagram

In the rear, immediately after coming through the back door, we find the kitchen—a unique arrangement in that everything is in an arm's reach. There is no walking from one cupboard to another or back and forth from sink to stove, as is necessary in most houses. In a trailer everything is compact, and yet all the kitchen necessities are there. We find a table-high cooking and heating stove across from the porcelain sink. Next to the sink modern trailers have a small electric refrigerator, but some older models have only an icebox. On the walls are cupboards, and in the rear wall two twenty-gallon steel water tanks are stored away. To the right of the back door is a toilet, small, I will admit, with a mirror and a shelf in the room but no wash basin, for the kitchen sink is used for bodies and dishes alike.

Coming forward a little we find a compartment, containing closets and pullman seats, that is used as a sitting room in the daytime. During meals this same room can be converted into a dining room by moving the seats forward and pulling down a table which is stored flat against the kitchen wall. The seats make up into a six-foot double bed, as does the studio couch in the front compartment. Both of these couch-beds run crosswise and just fit into the space allotted to them. Also in the front compartment, to the side, is a small table and a straight chair for writing.

The trailer is equipped with electric lamps and wall connections, a radio, from six to eleven safety-glass windows, and two roof ventilators. In every available space there are closets or small shelves, the latter connected to the walls in such a way that they can fold back and lie flat when they are not in use. The majority of trailers are now constructed of steel, with about an inch and three-quarters of dead-air space in the walls for insulation.

Contrary to what most people think, a great deal is contained in this little space, in this house-on-wheels. In fact, almost everything needed for a short vacation is included in some nook or corner.

Typical information papers

The articles already quoted in this chapter illustrate some of the subjects and methods of typical information papers. In newspapers and magazines these are often called feature articles. To be published, a feature article has to be not only informative but interesting to a number of readers–it is openly competing for their attention. Such articles are read partly for enlightenment–as a people Americans have an insatiable appetite for facts–and partly for interest. The range of possible subjects is as wide as human experience and human knowledge.

You certainly have some interesting information that you can write up as a feature article, whether it concerns jobs, hobbies, sports, places, the actions of people, clubs, institutions, or college courses. A few sample subjects may suggest some specific topic you could write about:

Explain the steps in a job.
Describe the structure of a college organization.
Give directions for making a gadget.
Explain a method of dieting.
Analyze a television program.
Point out the effects of a new road.
Explain a special type of insurance.
Make a study of clipped words in headlines.
Explain how to raise some kind of plant or animal.
Give directions for some sport.
Describe a superstition or local custom.
Describe the activities or rules of a club.
Analyze the method of studying you follow.
Explain the political viewpoint of a local paper.

These and others that have been noted in this chapter should make it easy for you to draw up a list of possibilities.

A typical pattern for a feature article is shown in the following discussion of jobs. It is, to be sure, a professional piece, based on a compilation of facts from reporters all over the country. But you might do a comparable paper of two or three pages based on your own or your friends' experiences in getting jobs. Note that the opening statement summarizes the facts–it is not an opinion. The paragraphs are short and journalistic and the style is direct, but the article still manages to incorporate a good many figures.

People looking for work and those who would like to change occupations are finding that jobs are not always where they used to be. A gradual change has been taking place in the job pattern of the United States.

The shift generally is away from the producing industries to the service industries. Producing industries include manufacturing, farming, mining, forestry, fishing, and construction. In the group known as service industries are to be found professional people, such as physicians, dentists and lawyers, automobile mechanics, salespeople and many others.

A survey by the Economic Unit of "U.S. News & World Report" shows the shift in the job pattern that has been taking place in recent years. It shows, too, the types of work now being performed by the 65 million persons who hold jobs in this country.

As recently as 1940, the producing industries accounted for 51 per cent of the work force, but now are down to 44 per cent. In that period the proportion of workers in the service industries jumped from 49 per cent of the labor force to 56 per cent.

[*Brief paragraphs in the body of the article describe the situation in fourteen different areas. For example:* Farming accounted for many of the jobs lost in the producing division. Where agriculture, lumbering and fishing had 18 per cent of the total work force back in 1940, they have only 8.5 per cent at present. The three industries had about 10 million workers in 1940, but now are down to 5.8 million. This represents a drop of almost 43 per cent.]

Thus, with the two exceptions noted above, the service trades are giving more work opportunities than they did in 1940, and indications are that there will be continued expansion in this industry, as more gadgets need repairs, as people spend more money on travel and resorts.—"Jobs Aren't Where They Used to Be," *U.S. News & World Report,* July 12, 1957, pp. 89-90

Writing a process paper

A particular kind of information paper—the process paper—usually describes a systematic series of actions. Because its organization is fairly simple, the process paper is a common assignment in composition courses. Magazine articles and even books are often written to describe how something is done or how something works. These descriptions resemble other kinds of factual writing except that they place more stress on *how* than *what*. With the popularity of do-it-yourself projects, process papers have become familiar to all of us.

Directions

A paper that tells the reader how to do something follows a fairly simple plan. The opening sentences usually identify or describe the process, indicate its usefulness, define any technical terms, and specify the tools, conditions, and materials necessary. The extent of the introduction will depend on the complexity of the process and the reader's probable knowledge. The body of the paper follows the major steps in the order in which they are performed. Often a diagram or a sketch will help make the steps clear. This simple example is typical in its identification of the process and its step-by-step arrangement:

> If it's a sunny day and you have a watch and your watch is reasonably on time, you can locate directions by following these steps:
>
> Place the watch on your wrist with the flat surface parallel to the ground. Keeping it parallel to the ground, rotate it until the *hour* hand points in the general direction of the sun.
>
> In the morning, south lies about halfway between the hour hand and twelve o'clock, measuring clockwise. In the afternoon, south lies about halfway between the hour hand and twelve o'clock, measuring *counter*-clockwise.
>
> North, of course, will be on the same line, in the opposite direction.
>
> This method isn't entirely accurate, but if you're wondering which way to turn at a highway crossroad, for example, it may serve to give you the approximate direction you need.–*Good Housekeeping,* July 1957, p. 45

This student paper makes a good start on a considerably more complicated process:

> Break Your Own Horse
>
> There was a time when horse-breaking was a simple, everyday affair. All you needed was a horse, saddle, halter and buckrein, or hackamore, and enough courage to climb on. However, times have changed, and the methods of horsebreaking have changed with them. There are several methods now in use, but this is the one I have found to be most successful.
>
> The best time to start breaking a horse is while he is still a colt, not over three or four years old; a horse older than this may be broken, but it is much more difficult. If the horse has been raised in a barn, this first step has probably been completed, but if he is a range pony, the first step in his training is breaking him to lead and gaining his confidence. Never yell or make any quick movements around a green horse, for it is all new to him and he'll scare easily. Talk to him in a low, gentle voice and pet him around his neck and shoulders. To break him to lead, take an extra piece of rope and run it around his rump or around a fore-foot and pull on this rope and the halter rope at the same time. If you run the rope around his rump, don't pull too hard or he may be on top of you before you know what's happening. Never use a halter rope alone when you're first breaking a horse to lead because he'll just pull against you, and you'll have a hard time breaking him of this habit.
>
> After the horse leads well, the next step is breaking him to the bit. The best type of bit is a broken snaffle or a straight buggy or work bit.

This part of the training acquaints the horse with the feel of the bit in his mouth, and the horse will hold his head up where it belongs when you start to ride him. To bit him up tie the reins to the saddle, or use a driving harness, and apply a small amount of pressure against the bit. Leave this on for about fifteen minutes the first day, half an hour the second day, and so on until it can be left on for about two hours a day.

After the horse has been bitted up for about a week, it is time to start ground driving him. This is to train the horse to stop and turn in each direction. A driving harness may be used for this, but I prefer a saddle, because the horse gets used to the saddle and the flapping of the stirrups, and it makes things easier when the time comes to ride him. If the saddle is used it is wise to attach a ring, at least one inch in diameter, to the dee ring on each side of the saddle, and run your reins through these. They will keep the reins free from the saddle, and pressure will be applied from the proper direction. You should also have a pair of reins about thirty feet long, a buggy whip, and a circular corral about fifty feet in diameter.

If you don't have leather reins a length of clothesline will do and if a circular corral is unavailable a square one will serve you just as well. Drive the horse in a walk, trot, and lope, stopping him now and then to reverse his direction.

After the horse has been ground driven for a week, it is time to mount and ride him. I prefer to ride a green horse snubbed the first two or three times, for although he should be used to a saddle by now, the extra weight of the rider and having a man on his back may cause him to buck, and I believe a horse is better if he doesn't know what a buck is. Also, you should mount and dismount several times at the beginning and end of each ride to get him used to it.

After the third day it is safe to ride him unsnubbed, and it is time to concentrate on his reining again. The ground driving was the preliminary for this part of the training. When the horse becomes so bridlewise that he responds to a gentle pull on the reins, it is time to break him to neckrein. The easiest way to do this is to cross the reins under his neck. This will cause pressure on the bit as well as his neck at the same time, and he will soon associate the two and the reins may be uncrossed.

If a person has a slight knowledge of horsemanship, and a great deal of patience, and follows these directions, it is not at all difficult to break a horse to ride, and the personal satisfaction of riding a horse you have broken yourself is well worth the time and effort.

Description

A slightly different type of process paper describes how something works. The preliminaries are similar to those in directions: the use and main parts of the mechanism are identified, and any unfamiliar terms are defined. The body of the paper describes the main parts of the mechanism or activity and the function of each. This excerpt is from a rather technical description of parts of a loudspeaker:

> Practically all modern loudspeakers are of the permanent magnet dynamic type. The dynamic speaker is one whose diaphragm is energized by a moving coil attached to it. The designation "permanent magnet" refers to the fact that the speaker's magnetic field is supplied by a permanently magnetized and highly magnetic alloy, in place of the iron-cored coil used in earlier dynamic speakers.
>
> The permanent magnet dynamic speaker consists of a very light coil of wire cemented to a cone-shaped diaphragm. The coil is free to move in the field of a strong permanent magnet. Electrical impulses from the amplifier are applied to the coil, referred to as the voice coil. Because the impulses from the amplifier are constantly changing in direction and intensity, a changing magnetic field is set up in the voice coil. This changing magnetic field reacts with the steady magnetic field produced by the permanent magnet, with the result that the voice coil is alternately attracted and repelled by the permanent magnet. Each time the voice coil is repelled, it moves forward and the cone moves with it. This forward movement compresses air in front of the cone and produces sound waves. When the voice coil is attracted by the permanent magnet it moves backward, and so does the cone, compressing air at the rear of the cone. In this way, the electrical impulses are converted into sound waves. The rapidity of vibration of the voice coil and cone depends upon the pitch or frequency of the signal from the amplifier. The distance that the cone moves is dependent upon the strength of the signal.—WILLIAM R. WELLMAN, *High Fidelity Music Systems,* pp. 21-3

This student paper outlines the process of logging:

> A great deal has to be done before actual logging operations can begin. Roads must be built, a landing cleared, and a spar pole constructed. Since logging is often done in swampy places, building roads strong enough to support a heavy truck loaded with logs can become quite a problem. These roads are laid to the center of the area to be logged, and there the landing is prepared. The landing is a cleared area large enough for a truck and cat to maneuver and for the logs to be piled. The spar tree is constructed in the middle of the landing. This is the center of all operations; it consists of a tree which has been topped and limbed and rigged out from the top with four guy wires for extra support. Logs are lifted onto the trucks by means of a cable through a pulley at the top of this tree.
>
> The job of felling the trees has changed a great deal in the past ten years. It used to require an axe, a bucksaw, and a lot of hard work. The axe is still used to make the undercut and limb the tree, but the bucksaw has been replaced by the modern power saw. This speeds up the feller's part of the operation and eliminates much of the work. Now fellers are usually special crews hired solely to fell the allotted number of trees.

Getting the logs from the woods to the spar tree requires a lot of cooperation between the cat driver and the choker. First the cat driver maneuvers close to the downed trees. Then the choker drags the main line, which is on a drum at the rear of the cat, to the logs. He connects this line to the chokes which he has previously secured to the ends of the logs. The cat driver then snakes them out. If the downed trees are behind standing trees or stumps, it is sometimes necessary to move the chokes a number of times. It takes much experience to be a good choker.

Loading the logs onto trucks is the most dangerous job connected with logging. One end of the hoisting cable is divided into two sections, each about twenty feet long and hooked at the end. The hooks are held at each end of the log, and when the cable is raised they tend to bury themselves in the wood. But these hooks sometimes break, and the loose end of the cable, acting like a giant scythe as it whips through the air, could easily cut a person in half. Once the log is raised into the air, the truck backs in under it and it is then lowered onto the trailer. After the trailer is completely loaded, the logs are secured and taken to the mill pond or to the log dump.

These are the main steps in a logging operation. To have an efficient organization, and to obtain the greatest degree of safety, each division must work in close cooperation with the rest.

The same general method of description may be used for a non-mechanical process—for example, referendum in political science, conditioning in psychology, or urbanization in sociology.

Writing a profile

Although it will probably contain more interpretation and judgment than the papers just discussed, a "profile" is an information paper. Its aim is to tell readers enough about a person so that they will feel they have met him and in a sense know him. It differs from a biography in that it is usually not organized chronologically. It is a "character sketch" written with purpose and direction, arranged somewhat informally by topics.

The subject of a profile should be interesting and distinctive in some way, either in his characteristics or in what he does. To write a profile, you need a rather full knowledge (first-hand knowledge is best) of the person, more than can be got from reference books or casual acquaintance. Information can be collected by talking with him, if he is available, and by talking with people who know him. Sometimes there is material in print, perhaps in newspapers or in the campus paper if he is a student. But these secondary sources cannot take the place of your first-hand knowledge; consequently, the best profile is written about a person you know, a grandfather, a family friend, a teacher, a teammate, or someone you have worked with.

Profiles in magazines follow a typical plan. The first paragraph or two gives a glimpse of the person and tells why he is distinctive in terms of a character trait, often shown in a direct quotation, or of an occupation. Something about his appearance may come here. The second block usually gives further details of his distinctiveness. Then the profile often goes back to his beginnings and gives a brief biography, amplifying incidents that are especially revealing. This chronological patch leads back to the present so that the last part gives some further details of him today and ends either with a brief summary or more often with another glimpse of him in action.

A profile of the great photographer Edward Steichen shows most of these characteristics of the type. It is about 3000 words long, in twenty-eight paragraphs. The title is "Steichen: Dissatisfied Genius," and most of the parts contribute to the keynote of dissatisfied genius.

1. The first topic (five paragraphs) gives a glimpse of Steichen at work, places him, and establishes the keynote. It begins:

> A friend came upon Edward Steichen recently crouching in the sculpture garden of the Museum of Modern Art in New York. His abundant, silvery hair blew in the soft wind as he moved quickly about the garden, shooting from different angles the massive, glowering statue of Balzac by Rodin. When he saw his friend Steichen looked up delightedly and beamed.
>
> "I first photographed that statue by moonlight in Rodin's garden in Paris more than fifty years ago," he exclaimed enthusiastically. "But this background is terrible! These skyscrapers...." Then he returned to his camera, grumbling and seeking a better angle.
>
> The incident gives a sharp snapshot of a man considered by many to be the greatest living photographer....

There is a bit of advice from Rodin with the comment: "Those consoling words have guided Steichen through a lifetime of achievement without a real moment of satisfaction."

2. The second topic devotes six paragraphs to one of his chief accomplishments, selecting from two million photographs the 503 that formed the exhibit, later published as a book, *The Family of Man*.

3. The next three paragraphs sketch his early years and the beginning of his painting and photography.

4. Then five paragraphs take him through his years in Paris, his painting, his final turn to photography, his hobby of raising delphiniums, and his work as an Army photographer in World War I.

5. The next five paragraphs cover briefly his career in photography, including his famous picture of J. P. Morgan, and various significant details of his work.

6. The last topic, four paragraphs, gives an anecdote from his work as a naval combat photographer in World War II and ends with a paragraph that returns to the present, concluding with another statement of the quality that has been stressed all along:

> When he was named photographic director of the Museum of Modern Art in 1947, Steichen gave up his own photography in order to maintain complete objectivity toward the works he must judge. But the urge to create with a camera lens grew too strong, and recently he has resumed practice—beginning what he calls his third apprenticeship in photography, while at the same time working on a new exhibition. At seventy-eight Steichen remains as restless and searching as when he first began his ceaseless quest for perfection.—LENORE CISNEY and JOHN REDDY, "Steichen: Dissatisfied Genius," *Saturday Review,* Dec. 14, 1957, pp. 9-12, 28

A profile of a less known person would be shorter but could be organized in much the same way, with direct glimpses, quoted remarks, incidents, and some interpretation. The purpose would be the same: to *show* the person to readers so that they could draw their own conclusions about him and feel they had really become acquainted with him.

Writing essay examination answers

Although essay examination questions may call for judgments and "reactions," typically they call for information and require the accuracy and clear organization of good information papers. The subject is specified or at least limited, though the question has to be interpreted; the material is from memory, though it may be combined from textbook and lectures or other sources; your work, from the point of view of composition, is chiefly in planning and writing.

Analyzing the questions

Too many students take a quick glance at the heading of an examination and then begin dashing off an answer to the first question. You will do better if you spend a few minutes reading over the entire examination. When you know all the directions and questions, you can avoid overlapping answers, and a detail in one question may jog your memory or suggest an approach to use in answering an earlier question. If a choice of questions is offered, cross out the ones that you know least about and, unless you have a very good reason for changing, stick to your decision. If the questions have different values, apportion your time accordingly. A question weighted at 10% is not worth 25% of the examination time, since you can earn no more than the maximum value of a question. Try to save enough time at the end of the period to read over your answers.

After scanning the whole examination and setting time limits, read each question closely before writing your answer. Decide what kind of answer is expected. In most examination questions there is at least one key word. In the following, for example, each of the nouns would call for a quite different answer:

Discuss the adoption / provisions / shortcomings of the Articles of Confederation.

Usually the verb is the significant word in a question. These verbs are often used:

analyze: give main divisions, or aspects, emphasizing essential features
compare: point out likenesses
contrast: point out differences
define: explain the meaning, distinguish from similar terms
discuss: examine in detail
evaluate: judge, give your opinion of the value or validity
explain: make clear, give reasons for
illustrate: give one or more examples of
interpret: give the meaning or significance
review: examine on a broad scale
summarize: examine concisely, reduce to essentials

Often, using the key word or a derivative (*analyze–analysis*) in the first sentence of your answer will hold you to the question.

Writing the answers

After you determine your approach to a question, you are ready to write. If you are permitted to answer questions in any order, it is wise to begin with the one you know best. Answering it will increase your confidence and may recall information useful in answering later questions. The only danger is wasting valuable time by writing too much.

Students are sometimes misled by the general nature of a question. An instructor may ask fairly broad questions so that every student can discuss some aspect of each, especially in a course based on outside readings rather than on a textbook. But a general question usually requires a specific answer. Choose your approach and your main points before you begin to write. If necessary, make a rough outline on a piece of scratch paper or at the top of the page. Stick to your plan and develop your ideas neatly, accurately, and systematically.

An organized answer is so rare in a set of examination papers that it is likely to receive even more credit than it deserves. The typical answer is a hodgepodge of unrelated statements set down in the order in which they came to mind, plus an afterthought or two from a previous question. In a good answer the sentences all relate to the question, and they proceed in an orderly, sensible manner.

One reason for the vague, general phrasing in many answers is that the student thinks to himself, "He'll know what I mean." An examination is almost the only writing situation in which you are aware that the reader knows more about the subject than you do. To rely consciously or unconsciously on your instructor's knowledge is a fatal error. He may know what you mean to say, but he can grade you only on what you do say. Vagueness is also caused by an inability to use the terminology of a field. If you avoid using technical terms such as *hydrolysis, sovereignty,* or *sestet* because you are unsure of the meaning or the spelling, you are certain to be wordy and you will probably be inaccurate.

The quality of your answer will be improved if you proofread it carefully. Examination jitters can cause some incredible blunders–the omission of a "not," for example, which changes the whole meaning of an answer. Corrections should be made neatly above the line or in the margin.

An examination answer should be written in acceptable General English. Instructors who lower grades for poor English often penalize a paper most heavily for misspelling. Although spelling seems less important than factual information and misspelling a less flagrant error than sentence fragments or faulty agreement, it is the most noticeable kind of mistake, and it is understandable that an instructor will be disturbed when a student misspells a term that has been used throughout the course. Take time to check the spelling in your examination answer and also to revise vague or faulty sentences.

Specimen answers

Typical answers from examinations in biology, history, and philosophy are contrasted below. After comparing each pair of answers yourself, read the comments that follow.

Question: *Differentiate between the arrangement and the orientation of leaves.*

A.

The arrangement and orientation of leaves means the way they are arranged on the stem. This is the same for any type of plant. When there is a single leaf at each node and the nodes form a spiral up the stem, the arrangement is alternate. When there are two leaves at a node across the stem from each other, the arrangement is opposite. When three or more leaves encircle the stem at the node, the arrangement is whorled. When the leaves occur in clusters or bundles, the arrangement is fasicled. Leaves are arranged so that they will receive a maximum amount of sunlight.

Although Answer A is clearly written except for the second sentence and contains correct factual information it is not successful. The question calls for a contrast; but the student either overlooked the key word, "differentiate," or did not know the meaning of "orientation." He has defined the two terms as if they were synonymous.

B.

The arrangement of leaves is fixed by heredity and is not affected by environmental conditions. The orientation of leaves is their change of position to suit light conditions and is determined largely by environment. Thus, two vines of the same species must have the same arrangement, but they may differ in orientation. The most common arrangements are as follows: alternate (a single leaf at each node), opposite (two leaves opposite each other at the same node), and whorled (three or more leaves at the same node). Orientation varies more because it is the specialized adaptation of a plant to light conditions. Vines on a wall spread their leaves to receive maximum sunlight. Mullein leaves form a rosette. Some desert plants have leaves that are tilted so that they receive early and late sunlight but escape the intense midday sun.

Answer B is satisfactory. The two terms are differentiated in the first three sentences; then examples of each are contrasted. The descriptions of leaf arrangements are not so detailed as in Answer A, but here they are a subordinate part of the answer.

Question: *Explain the increased power of the British Parliament in the early 18th century.*

A.

The British Parliament became much more powerful in the early 18th century. After the Revolution of 1688 Parliament passed a Bill of Rights. It denounced despotic rule by a king. Other acts made the army dependent on annual grants by Parliament and

B.

The power of Parliament increased in the early 18th century because of political and social changes in England. Politically, the two revolutions of the 17th century showed the power of Parliament and ended with the crowning of William III. Because he made it impossible for the king to remove judges from the bench. A king could no longer rule without Parliament. In France, however, which had not advanced so far from feudalism, the king was still supreme. Louis XIV was an absolute monarch. Colbert and other ministers ruled the country under his direction. Even in England few people were able to vote, and the common people had no more to say about the way they were governed than the people of France.

Answer A was written by a half-informed student who apparently forgot the question as soon as he read it. The first five sentences are correct in themselves, but they are evidence of the increased power of Parliament, not reasons for it. Effects are confused with causes. The discussion of France is irrelevant padding. The last sentence returns to the question but is still far from the point and actually contradicts the basic idea of the question.

was a foreigner and was interested in continental affairs, he did not object to the Bill of Rights and other acts that reduced his power. The first two Georges also ignored most domestic affairs. Arguments over the succession led to the forming of political parties, and they naturally accumulated power for themselves and reduced the king's power. Socially, the growth of the middle class led to an increase in parliamentary power. The Industrial Revolution began early in England. Colonial trade also made the nation prosperous. The increasing middle class wanted power, and its wishes were made known through the members it elected to Parliament.

Answer B is organized and unified. All the reasons are not given, but the major ones are discussed in two groups. Each sentence advances the development and relates to the question.

Question: *Discuss John Locke's theory regarding the source or origin of knowledge.*

A.

Lock said that the source of all knowledge is in the mind. All a person knows is what he knows from his own thoughts, and there is no such thing as inate ideas, the mind of a baby when it is just born is like a blank tablet. Which gets filled in as the baby gets older. Lock died in 1704. Some of his ideas are found in the Declaration of idependance. His ideas were very important in the growth of the United States. Lock's origion of knowledge is in the mind. Kant didn't believe this. He thought the mind was more impassive. Lock thought it was passive.

B.

John Locke believed that all knowledge originates in experience. The mind of a new-born baby is a blank tablet on which experience registers impressions; there are no innate ideas. Instead, ideas come from sensation or from reflection. Ideas coming through the senses are indirect knowledge. They represent objects in the external world. Other ideas originate in reflection as the mind observes its own operations. This direct knowledge comes from the activity of the mind itself, or introspection. Also, the mind may compare these simple ideas and

Answer A is a failing answer. Seen in cold type, it may appear exaggerated, but it is not an extreme example of an answer written by a careless, poorly prepared student. Nonstandard errors and obvious padding are the main faults. It becomes less coherent toward the close. An instructor might find the misspelling of "Locke" most offensive.

unite them into complex ideas. But the primary source of all knowledge is experience.

Answer B is not perfect, but compared to Answer A it deserves well. The first two sentences are a general response to the question. The third sentence introduces two subdivisions, each of which is developed in an orderly way.

Information papers of all types—including examination answers—are excellent for practice in the actual process of writing, especially in selecting material and shaping it purposefully and interestingly for readers. Because the material is specific, they encourage a direct, concrete style, and because you are familiar with the material, you can write with confidence. These qualities may then carry over into the other writing that you do.

Chapter 11

SUGGESTED STUDY AND WRITING

1. For each of the following general subjects write out a good topic for an information paper of a definite length and for a particular audience (specify both).

Job or sport	Topic from a college course
Hobby	Person
Place	Social situation

2. Select an informational article from a magazine or from the book of readings for this course. Study it and then write a paragraph on the sources of the writer's material. What in his article seems to have come from his own experience and observation? From interviews? From reading?

3. Write a short process paper giving directions for doing something or explaining how something works. In selecting a topic for your paper try to choose one you know more about than most of your classmates. (Avoid topics that are too simple or trivial.)

4. Analyze the following student paper. In your opinion, are the directives sufficiently full and clear? How might the paper be improved?

The Caulking Problem

To be sure, there is a right and a wrong way to do everything and unfortunately some things done wrongly simply have to be redone. The calking of a boat is no exception to this rule. A good calking job is easily done, and if successful, makes it possible for the boatman to enjoy a carefree season. However, if the poor yachtsman fails to use proper materials, or spends too short a time on the job, a leaky hull and perhaps a mid-season lay up can be expected.

The job in itself requires nothing but time, patience, and a limited amount of skill. Luckily enough the materials are comparatively inexpensive, consisting mainly of calking irons, hammer, reamer, calking cotton and perhaps a little calking compound. The process can be classified into two big steps, the first being to clean out the seams, removing the old cotton and paint, and the second being to replace the old cotton with new. This in itself presents no problem since it is a knack which can easily be learned. The whole process involves reaming out the seams, being careful to get out all the old cotton, then taking some new cotton, rolling it up into thin strands, and with hammer and iron, inserting these strands firmly between the seams. However in this there is danger, danger of putting so much cotton in the seam that it can't close up properly after the swelling process is started. This results either in a split bottom plank or bent ribs. To avoid this, the boatman must see to it that his seams are filled with cotton to the extent that it can't be pushed out easily with a knife, but not so firmly imbedded that even a reamer has difficulty in removing it. A solution to the problem can be found by using a limited amount of cotton and placing a little non-hardening calking compound as a background for the cotton. This completes the calking job.

If possible, the engine should be left out of the boat at the launching. Chances are ten to one that if the boat is calked really properly, it will sink and stay under water for at least a two day period. In this period, from the time the bottom first hits the water to the time the boat is rehauled up the ways, the seams will have had time to swell so that the cotton is made sufficiently tight to keep the hull dry. Also, the soft compound which formed a temporary filling will have been completely pushed out of the seams. Of course, this method of temporary sinking is impractical for a larger boat. It must be placed on strong supports, and the bottom filled with from two to three inches of water, enough to do the swelling from the inside out. It will be found that the above method is perhaps more desirable. It permits the hull to swell without the danger of buckling, and it makes for stronger seams, since all the calking is cotton, and none of it is the soft compound.

5. Select a person who has an interesting occupation or hobby and arrange an interview with him. (You may want to note down a few questions beforehand.) Then write a short paper based on the interview. Try to get across the personality of the person you interviewed as well as the facts you learned from him.

6. Read two or three magazine articles on a topic in which you are interested. Then write a short paper on your topic, weaving in quoted and summarized material from the articles and mentioning the sources of your information informally rather than by footnotes.

7. Find an example of a profile in a recent magazine. Study its organization and make a summary similar to the one in this chapter pp. 315-316. Be prepared to present your summary in class.

8. Find a passage written for a specialized audience–perhaps a paragraph from a textbook for one of your other courses. Rewrite it for general readers, people who have no special knowledge of the subject. Use a dictionary if necessary to find simpler terms for those which are likely to be unfamiliar to your readers.

9. Select a magazine for which you might like to write an informational article.

A) Study it carefully to get an idea of its readers. Notice the style of its articles, the type of advertisements it carries, its correspondence column. Write a summary of your analysis and suggest several topics of probable interest to the readers of the magazine.

B) Write a short informational article for the magazine you selected.

[Opinion:] A judgment formed or a conclusion reached;
especially a judgment formed on evidence that does not produce
knowledge or certainty; one's view of a matter;
what one thinks, as distinguished from what one knows to be true.

CENTURY DICTIONARY

Chapter **12**

Opinion papers

Genuine opinion is neither cold, logical judgment

nor irrational feeling. It is scientific hypothesis,

to be tested and revised as experience widens.

Opinion is a view of a situation based on grounds short of proof.

In a valid opinion they must be just *short of proof.*

RANDOLPH BOURNE

The two preceding chapters considered papers on matters of fact, papers consisting principally of details from experience and observation and presented as factual or true. This chapter discusses papers centered on opinions, on matters that are less certain than fact but that can be demonstrated as reasonable or plausible. While the categories of fact and opinion are practical rather than precise or scientific, we are aware of the distinction between them and realize that our treatments of the two sorts of statement differ, or at least should differ. (Compare Ch. 6, p. 139.)

Opinions, themselves, differ in their closeness to facts, as we can see if we consider three general types: *interpretations, evaluations,* and *generalizations.*

An *interpretation* is the type of opinion that is closest to fact. It answers chiefly the question *What does it mean?* The subject may be a word (for example, *democracy*), a statement, an event, or a poem—anything that the writer believes should be clarified. The meaning attributed to the word or statement or event is not a part of any of these but is an opinion, the result of someone's observation and reflection. The interpretation often involves comparing the subject with other similar things or supplying background of some sort; thus a news commentator may interpret a crisis in the French government by referring to specific current events, to individual politicians, to previous crises, to party alignments. Statements of probable or expected results, except when they are quite certain, are also best regarded as interpretations. An interpretation, then, may be close to fact, but it is not a fact, because a different but equally plausible interpretation is usually possible.

The most characteristic level of opinion is an *evaluation,* a judgment of some particular item. An evaluation answers questions like What is it worth? Is it good or bad? Effective or ineffective? In a single day we make scores of informal, offhand evaluations: This coffee is terrible. Our team is weak on defense. My grade was too low, or just what I deserved, or better than I deserved. Although many are snap judgments, others may represent a careful series of comparisons or a consideration of other opinions, or they may be based firmly on some general principles, especially on ideals or standards. In evaluating the grading in a large course, for example, you first might consider the grades you have received in that course, then compare them with the grades of other students in the course and with the grading in other courses, and finally apply a standard based on some general notions of what a satisfactory grading system might be.

Generalizations are more complex than the other types of opinions and usually include interpretations and evaluations. An evaluation might be made of a single TV program or series, or of a type of program (westerns, situation comedies, variety shows). But to consider the relative values of these types as commercial ventures or as entertainment or as art would require greater reflection and a greater range of information. Much of the material in such a paper would be specific details, but obviously the topic would demand more summaries of facts, a number of interpretations and evaluations, and probably some discussion of general principles (ideas and ideals of entertainment or of art). To be worth while, a generalization must be longer and must be given more thought than a paper centered chiefly on interpretation or evaluation. (See Ch. 6 for a discussion of the uses of interpretations, opinions, and generalizations in the development of paragraphs.)

Although most of our opinions are borrowed outright from other people, in the process we may relate them to our own experience. Sometimes, just to be different, we adopt opinions that are the opposite of those held by others. Some opinions we form for ourselves, by putting two and two together from our experience and observation. A few are so close to our interests and knowledge that we work and rework them, taking account of other views, adapting and adding from whatever source we can. We think in terms of our opinions and to a certain extent guide our conduct by them. Since we talk about them, we can also write about them.

Subjects for opinion papers

The contents of many current magazines show that people are interested in—or at least writers write about and editors publish—opinions on almost every conceivable subject. You also have opinions on many subjects, opinions that you air freely in conversation and that with a little further reflection you might write about. The following list suggests some areas that you might consider for possible subjects of opinion papers.

1. *Manners and customs:* reactions to dress and fashion, home or office or school etiquette, dating, engagements, bringing up children or bringing up parents
2. *Social affairs:* an examination of family relations, weddings, holiday celebrations, entertainment, education, movement of people from farms to cities or from cities to suburbs, relations between groups of people
3. *Organizations and institutions:* interpretations and evaluations of clubs of all sorts, such as a lodge, a labor union, a church or one of its affiliated organizations
4. *Politics:* your own or your family's conclusions about a campaign or a political party, the conduct of elections, the duties of some office, the performance of a person in office
5. *Farming:* comparisons of methods, crops, machinery, soils; the reasons for the prices of farm products; evaluations of gardens and flowers for pleasure or profit; reflections on farming as a way of life
6. *Economics and business:* an examination of pricing, advertising and selling, qualities of products (from a consumer's point of view), buyers (from the point of view of the seller), tricks of the trade
7. *Technology and production:* comparison and evaluation of two or more processes, methods, materials, designs; interpretation of some trend in engineering, architecture, or any other special field.
8. *Health and medicine:* an examination of a popular notion or of one with supposedly scientific backing; the need for some new medical development; opinions arrived at from a person's experience with illness or from nurses' training or premedical studies
9. *Science:* interpretations of new developments, methods, applications, hypotheses, and theories
10. *Literature and the arts:* interpretations of and preferences in literature, painting, sculpture, music—of particular works, of the works of one person; discussion of methods or styles in painting; attitudes toward certain aspects of the "popular arts" of movies, television, folk music

These are general subjects rather than specific topics for opinion papers. To explore the possibilities in one field in more detail, consider the general subject of education. You have plenty of opinions about it that you have formed from your experiences in grade and high school, and you are rapidly acquiring opinions from your college life—possibly beginning with your first reading of the admission requirements. Some of these opinions are not much more than pet peeves, but many of them could be developed into interesting papers. In considering possible subjects, don't limit yourself to grievances. Although it may be easier to write in a lively way of faults and matters that need improvement, it is also worth while to write of things you approve of or are enthusiastic about. It is impossible to avoid topics that others have discussed, but you should shun the hackneyed ones (like the advantages of fraternity life, the importance of athletics as a preparation for life, the advantages of a small college over a large one or vice versa), unless you have a new approach to the matter and fresh, personal examples.

The list below suggests only a few of the subjects that can be chosen from the general field of education. The blanks in the statements can be filled in various ways; a question allows for the development of several possible answers; the opposite of the definite statements may be supported. Your stated opinion should be prefaced by "I think," "I believe," "I would like to see," "I recommend," or some other such personal qualification. Papers on these or similar subjects may range from evaluations of specific situations through suggestions and recommendations to more inclusive discussions of complex situations.

1. The hardest grade to teach must be the _______.
2. What are the reasons for the bad behavior of some students?
3. Do the poorer students limit the work of the better students?
4. Why do some students resist school instruction?
5. What happens in school to the natural curiosity of youngsters?
6. The trouble with "progressive education" is that it has been more written about than practiced.
7. High school work would be more effective if the classes were smaller.
8. The literature read in high school should be chosen _______.
9. More of the contemporary poets should be presented in high school.
10. The natural sciences are better taught than the other subjects.
11. Our college catalog makes selecting courses unnecessarily difficult.
12. This institution should have more courses in _______.
13. It is hard to choose a major department.
14. The system for advising students on courses needs _______.
15. The presentation of (some social situation) in (a specific course) bears little relation to life as I know it.
16. _______ is a model (an impossible, a pretty good) textbook for an introductory course.
17. What is the difference between a major and a minor sport?
18. Student government is not a government but a sort of buffer set up between the administration and the student body.

19. Graduates of liberal arts colleges get jobs as easily as graduates from the vocational colleges.

In addition to these more or less continuing subjects, you may have some contribution to make to one of the topics about education being currently discussed in newspapers and magazines. These will vary from year to year. Some suggested by recent discussions are:

1. Children still learn to read.
2. One reason for poor reading is the material students are asked to read.
3. Why should our public education imitate Russian education?
4. Requiring more mathematics and science of high school students will probably ________.
5. My suggestions for helping superior students are ________.

The collections of readings used in composition courses generally include a group of articles on education that will contain specific points that you might want to question or disagree with or for which you can give further evidence from your experience. More complex questions about education will involve reading and study and would make good subjects for reference papers:

1. What are the most reliable estimates of the number of students who will be in college in five years?
2. What do the English think of their system of education?
3. What are the facts and issues in the argument over federal support of higher education?

The purpose of considering these subjects is to show that you can find some topic on which you have opinions and the material to back them up. The paper should not sound like an article by a specialist in education or an address by a college president, but like the work of a student who has thought about the subject and, since he is in the actual educational process, has something to say that can make a small contribution to the general discussion.

Some special considerations

We often hear or say, "Everyone has a right to his opinion." This is fair enough for a person as an individual, but anyone who is going to express his opinions in writing for others to read has a responsibility to examine them closely, to consider his reasons for holding them, and to judge how convincing they will seem to others. The basic method is to question the material. Will a careful, intelligent reader, who perhaps does not agree with me, understand and possibly agree with my presentation? Can I say this? Should I say this? Must I say this?

An opinion can be stated in a sentence or two, but its bare statement may not, and ordinarily will not, make it acceptable to others. To make your opinion understandable and, even more, to make it convincing, you need evidence, for the most part facts that support your opinion. To produce a good opinion paper, you need to be careful in *using facts*, but you also must be careful in *using generalizations, indicating relationships,* and *taking account of other views*. This section will consider these points in some detail.

Using facts

Actually the larger part, often more than three fourths, of an opinion paper consists of facts, details selected to explain why the writer thinks as he does and to prove the validity of his opinion.

Accuracy is obviously fundamental. You need to be scrupulous in reporting your own observations and experiences, and you need to check the information you get from others. In using material from published sources, you need to draw upon sources that are recent and known to be authoritative.

The details should be stated as specifically as possible. Vague phrases like "a considerable number" or "somewhere in the Midwest" should be replaced by concrete information, for example, "10,500" or "Elkhart, Indiana." The writers of the following passages started out with the same data, but one has translated his knowledge into much sharper language:

Vague	*Exact*
One of the most desirable properties of the metal known as aluminum is its lightness. It is much lighter in weight than other widely used metals. People are conscious of the fact that this quality means that they get more for their money when they buy products that are made of aluminum.	One of the most desirable qualities of aluminum is its lightness; it is about one third as heavy as copper, brass, or steel. Therefore, if a man buys a pound of aluminum nails, he gets three times as many as he would get if he bought a pound of steel nails.

There should be sufficient facts. The amount of evidence needed depends upon the complexity of the problem. A new or unpopular idea usually needs more particulars to support it than one that is widely held. A few well-chosen details may make an opinion seem plausible; more might make it seem really convincing. When you appear to be forming your opinion on the basis of specific instances (a process called *induction*), you need to give enough data to convince the reader that you have not just chosen a few instances which happen to fit your case. Although it is impossible to put in enough details for absolute proof, a good sample of typical or crucial details will "make the point."

A sufficient number of details will keep you from oversimplifying the problem and thus settling on a too easy solution. You may feel, for example, that students misbehave because they are bored by the subject matter of the course and propose as a solution that more interesting subject matter be offered. A fuller investigation of the situation may reveal (a) that some students because of poor background or training or low mentality feel inferior and misbehave to get recognition; (b) that some students suffer from severe emotional disturbances that in part explain their behavior; (c) that some students because of physical disabilities–poor eyesight or deafness–are unable to read the blackboard assignments and explanations or cannot follow the classroom discussions. Since more interesting subject matter would not necessarily change the behavior of these students, you could not be satisfied with your original solution.

A number of details will also prevent you from "stereotyping," from using loose general labels that ignore the individual differences that actually exist. Much intolerance–insofar as it has any basis at all in reason–is founded on broad generalizations about groups, generalizations that may be false if applied to single members of the group. There are stereotypes for almost any group–for Swedes, school teachers, blondes, Indians, Baptists, Rotarians, movie stars, Texans, scientists, and so on. Remember that the fact that an individual belongs in a certain group does not determine his whole make-up and that his thousand other characteristics make him, in some respects at least, different from any other person. For example, it would be foolish for you to decide on the basis of one experience that all teachers of small country schools are poorly educated and have limited backgrounds. Visiting various country schools or checking with people who have had more experience with them (county superintendents, state school inspectors) would undoubtedly give you a quite different opinion.

The facts or details you use must be relevant to the question and to your view of it. Of course there are degrees of relevance. If you are trying to show that the college advisory program is understaffed, that more faculty members are needed to help students make out their course programs, you would certainly want to mention the number of students being handled by individual advisors as well as the amount of time the advisors have available for their work. You would probably describe their attitudes and their knowledge of the courses available in all departments. You might mention the institution's course requirements and department requirements for majors if they showed how large an area of choice remained in which advice might be helpful. But there would be no point in giving details which concerned paying tuition, even though tuition payment might be a part of the process of registration. Relevance is a matter of judgment, of the relationship between the details and your opinion.

You must be careful in using comparisons or analogies (extended comparisons). Sometimes they are used chiefly to emphasize a point, as part of the exposition, as in this:

> If we imagine the earth's atmosphere as a great unknown ocean, we can recognize the experiments of the International Geophysical Year as cosmic counterparts of the Atlantic voyages of Christopher Columbus. Astronomers of Columbus's day knew very well, from mathematical calculations, that the earth was round. But they didn't know what lay beyond their immediate horizon. Today's geophysicists are in much the same position regarding the horizon of space.—*Saturday Review*, July 6, 1957, p. 41

For such a use often a single point of similarity (here, a voyage into the unknown) may suffice. But when comparisons or analogies are used as evidence, you should be sure that the points of likeness are actual and that important, contradictory differences are not overlooked. The argument that because a sick adult is cured by taking a certain medicine, a baby with the same illness will also be cured by it fails to take into account vital differences. Although both the adult and the baby are human beings suffering from the same illness, the comparison would be justified as evidence only if their physical reactions to the medicine are alike. Even when a comparison is sound, it is only partial evidence. No matter how similar two situations may be, there are always differences, some of which we may not know about.

To test the value of particular facts as evidence, consider them in terms of these questions: Are the facts directly related to my opinion? Are there enough of them to support it? Have I stated the facts exactly? And, above all, are they accurate?

Using generalizations

Although the generalizations you use in a paper will not bulk so large in space as the specific facts, they are of great importance. In addition to generalizations you arrive at yourself, you may want to use some existing generalizations to help make your opinion more convincing. These generalizations range from popular beliefs (Spare the rod and spoil the child) through widely accepted ideas (Language is a unique ability of man) to all sorts of general beliefs (about why people act as they do or about philosophy and religion) and even to the hypotheses and theories of various sciences (atomic structure the nature of light, the origins of life or of the universe).

If you use such generalizations as support for your own opinion you must not content yourself simply with stating the generalization—unless you think your readers will all agree with it, and even then you may be taking too much for granted. For example, a good many people do not believe that a child is spoiled if he is not punished physically (Spare the rod and spoil the child). In fact, many people are strongly opposed to the use of physical punishment in correcting a child. To make use of an existing generalization, you need to do two things. First you must state the generalization clearly and fully and show its significance and perhaps something of its basis. Second you must bring your own opinion in touch with it.

Suppose you are developing one of your ideas about higher education: that only superior students (or, on the contrary, that almost all young people) should be admitted to a university, or suppose you want to show that vocational preparation is (or is not) a proper aim of college training. You would discuss students, their needs and desires and abilities as you see them, and perhaps the curriculum of some specific institutions. These would be your facts. But you would also use some generalizations as a framework for your reasoning and as support for your ideas. There are plenty of generalizations about that you might draw on. For example:

1. One of the aims of higher education has always been to prepare students for vocations.

2. The principal aim of higher education is to further the individual development of each student.

3. "The justification for a university is that it preserves the connection between knowledge and the zest for life, by uniting the young and the old in the imaginative consideration of learning."—A.N. Whitehead "Universities and Their Function," in *The Aims of Education*, p. 139

The simple statement of one of these generalizations would not be much help to an argument. Not many people, for instance, would immediately accept number 1, though it is the most specific and factual of the three. A sampling of evidence for it would be necessary to make it useful. Professor Whitehead uses it in the essay from which number 3 is taken and (between statements of his own generalizations about education for business) gives relevant facts in support of it:

The novelty of business schools must not be exaggerated. At no time have universities been restricted to pure abstract learning. The Univer-

> sity of Salerno in Italy, the earliest of European universities, was devoted to medicine. In England, at Cambridge, in the year 1316, a college was founded for the special purpose of providing "clerks for the King's service." Universities have trained clergy, medical men, lawyers, engineers. Business is now a highly intellectualized vocation, so it well fits into the series.—pp. 137-8

Even though the few details given do not prove the generalization, they would suggest to a reader who didn't believe it that perhaps his idea of what higher education used to be was too narrow. Then the generalization might help you in a plea for recognizing vocational education, but since it properly begins "One of the aims," you could not use it as your only argument.

The second generalization could be used to support a different point, perhaps an emphasis on general as contrasted with specialized or vocational education. Preparing it for use, amplifying it, would probably mean analyzing the terms *principal aim* (What are some of the other aims?) and *individual development*. This latter term might involve some definition of maturity, of the use of the fruits of education in a person's leisure time and in his position as a member of society. These particular points could then be brought into relation with your specific opinion.

The third generalization is somewhat different from the first two. Quoting it would let you borrow something of the prestige of a well-known and respected philosopher. The phrasing is appealing and thought provoking. But despite the prestige of the source and the excellent expression of the idea, this generalization would not necessarily be accepted by your readers. ("Zest for life," huh, where is it in these classes? What does he mean, "uniting the young and the old" or "*imaginative* consideration of learning?") It is a statement of an ideal, one of the possible ideals, and consequently harder to relate to actual experience. But it could be used to suggest or to emphasize qualities of personal relations and of liveliness you might think desirable in education.

This all suggests that in using the generalizations of others, we need to look at them carefully, as carefully as at our own. For example, we must not rely too readily on someone else, even on someone we regard as an authority. We should question his authority. Is he qualified in this particular field? Competence in one field does not guarantee competence in another: an atomic scientist may not be an authority on international relations. Do others in his field recognize him? It he relatively objective? A labor leader's views on picketing should be taken as representing one side only and possibly should be balanced by an employer's view.

We must remember, too, that many generalizations involve other generalizations, or assumptions. One way to test your own generalizations or those of others is to look at the assumptions, which often are implied rather than stated. For example:

> If he didn't steal my billfold, then somebody else must have. (*Assumption:* There is only one possible cause for the disappearance of my billfold: it has been stolen.)
>
> To prevent a serious depression we must either cut taxes or subsidize industries. (*Assumption:* These two ways are the only possible ways to prevent a serious depression.)
>
> There wouldn't be any juvenile delinquency if mothers stayed at home instead of working for pretty clothes and television sets. (*Assumptions:* The employment of mothers is the cause of juvenile delinquency; all employed mothers work in order to buy selfish luxuries.)

It is safer—that is, you will make more convincing statements—if you look for the implied assumptions in your statements, and in the statements of others that you may want to quote, and then present them openly, so that your reader can also examine them. A careful examination of the implied assumptions may suggest revision or even complete rejection of your original generalization. (See *Logic.)

Finally, you should be as scrupulous in stating your generalizations as in stating your facts, even though it is more difficult to do. In conversation we generalize hastily and too sweepingly: "Fishing is no good in this lake; I haven't had a bite for three hours." (Certainly more evidence is necessary.) Statements with *all, every, always, never, only, nothing but, either . . . or* should be carefully examined, because one small bit of evidence to the contrary will weaken them or perhaps even refute them. Most generalizations require abstract words, and these should be defined and illustrated whenever possible by specific instances. (See Ch. 8, p. 219.) You may feel intensely about your subject, but you need to remember that your reader may not and may indeed think quite differently. Careful preliminary examination of generalizations—your own and those of others—even if it means making less sweeping claims, should lead to a more persuasive paper.

Considering relationships

If you are to convince your reader, it is especially important for him to see the relationship between your ideas, and that means that you must first see them yourself. Making relationships clear is in part just a matter of continuity of statement, as discussed in paragraph development (see Ch. 6, p. 159). Most of the relationships are simple —a particular situation as an example or illustration of what you mean, or a comparison or contrast to clarify and emphasize. But a few special points need to be made about three relations: *analysis, reasons, cause and effect.*

Often the subject of your opinion (a book, an occupation, a social situation) needs to be *analyzed,* to be divided into its component parts. The basis of the analysis should be suited to your actual purpose. In discussing safety features of new automobiles, you might group cars according to their relative safety or you might base your classification on types of driving hazards; in discussing their cost, you might divide automobiles into four price ranges; in discussing their appearance, you might group comparable models. The basis should be consistent. You might laugh at a misgrouping like "cars, trucks, and Fords" but might not see the same error in "encyclopedias, magazines, and reference books," which should be "magazines, encyclopedias, and other reference books." The groups should be actual divisions, not overlapping units:

Inconsistent	*Consistent*
Universities	Universities
Liberal arts colleges	Liberal arts colleges
Church institutions	Separate professional schools
Teachers colleges	(Including teachers colleges
Junior colleges	and others if subdivided)
Separate professional schools	

(Junior colleges and church-supported institutions belong in a different division altogether.)

And the groups together should add up to the whole: "The primary colors in painting, red and yellow" is not a satisfactory classification because it omits the blue group; an analysis of "minority groups in the United States" would be inaccurate if it included only two or three. Sometimes a qualification like "some" will show that you do not intend to be complete, or you can make the flat statement that there are "others."

In giving *reasons,* which are important for demonstrating an opinion, you should remember that there are two sorts that may possibly apply—the reasons why you hold the opinion and the reasons why people in general might hold it. These may be the same, but they may not be. You may believe one political party has the better program for the United States because your parents believe so or because something in your own experience leads you to believe it. There is no harm in saying this, but you must remember that these are not reasons why people in general might hold the opinion and that they will not do much to convince your readers. The more important reasons answer or seem to answer the question *Why is this so?* In an article "The Fuss About Eggheads," in the April 1957 issue of *Encounter,* Seymour Martin Lipsit asks "Why then do American intellectuals *feel* that they are looked down upon?" and proceeds to give three principal reasons:

1. American intellectuals' feeling of inferiority comes from using the situation of European intellectuals as a point of reference. Two specific aspects of the Europeans' situation are discussed: European intellectuals are given more recognition by other groups (6 paragraphs), and they have more influence on popular culture (2 paragraphs).
2. There are so many American intellectuals in specific professional groups that they tend to stay in small groups and do not form a large, single group of intellectuals (3 paragraphs).
3. The income of American intellectuals is relatively lower than that of other groups (1 paragraph).

Perhaps the most important point to remember in giving reasons is that since there is rarely just one reason for a view, giving several will not only be more accurate and more convincing but will indicate that you have thought seriously about the subject. (See Ch. 6, pp. 145-147.)

One of the most important relations is of *cause and effect*. We reason both from cause to effect and from effect to cause. For example, if you drive over broken glass (effect), you decide that someone has broken a bottle on the highway (cause). A minute later, the glass becomes a cause as you hear air hissing from a punctured tire (effect). Such immediate cause-effect relations are simple but in a complex issue they become more complicated. There are usually many factors operating to produce a given situation; most of these factors cannot be tested in isolation, but our knowledge of events can show pretty certain relations. For example, the birth rate tends to fall in a period of economic depression and to rise in boom years. From this evident relationship we conclude that economic factors affect (are at least one of the causes to be considered in discussing) the birth rate.

Sometimes the statement of the cause or the effect is too sweeping:

> No single individual was responsible for the basketball scandals, which resulted from the deterioration of morals and ideals in our colleges. (Cause too sweeping)
>
> End the H-bomb Tests–Save humanity. (Effect too sweeping)

You can test the soundness of your statement of this relationship by asking yourself a number of questions: Is the cause sufficient to produce the effect? Does the effect regularly and necessarily follow the cause as stated? Could there be other important causes? (See Chapter 6, page 145.)

Taking account of other views

Since you are presenting an opinion rather than facts, there are presumably other possible opinions, often held by people as well informed as you are. Considering them is part of the preparation for stating your own. They will frequently remind you of something you might (or might like to) overlook. They will often lead you to qualify your view, make a less extreme and so a more defensible statement.

Judgment differs about the wisdom of actually presenting differing opinions in your paper. It is often useful to open with an opinion with which you disagree, if you believe you have a better case and can refute it. It would ordinarily be bad tactics to end with other opinions, since that might leave the reader with active questions or even with a preference for the other opinions. But some consideration of differences along the way has advantages. It shows that you have actually thought about the matter from various points of view and that you have confidence in your own conclusion. It will help establish your right to discuss the subject. It will also give an impression of fairness if you deal frankly with differing opinions and do not take the unfair way of simply dismissing them, or, even worse, of insulting those who hold them. Perhaps the best reason for including different views is that if you handle them well the reader too will be led to see their weakness, and if he later meets with them he is inoculated against them.

In the following paragraph from "News and the Whole Truth" (*Atlantic Monthly,* Aug. 1952), Elmer Davis reminds us of a principle followed by most American newspapers and then suggests some of the arguments against the principle:

> There was not much objectivity in the American press through most of the nineteenth century; if a story touched on the political or economic interest of the editor or owner, it was usually written so as to make his side look good. Some papers still follow that practice; but most of them, for some decades past, have accepted the principle that they ought to try to be objective in the news columns, leaving argument to the editorial page. Publish everything that is said on both sides of a controversial issue, and let the reader make up his mind. A noble theory; but suppose that men who talk on one side (or on both) are known to be lying to serve their own personal interest; or suppose they don't know what they are talking about. To call attention to these facts, except on the editorial page, would not, according to most newspaper practice, be objective. Yet in the complex news of today how many readers have enough personal knowledge to distinguish fact from fiction, ignorance from knowledge, interest from impartiality?–pp. 34-5

Writing an opinion paper

Since the last three chapters have discussed various general and specific problems of writing papers, only a few points particularly important in writing opinion papers will be stressed here.

First of all, you must keep clearly in mind your purpose in writing. One purpose of an opinion paper is to present your view with enough evidence so that readers can see what you think and something of why. Another purpose is to influence readers, either to convince them, to get them to agree with your idea, or to persuade them, to get them to do something, as in a "plea for action." To do this you must consider what various readers now think or do, or may want to do. The basis for a persuasive paper still is a reasonable opinion and plenty of specific evidence for it. But the tactics noted in the previous section and in this one are also extremely important.

Limiting the subject

Limiting the subject is essential if you are to say anything that will really influence a reader's thinking. The vast arguments over heredity versus environment or science versus religion require very long treatments and a good deal of thought and specialized information. Smaller, more particular situations are better subjects for papers. In a short paper, you might, for instance, evaluate only one aspect of the campus newspaper–its editorial policy, its humor, the letters to the editor, its news coverage of student affairs, its typography and appearance. You can then concentrate your material on the area that is your central point.

Supplying transitions

The plan of the essay must not only be clear in your mind but must be clearly indicated in your paper by careful transitions. (See Ch. 6, p. 159.) Abstract markers like *nevertheless, for example,* and *however* are essential in papers about ideas. At the beginning of a new block of material, a key word may echo the preceding unit, or a pronoun may help tie two units together. Sentences in parallel form emphasize the pattern of thought. Mechanical markers like Arabic numerals or lower case letters are sometimes helpful, though it is less obvious and often more appropriate to use words like *second* or *next*. Whatever the transitional markers used, they should be varied. Opinion papers may need more elaborate transitions than narrative or factual papers, but the markers should never be conspicuous.

Opening and concluding paragraphs

The beginning of your paper should be strong. You can ask a question that will lead to your opinion; or you can give a widely held opinion that you intend to replace with a better one; or you can state your opinion firmly and go on to give evidence for it; or, especially if the subject is familiar, you can begin with details. For example, you could begin to discuss the campus paper by quoting or describing some particular stories in it.

The ending should be strong, too. You can save a telling bit of evidence for that position, or, more often, you can make an emphatic restatement of your opinion or show what the consequences of your view are.

Keeping your readers in mind

It is especially important to think of your readers as you write, because you want them at least to see that it is reasonable for you to think as you do, and more likely you want them to agree with you. You should keep their probable opinions in mind and use examples and comparisons and evidence that will be convincing to them. Persuasion requires more tact, more careful use of language, more systematic marshaling of material, and in general more awareness of readers than most other types of writing.

Avoid the temptation of repeating your opinion without advancing it in some way. Tie restatements to bits of new evidence so that the reader will feel the paper is advancing rather than going in a circle.

And finally, revise your paper for the quality of individual statements, seeing that they are accurate and vigorous but not too dogmatic or "emotional." If you find unfairly loaded words, or unanalyzed slogans, or "glittering generalities," try to make them more reasonable, appealing to your readers' better judgment. If the paper represents your actual view of the matter when you are seriously considering it, you can be firm enough and fair at the same time. See Chapter 8 for a discussion of slanted words, responsible use of words, etc.

The first part of this chapter has discussed general points applying to the writing of opinion papers; the last part will consider and illustrate some common types of opinion papers—corrections and refutations, and reviews and book reports.

Corrections and refutations

People steadily write letters-to-the-editor and articles correcting or refuting some generally held idea. We all have some beliefs that we feel are superior to what some other people hold or some special information that might puncture a common belief or "superstition." Such material makes a good opinion paper.

Here are three examples of such pieces that may suggest a topic to you. The first is confident and vigorous, because the writer was sure of his point (and had in fact given more detailed evidence earlier in the book from which this passage is taken):

> It is the point of view of this report that *a study of the real grammar of Present-day English has never been used in the schools* and that the conclusions concerning its effectiveness relate only to the type of "grammar" that has been tried. The "grammar" hitherto used in the schools has been either the logical analysis of sentences and "parsing," most often illustrated by the various methods of diagramming, or a learning of rules and definitions which were assumed to be the measures of correct language. As indicated in the first two chapters of this book, this use of grammar assumes that the problem of language usage is a simple one of *correct* forms and *mistakes* which can easily be separated according to the rules. The teaching efforts that have been devoted to this type of grammar have therefore been directed toward making pupils "conscious of the rules" by which to determine correctness.
>
> In the light of the principles which underlie our investigation this customary use of "grammar" is fundamentally unsound. First, language usage cannot thus be separated into two simple classes. Instead, our usage presents a complex range of differing and changing practices which must be understood in relation to the feelings of an indefinite number of social groups. Second, sensitiveness to usage–a richness of assimilated experience through which one becomes aware of the suggestions attaching to words and constructions because of the circumstances in which they are commonly used–is the only condition upon which good English can be won. All the effort which goes to make one *conscious* of "rules of grammar" serves to deaden this sensitiveness to one's speech environment and to turn one's attention away from the only source of real knowledge.–C. C. FRIES, *American English Grammar,* pp. 285-6

The second example is an article by Arthur Ames, "The Beleaguered Wagon Train" (*The Pacific Spectator,* 1950, IV:320-322). It is more tentative, really only raising the question of the historical accuracy of "a very beautiful and revered American legend."

> I scarcely need to offer a description. The covered wagons have been driven into a circle, women and children, oxen and horses sheltering inside. From between the spokes, the men shoot outward with their long rifles, and on the outside of the circle, the Indians gallop, shooting their arrows at the wagons from underneath the necks of ponies.

Major Ames then gives four reasons for his doubt:

> 1. Lack of first-hand evidence. "I have never found in a historical work, or in an original diary of covered-wagon travel, any such actual occurrence."

2. Difficulty and unlikelihood of the maneuver. "To ride round and round, trying to get to effective bow-and-arrow range while riflemen under cover picked you off, was not a sound military maneuver, and the Plains Indians were excellent tacticians," who would certainly have attacked while the train was in a line.

3. Unlikelihood that the Indians could approach without being seen or heard and so surprise the train.

4. Improbability in the light of the general history of the time. Between 1842 and 1860, the period of the migration, the Plains Indians were at peace with the whites, and though the Indians of the Great Basin gave some trouble, they never fought on horseback.

He then gives some suggestions to explain how the legend arose and ends still "a reluctant skeptic," with the reader joining in his skepticism.

Even larger topics can be approached in this way, but the aim is rather to raise questions than to offer "proof." In *Harper's Magazine* for March 1952, Joyce Cary wrote on "The Mass Mind: Our Favorite Folly" (pp. 25-27). This is a large idea, and holding for or against it is more a matter of temperament than of reason. In the first paragraph Mr. Cary states the belief that he opposes:

> We are all told constantly that people are becoming more and more standardized. That mass education, mass amusements, mass production, ready-made clothes, and a popular press are destroying all individuality —turning civilization into a nice, warmed, sterilized orphan asylum where all the little lost souls wear the same uniforms, eat the same meals, think the same thoughts, and play the same games.

Then follow four reasons why Mr. Cary does not hold this belief:

1. As an administrator in an African tribe, he had found "more truly a mass mind than anything I had known in Europe." In breaking with tribal customs and taking on European ways, the people were becoming more independent.

2. Education is a principal means to variety. "The more education a man has the more likely he is to be independent in his views and obstinate in sticking to them. A committee of professors, I can assure you, is much harder to manage than a council of African chiefs." The increase in law and regulation is evidence "of a growing number of people who think and act for themselves."

3. The large numbers taking part in any popular entertainment "have freely chosen to join that crowd and will join a different one tomorrow."

4. As education increases—as, for instance in Russia—it is more difficult to control the people. This leads to the last short paragraph: "The 'mass mind' is a delusion. How many dictators have been amazed when their rule, which seemed so strong, has collapsed in a few hours, without a friend?"

Although this article obviously does not "prove" that a mass mind does not exist, when read in its vigorous entirety, it is enough to raise questions about the belief, even in people who hold it.

You certainly have some bits of information or reasoning or belief that you feel are superior to what at least some people believe. Setting them out—perhaps with four reasons like the last two articles described—can make an interesting and perhaps illuminating paper.

Reviews and book reports

A review is a description and evaluation of something new. When we think of reviews we think first of evaluations of books, movies, and plays, but actually reviews are published of a large variety of things—of TV programs, concerts, recitals, recordings, art exhibitions; of new buildings; of new medicines and other chemical compounds from fertilizers to weed killers; of new machines of all sorts, including each year's crop of new cars. Many of these reviews appear in specialized magazines and go into considerable technical detail, but many are published in periodicals for general circulation and give the information that a fairly intelligent person with some interest but not a great deal of specialized knowledge might want. The purpose of a review is to inform the reader of the existence of the new thing and to give him some description and evaluation of it, so that if he is interested he can decide whether he wants to investigate it further for himself.

A review makes a good paper in a composition course because the subject is necessarily fresh, because you can find something you are actually interested in and would like to express your opinion about, because the subject is definite and easy to gather material about by actual observation, and because the review itself calls for compact, readable expression.

Typical content of reviews

The content of reviews, at least their essential points, has been pretty well standardized. It is customary to identify, classify, describe, and evaluate the subject.

Identifying the subject. A review should identify its subject specifically enough for a reader to find it (unless it is of a single occurrence, like a concert). For a book this means giving title, author, publisher, and usually the number of pages and price; for a movie—title, principals of the cast, theater where playing, and often the producer, director, and company; for a concert—time and place, principal performers or organization sponsoring it; for a product—its name (often a trade name), the model or type and perhaps catalog number, manufacturer, price, and often where it can be obtained if distribution is limited. In periodicals that regularly feature reviews this information is usually presented in a standardized form at the head of each review, though it may sometimes be stated in a sentence or two at the beginning of the text.

Classifying the subject. Usually you will tell what sort of thing your subject is, for instance, whether a movie is a western, a musical, a comedy, a mystery, a serious drama, a documentary, or what. This will ordinarily take only a phrase or two, but it helps the reader place the subject and suggests what it may be compared with. Some incidental facts like "the writer's third novel," "the fourth annual exhibition," "the 1959 version of the model" also relate the subject to other similar things.

Describing the subject. The bulk of your review will be details about the subject, either given in a block of description or scattered as evidence for your opinions. Gathering the material for a review simply calls for attentive observation–reading a book, seeing a movie, inspecting (and perhaps driving) a car, looking closely at whatever you are to discuss. Previous experience with things of the same sort guides you in what to look for, what is important. Of course the more specialized information you have, the more illuminating you can make the review, but anyone's careful attention can provide enough details to make a worthwhile paper.

Reviewers of books become very skilful in summarizing a story without giving its outcome away and in sketching sample scenes that are either representative or especially successful or unsuccessful. Something of the same sort is appropriate for a review of a movie. For the movie review you would also mention such technical features as the acting, the setting, lighting, and photography. For a review of an automobile there are details of appearance, of the body and accessories, of the motor, and of performance. Sometimes, especially in reviewing a book or a movie, you may be inclined to give too much description or to provide just description without an opinion, but a good eye for detail and for analysis is fundamental to a good review.

Evaluating the subject. The important feature of your review is your opinion, even though it may be stated briefly. It may range from an informal expression of your immediate reaction to a judgment based on considerable study and reflection. Ordinarily you will state it directly, but you may suggest it by the tone of your statements. It should sound like a genuine opinion, arrived at by observing the subject, not like what you think you are supposed to say. As with other opinion papers, you should be able to give reasons that will make your evaluation plausible. These will for the most part be specific facts about the subject but will sometimes be relevant generalizations. There is a temptation to take refuge in vague or in sweeping verdicts: "I liked it," "Perhaps it is as good as we can expect," "It is the best...," "It is the poorest...." One way to avoid this is to give (in addition to your general opinion of the subject) some specific verdicts on particular aspects or parts (as of the various aspects of a movie), some of which will undoubtedly be more successful than others.

You will find comparisons very helpful in making such discriminations. The comparison (or contrast) may be with something similar—with other books by the same writer or of the same type, with last year's model or with another make of this year's automobiles, with another building of the same type or by the same architect. Or the comparison may be with your ideal of what such a thing should be or with some example that is generally regarded as a standard. Making such comparisons is an automatic part of forming your opinion, and often, if they can be stated briefly, they help a reader see or understand the subject by associating it with something he already knows.

A review sometimes includes other matters (for interest or for what light they throw on the subject), especially *background facts,* something about the making of the subject, and *generalizations,* the reviewer's general beliefs about the sort of thing being reviewed, about its proper function, or about its place in society. But the body of short reviews will be the description and evaluation.

You will find the essential elements in this review of a book on education:

> Though Irving Adler's *What We Want of Our Schools* (John Day, $3.75) was published a month before the first sputnik was launched, the launching makes it more rather than less cogent, because Adler speaks to the times. Most of the recent popular critics of American public education have been conservatives trying to guide education back to the path they knew when they were young; most of them have been trained in the liberal arts, with at most a limited interest in innovation in general and in technological innovation in particular; and often their firsthand experience of public schools has been slight. Adler, on the other hand, is a radical, a man who wants to make changes that are not a return to old ways; his education is in science and mathematics, he is deeply interested in technology, and he has experience as a teacher of mathematics in public schools.
>
> On many points Adler seems to me very interesting and quite wrong. His conception of man as *only* a technological animal is too narrow: "man's characteristically human activity is directed toward control of his environment." Man is engaged in just as "human" an activity when he is controlling himself as when he is controlling his environment, possibly more so.
>
> In describing the social and economic pressures on public education, Adler undertakes a useful kind of analysis, but it is much too

crude to do justice to the facts. He sees the schools as squeezed between two groups: first, a small privileged class who want to keep school budgets low (to save taxes) and the quality of teaching poor (to assure a labor force that knows just enough to do its work but not enough to make any trouble), and second, "the common people" who want good schools for their children. Actually, in between these two groups stand most of the American people, who are and think of themselves as middle class; they run the schools because they supply most of the teachers and administrators, most of the members of PTA's and school boards, and most of the funds. They are not as rich as the members of the NAM, but they have a great many more votes. Those in the middle class are by no means united on what they want of the schools, except, to do them justice, most of them want the schools to be "good."

Adler's argument for academic freedom is also open to exception. He says that he believes that all points of view should be represented, though his chapter on the Negro and education suggests that he would not care to have his children taught by a white supremacist, and his (very good) discussion of teaching methods suggests that he would not care to have them taught algebra by anyone who believes in the theory of "incidental learning" (the theory that a subject can be picked up incidentally while the student is engaged in other projects or activities).

But, however that may be, the fact is that all points of view *cannot* be represented, and if academic freedom depended on such representation (as it does not), then academic freedom would be impossible. Think, for example, of the study of Shakespeare in college. Think of how many different courses you would need to have to represent all points of view on the authorship alone–you would have to have a Baconian, an Oxfordian, a Marlovian, a Dyerite, and so on and so on; you would even need a Shakespearean. Then think of all the other courses you would need to represent all points of view on the chronology, the text, and the interpretation of the plays. It is impossible. No philosophy department in America is large enough to include a spokesman for every philosophy; no economics department is large enough to include a spokesman for every economic theory; and none needs to be. What Adler means is that he thinks Communists should be permitted to teach. There is a fairly good argument on his side, but it does not depend on the principle that all points of view should be represented.

Yet if there were nothing else of value in Adler's book (and there is a good deal), it would be worth reading for one chapter alone, a chapter called "The I. Q. Hoax." This is a discussion which, if taken seriously, could make an important change in our estimate of the resources of human intelligence available to us. For Adler persuasively argues that the I. Q. has come to be regarded as a measure of *innate* ability, as a fixed limit on what can be expected of the child, and is used by the schools to excuse their own failures. He believes that schools should entirely stop using I. Q. tests and use only achievement tests, and that they should stop having "second track" curriculums to which students with low I. Q.'s are permanently condemned and instead set up "feeder courses" in which those with low scores on achievement tests would be specially trained until they were ready to enter the "first track." Adler is so intent on maintaining that all God's chillun must have shoes that a careless reading might give the impression that he thinks they all have feet of the same size. But in fact Adler does not deny that there are differences in human intelligence; he only argues that since we have found no reliable way of measuring those differences we have no business setting up an educational system based on them.—PAUL PICKREL, *Harper's Magazine*, Jan. 1958, pp. 87-8

It will help you select and focus the material for your review if you keep in mind that you are not only expressing your opinion but doing something for your readers by telling them about something that is new to them. The details from the description can help them decide whether they want to follow up the subject by themselves or ignore it, and your opinion may give them some guidance, whether or not they agree with it. Anything that shows what kind of people can benefit from the subject reviewed or that points out what they can expect to get from it is good material for the review. (Recall your conversations intended to get a friend to go to or to keep away from a certain movie.) Even a modest effort may help someone see more in something than he would see by himself. Reviews are not definitive evaluations but useful contributions to the understanding and circulation of new things.

Course book reports

A report on "outside reading" for a college course in some respects resembles a review. But since the book or article is generally not new and the reader (the instructor) presumably has read it, your report is primarily a record of your experience in the reading. The selection of the book, the nature of the report, and usually its form, are closely conditioned by the course. The particular aspects to be covered are usually specified or suggested by the subject and by the methods of the course. In a good report a book and a student are working together within the frame of a course.

The report may be a summary only, in which the scope of the book —what it covers—is clearly indicated and some specific points are selected for detailed presentation. These points would usually be selected because they add to material presented in the course or differ from it, or because they are especially well presented, show methods of work in the field, or make some definite contribution to the general area of knowledge. Unless a complete summary of the book is called for, a purposeful sampling of points makes the best report.

Sometimes you will need to add background material—something about the author of the book, or his reputation in the field, or reviews of the book by other authorities—though this kind of approach resembles that of a reference paper (Ch. 13). You may be asked to express some opinion of the book, some judgment of the accuracy of the information presented, of the interpretation of facts, of the method. Although it would take a good deal of experience to do this with authority, the course will have given you some background, and you can go quite a way by looking at the book itself—its convincingness, the support of its generalizations by facts, its conspicuous omissions, overelaborations, contradictions, extreme statements, and so on.

In a literature course a report of outside reading, say of a novel, usually involves some interpretation and evaluation, at least some individual response to the book. It is unlikely that you will come up with a new interpretation of a well-known poem or of a Dickens novel or that your evaluation will alter existing estimates of a Shakespearean play. But on most works there is considerable variation even among the experts, so that a direct statement of what you see in a work and of how it appeals to you, both supported by direct references to the text, has its place and is usually the goal of the reading. The interaction of description, interpretation, and evaluation that characterizes a review would be appropriate. The course will have established the important points to look for: in an elementary course—the content and meaning, mood, convincingness, social and personal bearings, and so on; in more advanced courses—more complex matters of method, structure, and style. Usually you are expected to show in a report that you can apply to your individual reading the methods appropriate to it which have been used in discussing class assignments.

In your report the work you used should be exactly identified, including the edition. Your writing should be clear and direct, neither apologetic nor pretentious. You should include many specific references to the book and a good deal of direct summary, with page references in parentheses unless footnotes are specified. So far as possible the material should be translated into your own words, though some quotation is usually needed—of points that are centrally important or that are distinctive in content or expression. Try to keep them short and where possible build them into your own sentences.

Although a book report is actually a course exercise rather than a piece of individual communication, it can help your composition by developing your judgment in selection of material, in summarizing a good deal in a short space, and in clear, compact expression.

Opinion papers force you to test your facts, to clarify your ideas, and especially to see the relationship between them—whether the opinions are actually supported by the facts. There is some truth in the common saying "I don't know what I think till I write it down," because the act of writing forces you to phrase, more or less exactly, what may have been the characteristic flux of your "mind." But this is writing notes to yourself, a useful stage perhaps but only a preliminary stage in actual composition.

For the purpose of written composition, as of conversation, discussion, and speeches, is communicating, sharing ideas with readers. A writer may present his ideas informally, seemingly for their own sake, or perhaps for his own gratification, as in a "personal essay." But few essayists would take the pains to express their ideas so well unless they to some degree expected or hoped for readers.

For a particular paper take one of your opinions that falls within the assignment and that can be adequately treated in the expected length, something manageable in two pages or six or whatever, and present it purposefully. In the actual writing you may find both the pleasure of extending the currency of one of your ideas, of representing something of yourself, and the pleasure of contributing to the responsible discussion of ideas that should characterize educated people.

Chapter 12

SUGGESTED STUDY AND WRITING

1. Look at the contents of two current magazines, and after browsing through the articles (not the stories), list the ones that are primarily information and those that are primarily opinion. What fields of interest do the opinion articles represent?

2. Study one or more opinion articles assigned by your instructor in your reading volume, applying the points about details, generalization, and relationships made in this chapter (pp. 329-337).

3. Cut out a review from a newspaper or magazine and paste it in the center of a sheet of paper. In the space at the right label the content of each sentence (identification, classification, description, evaluation) and at the left note any devices or traits of style or indications of tone.

4. Make a list, in the form of complete statements, of some opinions that you might develop in papers, indicating for each about the length you think an adequate presentation would be.

A) Your preference between two things (two books, two college courses, two political candidates, two cameras, two types of dress)
B) A popular notion that you might refute (pp. 339-342)
C) Something new that you might review (pp. 342-348)
D) One opinion for each of three of the fields listed on page 326
E) Two opinions in the field of education

5. Make some notes of good reasons for holding two opposing or at least differing opinions of the same thing, and write a paper developing the one you prefer, taking due account of the more important reasons for the other view.

His [the teacher's] problem is to protect the spirit of inquiry,
to keep it from becoming blasé from overexcitement,
wooden from routine, fossilized through dogmatic instruction,
or dissipated by random exercise upon trivial things.

JOHN DEWEY

Chapter **13**

Reference papers

...an honest and industrious manufacturer,

who has fairly procured the raw materials,

and worked them up with a laudable degree of skill and success.

EDWARD GIBBON (of himself as historian)

A college library is for fun and for work. It furnishes books and periodicals for leisure reading and for supplementing laboratory work, lectures, recitations, conferences, and textbooks in the main work of education—furthering the individual's intellectual development.

Although probably larger and more complexly organized, the college library is not fundamentally different from the school and public libraries you have been using. It has its staff of specialized librarians, stated hours, rules for the circulation of books, system of classifying and arranging books, card catalog, stacks filled with books, and various special collections. All these a student needs to know about, because self-reliant use of the library is absolutely necessary in carrying on college work. This training is also valuable in later life. A college graduate isn't expected to know everything, but he should know how to find out about almost anything.

For both your leisuretime and worktime use of the library, you need to know its general rules, the best method of finding books by using the card catalog, the location of recent periodicals, the new book shelf, the fiction section, the location of any particular sort of book that specially interests you, the provisions for browsing and casual reading, the most comfortable chairs, and the best lighting. You also need to know the difference between rapid reading and close reading—when to read fifty to a hundred pages an hour, getting the gist of some light book or article, and when to read thoroughly, digesting carefully all that the writer says.[1]

---

[1] For helpful suggestions for the former, see C. Gilbert Wrenn and Luella Cole, *How to Read Rapidly and Well* (Stanford University, 1935), and for the latter, Mortimer J. Adler, *How to Read a Book* (New York, 1940), Part 2.

This chapter does not deal with leisure reading but with one phase of library *work*—using material drawn from close reading to write a paper, called variously a library paper, term paper, research paper, source paper, investigative paper, or reference paper.

Purposes of a reference paper

Most undergraduate reference papers are a record of intelligent reading about a particular subject in several sources. Genuine, or "original," research is the discovery and discussion of material that has not been generally known; undergraduate research is usually based on published information that has been gathered by someone else.

Since much college work consists of acquiring and discussing the information and ideas of others, standard methods of finding material, taking notes on it, and presenting it have been developed. Preparing a reference paper will give you practice in using these methods. In a composition course the method and form of the reference paper are often emphasized to give the student the preparation he will need to do papers in later courses. Advanced work, especially in literature, history, and the social sciences, depends on this sort of study, and in sciences a laboratory experiment is often supplemented by research in records of previous experiments. These same methods, more elaborately developed, are the basis of graduate work in the various professional schools, where theses, dissertations, and monographs are required; they are also the basis of many sorts of reports and industrial studies. A glance at the "learned journals" in a college library shows that in every field of knowledge there are periodicals containing research articles written by specialists for other specialists. A freshman reference paper is a start on the road of scholarship that extends through the advanced courses in college to the work of professional people who are steadily adding to our knowledge of the past and the present. It is also practice for research that you may do later for some club or special group, as part of a business project, or as an investigation of questions raised in your day-to-day experience.

Besides offering training in research methods, a reference paper clearly shows the various stages of the writing process (see chart, p. 247). Because of the length of a reference paper and the complexity of its material, each stage becomes particularly important. Choosing an appropriate subject is crucial, because a poor selection will make all later work a tiresome chore; gathering the material is by far the largest part of the task; selecting material and planning the paper are important because you cannot put in the paper all that you find; and preparing the manuscript requires special attention because of the footnotes and bibliography. Each stage requires time and judgment.

At first thought your own contribution to a reference paper may seem slight. The material comes from sources outside your experience, the style is impersonal, the language is rather Formal, and the intention is primarily to inform rather than to entertain or persuade. But actual work on a paper will show how large a part you actually play. You choose a subject related to some interest of your own. You not only uncover the material (a process often calling for ingenuity), but you constantly use your judgment in selecting which of dozens of facts fit your purpose. This purpose you have defined for yourself, and you must also arrange your points in a plan that will accurately emphasize your sense of their relative importance. Although the methods of gathering material have been worked out by thousands of research workers before you, and although the form of the manuscript has been standardized, the actual content and organization of your paper represent your own interest and judgment.

Furthermore, a reference paper is not just a series of facts. Facts must be *interpreted,* for only the most common knowledge can stand without some comment on its meaning. Questions of causes, of results, of significance are not settled by recording data; a mind must work on the facts and ideas to find their proper relationships and to see their meaning in perspective. You cannot gather and present research materials intelligently without leaving your mark on them.

The main purpose of a reference paper, from the point of view of a composition course, is to give training in college writing: in gathering, organizing, and putting into readable form material gained from study. But for the writer, much of the interest as well as the profit comes from the material itself, from acquiring knowledge and becoming something of an authority in a small field.

Choosing a subject

You can write on almost any subject, but if you choose "almost any subject" at random, you will regret it. Preparing a reference paper is a long job; it will become a bore or at least a waste of time unless you pick a subject that interests you and that will add something useful to your stock of knowledge. It is a good idea to make your selection only after a comparison of the merits of two or three possible subjects.

Choosing a field

The natural way to begin choosing a topic for research is to consider a field in which you are really interested. It may be business or medicine or engines or dress design or anything else. It may be a field that you are studying in another course–chemistry, history, sociology, or language; any course touches briefly on subjects that you would like to know more about, raises questions that it does not fully answer.

Your own experience has raised many questions that can be answered with a little study. You may have worked or traded at a chain store and wondered about the organization of chain stores, the amount of the country's business they handle, or the reasons for special taxes on them in some states. You may be interested in some person, living or dead, and want to know more about him. You may have wondered about something referred to in the newspapers–the British Labour Party, UNESCO, the cost of living index, French impressionist painting. You may play a saxophone and want to know something of its origin and rise to popularity. You may be interested in some recent development in technology (transistor radios, new vaccines, atomic power in industry) or in some organization (a government agency, the Society of Friends, the Associated Press). These subjects only suggest the range of possibilities. Books and periodicals can furnish information for a reference paper about any one of them.

A good paper can also be developed by taking an opinion you hold, or think you hold, and doing some reading to find evidence to support it. You may approve or disapprove of "right to work" legislation, or of hazing in colleges, or of pay television. But if you start with a strong opinion, make a special effort to maintain an open mind, or you may find yourself selecting only material that fits your case. Looking for sound factual evidence will probably result not only in a more valid opinion but in a better understanding of the problem.

Although any topic is possible, there are some that you should be warned against. It is good sense to avoid topics that are too commonly chosen or that do not represent a genuine personal choice, the kind that students fall back on as a last resort–the history of baseball, juvenile delinquency, the American Indian. Your instructor can tell you what topics he has found to be unsuitable. Topics for which material is uncertain, like treatment of cancer, or for which the material is likely to be biased or emotional, like communism, are difficult because you need unusual judgment to handle them. A topic that you already know thoroughly may prove boring. Your instructor's advice will be useful in finding a topic that not only will promise a good paper within the purpose and limitations of the assignment but will be good for *you*.

Defining the subject

Some of the subjects just mentioned are narrow enough to be treated in two or three thousand words, but most of them are *fields* that include many subjects for papers. Each needs to be limited to a topic that can be treated adequately, treated with enough detail so that you can really inform a reader and do something besides enumerate the commonplace facts that most people already know. After a little general reading in a field, you can focus on a particular topic, always keeping in mind the approximate length of your paper. Better than "the Associated Press" would be the origin of the Associated Press, or its present organization, or its chief services; instead of "airplanes" or "aviation," the safety devices in airplanes or air freight lines. Sometimes the library yields information on one phase more readily than on another. Perhaps you will find a topic just to one side of the one you started on, perhaps not "sources of pigments for oil painting" but "tempera as a medium of painting."

As quickly as possible you should narrow your subject to a workable topic, usually while gathering your working bibliography or at least in the very early stages of note-taking. Your instructor can offer suggestions for the final selection of a topic, especially if you indicate the sort of material that interests you. Thoughtful and early attention to the definition of your subject will make all later stages of the work easier and more profitable.

Sources of references

Almost everyone starts work on a paper with one or two sources in mind—a discussion in a textbook, a magazine article, the name of a writer, the title of a book. Very often preliminary reading furnishes references to other works, and these make a natural starting point for the working bibliography. But a businesslike assembling of possible useful sources depends on intelligent use of the resources of the library. There are several aids planned specifically to direct you to books and periodicals that you can use.

The card catalog

The library card catalog lists all the books in the library by *author,* by *title,* and by *subject*. Some books, of course, are cataloged under more than one subject heading. If you know the name of a man who has written on your subject, look up his name in the card catalog. If you know the title of a book dealing with your topic, look up the title in the catalog. Look up also the subject heading that you are writing about, remembering that your exact subject may not be given but that another heading may include it. You may not find the heading *Skyscraper*, for example, but under *Architecture* or *Building* you may find books that deal with skyscrapers. The library subject card below (*Public Welfare* is the subject heading) illustrates the information given about a book. Items 2, 3, 4, and 5 would be transferred to a bibliography card. The entry on the bibliography card should resemble that in the final bibliography as closely as possible (pp. 378-379, 399). Then making the final bibliography will be simply a matter of arranging the cards alphabetically and copying the entries, inserting conventional punctuation.

1. Card catalog subject heading
2. Library call number
3. Author
4. Title
5. Facts of publication
6. Miscellaneous facts about the book
7. Subject index
8. Information for librarians

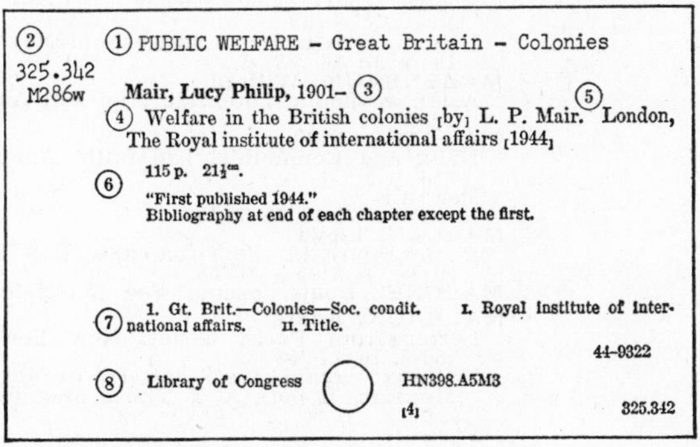

(2) 325.342 M286w
(1) PUBLIC WELFARE - Great Britain - Colonies

Mair, Lucy Philip, 1901- (3)
(4) Welfare in the British colonies [by] L. P. Mair. (5) London, The Royal institute of international affairs [1944]

(6) 115 p. 21½cm.
"First published 1944."
Bibliography at end of each chapter except the first.

(7) 1. Gt. Brit.—Colonies—Soc. condit. I. Royal institute of international affairs. II. Title.

44-9322

(8) Library of Congress HN398.A5M3
[4] 325.342

Library Subject Card

1. Topic of paper
2. Call number
3. Author
4. Title
5. Facts of publication
6. Pages on the specific subject (added from the book)

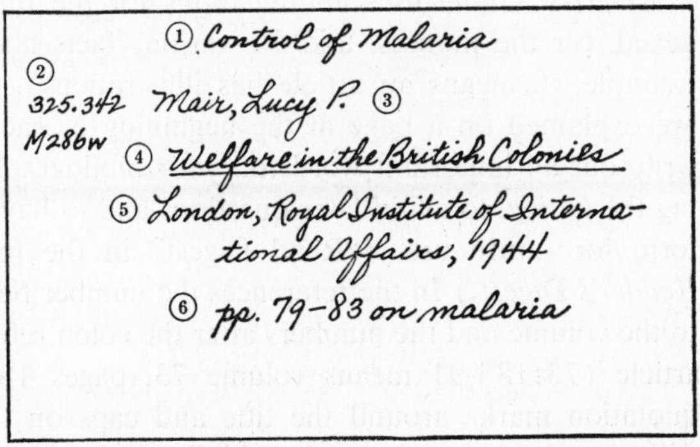

(1) Control of Malaria
(2) 325.342 M286w
Mair, Lucy P. (3)
(4) Welfare in the British Colonies
(5) London, Royal Institute of International Affairs, 1944
(6) pp. 79-83 on malaria

Bibliography Card

Periodical indexes

Next to the card catalog the most useful sources of references are *Readers' Guide* and other periodical indexes.

Readers' Guide. This reference source, which indexes magazines published since 1900, gives, under author entries and subject entries (see illustration below), references to articles in some 200 current magazines of general interest. It is published in paperbound booklets twice a month except in July and August, when it appears monthly, and later in cumulative volumes covering one or more years; it is consequently one of the most valuable sources for topics that are of current interest. The following excerpt from *Readers' Guide* for July 1958 shows typical entries:

MALARIA
Prevention and control
All-out attack on malaria. O. K. Armstrong. il Read Digest 73:188-91 Jl '58
Venezuela expects no malaria by 1960. Sci N L 73:377 Je 14 '58
MALCOLM, Donald F.
Books (cont) New Yorker 34:96-8+ Je 21; 86+ Je 28 '58
Eminently reasonable suggestion. New Repub 138:9 Je 16 '58
MALENBAUM, Wilfred
Asian economic potential. Ann Am Acad 318: 18-26 Jl '58
MALETER, Pal
Nagy and Communist bad faith. America 99: 386 Jl 5 '58
Portrait
Time 71:19 Je 30 '58
MALLAN, Lloyd
Photography in the space age. Pop Photography 43:51-5+ Jl '58
MALONE, Louis, pseud. See MacNeice, L.
MALRAUX, André
Letter from Paris. Genêt. New Yorker 34: 100-3 Je 14 '58
Malraux: again from letters to action. C. Mauriac. il pors N Y Times Mag p9+ Jl 6 '58
Portrait
Bsns W p29 Je 7 '58
Vision of victory. por Time 72:20 Jl 7 '58

Readers' Guide uses abbreviations for the titles of magazines indexed, for the months, and for various facts about the articles (for example, *il.* means an article has illustrations). These abbreviations are explained on a page at the beginning of each issue. You should write out all important words on your bibliography card before leaving the *Guide,* to avoid later questions and to have the data in correct form for future use. ("Read Digest" in the first entry stands for *Reader's Digest.*) In the references the number before the colon refers to the volume and the numbers after the colon refer to the pages of the article (73:188-91 means volume 73, pages 188 to 191). Putting quotation marks around the title and caps on the important words will give the entry the proper bibliographical form. A bibliography card for the second item of the second entry shown follows:

1. Topic of paper
2. Author
3. Title
4. Facts of publication
5. Description of content

(1) Traffic deaths in the United States
(2) Malcolm, Donald F.
(3) "Eminently Reasonable Suggestion"
(4) New Republic, June 16, 1958, 138:9
(5) (Satiric comment on number of unnescessary traffic deaths)

Bibliography Card from a *Readers' Guide* Entry

Other Magazine Indexes. A number of indexes list articles from specialized periodicals which are not covered by *Readers' Guide.* Most of them appear annually. The ones marked with a † in this list are the most generally useful and should be known by everyone:

Agricultural Index, 1916- . Subject index to a selected list of periodicals, books, bulletins, documents

Annual Magazine Subject Index, 1907- . Subject index to a selected list of American and English periodicals and historical society publications

Art Index, 1929- . Author and subject index to fine arts periodicals and museum bulletins

Bibliographic Index, 1937- . Subject index to bibliographies in books and periodicals

†*Biography Index,* 1946- . Subject index to biographical material in books and periodicals

†*Book Review Digest,* 1905- . Author, subject, and title index to published book reviews. Gives extracts and exact references to sources

Catholic Periodical Index, 1930- . Subject index to a selected list of Catholic periodicals

Dramatic Index, 1909- . Index to articles and illustrations concerning the American and English theater

†*Education Index,* 1929- . Author and subject index to educational periodicals, books, and pamphlets

Engineering Index, 1884-1905; 1906- . Subject index to technical periodicals; transactions and journals of engineering and other technical societies; reports of government bureaus, engineering colleges, research laboratories

Index to Legal Periodicals, 1926- . Author, subject, and book review index to legal periodicals

†*Industrial Arts Index,* 1913-1957. In 1958, it became two separate indexes: *Applied Science and Technology Index,* and *Business Periodicals Index.* Subject index to a selected list of engineering, trade, and business periodicals

†*International Index to Periodicals,* 1907- . Author and subject

index to periodicals from various countries; devoted chiefly to the humanities and the social sciences.

†*Nineteenth Century Readers' Guide,* 1944- . An index to periodicals, 1890-1899 and to some omitted from *Readers' Guide,* 1900-1922

Poole's Index to Periodical Literature, 1802-1906. Subject index to American and English periodicals, many of which are no longer published but are still important; precedes coverage of *Readers' Guide*

†*Public Affairs Information Service,* 1915- . Subject index to books, periodicals, pamphlets, and other materials in economics, government, and other public affairs

Quarterly Cumulative Index Medicus, 1927- . Author and subject index to medical literature in many languages

Subject Index to Periodicals, 1915- . An English index which includes some American periodical references

United States Government Publications; Monthly Catalog, 1895- . A bibliography of publications issued by all branches of the government

Ulrich's Periodical Directory (8th ed., 1956) lists periodicals under subjects they treat, answering the question: What periodicals are there in this field? It also tells where each is indexed so that it becomes an indirect guide to the contents of all magazines.

The New York Times Index. Most libraries have *The New York Times Index,* which now appears semimonthly and runs back to 1913. Although this index covers only *The New York Times,* it will serve as an index to other papers on matters of general importance because it gives the dates of events which would presumably be covered in all papers of the same date. Through this index you can find many speeches and important documents as well as the news stories of events.

Special bibliographies

Besides these periodical indexes there are many annual bibliographies in the learned journals in special fields and many bibliographies in one or more volumes that survey a complete field. Most of these are more elaborate than you will need for your practice reference paper, but when you begin to work in detail in a particular field, as in a college major subject, you should know the special bibliographies that serve it.

The key to these special lists is Besterman: *World Bibliography of Bibliographies* (2nd ed., 3 vols., 1947-1949), a standard and comprehensive work, or the shorter Ireland's *An Index to Indexes* (1942). The following standard bibliographies in the fields of history and literature show the extent of bibliographical aids available in many fields of study:

Articles on American Literature, 1900-1950 (Leary), 1954
Bibliographical Guide to English Studies (Cross), 10th ed., 1951
A Concise Bibliography for Students of English (Kennedy), 3rd ed., 1954
Bibliography of Writings on the English Language . . . to the end of 1922 (Kennedy), 1927 and supplement
Cambridge Bibliography of English Literature, 1940, 4 vols.
Literary History of the United States (Spiller and others), 1948, 3 vols.; Rev. ed. in 1 vol., 1953
Contemporary British Literature (Manly and Rickert), 1935
Contemporary American Authors (Millett), 1940
Literature of American History (Larned), 1902 and supplement
Bibliographies in American History (Beers), 1942
Guide to Historical Literature (Dutcher and others), 1931; repr. 1949

The following miscellaneous indexes are of frequent use to anyone engaged in reference work:

Vertical File Service Catalog, 1932- . An annotated subject catalog of pamphlets, booklets, brochures, leaflets, circulars, folders, maps, posters, charts, mimeographed bulletins, etc.
United States Catalog: Books in Print (1899-1934) Four editions and their supplements, constituting a comprehensive record of American book publication from 1898 to 1934
Cumulative Book Index, 1898- . Supplement to the *United States Catalog;* since 1930 an author, subject, and title index to books printed in English
Catalog of the Public Documents of Congress and of All Departments of the Government of the United States for the Period 1893-1940 (1895-1945, 25 vols.)
Biography Index, 1946- . A quarterly index to biographical material, with annual cumulations
Essay and General Literature Index, 1900- . Author and subject index to essays and articles in collections and miscellaneous works
Granger's Index to Poetry and Recitations (1904-1944) Author, title, and first line index to poetry in collections; 4th ed., 1953 (recitations dropped); supplement, 1957
Play Index, 1949-1952. Augments but does not supersede the *Index to Plays*
Short Story Index, 1953- . Index–by author, title, and in many cases by subject–to some 60,000 stories published in 1949 or earlier; supplement, 1953
Song Index (1926-1934) Author and title index to more than 19,000 songs in collections
Index to Plays (1927-1935) Author and title and subject index to plays in collections or separately published from 1800 to 1935
Index to Reproductions of American Paintings, 1948
Portrait Index (1906) Subject index to portraits of persons in books and periodicals; *Readers' Guide* and other periodical indexes now indicate portraits in periodicals

Reference works

The reference department of a library has a large number of general and special works which furnish varied and plentiful information. Often it is a good plan to see what one of these has to say about your subject before you do any extensive searching, because it can help you find your way around more intelligently. Since the articles in reference works almost always refer you to authoritative specialized works, they are a good starting point for compiling a bibliography.

The general guide to reference books is *Guide to Reference Books,* by Constance M. Winchell, 7th edition, 1951, based on 6th edition by Isadore G. Mudge, with supplements from 1952 to 1955.

General Encyclopedias. Everyone needs to use these great storehouses of information. They are frequently revised and each publishes an annual supplement bringing its topics up to date.

Encyclopedia Americana
Encyclopaedia Britannica
New International Encyclopaedia, 2d ed., 1922. Supplements to date.

Special Reference Works. Less well known but even more important for college work are the encyclopedias and general reference works in various specific fields. Their articles usually go into further detail than those in the general encyclopedias, and their approach is more specialized. They also give brief, carefully selected bibliographies.These works are usually shelved in the reference department of the library but are sometimes kept with the books in their respective fields. An early acquaintance with those which you expect to use will be valuable. Some of the best known are:

Agriculture: *Cyclopedia of American Agriculture* (Bailey), 1907-1909, 4 vols.

Architecture: *A History of Architecture* (Fletcher), 14th ed., 1948

Art: *Harper's Encyclopedia of Art,* 1937, 2 vols.

Bryan's Dictionary of Painters and Engravers, 1903-1905, 5 vols.

Biography (American): *Dictionary of American Biography,* 1928-1937, 20 vols. and index

Who's Who in America, biennially since 1899

Who Was Who in America, Vol. I, 1897-1942, Vol. II, 1943-1950 (*Who's Who* subjects dropped during those years)

Biography (British): *Dictionary of National Biography,* 1885-1940, 22 vols. and supplements

Who's Who, annually since 1848

Biography (General): *Current Biography,* monthly since 1940, with annual cumulation

International Who's Who, 1935-

World Biography, 5th ed., 1954

Business: *Encyclopedia of Banking and Finance* (Munn), 5th ed., 1949; supplements up to 1955

Chemistry: *Thorpe's Dictionary of Applied Chemistry,* 4th ed., 1937-1949, 9 vols.; Vols. 10-12, 1950-1956; 12 vols.

Education: *Cyclopedia of Education* (Monroe), 1911-1913, 5 vols.

Encyclopedia of Educational Research (Monroe), rev. ed., 1950

Government: *Cyclopedia of American Government* (McLaughlin and Hart), 1914, 3 vols.

History (General): *An Encyclopedia of World History* (Langer), 3rd ed., 1952

Cambridge Ancient History (Bury and others), 2d ed., 1923-1939, 12 vols. of text and 5 vols. of plates

Cambridge Medieval History (Bury and others), 1911-1936, 8 vols., 1 vol. of maps

Cambridge Modern History (Ward and others), 2d ed., 1926, 13 vols. and atlas

History (American): *Dictionary of American History* (Adams), 2d ed., 1942, 5 vols. and index

Literature (General): *Dictionary of World Literature* (Shipley), new ed. 1953

Columbia Dictionary of Modern European Literature (Smith), 1947

Literature (Classical): *Oxford Companion to Classical Literature* (Harvey), 1937

Oxford Classical Dictionary (Cary and others), 1949

Literature (English): *Cambridge History of English Literature* (Ward and Waller), 1907-1927, 15 vols.

Oxford Companion to English Literature (Harvey), 3d ed., 1946

Literature (American): *Cambridge History of American Literature* (Trent and others), 1917-1921, 4 vols.

Oxford Companion to American Literature (Hart), 3rd ed., 1956

Literary History of the United States (Spiller and others), 1948, 3 vols.; 5th ed., 1956

Twentieth Century Authors (Kunitz and Haycraft, eds.), 1942; first supplement, 1955

Music: *Grove's Dictionary of Music and Musicians,* 5th ed., 1954, 9 vols.

International Cyclopedia of Music and Musicians (Thompson), 7th ed., 1956

Philosophy and Psychology: *Dictionary of Philosophy and Psychology* (Baldwin), 1910, 3 vols.

Encyclopedia of Psychology (Harriman), 1946

The New Dictionary of Psychology (Harriman), 1947

Quotations: *Bartlett's Familiar Quotations,* 13th ed., 1955

The Home Book of Bible Quotations (Stevenson), 1949

The Home Book of Shakespeare Quotations (Stevenson), 1937

The Home Book of Quotations, Classical and Modern (Stevenson), 5th ed., 1947

Religion: *Catholic Encyclopedia,* 1907-1922, 17 vols.

Universal Jewish Encyclopedia, 1939-1944, 10 vols.

Encyclopedia of Religion and Ethics (Hastings), 1908-1927, 13 vols.
New Schaff-Herzog Encyclopedia of Religious Knowledge (Jackson), 1908-1914, 12 vols. and index
Dictionary of the Bible (Hastings), 1898-1904, 5 vols.
Science: *Dictionary of Scientific Terms* (Henderson), 6th ed., 1957
Hutchinson's Technical and Scientific Encyclopedia (Tweney and Shirshov), 1935-1936, 4 vols.
Space Encyclopedia, 1957
Van Nostrand's Scientific Encyclopedia, 3rd ed., 1958
Social Sciences: *Encyclopedia of the Social Sciences* (Seligman and Johnson), 1930-1935, 15 vols.

General and special dictionaries are described on pages 210, 215-216.

Yearbooks, etc. For facts and figures, various annual publications are valuable for the information they contain or can direct you to:

World Almanac and Book of Facts, 1868- . This is the one general reference work that an individual can afford to own and one anyone with a serious interest in affairs can hardly afford to be without.
Information Please Almanac, 1947- .
The American Yearbook, 1910-1919, 1925-1950. Annual record of events in the United States
The Americana Annual, 1923- . Annual supplement to the *Encyclopedia Americana*
The Britannica Book of the Year, 1938- . Annual supplement to the *Encyclopaedia Britannica*
The New International Yearbook, 1907- . Annual supplement to the *New International Encyclopaedia*
Statistical Abstract of the United States, 1878- . Summary statistics on the industrial, social, political, and economic organization of the United States
Social Work Yearbook, biennially since 1929. Social work and related fields
Statesman's Yearbook, 1864- . Descriptive and statistical information about world governments
Reference Shelf, 1922- . Reprints of articles, bibliographies, and debates on topics of current interest
University Debaters' Annual, 1915- . Constructive and rebuttal speeches from college and university debates
Yearbook of the United Nations, 1956

Besides these specific sources that must be covered, you will always find some references by chance. Almost every article or book will mention some other source or give some clue that you can follow up. You can glean material rapidly from books by checking your topic in the indexes; often an important side light on a topic will be given in a book on a related subject. Talking with experts in the field will produce suggestions. The sources of material spread out like a fan—one source leads to another, and if you work long enough in a field, friends and sometimes even strangers may give you clues without being asked. Because one reference leads to another, it is usually safe to start work on a subject if you can first turn up two or three works that contain good relevant material. Systematic work and ingenuity in following up hunches will almost always enable you to find enough to finish the job.

Since one reason for the assignment of reference papers is to train students in research methods, you should do as much as possible without help. The library has reference librarians, but you should not bother them until you have exhausted your own resources.

The working bibliography

Before you concentrate on gathering material for the topic you have selected, you need to compile a *working bibliography* of sources that you expect to consult. You should see if any of the reference works listed in the preceding section relate to your topic, and you should consult the appropriate subject headings in the card catalog and the periodical indexes. To make sure that enough material on your specific subject is available in the library, you should compile the working bibliography before actually starting to take notes. This preliminary survey of materials saves time and worry in the actual reading and makes possible intelligent selection of books and articles. It also adds to your confidence, for finding several promising references shows that you will be able to go through with your subject.

Materials

Everyone should have a consistent method of keeping track of references and of taking and keeping the notes from which he works. For casual study, notebooks and odd sheets may do, but for large and important jobs and for training in research methods, the most flexible and efficient materials are standard filing cards or slips, either 3x5 or 4x6 inches. The 4x6 size is probably more convenient, since it can hold more than the 3x5 and allows for more generous spacing and labeling of material. *A separate bibliography card should be prepared for each reference.* Later, note cards on the content of the reference will be added to your file of material for the paper.

Form of bibliographical entries

The purpose of the bibliography card is to record all the facts about a book or an article that you will need to identify it, to find it in the library when you are ready to use it, and to make the formal bibliography that will appear at the end of the paper. Each card, therefore, should carry these facts:

For the formal bibliography:

1) *The author's name,* with last name first. If the book is edited, use the editor's name, followed by *ed.*

2) *The title* of the article (in quotation marks) or of the book (underlined to represent italics)

3) *The facts of publication:*

(a) Of a book, the city and date, and the name of the publisher if you need to use it.

(b) Of a magazine, the name of the magazine (underlined), the volume, the date, the pages on which the article appears.

(c) Of a newspaper story, the name of the paper (underlined), the date, the page, and, if you wish, the column number.

For your own use:

1) *The library call number* or location–preferably in the upper left corner, as it is in the card catalog

2) *Any other facts* that relate to the use of the reference, such as the pages that treat your subject or the value of the source–preferably at the bottom of the card

3) *A subject heading,* a phrase for the particular part of your topic that the reference pertains to, at the top center of the card. This label is familiarly known as a *slug.*

4) *A code reference* in the upper right corner. This reference may be a number, a letter, or the author's last name. It is used instead of a full citation on each note card taken from this source and saves a great deal of needless copying.

The form and arrangement of bibliography cards are illustrated on page 365.

Bibliography cards

Your bibliography cards should be kept in alphabetical order according to author, or first important word of the title if no author is given. If you have only a few, they can be held together with a paper clip or kept in an envelope or an expanding pocket file. For large accumulations there are boxes and filing drawers of various sizes.

Students always ask how many references they should have for a paper. Graduate research papers are expected to show all the pertinent material; undergraduate papers are supposed to represent adequate coverage of the subject. You will probably want to glance at all available sources and select those which are neither too technical nor too general for your purpose. No paper should be written from only one or two sources, but of course for a short paper done in a limited time, a student can easily be weighed down by too much material. Papers that run from 2000 to 5000 words have typically from six to fifteen or twenty sources, depending on the nature of the subject and the length and thoroughness of the work.

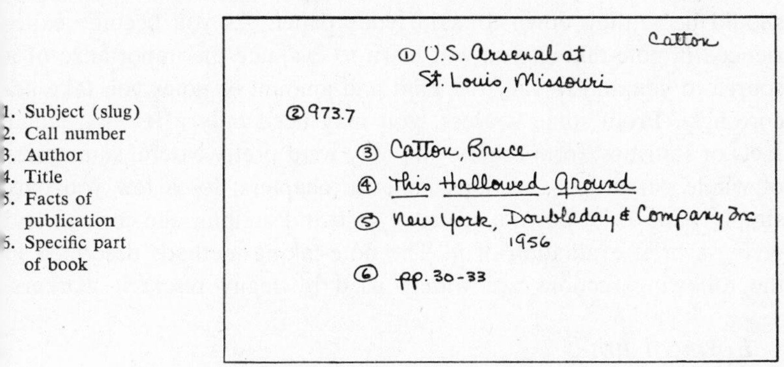

Bibliography Card for a Book

1. Subject (slug)
2. Author
3. Title
4. Facts of publication

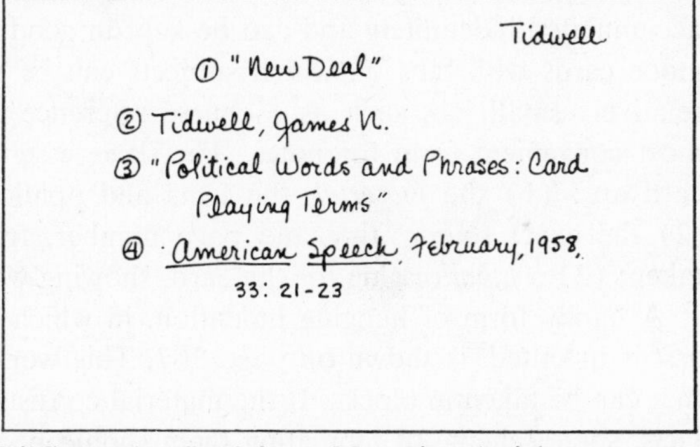

Bibliography Card for a Magazine Article

1. Facts of publication
2. Headline
3. Description of content

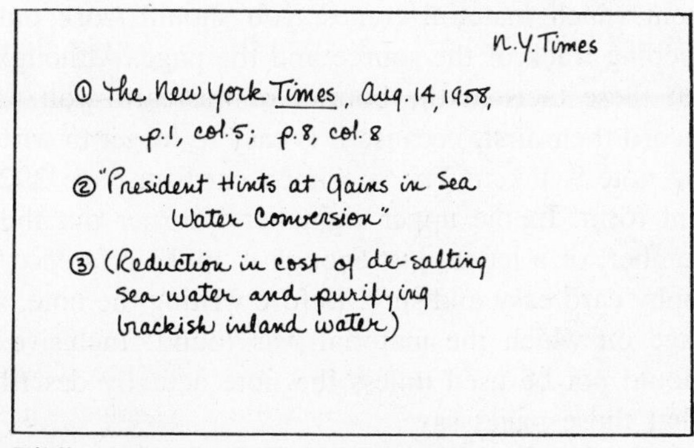

Bibliography Card for a Newspaper

Taking notes on reading

Good notes are crucial in the preparation of a reference paper. Illegible handwriting, meaningless phrases (clear when the note was taken but not when it's "cold"), and inadequate labeling of the source may send you back to the library for extra work when you should be settling down to write your paper. As you become experienced in note-taking, you will learn to evaluate the importance of a source to you and to vary the kind and amount of notes you take accordingly. From some sources, you may need only a few particular facts or statistics; from others, you may want pretty careful summaries of whole paragraphs, sections, or even chapters; for a few you may simply want to jot down a sentence or two describing the content and giving a brief evaluation of it. The note-taking methods described in the following sections are widely used by many research workers.

Form of notes

Most research workers take their notes on 3x5 or 4x6 slips or cards because they are easy to sort, discard, and rearrange. They can be accumulated indefinitely and can be kept in good order by the use of guide cards with tabs on which subjects can be written. Even for a relatively small job, such as a course reference paper, they are the most convenient form for notes. The three essential parts of a note card are: (1) the *material,* the facts and opinions to be recorded; (2) the exact *source,* title and page number, from which they are taken; (3) a *label* or slug for the card, showing what it treats.

A handy form of hanging indention, in which every line after the first is indented, is shown on page 367. This works well for material that can be taken in blocks. If the material consists of small particular facts, some scheme of tabulating them should be worked out.

Since the final paper will have footnotes referring to the exact page from which material comes, you should work out some system for keeping track of the source and the page. Although some note-takers put these facts at the bottom of the card, you will find it safer to record them first, because it is easy to forget to write them down after the note is taken. The specimen card on page 392 shows a convenient form. In the upper right hand corner put the author's name, a number, or a letter–just enough to make reference to the full bibliography card easy and sure. Before writing the note, set down the exact page on which the material was found. Inclusive pages (as 87-92) should not be used unless the note actually describes or summarizes what those pages say.

Label

Notes with page references

First Harvard Commencement Morison, Founding of Harvard Coll.

257 1st Harvard Commencement Sept. 23, 1642
Gov. Winthrop, his guard, the magistrates of the Colony come from Boston by ferry or barge

258 By 9 or 10 a.m. audience on benches in the college hall. 9 in graduating class. Splendid formal procession. (Details given)

259 Long extemporaneous prayer in Latin; Latin salutatory oration; one of the graduates gives oration in Greek; exercises in Hebrew

Specimen Note Card

The slug is most conveniently placed in the upper left corner, where it can be instantly seen. It should label the subject matter of that particular card. This procedure makes it possible for you to sort the cards when you get ready to outline and write the paper.

It is well not to put too much on a single card; students tend to crowd their notes, making them hard to use. A card should contain only one point or a few closely related facts. Try to visualize the paper while you are taking notes, and do not put two facts on the same card unless you are sure that they will be used in the same part of the paper.

Use only one side of the card. Cards written on both sides are difficult to handle, and you will certainly forget to turn some over if you use both sides. If only a few words remain at the end of a statement they can be written on the back, but *over* should be put on the front as a reminder.

Notes need not be taken in full sentences—words, phrases, and topics are enough, if you are sure the note will be meaningful after you have laid it aside for a while. Take workable notes, in ink, as you do the reading, but don't bother to copy them except for some very good reason. They are means to an end (a good paper), not works of art themselves.

General suggestions for note-taking

First read the article or chapter once through rapidly to see what it contains for your purposes. Then go over it again, taking down the necessary notes. Use cards freely, leaving space for later notes. From your first few references you may need to take a good many notes, but after you have accumulated quite a bit of material, a long reference will sometimes give only a few additional facts.

Rules for what to take cannot be laid down. Your judgment will improve as you go on, and the guidance of your instructor is often necessary at the start. Here are three general points that apply to all topics.

1. *Distinguish between the author's facts and his opinions.* Label the opinions "So-and-so thinks. . . ." In general pay most attention to the *facts* presented (unless of course your topic is opinions, as in a paper on "What reviewers said of Hemingway's short stories"). You will need the facts as the basis of your own opinions and as evidence to support them in the paper.

2. *Distinguish carefully between direct quotation and summary, and take as little quotation as possible.* Quotations should be carefully inclosed in quotation marks; it is easy to forget to close a quotation that is part of a longer note. A quotation should be taken down exactly as it appears. After an obvious error put *sic* (thus) in brackets to indicate that the error was in the source. Actually [*sic*] is seldom necessary in student papers, but you should know what it means when you find it in your reading. Quotations should be taken only for good reason: unusually important material, crucial for your paper; a striking statement that you want to quote for its vividness or its conciseness; controversial or difficult material that you need to think about before deciding exactly what it means for your subject. Almost everything else should be digested in your own words and so reduced to the scale of your paper. The time to do this is when you take the notes, but in putting the paper together you will convert some quotations you have taken into summaries.

3. *Distinguish between what you take from a source and any comments of your own.* Put the latter in brackets or encircle them and write your initials alongside. If there is any possibility of confusion, it is better to put your own comments on a separate card.

Suggestions for the summarizing note

Since the summary is one of the most useful kinds of notes, and perhaps one of the most difficult to do well, you may need the following suggestions. Any selection to be summarized must be read more than once. The number of readings necessary will depend upon the difficulty of the selection and the use to be made of the material. In

your first reading, watch for the main ideas and the way each is developed. If you own the book or magazine, underline the main ideas; otherwise, make notes. You can use a decimal system for recording a location on a page. For example, if a key passage occurs about one third of the way down page 344, mark it 344.3 in your notes. In reading an article to summarize it, you work from the general to the specific; that is, you try first to determine the overall meaning and then the main points (usually from three to five) and then the subdivisions supporting each main point. The author's transitional expressions are useful clues to the pattern of his ideas. As in any other note-taking, you must be sure you understand and write down the author's ideas, not your own, even though you disagree violently with the author's point of view. Your summary should not be interrupted or distorted by your personal opinions.

Your success in producing a good summary will depend partly on the care with which you read the original and partly on your skill in cutting unnecessary passages and in condensing the author's language. Condensation is accomplished mainly by eliminating nonessentials—anecdotes, descriptive details, digressions, illustrations, and all kinds of repetition. Elimination is the chief means of reducing the bulk of an article, but it can also be reduced by substituting shorter expressions for the author's phrasing. Useful expressions for reducing a selection are appositives, series, and verbals:

Original	*Summary*
Louisiana leads the nation in fur production and in conservation of fur resources. The state realizes about 5 million dollars annually from its raw fur crop and collects more than $200,000 a year in fees and dues of various kinds for use in maintaining the fur business.—Ruben L. Parson, *Conserving American Resources,* p. 279	Each year Louisiana, the national leader in production and conservation of raw furs, realizes about 5 million dollars from raw furs and over $200,000 from fees charged the fur industry.
Government is the "benevolent despot" of conservation, and no one else can play that important role. None but the national government could adequately preserve our aesthetic resources. Only government can prescribe and finance conservation of such scope as flood prevention, forest fire protection, and range restoration. Only government can	Only the national government can preserve our aesthetic resources, conduct large-scale conservation, and control water- and air-pollution.

establish and enforce regulations
for cleansing our streams and
purifying the air we breathe.
–*Ibid.*, pp. 8-9

Simply by coincidence, many words from the original are certain to reappear in your summary. But if you deliberately use a phrase exactly as it appears in the original, inclose it in quotation marks and cite the page number in parentheses or in a footnote. Quoting a key phrase is often an effective means of suggesting the style of the original. Such quotations should be blended as smoothly as possible into your own sentences. A good summary reproduces as faithfully as possible the ideas, the structure, and the spirit of the original.

Evaluating material

Because composing a reference paper is largely an exercise of judgment, it is important to evaluate the sources being used. "I found a book in the library that said . . . ." is a confession of uncritical work. Your aim should be to find the best books and articles, the most recent authoritative material on the subject. Since most of us cannot evaluate references until we have done a good deal of work in a field, we must at first rely on the opinions of others. In reading several sources you are likely to find remarks about other sources–that one is the recognized authority, that another misinterprets facts, and so on. These criticisms should be noted and if they seem reasonable should be taken into account.

For recent books it is often possible to find reviews that will be some indication of their value, though many reviews in newspapers and general periodicals discuss the interest rather than the accuracy of a book. The best sources of reviews of serious works are the learned journals–the *American Historical Review* for historical works, for instance. The *Book Review Digest* will lead you to reviews of less specialized works.

After you have worked awhile on a subject, you can evaluate a good deal of the material yourself, and your considered opinion should influence your choice of materials. It is often helpful to enter a brief critical note on a bibliographical card.

Sources are often classed as *primary* (or *original*) and *secondary*. A primary source is a first record of facts or the closest that a person writing now can come to the subject he is discussing; a secondary source is something written by someone else using original sources. In a paper on a literary subject, for instance, the primary sources are the works written by the man you are discussing–letters, diaries, and so on written by him or by others who knew him; secondary sources are what a critic or historian has written about him and his work. In a science, primary sources are records of observation or experiments; secondary sources are discussions of such records. In history, primary sources are records of all sorts or reliable reproductions of them–letters, diaries, documents–and remains such as coins, tools, or buildings; secondary sources are historians' accounts based on this evidence. Textbooks and reference works are all secondary sources.

Graduate research relies chiefly on primary sources. Undergraduate papers are drawn principally from secondary sources, but a student who is trying to do a thorough job should use some original sources. He certainly should come as close as he can to the first record of the facts he is to use, and in choosing his material he should try to find the most reliable facts available.

The material needs careful sifting for its usefulness in the particular paper you are going to write as well as for its accuracy. It is a good idea to read through all the notes you have taken to see what there is, how the information shapes up, and whether there are some spots for which you need more material. This overall view of your material should lead to an exact formulation of the subject and purpose of your paper. If you haven't done it already, you should state the scope of the paper in a full sentence. Such a statement, usually called a *thesis sentence,* enables you to see the emphasis of your ideas more clearly and makes your research more purposeful. It is often a difficult sentence to write, requiring considerable juggling and cutting of ideas, and will probably be rewritten more specifically during the planning phase. For the specimen paper, "The Cowboy Legend," pp. 385-399, the thesis sentence is: "Although some of the characteristics that have popularized the cowboy as a legendary hero are based on reality, others are imaginary."

With such a statement it is easy to select the particular parts of your material that will relate to it. If you have done a good job of research, you will have considerably more material than you can use. As you survey your notes and make your outline, you will be sorting your facts into those that must be used, those that will probably be used, those of incidental importance or interest that may be used, and those that clearly do not belong. It is a good idea to mark in the margins of your note cards the most important points, using a # or some other sign. You may want to sort your note cards into four groups: *Must, Probably, Maybe,* and *No.* Of course, the final selection of material takes place during the actual writing, but the clearer the plan you have in mind before you begin writing, the more easily the paper will move and the more satisfactory it is likely to be.

Planning the paper

After the material has been gathered, the work of planning and writing a reference paper resembles that of any other paper (see Ch. 9, pp. 253-265). But the material, gathered from study instead of from memory or observation, will probably seem more objective, and with your notes you will find it easy to review, to think about as *material,* and to manipulate.

Because of the amount of material and the length of the paper, you will have to make some sort of outline before writing. You should try to group the material in from three to six stages—not more unless the paper is unusually long. As in any paper, the main divisions grow out of the material you have collected. To check the plan and to enable your instructor to examine it and make suggestions, you should cast it in one of the standard outline forms. (See Ch. 9, pp. 253-259.)

If you have the time, it is wise to keep the outline around for a few days and look at it closely to see if it is a really systematic grouping of your facts and ideas, one that your reader can follow easily and one that represents your understanding of the material and your intended emphasis.

There is a tendency in reference papers to compose an "introduction" that really does not advance the subject. A history of the subject is usually unnecessary. Every main head, including the first, should tell the reader something. Pick a natural starting point that is related to the thesis and then advance by clear-cut stages to the final and most important point.

Writing the first draft

By this time you should be thoroughly familiar with your material. Even though you have been reviewing it as a whole and thinking it over in the last two steps, you should read your notes through once or twice more to get them fully in mind. Then you can deal with them thoughtfully instead of just transcribing from note cards to paper.

This review of the material will also help you put it into your own words, get it away from the form in which you found it, and work it into the proportion suitable to your paper. Digesting the material into your own words is important. If you are inclined to be lazy or hasty, you will tend to follow your sources too closely. It is the intention of the assignment that you are to take information from various sources and work it over into a form of your own, not just reproduce it. Direct quotation should be kept to a minimum and should always be indicated by quotation marks or, if it is more than three lines long, by indention as a "display quotation." (See p. 395.) Often a part of a sentence will be all that is worth quoting; the rest of the material will be summarized in your own words. The purpose of this advice is not just to prevent copying but to encourage the proper method for producing a reference paper, which is to learn something new through careful reading and then to write about it.

Because the finished paper gives credit in footnotes to the sources from which you have taken your facts, you will have to devise some way of including the sources in the first draft. A simple method is to put in parentheses after a statement an abbreviated reference to the source used. (See the draft reproduced on p. 396.) Or the reference may be written in the margin of the paper. The most complicated method is to put a number after each borrowed statement and keep the sources on a separate sheet. Using any of these methods, you can transfer the data to a footnote at the bottom of the page when you make your final copy.

The traditional style of reference papers is Formal and impersonal. It is not usually necessary for the writer to refer to himself at all, and if he does, the reference should be brief. But impersonal writing does not have to be dull. Simply put down your material as compactly and directly as possible–you may find yourself writing more concretely and more concisely than the sources you are using.

There is a question of the audience to which the paper should be directed. "Term papers" for advanced college courses are ordinarily written for a specialist in the field and their reader-audience is usually the instructor. But in a composition course, where all sorts of subjects may be treated, the approach may vary from that of a specialist, if you are very much at home in the field of your subject, to that of a writer for a general magazine. Your instructor will explain the approach most appropriate for the course and for the subject. Usually, the best approach is to direct your paper to an intelligent reader who knows very little about your subject but has some desire to learn more, a reader serious enough to prefer accurate information to sensational appeal. Then you can use all your skill in expression explaining to him the subject as you understand it.

Footnotes: crediting sources

Any paper based on the writings of others should acknowledge the sources used. Not only is it common courtesy (or honesty) to give credit where credit is due, but it is a sign of scrupulousness to tell the source of a statement, so that a reader can judge for himself the evidence it is based on. It also allows an occasional interested reader to turn to the sources for further information. College students are expected to draw their materials from various sources, and a frank acknowledgment of sources is expected.

In formal academic papers–reference papers, term papers, theses, dissertations–it is conventional to give exact references in footnotes. The forms differ slightly, but the aim of all is the same–*to record in some brief and consistent form the author, title, facts of publication, and exact page from which each quotation and each fact or opinion is taken.* Giving these facts about sources of material is called *documentation.* The style of footnotes and bibliography suggested in this chapter is suitable for documentation in a college reference paper. This style follows the recommendations of the *MLA Style Sheet,* revised edition, which has been adopted by most journals in literature and history and by many university presses. Other styles differ slightly from this one in placement, content, and punctuation. Some variant forms are illustrated in the notes on the sample paper at the end of this chapter. Two styles of reference often used in scientific papers are given in the Index article *References in scientific papers. If your instructor prefers that you follow any of these alternative forms, check his preferences and copy them into your notebook to use as a guide. *Be sure to learn from your instructor what style of documentation he wants you to follow.*

Handling footnotes

Footnotes are needed *for all direct quotations* (except well-known bits from the Bible or other literature that are used for style rather than content) *and for all important statements of facts or opinions that are summarized from written sources.* Obviously statistics, dates, descriptions of situations, scientific data, opinions, and the like that are not common knowledge and that are presented to advance the theme of the paper need a stated source.

Although the number of sources referred to in a paper must vary with the type of subject and the kind of sources used, a typical student reference paper might have from two to five footnotes to a page of typewritten manuscript.

Material from conversation, from lectures, or from any other source that a reader cannot turn to is best acknowledged in the text of the paper or in a prefatory note. The source of a diagram, map, table, or other illustration is not given in a footnote but under the illustration (see p. 10).

The reference figure is placed slightly above the line after the summary or quotation whose source is being given. It follows the end punctuation of the material to which it applies.

The notes are numbered from 1 up throughout a short paper. They may be numbered from 1 up on each page, but this practice is rare except for papers with a very large number of notes.

The footnotes are placed at the bottom of the page on which they belong. In preparing the final paper, look ahead in the rough draft to see how many footnotes will be needed on a page; put a light pencil mark where you should begin the footnote series.

The first line of each footnote is indented like a paragraph; following lines, if any, begin flush with the left margin. The reference number may be slightly raised above the line as in the text, but this is not necessary. If elevated, the number is not followed by a period.

Form of footnotes

The purpose of a citation footnote is to tell the reader the exact source from which a statement has been taken. Uniformity is a convenience for the reader, and one reason for assigning a reference paper is to give students practice in systematic footnote reference. The particular style you use is not so important as being consistent throughout a paper. This section gives a pattern for use in undergraduate papers and attempts to answer in advance most questions.

Books. The *first* reference to a book gives the author's name in normal order (first name first), the title underlined, the place and date of publication, and the page or pages. Note the following example:

[1]Everett Dick, Vanguards of the Frontier (New York, 1941), p. 450.

For *later* references to the same book use a short form, enough to identify the work in the bibliography; the author's last name is sufficient if only one work by the same man is used:

[2]Dick, p. 128.

One or two key words from the title must be included if more than one source by the same man is used:

[3]Dick, Vanguards, p. 128.

Pamphlets and government bulletins are referred to in the same form as books. The items always appear in the same order (author, title, place, date, page). Unavailable details are simply omitted.

Magazine articles. In the *first* reference to a magazine article, give the author's name in normal order, the title of the article in quotation marks, the name of the magazine underlined, the volume in Roman numerals, the year in parentheses, and the page or pages without abbreviations:

[4]David B. Davis, "Ten-Gallon Hero," American Quarterly, VI (1954), 114.

For magazines that number pages separately in each issue (instead of consecutively through a volume), give the complete date of issue and page:

[5]Bernard DeVoto, "Birth of an Art," Harper's Magazine, CCVII (Dec. 1953), 8.

It is permissible to omit volume numbers with weekly or monthly magazines. No parentheses are used and *p.* precedes the page number.

[5]Bernard DeVoto, "Birth of an Art," Harper's Magazine, December 1953, p. 8.

A later reference to a magazine article may be shortened to the author's last name, the name of the magazine, and the page:

[6]DeVoto, Harper's, p. 12.

Newspapers. Reference to a news story includes the name of the paper underlined, the date, and the page. The column number may be given. If there are sections paged separately, the section should also be given. Headlines are not ordinarily given because they are often changed from edition to edition.

[7]The New York Times, Nov. 30, 1957, Sec. II, p. 1, col. 6.

Ibid. In a footnote *Ibid.* means "in the same place"–that is, in the same book or article as the preceding footnote. It is used to refer to the work cited in the immediately preceding footnote. Though useful, it should not appear very many times in a good paper; a long succession of *Ibid.*'s shows excessive reliance on one source.

[8]Edward Everett Dale, Cow Country (Norman, Oklahoma, 1945), p. 53.
[9]Ibid., p. 96.

Ditto marks are not used in footnotes or in the bibliography.

Author not known. When an author's name is not given in the source, the title becomes the first item of the note. "Anonymous" and such substitutes for a name are not used.

[10]"Just Wild About Westerns," Newsweek, L (July 22, 1957), 51.
[11]History of Old Pembina 1780–1872 (Larimore, North Dakota, 1917), p. 21.

Unsigned encyclopedia articles may be given by the title of the article or simply by the name of the encyclopedia:

[12]"Rhetoric," Encyclopaedia Britannica (Chicago, 1945), XIX, 248.
[12]Encyclopaedia Britannica (Chicago, 1945), XIX, 248.

Unsigned publications of organizations are listed by title:

[13]American Education and International Tension (Washington, National Education Association, 1949), p. 32.

Material at second hand. When your material comes at second hand—that is, when it is quoted or summarized in the source you are using—you should give the original source first and then the source in which you found it:

[14]William Caxton, Preface to Eneydos (1490), quoted in Albert C. Baugh, A History of the English Language (New York, 1935), p. 241.

A similar form is used for an article that is part of an anthology or a collected volume:

[15]Frank Luther Mott, "Trends in Newspaper Content," in Wilbur Schramm, ed., Mass Communications (Urbana, 1949), p. 339.

Split note. If part of a reference is given in the text of the paper, it need not be repeated in the footnote. For example, if the author's name is in the text, the footnote may begin with the title; or if author and title are in the text, only the facts of publication and the page are in the footnote. This system can be used for material at second hand; if you give the original source in the text, you give the secondary source in which you found it in the footnote.

Informational footnote. Occasionally an additional fact, a statement of a different opinion, a quotation, or a reference to other sources is given in a footnote, but this sort of thing should be kept to a minimum. In college writing it is well to use footnotes only for citations of sources. If something is worth including, it belongs in the text.

Law cases. The following form is used to cite law cases: the plaintiff's last name, *v.* (*versus,* meaning "against"), the defendant's last name, the volume number of the reports where the case is given, an abbreviation for the report series, the page on which the case begins, and the year in which the decision was rendered:

[16]Lochner v. New York, 198 U.S. 539 (1905).

Bible. Books of the Bible are not underlined. The reference form is name of the book, chapter, verse:

[17]Genesis 4:16 (or 4, 16).

Common abbreviations. The following abbreviations are commonly used in footnotes. Although you are not likely to use them all, you should recognize them when you find them in your reading. Those that come from Latin should be underlined in your paper to represent italics.

art.—article
c.—copyright
ca. or *c.* (*circa*)—around a given date (*ca.* 1480)
ch. or chap.—chapter; chs. or chaps.—chapters

col.—column; cols.—columns
ed.—edited by; edition (2d ed.)
f.—following (one following page: 286f.); ff. (more than one following page: 286ff.) Exact references are preferable: pp. 286-7; pp. 286-91
ibid. (*ibidem*)—in the same place (see p. 376)
l.—line; ll.—lines
MS.—manuscript; MSS.—manuscripts
n.—note (to refer to a footnote in a source: p. 135n.)
n.d.—no date of publication
n.p.—no place of publication
n.s.—new series of a periodical
o.s.—old series of a periodical
p.—page; pp.—pages
tr. or trans.—translated by
vol.—volume; vols.—volumes (vol. and p. are not used when figures for both are given: vol. III; p. 176; but III, 176 or 3:176)

The following abbreviations were formerly in general use but are less common now:

cf. (*confer*)—compare (used to cite other related passages)
et al. (*et alii*)—and others (used for multiple authorship; English words are now more common: Maurice Frink and others)
infra—below (referring to something discussed later in the paper)
loc. cit. (*loco citato*)—in the place cited (referring to a passage cited in a recent footnote; not followed by a page number)
op. cit. (*opere citato*)—the work cited: Dick, *op. cit.*, p. 128; now a shortened form of the title is more common: Dick, *Vanguards,* p. 128
passim—here and there (indicating that a matter is discussed in several places in a book or an article)
q.v. (*quod vide*)—which see (used for cross reference; now generally replaced by "see")
seq. (*sequentes*)—following (replaced by *f.* and *ff.*)
supra—above (referring to something discussed earlier in the paper)
s.v. (*sub verbo*)—under the word (used to refer to an item in an alphabetical listing)
vide or *v.*—see (now replaced by the English word)

Any description of the form of footnotes makes their use seem harder than it really is. If you have good notes with the sources carefully recorded, it is relatively simple to keep track of the necessary citations in the first draft and then to place them in the final manuscript in proper form.

The final bibliography

A completed reference paper contains a bibliography of the sources actually used in its preparation—not all the items consulted but only those which have actually furnished material. This records the work that has been done, and it also enables a reader to identify the works cited in the footnotes.

The form of bibliographies has been pretty well standardized so that the necessary facts can be given economically and systematically. Observation of the bibliographies in books and magazines consulted for the paper will show slight variations in punctuation and content. Other forms are illustrated in *References in scientific papers; check any of them that your instructor prefers you to use. The forms recommended for a book and for a magazine are as follows:

Adams, Ramon F. Western Words. Norman, Oklahoma, 1944.
Davis, David B. "Ten-Gallon Hero," American Quarterly, VI (1954), 111-125.

Note that authors' names are inverted and hanging indention is used.

In short bibliographies all the items are run in one list, alphabetically arranged. When no author is given, the first important word of the title (omitting *a, an,* or *the*) is used as the key word for alphabetizing. Very long bibliographies are sometimes grouped by type of material: Primary Sources, Secondary Sources; Works by an Author, Works About Him; and so on. They should not be grouped according to type of publication, such as books and periodicals, except in a list of the works of a single writer.

The completed paper

Typically the completed paper would comprise these units (those in brackets are optional):

Title page: Give the title of the paper, the writer's name, the date submitted, and any other information required, such as course and section number.

[*Preface:* In a preface the writer talks about his work. Usually you will not need a preface, but a preface is useful if you wish to thank someone for special help, call attention to some unusual material, or note some point that you wanted to develop or should develop but are unable to. The preface stands on a page by itself.]

Outline: Make the type of outline assigned. Be sure that it conforms to the order of material in the finished paper. Check its form by referring to Chapter 9, pages 254-259. The outline can serve as a table of contents if you give at the right of each main topic the page on which it begins.

Text of the paper: This is the final copy of the paper, complete with footnotes and diagrams or any other illustrative material used. Put the title at the top of the first page and follow the manuscript form required by your instructor. Before making this final copy, go through pages 375-378 of this chapter and the sample paper on pages 387-399 to make sure that your footnotes follow the form suggested.

Bibliography: On a separate page, list in the form suggested on pages 378-379 the books and articles actually used in writing your paper.

[*Appendix:* Occasionally a paper needs a table of statistics too long to work into the body of the paper, or it may require a long quotation, such as part of a treaty or other document that much of the paper is based on. Such material can be placed in an appendix, but it is rather rare in student reference papers.]

A reference paper is usually the largest single job in a composition course. Done carefully, with close attention to each of the stages outlined in this chapter, it can be a satisfying activity as well as good training for later college work.

Alternate Instructions

Alternate Instructions

Chapter 13

EXERCISES AND SPECIMEN REFERENCE PAPER

Specimen reference paper

On the following right-hand pages a sample reference paper is presented in the style of documentation described on pages 375-378. On the left-hand pages are comments on the paper, possible variant styles in documentation, and, at the bottom of the page, further exercises. If your instructor asks you to use any of the variants in your paper, star them in the book and later copy them into your notebook for reference.

Exercises

1. The subjects in the following list are too broad or too general for successful treatment in a reference paper of moderate length. Select two that interest you and make up for each at least four topics which could be treated adequately in papers of the length assigned for your course.

American magazines
Artificial languages
Atomic Energy Commission
Blood bank
Books for children
Cartels
Chautauquas
Detective stories
Diamonds
Eskimos
Etiquette
Euthanasia
Frozen foods
Game laws
Golden Gate Bridge
Gypsies
Hemingway's novels
Hydroelectric plants
Hygiene
Israeli
Libel laws
Lewis and Clark
Map making
Metalworking
Metropolitan Opera Company
Modern productions of *Hamlet*
Music in industry
Nonobjective painting
Oregon Trail
Parent Teachers Association
Plastics
Postage stamps
Primitive peoples
Prison conditions
Public libraries
Radar
Satellites
Simplified spelling
Stereophonic sound
Teaching of poetry
Television
UNESCO
Volcanoes
Witchcraft

2. Choose a subject on which you would like to write a reference paper, and prepare brief answers on the following points:

1. Your reason for choosing this subject.
2. Your present knowledge about the subject and the gaps you would have to fill in.
3. The audience you have in mind and the information you assume this audience already has about the topic.
4. The bibliographies, indexes, and other reference works that would be most useful for the topic you have selected.
5. The method and the particular kinds of material–books, periodicals, pamphlets–most useful for developing your paper.

Comment

The outline below is a preliminary version of the outline of the paper, as given on the opposite page. Study it and prepare to answer the questions in Exercise 3 below.

The Cowboy Legend (rough outline)

The cowboy is a popular hero, and his popularity is largely due to characteristics that are not authentic.

I. The cowboy and his horse
   A. Horses in the movies
   B. Actual cowboys were hard on horses.
   C. Tom Mix and Tony
II. The Virginian
   A. Published in 1902
   B. Set a pattern that is still popular
   C. High Noon
III. W. S. Hart
   A. Continued the Virginian type of hero
IV. The life of the cowboy in the 1870's is the basis of most movie cowboys.
   A. By 1890 this life had changed.
   B. An employee of a corporation
   C. In the 1870's he was carefree and adventurous.
   D. Reasons for the change in his way of life
   E. The blizzard of 1887
V. Cowboy costumes
   A. Movie costumes
   B. Expensive buckskin vests
   C. Actual cowboys
VI. Singing cowboys
   A. Gene Autry
   B. Songs of actual cowboys
   C. Sentimental songs
VII. Gunplay
   A. Marksmanship exaggerated
VIII. Cowboys and homesteaders
   A. Early drives
   B. Movie plots
   C. Johnson County War
IX. Conclusion

Exercises

3. Compare the outline above and the one on the opposite page and analyze the changes that were made.

A) Answer the following questions about the above outline: Why is the revised thesis sentence more satisfactory? Why has the order of topics been changed? Which sections of the original outline overlap? Why is "Conclusion" unnecessary in the outline?

B) Convert the sentence outline on the opposite page to a topic outline, making each item a noun phrase.

The Cowboy Legend

Although some of the characteristics that have popularized the cowboy as a legendary hero are based on reality, others are imaginary.

I. The cowboy hero is an anachronism.
   A. The cowboy's free and easy life flourished in the 1870's.
   B. By 1888 his life had changed.
   C. In the legend his life has been made more pleasant.

II. The Virginian set the basic pattern.
   A. Owen Wister thought that he was describing a vanishing American.
   B. W. S. Hart continued the Virginian tradition.
   C. The Virginian type is still popular.

III. Tom Mix popularized two aspects of the cowboy hero.
   A. The devoted horse is not wholly authentic.
   B. The elaborate costume is also exaggerated.
   C. Actual cowboy dress was more functional than decorative.

IV. The singing cowboy like Gene Autry has become familiar.
   A. Actual cowboys sang on night guard or around the campfire.
   B. Their singing was very different from movie versions.

V. Miscellaneous aspects of the legend are also a mixture of fantasy and reality.
   A. The cowboy's proficiency with a gun is exaggerated.
   B. His difficulties with homesteaders have some basis in fact.
   C. His recreations have been revised considerably.

Comment

In a manuscript prepared for a printer, footnotes should be placed on a separate page, following the bibliography, and this form may be used for course papers. Sometimes footnotes are included in the text and set off by two horizontal lines. For example, footnote 4 on the opposite page would come immediately after the line in which its reference number appears and would be set up as follows:

much in New York if a way could be found to get it there.[4]

---

[4]Everett Dick, Vanguards of the Frontier (New York, 1941), p. 450.

The railroad provided the way. Young Americans, many of

Most students and instructors feel that drawing or typing so many lines across the page is a waste of time. The natural place for footnotes is at the bottom of the page, where the eye can pick them up easily and relate them to the material in the text.

The first line of a footnote is usually indented, but it may be written flush with the left margin, in which case the reference number is even with the line:

4. Everett Dick, Vanguards of the Frontier (New York, 1941), p. 450.

A line across or partially across the page may be used to separate the footnotes from the text. An extra space, however, is usually considered adequate (see opposite page).

Variant forms for a footnote to a book differ mainly in content. Sometimes the publisher is included; sometimes the place and year are omitted:

[4]Everett Dick, Vanguards of the Frontier (New York: D. Appleton-Century, 1941), p. 450.
[4]Everett Dick, Vanguards of the Frontier, p. 450.

In some styles the year precedes the volume number of a magazine, and the volume number may be in ordinary (Arabic) numerals:

[2]David B. Davis, "Ten-Gallon Hero," American Quarterly, 1954, 6:114.

Exercises

4. If you are using a style of documentation in your paper which differs from the one followed in this sample paper, rewrite the footnotes on pages 1 and 2 of "The Cowboy Legend" in the form specified.

The Cowboy Legend

The cowboy is the most popular legendary hero America has produced. Evidence of his popularity surrounds us all day long; a grim-faced cowboy stares from a box of morning cereal, and his twin brother gallops through the late movie. His appeal is sometimes explained as a modern longing for the days when life was simple.[1] David B. Davis believes that the cowboy is a symbol of our national adolescence, "the last image of a carefree life."[2] A Swedish critic calls westerns the American mythology and explains their similarity by saying that any myth requires repetition and "a ritualistic passivity" in the audience.[3] Whatever the reasons, the cowboy's popularity is indisputable and must be mainly due to the cowboy hero himself. His characteristics are partly inventions and partly distortions or exaggerations of actual traits.

The cowboy of movies and television is an anachronism. He represents life on the cattle range in the 1870's and early 1880's. After the Civil War the industrial North offered a market for Texas cattle, which outnumbered people six to one and were of little value. A steer worth three to five dollars in Texas would bring ten times as much in New York if a way could be found to get it there.[4] The railroad provided the way. Young Americans, many of them former soldiers, assumed duties once performed by Mexican herders. The northern drives to the railroad and to grazing lands in Montana and Wyoming are the cowboy's heroic age. Round-ups, river crossings, stampedes, the chuck wagon, and the wandering cowboy date from this period. As early as 1888 Theodore Roosevelt wrote that "In its present form stock-raising on the plains is doomed, and

[1]"Just Wild About Westerns," Newsweek, L (July 22, 1957), 51.

[2]"Ten-Gallon Hero," American Quarterly, VI (1954), 114.

[3]Harry Schein, "The Olympian Cowboy," tr. Ida M. Alcock, American Scholar, XXIV (1955), 311.

[4]Everett Dick, Vanguards of the Frontier (New York, 1941), p.450.

Comment

Quotations can often be blended more smoothly into the text and reduced in bulk by the use of the *ellipsis(...). In citation 5 the quotation itself seemed necessary because of the authority carried by Roosevelt's actual words. The following was omitted: ... *with their barbarous, picturesque, and curiously fascinating surroundings, mark a primitive stage of existence as surely as do the great tracts of primeval forests, and like the latter....* Since these words add nothing to the student's paper, he is free to cut them as long as he does not distort the meaning of the original. Short quoted phrases like those in the first paragraph of the sample paper do not require an ellipsis.

Note 5: In the citation of a book or an article by two authors, both names are given.

Note 6: A book by more than two authors may also be cited as follows:

[6]Maurice Frink, W. Turrentine Jackson, Agnes Wright Spring, When Grass Was King (Boulder, Colorado, 1956),p.58.

[6]Maurice Frink et al., When Grass Was King (Boulder, Colorado, 1956), p.58.

Note 7: The first reference to a book or an article should be complete enough to enable the reader to find it. Later references should be condensed. Note 7 could also be handled as follows:

[7]Brown. op. cit., p.130.

[7]Brown, Trail Driving Days, p.130.

If lengthy, the title may be shortened but not abbreviated; *Days* would be acceptable. The use of *op. cit.* (work previously cited) is decreasing. If one book is used, the author's last name (see example) is adequate. If two books by the same author are used, a shortened title is necessary to indicate which one is being cited.

[7]Brown, Days, p.130.

Exercises

5. Bring to class a quotation of about three sentences from a source that you are using in your paper.

A) Summarize it in your own words.

B) Reduce it by leaving out words and inserting an ellipsis.

C) Pick out a brief usable phrase and blend it into a sentence of your own.

can hardly outlast the century. The great free ranches... must pass away before the onward march of our people."[5]

The end of an era is difficult to pinpoint. Perhaps the cowboy's way of life began to change with the invention of barbed wire in 1874. Its use spread widely; 80,500,000 pounds had been sold by 1880.[6] It brought the small farmer, closed off the northern trails, and forced cattlemen to grow hay for winter feed. The open range was doomed. The passing of the early cowboy might also be dated from the blizzard of 1886-1887. Millions of cattle starved or froze to death. The next spring many unemployed cowboys became homesteaders; others went to work for the large corporations that survived the debacle. The carefree cowboy became a cowhand, who spent much of his time stretching fence, haying, digging wells, and dehorning cattle. In the late 1880's on the huge new XIT (ten counties in Texas) ranch, drinking, gambling, and carrying firearms were forbidden.[7]

Creators of the movie cowboy have eliminated most unpleasantness from his existence. The loneliness and boredom of a life in which memorizing labels on tin cans was a major recreation[8] are seldom shown. The swirling dust in the face of a cowboy at the rear of a cow column, the prairie dog holes into which his horse might stumble, the swift current that imperiled a man riding downstream of a swimming herd--such hazards have been cut in favor of melodramatic encounters with rustlers and bandit-leaders masquerading as respectable bankers. The legendary cowboy

[5]Quoted in Dee Brown and Martin F. Schmitt, Trail Driving Days (New York, 1952), p. 231.

[6]Maurice Frink and others, When Grass Was King (Boulder, Colorado, 1956), p. 58.

[7]Brown, p. 130.

[8]Philip Ashton Rollins, The Cowboy (New York, 1922), p. 185.

Comment

Note 9: A lengthy title may be shortened in the first citation if the full title is given in the bibliography.

Note 10: The author's name and title of the book are given in the text. Only what is not given in the text is presented in the footnote. If the book had been cited previously, only the page number would be needed, and it might be given in the text in parentheses. The small Roman numeral indicates a page in the preface.

Note 11: When two sources supply information for the same sentence, they are cited in one footnote and separated by a semicolon. The necessity for this type of note seldom arises.

Note 12: The author's name is not repeated because it appears in the text.

Exercises

6. Draw a floor plan of the reference library, or that part of the library where you will be gathering material, and show the location of the following reference works, and any others assigned, using the numbers as listed below. If you are unable to locate some of the references, consult the card catalog to see whether your library has them.

1. *Readers' Guide*
2. *International Index*
3. *Encyclopaedia Britannica*
4. *Encyclopedia Americana*
5. *New York Times Index*
6. *Oxford English Dictionary*
7. *Current Biography*
8. *Dictionary of National Biography*
9. *Britannica Book of the Year*
10. *Dictionary of American Biography*

7. Read at least two articles in general encyclopedias on your topic and one in a special encyclopedia. (See the list on pages 360-362.) Contrast these articles as to (1) date of publication; (2) completeness of treatment; (3) emphasis, or possible bias; (4) approach, whether popular or technical; (5) interest and general value of the articles for your purpose.

has been raised to an enviable status which inspires respect but requires no work. Cowboy movies in which cattle are not even seen are common.

In 1902, when the cowboy seemed a vanishing American, Owen Wister wrote a novel that standardized the legendary cowboy's personality. The Virginian has sold more than 1,600,000 copies[9] and has been popular as a play and as a movie. In his preface to the novel, Wister announced that the cowboy had disappeared and "rides in his historic yesterday."[10] The real-life cowboy, perhaps; but the soft-spoken Virginian galloped straight into the plot of High Noon and a thousand other movies.

Although Broncho Billy, the first movie cowboy, began making short films in 1908, William S. Hart was the first to number his fans in the millions.[11] A former stage actor, he continued the Virginian tradition of a taciturn hero, honest and upright and true.

The Virginian is as reluctant to fight as Achilles. He endures insults and indignities but sets a limit which must not be passed: "When you call me that, smile." He postpones his wedding while he walks out to meet the villain who killed his pal. Of course, he lets the villain fire first. His phlegmatic chivalry and devotion to a friend set a pattern for his successors. Bernard DeVoto called the Virginian "a sun god in leather pants" but complained that because of "caste snobbery" Wister put his hero on the side of the cattle barons.[12] Whatever his allegiance may be, the Virginian, erect on his beloved

[9]Seth M. Agnew, "Destry Goes On Riding...," Publishers' Weekly, CLXIX (August 22, 1952), 746.

[10](New York, 1902), p. x.

[11]S.P., "50 Years Going That-a-Way," New York Times Magazine, April 5, 1953, pp.20-21; Daniel Blum, A Pictorial History of the Silent Screen (New York, 1953), p.10.

[12]"Birth of an Art," Harper's Magazine, CCVII (December 1953), 8.

Comment

As is shown in the specimen note cards below, the page number is written first to prevent memory lapses. On the first card, a part of a sentence is taken as a quotation in case the author's words are wanted in the paper. In quoting, use an author's exact words and be sure to inclose them in quotation marks; in summarizing, do not use his words.

In the second specimen card, several facts have been taken on the same card because they will obviously be used at the same point in the paper. Note that they were not used in the same order in which they were found and that the second point was not used at all. The hanging indention makes it easy to pick out separate points. Single quotes around the last point indicate a quotation in the original.

Slug — Source

Page Notes

Horses — Rollins

275 – One pony good at cutting out, another at driving stock, another at roping, etc.

There, "to an efficient cowboy on a large ranch were assigned several ponies, one animal for one class of work, another for another"

Slug — Source

Page Notes

Clothes — Rollins

105 – hat used for eye-shade, water bucket, fan for campfire, pillow, etc.

106-7 – bandana pulled over nose and face in dust or cold

109 – vest always worn (ordinary civilian type), pockets for matches and tobacco, left arms free

114 – two-inch heels kept heels from slipping through stirrups

117 – cattle country thoroughly masculine; "hung its clothes on the floor, so they couldn't fall down and get lost." 'Only saddles, bridles, lariats, and firearms received considerate care.'

Use of *Ibid.*: Because footnotes 14 and 15 refer to Rollins, *Ibid.* (in the same place) is sufficient.

Exercises

8. Bring to class three note cards and be prepared to discuss how the information may be used in your paper.

"hawss," is the original legendary cowboy.

Although the cowboy's horse was essential in life, it is indispensable in legend. Tom Mix, who rose to fame about the same time as W. S. Hart, popularized the devoted, intelligent horse that can pick a lock, untie knots, and anticipate every thought of his cowboy costar. To some extent, the mutual affection of cowboy and horse is a substitute for a love-plot, which most patrons of cowboy movies would find objectionable. Beautiful palominos and Arabians, the movie horses are far different from actual cow ponies. In fact, a cowboy had a string of horses, each valued for a particular skill such as cutting out or night herding.[13] At round-up and on a long drive he was hard on horses and used them up fast. If he felt a special fondness for one horse, it was often a memory of a horse he had once owned.

Tom Mix is also chiefly responsible for the elaborate cowboy regalia. His white sombrero, white gloves, and jewelled spurs have been imitated by most of his successors. Although an actual cowboy might take pride in his appearance when he left the ranch, he ordinarily was careful only of his saddle, bridle, lariat, and gun. In the cattle country clothes were hung on the floor "so they couldn't fall down and get lost."[14]

The dress of an actual cowboy was functional. Every item of his apparel had its purpose—from the two-inch heels, which enabled him to brace against the stirrups when roping a calf, to the sombrero, which he could use to fan a campfire or to carry water to his horse.[15] His cloth "civilian" vest, which left his arms free and provided

[13]Rollins, p.275.
[14]_Ibid._, p.117.
[15]_Ibid._, p.114; p.105.

Comment

A quotation of three or more lines may be indented and single-spaced; it should not be inclosed in quotation marks unless the quotation marks appear in the original source, as they did in the two notes on the opposite page.

Long blocks of quoted matter often indicate too much reliance on sources. Some research papers use no quoted matter at all. Three on a single page (see the page opposite) is rather unusual, but the quotations are appropriate to the material. There is no set way of introducing a display quotation. Compare the three ways used in the sample paper.

Note 16: *Ibid.* would be suitable here, but the author's name is just as easy to write and saves the reader the trouble of turning to the preceding page.

Note 18: At least once in a reference paper a situation will arise which does not fit any of the conventional forms. The citation of an unusual source like a phonograph record (Note 18) or a mimeographed pamphlet should resemble as closely as possible the style used for other footnotes. It should ordinarily describe the unusual source briefly in parentheses.

Exercises

9. Write out in full these entries from the *Readers' Guide,* using the form recommended by your instructor. Consult a recent volume of the index for the meaning of any unfamiliar abbreviations. What information in these entries would you omit in your footnotes and bibliography? What additional information might you need?

NORTH Atlantic treaty organization
Breaking the stalemate. H. S. Reuss. Commonweal 68:295-8 Je 20 '58
Re-appraisal; weakening of the West. New Repub 138:3-4 Je 2 '58
Sword and the shield. R. Hotz. Aviation W 68:13 Je 30 '58

SHAKESPEARE, William
Hamlet
Reform it altogether. H. Hewes. Sat R 41:22 Jl 5 '58
Theatre; American Shakespeare festival theatre's productions. H. Clurman. Nation 187:19-20 Jl 5 '58

MARTZ, Louis Lohr
Wallace Stevens: the world as meditation. Yale R 45:517-36 Je '58

MOVING picture sound recording
Add sound with pocket-size tape recorder. L. Barry. il Pop Photography 43:104+ Jl '58

pockets for matches and tobacco,[16] contrasts sharply with the embroidered, pearl-encrusted garment for which a movie cowboy may pay several hundred dollars.

To the legend established by the Virginian and glamorized by Tom Mix, Gene Autry added a new element--singing. Actual cowboys sang on night guard because of a superstition that cattle were soothed by the sound of a human voice.[17] They sang also to let off steam on their rare trips to town and to pass the time around the campfire. The last is most like a Gene Autry situation.

> "Well, after they'd tied up their night horses, and the day's work was done, why, they'd always build up a campfire and sit around till they was ready to go to bed. Then they'd always see which was the finest singer and knew the most songs."[18]

Their songs and their manner of singing were far different from the movie hero with a guitar slung from his saddle who bursts into song at the drop of a rustler. The songs were of all kinds, but some of the favorites were surprisingly sentimental like the following:

> Close the brown eyes gently,
> Beautiful Mable Clare,
> For no more shall I gather wild flowers
> To braid in your shining hair.[19]

No one seems to describe the singing as melodious. According to one cowboy,

> "...the average puncher's voice and the songs he sings ain't soothing. Mostly he has a voice like a burro with a bad cold, and the noise he calls singin'd drive all the coyotes out of the country."[20]

The cowboy's proficiency as a gun-slinger is probably as exaggerated as his ability as a ballad-singer. He usually wore one forty-five and carried a rifle to protect

[16]Rollins, p.109.

[17]Edward Everett Dale, Cow Country (Norman, Oklahoma, 1945), p.53.

[18]Harry Stephens of Denison, Texas, in a recorded interview with John A. Lomax, Cowboy Songs, Ballads, and Cattle Calls from Texas, ed. Duncan Emrich (Record L28, issued by Music Division, Library of Congress).

[19]Dale, p.128.

[20]Ramon F. Adams, Western Words (Norman, Oklahoma, 1944), p.144.

Comment

A rough draft should be triple-spaced or written with wide margins to leave room for revisions. Notice in the sample rough draft below that a brief citation in parentheses records temporarily the source of material used. If footnotes are put at the bottom of the page in a rough draft, one or two may be overlooked because the draft and the final copy will not correspond page for page.

In the sample below, the writer was carried away by his interest in a phase of his subject irrelevant to his purpose and gave it more space than it deserves. Notice the condensation and the single footnote to cover a summary of four pages in the sample paper.

animosity between / based on fact

The ~~dislike of~~ cowboys and homesteaders is ~~factual~~.

Kansas and Missouri / f / n / d / in 1866

Farmers ~~to the North~~ did not like the first Northern Drive

because of their belief that cattle carried "Spanish

also / m

fever." (Brown, 6) Many cowboys ~~also~~ came from the South,

Yankees transplanted

and their ways probably shocked the ~~northerners~~ in the farm

warfare ~~broke~~ between stockmen and homesteaders broke out in Johnson County, Wyoming. (Brown, 228-31)

states. In 1892 ~~cattlemen in Johnson County, Wyoming~~

~~formed a society known as Regulators to attack the home-~~

~~steaders. (Brown, 228) They arrived in Caspar Wyoming, on~~

~~April 7 and moved into Johnson County. (Brown, 229) They~~

~~attacked the ranch of Nate Champion, a leader of the home-~~

~~steaders. The homesteaders organized an army and moved~~

~~against them, and fighting was stopped only by the arrival~~

~~of the U. S. cavalry. (Brown, 231)~~

Exercises

10. Bring your rough draft to class and be prepared to explain your methods of revision. In the margin star any points about which you want to ask your instructor's advice.

the herd from wolves, but he was "only a fair marksman with a pistol."[21] The movie cowboy firing from the hip with both hands has often been repudiated, and the legend of "fanning" a hammer is even less credible.

The animosity between cowboy and homesteader is based on fact. Kansas and Missouri farmers opposed the first northern drive in 1866 because of their belief that Texas cattle carried "Spanish fever."[22] Also, many cowboys were Southerners, and their ways probably shocked the transplanted Yankees in the farm states. In 1892 warfare between stockmen and homesteaders broke out in Johnson County, Wyoming.[23] It is doubtful, however, that every homesteader had a daughter to fall in love with a cattleman, as in most movie treatments, and thus resolve the feud.

The cowboy's recreations have been revised drastically. His drinking habits have been toned down. When he was paid off and came to town, a real cowboy's drinking was uninhibited and rapid.[24] The hero calling for sarsaparilla or milk must have been far less common than in western movies. The movie cowboy is hedged in by a long list of taboos: he cannot spit, swear, chew tobacco, drink whisky, or kiss the heroine. He has, however, been granted wider latitude in gambling. Although gambling was widespread in the cattle country and there are stories of ranches being lost on the turn of a card, poker games for high stakes must have been rare among ordinary cowboys. The fact seems indisputable when one learns that a cowboy's monthly wage was from thirty to thirty-five dollars.[25]

While the cowboy on America's movie and television screens may ride the old range and fight the old fights, he is as different from his historic counterpart as exaggeration, distortion, and invention can make him. But to his millions of fans this fact will hardly make a difference—he represents what cowboys should have been like, whether they were or not.

[21]Dale, pp.122-123.
[22]Brown, p.6.
[23]_Ibid._, pp.228-231.
[24]Rollins, pp.187-188.
[25]Frink and others, p.10.

Comment

The sample bibliography cards are for entries 6 and 8 in the bibliography on the facing page.

Note that the bibliography does not give publishers. If the publishers were given, the first entry might read:

```
    Adams, Ramon F. Western Words. Norman, University of
Oklahoma Press, 1944.
```

Note that the two entries without authors are put in alphabetical order, according to titles, with those entries with authors.

	Call Number	Slug	Code
	F 596 D25	singing	Dale
Author	Dale, Edward Everett		
Title	Cow Country		
Publication data	Norman, Oklahoma, 1945		
Comment	singing and night-herding, pp. 52-54		

Book

	Location	Slug	Code
	west stacks	Virginian	DeVoto
Author	DeVoto, Bernard		
Title	"Birth of an Art"		
Publication data	Harper's Magazine CCVII (December 1953), 8-9		
Comment	pretty anti-Wister; Virginian set pattern for western movies		

Magazine

7.

Bibliography

Adams, Ramon F. Western Words. Norman, Oklahoma, 1944.

Agnew, Seth M. "Destry Goes On Riding--or--Working the Six-Gun Lode," Publishers' Weekly, CLXIX (August 22, 1952), 746-751.

Blum, Daniel. A Pictorial History of the Silent Screen. New York, 1953.

Brown, Dee and Martin F. Schmitt. Trail Driving Days. New York, 1952.

Cowboy Songs, Ballads, and Cattle Calls from Texas, ed. Duncan Emrich (Record L28, issued by Music Division, Library of Congress).

Dale, Edward Everett. Cow Country. Norman, Oklahoma, 1945.

Davis, David B. "Ten-Gallon Hero," American Quarterly, VI (1954), 111-125.

DeVoto, Bernard. "Birth of an Art," Harper's Magazine, CCVII (December 1953), 8-9.

Dick, Everett. Vanguards of the Frontier. New York, 1941.

Frink, Maurice and others. When Grass Was King. Boulder, Colorado, 1956.

"Just Wild About Westerns," Newsweek, L (July 22, 1957), 51-54.

Rollins, Philip Ashton. The Cowboy. New York, 1922.

S.P. "50 Years Going That-a-Way," New York Times Magazine, April 5, 1953, pp.20-21.

Schein, Harry. "The Olympian Cowboy," tr. Ida M. Alcock, The American Scholar, XXIV (1955), 309-320.

Wister, Owen. The Virginian. New York, 1902.

11. Put the following references to source material in consistent footnote form as they would appear in a reference paper. Keep them in the present numerical order.

1. To page 225 of this book.
2. To an editorial in the Boston Traveler on December 2, 1940, entitled The Responsibility of the Press.
3. To pages 139 and 140 in the second volume of a book by George Philip Krapp called The English Language in America. The book was published by the Century Company of New York and the date on the title page reads MCMXXV.
4. To pages 228 to 231 inclusive of the book mentioned in 1.
5. To an unsigned article called Baby Bombs in volume LV of Time for May 22, 1950, page 69.
6. To page xvii in the Introduction of a book called Burke's Politics. The book has a subtitle Selected writings and speeches of Edmund Burke on Reform, revolution and war. It was edited by Ross J. S. Hoffman and Paul Levack, and was published in 1949 by Alfred A. Knopf in New York.
7. To an article entitled Letters to the Editor as a Means of Measuring the Effectiveness of Propaganda, written by two men, H. Schuyler Foster, Jr., and Carl J. Friedrich and printed in The American Political Science Review for February 1937, pages 71 to 79. This issue was part of volume 31.
8. To the same pages of the article mentioned in 7.
9. To a quotation by Dr. Raymond B. Nixon in the June 1945 issue of Journalism Quarterly, quoted on pages 78 to 79 of The First Freedom, a book by Morris L. Ernst published in 1946 in New York by The Macmillan Company.
10. To an unsigned article called Isle of Man in the 1941 edition of the Encyclopedia Americana, a thirty volume work published in New York and Chicago by the Americana Corporation. This article appeared on page 414 of volume XV.

12. Put the items in the preceding exercise in proper form and order for a bibliography.

13. Prepare to write a brief report in class on one of the following or similar topics. Bring your bibliography and note cards with you for reference.

1. A summary or précis of your paper, giving the essential ideas and the emphasis of the original.
2. Different methods by which you could have developed your paper, and why you chose the one you did.
3. The sources you found most useful and why.
4. Some problems you encountered in organizing your paper and how you solved them.
5. The material you omitted from your rough draft and why.
6. Some interesting by-products of your research–information you have gained about finding material, about the subject itself, or about further areas for investigation.

14. Evaluate the sample paper as a piece of writing–opening and closing paragraphs, emphasis, transitions, sentence variety, and so on.

Part Two INDEX TO ENGLISH

To make the maximum use of this Index, *it would be well to read first Chapter 1 of the* Guide *so that you will understand the general principles involved, and then to read a few consecutive pages of the* Index *articles (or a selection of them, such as those referred to below) to see those principles applied, to get the feel of the articles, and to see how they fit with your present usage. With this preparation the articles should prove of immediate and convenient use in your actual speaking and writing.*

References to the sources most used in gathering the material for this book are usually made to author's name only. The exact titles of these sources will be found in the Bibliography on pages xiv-xv.

*A full discussion of the symbols by which pronunciation is represented appears in the article *Pronunciation §1.*

This *Index* contains entries in alphabetical arrangement that fall roughly into four categories:

a) **Entries on particular words and constructions,** such as *continual, continuous; *fiancé, fiancée; *get, got; *like–as; *route; *shall–will; *so . . . that; *very. Information about their standing in current usage is given. Since in these discussions classifying labels like Informal, General, and Formal are used, you should read Chapter 1 of the *Guide* in order to make certain of the meaning of these terms as they are employed in this *Index*. These entries are not capitalized.

b) **Entries for correction and revision of papers,** indicated by longhand abbreviations before the entry word. A list of these entries is given at the end of the book. These subjects are so important that they are likely to be studied in class and so are usually treated most fully in the chapters of the *Guide;* but for convenience in revising papers the basic points are given in the *Index* entry, with a page reference to the fuller treatment in the chapter.

c) **Articles on English grammar** giving definitions and examples of such matters as *Case, *Conjunctions, *Plurals, *Principal parts of verbs.

These are necessary for a full description of the language but are not of immediate use at the time of writing.

d) **Articles on various facts of language,** such as *American and British usage, *Foreign words in English, *Linguistics, that are designed more for general information than for immediate application.

A

The letter *a* represents several different sounds, which are also spelled by other letters. They are listed here by their traditional names because these are well known though not linguistically accurate:

1. *"Short a,"* the (a) of *hat* and *stack,* differently spelled in *plaid.*

2. *"Long a,"* the (ā) of *game* and *famous;* other spellings occur in *aid, gauge, say, break, vein, weigh,* and *they.*

3. *"Broad a,"* the (ä) of *hard, father,* and *calm,* differently spelled in *heart* and *sergeant.* In Southern British English and by some speakers in the United States and Canada this vowel is used in a fairly large group of words like *ask, bath, craft, demand, half,* and *laugh.* In eastern New England these words are often pronounced with a vowel between (a) and (ä), known as "intermediate *a.*" But the great majority of Americans and Canadians pronounce "the *ask*-group" with the (a) of *hat.*

Some speakers try to substitute the "broad *a*" or "intermediate *a*" for their natural "short *a*" in these words. But this attempt to imitate a type of pronunciation which one has not acquired naturally in childhood usually calls attention to itself, especially since the imitated vowel may be introduced into the wrong words: British *glass* (gläs), for example, may lead to (läs) for *lass,* which British speakers pronounce (las). The best practice is to pronounce this group of words in the fashion that is usual among educated speakers in your own region.

4. The (ã) of *care* and *parent,* differently spelled in *fair, pear, prayer, their,* and *where.* In these words the vowel varies regionally between the (ā) of *gate* and the (a) of *hat.*

5. The (o) of the first syllable of *swallow* (swol'ō, rhyming with *follow*), more commonly spelled with *o,* as in *rock* and *novel.* Many speakers have (ä) in these words.

6. *"Open o,"* the (ô) of *tall* and *warm,* differently spelled in *broad, maul, draw, soft, taught,* and *thought.* Here, too, pronunciation varies in different regions; many use this vowel only before *r,* pronouncing the other words so that *stalk* and *stock, caller* and *collar* are identical.

7. The *"schwa"* (ə) of *soda* and *about*. This *neutral vowel sound occurs only in unstressed syllables and is also spelled with the other vowel letters, as in *society, pencil, lemon, circus.*

Reference: *Webster's New International,* "A Guide to Pronunciation," §§ 76-96.

a- *A-* as a prefix from Greek meaning *not* is used in forming many words in the Formal and scientific vocabularies (*amoral, asexual, asymmetrical, atypical, achromatic*). It is usually pronounced ā (ā si met′ri kəl) though "short *a*" is heard, especially in *amoral* and *achromatic.*

A prefix *a-* from various Old English origins is found in many words (*abed, aloud, asleep*) and survives regionally in phrases like *going a-fishing, a-hunting.* See dictionaries for details of origin and use.

a, an 1. The choice between *a* or *an* depends on the initial sound of the word that follows:

A is used before all words beginning with *a consonant sound*—that is, before all words spelled with initial consonant letters except silent *h,* as in *hour*—and before words spelled with initial vowel letters that represent combined consonant and vowel sounds, as in *eulogy, unit* (yo͞ol′ə ji, yo͞o′nit): *a business, a European trip, a D, a usage.*

An is used before all words beginning with *a vowel sound,* including words spelled with initial silent *h* (see *H): *an apple, an F, an hour apart, an honor.*

Questions sometimes arise over words beginning with *h* but not accented on the first syllable, as in *histo′rian.* Formerly this *h* was not pronounced, so that *an* was used. Although the *h* is now often pronounced, some people continue to say and write *an histor′ical* event (but *a his′tory*). In contemporary usage *a* is the more common in such locutions, but an individual is free to choose whichever he prefers.

2. Repeating *a* or *an* before each noun of a series tends to keep the various words distinct and make the expression emphatic: *a pen, a sheet of paper, and an envelope* (*a pen, sheet of paper, and envelope* would be less emphatic).

3. *Awhile, a while.* The adverb *awhile* is written as one word (He came *awhile* ago)but not the noun (He came for *a while*). The *a* is also separate in *a lot, a bit, a little.* (See *half for *a half hour, half an hour,* etc. For *kind of a, sort of a* see *kind of [a], sort of [a].)

Ab **Abbreviations** Revision: Write in full the abbreviation marked.

1. *Appropriateness.* Abbreviations belong most appropriately to manuals, reference books, business and legal documents, scholarly footnotes, and other works in which saving space is important. They also fit in Informal writing—notes for one's own use, letters to friends.

In literature and most Formal writing, abbreviations are held to a minimum, though modern General style is much less strict.

Shoptalk, familiar conversation, and slang use many abbreviations for the names of things frequently mentioned: *t.b.* (*tuberculosis*), *d.t.'s* (*delirium tremens*), *b.o.m.* (newspaper: *business office must*), *b.f.* (*boy friend*), *g.f.* (*girl friend*).

2. *Standard abbreviations. Dr., *Mr., *Mrs., *Messrs.* are always abbreviated when used with names. A number of abbreviations, such as *St.* (**Saint*), **a.m.* and *p.m., S.E.C., T.V.A.,* and abbreviations for other government agencies, are generally used. In Formal writing, titles like *Reverend, *Professor, President, and Senator would not be abbreviated at all, but in most other writing they are found abbreviated *when initials or given names are used:* not *Prof. Hylander,* but *Professor Hylander* or *Prof. G. W. Hylander.*

English still has many abbreviations of Latin words:

A.D.	*Anno Domini*–in the year of our Lord (*Centuries)
cf.	*confer*–compare (for which *see* may be used)
e.g.	*exempli gratia*–for example
*etc.	*et cetera*–and so forth
ibid.	*ibidem*–the same (used in footnotes)
i.e.	*id est*–that is

Such abbreviations are not italicized, unless there is a special reason for italics (as when *ibid.* represents the title of a book), since they are regarded as English words. Less commonly used abbreviations from Latin are usually italicized: *c.* or *ca.* (*circa,* about, used with uncertain dates), *seq.* (*sequentes,* following).

Dictionaries give frequently used abbreviations in the main alphabetical list of words or in a special list. (See Ch. 13, p. 377 for abbreviations used in footnotes of reference papers.)

3. *Period with abbreviations.* An abbreviation is normally followed by a period; omitting it is a careless slip.

Some publishers do not use a period after an abbreviation that is to be followed by a colon (as *i.e:*). Only one period is used when an abbreviation falls at the end of a sentence.

There is a tendency today not to use a period after an abbreviation that ends with the last letter of the word abbreviated: *Dr, Mr, Mrs, vs, Wm.* This is more common in British than in American usage.

Periods are frequently not used with the abbreviations of names of government agencies (SEC, TVA, FBI) and of other terms if the abbreviation is generally used instead of the name (AFL-CIO, NATO, CBS), and of phrases like *mph, hp, kwh, rpm* in scientific contexts or when used with figures (*780 rpm*).

Abbreviations that are pronounced as words (*Wac, Nazi, UNESCO*) are called *acronyms.*

Compare *Contractions, *Origin of words § 3c.

ability (to) The idiom with *ability* is *to* and an infinitive (ability *to do,* not *of doing*): He has the ability to design beautiful buildings. The idea is often better expressed by an adjective or verb: He is able to (He can) design beautiful buildings. He designs (is designing) beautiful buildings.

able to *Able to* is rarely followed by a passive infinitive (like *to be done* or *to be ended*) because the construction sounds awkward.

Awkward: This was not able to be done because of lack of time.
Improved: This could not be done because of lack of time.
Or: They were not able to do this because of lack of time.

-able, -ible These two suffixes, alike in meaning, cause trouble in spelling because we pronounce them alike. In earlier English they were pronounced differently, as they are in Latin and French, but the English tendency to obscure the vowels in unstressed syllables has obliterated the distinction. Since pronunciation is of no help, we must learn the spelling of each word. Points to remember are that *-able* is by far the more common form and that it should be used in coining occasional words like *jumpable* or *come-at-able.*

1. *-able.* This list contains a few of the many words ending in *-able:*

advisable	imaginable	movable	teachable
applicable	incurable	noticeable	tolerable
changeable	indispensable	perishable	unbearable
comfortable	inseparable	presentable	unbelievable
desirable	intolerable	receivable	unmistakable
detestable	justifiable	serviceable	unpronounceable
eatable	laughable	sizable	unspeakable
excusable	lovable	suitable	usable

2. *-ible.* The following rather common words have *-ible:*

accessible	discernible	indefensible	possible
audible	divisible	indelible	reducible
combustible	edible	inexhaustible	repressible
compatible	eligible	intelligible	responsible
comprehensible	feasible	invisible	reversible
contemptible	flexible	irresistible	sensible
convertible	forcible	legible	suggestible
corruptible	gullible	negligible	susceptible
credible	horrible	perceptible	tangible
destructible	impossible	permissible	terrible
digestible	incredible	plausible	visible

3. *-able or -ible.* Several words are found with either *-able* or *-ible.* The more common form is put first: *collapsible–collapsable, collectable–collectible, preventable–preventible.*

above *Above* is primarily used as a preposition (*above* the clouds) or adverb (dark *above* and light below). Its adverbial use in such phrases as "the evidence cited above" is common in contemporary prose; but many writers prefer "the evidence already cited" or some such expression. The use of *above* as an adjective (the *above* prices) or as a noun (the *above* is confirmed) is often found in commercial and some journalistic writing but is usually avoided elsewhere. (Reference: Pooley, pp. 128-130.)

Absolute phrases Absolute phrases, like *the narrows passed* in "The narrows passed, we went along at a fairly good speed," modify the sentence as a whole. They are "absolute" not because they are independent but because they lack connectives defining their relationship to other sentence elements, being joined to the rest of the sentence only by their position, by contact.

When such phrases precede the main clause, they often seem unidiomatic: *"The discussion having been concluded,* the chairman brought the meeting to an end." More natural English would use a subordinate clause: "When the discussion had been concluded. . . ." A few instances of the construction, however, like "Other things being equal . . ." are well established and are used freely in all varieties of English.

When absolute phrases follow the main clause, they are a convenient way of adding details, as in the following sentence, where everything except the main clause, *She walked slowly,* is in what are usually known as absolute phrases:

> She walked slowly, big flakes falling on her lamb coat and clinging to hair over her ears, the lazily falling snow giving her, in her thick warm coat, a fine feeling of self-indulgence.—MORLEY CALLAGHAN, *A Native Argosy,* p. 135

See Chapter 2, "Absolute verbid phrases," page 65, *Participles § 3, *Infinitives § 5. Reference: Francis Christensen, *College English,* 1950, 11:401-403.

Abstract and concrete words Revision: Change the abstract expressions marked to concrete ones. *Abst*

Nouns that name qualities, conditions, actions, summaries of particular facts are abstract: *love, civilization, danger, age, flying.* They contrast with concrete nouns, which name persons and things that can be seen and touched: *girl, schoolhouse, tree.* Abstract nouns are necessary in discussing ideas but are often used where specific, concrete words would be more exact and forceful. (See Ch. 8 "Concrete words," p. 217, and "Abstract words," p. 219; and compare Ch. 6, "Details and generalizations," p. 139.)

Academic writing One conspicuous trait of academic writing—that is, the publications of teachers and scholars and others engaged in research and in originating ideas—is its documentation, the devices of bibliography and footnote reference that give the sources of material used in preparing the paper. Scrupulousness in giving exact references to those materials sets scholarly writing off from popular books and articles. (See Ch. 13, "Footnotes: crediting sources," p. 374.)

Another trait of academic writing is its Formal style. When scholarly articles and monographs deal with the results of experiments, of historical research, or of special investigation in any field, they naturally show the specialized vocabulary, compactness, and impersonality of *scientific and technical writing. Less specialized academic writing, too, tends to be dignified and Formal.

Partly because many works by professors and research workers are written more impersonally than they need be, "academic" is often used to describe writing that is unpleasantly abstract, distant, and dry, and to describe the style of many books supposedly for general reading that do not show sufficient adaptation to the desired readers. But such failures in communication should not hide the importance of academic writing. Very often the men engaged in discovering new facts, in originating interpretations of facts, are not particularly interested in popularizing them and leave that task to others. This passage, itself in the Formal style of academic writing, discusses the language of specialists:

> The truth is that the language of science and scholarship and that of ordinary literature are different engines of communication, though they have something in common. It is essential for academics to write as far as possible in normal language, and desirable for them to write well. It is essential for them to explain what they are doing to non-specialists and this task, if it is to be carried out adequately, requires them to write well. But they will not themselves judge the value of academic writing by literary standards. When a mathematician or nuclear physicist speaks of beauty and elegance–and he speaks of both as often as the composer or chessplayer, and may strive for both as hard as the poet –he has not in mind the proper ordering of words, but of ideas. And for him, as for Spinoza, their beauty may be so great that it altogether dwarfs the lesser beauties of the word. But those of us who do not share his aesthetics, and perhaps cannot understand them, are ill at ease.–"The Language of Scholarship," *The Times Literary Supplement,* Aug. 17, 1956, p. viii

Accent Accent–or stress as it is called in this *Guide-Index*–is the prominence given to certain syllables in speech; in English it results from greater force of exhalation. (See *Pronunciation § 2, a and b.)

Accent marks French words in English sometimes keep the accent marks with which they are spelled in their original language:

Acute: café outré attaché fiancée
Circumflex: crêpe tête
Grave: frère suède

The accent marks are regularly used in Formal writing and Formal publications. In General writing the marks are usually dropped, though both forms of some words are found–for instance, *fete* and *fête, role* and *rôle*. Most newspapers do not use accent marks. (See *Foreign words in English, and for particular words consult a recent dictionary.)

Accusative case In English six distinctive pronoun forms have survived which are often called accusative (or objective) forms and usually occur in the object function (but see *It's me): *me, her, his, us, them, whom. You* and *it* do not have such distinctive forms. Nouns do not have a special form for the accusative; noun objects of verbs and prepositions are in the common case form. (See *Case; *Objects; *Infinitives § 5; *Gerund § 2; *who, whom.)

ad *Ad,* the clipped form of *advertisement,* has only one *d* and should not be followed by a period. Like other clipped words it belongs to General and Informal speech and writing. (Reference: *College English,* 1954, 15:418.)

address As a verb, *address* is stressed on the second syllable: ə dres′; as a noun, stress is divided: a dres′ (ə dres′) or ad′res; in the word's commonest sense (the address of a letter, package, etc.) ad′res is most used.

> Mr. Thorpe was to address [ə dres′] the meeting.
> Mr. Thorpe then addressed [ə drest′] the meeting.
> Mr. Thorpe's address [ə dres′ or ad′res] was almost an hour long.
> The letter's address [ad′res or ə dres′] was illegible.

Addresses When the various parts of a person's address are written on the same line, they are separated by commas:

> Miss Louise Finney, 48 Adirondack View, Middlebury, Vermont
> Mr. Davis was a native of Carroll County, Virginia, and a graduate of the College of William and Mary.

(See *Letters § 1, b and c for addresses in and on letters.)

Adjectives in use Adjectives should add something to the exactness of a writer's statement or to the definiteness of his picture. As Herbert Read puts it, "appropriate epithets may be either exact or happy." In *briny* ocean, the *briny* does not add, because all oceans are briny; *stark* does not add much to the meaning of *tragedy,* or of *madness* either. Very general adjectives like *good* or *bad* or *beautiful* or *wonderful* do not as a rule add; the reader wants a more specific detail, a particular sort of *good* (*generous, affable, efficient*). Many adjectives that are exact enough have been used too often with certain nouns (*fond* farewell, *beady black* eyes) and are merely trite. Because most people do not use exact adjectives in conversation, they often fall back on these flat and stale modifiers in writing–and professional writers sometimes fall back on them too. (See Ch. 8, "Trite words," p. 225.)

A writer may try too hard to make a picture exact. Most of the adjectives in the following paragraph from a student theme are exact–that is, they add clearly to the meaning. But there are too many of them; the writer has been too conscientious. The passage would be more readable if those in brackets, and probably others, were taken out.

> In a hotel dining room there is not the [*clamorous, raucous*] bedlam of its *immediate* surroundings, but a *refined, subdued* atmosphere, pervaded by *distinct,* faintly *audible* sounds. The orchestra, with a barely *perceptible* diminuendo, concludes the [*melodic,*] *slow-tempo* arrangement, climaxed by the [*beautiful*] strains of the "Merry Widow" waltz —*rising, falling, fading* with *plaintive* supplication. Then later, while a *modern, rhythmic* melody is being played, the *hushed* clash of cymbals, the [*musical*] tinkle of the chimes, and the *muted* blare of brass blend harmoniously with the [*pulsing,*] *vibrant* voice of the *featured* soloist, only to be anticlimaxed by the *perfunctory* applause of the diners. The [*constant,*] *relentless* shuffle, shuffle, shuffle of *dancing* feet becomes *monotonous* with its [*endless*] repetition and *imperceptible* variation, while *trite* conversation is often interrupted by the *affected* voice of the *solicitous* waiter. The whispers and [*gay*] laughter, the *discordant* clatter of dishes upon trays, and the [*careless*] scraping of chairs blend into the room's *distinctive* personality.

But a sensible and sensitive use of adjectives is necessary. In most exposition the first requirement of adjectives is exactness; they must answer the needs of the material, like the italicized words in the next two paragraphs:

> *Many* counselors on *public* relations had *one* foot in commerce and the other in politics—even *international* politics. The most *eminent* figure in *this* class was the *late* Ivy Lee. It seems a pity that he died silently, leaving behind, so far as anyone knows, no *real* record of *his* activities. The *candid* reminiscences of Ivy Lee would be as *useful* to a *future* historian as Pepys' Diary—and perhaps as *interesting* to the student of *human* souls. He began *his larger* career as counselor for *certain* Rockefeller interests. He was *careful,* nevertheless, not to identify himself with the Rockefellers or *any other* group, so leaving himself *free* to serve *all* clients. He had a hand in an agitation for recognition of Russia as a means of increasing our *export* market. Indeed, he may have directed *this* campaign. So, too, when an element among the bankers decided that cancellation of *European war* debts would benefit *American* finance, they used Lee's talent for sweetening *unpopular* causes. And in the *last* year of his life he was advising the *new German* government on ways and means for making *Nazi* principles and methods less *hateful* to the *average American* citizen.—WILL IRWIN, *Propaganda and the News,* pp. 267-8

In writing that makes a definite attempt to capture the feelings and sensations of the reader, the adjectives must be exact (as they are in the following paragraph) but they must also deserve the epithet "happy"; that is, they must seem to fit and at the same time to contribute an accent, to lead the reader to the writer's feeling; perhaps they may make an imaginative appeal. In describing an actual experience Ernest Hemingway presents a picture rather than a series of facts:

> In the *five* days I saw a *dozen* or *more kudu* cows and *one young* bull with a string of cows. The cows were *big, gray, striped-flanked* antelope with ridiculously *small* heads, *big* ears, and a *soft, fast-rushing* gait that moved them in *big-bellied* panic through the trees. The *young* bull had the start of a spiral on *his* horns but they were *short* and *dumpy* and as he ran past us at the end of a glade in the dusk, *third* in a string of *six* cows, he was no more like a *real* bull than a *spike* elk is like a *big, old, thick-necked, dark-maned, wonder-horned, tawny-hided, beer-horse-built* bugler of a bull-elk.—*Green Hills of Africa,* p. 138

Notice that the relatively insignificant *glade, dusk,* and *trees* are not modified but that the *gait* is *soft, fast-rushing.* The gait needed to be described; the dusk and the trees are merely part of the background.

Adjectives sometimes tend to make a slow movement in writing partly because many of them have a falling rhythm—that is, the stressed syllable is followed by one or more unstressed syllables. They may contribute to a leisurely, relaxed effect:

> The sheltering trees only emphasized the ashen deadness of the wrinkled clapboards.

Too many of them may result in an excessively slow movement.

Carl Sandburg has been credited with advising a writer, "Think twice before you use an adjective." This is probably sound advice for anyone who is writing a good deal and tends to let thoughtless adjectives slip in. But it is also important for a writer to fix his eye on his subject and write about it as he really sees it. Without stuffing in adjectives he should fill in the qualities that are needed for the reader to re-create the picture or idea for himself. The adjectives then should be at least exact, and some of them may be happy.

Compare *Adverbs in use.

Adjectives, types and forms 1. *Forms.* Many adjectives can be identified by the fact that they are compared by adding *-er* or *-est* to the positive (or base) form or by preceding the positive form with *more* or *most:*

Positive	*Comparative*	*Superlative*
warm	warmer, more warm	warmest, most warm
talkative	more talkative	most talkative

(See *Comparison of adjectives and adverbs for further examples and discussion of use; see also *unique.)

Many adjectives have come down from an early period of the language (*high, handsome, civil*) without a distinctive adjective form, but many have been made and are still being made by adding a derivational ending or *suffix to a noun or verb. Some suffixes that are still active are:

-able (*-ible*)—translatable, edible
-al—critical, hypothetical
-ed—sugared, four-footed
-ful—playful, soulful
-ish—darkish, womanish
-less—harmless, fearless
-ous—callous, ferrous
-y—cranky, dreamy, corny

2. *Position of adjectives.* We recognize adjectives in sentences chiefly by their position in relation to the nouns that they modify, especially by the fact that they can stand between an article (*a/an, the*) or words like *our, this, some* and a noun: an *old* parka, our *youngest* son, this *characteristic* gesture, some more *favorable* opportunity.

According to its position in a sentence, an adjective is either *attributive* or *predicate:*

a) *Attributive* adjectives are placed next to their nouns, usually preceding, as in *tiny* brook, *horseless* carriages. Sometimes there is good reason for placing an adjective after its noun:

a woman *sweet, simple, home-loving* (Two or more adjectives often follow the noun.)

the outfit *complete* (For emphasis)

court *martial,* attorney *general* (Following French patterns)

a good plan *gone* wrong (Participle modified by adverb)

a plan so *complicated* no one could follow it (The adjective modified by other words)

a *white* cap, *small* and beautifully *made* (Avoiding an awkward piling up of adjectives before the noun)

b) *Predicate* adjectives come after some form of the verb *be* or some other linking verb (*taste, feel, turn*), except in inverted sentence order (*Silent* was the night).

The day is *warm*.
The train was *crowded.*
That pie smells *good.*
For a while I felt *bad.*

(See *Predicate adjective, Predicate noun.)

3. *Types of adjectives.* Adjectives are conventionally regarded as of three types according to their meaning or the character of their modification:

a) *Descriptive* adjectives, the most common type, modify the noun by naming a quality or condition of the object named: a *gray* shutter, *vivid* colors, *difficult* words. Descriptive adjectives are ordinarily compared and may themselves be modified by intensive and qualifying adverbs, words like *almost, very, quite.* Participles (*laughing, wrecked*) function as descriptive adjective modifiers but usually are not compared or modified by qualifying or intensive adverbs.

b) *Limiting* adjectives, a loose and not very numerous group of words, placed in other categories by some grammarians, point out in some way the object named (*this, that, his, other, former*) or indicate quantity or number (*two, second, both*). Several of the first group are pronouns regularly used in the function of adjectives. The articles *a, an,* and *the* are often included in this group. Limiting adjectives cannot ordinarily be compared or modified by other words.

c) *Proper* adjectives, derived from proper nouns, originally are limiting adjectives: *French* possessions, the *Puritan* colonies—but often become descriptive: *French* culture, *Puritan* manners. Sometimes they mingle both functions, as *Elizabethan* in the *Elizabethan drama* both limits drama to a period and brings to mind qualities of a group of plays.

Often a proper adjective is used so frequently in a merely descriptive sense that it loses its relation to the proper noun from which it came and becomes a simple descriptive adjective, written without a capital: *bacchanalian, pasteurized, diesel, india* ink, *paris* green.

4. *Adjective phrases and clauses.* Phrases and clauses are used in the function of adjectives:

> The man *with his hat on* is Harry.
> I like the one *on the end* best.
> a bird *with a long bill* (=a *long-billed* bird, a descriptive adjective)
> a bird *in the hand* (a limiting adjective)
> Everyone *who approves of this* will please raise his right hand.
> That was the summer *we went to Yellowstone.*
> He asked the first man *he met.*

(See *Clauses § 2, *Restrictive and nonrestrictive for further examples and discussion.)

5. *Other parts of speech as adjective modifiers.* One of the outstanding traits of English is the use of nouns in the adjective function: a *glass* jar, the *Churchill* government, a *hurry* call, *store* bread, *ski* pants, *adjective* modifier, the *high school* course, a *stretcher* case, the *horse and buggy* days. (See *Parts of speech.)

Participles are the adjectival parts of verbs: a *coming* man, a *deserved* tribute.

6. *Adjectives as subjects and objects.* Preceded by an article, words that are ordinarily adjectives occur in the functions of nouns: *the just, the rich, the unemployed, a high* (of weather), *an* all-time *high, a* new *low*. As a rule such words do not have genitive or plural forms.

References: Curme, *Parts of Speech,* Chapters 3, 11; *Syntax,* Chapters 5, 13, 14, 25; Roberts, Chapters 4, 14.

Adverbs in use What has been said about the use of adjectives (*Adjectives in use) can be said again about the use of adverbs: adverbs, too, should be either exact or happy or both. When an amateur writer wants to portray rapid or violent action, he is quite likely to make too free a use of adverbs and kill the whole effect. In this paragraph we would be relieved—and see the picture more clearly—if the student writer had abandoned his adverbs:

> Shrill horns scream *threateningly*. Automobiles careen *wildly*. Giant buses lumber *dominantly* along. Policemen shout *warningly* and then *desperately*. Pedestrians scurry across the broad avenue. And then more squeaky, impatient cars, more terrifying trucks, and more lumbering buses.

Some writers tend to qualify too much, to make a statement and then draw part of it back with such words as *probably, apparently:*

I shall [probably] try to read your paper tonight.

It is better to choose the most accurate word available and use that.

Many of the longer adverbs are unemphatic because they are unstressed toward the end, and when two or more of them come close together they make a clumsy or unpleasant sounding phrase. The repetition of the *-ly* is especially enfeebling:

. . . she sang *resonantly,* if *slightly nasally,* between the towering walls of the adjacent buildings.

They each respond to recurrent temperamental differences, and to analogous though *chronologically distantly* separated social conditions.

Because of the tendency in conversation to use superfluous adverbs, a writer needs to watch out for adverbs that add nothing to his meaning:

We found [out] that what had looked like snow was a mound of quartz.

The college student meets [up with] a different type of instructor in English than he had in high school.

Sometimes writers use an adverb plus an adjective or a verb when an accurate adjective or exact verb would be neater and just as expressive.

Scholarships should be kept for those who are *studiously inclined* [that is, for those who are *studious*].

When no one was looking I took the goggles and *swiftly made my way* out of the store. (Even *hurried* would say as much and a verb like *scurried* might say more.)

See *Prepositions § 3b; *very.

Adv **Adverbs, types and forms** Revision: Make the adjective marked an adverb by adding *-ly*. (§ 1.)

1. *Forms of adverbs.* 2. *Functions of adverbs.* 3. *Adverbs grouped by meaning.* 4. *Other constructions as adverbial modifiers.* 5. *Position of adverbial modifiers.*

Traditionally the parts of speech category of adverbs has been a sort of rag bag, including a variety of words that modify verbs, adjectives, other adverbs, and whole clauses and sentences. (Some words in the category, like *almost, very, quite, yes, no,* obviously differ in certain respects from typical adverbs—they cannot be compared—and could be set off as different parts of speech; but because some of their functions resemble those of adverbs, they can also be regarded as subgroups of adverbs.) Grammarians are experimenting with setting off various of these words in other categories, but there is no widely accepted grouping as yet, so that this article follows the traditional grouping.

1. *Forms of adverbs.* Most adverbs are adjectives or participles plus the ending *-ly: badly, deservedly, laughingly, surely.* Some adverbs have developed from Old English forms without a special adverbial sign: *now, quite, since, then, there, where.*

There are a number of adverbs with the same forms as adjectives, most of them in use for hundreds of years. Some of these are:

bad	doubtless	hard	much	slow
better	early	high	near	smooth
bright	even	late	new	straight
cheap	fair	loose	right	tight
close	fast	loud	rough	well
deep	first	low	sharp	wrong

Most of these also have forms in *-ly,* so that we can write "He sang *loud*" or "He sang *loudly*." The *-ly* forms are likely to be preferred in Formal English and the shorter forms in speech and Informal writing. The choice between the two is chiefly a matter of style. The shorter forms are often more vigorous than the longer:

> Go *slow*. Don't talk so *loud*. It was so windy that I had to hold on *tight* to the iron stand to keep from being blown away.

In speech and Informal writing some other short forms of adverbs are used: Take it *easy*. It came *easy*. He talked *big*.

In Nonstandard and careless usage there is a tendency to drop the *-ly* from commonly used adverbs, such as **real, special, considerable* for *really, specially, considerably*. This should be avoided. When in doubt consult a good dictionary.

Most adverbs are compared, either by adding *-er* and *-est* or by preceding them by *more* and *most*. (See *Comparison of adjectives and adverbs.)

2. *Functions of adverbs.* Adverbs are used typically in four functions:

a) Modifying a single word or sentence element:

> He will come *today*. (Modifying verb *come*)
> She was *rather* shy. (Modifying adjective *shy*)
> *Almost* immediately we saw them. (Modifying adverb *immediately*)

b) Modifying whole sentences:

> *Perhaps* he will come today. *Unfortunately* there were no more left. *Later* I was sorry. *That evening* I was sorry. *As soon as I said it,* I was sorry.

c) Connecting clauses and also modifying their meaning (see *Conjunctive adverbs):

> We agreed to call the matter closed; *however,* they were by no means convinced.
>
> The museum, we discovered, was closed on Fridays; *consequently,* we drove on to the next city.

d) Introducing questions:

When did you begin to feel this way?
Where was the car when you first saw it?

3. *Adverbs grouped by meaning.* Adverbs can be rather simply identified by considering their meaning, according to what question they answer:

a) How? (Adverbs of manner)

alike so worse keenly openly painstakingly

b) When? In what order? (Adverbs of time and succession)

afterwards when finally late lately never soon

c) Where? (Adverbs of place and direction)

below far north there upstairs

d) How much? To what extent? (Adverbs of degree and measure)

all almost less little much quite completely equally

e) Why? (Adverbs of cause and purpose)

consequently therefore

f) Yes or no. (Adverbs of assertion, condition, and concession)

yes no certainly doubtless not perhaps possibly surely
Informal: O.K. nix absolutely

4. *Other constructions as adverbial modifiers.* Nouns may be used in the function of adverbs (see *Genitive case, § 2):

He came *mornings.* He plans to stay a *month.*

Phrases may have the functions of adverbs (*Phrases, § 1):

He came *in the morning. After the examination* he had stopped studying.

Clauses may have the functions of adverbs:

When it came time to go, he didn't know what to do. He stayed on and on *because he didn't know how to leave.*

5. *Position of adverbial modifiers.* Unlike the position of adjectival modifiers, the position of adverbial modifiers in a sentence is variable and cannot be used as a way of identifying them with certainty. They should be placed in a position that is natural for a native user of the language and that will represent his desired emphasis.

Single word adverbs modifying single words tend to be placed next to the word modified: the *almost* perfect state, the *most disagreeably* certain result, they *certainly* tried, they all worked *hard.* Adverbial phrases and clauses usually precede or follow the main construction. These versions of the same sentence show some typical variations in the position of adverbials:

1. *When the tide turned,* all the boats *hurriedly* headed *for the channel.*

2. All the boats *hurriedly* headed *for the channel when the tide turned.*

3. All the boats headed *for the channel hurriedly when the tide turned.*

4. *Hurriedly* all the boats headed *for the channel when the tide turned.*

5. All the boats, *when the tide turned, hurriedly* headed *for the channel.*

6. All the boats headed *for the channel when the tide turned hurriedly.*

All of the first five would be possible, though four and five only if special emphasis was wanted on *hurriedly* or *when the tide turned.* Six is impossible because from its position *hurriedly* seems to go with *turned.*

Reference: Curme, *Parts of Speech,* pages 73-86, and all books on English.

advertisement Ad vûr′tiz mənt (or ad vûr′tis mənt) is winning out over ad′vər tīz′mənt and is now the more common pronunciation, though the latter is still heard.

adviser, advisor Advis*er* has been the more common spelling, but the *-or* form (from advis*ory*) is increasingly used. Either is acceptable.

-ae-, -oe- Words from Greek and Latin that contain the digraphs *-ae-* and *-oe-* have been for a long time variously spelled in English. (Most printers do not now use the ligatures—*æ, œ*—except in works dealing with the ancient languages.) Both *-ae-* and *-oe-* are pronounced as though written *e* (either long or short). Many spellings have been simplified in the past: *economics, pedagogy, penal* were formerly *oeconomics, paedagogy, poenal.*

The present trend is to hasten this simplification. Medicine, for instance, has adopted many of the simpler forms, like *anesthetic* (for *anaesthetic*). The long series of words beginning with *haem-* (meaning "blood") now preferably begin with *hem-* (*hematic, hemoglobin, hemorrhage,* and so on). The American Historical Association long ago adopted *medieval.* Dictionaries now give such words as *ameba, cesura, dieresis, esthetic, subpena* either as preferred or alternate spellings. For a particular word consult a recent authoritative dictionary. Formal style tends to keep the older form with the two letters, General to use the simple *e.*

Latin plurals in *ae* still keep the two letters: *alumnae, antennae, formulae* (see *Plurals § 4); and in Greek and Latin proper names the two letters are kept: *Boeotia, Caesar, Oedipus.*

affect, effect Since most people make no distinction in pronouncing the first vowel of these words (ə fekt′), the spelling is likely to be carelessly confused.

Affect is usually a verb, meaning to "influence" or "put on" (compare *affectation*): This will *affect* the lives of thousands. He *affected* a stern manner.

Effect is most commonly a noun, meaning "result": The *effects* of this will be felt by thousands. What would be the *effect* of doubling the amount?

Effect is also a verb in Formal English, meaning to "bring about": The change was *effected* peaceably.

Affectation We learn our language as children by imitating the speech of people around us, and we change our language later in life by imitating what we hear others say or what we find in reading. So long as these changes furnish us with more varied and more exact ways of saying things, they are proper and necessary and represent a healthy growth. But sometimes we are led to adopt different pronunciations or different words or different constructions not so much to make our speech more effective as to make it seem more elegant, or even for the effect of the language itself rather than the effect of what it is conveying. Such changes are affectations and are unpleasant. Writing is more precise than speech, but writing in a style quite different from one's speech is affectation.

Affectation is most easily spotted in pronunciations. In some parts of the United States bēn (for *been*), rä′thər (for *rather*), and ī′thər (for *either*) are common pronunciations, but consciously adopting them is affectation in regions where bin, ra′thər, or ē′thər are usual. For many people expressions like the following are affectations: *aren't I—one should, shouldn't one;* Briticisms like *no end—that which* for *what*. Using slang except for humorous effect is an affectation for a person who knows little slang and seldom uses it in natural speech.

The line between natural and affected speech is hard to draw, since it depends chiefly on motive. In general, picking up expressions not commonly heard from the educated people of a community is dangerous. Increasing the expressiveness of one's speech is praiseworthy, but just trying to be "different" will usually result in bad English. The way to avoid affectation is to consider the appropriateness and expressiveness of language and to shun "big words." (See Ch. 1, The Varieties of English, pp. 4-35; *Pronunciation § 3.)

again, against The general American pronunciation is ə gen′, ə genst′; ə gān′, ə gānst′ are in general British use but uncommon in the United States.

aggravate In Informal usage *aggravate* means to "annoy" or "irritate": "I was never so aggravated in my life." In Formal and usually in General English *aggravate* means "to intensify or increase something unpleasant," as to *aggravate suffering* or *a wound* or *a crime*. The same distinction is made with the noun, *aggravation*.

Agr **Agreement** Revision: Make the pronoun or verb marked agree grammatically with the word to which it is related: its antecedent if it is a pronoun, its subject if it is a verb.

Certain parts of speech, which vary in form for gender, person, or number should agree when they stand in relationship to each other:

1. *Subject and verb* agree in number (The *man is* old—The *men are* old) and person (*I go* tomorrow—*He goes* tomorrow). See Chapter 2, "Agreement of subject and verb," page 60; *Subject and verb, *Collective nouns.

2. *A pronoun* agrees with its antecedent in gender (The *man* found *his* keys–The *girl* found *her* keys), in number (The *boy* had lost *his* way–The *hikers* had lost *their* way), and in person. See Chapter 3, "Checking pronouns," page 84; *Reference of pronouns, *each, *every and its compounds.

3. *A demonstrative adjective* usually agrees in number with the noun it modifies. (*That coat* is expensive–*These shoes* cost more than my old black suede pair did.) See *Demonstrative adjectives, *this, *kind, sort.

The chief cause of failure in agreement is that we do not hold our grammatical patterns in mind very well. If several words intervene between the two that should be in agreement, we seem to forget the way we started out. This is especially true if the subject is a collective noun or pronoun or if several words, some of them plural, come between a singular subject and its verb, so that we are tempted to use a plural verb.

In Formal English, grammatical agreement is quite strictly followed, but there are many locutions in which variations in agreement have become acceptable in General and Informal English. See, for example, *either, *one of those who, *who, whom.

agree to, agree with One agrees *to* a plan and agrees *with* a person. One thing agrees *with* another. Other idioms are: I agree *in* principle; we agreed *on* a plan of attack.

ain't *Ain't* is one of the commonest and most easily identifiable Nonstandard words, and prejudice against it among educated people has been almost unanimous for the last half century or so, though it is directly descended from formerly accepted contractions. In actual conversation it is inconspicuously pronounced (often *ant* or *nt* rather than *ānt*) and could be an economical single form for *am not, is not, are not, has not, have not* if the social objection could be relaxed, but the schools continue their effort to eliminate it.

Used in the first person, especially in question form (*ain't I*) where there is no easy natural contraction–*amn't* is hard to pronounce–*ain't* is occasionally heard among educated speakers and was marked "disputable" and "almost established" in the Leonard study of 1932. *Aren't* is often used in this construction, especially in England: "I'm making real progress, aren't I?" In the first person, both *ain't* and *aren't* may be regarded as Informal, other uses of *ain't* as Nonstandard. (See *Divided usage. References: Curme, *Parts of Speech,* p. 248; Marckwardt and Walcott, pp. 48, 95-96.)

airplane–aeroplane For several years these two words competed for general usage, but in the United States at least, *airplane* is now both the official and the popular form. *Aeroplane* (pronounced er′ə plān) is more commonly used in England.

a la *A la* is regarded as an English preposition, meaning "in the manner of": a la Whistler, a la *The New Yorker*. In Formal writing and modish advertising (as of cosmetics and fashionable clothes), the accent mark is usually kept (*à la*); elsewhere it is written *a la*. We do not use the other French forms, *à l'* and *au,* except in borrowed phrases (*au gratin*). *Alamode* (whether meaning "in the fashion" or referring to ice cream on pie) is usually written as one word without the accent mark. The French form (*à la mode*) is now rarely found.

alibi In Formal English *alibi* means "a defense on the ground of having been in another place"; in General English *alibi* refers to any excuse. (Reference: *College English,* 1955, 17:55.)

all and its compounds The following words and phrases should be watched carefully:

all ready (adjective phrase): At last they were *all ready* to begin.
already (adverb of time): They had *already* begun.
**all right* (adjective phrase): The seats seemed *all right* to me.
all the farther (adverb, equivalent to as far as) is a localism: That's *all the farther* I'll go.
all together (adjective phrase): We found them *all together* in an old trunk. There were six *all together.*
altogether (adverb, equivalent to *wholly*): That's *altogether* another matter.

Alliteration Alliteration is the repetition of the same sound at the beginnings of several words in a series or at the beginnings of stressed syllables within several words close together. Besides contributing to the pleasure that a reader may find in the similar sounds, alliteration serves to bind the phrase, or sometimes a whole series of phrases, into a unit:

. . . the *c*rowded, *c*loistered *c*olleges of Oxford.—PAUL ELMER MORE.
. . . ran over the *s*tarry *s*moothness of the lagoon, and the water between the piles lapped the *s*limy timber once with a *s*udden *s*plash.—JOSEPH CONRAD, "The Lagoon," *Tales of Unrest,* p. 199

Alliteration is one of the figures of sound that contribute to the musical effect of poetry, though not one of the most important:

Here I am, an old *m*an in a dry *m*onth,
Being *r*ead to by a boy, waiting for *r*ain.
T. S. ELIOT, "Gerontion"

All *d*ay within the *d*reamy *h*ouse,
The *d*oors upon their *h*inges creaked;
ALFRED, LORD TENNYSON, "Mariana"

In ordinary expository prose conspicuous alliteration is usually out of place because it tends to attract attention to the expression at the expense of the idea. Its use in Formal prose, especially in prose with an oratorical or poetic background, is more appropriate.

At present, alliteration is one of the chief weapons of advertising sloganeers and makers of flashy titles, who simply push to a conspicuous point the natural binding power of the figure:

*B*rush *b*ad *b*reath away.	*P*otatoes *P*romote *P*rosperity
*S*weethearts in *sw*imsuits	*M*ealtime *M*agic with *M*ilk
*F*ilter, *fl*avor, *fl*ip-top box	*L*and of *L*incoln

Alliteration is also characteristic of humorous verse and prose and of any mannered writing on the light side:

Tell me, what is a man to do
When the *l*ady his *l*ife is based upon
*L*ikes to be *w*ooed but *w*on't be *w*on?

OGDEN NASH, *Hard Lines,* p. 58

all (of) In General and Informal usage *all* is followed by *of* in many constructions where the *of* would not be used in Formal writing:

All *of* the milk was spilled.
They passed all *of* the candidates.
You can't fool all *of* the people all *of* the time.

All of is used with a pronoun in all varieties of usage:

All of them went home.
They wanted *all of it* but got only half.
He gave *all of us* some candy.

all right–alright *All right* is the spelling of both the adjective phrase (He is all right) and the sentence adverb, meaning "yes, certainly" (All right, I'll come).

Alright is a natural analogy with *altogether* and *already* but at present is found only in advertising, comic strips, in unedited writings, and, rarely, in fiction. It will be worth watching to see if *alright* makes its way into General English. In the meantime, be on your guard.

all-round is usually hyphened: an *all-round* athlete, an *all-round* education.

-al ly English has a number of adjectives with the (Latin) endings *-al* and *-ical: fatal, final, medical, historical, political.* Usually an adverb is made by adding *-ly* to this ending. This should be remembered in spelling these words, especially since the unstressed final sounds give the impression that there are fewer syllables than must be spelled.

ment*al*	ment*ally*	fundament*al*	fundament*ally*
accident*al*	accident*ally*	incident*al*	incident*ally*
politic*al*	politic*ally*	practic*al*	practic*ally*

Several adjectives ending in *-ical* show a tendency to drop the *-al: alphabetic, biographic, geographic, grammatic, philosophic* are becoming more common, following the course of *academic, frantic, emphatic, poetic,* and others that have already shed the final syllable.

Although *frantic* and *public* and a few others have adverbs without the *-al-* (*franticly, publicly*), most of these words reinstate that ending before the *-ly:*

academic*ally*	dramatic*ally*	prolific*ally*
athletic*ally*	heroic*ally*	specific*ally*
automatic*ally*	idiotic*ally*	terrific*ally*

alma mater An anglicized Latin term ("fostering mother") meaning one's school or college; likely to be pretentious in General writing. Pronounced al′mə mā′tər, äl′mə mä′tər, al′ma ma′tər.

also is a weak connective; ordinarily *and* will do its work better:

He came with tents, cooking things, *and* [better than *also*] about fifty pounds of photographic equipment.

(See *Conjunctive adverbs.)

alternative comes from the Latin *alter,* "the second of two"; some Formal writers, in deference to the word's origin, confine its meaning to "one of two possibilities," but it is commonly used to mean one of several possibilities, and is so defined in dictionaries.

although *Although* and *though* connect with the main clause an adverbial clause of concession—that is, a statement in opposition to the main statement but one that does not contradict it. *Although* is more likely to introduce a clause that precedes the main clause, *though* one that follows:

Although [Though] the rain kept up for almost three weeks, we managed to have a pretty good time.

We managed to have a pretty good time, though [although] the rain kept up for almost three weeks.

There is no distinction in meaning; the choice between the two may be based on sentence rhythm. *Although* is a heavier and slightly more Formal word.

Often one of two clauses connected by *but* can be thrown into an *although* clause with greater accuracy of meaning and with greater variety in the sentence pattern:

We had rehearsed that act time and time again, but we all missed our cues the first night.

Although we had rehearsed that act time and time again, we all missed our cues the first night.

The spelling *altho* has made more headway than *tho* and *thru* and is appropriate in Informal writing, and in some General writing (if editorial or course policy approves), but would not be used in Formal writing. (See *but. Reference: Curme, *Syntax,* pp. 332-340.)

alumnus In spite of their clumsiness four Latin forms of this word are kept in English:

One male graduate is an	alumnus (ə lum′nəs)
Two or more male graduates are	alumni (ə lum′nī)
One female graduate is an	alumna (ə lum′nə)

Two or more female graduates are alumnae (ə lum′nē)

By common practice *alumnus* and *alumni* are used for graduates of coeducational institutions. Because of this complication of forms, *graduate* and *graduates* are increasingly used. *Alum* (ə lum′) is used in some institutions.

a.m. and p.m. These abbreviations (for *ante meridiem,* "before noon," and *post meridiem,* "after noon") are now usually written in small letters except in headlines and tables. They are most useful in tables and lists of times. In General writing they are used only with figures for specific hours: "from 2 to 4 p.m." The periods are sometimes omitted in reference style.

M. is the abbreviation for noon: "12 m." There is no corresponding abbreviation for midnight.

Ambiguity Revision: Make the meaning you intend unmistakable. *Amb*

1. *Inexact reference of pronouns.* 2. *Modifiers.* 3. *Incomplete idioms.* 4. *"Yes" or "no" after negatives.* 5. *Intentional ambiguity.*

Although inexact writing is common enough, actually ambiguous writing, in which there is possibility of confusing two meanings, is relatively rare. The context usually shows which of two possible meanings must be taken. The most common sources of actual ambiguity are:

1. *Inexact reference of pronoun,* especially in *indirect discourse:

He told his father he had been talking too much.

Such a sentence usually needs re-forming, perhaps as:

"I've been talking too much," he told his father.
"You've been talking too much," he said to his father.

(See *Reference of pronouns.)

2. *Modifiers*

a) Squinting modifiers that may refer to either of two words or constructions:

I said *when the game was over* that I would go. (When the game was over I said that I would go. Or: I said that I would go when the game was over.)

Some people *I know* would go there anyway. (Some people whom I know. . . . Or: Some people would go there anyway, I know.)

b) *Modifiers temporarily misleading,* as in headlines:

Police repair man killed by car
Horse bites off ear of owner–Man says he will keep biting mare despite attack

Such sentences are usually clear in spoken English, and even in writing the intended meaning can be wrung out by rereading. But the writer should not require his reader to be a detective.

3. *Incomplete idioms,* especially in comparisons:

"I like Alice as well as Will" might mean "I like Alice as well as Will does," "I like Alice as well as I do Will," or "I like both Alice and Will."

4. *"Yes" or "no" after negatives.* *Yes* or *no,* in response to a negative question or in commenting on a negative statement, often needs a clause to make the meaning clear.

> You haven't any more red ink, have you? (Answer, "Yes, I have" or "No, I haven't.")
>
> Let's not use such a long quotation. (No, let's not.)

5. *Intentional ambiguity.* Incomplete or ambiguous statements are sometimes intentional, like the sign in an airport limousine, "Tipping for this service not required," which drew tips from most passengers.

American Since it is inconvenient to form an adjective or a compound with *-man* (English-man) from *the United States, American* is ordinarily used. It is obviously inexact, since Canadians and Mexicans are as American as we are. But it is no more inexact than many other words and is generally used in this sense. Perhaps we can take an Englishman's judgment:

> The use of *America* for *the United States* & *American* for *(citizen) of the U. S.* is open to as much & as little objection as that of *England* & *English(man)* for *Great Britain* (& *Ireland*), *British,* & *Briton.* It will continue to be protested against by purists & patriots, & will doubtless survive the protests.—H. W. Fowler, *Modern English Usage,* p. 18

It is more exact to use *the United States* as the name of our country, but the use of *America* is common. Use *American* as the adjective and the name of an inhabitant. (Reference: H. L. Mencken, "Names for American," *American Speech,* 1947, 22:241-256.)

American and British usage There are several reasons why the spoken and written English of the United States differs from that of England. Since the seventeenth and eighteenth centuries, when the English language was brought to North America, the language used on both sides of the Atlantic has changed noticeably, and naturally in somewhat different ways. For the past few generations first-hand contacts between Americans and Englishmen have been confined to a handful of the upper classes of both nations, in contrast to the rather frequent movement back and forth among the citizens of the British Commonwealth, so that there has been little chance for the pronunciation of one to affect the other. Even the stationing of American troops in England during World War II did not have widespread effect, though their presence, as well as the popularity of American movies in England, has probably made it easier for the English to understand American speech than it is for us to understand British speech. The people in the United States and England live under different governments; they are educated in different school systems. Social stratification, affecting the ideals and habits of large classes of people, is considerably different. In spite of the mutual circulation of publications, visits of lecturers, professors, and ministers, and interchange by way of the movies and the radio, many of the factors that tend to keep the speech within the British Commonwealth like that of England cannot operate as effectively between England and the United States.

The differences in language have led to interesting emotional attitudes on both sides. There has been considerable arrogance. Britishers scorn "vulgar Americanisms," partly from dislike of differing language habits, partly from a feeling of superiority in customs and manners: The maker of the glossary to the London edition of Sinclair Lewis' *Babbitt* went beyond simple definition when he wrote for *ice cream soda* "Ice cream in soda water. A ghastly American summer time drink." Fowler says that the realization that Americans had dropped the *u* from words ending in *-our* stopped the British from making the same change. Many Americans look upon British accent and vocabulary as ludicrous or at best snobbish. The average American's dislike for Briticisms has been intensified by affectation of British pronunciations and British words by some Americans. Yet despite the British criticism of us for "debasing" the language, many of them seem to have a sneaking fondness for the "vigor" of American speech, and many Americanisms find an easy adoption as a result. The introduction to *Everyman's English Dictionary,* London, 1942, says: "Special attention has been given to the wealth of colourful American coinages with which the English language is in process of being enriched."

In the written language some spelling differences stand out. The British tend still to prefer *-re* to *-er* in words like *center* and **theater,* though they use both forms; they still keep *-our* in a number of words, though they are gradually simplifying; they use *x* in a few words like *inflexion;* they tend to double more consonants, as in *traveller, waggon;* and there are various individual words that differ, such as *tyre* (automobile *tire*). But these distinctions do not affect a large number of words, and actually for most of them usage is divided in both countries. They are just enough to show that a book is of British or American origin, but they do not interfere with reading except among fanatics in one country or the other. They really are one of the better arguments for allowing more individual freedom in spelling, but offer a problem to a publisher who wishes to circulate a book in both countries.

For a number of years scholars in the United States have been at work discovering and describing our speech. The magazine *American Speech* (founded in 1925) has published specific observations of usage and more general articles. Professor George Philip Krapp's *The English Language in America* (New York, 1925) and John S. Kenyon's *American Pronunciation* (Ann Arbor, 1935) are scholarly works. The four editions of H. L. Mencken's *The American Language* (New York, 1919-1936) have given a sturdy defense of American as against British usage. Mencken is not quite fair in that he usually pits American vulgate against formal British, but his main point, the existence of a distinctive popular speech in the United States, is well proved (though not his implication that there is a distinct American language). *The Dictionary of American English* presents the record of many words as they have been used in the United States.

There are of course several varieties of English in use on both sides of the Atlantic, and Great Britain presents a greater variety than the United States, in part because of sturdy remains of older dialects in the various counties, in Scotland, and in Wales. But standard British English is likely to be more uniform in pronunciation than standard American English, which has at least three great regional varieties. (British "Received Standard," incidentally, is a relatively recent development; American pronunciation is in many respects closer to that of the England of 250 years ago.) Among Englishmen and Americans of average education and social position, differences in pronunciation are likely to be particularly striking. There are different intonations, different values for the vowels, differences in particular words like the British trā (*trait*), prō cess, con tents′, lef ten′-ənt (*lieutenant*), ral′i for the American rô′li (*Raleigh*), and in general a more rapid speech and tendency to slur syllables (such as -*ar* in *dictionary*). The slower, fuller pronunciation of Americans seems wasteful and provincial to a Britisher.

Everyone knows some of the differences in vocabulary in certain common words: In England an *elevator* is a *lift, radio* is *wireless, crackers* are *biscuits* (*cakes* and *muffins* are also different from those in America), a *sit-down strike* is a *stay-in strike,* a *run* in a stocking is a *ladder, daylight saving time* is *summer time, installment buying* is the *hire-purchase system, white-collar* workers are *black-coat* workers. From the group word *tin can* the British have taken *tin,* Americans *can.* A *truck* is a *lorry,* an *automobile* is a *motor car* (though both are compromising on *car*), *gasoline* is *petrol,* sold in a *gallon* of five quarts. A *billion* is a thousand million in America (and France) and a million million in England (and Germany).

There is a vulgate speech in both England and America, a vast array of slang that baffles readers on the opposite side of the Atlantic, and many colloquialisms unique to each. In a book or play *no end* and rä thûr′ are supposed to identify an Englishman as clearly as *guess* or *reckon* is supposed to identify an American. One reason for careful study of the differences between the two speeches was the increased vogue of realistic fiction, which necessarily made use of more colloquial English and more colloquial American. In fact, the increased informality of modern prose in both England and the United States tended to emphasize the distinctions between the two.

The grammar of the popular levels of English and of American differs somewhat–contrast the speech of ordinary people in novels of the two countries. But in the General writing of the two there is less difference in grammar than in vocabulary. Collective nouns are more likely to be plural in British usage (*the government intend*); British writers differ in small matters like the position of **only,* the proper preposition with **different,* and various other idioms. (See Stuart Robertson, "British-American Differentiations in Syntax and Idiom," *American Speech,* 1939, 14:243-254.)

A fairly long catalog of such minor differences between these two branches of English could be drawn up, but their importance should not be exaggerated or allowed to obscure the fundamental fact that the resemblances far outnumber the differences and that the speech of the two countries represents two different strands of the English language. With patience a citizen of one country can understand the speech of the other, and with tolerance for small differences one can read the other's books and periodicals without trouble. An Englishman should write for Englishmen and an American for Americans. Too much concern for an "American language" may be mistaken patriotism. It is better to regard our speech as one of several branches of the great English language.

For an American there is no virtue in consciously cultivating British pronunciations or adopting British words and idioms (Briticisms). If he uses generally accepted American English he will reach his proper public, and if what he writes is interesting or important enough he can reach British readers too. (Many particular entries in this *Index* note differences between British and American usage.)

amount, number *Amount* is used of things viewed in bulk, weight, or sums; *number* is used of things that can be counted in individual units:

an *amount* of milk (but a *number* of cans of milk)

an *amount* of beets, corn, oats, wheat (but a *number* of bushels or carloads of any of these)

a *number* of seats, a *number* of people, a *number* of mistakes

an *amount* of money, an *amount* of humor

There is some tendency for *amount* to replace *number,* as in "The amount of people in the room . . ."; but this is as yet a usage to be avoided.

ampersand is the name for the **&** sign (originally a linking of the letters of *et*), called also *short and.* Its primary use, obviously, is to save space. It is used chiefly in business writing and in reference works. In addressing firms, use the form they habitually use (. . . and Company or . . . & Company), and in quoting, follow your original carefully.

Analogy in language *Analogy* is the name for the natural tendency in users of a language to make their speech more regular by forming new words like some existing ones, bringing old words closer together in form, or bringing constructions in line with familiar patterns. It results from the fact that, in general, language is a complex of consistent patterns (noun plurals end in *-s,* past tenses in *-ed,* etc.). It is easiest to watch analogy in the attempts of children to master their language. Before they learn the forms conventionally used by grown-ups, they manufacture forms like those they are familiar with: Most children for a time say *mans* before they learn to say *men;* they experiment with verb forms, usually making verbs regular, *singed* for *sang* or *sung, digged* for *dug,* or they may say *dag* instead of *dug.*

Analogy is the force that has disposed of many irregularities in the main body of the language. Out of various plural forms used in Old English, *-s* has won in all but a few words, and analogy is still bringing more words to that form, like **formula, formulas.* Words occasionally are changed in spelling by analogy, as the *-b* was rather recently added to *crumb* and *thumb* from analogy with *comb, dumb,* and so on. *Cole slaw* is often replaced by *cold slaw.* **Adviser* is now changing to *advisor* from analogy with *advisory* and words like *inspector, distributor. Alright* is slowly making its way from analogy with *already* (see *all right). New words are formed on analogy with old ones, like *avigation, aerobatics.* Since **who* is the form that usually stands before a verb, as its subject, people ordinarily say *who* instead of *whom* when the object precedes the verb (*Who* were you with?). The extension of *was* to the plural—a common form in Nonstandard English, based on the analogy of most English verbs in the past tense (I did—we did; he went—they went)—illustrates not only the force of analogy but the fact that the result, however logical and consistent, is not necessarily acceptable. To be accepted the analogical form must be frequently used by educated writers and speakers—and "we was" is not. (See *Change in language, *due to, the words starred in this article, and various other examples of analogy treated in particular *Index* entries. Reference: E. H. Sturtevant, *Linguistic Change* (Chicago, 1917), p. 38 ff., Ch. 6. See also the indexes of most works on language for their treatment of analogy.)

-ance, -ence (-ant, -ent) Two of the most troublesome groups of words in English spelling are those ending in *-ance* (*-ant*) and *-ence* (*-ent*). Most of them are nouns and adjectives descended from verbs of different Latin conjugations whose vowel signs are generally represented in these endings. There is no difference in our pronunciation of the endings—both get the neutral vowel ə (di fen′dənt). There is a slight tendency to adopt the ending with *e,* but for the present all we can do is learn the individual forms by memory or frequently consult a dictionary, either of which is an unconscionable waste of time.

Here are some of the commoner words of these types:

-ANCE, -ANT

appearance	descendant (or descendent)
attendance, attendant	extravagance, extravagant
balance	intolerance, intolerant
defendant	reluctance, reluctant

repentance, repentant	significance, significant
resemblance	tolerance, tolerant
resistance, resistant	vigilance, vigilant

-ENCE, -ENT

competence, competent	innocence, innocent
confidence, confident	insistence, insistent
consistency, consistent	obedience, obedient
dependence (-ance) dependent (-ant)	persistence, persistent
existence, existent	reverence, reverent
independence, independent	turbulence, turbulent

A group of similar nouns end in *-ense:*

defense dispense expense offense pretense suspense

and **1.** *Use of "and." And* is the most used connective, joining two or more elements in a series. In its typical use, the elements are of equal grammatical rank:

Adjectives: a *pink* and *white* apron; a *blue, green,* and *white* flag

Adverbs: He drove *fast* and a little *carelessly*.

Nouns: *trees* and *shrubs; trees, shrubs,* and *plants*

Verbs: I *found* the book and *opened* it at the exact place.

Phrases: *in one ear* and *out the other*

Subordinate clauses: *While the boys were swimming* and [*while*] *the older folks were resting,* I was reading.

Coordinate clauses: *The first generation makes the money* and *the second spends it.*

2. *Misuse of "and."* In careless writing, elements of unequal grammatical value are sometimes connected by an unnecessary *and:*

Main verbs and participles: Three or four men *sat* on the edge of the lake with their backs to the road, [and] apparently *watching* the ducks.

Main and subordinate clauses: *A contract has been let to install new copper work on the Post Office* [and] *which will require 4500 pounds of lead coated copper*. (See * which, § 4.)

And is often used in amateur writing where no connective is needed or where some other connective would be more accurate:

All the passages inside the muskrats' house tended to head upward and we pushed the traps far enough in to reach dry ground. (Since all the passages . . . , we pushed . . . .)

At prep school we had certain hours for study and during that time [during which time] the dormitories were quiet.

The freshmen have a number of required courses and [but] the upperclassmen almost none.

3. *At beginning of sentence.* In current writing, especially Informal writing with rather short sentences, *and* often stands at the beginning of sentences. If this usage becomes conspicuous, some of the *and*'s should be dropped or two sentences put together as a compound sentence.

4. *Omission of "and."* In some compact writing *and* is omitted between series of items. Judiciously used, this omission makes for economy, but used very frequently it is a mark of a "telegraphic" style, which is usually inappropriate for General writing.

These *Index* articles involve *and:* *Compound predicate, *Compound sentences, *Compound subject, *Conjunctive adverbs, *Coordinating conjunctions, *between you and me, *which (*and which*), *Series, *try and–try to.

and/or is primarily a business and legal locution. It is useful when three alternatives exist (*both* circumstances mentioned or *either one* of the two): *fruit and/or vegetables* means "fruit" *or* "vegetables" or "fruit and vegetables."

The use of *and/or* in General writing is objected to by many people because of its business connotation and odd appearance, but it is increasingly seen:

> There is something in the power of "great" personalities, but to found a theory of history on it is to deny the demonstrated existence of surrounding circumstances which condition and/or determine the conduct of leaders, heroes, and dictators.–C. A. BEARD, *The Discussion of Human Affairs,* p. 107

angle *Angle* is often *deadwood and suggests a colloquial or business phrase that is out of place in General writing:

> In a preparatory school the masters go at the matter from a different angle [that is, *differently*] and make the same kind of literature more enjoyable.

Antecedent An antecedent is the word or statement to which a pronoun or *pronominal adjective refers. It may stand before or after the pronoun:

> We did not hear their call again and when we found the Thompsons they were almost exhausted. (*The Thompsons* is the antecedent of the pronominal adjective *their* and the pronoun *they*.)

(For relations between antecedents and their pronouns see *Reference of pronouns.)

antenna In zoology the Latin plural *antennae* is usually kept, but this is too foreign a form for most of us in talking about television, so that the customary plural form of the television antenna is *antennas.*

anti-, anti The prefix *anti-,* meaning "against" in its various senses, is hyphened only before root words beginning with *i* and before proper nouns:

anticlimax	antifreeze	antimonarchic	antisocial
anti-imperialistic	anti-intellectual	anti-British	anti-Semitic

Anti- is pronounced an′ti or often an′tī.

Anti is an Informal noun, meaning "a person opposed to something"; plural *antis:* The supporters of the plan spoke amid boos from the antis.

Anticlimax Arrangement of a series in order of descending importance of the elements. It may be intentional, as a form of humor (as in

Pope's "Men, monkeys, lap-dogs, parrots, perish all"), or unintentional because of a lapse of judgment that should be corrected. (See the discussion of climax and anticlimax in Ch. 7, "Position," p. 195.)

Antonym An antonym is a word that means approximately the opposite of another word: *hot, stingy, boring* are antonyms of *cold, generous, entertaining*. Most books of synonyms also give antonyms, as do the synonym entries in dictionaries.

any, and compounds with any **1.** *Any* is used primarily as an adjective (*any* member of the family; *Any* dog is a good dog) but also as a pronoun (*Any* will do).

In comparisons of things of the same class, *idiom calls for *any other:* "This book is better than *any other* on the subject"; but: "I think a movie is more entertaining than *any* book" (not the same class of things).

2. *Compounds with "any." Anybody, anyhow, anything,* and *anywhere* are always written as single words. *Any rate* is always two words: "at *any rate.*" *Anyone* is written as one word when the stress is on the *any* (*Anyone* [en′ i wun] would know that), and as two when the stress is on the *one* (I'd like *any one* [en′ i wun′] of them).

Anyway is one word when the *any* is stressed (I can't do it *anyway* [en′i wā]) and two when the stress is about equal (*Any way* [en′i wā′] I try, it comes out wrong). If the word *whatever* can be substituted for the *any* (*Whatever* way I try, it comes out wrong), *any way* should be written as two words.

3. *Pronouns referring to "anybody," "anyone." Anybody* and *anyone* are singular in form and take singular verbs (Anybody [Anyone] feels bad at times). They are referred to by *he, his, him* (Anybody knows what he deserves), or, since they are often felt to be collectives, Informally they are referred to by a plural pronoun:

> . . . and a top that goes up and down without anybody losing their temper.—THORNTON WILDER (letter), *Theatre Arts,* Nov. 1940.

(See *Divided usage. Compare *every and its compounds; Fries, *AEG,* p. 50.)

4. *Informal forms. Any place* is Informal for *anywhere* (He wasn't *any place* I looked). *Anyways* is regional for the generally used *anyway,* and *anywheres* Nonstandard for *anywhere.*

Apostrophe (') Revision: Insert an apostrophe where it belongs in the word marked; or take out a wrongly used apostrophe. *Apos*

1. *In genitives.* The most common use of the apostrophe is in spelling the *genitive (possessive) case of nouns and of the indefinite pronouns (*anyone, nobody, someone*—See *Pronouns § 8): *Dorothy's* first picture, The *companies'* original charters, *Everybody's* business is *nobody's* business.

It should be kept in singular genitives of time even though they carry no idea of possession: a *day's* hike, this *month's* quota.

It is often omitted from plurals that can be regarded as nouns used in the function of an adjective: teachers college, a girls school. (See *Genitive case for discussion of special examples of possessive form.)

2. *In contractions.* The apostrophe is used to show the omission of one or more letters in contractions: *can't, I'm, I'll, it's* [*it is*]. (See *Contractions.)

3. *In plurals.* An apostrophe is ordinarily used in plurals of figures, letters of the alphabet, and words being discussed as words: *three e's, the 1920's, the first of the two that's.* But there is a growing tendency to omit this apostrophe:

> The legendary Miss Millay, the feminine Byron of the 1920s. . . .
> —LOUIS UNTERMEYER, *Modern American Poetry*, p. 485

4. *In representing speech.* An apostrophe may be used to show that certain sounds represented in the usual spelling were not spoken:

> Good mornin' He was goin' to see fer himself.
> "An' one o' them is the new schoolmaster," he shouted.

This is a legitimate use, but too many apostrophes make a spotted page and confuse the reader. It is better to suggest occasional pronunciations of this sort than to try to represent them conscientiously.

5. *Personal pronouns.* Apostrophes are not used in the genitive of the personal pronouns (*his, hers, its, ours, theirs, yours*).

6. *Simplified spellings.* No apology is needed for simplified spellings that are entered in the dictionary: (*altho,* not *altho'; thru,* not *thro'*. And *till* is a word, equivalent to *until,* not *'til*). The apostrophe is one of the most useless anachronisms in our traditional system of spelling, as Bernard Shaw demonstrated in his printed works; but you must know how to use it.

appearing is an inflated (or unnecessarily Formal) substitute for *looking:* a comfortable *looking* (better than *appearing*) street, a fine *looking* (better than *appearing*) house.

appendix The English plural *appendixes* has overtaken the Latin *appendices* and is the better form except in quite Formal usage; it is the only plural form used in referring to the appendix of appendicitis.

Apposition, appositives Apposition is the placing of a construction next to another so that the second complements or supplements the first. The complementary relationship is called close or restrictive apposition because the second element completes the first; it is not set off by commas. The supplementary relationship is loose or nonrestrictive; it is usually set off by commas.

Close (restrictive, complementary)	*Loose (nonrestrictive, supplementary)*
Coach Bradley	Our coach, Bradley,
William the Conqueror	William I, conqueror of England,
My aunts Mary and Agnes (He had more aunts.)	My aunts, Mary and Agnes, (He had only two.)

Fletcher the grocer	Fletcher, our grocer,
The fact *that he had been over the road before* gave him an advantage.	This fact, *that he had been over the road before,* gave him an advantage.

Close: Washington *the Capital* is a symbol of democracy and America. Washington *the city* is a symbol of almost everything that sincere and thoughtful men know is wrong with democracy and America.—ALDEN STEVENS, "Washington: Blight on Democracy," *Harper's Magazine,* Dec. 1941

Loose: Literary critics have repeatedly called attention to the pathetic fallacy, *the reading of emotion in emotionless things.* . . .—IRWIN EDMAN, *Four Ways of Philosophy,* p. 29

An appositive pronoun agrees with its headword in number and case:

He called the two of us, *John and me* [object].
The two of us, *John and I* [subject], were going together.

(Reference: Curme, *Syntax,* pp. 88-92; Jespersen, pp. 93-95; articles in *American Speech,* vols. 27-31.)

as *As* is one of the most versatile words in English and one of the most frequently used. Some of its uses are:

1. *Conjunction. As* occurs most commonly as a conjunction, introducing several kinds of clauses.

Degree or manner: . . . as far *as* I could.
Time (=while): *As* I was coming in he was going out.
Cause: *As* it was getting dark, we made for home.

Such a handy word is of course much used in speech, which often prefers *counter words to more exact ones. But the very variety of possible uses makes *as* a problem in written English. It is necessary in comparisons (We went as far *as* he did) and for attendant circumstance (*As* we walked along he told us stories) though *while* is preferable if the emphasis is on the time or the action (*While* we were walking along he told us stories).

As is weak in the sense of *because.* Usually *since* or *because* would be better in writing and certainly better in Formal English:

Informal: *As* it was almost time to go, we were getting more and more exasperated.

More exact and emphatic: *Since* it was almost time to go, we were getting more and more exasperated. Or: *Because* it was almost time to go, we were getting more and more exasperated.

2. *Preposition. As* occurs as a preposition with the meaning "in the position of" (She had a job *as* stenographer); "in the role of" (He was in the cast *as* Mercutio). In the Informal construction "I don't like him as well *as her*" (meaning "I don't like him *as well as I like her*"), *as her* may be construed as a prepositional phrase: Who would want to go with such a poor skater *as me*? (Formal usage would often have "... with such a poor skater *as I* [*am*].")

There is a growing tendency to use *as* as a preposition where *like* or *such as* would be preferable: Some writers, *as* Faulkner, take their material from a particular region.

3. *Adverb. As* occurs as an adverb of degree: I came *as* soon as I could. It also introduces appositives: There were several kinds of shellfish, *as* scallops, oysters, crabs, lobsters.

4. *Pronoun.* In Formal English *as* occurs as a pronoun usually with *same* or *such* as antecedent: It was such a day *as* one rarely sees.

As a common Nonstandard relative pronoun, it takes the place of *who* and *that:* Everyone *as* has his ticket can go in.

Compare *like–as. References: Curme, *Syntax,* pages 269-271; *Parts of Speech,* pages 78-82, and index references in both books.

as . . . as 1. *In double comparisons* we sometimes fail to complete the first construction with a second *as:* He is fully as tall if not taller than his older brother. This reads more accurately if completed: He is fully as tall *as,* if not taller than, his older brother. But since the interrupted sentence movement is undesirable in General English, it is usually better to complete the first comparison and then add the second: He is fully as tall as his older brother, if not taller.

2. *In negative comparisons* Formal English sometimes prefers *not so . . . as:* The winters are *not so* long or so cold *as* they used to be. The winters are *neither so* cold *nor so* long *as* they used to be. General English does not as a rule make this distinction: The winters are *not as* long or as cold *as* they used to be. Which idiom is to be used depends on the formality of the context and the taste of the writer.

as if (as though) In Formal English the *subjunctive is used after *as if* or *as though:* He acted *as if* (*as though*) *he were* losing his temper. In General English the subjunctive would not usually be used: He acted *as if* (*as though*) *he was* losing his temper. Often in Informal English and sometimes in General, *like* is used instead of *as if:* He acted *like he was* losing his temper. The subjunctive is never used with *like.*

asset Something of value, currently overused for *advantage, aid, benefit, property,* and so on.

Assonance refers to the like sound of vowels in syllables having different consonants (*brave–vain, lone–show*). It is a common and effective sound element in verse and is also common in prose, especially in an emotional or heightened style:

> "that id*e*al country, of gr*ee*n, d*ee*p lanes and high gr*ee*n banks."—OSBERT SITWELL, *Trio,* p. 89

Asterisk (*) Except in reference works, the asterisk or star is not used so much now as formerly, because it is a conspicuous mark and attracts more attention than is necessary.

1. In works which have very few footnotes, an asterisk may be used as a reference mark, placed after the statement calling for the note and again at the beginning of the footnote; but numbers are more common. (See Ch. 13, "Footnotes: crediting sources," p. 374.)

2. Asterisks are sometimes used to indicate a rather long omission in a quotation, as of a stanza or more from a poem, or a paragraph or more from prose, though now spaced periods are more in favor. (See *Ellipsis.)

3. In fiction a group of asterisks has been used to suggest that action is omitted or to indicate passage of time between movements of a story, but here again a line of spaced periods or extra space between the movements is more common. (See *Ellipsis.)

4. In this book, where frequent cross references are needed, the asterisk is used to refer to *Index* articles.

as to *As to* is often a clumsy substitute for a single preposition, usually *of* or *about:*

> Practice proves the best teacher as to [in, for, of] the use of organ stops.
>
> If the question contains words as to the exact meaning of which [of whose exact meaning] you are uncertain, by all means get out your dictionary.

athlete, athletic, athletics Watch your spelling and pronunciation of these: ath′lete, ath let′ic, ath let′ics.

When *athletics* refers to sports and games it usually takes a plural verb and pronoun: Our athletics *include* football, basketball, and baseball.

When *athletics* refers to skill or activity it usually takes a singular verb and pronoun: Athletics *is* recommended for every student.

Attributive An adjective that stands next to its noun is attributive (a *blue* shirt; a shirt, *blue* and *clean*), as contrasted with a predicate adjective that is related to its noun by a *linking verb (The shirt is *blue*). A noun modifying another noun (*horse* race, *football* field) is used *attributively.*

aunt The usual pronunciation is ant; in the East also änt.

Auxiliary verb A verb used with another verb to form a phrasal tense or voice is called an *auxiliary verb* or *helping verb:*

> I *am* going. He *will* go. They *were* lost. He *should* watch out.

Be, do, have are the commonest auxiliaries; *can, may, shall, will, must, ought, should, would, might* are frequently used as auxiliaries; *get, let, need,* and *used* sometimes. See *Index* entries on these verbs and the general article *Verbs.

awful In Formal English *awful* means "inspiring with awe." In Informal English it is a convenient utility word of disapproval—"ugly, shocking, ludicrous" (*awful* manners, an *awful* run in my stocking).

As a result of this contamination the word is seldom used in General writing. *Awfully* is common in speech as an intensive, but in writing it is an example of *schoolgirl style.

awhile, a while *Awhile* is an adverb (They talked *awhile*). Strictly, a prepositional phrase in which *while* is a noun should be in three words (for *a while, in a while*), but *awhile* is sometimes found.

Awk (*K*) **Awkward** Revision: Rewrite the passage marked.

A rather general word of disapproval sometimes used in correcting themes. It may refer to clumsy phrases, unnatural word order, unnecessary repetition of a word or phrase, or other phrasing that attracts unpleasant attention or handicaps a reader. The remedy is to recast the sentence or passage.

aye Used for *yes* in voting; pronounced ī.

B

The letter *b* occurs frequently in English spelling as a *silent letter and therefore a possible snare in spelling and sometimes in pronunciation. Many silent *b*'s, especially after *m,* represent *b*'s that were pronounced in Old English but perhaps have not been generally sounded for hundreds of years: *climb* (klīm), *comb* (kōm), *dumb* (dum), though the *b* is pronounced in the Formal or archaic *clamber,* in *limber,* and in a few other words. A *b* has rather recently been added in *crumb* and *thumb*. Other silent *b*'s represent sounds that had been in the Latin ancestor words but that were dropped as the sound disappeared in Old French, from which the words came into English: *debt* (from *debitum*), *doubt* (from *dubitare*), *subtle* (from *subtilis*). Some of these *b*'s were inserted by Renaissance scholars because they wished to tie English closer to Latin: Chaucer wrote *det* but we cannot.

When *b* comes next to *p* the two sounds sometimes are assimilated to one: *cupboard* (kub′ərd), *subpoena* (sə pē′nə).

bad, badly *Bad* is an adjective of varied application: a *bad* man, a *bad* cold, a *bad* night, a *bad* accident, *bad* weather, *bad* news, a *bad* light, a *bad* taste.

In "I feel bad about it," "She looks bad," *bad* is a predicate adjective. *Badly* also is an adjective in the predicate position: I feel badly. (See *Linking verbs.)

Both *badly* and *bad* are also used as adverbs, the latter only in Informal usage:

> He draws badly. The starter has always worked badly [Informal: bad].

(Reference: Lillian M. Feinsilver, "How Bad(ly) Do You Feel?" *American Speech,* 1949, 24:161-170.)

Worse, worst, the comparative and superlative of *bad,* of course come from a quite different root. They were earlier used in comparing *evil* and *ill,* and when *bad* acquired the meaning of those words, *worse* and *worst* were used for it too.

Bad grammar *Bad grammar* is used as a term of reproach and is applied to all sorts of locutions. It is too vague and emotional a term to be useful. (See Ch. 1, pp. 24-35; Ch. 2, pp. 54-71; Ch. 3, pp. 81-92; and *Grammar.)

Basic English A simplified form of English devised by C. K. Ogden and intended to facilitate international communication. It has a vocabulary of only 850 words. (Reference: C. K. Ogden, *The System of Basic English,* New York, 1934.)

be **1.** *Forms.* The English verb *be* has forms from three originally separate verbs (as in *are, was, been*), but we use the verb so much that the various forms give little trouble:

Present: I am, you are, he is; we, you, they are
Present subjunctive: I, you, he, we, you, they be
Past: I was, you were, he was; we, you, they were
Past subjunctive: I, you, he, we, you, they were
Infinitive: be; Present participle: being; Past participle: been

Some old forms survive in stock phrases ("the powers that *be*") and in the Nonstandard "You ain't (sometimes *be'n't*) going, *be* you?" Nonstandard also uses *was* in the plural ("*Was* the Adamses there?"), leveling the past tense to one form (*was*), like the past of other English verbs.

2. *As a linking verb. Be* is the most common *linking verb, joining, without adding specifically a meaning of its own, a subject and a predicate nominative or adjective:

Jerome was the secretary. (Predicate nominative)
She is sick. (Predicate adjective)

With the finite parts of *be* the predicate noun or pronoun is in the nominative case in written English:

It was *he.* (Informal: It was *him.*)

"It's I" is Formal for the General *"It's me."* (See *It's me.)

When the infinitive has a subject and complement, both are in the objective form: I wanted *him* to be *me.*

When the infinitive has no subject, Formal usage has a nominative as the complement (I wanted to be *he*), but General usage would more often have an accusative (I wanted to be *him*).

3. *As auxiliary verb.* Forms of *be* are used with the present participles of other verbs to form the progressive tense form:

I am asking   he was asking   you will be asking

Forms of *be* with past participles form the passive voice:

I am asked   you will be asked   he was asked

4. *As verb of complete predication. Be* is a verb of complete predication when indicating states or positions:

He *was* at home anywhere. The fire *was* just across the street.

In the sense of "exist," "live" (Hamlet's "To be, or not to be," "Can such things be?"), *be* is now rather rare. (See *Subjunctives; *Subject and verb; *ain't.)

beau The plural is *beaus,* or Formally, *beaux;* both are pronounced bōz.

because introduces a subordinate clause giving the reason for the independent statement:

Because we were getting hungry, we began to look for a convenient restaurant.

Since and *as* can be used in such clauses, but they are less definite, more casual, and more characteristic of easy speech than of writing:

In a small rural school these young children have to stay for the rest of the day's session, because [more definite than *as* or *since*] there is no one to take them home.

For, which also introduces reasons, is a more Formal word, rather rare in conversation and General writing. It also often has the sense of giving evidence for the statement, for the writer's knowledge of the fact stated, rather than for its cause:

General: I know he is reliable, because I have traded with him for years.

More Formal: I know he is reliable, for I have traded with him for years. ("He is reliable because [or *for*] I have traded with him for years" would not be exact.)

(See *reason is because, *for, *as.)

been Usually pronounced bin; rarely bēn in the United States but more commonly in England.

Beg **Beginning paragraphs** Revision: Revise the opening paragraph to make it lead more directly into your subject and if possible to arouse your reader's interest.

For discussion of qualities of beginning paragraphs and examples, see Chapter 6, "Opening paragraphs," page 165; Chapter 10, "The opening," page 286; Chapter 11, page 305.

beside–besides *Beside* is a preposition referring to place, "by the side of," as in "beside the road," "beside her," and is used figuratively in a few rather Formal idioms like "beside the point," "beside himself with rage." (*Beside* is less commonly used as an adverb, with the meaning of *besides.*)

Besides is an adverb or preposition meaning "in addition to" or "except":

We tried two other ways *besides.* (adverb)

Besides our own members, . . . (preposition)

He said that his wife was a regular farm wife who helped him milk the cows *besides* raising five fine healthy children. (preposition)

It is also used as a conjunctive adverb: He didn't think that he ought to get into the quarrel; *besides,* he had come to enjoy himself.

between, among *Among* implies more than two objects: They distributed the provisions *among* the survivors.

Between is most strictly used of only two: They divided the prize *between* Kincaid and Thomas. But the attempt to limit *between* to use only with two items has failed. The *Oxford English Dictionary* says that from the first it has been used of several. So used, *between* tends to suggest the individuals involved more than the situation: The family of seven hadn't a pair of shoes *between* them. (Reference: Pooley, pp. 135-137.)

between you and me Since the object of a preposition is grammatically in the accusative case, the expected form is *between you and me, for you and me, to you and me* (or when the pronouns are objects of a verb, "He will take *you and me*").

Between you and I is frequently heard–reversing the usual tendency in speech to use *me* (as in *It's me), perhaps because the speakers remember the prejudice against *It's me* and carry over the taboo to a different construction.

Bible, bible *Bible,* referring to the Christian Scriptures, is capitalized but not italicized: "You will find all that in the Bible, and more too." In the sense of an authoritative book or a book much consulted or quoted, *bible* is not capitalized: "Gray's *Manual,* the botanist's bible, . . ."

The usual form of particular references to parts of the Bible is:

the Old Testament
the New Testament (capitalized but not italicized)
The Ten Commandments are in Exodus xx (or: in Exodus 20).
The Ten Commandments are in Exodus 20:3-17.
I Corinthians 4:6

The adjective *biblical* ordinarily is not capitalized.

Big words Revision: Use a simpler, more natural word instead of the Formal or heavy one marked.

Big W

Good writing uses direct and ordinary words instead of "bigger" ones–*home* rather than *domicile, think* or *believe* rather than *deem, happen* rather than *transpire,* and so on. For full discussion of big words and suggestions for avoiding them see Chapter 8, "Big words," page 228.

biography Pronounced bī og'rə fi or bi-. A biography is the life of a person written by someone else; an autobiography is the life of a person written by himself. (Compare Ch. 10, "Writing a profile," p. 314.)

Blanks for names and dates have gone out of fashion. The present style is all for specificness. Don't write "In 18–" but, if the exact date isn't to be given, "About ninety years ago."

Similarly, "Mr. ——" or "Mr. X" or "A man whom I shall call Mr. Wheeler, though that is not his name" would be avoided. Real names are used wherever possible, or if they cannot be used, the avoidance is made as inconspicuous as possible by "A man," "Someone," or some such expression.

Blend A word made by fusing two words, often with a syllable in common: *paratroops, cinemactress, imagineering, smog, motel, beautility, snoopervise*. (See *Origin of words § 3b.)

Until a blend has made its way in the language, as *electrocute* (from *electric* and *execute*) has, it is usually more appropriate to Informal and General than Formal writing.

blond, blonde As a noun, *blond* is used of a man, *blonde* of a woman:

He is a blond. She is a blonde. a peroxide blonde (or blond)

In its adjective use, the *-e* is gradually disappearing and in General writing *blond* can always be used. Some write *blonde* when it refers specifically to a woman (a blonde Helen) and *blond* elsewhere, including *blond hair*.

Brunet, brunette are in the same situation: masculine noun *brunet,* feminine noun *brunette,* with perhaps a tendency to use *brunette* as the adjective (to help represent the accent on the second syllable).

Boners Confusion of two similar words, mistaken constructions, combinations of ideas that don't belong together have always been a source of fun for everyone except the persons who made them. Volumes of these boners have been gathered and several periodicals run specimens that they find in other publications. Here are a few that have cropped up in themes:

My papers have a decided tendency toward longevity.

He is descended from one of the most virulent [really *poisonous?* or merely *virile?*] families in the U. S. A.

Jean is no plastic saint.

For the lowly freshmen are moved by sediment rather than by intellect in their voting.

The arduous loves of movie stars are not always convincing.

Many times I started for the library to do some research on Gestalt's psychology.

[Of the cross country team, running on back roads:] Not even the sharp stones can dampen their spirits.

Keep your eye out for boners in manuscript and in print and get what fun you can from them—but most of all scan your own writing to catch them before they come to anybody else's attention

born, borne **1.** The past participle of *bear* in most of its senses is *borne:*

They had *borne* this poverty without complaining.

The ship, *borne* along by the breeze, was soon out of sight.

Bear in most of these senses is somewhat Formal; *carry* or *endure* would be more common. But in "It was more than I could *bear,*" *bear* is less Formal than *endure* would be.

In the sense of "give birth to," the past participle of *bear* is spelled *borne* except in the (very common) passive when not followed by *by:*

She had *borne* five children.
Of the four children *borne* by his first wife. . . .
He was *born* in 1891.   A *born* liar.
The children, *born* in Chicago. . . .

2. In autobiographical papers students often become self-conscious or humorous in giving the facts of their birth: "I saw the light of day first on June 28, 1940"; "No planets blazed on the night of June 28, 1940, when a squally infant appeared in the home of Mr. and Mrs. . . ." None of these is any improvement over the simple and natural statement "I was born June 28, 1940."

both *Both* is a favorite way of emphasizing two-ness:

The twins were both there. They are both alike. Both Harry and his brother went.

Strictly speaking, all these *both*'s are redundant but they give legitimate emphasis. A sentence like "The both women got along well enough together" is a localism for "The two women got along well enough together." "The both of them" is a fairly common spoken idiom.

Brace { or } A brace is the mark used to group two or more lines of writing. Its use is chiefly in technical writing, especially in tables and formulas. Examples of braces will be found in the article *English language.

Brackets [ ] Brackets are rarely used in General writing and are not in the standard typewriter keyboard, but in much academic and professional writing they have specific and convenient uses. If they are needed in typing, you can make them by using a diagonal and two underscores (/̲ /̲), or you can put them in by hand.

Brackets are primarily editorial marks, used to show where some explanation or comment has been added to the text, especially to quoted matter:

The preposition *due to* is not more incorrect than the preposition *owing to,* which is approved by the same dictionary [the *Concise Oxford Dictionary*], but it is not yet so thoroughly established in the language. –G. O. Curme, *Syntax,* p. 561

. . . and by the Accounts thereof, made up by Mr. Peirce, Master of the said ship, and [*torn*] Agent for Mr. Craddocke, one of the Owners; being al [*torn*] by Mr. Peters. . . . '–S. E. Morison, *The Founding of Harvard College.*

If the torn word had been filled in by the editor, the conjectured letters would be in brackets: being al[lowed] by Mr. Peters. . . .

In quoting material, *sic in brackets is sometimes used to indicate that an error in the original is being reproduced exactly: "New Haven, Conneticut [sic] . . ."; or a correction may be inserted in brackets: "When he was thirty-eight [Actually he was forty-three] he published his first novel."

Brackets are used as parentheses within parentheses. They are likely to be found particularly in legal documents or in footnotes to theses, etc.

In this *Index,* brackets are used in examples of faulty writing to inclose words that might better be left out or to suggest an improved expression:

> Throughout [the course of the year] I read such books as *Oliver Twist* and *Boots and Saddles.*
>
> The continuously moving belt makes a noise *similar to* [*like*] a cement mixer.

bring up is the General idiom (that's the way I was *brought up*) for the more Formal *rear* or *nurture;* it also means *to introduce* (a subject).

broadcast The past tense and past participle of *broadcast* are the same: *broadcast* (or *broadcasted*).

Broad reference A pronoun referring to a preceding idea rather than to a particular antecedent is said to have a broad reference. (See *Reference of pronouns § 1.)

bunch In Formal English *bunch* is limited to objects that grow together or can be fastened together (a bunch of carrots, roses, keys). General English holds to the older usage of *bunch,* applying it to a small collection of anything–including people.

buoy Pronounced boi or bo͞o′i.

-burgh In Scottish place names pronounced like *borough* (Edinburgh); in British use often reduced to brə; in this country, berg, whether spelled with a final *h* or not.

burst, bust The principal parts of *burst* are *burst, burst, burst:*

> One *bursts* almost every day. Two tanks *burst* yesterday. One tank had *burst.*

Bust, in origin a variant pronunciation of *burst,* has the principal parts *bust, busted, busted.* It is used in Nonstandard English in the sense of *burst.* But it also occurs in Informal English in the sense of "being broke" or "being demoted," and in General English in the sense of "busting a broncho" or "busting a trust."

bus The plural is spelled *buses* or *busses,* the first much more common American usage.

Business English The writing of business English has attained a very high standard of mechanical form. The layout, spacing, and mechanics of most business letters and reports are excellent, reflecting the skill of professional typists; and the skill of layout men and printers is available for printed matter.

But the usage and style of business communications vary considerably. Most firms at present pay a good deal of attention to the style of their written and printed matter. The old clichés–*in re, the above, Yrs. of 23d inst. rec'd and contents noted, and oblige*–have practically disappeared. Naturally all degrees of Formality and Informality are found. The prime virtues of good business writing are *directness* and *adaptation to reader*. Adapting the style to the reader is especially difficult in writing advertising and business letters, since usually the writer is not acquainted with his reader and in spite of elaborate market analyses may not visualize him rightly. If the letter is sent to many people, there is the difficulty of making it *seem* personal when it really cannot be personal. For most purposes "business English" is merely good English applied to the specific needs of industry and trade.

Business people have adopted a General style and have handled English with the freedom a living language deserves. They have pioneered in the much needed shortening of our spelling. Business writers have used all the native resources of the language in making new names and in brightening style–outright coinages like *kodak, vaseline, fabrikoid,* blends like *servicenter, unisteel, sunoco,* compounds and respellings like *cutex, denticuring* (preventive dentistry), *tudor* (cars), *lubritory*. Though many such words are ludicrous or overcute or in poor taste, some are expressive and are normal language developments. They are much better than attempts at false dignity (*client* for *customer, favor* for *letter,* **business world* for *business, cheque* for **check*).

The question of fitness arises when certain words with obvious business connotation are used in other contexts. Some are frequently borrowed and are useful: *deal, asset, feature, bank on,* and *take stock in* are in General usage. But many people, who perhaps do not like to be reminded that they live in a society primarily commercial, are offended by *advise, *angle, *and/or, *contact, *realtor*. Such words are out of place in Formal writing and in discussions of ideal rather than practical affairs; but in General writing business locutions are often useful. H. S. Canby used ordinary business terms to point up a comment on current literature:

> No; public taste, ease of publication, variety of interest, even editorial capability, have all risen with the intellectual development of the country; only the professional writers, as a class, have not progressed. They have become astonishingly clever, as clever as the mechanism of a Ford; but as a class they have not moved ten feet towards literature. *They have standardized their product without improving the model.–Saturday Papers,* p. 56

(See *Letters; *Reports; *Shoptalk; Ch. 8, "Euphemisms," p. 227.)

business world is an inflated term for *business* or *businessmen:* I expect to enter the business world (I expect to go into business).

but *But* is the natural coordinating conjunction to connect two contrasted statements of equal grammatical rank. It is more natural than the Formal **however* or **yet,* and more emphatic than *although.

1. *Connects equals.* The locutions connected by *but* should be of equal grammatical weight:

Adjectives: not blue but green.

Adverbs: He worked fast but accurately.

Phrases: He didn't come in the forenoon but in the early evening.

Clauses: We just rested the first day, but the second we got down to real work.

Sentences: Enigma of the semitropics, the Rio Grande defied the best engineering minds of two countries for a century. But $10,000,000 in flood control work has harnessed the treacherous stream.

(See *which § 4 for comments on *but which.*)

2. *Connects statements in opposition.* The statements connected by *but* should be actually in opposition; contrast the first example with the second and third:

He knows vaguely that the nation is not much good any more; he has read that the crust of the earth is shrinking alarmingly and that the universe is growing steadily colder; but he does not believe that any of the three is in half as bad shape as he is.—JAMES THURBER, *My Life and Hard Times,* Preface

He supported a wife and three children on this pittance *and* [not *but*] he seemed very proud that he wasn't on relief.

Our view was limited to about twenty yards down Tuckerman Ravine; [not *but*] beyond that everything was in clouds.

3. *"But" with "however." But* should be used efficiently, carrying its real meaning. It should not be doubled by a *however* which can add nothing:

The students wanted to extend the Christmas vacation a day beyond New Year's, but [*however* not needed] the Administration couldn't see their point of view.

4. *At beginnings of sentences. But,* like **and,* often stands at the beginning of sentences, especially if the sentences are short; but it should not be overused.

5. *Punctuation.* Two clauses connected by *but* should ordinarily be separated by a comma. The contrast in idea suggests the use of punctuation even when the clauses are relatively short.

I couldn't get the whole license number, but it began with A30.

But is part of the clause in which it stands and should not be separated from it by a comma. A parenthetical phrase following the *but* may be set off by commas, especially in Formal English:

His speech was supposed to be extemporaneous, but he had really been practicing it for a week.

His speech was supposed to be extemporaneous, but, to be quite truthful, we must add that he had practiced it for a week.

6. *Minor uses of "but."*

a) As subordinating conjunction, after *no doubt,* in questions with *know,* and in a few other constructions:

There is no doubt but [or *but that,* or more Formally, *that*] he had tried his best.

Who knows but everything will come out right?

Nothing would do but I must spend the night with them.

b) As a preposition, equivalent to *except* (no comma preceding):

We didn't get anything but a couple of shad.

No one could have done it but me.

c) As a rather Formal adverb, equivalent to *only:*

If he but stops to think, he can interpret his own reactions.

d) With "not." *But* is sometimes used after *not* in Standard usage, especially in speech: There aren't but three eggs left.

References: Fowler, article "but"; Curme, *Parts of Speech,* index references.

but that–but what *But that* is the usual conjunction in written English; *but what* is Informal.

He didn't know but that [Informal: *but what*] the other car could still turn out.

General: I don't doubt but that he will come.

Informal: I don't doubt but what he'll come.

Formal: I do not doubt that he will come.

C

In Old English *c* represented two sounds: Usually it was *k*—*cruma,* "crumb," *cempa,* "warrior," *cyning,* "king"; but before *e* or *i* it often represented *ch* (*ceosan, ciepan, cild*). This second sound is spelled *ch* in Modern English: *choose, cheap, child.* The Norman Conquest complicated *c,* for it brought in many French words in which *c* spelled the *s* sound. Today *c* is an unnecessary letter, doing work that could more clearly be done by *k* and *s*. Many words spelled with *c* must be respelled with *k* or *s* to show pronunciation: sit′i (*city*), sel (*cell*), fōrs (*force*), kōld (*cold*), kum (*come*), ärk (*arc*).

Before *e, i,* or *y, c* regularly represents *s: cent, civil, cynic;* before *a, o, u,* and any consonant but *h, c* is regularly *k; can't, coffee, cute, fact*. Marked with a *cedilla, as in *façade, c* has the *s* sound before *a, o,* or *u*.

C may represent *sh: ocean* (ō′shən), *conscience* (kon′shəns), *special* (spesh′əl); and *ch: cello* (chel′ō).

C is silent in *czar, indict, muscle,* and a few other words.

Before *e* or *i, cc* spells *ks: accident, occident, success, vaccine;* otherwise it is *k: acclaim, accommodate*. The pronunciation of *cc* as *s* in some words like *accessory* and *flaccid,* though widespread, is objected to by many cultivated speakers. (See *ch.)

calculate, guess, reckon *Calculate* (cut in Nonstandard to kalk′lāt or even to kal′āt), *guess, reckon* are localisms for the *think, suppose, expect* of General English. (Which is the word in your region?)

can–may (could–might) 1. *In General English.* In General usage *may* occurs rather rarely except in the sense of possibility:

It may be all right for her, but not for me.

Can is generally used for both permission and ability:

Can I go now? You can if you want to.
I can do 80 miles an hour with mine.

This is in such widespread usage that it should be regarded as Standard English in speaking and in writing.

Can't almost always takes the place of *mayn't* in the United States:

Can't I go now? We can't have lights after twelve o'clock.

2. *In Formal English.* In Formal English a distinction is sometimes made between the auxiliary *can,* with the meaning of ability, "being able to," and *may,* with the meaning of permission.

You may go now. He can walk with crutches. You may if you can.

The distinction makes possible the classic dialog at many tables:

"Can I have some more meat and potato?"

"You *may* [with a withering accent] have some more meat and potato."

May also indicates possibility: He may have the right one.

3. *Might and could. Might,* originally the past of *may,* and *could,* the past of *can,* are now used chiefly to convey a shade of doubt, or a smaller degree of possibility.

It might be all right for her, but it isn't for me.
It might have been all right for her, but not for me.

Adverbs are likely to be used instead of *may* or *might* in such constructions, especially for the past tense:

Perhaps it was all right for her, but not for me.

Can and *could, may* and *might* are often interchangeable, except that *could* and *might* are perhaps more deferential or tentative; compare:

May I help you?	Can you help me?
Might I help you?	Could you help me?

Could also suggests doubt or qualified possibility:

Perhaps I could write a poem, but I doubt it.
I could do 80 miles an hour in mine, too.

Be able to tends to replace *can* and *could* when the idea of ability needs emphasis:

I am able to live on my income.

(See *Divided usage. Reference: Gladys D. Haase, *College English,* 1950, 11:215-216.)

cannot, can not Usage is divided with *cannot* the more common.

 can't help but There are three possible idioms:

Formal: I *cannot but feel* sorry for him.
General: I *can't help feeling* sorry for him.
General: I *can't help but feel* sorry for him.

The last is an established idiom, though avoided by many writers. (Reference: Marckwardt and Walcott, pp. 98-99; Russell Thomas, *College English,* 1948, 10:38-39.)

Capital letters Revision: Capitalize the word marked, for one of the reasons shown in this article; or, if the word marked is written with a capital, make it a small letter. *Cap*

1. *Sentences.* 2. *Proper names.* 3. *Lines of verse.* 4. *Titles.* 5. *"I," "O."* 6. *Names of relatives.* 7. *Deity.* 8. *Street, etc.* 9. *Abstract nouns.* 10. *Stylistic capitals.*

*Proofreading marks can be used for correcting themes. Three lines under a small letter means: make this a capital. A slanting line drawn through a capital means: make this a small letter.

march 15 He came from West of Buffalo.

Certain uses of capitals, as at the beginning of sentences or for proper names, are conventions followed by everyone; certain others show divided usage or are matters of taste. In general, Formal English tends to use more capitals than General English, and newspaper usage tends to cut them to a minimum.

This article summarizes the principal uses of capitals in current writing. Further discussion and examples will be found in the articles marked by asterisks.

1. *Sentence capitals.* The first word of a sentence is capitalized. In quotations, the first word of a quoted sentence or part of sentence is capitalized, but when the quotation is broken, the second part is not capitalized unless it is a complete sentence:

He said, "The first time I came this way almost none of the roads were hard surfaced."

He said, "Perhaps," and went on.

"The first time I came this way," he said, "almost none of the roads were hard surfaced."

"That was your last chance," she said. "Don't ever ask again."

Complete sentences that stand in *parentheses are capitalized always if they stand between other sentences, but if they stand within sentences they usually are not.

The men were very stiff and self-conscious in their swallowtail coats (the dinner jacket had not been invented), bulging shirt fronts, white kid gloves (which often smelled of naphtha), and the enormously high "poke" or "Piccadilly" collars....—E. ALEXANDER POWELL, *Gone Are the Days,* p. 138

A complete sentence standing after a *colon is not capitalized if it is short and closely connected to the preceding words, but may be if it is long or if for some reason the writer wants to emphasize it or keep it distinct:

Charles Sumner wanted to know his opinion on European law journals: what should he say?—H. S. COMMAGER, *Theodore Parker,* p. 109

Possible explanation: The nestlings were struck by an eastern Arctic storm which only the older birds were able to escape.—*Time,* Nov. 7, 1938.

2. *Proper names.* Proper names and abbreviations of proper names are capitalized: names of people, places, races (Indian, Negro, Caucasian), languages (French, Latin), days of the week, months, companies, *ships, institutions, fraternities, religious bodies, historical events (the Revolutionary War), documents (the Constitution), *course names.

The names of the *seasons (*summer, fall, midwinter*) are not capitalized except for emphasis or stylistic reasons.

The points of the compass (*north, southwest*) are not capitalized when they indicate direction, but are usually capitalized when they denote a region (though this practice is now declining):

His grandfather had come west in 1849.
He was much more popular in the West than in the East.

Army, Navy, and so on, are not capitalized unless they refer to the organized forces of a particular nation: United States *Army,* the British *Navy,* and even *the Army* when referring to that of a particular nation. Also:

He went to college.
He went to Beloit College.
He went to the College (if a particular college is clearly intended from the context).

Proper nouns that have become common nouns (*tweed, sandwich, burnsides, plaster of paris*) are not capitalized nor are proper adjectives in senses that no longer suggest their origin: *Paris fashions* (fashions originating in Paris), but *paris green.*

3. *Lines of verse.* The first letter of a line of verse is capitalized unless it was originally written without a capital, as in the second example below:

These lovely groves of fountain-trees that shake
A burning spray against autumnal cool,
Descend again in molten drops to make
The rutted path a river and a pool.

ELINOR WYLIE, "Golden Bough"

Ecstatic bird songs pound
the hollow vastness of the sky
with metallic clinkings—
beating color up into it
at a far edge,—

WILLIAM CARLOS WILLIAMS, "Dawn"

4. **Titles of articles, books, etc.* The usual convention is to capitalize the first word, all nouns, pronouns, verbs, adjectives, and adverbs as well as prepositions that stand last or contain more than four (sometimes more than five) letters:

With Malice Toward Some	*The Book of a Naturalist*
You Can't Take It with You	*Pity Is Not Enough*

5. *"I," "O."* The pronoun *I* is capitalized (not from any sort of egotism, but simply because a small *i* in manuscript is likely to be lost or to become attached to other words). The exclamation *O is capitalized, but not *oh* unless it begins a sentence or is to be especially emphasized.

6. *Names of relatives, individuals.* In personal and Informal writing, as a matter of courtesy, and in General writing, when they are used as proper names, names for members of one's family are often capitalized:

> She talked it over with Father, however, just to see what he'd say. –CLARENCE DAY, *Life with Mother,* p. 117

They are not usually capitalized when used as common nouns: My sister and two brothers are older than I.

President referring to the President of the United States is always capitalized, and ordinarily titles of people in high office when referring to an individual (the Senator). Other titles may be capitalized when referring to individuals (The Colonel was there).

7. *References to Deity. God, Jesus,* nouns such as *Savior,* and pronouns referring directly to them are capitalized–though practice is divided on the pronouns:

> Webster for the first time in an English Bible rendered Jesus's saying as He said it.–HARRY R. WARFEL, *Noah Webster,* p. 411
>
> As we think of him [God], do we think of what he has done or what he can do for us? Do we love him so much that we would keep him for ourselves?–S. K. YEAPLE, *Your Money and Your Life,* p. 30

Pronouns referring to pagan deities (Zeus, Jove, Venus) are not capitalized.

8. *Street, river, park, etc.* Usage is divided over capitalizing such words as *street, river, park, hotel, church* when they follow a proper name. Typically, books and conservative magazines would use capitals; General writing, as in many magazines and most newspapers, would not:

Formal:	the Mississippi River	Thirty-second Street
General:	the Mississippi river	Thirty-second street

An organization is likely to capitalize more words pertaining to its functions than an outsider would, as the Government Printing Office capitalizes many words having to do with government.

9. *Abstract nouns.* Abstract nouns are likely to be capitalized, more often in Formal writing than in General, when the concept they refer to is personified or when they refer to ideals or institutions: The State has nothing to do with the Church, nor the Church with the State.

10. *Stylistic capitals.* Some writers, usually in a rather Formal style, use capitals as a form of emphasis, to lead the reader to stress certain words a little or give them more attention:

My Mission

> But when in modern books, reviews, and thoughtful magazines I read about the Needs of the Age, its Complex Questions, its Dismays, Doubts, and Spiritual Agonies, I feel an impulse to go out and comfort it, to still its cries, and speak earnest words of Consolation to it. —LOGAN PEARSALL SMITH, *Trivia,* p. 34
>
> And a woman is only a woman, but a good Cigar is a Smoke.—RUDYARD KIPLING, "The Betrothed"

For more details of general practice, consult the stylebooks of periodicals and publishers, such as the *GPO Style Manual.*

C **Carelessness** Revision: Correct the obvious and apparently careless mistake marked.

Conferences with students on their themes show that well over half the mistakes and slips that an instructor has to mark are due not to ignorance but to carelessness. Everyone is liable to careless lapses in hasty work. But a course paper is not supposed to be hasty work. Slips like *it's* for *its* (or the other way around), *detract* for *distract,* most *comma faults and *fragmentary sentences, and scores of others are due to lack of attention in the final stages of preparing a paper. An instructor can sympathize with lack of knowledge but not with lack of care; in fact, he should refuse to read an obviously careless paper.

One of the best investments is a careful reading of your final manuscript. It will make the paper more presentable (and worth a better grade), as well as give you the satisfaction that comes from seeing a job through to the best of your ability. See Chapters 2 and 3, especially the suggestions for proofreading.

Caret (∧) This inverted v-shaped mark put in or under a line of manuscript shows that something between the lines or in the margin should be inserted at that point:

```
     Yes, they were smart, but there wasn't any reason why they
           because
shouldn't be, all they did was study.
              ∧
```

This is a respectable way to revise papers and should be used to improve a paper to be handed in or to make a correction suggested by an instructor, though too frequent use shows lack of care in the preliminary writing and revision.

A caret may be used by an instructor as a correction mark to show where something should be inserted.

Case One of the relationships between a noun or pronoun and another element in a sentence is called case. In languages like Latin and

German, whose nouns and pronouns (and adjectives too) are elaborately declined, the case endings of the nominative, genitive, dative, and accusative (and ablative in Latin) are important clues to the relations of the words in the sentence. In English, the forms are a much less useful factor in grammar. Our adjectives do not take any endings; nouns are reduced to two forms, a genitive and a common form that serves for all other relationships (*soldier's–soldier*), and the personal pronouns are reduced to three, a nominative, genitive, and accusative (*I–my–me*), or two (*you–your–you*).

We express the relation of nouns and pronouns to other sentence elements through *word order* (an object following its verb or preposition, for example) and by means of *prepositions* (*to Fred* instead of a dative ending). The few problems in case that we have come chiefly from the surviving accusative form of pronouns (*It's me; *who, whom).

This *Index* has articles on four cases to call attention to the few functions in which the case forms are significant, to note problems in usage that are due to case forms, and to make possible some comparison between English and the languages which rely more definitely on case forms to express relationship between words:

*Nominative (or subjective)–the subject of a verb, complement of a linking verb

*Genitive (or possessive)–indicating not only possession but various adjectival and adverbial relations

*Dative–principally notions of interest or location or "indirect objects"

*Accusative (or objective)–the object of a verb or preposition

Fuller accounts of the grammatical points involved will be found in the articles on the various functions indicated: *Subject and verb, *Objects, *Infinitives § 5, *Linking verbs, *Gerund § 2, *Nouns, *Pronouns, *Word order. For more complex treatments of problems of English cases, see Jespersen, Chapter 14 (the two-case system); Curme, *Parts of Speech,* pages 127-136 (the four-case system).

case Some of the commonest bits of *deadwood in writing are various locutions with the word *case*. They are wordy and keep the real person or situation or thing (whatever the "case" stands for) one construction away from the reader.

These quotations, from student papers and published articles, show how easy it is to let an unneeded *case* slip into careless writing.

> Drinking went on very moderately except in a few scattered cases. (Written of a convention. The "cases" would be delegates?)
>
> . . . but that does not happen to be the case [but that isn't true].
>
> In many cases a corporation may wish to carry on only one type of business and in such a case it is necessary for such a charter to be obtained in a state where this particular line of work is to be carried on.

(If a corporation is to carry on only one type of business, it must secure a charter in the state in which it will operate.)

catalog–catalogue Spelling is divided, with the shorter form gaining. Over half the colleges now use *catalog* as the name of their annual bulletin of announcements.

-ce, -ge A few special spelling problems arise from the use of *c* for the sound of *s,* and of *g* for the sound of *j.*

A word ending in *-ce* (pronounced *s*) or *-ge* (pronounced *j*) keeps the final *e* before suffixes beginning with *a, o,* or *u* to indicate the pronunciation: *courageous, noticeable, peaceable, vengeance* (but *mortgage, mortgagor* or *mortgager*). Before a suffix beginning with *e* or *i* the final *e* is dropped: *diced, noticing, encouraging.*

Usually a word ending in *-c* (pronounced *k*) adds a *k* before an ending beginning with *e* or *i* or *y* so that it will still be pronounced *k: colic, colicky; mimic, mimicking; picnic, picnicked, picnicking.* (See also *-ei-, -ie-.)

Cedilla is a mark under the letter *c* (ç) to show that the letter is not sounded as *c* normally would be in that position. In English spelling it is used to show the sound of *s* in words originally French: façade, Français, Provençal, garçon, aperçu, soupçon.

center around (or about) *Center around* (The story *centers around* the theft of a necklace) is the General idiom. The Formal idiom is *center on* or *upon.*

Centuries Remember that the fifth century A.D. ran from the beginning of the year 401 to the end of the year 500, the nineteenth century from January 1, 1801, through December 31, 1900. Thus to name the century correctly, add one to the number of its hundred. It will help to remember that you live in the *twentieth* century.

Popularly the distinction is not closely kept, since people feel that the century changes when the figure for the hundreds changes: there were celebrations for the beginning of the twentieth century on January 1 of both 1900 and 1901. (Compare the debate over whether the second half of our century began with 1950 or 1951.)

Partly because of the frequent errors made in this scheme of indicating centuries, the practice of naming the hundred is becoming more and more used, even in Formal writing (the seventeen hundreds, the nineteen hundreds . . .).

The abbreviation A.D. if strictly applied would come before a date and would not be used with centuries, since it stands for *anno Domini,* "in the year of our Lord." But like B.C. (before Christ) it commonly follows the year (431 B.C., 1681 A.D.), and even historians use it to designate centuries (the fifth century A.D.).

ch *Ch* usually spells the sound *tsh* (pronunciation symbol *ch*), as in *arch, bachelor, chatter, check, cheese, child, church.* When the sound is not at the beginning of a word, it is often spelled *tch* (*batch, watch*) and *ti* in such words as *question, Sebastian.* Compare also *righteous* (rī'chəs) and *literature*. It is spelled *c* in cello.

In some words from French, *ch* has the French sound of *sh: champagne, chagrin, mustache, machine.*

In a number of words from Greek, *ch* is sounded *k: chemist, chimera, chorus, echo.*

chairman, chairwoman Although *chairwoman* is entered in some dictionaries, it is no more necessary to indicate the sex of a presiding officer than of a beginning college student (*freshman*); *chairlady* is not in good use.

Change in language (oral and written) All languages whose histories have been traced show change. Sometimes changes are relatively sudden and far-reaching, as after an invasion, but ordinarily they are slow–the accumulation of slightly different pronunciations, unconscious or designed changes in the meanings of words, and gradual shifts in grammatical forms and constructions. Vocabulary tends to vary more rapidly than the basic structure of a language.

English shows many changes during the centuries in which it has been recorded. (See *English language.) When we think of the millions of people using our language and of the wide territory over which it is spread, the wonder is that change is not more rapid. Although schools, radio and television, books, periodicals, and newspapers tend to stabilize the language somewhat, English is still changing. One of the fundamental principles of linguistics is that this change in language is natural and inevitable.

Attempts to direct the course of English have not been very successful. In the eighteenth century the speech and writing (or at least the writing) of a small and influential group were modified by the application of a formal grammar, but the language of the majority of English users was unaffected. Even today's simplified spelling movement, which attacks only the transcription of the language, has had much less effect than we might expect from such a sensible and needed effort. At present, advertising is the chief source of spelling change, though some teachers and nearly all linguists believe that our spelling should be modified. In general, schools and publishing houses have taken a pretty firm stand against change, some of them even now presenting usage of the middle nineteenth century. It is possible that this will not always be true.

A person interested in writing needs to be aware of the naturalness and necessity of change in his language and should cultivate the habit of watching the small signs of change that he hears and sees in speech and writing. He needs also to decide whether he is going to oppose change, to welcome it in all its forms, or to try to discriminate, adopting in his own work those new words and forms and constructions that seem to be more convenient and more expressive than older forms. Following the direction in which English has already been moving (as the increase in nouns making their *plural with *-s*) is a good general principle to follow.

Several discussions in this *Guide-Index* treat points of change in current English. Reading them will suggest what to watch: The meaning of words (Ch. 8, p. 216), *Origin of words, Spelling (Ch. 4, p. 102), and specific articles like *all right–alright, *-al ly, *due to, *like–as, *shall–will.

The study of the changes that have taken place in English and the reasons for them is fascinating, and ample materials exist for carrying it on. The *Oxford English Dictionary* gives the history of individual words from their first appearance in the language, recording their changes in form and in meaning. Histories of the language, like those by Albert G. Baugh and Stuart Robertson, tell the story in detail. The general and orderly process of change is described in Otto Jespersen, *Language,* Part IV, and in E. H. Sturtevant, *Linguistic Change* (Chicago, 1917). See also Bloomfield, Chapter 20 ff.

chaperon Sometimes found with a final *e* but most commonly *chaperon.* Pronounced shap′ər ōn.

Chapters Chapters are numbered in Roman (I, II, III) or Arabic (1, 2, 3) numerals, the latter increasingly used. In bibliographies lower case Roman numerals (i, ii, x) are now more common than capitals (I, II, X), and Arabic are more common still.

In Formal book style, references to titles of chapters are quoted. In General writing they are simply capitalized.

> Formal: Kennedy, Chapter XIV, "Improvement of the English Language."
>
> General: Kennedy, Chapter 14, Improvement of the English Language.

check–cheque *Cheque* is the regular British spelling, but its use in the United States is Formal or pretentious.

Chinese Preferred by natives of China (and others) to *Chinaman, Chinamen,* because of the belittling connotation of those words. Say *a Chinese, the Chinese.* In Formal compounds *Sino-* (sī′nō or sin′ō) is used: *the Sino-Japanese War.*

Cities The name of the country or state need not be given with the name of well-known cities: Athens, Berlin, Chicago, Hollywood, London, New York, Rome, San Francisco. Many American cities and towns bearing the same names need identification if used in writing that is to circulate outside their states: Athens, Georgia; Berlin, New Hampshire; Roanoke, Illinois. (See *Proper names, *Comma § 9b.)

Clauses 1. *Definition.* A clause is an element of a compound or complex sentence that ordinarily has a subject and a finite verb. (But see § 3 and § 4.) By means of a conjunction or of an implied connection the clause construction is related to the rest of the sentence. A simple sentence, like "The bird flew higher and higher in slow easy circles," is usually not called a clause.

Compound sentences have two or more coordinate clauses of grammatically equal value, connected usually by *and, but, or, for,* or another *coordinating conjunction. Complex sentences have at least one main (or independent) clause, grammatically capable of standing alone, and one or more subordinate (or dependent) clauses, joined to the main clause or clauses by *as, because, since, when,* or some other *subordinating conjunction, or by a *relative pronoun, such as *that, who, which.*

> [Compound sentence, first coordinate clause:] A government as totalitarian as the Chinese has to maintain a vast army of officials, [Second coordinate clause:] and it is far in excess of the number of educated men available. [Complex sentence, subordinate clause:] Although all have nominally some knowledge of the basic principles of Communism, [Main clause:] their acquaintance with them is often hazy or perverted.–GUY WINT, *Spotlight on Asia,* p. 87

2. *Functions of subordinate clauses.* Subordinate clauses are classified according to the grammatical function they serve in the sentence:

a) Noun clauses are subjects and objects of verbs or objects of prepositions:

> [Subject, usually Formal:] *That herons fed at night* was not news to him.
>
> No one knew [Object:] *which way they had gone.*

b) Adjective clauses modify nouns:

> The man *whom they met* [or: The man *they met*] did not return.
>
> The cement road turned into a macadam road, *which in time turned into a clayey unsurfaced road.*

c) Adverbial clauses add notions of time, place, cause, effect, concession, etc.:

> *When they finally got that straightened out,* it was too late to go on.
>
> They were discouraged *because they had tried very hard.*

Here is a passage of 19 sentences in which four (6, 7, 9, 18) are simple, two are compound-complex (11, 16), and the others complex. The subordinate clauses are in italics, and at the end of the passage are the conventional grammatical interpretations of them.

> (1) Without question a young man *who is not a radical about something* is a pretty poor risk for education. (2) The relevant question to ask is, *What does this young man's radicalism express?* (3) In general, *if it is doctrinaire,/if he has learned all the answers to the world's problems out of a book or from a wise guy outside,* the worth of his beliefs is slight, both to him and to society. (4) The cut-and-dried patter must first be got out of him *before his mind will give a clear tone.* (5) It is true *that the reasons for the early adoption of ready-made beliefs often deserve sympathy.* (6) Poverty, injustice, a sense of wrong connected

with a physical or other defect, are predisposing causes. (7) In other instances it may be great intellectual curiosity coupled with a yearning for absolute truth. (8) This is *why students–though the Trustees do not trust it–can go so easily from the doctrine of Karl Marx to the doctrine of Saint Thomas.* (9) By means of these systems, converts can act out their dissent from the regular way and secure the comforts of a vast intellectual edifice.

(10) But dissent of a different type remains the really fruitful element in undergraduate thought; *though here again quality is important.* (11) Dissent from teacher *because he is an authority* is meaningless, but the defiant conviction *that it is no atrocious crime to be a young man, born later, with a different world impressed on the mind, with the consciousness of untried powers and unlimited courage*–that form of dissent is without doubt the one quality to nurture when found and to shield *if need be* against all literal conformity. (12) For *what it fulfills* is the solitary truth rattling through the empty periods of the Commencement orator *when he says:* "Young man, the future is in your hands."

(13) Imagine a generation of young men *who did not think/they could govern better than their fathers,/who did not want to revolutionize the world with new inventions or make T. S. Eliot's laurels fade.* (14) *If they do not believe/they can do this,* who will tell them? (15) Certainly not the institutions *that rightfully nurse a Tradition.* (16) But a tradition lives by being added to, and it is the young men *who must make the effort of creation.* (17) It is irrelevant to suggest *that this ambition moves thousands of hearts every year and ends in workaday routine and indolence.* (18) That is to look only at the husks. (19) *As long as we cannot prophesy/who will turn out a winner,* we have no right to question initiative and self-dedication.–JACQUES BARZUN, *Teacher in America,* pp. 238-9

1. Adjective clause modifying *young man*
2. Noun clause, complement of *is*
3. Two adverbial clauses (condition), modifying the main clause
4. Adverbial clause (time), modifying the main clause
5. Noun clause, postponed subject of *is.* (Obviously here the "main" idea is in the "subordinate" clause.)

8. Noun clause (*why* . . .), complement of *is;* adverbial clause (*though* . . .), modifying the *why* clause

10. Adverbial clause modifying the main clause (though it has the value of a coordinate clause, as is borne out by the punctuation)

11. Adverbial clause of reason (*because* . . .) on the face of it (but what does it "modify"?); noun clause (*that* . . .), in apposition with *conviction;* adverbial clause of condition (*if* . . .), modifying *to shield. When found* could be regarded as a subjectless clause of time.

12. Noun clause (*what* . . .), subject of *is;* adverbial clause of time (*when* . . .), modifying the main clause, or it could be regarded as modifying the quotation. A quotation is conventionally regarded as a noun clause, object of the verb of saying.

13. Two adjective clauses modifying *young men;* noun clause (they could . . .) object of *think*

14. Adverbial clause (condition), modifying the main clause; noun clause, object of *do believe*
15. Adjective clause, modifying *institutions*
16. Adjective clause, modifying *young men*
17. Noun clause, object of *to suggest*
19. Adverbial clause of time, modifying main clause; noun clause, object of *prophesy*

(The coordinate-subordinate category is not as important as it was once supposed to be—not as important as the functional classification of subject, object, modifier, for instance—but it is continued here as a convenient familiar classification.)

3. *Verbless clauses.* The typical clause has a subject and verb, but just as there are verbless sentences (see Ch. 2, "Verbless sentences," p. 53), there are clauses without finite verbs. They are of two types:

a) Elliptical clauses, in which the verb can be supplied from another part of the sentence or can be added with certainty because of the frame of the sentence:

I don't believe it any more than you [Supply: *do,* or *believe it*].
When [Supply: *he was*] sixteen, he had gone to work.

b) Genuine "abridged clauses" in which no verb element stands (or ever has stood). These should not be construed as elliptical clauses, since no verb ever enters the speaker's or listener's mind. Two familiar sayings illustrate the abridged clause:

The more, the merrier.
The better the day, the better the deed.

4. *Clause and phrase.* Dictionaries define clause approximately as in § 1 above and phrase as in the *Index* article for that term. But since phrases centered on verbal elements function much like clauses, it has been argued that they should be classified as a kind of clause. (See *Phrases and *Verbid.)

See Chapter 2, "The favorite English sentence," page 43, and Complex sentences, page 50, *Subordination, *Restrictive and nonrestrictive. References: Curme, *Syntax,* Chapter 10; Roberts, pages 343-345.

Clearness is one of the fundamental virtues of writing, perhaps the fundamental virtue, but it is a little hard to discuss helpfully. No accumulation of small virtues or banning of particular faults will produce essential clearness. It is true in writing that pronouns should match their antecedents, that verbs and subjects should agree, that constructions should not be wantonly shifted. These are traits which, though often ignored in speech, require care in writing.

True clearness will be gained not merely by paying attention to these details but by determining to convey to the reader the ideas and feelings you wish him to find in what you say. Clearness is the chief virtue of writing because it enables writing to carry out its fundamental purpose, communication. But writing has other purposes too—influencing people, entertaining them—and expression also has other virtues. Even in exposition, where clearness is the first demand, it is not the only one. Preoccupation with clearness for its own sake will produce writing that is clear—but also cold and dry. Without clearness a paper will certainly be bad, but with clearness it may not be particularly good. There are overtones demanded by certain situations; there are special considerations of the sensibilities of readers; there are small signs of the writer's own sense of the matter, even his sense of himself. All of these elements may detract in some small way from immediate clearness and yet add importantly to a complete understanding of the whole and so be intrinsic to good English. A piece of writing is clear because the writer has thought his subject and its implications through, has decided on the relation of the parts to the whole, and has tried to write "with the reader looking over his shoulder."

Clothes The usual pronunciation of the noun is klōz and of the verb, klōt͟hz.

Cognate *Cognate* means "related, of the same family." It is applied to languages that are from the same stock, as Spanish and French are both descended from Latin. *Cognate* is often used of words in different languages which are modern forms of some one word in an older ancestral language: German *Wasser,* English *water.*

Coh **Coherence** Revision: Make the relation between the parts of this sentence or between these sentences or paragraphs exact and clear to a reader.

Coherence—the traditional name for *relationship, connection, consecutiveness*—is a difficult and necessary virtue in writing. It is necessary because a reader does not have the same mind as the writer, does not see the same relationships, and consequently must be led through a line of thought, guided from one stage, from one sentence, to another. It is difficult because a coherent piece of writing is a triumph over natural human casualness; it represents an editing of a writer's thought so that it can be grasped by others.

Coherence is the name of a quality of finished writing and is to be checked finally in revision. A writer cannot be always worrying about the connection between his statements while he is at work. There is always some relation between his consecutive "thoughts," but the relation may be entirely personal. Carefully thinking over material before beginning to write should help prepare a coherent paper, especially if some sort of plan, arranging the different stages in a natural and sensible order, is drawn up. But coherence must be tested after writing. The writer should go over his copy as impersonally as he can to see if what he has written not only hangs together for him but will hang together for those he wants to read it. He should ask himself, "Is the relation between these statements clear? Can a reader pass from this sentence or from this paragraph to the next, without feeling a break?"

A natural arrangement of material is not enough for this; there must often be signs of the relationship between sentences and paragraphs. These signs, various suggestions pointing toward coherence, and examples of successful and unsuccessful attempts at coherence are discussed in this *Guide-Index,* especially in *Conjunctions, *Prepositions, *Reference of pronouns, Chapter 6 (Paragraphs), Chapter 7 (Sentences), and Chaper 9, "Planning the paper," page 253.

Collective nouns Revision: Change, according to the principles of this article, the verb and/or the pronoun to agree with the collective noun marked. *Coll*

1. A collective noun is a noun whose singular form names a group of objects or persons or acts. Some common collective nouns are:

army	company	gang	*number
*athletics	contents	group	offspring
audience	*couple	herd	politics
band	crowd	jury	*public
class	dozen	majority	remainder
*committee	flock	mankind	team

When a writer means the group as a whole, a collective noun takes a singular verb and singular pronoun; when he means the individuals of the group, the noun takes a plural verb and plural pronoun:

The *crowd* that *has* been noisily engaged in finding *its* seats *settles* down and the incessant murmur of voices slowly quiets.

The *crowd* that *have* been noisily engaged in finding *their* seats *settle* down and the incessant murmur of voices slowly quiets.

The first *couple* on the floor *was* Tom and Janet.

One day when we were near where the old *couple were* living, we dropped in to see *them.*

The rule is simple enough; its application is more complicated because (1) some collectives have regular plural forms (army, armies), others do not (athletics, offspring); (2) even in the same sentence the sense may shift from singular to plural (see § 2 and § 3 below); (3) words which are not ordinarily collectives may be so used (the baseball *nine* were . . .); (4) some collectives more commonly take singular verbs (herd, mankind), others, plural verbs (people).

British and American practice differ somewhat; for example *government* and *party* as referring to political groups are plural in England, singular here.

2. In writing, especially Formal writing, a collective should not be treated as both singular and plural in the same context:

The *company was* organized and immediately sent out *its* [not *their*] representatives.

Mess is over and the guard *have* [not *has*] a busy morning ahead of *them* [not *it*].

There is often a temptation to use a collective noun and try to keep it singular when the meaning really calls for a plural construction. Often the writer slips unconsciously from singular to plural in such a passage:

Into the church troops the entire town, seats itself on the uncomfortable wooden benches and there remains for a good two hours, while an aged curé preaches to *them* [consistency demands *it*] of their [*its*] wicked lives and awful sins. (This might better have started "Into the church troop all the people, seat themselves. . . .")

In making constructions consistent you will often find, as in the sentence above, that it is the first member, the collective subject, that needs to be changed, rather than the pronouns referring to it.

3. In speech (and consequently in some Informal–and much unedited writing) our tendency not to continue constructions across intervening words usually operates: The verb, which comes close to the noun, is singular, but a pronoun some words away tends to refer to the individuals, in the plural.

Spoken: The team *was* called together for last minute instructions and sent out to *their* positions.

Written: The team *were* called together for last minute instructions and sent out to *their* positions.

Spoken: The election committee *has* from the beginning misused *their* rights in issuing false instructions for absentee ballots.

Written: The election committee *has* from the beginning misused *its* rights in issuing false instructions for absentee ballots.

4. The plural of a collective noun signifies different groups:

The audiences of New York and Chicago differed in their receptions of the play.

5. In measurements and amounts a plural noun is often followed by a singular verb:

Eighteen inches is half a yard.
About 80 pounds of carbon disulfide is [or *are*] added.

See *Subject and verb § 2; *every and its compounds § 1. References: Curme, *Syntax,* pages 539-540, 50-51; Fries, *AEG,* pages 48-50, 54, 57-59; Jespersen, pages 210-212; Pooley, pages 85-88.

Colloquial English Usage that is more characteristic of speech than of writing is *colloquial.* In modern style there is not a sharp division between what is spoken and what is written, but some distinctively spoken usages may be inappropriate in some writing, especially in Formal English.

For discussion of the traits of colloquial English see *Spoken and written English and Chapter 2, "Informal English," page 22.

Colon (:) Revision: Use a colon here.

Colon 1. *Anticipatory use.* 2. *Between clauses.* 3. *Conventional uses.* 4. *Stylistic use.* 5. *Capitals following.*

The colon is a mark of anticipation, directing attention to what follows. Its use differs from that of the semicolon, which is a stop, almost a period. Students do not use as many colons as they should, and often use a semicolon instead:

> Yesterday I received a clipping from home, the essence of which is as follows: [not ;]. . . .

The principal uses of the colon are:

1. *Anticipatory use.* A colon is used after an introductory expression, as in the second line above, and after the salutation of formal letters:

> Dear Sir: (Contrast the comma in informal letters: Dear Fritz,)

It is generally used to anticipate quotations in factual writing (not in fiction), especially if the quotation is a complete grammatic unit and runs to more than one sentence. Whether or not a colon is appropriate with shorter quotations depends in part upon the formula with which it is introduced. If the quotation is closely built into the sentence, a comma is usual (*says,* in the quotation below); if the introduction is more formal, a colon is usual (below, *was added:*).

> A card made out at 10:45 P.M. on Nov. 4, 1928, says, "Arnold Rothstein, Male, 46 years, 912 Fifth Avenue, gunshot wound in abdomen, found in employee's entrance, Park Central Hotel, 200 West Fifty-sixth Street. Attended by Dr. McGovern, of City Hospital. Removed to Polyclinic Hospital. Reported by Patrolman William M. Davis, Shield 2943, Ninth Precinct." Two days later the word "fatal," in parentheses, was written in after the word "abdomen," and a second report, with more detail, was added: "Rothstein apparently had been engaged in card game with others in Room 349 on third floor of Park Central Hotel when an unknown man shot him and threw revolver out of window to street. Body found by Lawrence Fallon of 3164 Thirty-fourth Street, Astoria, employed as house detective for the hotel."—MEYER BERGER, *The New Yorker,* Nov. 26, 1938

2. *Between clauses.* A colon is used between clauses when the following one is either an illustration, a restatement in different terms, or an amplification of the first:

> If a gunnery officer can't explain what he wants done, one of two things is going to happen: either the gun won't be fired or he'll have to do it himself.

> Lazy minds give up in despair: "I can't write anyhow," say students to me year after year; they mean that they won't think.—BARRETT WENDELL, *English Composition,* p. 136

> The supposition that words are used principally to convey thoughts is one of the most elementary of possible errors: they are used mainly to proclaim emotional effects on the hearers or attitudes that will lead to practical results.—H. R. HUSE, *The Illiteracy of the Literate,* p. 21

3. *Conventional uses.* There are a few conventional uses of the colon, though they vary among publishers:

a) Between hours and minutes expressed in figures:

11:42 a.m. 3:28 p.m.
(or, especially British: 11.42 a.m., 3.28 p.m.)

b) In formal bibliographies and formal citations of books:

Between volume and page–*The Atlantic Monthly,* 160:129-40
Between chapter and verse in citing the Bible–Genesis IX:3-5
Between author and title–Stuart Chase: *Men and Machines*
Between place of publication and publisher–New York: Holt, 1958

In the last two of these a comma would often be found.

c) In proportions when the numbers are written as numerals: Concrete mixed 5:3:1.

4. *Stylistic use.* Some writers prefer colons where most would use commas or semicolons:

> It [a castle] is a shut place that commands by its shutness the open place about it. A castle is builded of the stone of its world: it rises from the stone of its world: it *is* the stone of its world. A castle is austere toward the world which it defends. It is invariable, forbidding: its strength is that of a perpetual shutting-out of all which lies outside it. Sun beats on the castle wall: inside it is dark. Moon melts its bastion and bathes its county blue: it is harsh and rigid. Water and wind make song of the green hills: the castle is silent. It is the lord of its county because it is apart from it. A castle is hot in a cold land: a castle is cold in a hot land: a castle is high in a low land: a castle is full in a land of dearth: a castle is dry in a land of verdure.–WALDO FRANK, *Virgin Spain,* p. 108

This is a matter of taste rather than of correctness and is usually (as here) Formal. The mark ordinarily attracts some slight attention to itself when used this way.

5. *Capitals following.* After a colon either a capital or a small letter may be used. The capital is more usual when the matter following the colon is in the form of a complete sentence, a small letter when it is a subordinate element. That the deciding factor is largely the closeness of thought relation between the two parts of the sentence is suggested by the following quotations from a single article:

> Thus the task of democracy has always been a twofold one: to prevent political privilege from reëstablishing itself, and to make peaceful settlement of disputes possible in a society without privilege.
>
> Those who believe that fascism is simply a tool which Big Business created as soon as it found democracy dangerous overlook one important fact: the opposition of Big Business to democracy is much older than fascism.
>
> The ways in which the kings settled social disputes were very different, in spirit as well as in technic: The kings of France, after having subdued the rebellious nobles, protected the social privileges of the nobility to the point of subjecting both citizens and peasants to cruel oppression; the kings of Prussia, who occasionally liked to be called "kings of beggars," without fully living up to the implications of that

title, tried to restrict exploitation of the masses; so, much earlier, did Elizabeth of England.–CARL LANDAUER, in *The American Way,* by D. C. Coyle and others

column, columnist The usual pronunciation is kol′əm, kol′əm ist or kol′əm nist; kol′yum, kol′yum ist is often used humorously and for a newspaper "column" and is sometimes represented in the spellings *colyum, colyumist.*

Comma (,) Revision: Insert or remove a comma at the place marked, in accordance with one of the sections in this article.

Comma (C)

1. *Between coordinate clauses.* 2. *With subordinate clauses.* 3. *With nonrestrictive modifiers.* 4. *With interrupting and parenthetical elements.* 5. *In lists and series.* 6. *For emphasis and contrast.* 7. *For clearness.* 8. *With main sentence elements.* 9. *In conventional uses.* 10. *With other marks of punctuation.*

1. *Between coordinate clauses.* *C1*

a) A comma is used when the clauses are rather long and when it is desirable to emphasize their distinctness, especially if the clauses have different subjects.

> The frozen steel edges shrieked as they bit into the ice-covered turns, and the driving sleet slashed against their goggles and jackets with such force that it was impossible to keep clear vision.

A comma is not used when the coordinate clauses are short and closely related in meaning, especially in easy narrative:

> There was a knock at the front door [ ] and Mary ran to open it.

b) A comma is generally used between two coordinate locutions joined by *but* or *not,* to emphasize the contrast:

> I can remember Mother telling me that a book was one's best friend, but I couldn't understand how anyone could feel that way.
>
> Those who hold these ideas are to be pitied, not blamed.

A comma is generally used between clauses connected by the conjunction *for,* to avoid confusion with the preposition *for:*

> Conjunction: They are obviously mistaken, *for* all intercollegiate sports are competitive.
>
> Preposition: The English teacher had assigned us *Treasure Island* *for* a book report.

For commas between complete clauses that could stand as separate sentences, see Chapter 2, "Contact clauses," page 59, and *Comma fault.

2. *With subordinate clauses.* *C2*

a) A comma is used after a subordinate clause (or long phrase) that precedes the main clause or is not closely connected to it:

> If that lake wasn't frowning at something or other that night, I'll drink it down to the last drop.

Uses of the Comma

The following list of uses of the comma outlines the treatment in this article. The numbers and letters refer to sections and subsections. Brackets mean that a comma should be avoided.

1. BETWEEN COORDINATE CLAUSES
- **a)** Between rather long coordinate clauses
- **b)** Between clauses connected by *but, not, for*

2. WITH SUBORDINATE CLAUSES
- **a)** After subordinate clause or long phrase preceding the main clause
- **b)** Before a subordinate clause following the main clause and not closely related to it

3. WITH NONRESTRICTIVE MODIFIERS

4. WITH INTERRUPTING AND PARENTHETICAL ELEMENTS
- **a)** Around interrupting constructions
- **b)** Around conjunctive adverbs not standing first in their constructions

5. IN LISTS AND SERIES
- **a)** Between units of a list or series
- **b)** Between coordinate adjectives in the same relation to their noun
- **c)** [Not between two words or phrases joined by *and*]

6. FOR EMPHASIS AND CONTRAST

7. FOR CLEARNESS
- **a)** Before words of two possible functions (*for, but*)
- **b)** To prevent a noun being mistaken for an object
- **c)** To prevent wrong interpretation
- **d)** To separate consecutive uses of the same word

8. WITH MAIN SENTENCE ELEMENTS (S-V-O)
- **a)** [Not between a short subject and its verb]
- **b)** Sometimes after a long or heavily modified subject
- **c)** [Not between verb and its object]
- **d)** [Rarely between compound predicates]

9. IN CONVENTIONAL USES
- **a)** In dates **b)** In addresses
- **c)** After salutation of informal letters
- **d)** After names in direct address **e)** In figures
- **f)** With degrees and titles **g)** With weak exclamations
- **h)** [Not to show omission of a word]

10. WITH OTHER MARKS OF PUNCTUATION
- **a)** [Not with a dash] (*Dash § 6)
- **b)** With parentheses (*Parentheses § 5)
- **c)** With quotation marks (*Quotation marks § 4, b and c)

Although willing to use his athletic ability, he wouldn't study hard enough to become eligible.

When the preceding clause or phrase is short and closely related in thought to the main clause (especially when the subjects of the two clauses are the same), there is usually no comma following it:

Without a doubt [ ] Jack is the best linesman our school has.

When we had all gathered near the fence [ ] we could see that they were bums. (Subjects the same)

When appropriations are before the House [ ] he continually checks the Democrats' expenditures. (A close relationship between the statements)

b) A comma usually stands before a subordinate clause (or long phrase) that follows the main clause if it is not closely related in thought.

Kemal Ataturk's death had come as a blow to a nation of 14,000,000 people, though he reformed their social customs, their religion, and their economics with dictatorial zeal and speed.

They had tried four times to start it, the starter every time giving just a short whine.

3. *With nonrestrictive modifiers.* Modifiers which do not limit the meaning of a noun or verb but add a descriptive detail are nonrestrictive and are set off by a comma or commas. The expressions in italics are nonrestrictive:

From where I was standing, *almost directly above the treasure,* I could see many articles that had been lost. (The clause *that had been lost* is restrictive and so not set off by a comma.)

Pigeons breed in the spring and the hen lays two eggs, *one of which usually hatches into a cock and one into a hen.*

A restrictive modifier, one that is essential to a correct understanding of the word it modifies, is not set off by punctuation. The expressions in italics are restrictive:

Wouldn't it be as just to remove from his suffering a person *who has committed no crime* as to make suffer one *who has committed a crime?*

Great tracts were left, eaten bare of the grass *which had kept the soil in place.*

The best clue is that in reading aloud a nonrestrictive clause there is a slight pause and drop in voice; before a restrictive clause there is no such change of voice.

Many modifiers may be considered either restrictive or nonrestrictive, and their punctuation should follow the writer's sense of the closeness with which they limit the word they modify; this can be shown by the way he reads the sentence aloud. The expressions in italics in these sentences might be set off by commas, depending on the writer's intention:

A winding road *that seemed to lead nowhere in particular* passed through the village.

It was quite a satisfaction *after working a difficult logarithm problem* to know that something had been accomplished.

Further examples of restrictive and nonrestrictive expressions will be found in *Restrictive and nonrestrictive and in Chapter 5, "Before subordinate elements," page 122.

C4 **4.** *With interrupting and parenthetical elements.*

a) A phrase or clause that interrupts the direct movement of the sentence should be set off by commas, *two* commas:

Next summer, no matter what comes up, we will go to Europe.
The prank, I dare say, seemed amusing to you then.
Mr. Devant, as was customary with him, stopped at the tavern on his way home.

Usage is divided over setting off short parenthetical words and phrases like *incidentally, of course.* Setting them off with commas is more characteristic of Formal than of General writing, though there is often a difference in emphasis according to whether or not commas are used:

Mr. and Mrs. Crayton, of course, were late.
Mr. and Mrs. Crayton of course were late.
The speaker, naturally enough, was irritated by the interruption.
The speaker naturally enough was irritated by the interruption.

Adverbs that modify the verb or the statement closely should not be set off by commas when they are in their natural position:

Undoubtedly [ ] this package was intended for Smith.
This package was intended for Smith, undoubtedly.

b) When a *conjunctive adverb stands after the first phrase of its clause, as it often does, it is usually set off by commas, and often it is set off when it stands first in the clause:

His ridiculous proposal, nevertheless, was the one the committee adopted.
Furthermore, all leaves are cancelled until February 15.

But and other lighter conjunctions are a part of the clauses in which they appear and should not be set off:

Hart had received permission to finish his experiment after class. But [ ] he filed out with the others when the bell sounded.

C5 **5.** *In lists and series.*

a) The comma is the natural mark to use between the units of enumerations, lists, series (unless the units are long or contain commas within them, when semicolons would be used—see *Semicolon § 1).

There are, among others, an actor out of a job, a murderer, a Mexican dipsomaniac, a man obsessed with a philosophical concept of time, an Indian oil millionaire who prefers waffles to any other food, and assorted females, mostly tough.—*The New Yorker,* Nov. 26, 1938

Commas ordinarily are not used when conjunctions stand between the units of the series.

A bit of tarnish on the brass work [ ] or untidy life preservers [ ] or matches on the decks seem to be of little concern to him.

Usage is divided on the comma before the last item in a series: *celery, onions, and olives,* or *celery, onions and olives.* (See *Series.)

b) Adjectives in series. In the sentence

Although it was a hot, sticky, miserable day, Mrs. Marston looked cool in her fresh gingham dress.

there are commas between *hot–sticky–miserable* because each stands in the same relation to the noun *day.* There is no comma between *fresh* and *gingham* because *fresh* modifies *gingham dress* rather than just *dress.* A comma following *fresh* would throw more emphasis upon *gingham* and might sometimes be wanted. Compare these two versions:

The bright, red draperies showed to advantage against the dark, gray walls.

The bright red draperies showed to advantage against the dark gray walls.

Either version is correct, but in the first, *red* and *gray* stand out as separate modifiers of their nouns.

c) Two items connected by *and* are not usually punctuated:

Old Mrs. Clayton was always ready to watch over the young children in her neighborhood [ ] and to help their mothers with light housework.

C6 **6.** *For emphasis and contrast.* The pause indicated by a comma tends to keep distinct the constructions it separates and to emphasize slightly the construction that follows the mark:

The office manager was delighted with the prestige of his new position, and with the increase in pay.

This is especially true when a connective is omitted:

He repeated the story many times, repeated it when it no longer had any meaning.

In idioms like *the more . . . the greater,* Formal usage tends to have a comma, General does not:

. . . And the more meaning the Grammarian finds crowded into the verb [,] the happier he is.–P. B. BALLARD, *Thought and Language,* p. 87

C7 **7.** *For clearness.* Often a comma can guide a reader in interpreting a sentence and make it unnecessary for him to go back over it for meaning. In material that is likely to be read aloud, the writer should give special heed to this device. Two such constructions are especially helped by commas:

a) When a word has two possible functions. *For* or *but* may be either a conjunction or a preposition, and confusion may be avoided by using a comma before either when it is used as a conjunction:

The crowd hurried, for the river was rising swiftly. (To avoid reading "hurried for the river.")

b) When a noun might be mistaken for the object of a verb:

When the boll weevil struck, the credit system collapsed and ruined a great part of the landowners and tenants. (Not: When the boll weevil struck the credit system. . . .)

Soon after the inspector left, the room was crowded with curious onlookers. (Not: Soon after the inspector left the room . . . .)

c) Sometimes a faulty interpretation of word grouping can be prevented:

A great crowd of early shoppers milled around inside, and outside hundreds more were storming the doors.

d) Ordinarily when the same word occurs twice consecutively a comma should be used:

What Janice does, does not concern me.

C8

8. *With main sentence elements.*

a) Short subjects. Care should be taken not to separate short subjects from their verbs.

The first family to come [ ] sends word back to those left in the Old Country.

The six boys [ ] all came on the run.

b) Long subjects. When the subject of a sentence is a long phrase or a noun followed by modifiers–that is, when it is a locution of five or six words or more–Formal usage often puts a comma between it and the verb, but General usage does not.

Whether a program is appealing or not [Formal (,)] is quickly reflected in the sale of the sponsor's product.

Everything that I had picked out as a flaw to be pounced upon and criticized [Formal (,)] assumed a different meaning and became a vital part of the work.

c) Verb and object. There is some temptation to put a comma after a verb, separating it from its object or complement. This is especially true after verbs of saying. Such commas should be taken out in revision:

Since they know nothing whatsoever about their future occupation, they must start what might be termed [ ] a second schooling.

She always thought [ ] that I would never be a success.

d) Compound predicates. Usage is divided over separating the two verbs of a compound predicate. The better and more common usage is not to use a comma between the verbs unless the predicates are long or contrasted:

We watched television until seven [ ] and then hurried over to the auditorium for the first of the lecture series.

After the supervisor's lecture, the girls returned sullenly to their tasks [ ] and whispered furtively the rest of the morning.

C9

9. *In conventional uses.*

a) In dates, to separate the day of the month from the year: *May 26, 1958*. When the day of the month is not given, a comma may or may not be used: *In September 1958* or *In September, 1958.* The neater use is without the comma.

b) In addresses, to separate town from state or country when they are written on the same line:

Washington, D.C., is too hot and humid to be a nation's capital.
Chicago, Illinois Berne, Switzerland
Hamilton, Madison County, New York

c) After salutations in Informal letters: *Dear Dot, Dear Len,*

d) After names in direct address: *Jim,* try that one again.

e) In figures, to separate thousands, millions, etc.: 4,672,342.

f) To separate degrees and titles from names:

Elihu Root, Esq. Charles Evans Hughes, Jr.
Wallace W. Emmett, A.B. Wallace W. Emmett, A.B. '36

g) After a weak exclamation like *well, why, oh* when it does not carry much stress.

h) A comma is not now commonly used to show the omission of a word that is required to fill out a grammatical construction:

He must have taken the right-hand turn and I [,] the left.

10. *With other marks of punctuation.* *C10*

a) A comma is now rarely used with a dash. (See *Dash § 6.)

b) When a parenthesis comes within a construction that would be followed by a comma, the comma stands after the parenthesis. (See *Parentheses § 5.)

c) For use with quotation marks see *Quotation marks § 4, b and c.

Reference: Summey, index entries under *Comma.*

Comma fault **Revision: Revise the sentence marked by changing the comma to a semicolon or a period, or by inserting an appropriate conjunction, or by rephrasing to make it a more effective sentence.** *CF*

You should do more than merely remove the comma fault; you should make an effective statement.

A comma fault (comma blunder, comma splice, *fused sentence) is two or more statements in the form of independent sentences that are punctuated as a single sentence–that is, with a comma between them (or even run together with no mark at all). A few sentences of this sort are effective (see Ch. 2, "Contact clauses," p. 59), but here we are considering only those that are not effective, because of their form and the lack of thought relation between the clauses.

There are various remedies for a comma fault:

1) The easiest remedy, that satisfies the minimum requirements of conventional grammar, is to repunctuate, using a semicolon or a period instead of the comma, but this often leaves two weak sentences instead of one good one.

2) If the statements really belong together in one sentence, the clauses may be joined by a conjunction that shows the relationship, probably retaining the comma.

3) Often the sentence needs to be rephrased—perhaps a relative pronoun used instead of a *this* or *these*—or to be completely rewritten. Remember that the aim is to make an effective sentence.

The following examples show some common types:

Comma fault	*Suggested revision*
He took a couple of steps, stopped, reached out and turned a valve, as he did that he told us that all the valves were right-hand valves.	He took a couple of steps, stopped, reached out and turned a valve. As he did that he told us that all the valves were right-hand valves.
Two volumes of his great work are now completed, the first will be published next year.	Two volumes of his great work are now completed, the first of which will be published next year.
	Two volumes of his great work are now completed, and the first will be published next year.
	Two volumes of his great work are now completed. The first will be published next year.
Charley then crossed the room and threw a switch which started a motor, returning he wiped the perspiration from his forehead with the back of his hand.	Charley then crossed the room and threw a switch which started a motor. Returning he wiped the perspiration. . . .
They still produce aluminum tips for broken skis, these are very successful as a device for temporary repair.	They still produce aluminum tips for broken skis, which are very successful as a device for temporary repair.

Carelessly run-together sentences are one of the most serious faults in elementary writing. If you haven't yet learned to avoid them, you will need to take extra pains to eliminate them.

For a more complete discussion and more examples of comma faults and of successful run-on sentences, see Chapter 2, "Revising comma faults," page 56. See also *Contact clauses, *Conjunctions.

Commands and requests Direct commands (also called *imperatives*) are expressed by the simple (infinitive) form of the verb:

Hurry up! *Shut* the door, please.
Fill out the coupon and *mail* it today.

In speech the force of the command or request is shown by the stress and tone of voice, which are hard to represent on paper. Emphatic commands are punctuated with an exclamation mark, less emphatic with a period. The form with *do* is often emphatic (*Do* come!). Negative commands are expressed with *not* and the *do* form of the verb: Don't go yet.

Softened or more polite commands and requests depend on phrasing and usually involve auxiliaries or adverbs of courtesy. Often these commands and requests are in the pattern of a question, which would be written either with a period or a question mark, depending on the intonation intended.

Try to get them in on time.
You will write at least six pages.
Please think no more of it.
Would you be willing to take part in this program?
Would [or *Will*] you please close the window.
Let's go around and see what we can do with him.
Suppose we say nothing more about it.

In indirect discourse a command becomes an infinitive with *to* or a clause with *should:*

He told us to write a 5000-word paper.
Or: He said that we should write a 5000-word paper. (Direct form: "Write a 5000-word paper.")
He wired me to come at once. (Direct: "Come at once.")

(For further discussion of forms of commands see Curme, *Syntax,* pp. 419, 430-436.)

committee is a *collective noun, usually construed as singular but sometimes as plural when the writer is thinking of the several individuals who compose it. In the latter situation we are more likely to write *the members of the committee*. The singular would usually be the desired form.

The committee meets today at four.
The committee [or: the members of the committee] get together with difficulty.

comparative–comparatively–comparison–comparable So spelled in our inconsistent language. *Comparable* is pronounced kom′pə rə bəl.

compare–contrast *Compare* is used in two senses: (1) To point out likenesses (used with *to*); (2) To examine two or more objects to find likenesses or differences (used with *with*). *Contrast* always points out *differences.*

He compared my stories *to* Maupassant's [said they were like his].
He compared my stories *with* Maupassant's [pointed out like and unlike traits].

When the things compared are of different classes, *to* is used:

He compared my stories *to* a sack of beans.

In the common construction with the past participle, either *to* or *with* is used:

Compared *with* [or *to*] Maupassant's, mine are pretty feeble.
In comparison *with* [not *to*] Maupassant's, mine are pretty feeble.

Idioms with *contrast:*

He contrasted my work *with* [sometimes *to*] Maupassant's.
In contrast *to* [rarely *with*] Maupassant's, my stories are pretty feeble.

Note the difference in stress between *contrast* (kon′trast) the noun and *contrast* (kən trast′, kən tras′təd, kən trast′ing) the verb.

Comparison of adjectives and adverbs Revision: Change the form or construction of the adjective or adverb marked, in accordance with the section below that applies.

Comp

1. *Uses of the comparative.* 2. *Uses of the superlative.* 3. *Idioms with comparatives.* 4. *Comparison of absolutes.* 5. *Choice of forms.*

Adjectives and adverbs change their forms (see § 5) to show a greater degree of the characteristic named in the simple word (*long, longer, longest*). The forms are simple enough but a number of questions arise in using them.

1. *Uses of the comparative.* The comparative degree expresses a greater degree (It is *warmer* now) or makes specific comparison between two units (He was *kinder* [*more kind*] than his wife).

The two terms of a comparison should be comparable:

Comparable: His salary was lower than a shoe clerk's [Or: than that of a shoe clerk]. Not: His salary was lower than a shoe clerk.

Comparable: His face was round and healthy looking, like a recent college graduate's. Not: His face was round and healthy looking, like a recent college graduate.

With a comparative, idiom calls for *other* when the comparison is with something in the same class of things but not when the comparison is with things of a different class:

She is a better dancer than the other girls.
She is a better dancer than the boys [than any of the boys].

The comparative is frequently used absolutely, with no actual comparison involved (*higher education, the lower depths*), or the reader is left to supply a comparison (*Look younger–Live longer*). (Reference: Esther K. Sheldon, "The Rise of the Incomplete Comparative," *American Speech,* 1945, 20:161-167.)

2. *Uses of the superlative.*

a) The superlative is used to indicate the greatest degree of a quality among three or more people or things (He was the *jolliest* of the whole group; This is the *brightest* tie in the showcase). The form with *most* is also used as an intensive to indicate an extreme degree (You are *most kind;* She is *most clever*) in which no specific comparison is intended.

Superlatives are not completed by *other:*

The Egyptians had obtained the highest degree of cultivation in medicine that had up to that time been obtained by any [not *other*] nation.

b) In many instances the same idea may be expressed by the comparative and the superlative: *He was taller than the other boys. He was the tallest of the boys.* In Informal English a superlative is often a form of emphasis: *We saw the loveliest flowers when we visited her garden: Hasn't she the sweetest voice?* It is also used in comparing two items: *His new novel is the best of the two.* Fries says (p. 101): "The use of the superlative rather than the comparative for two, thus ignoring a dual as distinct from a plural, is a fact of Standard English usage and not a characteristic limited to Vulgar English." (Reference: Russell Thomas, "The Use of the Superlative for the Comparative," *English Journal* (College edition), 1935, 24:821-829.)

3. *Idioms with comparatives.*

a) *as much as if not more than.* People are likely to say "The styles vary as much if not more than the colors," but in writing both comparative constructions should be completed:

> The styles vary as much *as* if not more *than* the colors.
> The lobby is as strong *as* if not stronger *than* it was in 1955.
> Or: The lobby is as strong as it was in 1955, if not stronger.

b) *as . . . as.* Sometimes *than* is carelessly used for the second *as* in a sentence like this:

> I pay almost ten times as much for it *as* [not *than*] for the bigger bus ticket.

(See *as . . . as.)

4. *Comparison of absolutes.* Purists raise objections to the comparison of *black, dead, excellent, fatal, final, impossible, perfect,* **unique,* since their meaning is thought to be absolute: There are no degrees of *deadness* or *blackness* or *impossibility*. But in common use the meaning of these words is not absolute so that they are frequently compared: "This was even *more impossible*"; and the Constitution has ". . . to form a more perfect union. . . ." Many are used figuratively with less absolute meanings (This is the *deadest* town I was ever in), which naturally admit comparison. (See *Divided usage.)

5. *Choice of forms.* English adjectives and adverbs are compared in two ways:

a) By adding *-er, -est.*

	Positive	*Comparative*	*Superlative*
Adjective:	early	earlier	earliest
	hoarse	hoarser	hoarsest
	hot	hotter	hottest
Adverb:	fast	faster	fastest
	soon	sooner	soonest

b) By using *more, most.* The change in degree may be shown by prefixing *more* and *most* to the positive form. This form is generally used for adjectives and adverbs of three syllables or more, and for many of two syllables. But no absolute rule can be formulated. It may also be used with those of one syllable, so that for many comparatives and superlatives there are two forms.

	Positive	*Comparative*	*Superlative*
Adjective:	exquisite	more exquisite	most exquisite
	empty	emptier, more empty	emptiest, most empty
	able	abler, more able	ablest, most able

Adverb:	comfortably	more comfortably	most comfortably
	often	oftener, more often	oftenest, most often
	hotly	more hotly	most hotly

Words with a short vowel followed by a single consonant double the consonant to indicate the short sound (*thin, thinner, thinnest*). Words ending in *y* change the *y* to *i* before the endings: *dry, drier, driest; shy, shier, shiest* (sometimes *shyer, shyest*).

The meanings of the two forms (*-er* or *more; -est* or *most*) are the same, so that the one that sounds better can be used. But the *-er* or *-est* form necessarily places the stress on the root part of the word and so tends to emphasize the quality (kind′er), whereas the *more* or *most* form allows the stress to fall on the sign of the degree (more′ kind; you are most′ kind) so that there is some difference in the suggestion value of the two.

References: Curme, *Parts of Speech,* Chapters 11, 13; *Syntax,* Chapter 25; Fries, *AEG,* pages 96-101.

complement–compliment *Compliment* has to do with praise:

I *complimented* him on his progress.
His progress deserved a *compliment.*
"the *complimentary* close" of a letter

Complement means a number or amount that makes a whole, or an allotment (related to *complete*):

He had his full *complement* of good looks. *complementary* angles

Complement In this book *complement* refers to the noun or adjective completing the meaning of a linking verb and modifying the subject:

He was *busy*. He became *the real head* of the concern.

In some grammars *complement* is used to include direct and indirect objects. (See Ch. 2, "Subject–complement," p. 63, and *Linking verbs, *Predicate adjective, Predicate noun.)

Compound predicate Two or more verbs having the same subject are known as a compound predicate: The youngster *bawled* and *stamped* his feet; Ruth *wrote* and *mailed* three letters.

Compound predicates are one of the chief devices of economy in writing. Note how far removed these sentences are from the one-small-idea-to-a-sentence type so often used by immature writers:

> They (1) accepted the quinine and, in their gratitude, often (2) kissed the hygienists' hands. Heeding their advice, they (1) graveled the village roads, (2) began to drain their lands, (3) enlarged the windows of their dwellings, (4) built sidewalks, sanitary backhouses, and concrete platforms for manure, and so on.–LOUIS ADAMIC, *The Native's Return,* p. 318

For further discussion see *Subject and verb.

Compound sentences contain two or more complete statements (that is, each with a subject and complete verb) of coordinate grammatical value. (See Ch. 2, "Compound sentences," p. 49.)

1. *With coordinating conjunction.* Usually the clauses of a compound sentence are connected by one of the coordinating conjunctions, most commonly by *and, but, for, or,* and the combinations *either . . . or, neither . . . nor:*

> What a fool he was to be thus startled *but* always he had hated cats from childhood.—WALTER DURANTY, *Babies Without Tails,* p. 11
>
> *Either* you learned these simple things in high school *or* you will have to learn them in college.

2. *Without connective.* A compound sentence may stand without a connective (see *Contact clauses). Such sentences are usually punctuated with a semicolon:

> They are generous-minded; they hate shams and enjoy being indignant about them; they are valuable social reformers; they have no notion of confining books to a library shelf.—E. M. FORSTER, *Aspects of the Novel,* p. 33

Since each of these clauses could be written as a separate sentence, it is apparent that our traditional definition of sentence is somewhat arbitrary. (Compare Ch. 2, "Contact clauses," p. 59.)

3. *With conjunctive adverb.* The clauses of a compound sentence may be connected by a conjunctive adverb (*however, moreover, whereas, consequently, therefore . . .*):

> The F.B.I. had proved themselves expert in publicizing their solution of crimes; consequently some local police gave them only grudging support.

4. *Compound-complex.* Since one or more of the coordinate clauses of a sentence can be modified by subordinate clauses, we have the category of *compound-complex sentences:*

> He was an old man with a long beard, whose clothes were rags; but Mr. Kiddle had all the way wished to tell someone how proud he was of Ada, who did the running, so he was glad to have even a tinker to talk to.—T. F. POWYS, *Mr. Weston's Good Wine,* p. 66

This sentence has three main clauses (making it compound): *He was an old man . . . but Mr. Kiddle had all the way wished . . . so he was glad to have . . .*; and three subordinate clauses (making it compound-complex): *whose clothes were rags, how proud he was of Ada, who did the running.*

In current style there are more compound-complex sentences than compound ones.

Compound subject Two or more elements standing as the subject of one verb are called a *compound subject:*

> *Capitalists, militarists, and ecclesiastics* co-operate in education, because all depend for their power upon the prevalence of emotionalism and the rarity of critical judgment.—BERTRAND RUSSELL, *What I Believe,* p. 53

The verb following a compound subject is usually plural:

Christianity and humanity *have* gone hand in hand throughout history.

Some special cases are described under *Subject and verb § 2. See also Chapter 2, "Compound subjects," page 61.

Compound words Compound words in written English are combinations of two or more words which are written as one word or hyphened: *doorknob, notwithstanding, quarter-hour, father-in-law, drugstore.* But the conventions of writing ignore a large number of compounds which though written as separate words express more than the sum of the parts: the *White House, high school, post office.* In speech these are usually distinguished by the stronger stress on the first words: compare *a white house* and *the White House.*

Questions about the use of the hyphen in compound words are discussed in *Hyphen, and questions about their plurals in *Plurals § 5. See also *Group words.

Concluding paragraphs Revision: Revise the end of your paper to round out the discussion of your subject so that the paper ends strongly.

Concl

For discussion of concluding paragraphs and examples, see Chapter 6, "Concluding paragraphs," page 168; Chapter 10, "The close," page 291.

Concrete words Revision: Replace the abstract word or words by concrete ones.

Concr

Concrete words name persons and things that can be seen and touched (*bus, waitress, filing case*), in contrast to abstract words for acts, ideas, qualities, relationships (*flowing, theory, cleanliness*).

For discussion see Chapter 8, "Concrete words," page 217, and "Abstract words," page 219.

Conditions Conditional clauses state a condition or action necessary for the truth or occurrence of the main statement of a sentence. *If* is by far the most common conjunction for conditional clauses, with its negatives *if not* and *unless* (=*if not*), and *whether* (=*if . . . if, if . . . or if*). Somewhat more Formal words and phrases introducing conditions are *in case, provided, provided that, on condition that, in the event that.*

1. *Simple conditions.* Simple (or practical) conditions are statements of actual or reasonable conditions under which the main statement will hold. The indicative (ordinary) verb forms are used:

If the semaphore arm is horizontal, you know that a train is in that block of track.

He will be there *unless something happens to his car.*

Whether he comes or not, I shall go just the same.

An older type of condition survives in some proverbs:

Spare the rod and spoil the child. (If you spare the rod, you will spoil the child.)

In speech, we often express condition by a compound sentence:

You just try that and you'll be sorry.

2. *Less vivid conditions.* Less vivid (theoretical or hypothetical but still possible) conditions are usually made with *should . . . would* or with the past tense:

If he should raise his offer another $100, I would take it.

Or: *If he raised his offer,* I would take it.

If you revised your papers carefully, your writing would improve and would receive a higher grade.

3. *Contrary to fact conditions.* Conditions that cannot be met, or that are untrue, contrary to fact, are indicated by the past tense of the verb used in a present or future sense (If he *was* here [now], we would have seen him). In some Formal English, especially in writing, the plural form of the past tense is sometimes used in the third person singular, usually called a subjunctive (If he were here . . .). Formal English also sometimes uses a rather archaic inversion (*Were* he here . . .).

General: If I was going to be there, I'd be glad to help.

Formal: If I were President, I would change that.

General: If I had known what I do [or know] now, I would [I'd] never have let him go.

Formal: Had I known what I now know, I should never have let him go. (Inversion with no conjunction)

General: If he was only here, he . . . .

Formal: If he were only here, he . . . .

(See also *if, *Subjunctives. References: Curme, *Syntax,* pp. 317-332, 421-429; Fries, *AEG,* pp. 104-107; Jespersen, p. 254 ff.)

Conjugation The inflectional changes and phrasal forms of a verb or a group of verbs of the same type to show person, number, voice, and tense. See *Verbs, *Tenses of verbs, *Principal parts of verbs.

Conjunction *Conjunction* is the traditional term for a word which introduces and ties clauses together and joins series of words and phrases. In this *Guide-Index* conjunctions are discussed according to their conventional classification:

*Coordinating (*and, but, for,* etc.)

*Correlative (*either . . . or, not only . . . but,* etc.)

*Conjunctive adverbs (*however, therefore, consequently,* etc.)

*Subordinating (*as, because, since, so that, when,* etc.)

There are also articles on many of the particular conjunctions: **although,* **and,* **as,* **because,* **but,* and so on. The article *Contact clauses discusses joining clauses without connectives; pages 56-60 discuss in detail contact clauses and comma faults.

Since most conjunctions are derived from other parts of speech, especially from adverbs, identifying them as a part of speech is not always possible, nor is the distinction between coordinating and subordinating conjunctions always apparent. Professor Fries attempts a distinction as follows:

> Perhaps the most significant difference . . . lies in the fact that these function words of inclusion [subordinating conjunctions] at the beginning of a sentence look forward to a coming sentence unit [dependent clause], while the signals of sequence [coordinating conjunctions] look backward to the preceding sentence unit [main clause].–*Structure of English,* p. 253

(References: Fries, *AEG,* pp. 206-240; Roberts, pp. 231-242; Harold Whitehall, *Structural Essentials of English* (New York, 1956), pp. 65-77; all grammars have discussions.)

Conj **Conjunctions, use** Revision: Make the conjunction marked more accurate (§ 1) or more appropriate to the style of the passage (§ 2).

1. *Accurate conjunctions.* 2. *Weight.* 3. *Repetition of conjunctions.* 4. *Coordination versus subordination.*

1. *Accurate conjunctions.* An exact use of conjunctions in fitting together clauses is a sign of mature, practiced writing. In everyday speech we get along with a relatively small number–*and, as, but, so, when,* and a few others. We don't bother to emphasize shades of meaning and exact relationships, which are suggested by pauses, tones of voice, gestures. In writing, accurate connectives go a long way toward making up for the loss of these oral means of holding ideas together.

Accurate use of conjunctions needs to be stressed. There are some easy temptations, like using *but* when there is no contrast between the statements (see *but § 2). Some conjunctions vary in definiteness of meaning: *As* means *because,* but means it very weakly (*as § 1); **while* may mean *although* or *whereas,* but the core of its meaning relates to time. Such niceties in the use of these words are discussed in the articles on the particular conjunctions.

2. *Weight.* It is important for the conjunctions to be appropriate to other traits of style. Their weight should fit with the weight of other words and with the formality or informality of constructions.

The most common fault here is the use of the *conjunctive adverbs (*however, therefore, consequently . . .*) in General writing. These words are heavy and fit best in rather Formal style. *But* and *however,* for example, both connect statements in opposition, but one cannot always be substituted for the other. *But* fits in all varieties, but *however* is often too Formal or too heavy for General writing:

> The entrance and registration desk didn't strike me as beautiful. From here, however, I went upstairs and then I could see what they meant. (But from here. . . .)

The English language has a number of long connecting phrases that will weaken a written style when used in place of shorter, more compact conjunctions:

> At that time going to the movies was the usual evening pastime *in the same manner in which* [better: *as*] watching television is today.

(See *Conjunctive adverbs and *Function words.)

3. *Repetition of conjunctions.* Repeating a conjunction at the beginning of each element of a series gives distinctness to each element, avoids possible confusion, and gives the advantages of clear-cut *parallelism. This is more characteristic of Formal writing and often gives a definite rhythm:

> . . . designs of spears and shields and bastions and all the pomp of heraldry.—NORMAN DOUGLAS, *Siren Land,* p. 152
>
> For these five days and nights the Australians lived and ate and slept in that gallery of the mine of death, . . .—JOHN MASEFIELD, *Gallipoli,* p. 165

On the other hand, omitting *and* before the last member of a short series results in a crisp emphasis:

> High vacuums are essential not only to the distillation of vitamins but also in the manufacture of thermos bottles, radio tubes, X-ray apparatus, [ ] electric lamps.—*Time,* Nov. 28, 1938

(See *Series, *Telegraphic style.)

4. *Coordination versus subordination.* For discussion of this phase of the use of conjunctions see *Subordination and Chapter 2, "Complex sentences," page 50.

References: Curme, *Parts of Speech,* Chapter 7, and *Syntax,* §§ 19 and 21, and index references.

Conjunctive adverbs 1. A number of words primarily adverbs are used also as connectives. They are called *conjunctive adverbs* (or *transitional adverbs*). Their adverbial meaning remains rather prominent, so that they are relatively weak connectives. Used between clauses they are regarded as making compound sentences. The most common are:

accordingly	furthermore	*namely
*also (see *too)	hence	nevertheless
anyhow	*however	(*so)
anyway (colloquial)	indeed	still
*besides	likewise	*then
consequently	moreover	*therefore

> Adverb: No campaign, however violent, could make him vote.
>
> Conjunction: The results were poor; *however* we were not surprised.

2. *Weight and use.* The important fact about the conjunctive adverbs is that most of them are relatively heavy connectives. With the exception of *so* they are most appropriate in Formal writing, in sentences of some length and complexity, and in rather routine, stiff exposition, but are not so appropriate in General writing. They are now more used to connect the thought of separate sentences than the thought of clauses within the same sentence.

One of the duties of theme readers is to remove these stilted connectives from the ordinarily simple and straightforward writing of students. (They probably appear as a result of school exercises in the use of semicolons.) Note these appropriate and inappropriate uses:

It is, *therefore,* unfortunate that at a time like the present, which plainly calls for a Socrates, we should instead have got a Mencken. [Appropriate, as is suggested by the Formal sentence structure; connects with thought of preceding sentence]–IRVING BABBITT, *On Being Creative,* p. 205

When morning came, *however,* I was still sick; *nevertheless,* when the bugle blew, I got up. *Consequently,* I looked very white at breakfast. (Connectives much too heavy for the material and context.)

3. *Position.* Conjunctive adverbs are often placed within their clauses instead of at the beginning. This helps take the initial stress from them and gives it to more important words. When they are so placed, they are usually set off by commas as in the sentences in § 2 above.

4. *Punctuation.* The conventional rule of editors is that a clause introduced by a conjunctive adverb is preceded by a semicolon. This is generally true, but with *so* a comma is sufficient:

The whole forenoon had been a complete bore, *so* we wanted to make sure that we had a good time after lunch.

The advice sometimes given to strengthen *so* and *then* by adding *and* ("*and so* we wanted to make sure . . .") is usually wrong, since *and* adds nothing to the meaning of the connective. If the illustrative sentence above was to be really improved, it could be written:

The whole forenoon had been such a complete bore that we wanted to make sure we had a good time after lunch.

connected with, in connection with are wordy locutions, usually for *in* or *with:*

The social life in connection with a fraternity [in a fraternity] will be something you have never experienced before.

Construction A construction is a group of words which stand in some grammatical relationship to each other, as that of modifier and headword (*black cat*), preposition and object (*to* the *roof*), or subject and predicate (*They walked slowly*). A grammatical pattern may be spoken of as a construction, as in the phrases *sentence constructions, parallel constructions.* (For some of the commonest grammatical slips see Chs. 2 and 3.)

contact The objections to the use of *contact* in contexts like "Will you contact Mr. Hubble?" rest on the fact that the use came out of salesmanship–and many people have unpleasant associations with being "contacted" or with brokers' "contact men." Others object to using business terms in nonbusiness contexts. But the usage seems to serve a purpose in many fields besides business and must now be considered established in Standard English. (See *Divided usage. Reference: *College English,* 1955, 16:247.)

Contact clauses Two or more clauses of a sentence that stand together without a specific connective between them are known as *contact clauses.*

Many coordinate sentences are in the form of contact clauses, as in the famous "I came, I saw, I conquered" or in "But in him the pretence is justified: he has enjoyed thinking out his subject, he will delight in his work when it is done" (Max Beerbohm, *Yet Again,* p. 77). Clauses which in meaning seem subordinate are also sometimes set beside the main clause without connective:

> . . . and Soames lowered his eyes, he did not want to embarrass the girl.—JOHN GALSWORTHY, *Swan Song,* p. 103
>
> Give your decision, it will probably be right. But do not give your reasons, they will most certainly be wrong.—BERNARD HART, *The Psychology of Insanity.*

This very old type of sentence punctuation has been outlawed in the past by prescriptive grammar, though never quite abandoned by writers. In recent years it has re-emerged into literature from speech as an accurate transcription of a natural and common form of expression.

Contact clauses have a definite bearing upon one of the perennial problems of writing, the "comma fault," since many sentences containing clauses put together without expressed connectives are really effective as they stand and need no expressed connective. They are especially common and appropriate in rapid narrative where specific labeling of causes and results would slow up the movement, as in the sentence just quoted from Galsworthy. They are less common in straight exposition but occasionally occur. Many, of course, are the result of carelessness, but many also, as these examples suggest, are characteristic of a rapid and natural style. Deciding on the effectiveness of contact clauses is one of the more difficult problems of students and teachers.

Successful and unsuccessful contact clauses are discussed fully in Chapter 2, "Contact clauses," page 59. See also *Comma fault. References: Curme, *Syntax,* pages 170-173; Jespersen, pages 360-361.

content, contents *Adjectives:* The rather Formal *content* (He would be content with less) and the more common *contented* (He would be contented with less) are stressed on the second syllable: kən tent′, kən ten′təd.

Nouns: As a noun, *content* is used more as an abstract term (the content of the course) and in amounts (the moisture content); *contents* is rather more concrete (the contents of the box, the contents of the book). The nouns are pronounced kon′tent, kon′tents; kən-tent′ and kən tents′ survive only as variant British pronunciations.

Context The context is the discourse that surrounds and limits a word or passage that is being separately discussed: "The word sounds insulting, but in its *context* it could not possibly give offense."

1. The context is tremendously important in revealing the particular meanings of words. What, for instance, does the word *check* mean? By itself no one can tell even whether it is noun or verb or adjective, much less which of the forty dictionary senses of the word is meant. Yet in actual use, in definite contexts, it gives no trouble:

They were able to *check* the fire at the highway.
The treasurer's books *check* with the vouchers.
He drew a *check* for the entire amount.
The tablecloth had a red and white *check*.
He moved his bishop and proclaimed *"Check!"*
With difficulty he held his temper in *check*.
He had the *check* list on the desk in front of him.

And so on. *Check* has more senses than most English words, but a very large proportion of our words have more than one sense so that their exact meaning must be gathered from the context–and ordinarily it can be. Context is important not only in indicating the particular denotative sense of a word, as illustrated with *check,* but also in indicating the connotative value of the word, as suggested in the quotation in the first paragraph of this article.

2. Statements of ideas depend for full understanding upon the context in which they stand, and in quoting or alluding to a writer's thought we should be careful to take the context into account. Cardinal Newman's definition of a gentleman as a man who never inflicts pain is often referred to as though it represented Newman's ideal, but in its context (*The Idea of a University,* Discourse viii) he was showing that this gentleman is all very well but without religious conviction he falls far short of being an ideal type. Taking care that allusions and quotations are true to the context in which they occur, that they really represent the ideas of their authors, is a basic requirement of an honest writer. (See Ch. 8, "The use of connotative words," p. 222.)

continual, continuous *Continual* means "frequently or closely repeated," with little or no time between:

Dancing requires continual practice.
He continually interrupted the lecture with foolish questions.

Continuous means "without interruption," "unbroken":

A continuous procession of cars passed during the hour.
He has been continuously in debt for ten years.
But: He is continually running into debt.

Sometimes the context rather blurs the distinction: The roar of the planes overhead continually disturbed us (or: was continuously disturbing).

Contractions Since contractions are words from which an unstressed syllable is dropped in speaking, they belong to spoken English. In writing, contractions are appropriate in Informal English and usually in General English but are ordinarily out of place in treatments of dignified subjects and in a Formal style, whether in routine exposition (as in academic papers) or in more literary compositions. You could probably read through a chemistry textbook without finding a single contraction; but you would find the speech of a person who avoided contractions excessively stilted.

A more Formal style is not achieved merely by writing out the contractions of Informal speech. "I have not time" is not good Formal English for the Informal "I haven't time." For Formal writing another idiom is often needed: "I have no time."

In General English the fitness of a contraction is usually determined in part by the naturalness with which it falls into place, in part by the rhythm:

> I didn't always appreciate French cooking myself. It tasted all right, but it was dainty and there wasn't much of it.—CLARENCE DAY, *Life With Father,* p. 11

Did not and *was not* would slow up the movement slightly.

Contractions are necessary in reporting most conversation and in writing dialog for plays and stories:

> "Your mother has the damnedest number of friends I ever heard of," said Father. "She's everlastingly meeting some old friend or other wherever she goes. I never see people I know when I'm traveling. But there isn't a city in Europe where your mother wouldn't spot a friend in five minutes."—CLARENCE DAY, *Life With Father,* p. 114

An apostrophe ordinarily stands in the place of the omitted letter or letters (*doesn't, can't, shouldn't, he's*), though only one apostrophe is used in *shan't, won't,* and *ain't.*

Conversion The use of a word generally found as one part of speech in the function of a different part of speech is called *conversion* or *functional shift:* a *must* book; a *commercial* (adjective used in the function of a noun, meaning the advertising part of a television program); in the *know*. Sometimes a writer will use the noun form in preference to the adjective form:

> . . . affected by the *monster* growth of London. . . .—SIR CHARLES GRANT ROBERTSON, *England Under the Hanoverians,* p. 337

Although this practice is not peculiar to the English language it is facilitated by the absence of those distinctive forms for the parts of speech, so characteristic of Latin, for example. *Round* is identified in dictionaries as *adj., n., v., adv.,* and *prep.,* but there is nothing in the form of the word itself to identify it as any of those. (For further discussion see *Parts of speech.)

Coordinating conjunctions 1. The principal coordinating conjunctions are: **and,* **but,* **for, nor* (= and not), **or,* **yet. Only* (I'd come, only I have a class) and **while* (He's an expert, while I know nothing about the game) and other connectives are also used as coordinating conjunctions. The *conjunctive adverbs (*therefore, how-*

ever, and so on) are coordinating connectives, as are the *correlative conjunctions (*either . . . or, not only . . . but,* and so on).

2. Coordinating conjunctions are used between words, phrases, clauses, or sentences. It is important that the elements they connect should be equal in grammatical rank and substantially equivalent in thought:

Words: books and papers; books, pamphlets, and magazines; sugar or salt

Phrases: in one ear and out the other

Clauses: I would venture to say *that his description is perfect,* but *that there are some who would not agree with that verdict.*–BONAMY DOBRÉE, *Modern Prose Style,* p. 69

Independent clauses: What they talk of was in the books, but there was the stimulus of personality.–ARTHUR E. HERTZLER, *The Horse and Buggy Doctor,* p. 181

3. For different effects of repeating or omitting conjunctions in a series see *Conjunctions § 3 and *Series.

4. For coordination versus subordination see Chapter 2, "Compound sentences," page 49, "Complex sentences," page 50, and *Subordination. For various uses of coordinating conjunctions see *Conjunctions, *Clauses §1, and articles on individual conjunctions.

Coordination is the relationship between two or more elements regarded as of the same grammatical rank. See *Coordinating conjunctions § 2.

Copy Manuscript before printing is *copy.* For points of form see *Typewritten copy and Chapter 9, "Preparing the manuscript," page 262.

Correlative conjunctions 1. Some coordinating conjunctions are used in pairs:

both . . . and   either . . . or   neither . . . nor   not so . . . as
not only . . . but [but also]   whether . . . or

2. Except *either . . . or* and *both . . . and,* these correlative conjunctions are slightly Formal, showing a more conscious sentence planning than is common in Informal or General English:

Not only was the water muddy, but it had tadpoles swimming in it.

3. Since these correlatives are coordinating conjunctions, they provide the skeleton for two parallel constructions. In practice, especially in speech, the parallelism is not always complete (I wondered whether *I should go* or *to beg off*). Rhetoricians sometimes insist that in writing, the more complete the parallelism, the more satisfying the result is likely to be. This means not only that the elements connected by the conjunctions should be of equal value but also that the constructions linked by the conjunctions should have the same word order, as in the first part of this sentence. But a strict adherence to this principle makes for artificiality, and variations, such as the shift from active to passive in the last example below, are common:

Nouns: He said that both *the novel* and *the play* were badly written.
Adjectives: He must have been either *drunk* or *crazy*.
Phrases: They can be had not only *in the usual sizes* but also *in the outsizes.*
Clauses: Whether *the sale was for cash* or *a mortgage was given*, it seemed too much to pay.

See also *Parallel constructions. Reference: Lillian Mermin, "On the Placement of Correlatives in Modern English," *American Speech,* 1943, 18:171-191, and 19:66-68. For number of verb in constructions with *either . . . or,* see *Subject and verb § 2b, and as a reference, Dorothy J. Hughes, *College English,* 1941, 2:697-699.

Counter words Words that are used more frequently than their exact meanings warrant have been called *counter words.* They are especially words of general approval or disapproval. Their use is a matter of fashion and is related to slang, except that they are ordinary English words and lack the element of surprise that good slang has. In Elizabethan times *fair* was such a word; recently *fabulous, delicious, definitely, mixed-up* have had such currency. In ordinary speech *cute, fine, grand, lousy, lovely, gorgeous, poor* are samples, and in more educated circles words like *adjusted, creative, dynamic, structure, vital,* and often epithets like *red, radical, conservative, reactionary* are used as vague expressions of like or dislike without regard to more exact meaning.

In advertising and other more or less forced writing *super-, -conscious* (we are *air-conscious, flower-conscious, defense-conscious* by turns), *-conditioned, -type, -wise,* and at the moment *streamlined, bottleneck, propaganda* are all counter words. They are appropriate in Informal English (in which *certainly* has the sense of *yes*) but seem out of place in serious writing:

Today, the halfway spot in the two-week streamlined fair . . . .
Again, their spirit may be irrevocably broken, their lives turned into a streamlined hell.

couple 1. The primary meaning of *couple* is two persons or things associated in some way, typically as in "a married couple." In speech it is equivalent to the numeral *two:* a couple of pencils; or equivalent to *a few:* a couple of minutes.

2. This spoken usage has resulted in frequent obscuring of the following *of* and its omission in writing:

He'd had a couple drinks. I'll be gone only a couple days.
A couple boys were throwing stones at a dog.

This clipped idiom is finding its way into print in General writing:

Mr. Freeman's statement left unanswered a couple [ ] pertinent questions:—*The New Republic,* June 16, 1952, p. 15

Course names In general discussions, only the names of college subjects that are proper adjectives (the languages) are capitalized. In writing a list of courses including one or more of these proper adjectives, it is possible to capitalize them all for consistency (and courtesy), though the distinction would usually be kept, as in the first example:

> My program is biology, chemistry, European history, English composition, and French.
>
> My program is Biology, Chemistry, European History, English Composition, and French.

In referring to the various departments of an institution, all names would be capitalized, as they would also when preceding the number of a course:

the Department of Applied Psychology	Psychology 201
the English Department	English 101
the Department of History	History 347
the School of Biological Sciences	Biology 413

In newspaper style *department* and *school* would probably not be capitalized when they follow the proper name.

curriculum *Curriculum* still has the Latin plural *curricula,* though *curriculums* is becoming common. The adjective is *curricular,* and the compound adjective with *extra* is ordinarily written without a hyphen: *extracurricular. Curriculum* is also used as a modifier:

> . . . the guidance of college students, curriculum and instructional problems at the college level. . . .–*Current Issues in Higher Education,* 1955, p. 220

D

Besides its typical sound as in *die, do, addict, pod, addle, d* represents the *t* sound when it follows the sound of *f, k, p, s, ch, sh,* or *th* in the same syllable: *asked* (askt), *blessed* (blest, but bles′id), *kicked* (kikt), *raced* (rāst), *telegraphed* (tel′ə graft), *fished* (fisht), *matched* (macht), *toothed* (tōōtht). The *t* sound is produced exactly like the *d* sound except that in its production the vocal chords are not vibrated; it is voiceless, *d* is voiced. With the loss in Early Modern English of the vowel of *ed,* the *d* was next to a voiceless sound and lost its voiced quality.

In Standard English in the seventeenth and eighteenth centuries, *d* before an unstressed *i* or *y* sound usually became *j: grandeur* (gran′jər), *soldier* (sōl′jər). Spelling pronunciation has now restored the iə pronunciation in some of these words and the older *j* sound is heard only in the speech of some older or Nonstandard speakers: *Indian* (in′jən). British and American practice also differ: British English often has i mē′jit for *immediate* but kôr diəl for *cordial.* There are local extensions of the sound to stressed *u* syllables: jōō′ti (*duty*).

Dangling modifiers Revision: Revise the sentence so that the expression marked is clearly related to the word it is intended to modify. *DM*

A construction which from its position in a sentence seems to modify a word which it cannot sensibly modify is said to be "misrelated" or to "dangle" and should be avoided in writing. See Chapter 2, "Revising dangling modifiers," page 64.

A participle which is used in the function of an adjective should modify accurately either a noun or pronoun:

Looking further to the left, we saw the spire of a church. (*Looking* clearly modifies *we.*)

Defined in psychological terms, a fanatic is a man who consciously overcompensates a secret doubt. (*Defined* clearly modifies *fanatic.*)—ALDOUS HUXLEY, *Proper Studies,* p. 220

A verbid that precedes the main clause and does not relate to the subject of that clause is dangling:

Upon telling my story to the advisor, he stopped and thought. (For: When I told. . . .)

Motoring down Route 17 toward New York City, numerous signs read "Visit Our Snake Farm." (For: *Motoring* down Route 17 toward New York City, *we* saw numerous signs that read. . . .)

What if, forced to climb over this solid cloud bank, ice should form on the wings and force them down into the wild country? (The ice isn't forced to climb.)

Born in England in 1853, John MacDowell's seafaring activities began after he had emigrated to this country. (His seafaring activities were not born in England.)

Dangling participles should be avoided simply because educated readers do not expect to find them. As a rule there is no real question of the intended meaning of the sentence, though sometimes the faulty reference of a participle is ludicrous as in Professor Arthur Kennedy's gem: Having swelled because of the rains, the workman was unable to remove the timber.

Such dangling constructions should not be confused with *absolute phrases, in which the participial phrase is equivalent to a subordinate clause and is properly used, especially for adding details: He had worked for four hours, copy piling up quite satisfactorily. (See *Participles for further examples of these constructions. References: Curme, *Syntax,* pp. 158-160; Reuben Steinbach, "The Misrelated Constructions," *American Speech,* 1930, 5:181-197.)

Infinitive phrases may be dangling:

Faulty: To get the most out of a sport, the equipment must be in perfect condition. (The equipment does not profit from the sport.)

Improved: To get the most out of a sport, you must have your equipment in perfect condition.

This construction should not be confused with an absolute infinitive phrase which is well established in Standard English.

To judge from his looks, he can't be more than forty-five.

(See *Infinitives § 5.)

Phrases are sometimes similarly dangling:

At eleven, our family moved to Kansas City. (Clearer: When I was eleven, our family moved to Kansas City.)

Dash

1. *To mark sharp turn in thought.* 2. *Before a final summarizing statement.* 3. *Between compound clauses.* 4. *To inclose parenthetical statements.* 5. *Overuse.* 6. *With other marks.* 7. *Other uses.* 8. *Double dash.* 9. *En dash.*

Three dashes of varying lengths are used in printing: – (en dash), — (em dash, the usual mark), and —— (2-em dash). On the typewriter use a hyphen for the first, two hyphens not spaced away from the neighboring words for the usual dash, and four hyphens for the long dash.

The em dash, the one we have in mind when we say just *dash,* has aroused more discussion and more violent feeling than punctuation seems to deserve. Some textbooks and some publishers forbid its use generally, while others specify minute shades of meaning which they believe it indicates. Some writers rarely use it. Others, especially in matter not intended for publication, use it at the expense of other marks.

Most dashes are roughly equivalent to commas—that is, they separate units within a sentence—but if used sparingly they suggest a definite tone, usually a note of surprise, an emotional emphasis. Some other mark could always be substituted for the dash, but there would be a difference in movement and suggestiveness in the sentence. At its best it is a rather abrupt and emphatic mark.

1. *To mark sharp turn in thought.* The most typical use of the dash is to mark a sharp turn in the thought or construction of a sentence:

Of course, there is one place safe from lawyers—in heaven.—ARTHUR E. HERTZLER, *The Horse and Buggy Doctor,* p. 134

The danger of using terms like "romantic" and "classic"—this does not however give us permission to avoid them altogether—does not spring so much from the confusion caused by those who use these terms about their own work, as from inevitable shifts of meaning in context.—T. S. ELIOT, *After Strange Gods,* p. 27

2. *Before a final summarizing statement.* A dash is often used before an inserted or added phrase, usually one that summarizes what has just been said or that gives contrasting or emphasizing details of what has been said, or often a striking apposition. This dash has the force of a vigorous comma.

The waiting, the watching, the hundreds of small necessary acts about the sickroom—all this was past.

The elements of every story are these five: character, incident, nature, fate, and milieu–the social, historical, vital background.–D. H. PARKER, *Principles of Aesthetics,* p. 236

He [the Englishman of the 1870's and 80's] was strongly in favor of peace–that is to say, he liked his wars to be fought at a distance and, if possible, in the name of God.–GEORGE DANGERFIELD, *The Death of Liberal England,* p. 7

3. *Between compound clauses.* A dash is sometimes used between two compound clauses of a sentence, for abrupt separation:

The "womanly" woman became as obsolete as the buggy. The nurse must tend the children, the cook must order the meals–life must be spectacular, not frittered away in little household dullnesses.–IRENE and ALLEN CLEATON, *Books and Battles,* p. 92

4. *To inclose parenthetical statements.* Dashes are sometimes used to inclose parenthetical statements that are more Informal than parentheses would indicate, separating the expression from the context more than commas but less definitely than parentheses would:

The general effect upon readers–most of them quite uneducated–is quite different from what the serious messiah intends.–T. S. ELIOT, *After Strange Gods,* p. 36

5. *Overuse.* The overuse of dashes detracts from their special quality and proves that they are, as Mr. Dobrée says, "a sandy joint."

She [Marlene Dietrich] was turned into a static image of lorelei charm, frozen in a lovely pose–and to bring that image again to life, there seems to be no proposal except to point again to its over-publicized legs, and its–by this time–rubber-stamp "allure."

(See also *Schoolgirl style.)

6. *With other marks.* Formerly a dash was often combined with other marks, especially with a comma or a colon, but this use has declined. The dash adds nothing in the salutation of a letter (*Dear Sir:*–means no more than *Dear Sir:*) and adds a displeasing mark to the page. Within sentences the old comma-dash combination has very generally disappeared also, so that now we find either a comma, or if a desire for emphasis makes it useful, a dash alone.

7. *Other uses.*

a) In place of a colon when the statement ends with a question mark: How do you explain this?–"English 23, F."

b) To precede a credit line, as at the end of the quoted passages in this book.

c) After introductory words which are to be repeated before each of the following lines:

We recommend–

That a constitution be drawn up.

That it be presented to the student council. Etc.

d) To separate run-in questions and answers in testimony: Q. Did you see him?–A. No.

8. *Double dash.* Besides being used in some arbitrary places prescribed by particular publishing houses, the 2-em dash is used chiefly as an end stop in dialog when a speech is interrupted:

"... I can't say, of course, whether or not my layman's logic adds lustre to the gladsome light of jurisprudence——"

"Your reasoning is consistent as far as it goes," cut in Markham tartly. "But it is hardly complete enough to have led you directly to the linen-closet this morning."–S. S. VAN DINE, *The Greene Murder Case,* p. 220

9. *En dash.* A writer does not need to worry about the en dash, slightly longer than a hyphen, but printers use it between inclusive figures (*1837–1901*) and instead of a hyphen when one or both elements of an expression ordinarily requiring a hyphen are made up of two words: *the New York–Bar Harbor express.*

Reference: Summey, pages 101-104.

data Pronounced dā′tə or sometimes dat′ə or (affecting Latin) dä′tə. (See *Latin and English.)

Data is the plural form of the Latin noun *datum,* little used in English; *data* is the usual English form for both singular and plural. Its meaning is actually collective and may sometimes stress a group of facts as a unit and so be used with a singular verb. When it refers to the individual facts, *data* is used with a plural:

Singular idea: The actual data of history *consists* of contemporary facts in the form of remains and documents.–MORRIS R. COHEN, *Reason and Nature,* p. 381

Singular idea: Data concerning measurement of social attitudes *has* been included in the next chapter....–LUELLA COLE, *Psychology of Adolescence,* p. 102

Plural idea: When the data *have* been secured the task is to analyze, to sift, to select and to arrange those data which *bear* upon each particular phase of the object or event examined until at the end the scientist has what one might call a logical construct.–G. D. HIGGINSON, *Fields of Psychology,* p. 10

Either possible: These data are [This data is] unpublished.

The singular verb can be safely used in any but the most Formal writing. (Reference: A. Bartlett in "Current English Forum," *College English,* 1954, 15:417.)

date is Informal and General for "appointment, engagement" (I had a date for that evening) and slang in the sense of "person with whom one has an engagement" (After all, she was his date). *Blind date* is one of the more useful and economical Informal expressions, expressing in two syllables something that would take several words to express in Formal English.

Dates Unless you have good reason for some other form, write dates in the common method: August 19, 1950. The form *19 August 1950* is increasingly popular (partly as a result of its use by the armed services) and has a small advantage in that it makes a comma unnecessary.

Never write the year out in words except in formal social announcements, invitations, etc. Expressions like "January in the year 1885" are wasteful. *January 1885* is enough.

If saving space is important, or in business or reference writing, months having more than four letters should be abbreviated:

Jan. Feb. Mar. Apr. Aug. Sept. Oct. Nov. Dec.

In Informal writing, figures are convenient: 8/19/58, 11/27/58. (In England and other European countries the day of the month is usually put first: 27-11-58.)

Better style now usually omits the *st, nd, rd, th* from the day of the month: May 1 rather than May 1st, September 17 rather than September 17th.

In Formal style the day of the month may be written in words when the year is not given (September seventeen or September seventeenth).

Roman numerals are rarely used for the year except for decoration, as on the title page of a book.

See *Numbers § 1a; *Letters; *Social correspondence.

Dative case English has no distinctive form for the dative case and can hardly be said to have a dative case in any sense. A noun in a construction that in another language might have a dative is in the common case form and a pronoun is in the accusative case form. Usually we have a phrase made with *to, for,* or *on.* (See *Objects § 2.)

Deadwood Revision: Remove the meaningless word or words, revising the sentence if necessary.

Dead

Deadwood is a convenient label for a type of *wordiness in which a word or phrase adds nothing at all to the meaning of the statement.

In many *cases* students [Many students] have profited by this.

He was a handsome [looking] man.

The book is divided into various sections, all dealing with [the matter of] unemployment.

Many phrases of this sort make writing flabby and are a mark of amateur or careless writing. (For further examples and discussion, see Ch. 7, "Economy in sentences," p. 186, and *case.)

Declension is the change of form of nouns and pronouns (and in many languages the form of adjectives and participles also) to show number (singular or plural), gender (masculine, feminine, neuter), and case (nominative, genitive, accusative). The English noun has only two regular forms (the genitive and the common form, which is used for all other relationships), and the variations in pronoun forms are not regular; English has no declension in the sense that Latin has. (See *Case, the articles on the various cases, *Plurals, and the articles referred to there.)

definitely *Definitely* is one of the most frequently misspelled words. Remember there is no *a* in it and associate def i *ni* tion with def i *ni*te and def i *ni*te ly.

At present *definitely* is overused as a *counter word to give emphasis or in the sense of "certainly, quite" (I will not do it, definitely; He was definitely worse than usual; She definitely disapproves of those methods; But definitely!) instead of in its more limited sense of "clear-cut, in a definite manner."

Degrees Ordinarily a person's academic degrees are not given with his name except in college publications, reference works, and articles and letters where the degrees indicate competence in a particular field, as in a doctor's comment on a medical matter. When used, they are separated from the name by a comma and in alumni publications are often followed by the year in which they were granted:

Harvey J. Preble, A.B.　　Harvey J. Preble, A.B. '08
James T. Thomson, M.A.　　James T. Thomson, A.B. '21, A.M. '24
Robert Bernath, M.D., gave the principal address.
Royce Walton, B. Arch., discussed Wright's mile-high building.

As a rule, except in reference lists, only a person's highest degree in an academic or professional field needs to be mentioned.

If the institution granting the degree is named, the following forms are usual:

George H. Cook, A.B. (Grinnell), A.M. (Indiana), Ph. D. (Chicago)
D. C. Browning, B.A. (Oxon. [= Oxford])
J. H. Plumb, Ph. D. (Cantab. [= Cambridge])

Two kinds of degrees are granted by American colleges and universities. *Earned* ("in course") degrees are given at the completion of a required course of study. Some of the ones commonly granted are:

A.B. (*or* B.A.)–Bachelor of Arts
B.S.–Bachelor of Science
B.E.–Bachelor of Engineering
B.D.–Bachelor of Divinity
B. Mus.–Bachelor of Music
B. Arch.–Bachelor of Architecture
Ph. B.–Bachelor of Philosophy
LL.B.–Bachelor of Laws
A.M. (*or* M.A.)–Master of Arts
M.S.–Master of Science
M.E.–Master of Engineering
M.Ed. (*or* Ed.M.)–Master of Education
M.B.A.–Master of Business Administration
M.F.A.–Master of Fine Arts
M. Ped.–Master of Pedagogy (*or* M.Ed., Ed.M.–Master of Education)
Ed.D.–Doctor of Education
Ph. D.–Doctor of Philosophy
S.T.D.–Doctor of Sacred Theology
M.D.–Doctor of Medicine
D.D.S.–Doctor of Dental Surgery

Honorary ("honoris causa") degrees are given by institutions as a sign of respect. In the following list the four at left are the most common:

LL.D.–Doctor of Laws
D.D.–Doctor of Divinity
Lit(t). D.–Doctor of Literature *or* Letters
Sc. D.–Doctor of Science
D.C.L.–Doctor of Civil Law
L.H.D.–Doctor of Humanities
Eng.D.–Doctor of Engineering

British and other European degrees are similar but less numerous.

Delete means "take out, erase, remove." It is a direction to printers made by putting a Greek small *d* (δ–delta) in the margin and drawing a line through the matter to be removed. (See *Proofreading.)

To delete material in your manuscripts, simply draw a line through it (don't use parentheses or black it out completely).

Demonstrative adjectives and pronouns *This, that, these, those* are called demonstrative adjectives or demonstrative pronouns, according to their use in a sentence:

Adjectives: *This* car we bought in May.
Those fellows never think of anyone else.
Pronouns: *This* cost a good bit more than *those*.
That's a good idea.

(See *that, *this, *kind, sort.)

descendant *Descendant* is used as both adjective and noun; *descendent,* only as adjective. To be on the safe side, use descend*ant*.

detail Pronunciation is divided: di tāl′, dē′tāl, the first older, the second especially common in situations where the word is used a great deal (army life, architecture, composition, etc.).

Details Revision: Develop this topic more fully by giving pertinent details. *Det*

The development of a topic in writing usually comes from the use of details, small bits of observation, particular facts, and so on. They not only make the reader see clearly what you are discussing but are one of the chief sources of interest. (For the various uses of details see Ch. 6, pp. 139-147. See also Ch. 8, pp. 217-220.)

develop is the usual spelling for the verb and *development* for the noun; *develope* and *developement* are rare.

devil (and *hell*) seldom receive the courtesy of a capital except for stylistic emphasis.

Diagramming sentences Placing sentence elements in a traditional graphic organization to show their function in the sentence; of questionable value. (For a simpler, more useful method, see Ch. 2, pp. 44-47.)

Diagrams, graphs, etc. The function of diagrams, charts, graphs, and illustrations is to make a writer's meaning more clear and more concrete than his words alone could. They cannot be a substitute for a discussion in words, but they can make it easier for readers to grasp figures, to understand relationships, and especially to make comparisons between facts that can be graphically portrayed. They have also an incidental value for an article in that diagrams and charts attract attention and interest. It is part of a writer's work to prepare appropriate diagrams to accompany his text where they can be useful.

1. *Types of graphic devices.* Some of the commonest and most useful graphic devices (diagrams, charts, graphs, bars, and pictorial statistics) are illustrated on pages 494-496. Some general points in handling diagrams and charts are discussed on page 496.

a) Diagram. A schematic representation of the structure of something, a plan showing dimensions, direction for work, etc., as in the following diagram:

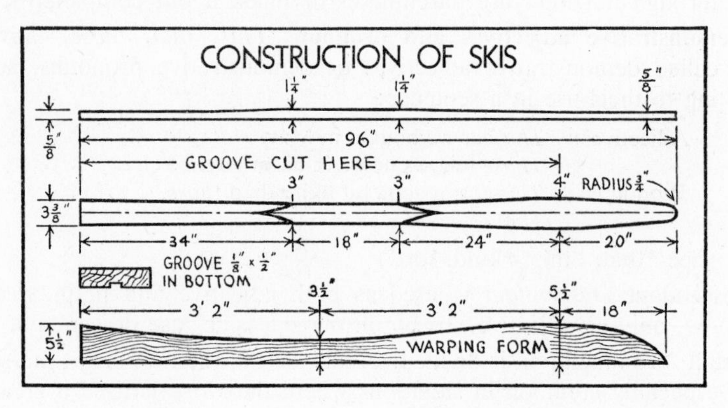

Science and Mechanics, February 1939

b) Chart. Showing organization and relationship:

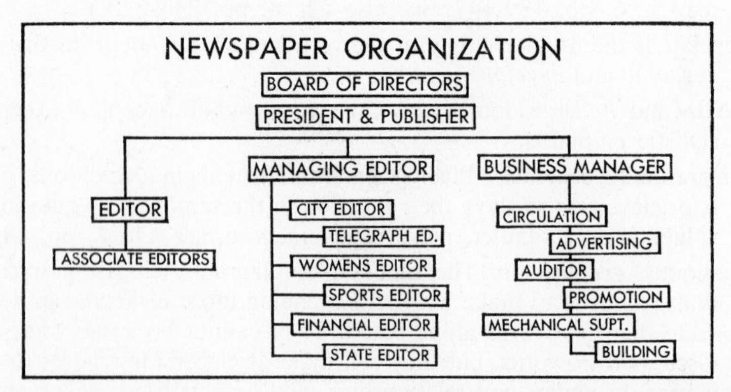

D. J. Hornberger and Douglas W. Miller, *Newspaper Organization,* Appendix B

c) Graph. Showing two or more variable facts:

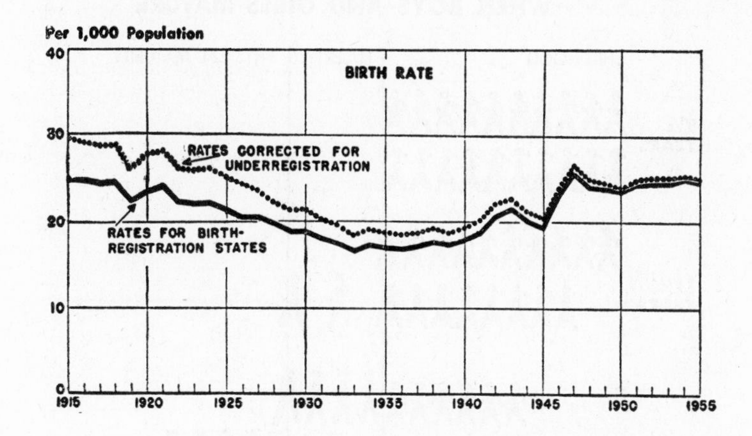

U.S. Bureau of the Census, *Statistical Abstract of the United States:* 1956 (77th ed.), Washington, D.C., 1956

d) Bars. To make comparison of amounts, etc.:

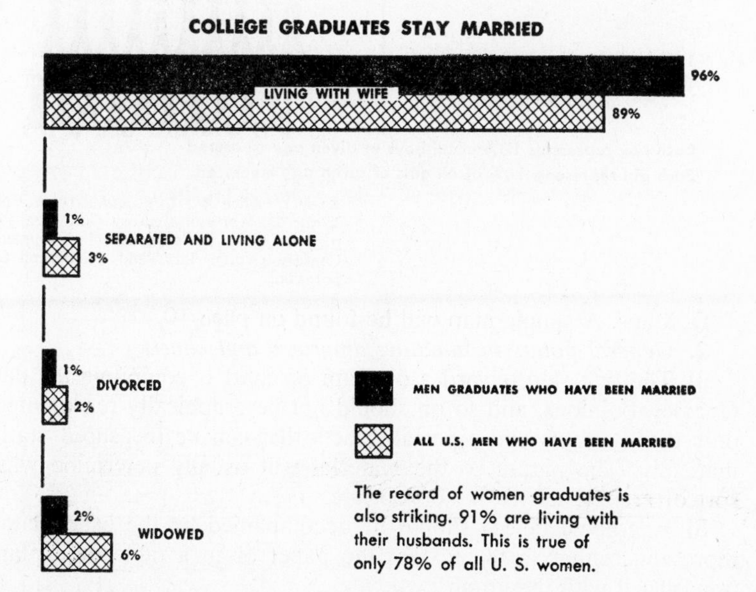

e) Pictorial statistics. Symbols to dramatize the material about which figures are given:

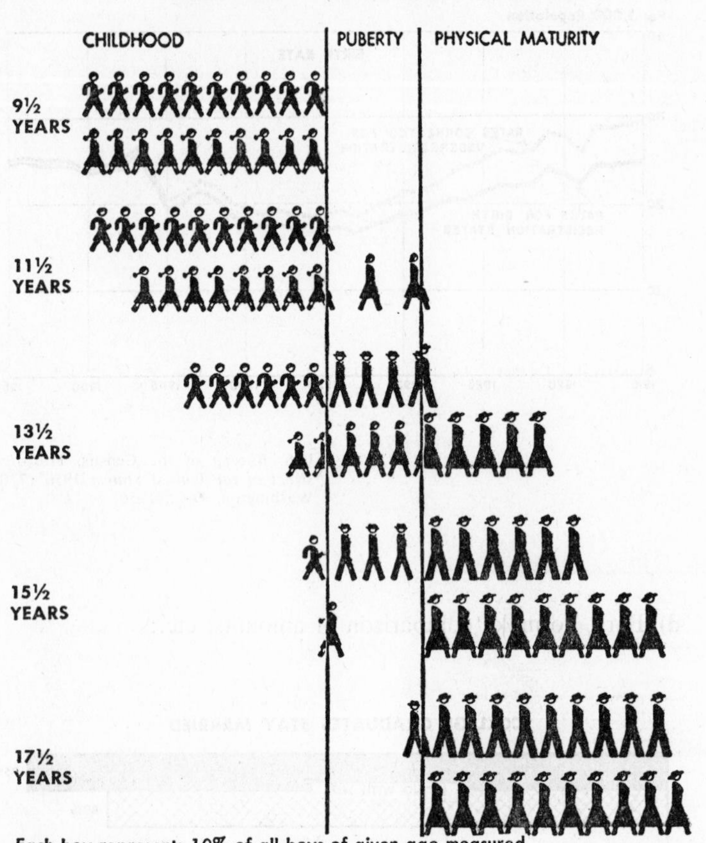

Keliher, Alice V. *Life and Growth.* New York: D. Appleton-Century Co., Inc., 1941, p. 159. Used by permission of Appleton-Century Crofts, Inc., and Pictograph Corporation.

f) Maps. A simple map will be found on page 10.

2. *General points in handling diagrams and charts.*

a) The first step toward a diagram or chart is compiling the data. Guesses, opinions, and so on should not be graphically represented—only definite facts and especially facts that can be measured mathematically. The nature of the material will usually determine which sort of graphic device is appropriate.

b) A graphic device should be accompanied by the exact data it represents, either in the text of the paper or in a table or explanation placed with the graph.

c) The graph should be made intelligible by clearly indicating the years, amounts, per cents, the scale it is drawn on, and so on. This is usually done at the bottom and along the sides.

(Compare *Illustration (Pictorial). References: Herbert Arkin and Raymond R. Colter, *Graphs–How to Make and Use Them* (New York, 1940); Frederick E. Croxton and Dudley J. Cowden, *Applied General Statistics,* 2nd ed., (New York, 1955), Chs. 4 and 6; and W. O. Sypherd, Alvin M. Fountain, and V. E. Gibbens, *Manual of Technical Writing* (Chicago, 1957), Ch. 7; chapters on graphic methods in other introductions to statistics.)

Dialects A dialect is the speech (words, sounds, stress, phrasing, grammatical habits) characteristic of a fairly definite region or group, or more accurately, it is speech that does not attract attention to itself among the residents of a region (*regional dialect*) or among members of a group (*group* or *class dialect*).

Localism is used in this book for a regional dialectal usage. Conspicuous dialectal words are usually out of place in Formal writing unless they are used to give a local flavor. They are more effective in speech, in fiction, and in Informal writing. (For description of dialects in the United States, see Ch. 1, "Variations due to place," p. 8, and for the use of localisms in writing, see Ch. 10, "Conversation," p. 289.)

Diction Revision: Replace the word marked with one that is more exact, more effective, or more appropriate. *D*

Diction here means primarily the choice of words in speaking or writing. Good diction means that the words seem to the reader or listener well chosen to convey the meanings or attitudes of the writer or speaker; faulty diction, that the words either fail to convey the meaning fully or accurately or do not satisfy the reader's expectation in some other way. Chapter 8, pages 204-241 discusses many problems of diction. Many specific words have articles of their own (*contact, *drunk, *hope, *however, *notorious, *try and–try to, *ye = the). Very often the solution to a question of diction will be found by referring to a dictionary.

Dieresis Two dots placed over the second of two consecutive vowels to show they are to be pronounced separately are referred to as a dieresis (dī er′ə sis): *reëxamine, coöperation.* A hyphen is often used to indicate that the vowels are to be kept separate, especially in words with *re-* (*re-enlist*). There is a tendency not to use either dieresis or hyphen in the more commonly used words, so that *cooperation* and *zoology,* for example, are now the more usual forms.

different The most common American written idiom with *different* is *from:*

> His second book was entirely different from his first.
>
> Sharon was so different from what we expected that we were all surprised.

But General usage is divided, with *than* commonly and *to* sometimes replacing *from* (*different to* is a common British idiom). *Different than* is especially common when the object is a clause:

> The house was a good deal different than he remembered it. (This idiom is neater than "different from what he remembered.")
>
> . . . as smart and vain and sweet a girl as Clyde had ever laid his eyes upon—so different to any he had ever known and so superior.—THEODORE DREISER, *An American Tragedy*, p. 225

Since many people still object to *different than,* students should avoid it in their Formal writing. (References: D. L. Bolinger, *The English Journal,* 1939, 28:480; Gladys D. Haase, *College English,* 1949, 10:345-47; Pooley, pp. 166-170.)

Digraph Two letters used together to spell a single sound are known as a *digraph.* English uses many digraphs:

ea as in *head* or *heat*	*ee* as in *seed*
ei as in *either* or *neighbor*	*oa* as in *coat*
oo as in *book* or *food*	*ph* as in *physics*
sh as in *shall*	*th* as in *then* or *thin*

dining *Dine, dined, dining, dining room* all have to do with eating—as does *dinner* with two *n*'s and a short *i; dinning* (short *i*) has to do with *din,* "noise."

Dine and *dining* are Formal words. *Dinner* is used in all varieties.

Diphthong A diphthong is a vowel-like sound made by moving the tongue, jaw, and lips from the position for one vowel to that of another while vibrating the vocal cords. The standard method of transcribing these glide sounds is to use two vowel symbols, which are to be interpreted as indicating where the diphthong begins and where it ends. The common distinctive diphthongs of American English are: ī (ä + i) oi (ô + i) ou (ä + oo) ū (i [y] + o͞o)

Most English vowels have some diphthongal quality. (For further details about American diphthongs, see J. S. Kenyon, *American Pronunciation,* § 327 ff, and the discussions of pronunciation in good modern dictionaries.)

Direct address is the term used to describe the construction in which persons (or objects) are addressed in speaking, reading, or writing:

> *My friends,* I wish you would forget this night.
> That's all right, *Mrs. Shephardson.*
> What do you think, *Doctor,* about his going home now?
> *Rain, rain,* go away.

As these examples show, words in direct address are separated from the rest of the sentence by a comma or, if they are in the middle of the sentence, by two commas.

disinterested From its first recorded uses in the seventeenth century, *disinterested* has been used in two senses: (1) impartial, not influenced by personal interest; (2) indifferent, inattentive, uninterested. (See *Oxford English Dictionary* and the 1933 *Supplement.*) As with other words with more than one sense, the context usually, though not always, makes clear which sense is intended:

> The rules [for criticism] may be given in one word: by being disinterested. And how is it to be disinterested? By keeping aloof from practice; by resolutely following the law of its own nature, which is to be a free play of the mind on all subjects which it touches; . . .—MATTHEW ARNOLD, "The Function of Criticism at the Present Time"
>
> Next was the question: Are modern students actually disinterested in reading?—RUTH DAVIES, "We Join the March of the Moderns," *English Journal* (College Edition), 1939, 28:203

Recently there have been a number of attacks on the use of *disinterested* in the sense of *uninterested.* Usage records the word in both senses, but stylistically (in part because of the honorific connotation of *disinterested,* which *impartial* and *objective* have not acquired) sensitive readers prefer the first sense. A writer should take their preference into account.

The noun *disinterest* means "lack of interest" (and is probably one reason for the increased use of the adjective to mean "uninterested"):

> He instances religious corruption, political corruption, and disinterest of the well-to-do.—*Times Literary Supplement,* June 28, 1957, p. 400

(Reference: Robert J. Geist, "Usage and Meaning," *College Composition and Communication,* 1955, 6:88-91.)

Ditto marks (") Ditto marks are used with lists and tabulations in reference works instead of repeating words that fall directly below. In typewritten manuscript, use quotation marks for ditto marks:

```
m, as in man, men, mine, hum, hammer
n,  "  " no, man, manner
```

Ditto marks are not used in consecutive writings nor in footnotes or bibliographies. In general they are much less used than formerly.

Divided usage Usage is said to be *divided* when two or more forms exist in the language, both in reputable use in the same dialect or variety. *Divided usage* is not applied, for example, to *localisms, like *poke* for *sack* or *bag,* or to differences like *ain't* and *isn't* which belong to separate varieties of the language. It applies to spellings, pronunciations, or constructions on which speakers and writers of similar education might differ.

There are many more of these divided usages within Standard English than most people are aware of. For instance, most dictionaries record these and hundreds of other instances of divided usage:

In pronunciation:

ab′domen—abdo′men	le′ver—lēv′er
adver′tisement—advertise′ment	ī′solate—is′olate

In spelling:

buses–busses | millionaire–millionnaire
catalog–catalogue | although–altho

In verb forms:

Past tense–*sing: sang* or *sung; ring: rang* or *rung*
Past participle–*show: shown* or *showed; prove: proved* or *proven*

It is hard for some careful users of the language to realize that others may speak or write somewhat differently from themselves and still be following Standard practice. Before calling a person to account, either seriously or playfully, for a usage, we should make sure that his is not a variant that is as reputable as the one we may prefer; that is, we should avoid emotional attitudes and useless disputes whenever possible. This is not always easy. Words (usage) can acquire powerful associations. For instance: The past tense of *eat* pronounced et is for many Americans associated with lack of education, though it is used by many educated Southerners. In England both et and āt are in widespread Standard usage, yet Fowler (entry for *eat*) is quite dogmatic: "The past is spelt *ate* (rarely *eat*) and pronounced ĕt (wrongly āt)." British dictionaries show that "wrongly pronounced āt" is not accurate; but Fowler evidently felt strongly about it. If he, a distinguished and competent lexicographer, could object so violently to a Standard pronunciation, other people, lacking his linguistic background, will have similar prejudices even less well-founded.

The point about divided usages is that *both* are acceptable. A person who has learned to say *It's I* does not need to change to *It's me* and one who says *It's me* does not need to change to *It's I*. When you have the opportunity to choose between variants of equal standing, choose the one that you use naturally, that is appropriate to your style, or, if you are taking pains to be tactful, the one that is common among the audience you are to reach.

The entries in this *Index* include a number of divided usages. When one or the other of two acceptable usages is likely to disturb many readers or listeners, likely to bring on emotional attitudes, evidence is usually presented: there is security in knowing what is dangerous ground. For examples of divided (and so perhaps disputed) usage, see:

Words: *can–may, *drought–drouth, *enthuse, *farther–further
Forms: *-ed, *It's me, *slow, slowly, *Principal parts of verbs
Pronunciations: *advertisement, *either, *route
Constructions: *different from, *due to, *like–as, *reason is because

Div **Division of words** Revision: Break the word at the end of this line between syllables.

Whenever it is necessary in manuscript or in print, a word is divided at the end of a line by a hyphen ("division hyphen"). But in preparing manuscript if you will leave a reasonable right hand margin, you will not be forced to divide many words. A good habit is to divide words only when the lines will be conspicuously uneven if the last word is completely written or completely carried over to the next line. In manuscript for publication most publishers prefer an uneven right margin to divided words.

When you are not sure how to divide a word, consult a dictionary. Both the divided parts should be pronounceable; words of one syllable, like *matched, said, thought,* should not be divided at all. English syllables are difficult to determine, but in general they follow pronunciation groups: *autocratic* would be divided into syllables *au to crat ic,* but *autocracy* is *au toc ra cy.*

The following words are divided to show typical syllables:

mar gin	ca ter	hy phen	chil dren	long ing
hi lar i ous	cat ty	ac com plished	ad min is trate	pitch er

Double consonants are usually separable:

ef fi cient com mit tee daz zling bat ted

A single letter is never allowed to stand by itself, that is, do not divide at the end of lines words like *enough* (which would leave a lone *e* at the end of a line) or *many* (which would put a lone *y* at the beginning of a line).

Words spelled with a hyphen (*half-brother, well-disposed*) should be divided only at the point of the hyphen to avoid the awkwardness of two hyphens in the same word.

Division of words is primarily a printing and editing problem and fuller directions than this book gives will be found in the stylebooks of publishing houses (like the *Manual of Style* of the University of Chicago Press).

do is one of the most important auxiliary verbs in English. Its conjugation follows the regular strong verb pattern (the past tense and past participle are formed by a change in vowel) except for the pronunciation of the third person singular *does* (duz) and of the contracted negative *don't* (dōnt).

1. *"Do" in verb phrases. Do* is used to form verb phrases with all verbs except *be* and the auxiliaries (*can, may, shall . . .*):

Present	*Past*
I, you do wish	I, you, he, she did wish
he, she does wish	we, you, they did wish
we, you, they do wish	

a) With *not* (In speech contracted to *don't, doesn't, didn't). This is the Standard way of negating all English verbs except the auxiliaries and usually *be.*

He did not feel well enough to go out. I don't expect to go.

b) In questions:

Do you think I was right?
Did you like the show as well as you expected to?

c) For emphasis:

I do′ wish he'd come. (Contrast "I wish he'd come.")
He did′ have his lunch, because I saw him go into Carter's.

2. *"Do" as a pro-verb. Do* is used to avoid repetition of a simple verb that has just been used:

I like him better than you do. (i.e., than you like him)

3. *"Do" in idioms. Do* has many idiomatic meanings and is part of many idiomatic phrases: A girl *does* her hair; a steak is well *done;* we *do away* with things; *do for* (which may mean "be enough"–That will do for you–or "put the finishing touches on"–That did for him–or, in some localities, "work for, serve"–She does for Mrs. Lawrence); *done for; do in; do over* (redecorate); *do up* (wrap up, launder, or in past, be used up).

Reference: Fries, *AEG,* pages 146-149, and *Structure,* pages 96-97, 149-151.

don't is the contraction of *do not,* universally used in conversation and often in writing when *do not* would seem too emphatic or when the rhythm seems more comfortable with the shorter form.

Until about 1900 *don't* equalled *doesn't* in Informal speech, and the usage still often finds its way into familiar speech and even into casual writing: "He don't look as well as he used to." Educated people now avoid it, though Atwood found that the *Linguistic Atlas* evidence for the Eastern states showed nearly half of the cultured informants using the construction. (References: Karl W. Dykema, "An Example of Prescriptive Linguistic Change: 'Don't' to 'Doesn't,' " *English Journal,* 1947, 36:370-376; E. B. Atwood, *A Survey of Verb Forms in the Eastern United States* (Ann Arbor, 1953), p. 28.)

Double negative 1. *In Standard English.* Two negative words in the same statement are not used in Standard English to express a single negation (Not "He could*n't* find it *no*where," but "He could*n't* find it *any*where" or "He could find it *no*where").

There are, however, occasional constructions in which one negative statement modifies another negative statement to give a qualified meaning or a meaning with some special emphasis. *In Informal and General English,* mostly in speech: "He is not sure he won't slip in at the last minute" does not mean "He will slip in at the last minute" but "He may possibly slip in. . . ." "And don't you think he isn't clever" stands for something more complex than "He is clever" –for "*I've* found out he's clever" or "You'd better believe he's clever (though I know you don't yet)." Other examples are: "I couldn't not invite her, could I?" "I couldn't just say nothing." *In Formal English:* "A not unattractive young woman." "Not for nothing did he sacrifice himself."

2. *In Nonstandard English.* Although double negatives are probably not so common in Nonstandard English as comic writers suggest in their cartoons and stories, two or more negatives are very often used to make an emphatic negative in this variety. "I do*n't* have *no*thing to lose" makes negative two parts of the idea and emphasizes the negative; if the *nothing* isn't stressed, it is a simple negative in two parts, as French uses *ne . . . pas*. Such a double negative is not a backsliding from the idiom of more Formal English but the survival of a desire for emphasis. In earlier English two negatives were used in all varieties of the language. Chaucer wrote:

> In al this world *ne* was ther *noon* him lyk.
> A bettre preest, I trowe that *nowher noon* is.

The objection to a double negative is not that "two negatives make an affirmative," for they do not–only a person being perverse would misunderstand one. The objection is simply that the construction is not now in fashion among educated people.

3. *Hardly, scarcely*. Students sometimes fall into a concealed double negative when using *hardly* or *scarcely*. *Hardly* means "not probably" and *scarcely* means the same a little more emphatically. Consequently in Standard English a sentence like "For the most part our college paper contains *hardly nothing*" should read "For the most part our college paper contains *hardly anything*," and "For a while we *couldn't scarcely* see a thing" should read "For a while we *could scarcely* see a thing."

Doubling final consonants 1. Words of one syllable ending in a single consonant following a single vowel (*brag, fat, win*) double the consonant before adding a syllable beginning with a vowel (*-able, -ed, -er, -ing, -y*):

brag: bragged, bragging	fat: fatted, fatter, fatty
win: winner, winning	scrap: scrapper, scrapping, scrappy

The consonant is not doubled in words with two vowel letters before the final consonant (*daub, daubed; seed, seeded*) or in words ending with two consonants (*help, helped; hold, holding*).

2. In words of more than one syllable ending in one vowel and one consonant, the final consonant is traditionally doubled if the word is accented on the last syllable. A few words so accented are very common:

con trol′: controlled, controller, controlling
re fer′: referred, referring
Also: confer′ equip′ excel′ infer′ occur′ prefer′

If the accent of the lengthened word shifts to an earlier syllable, the consonant is not doubled:

infer′–in′ference prefer′–pref′erence refer′–ref′erence

If the word is not accented on the last syllable, the consonant need not be doubled, and in American usage preferably is not doubled, though usage is divided on many words:

com′bat (or com bat′): combated or combatted, combating or combatting, but always com′ba tant

A few are never doubled:

ben′e fit: benefited, benefiting
o′pen: opened, opening   par′allel: paralleled, paralleling

Usage on *bias, diagram, kidnap, quarrel, travel, worship* is divided, but usually one consonant is preferred.

3. The part of the rule for doubling final consonants that applies to words of one syllable is useful, because it keeps distinct a number of pairs of words similar in appearance:

bat: batted, batting–bate: bated, bating
din: dinned, dinning–dine: dined, dining (but dinner)
grip: gripped, gripping–gripe: griped, griping
plan: planned, planning–plane: planed, planing
scrap: scrapped, scrapping–scrape: scraped, scraping

The boy who wrote "The scene in which she almost kills her husband is griping" did not say what he intended.

4. Words already ending in a doubled consonant keep both consonants before suffixes beginning with a vowel but may lose one consonant before suffixes beginning with another consonant:

enroll: enrolled, enrolling; but enrolment or enrollment
install: installed, installing, installation; but instalment or installment
fulfill: fulfilled, fulfilling; but fulfillment or fulfilment
skill: skilled; but skillful or skilful

doubt Idioms with *doubt:*

1. *Negative* (when there is no real doubt), *doubt that:*

Formal: I do not doubt that he meant well.
General: I don't doubt but that [sometimes: but what] he will come.

2. *Positive* (when doubt exists), *that, whether, if:*

Formal: I doubt whether he meant it that way.
I doubt that he meant it that way. (indicating unbelief really more than doubt)
General: I doubt if he meant it that way.

dove-dived The past tense of *dive* is *dived* or *dove.* The form *dove* is one of the few instances where a strong past tense form has developed (by *analogy with *drive*) for an Old English weak verb.

draft, draught The spelling of *draught* (from the Old English *dragan,* to draw) has gradually come to represent its pronunciation (draft). *Draft* is always the spelling for a *bank draft,* the *military draft,* a *draft of a composition;* usage is divided on the word in the sense of a maker of drawings–*draftsman* or *draughtsman*–or in the sense of a current of air–*draft* or *draught; draught* is more common for a *ship's draught,* a *draught of fish,* and for a *draught of ale* or *beer on draught* –though *draft* is rapidly gaining in both senses.

drought–drouth Both forms are in good use, *drought* probably more common in Formal English, *drouth* in General. Two pronunciations also occur, drout and drouth, which do not always correspond to the spellings.

> It is true the longest drouth will end in rain.—ROBERT FROST

drunk It seems to take courage to use this General word. We either go Formal—*intoxicated;* or grasp at respectability through euphemisms—*under the influence of liquor* or *indulged to excess;* or make a weak attempt at humor with one of the dozens of Informal phrases like *get plastered.* But *drunk* is the word.

due to The preposition *due to* is especially interesting as an illustration of the difficulties a new locution has in being recognized.

Due was originally an adjective and is still most strictly used as one: "The epidemic was *due* to the brown rat," in which *due* modifies *epidemic*. But *due to* as it is used in "The Mediterranean has its share of minority problems and they have become more prominent *due to* Italo-British tension in that area" (*Kaltenborn Edits the News,* p. 99) has long been popular, in magazine writing as well as in literature by Galsworthy and others of undisputed respectability. Advocates of strict usage have set themselves sternly against it, forgetting perhaps that *owing to,* which they have suggested should be substituted for it, has come from a participle to a preposition in exactly the same way.

An excellent example of a linguist's approach to a matter of divided and debatable usage is Professor John S. Kenyon's treatment of *due to* in *American Speech,* 1930, 6:61-70. He presents an imposing number of quotations from current writers, discusses the history of the phrase, and concludes:

> Strong as is my own prejudice against the prepositional use of *due to,* I greatly fear it has staked its claim and squatted in our midst alongside of and in exact imitation of *owing to,* its aristocratic neighbor and respected fellow citizen.

A more recent study reported by Professor Margaret M. Bryant shows that in some thousands of pages of books, periodicals, and newspapers, *due to* as a preposition occurred in 56% of the instances, *because of* in 25% and *owing to* in 19% ("Current English Forum," *College English,* 1954, 15:478). A person may not care to use *due to* as a preposition, but in view of actual usage today he hardly has the right to deny it to others.

E

1. The "long *e*" sound (ē) is found variously spelled in stressed syllables: b*e*, s*ee*d, rec*ei*ve, sh*ie*ld, m*ea*t, p*eo*ple, k*ey,* qu*ay*, *ae*gis, Ph*oe*be, mach*i*ne.

An unstressed or lightly stressed *e* may vary in pronunciation from long *e* in platform delivery (dē send′—*descend*) to a short *i* in ordinary speech (di send′); *hero* and *zero* may be hir′ō or hē′rō, zir′ō or zē′rō.

2. The "short *e*" sound (e) is also variously spelled, as in f*e*d, l*ea*ther, b*u*ry, m*a*ny, s*ai*d, l*eo*pard, fr*ie*nd, s*ay*s.

Before final *r* or *r* plus a consonant, short *e* represents the sound in *learn, fern, err,* marked û (lûrn, fûrn, ûr).

3. "Unstressed *e*" (as in *kindness, difference*) represents a slight and rather obscure sound in speech. It may represent short *i* (kīnd′-nis), or the neutral vowel sound represented in this book by ə (kīnd′nəs).

Before *l, m, n,* and *r* unstressed *e* is really a part of the consonant ("syllabic" *l, m, n, r*). In this book such syllables are represented by ə or by l̩ m̩ n̩ r̩: set′əl or set′l̩ (*settle*), wood′ən or wood′n̩ (*wooden*).

4. Miscellaneous sounds represented by *e: e* may represent *a* before *r,* as in *there* (t͟har); ä as in *sergeant* and many words in British usage which in the United States have û (*Derby, Berkeley, clerk*).

5. Silent or mute *e:* In general, words spelled with a final silent *e* drop the *-e* before additions beginning with a vowel and keep it before additions beginning with a consonant:

change: changed, changing; changeless (but changeable)
grease: greased, greaser; greasewood
like: likable, liking; likeness
pursue: pursuant, pursued, pursuing
use: usable, used, using; useful, useless
Exceptions: argument, awful, duly, ninth; judgment (or judgement)

A few other exceptions keep *-e* to indicate pronunciation, chiefly after *c* and *g* before suffixes beginning with *a* or *o:*

change: changeable   courage: courageous   notice: noticeable

(See *-ce, -ge.)

In a few words the *-e* is retained to avoid confusion with other words or to keep the connection with the root word obvious:

lineage (lin′ē ij) vs. linage (līn′ij)
singeing (sin′jing), dyeing (dī′ing)

each **1.** *Each,* though a singular, never occurs without an expressed or implied reference to more than one. Since the idea of plurality is always present when *each* is used, it inevitably attracts plural forms. In speech and increasingly in writing, *each* is regarded as a collective when the plural idea is uppermost (compare *every):

> *Each* of these peoples undoubtedly modified Latin in accordance with *their* own speech habits.—Baugh, p. 35

2. In Formal usage *each* is singular:

Each of the three has a different instructor.
Each ran as fast as his legs could carry him.

3. As an adjective, *each* does not affect the number of the verb; when the subject modified by *each* is plural, the verb is also plural:

Each applicant has to fill out the blank in full.
Three students, also from this county, each receive a scholarship.
They each feel keenly about it.

(Reference: Russell Thomas, "Concord Based on *Meaning* versus Concord Based on *Form*," *College English,* 1939, 1:38-45.)

each and every is a phrase which may have its place, but it has been greatly overused.

each other, basically used of two, is also in good use for more than two, though Formal usage frequently has *one another*.

> General: The men from farms on both sides of the river were shouting to each other.
> Formal: The men from farms on both sides of the river were shouting to one another.

(Reference: Russell Thomas, "'Each Other' or 'One Another'?" *College English,* 1957, 18:422-424.)

eat In Standard English the principal parts are *eat* (ēt), *ate* (āt), *eaten* (ē'tən). In Nonstandard usage, and in some Standard usage in the Southern United States and in England, the past form is pronounced et, spelled either *eat* or *ate*. (See *Divided usage.)

Echo phrases Sometimes it is convenient to form a phrase on the pattern of one well known or to echo one less known but apt. This is a type of allusion. The echo phrase may be either serious or light:

> I have seen American textbooks in which lesson after lesson is devoted to the lofty purpose of eliminating *got*. As though the fear of *got* were the beginning of wisdom. ["The fear of God is the beginning of wisdom."]–P. B. BALLARD, *Thought and Language,* p. 205
> ... but democracy means simply the bludgeoning of the people by the people for the people.–OSCAR WILDE, *The Soul of Man Under Socialism*

In General writing, echoes of common phrases usually fit, and in more Formal writing there is certainly no harm in a writer showing that he has read a bit, but a parade of echo phrases may seem pretentious.

economic Pronounced ē'kə nom'ik or ek'ə nom'ik; and so also *economical, economics; economist* is i kon'ə mist.

Economical means "saving, thrifty"; *economic* means "having to do with business or economics."

-ed A conspicuous spelling problem is the omission of *-ed* in past verb forms (§ 1) and in modifiers made from verbs (§ 2) and from nouns (§ 3). Students often raise questions about these forms, and teachers are much concerned about them. They must also be a problem for editors, who probably insert many *-ed*s in copy. The *-ed* is rarely omitted in published works, but it is frequently missing in unedited copy–in menus, in signs, and in letters.

To understand the situation it will help to consider the processes that have already led to many accepted forms without *-ed*. There has long been a tendency in speech for a final *d* sound to become a *t* sound, especially before voiceless consonants (*f, n, s, t...*): *a watched pot* (wôcht pot). Often the words in *-ed* come before *to* or other words beginning with *t* so that the two sounds are assimilated to one: *relieved to hear* (ri lēv tə hēr), *released time* (ri lēs tīm).

1. *In verb forms.* This trait of pronunciation has led to the complete loss of the *d* sound in the past tense and past participle of a few verbs, or to an optional form without the ending: *bet, burst, cast, knit, quit, wed.* (Compare the verbs in § 4 that are regularly spelled with a final *t.*)

But following this practice in the spelling of past forms of regular verbs is an annoyance to educated readers. In these verbs it is well to remember that in spite of omission or assimilation of the *-ed* in speech, *the written form of the past tense and of the past participle should have -ed.* In proofreading go by your eye rather than your ear.

> He was *unprejudiced* on the question.
> They were *surprised* to see so many present.
> I am *forced* to admit I *liked* the show.

(See *used to–the most common offender in this group.)

2. *In modifiers from verbs.* The past participle is commonly used as a modifier: *abandoned farms, dressed chickens.* The same features of pronunciation are at work here, and many fixed phrases without *-ed* are Standard usage: *frame house, grade school, ice cream, oil cloth, salt pork, skim milk.* (Many of these were opposed when they first appeared.) Others of the same type are sometimes found in print but are debatable: *advance headquarters, bottle beer, whip cream.* In all of these except *whip cream* the resulting form could be regarded as a noun used in the function of an adjective so that these expressions seem natural to English speakers.

A routine solution would be to go by a dictionary, but dictionaries will be found to vary, and many of the terms have not attracted the attention of dictionary makers. Two principles may help: (1) For a word group that is well established in speech, the oral form is likely to be appropriate in a written context reflecting its common use; (2) For others, appropriateness to other traits of style will be a useful guide. In Formal writing only those that have been generally accepted, as in the first group of the preceding paragraph, should be used. In Informal writing, especially if it suggests speech, more could stand. In General writing teachers and students may have to work out some compromise, though in academic writing the more conventional form with *-ed* is expected.

3. *In modifiers from nouns. -Ed* is frequently added to nouns to form adjectival modifiers: *barbed wire* (wire with barbs), *long-haired, moneyed, one-armed.* No verb is involved in the derivation of these terms. Consequently when the *-ed* is dropped the result is a noun used in the function of an adjective, a construction that is increasing in current English. In many group words the form without the *-ed* is well established: *one-arm bandit* and *barb wire* are alternative forms, and there are *blue-back speller, high-heel shoes, seven-room house, king-size cigaret, hard-surface road, wing chair.* (See *size.)

Established forms like these are certainly appropriate in writing and similar forms are also, if they can be taken as nouns used as modifiers. When a noun is not suggested or if the modifier is not conventionally bound to the headword, the *-ed* should be kept: *advanced courses, middle-aged, old-fashioned, one-sided.* (References: Curme, *Parts of Speech,* pp. 260-296; W. Nelson Francis, "More of the Lost *-ed,*" *Word Study,* Oct. 1954, pp. 6-7; Ralph H. Lane, "Passing Participles," *Word Study,* Feb. 1955, pp. 1-3.)

4. *-ed or -t.* In the past tense and past participles of verbs in which the *-ed* is (or may be) pronounced as *t,* simpler spelling has *-t.* A few words have been rather generally adopted with this sound and spelling: *crept, dreamt* (dremt), *leapt* (lept), *slept. Asked, jumped, shipped, spelled* are more common than *askt, jumpt, shipt, spelt.*

5. *-ed or 'd.* When *-ed* is added to words that are formed unusually, *'d* is sometimes used instead, as in *shanghai'd, ok'd.*

-ee is an ending denoting the one who receives or is directly affected by an act or grant of power, the opposite of nouns ending in *-er* (*payer,* one who pays; *payee,* one who is paid): *employee, draftee, grantee.*

> It takes two people to say a thing—a sayee as well as a sayer. The one is as essential to any true saying as the other.—Samuel Butler, "Thought and Language"

-ei-, -ie- Words with *-ie-* are much more common than words with *-ei-* and on the whole give less spelling trouble. The most common sound represented by *-ie-* is ē.

Some common words with *ie* are:

achieve	chief	friend	niece	shriek
belief	field	grieve	piece	siege
believe	fiend	hygiene	pier	sieve
cashier	financier	mischief	priest	view

Plural of nouns ending in *-y*: academies companies lotteries

Third person singular present of verbs in *-y*: cries fortifies fries

After *c, -ie-* is seldom used, but it does occur: *ancient, species.*

There are fewer words with *ei,* but their spelling needs careful watching. The most common sound spelled *ei* is ā:

deign	feint	neigh	rein	sleigh
eight	freight	neighbor	seine	veil
feign	heinous	reign	skein	weigh

A number of words spell the sound ē with *ei,* especially after *c:*

ceiling	deceive	leisure	perceive	seize
conceive	either	neither	receive	weird

And a few words spell other sounds with *ei:*

counterfeit forfeit height heir their

In some words *i* and *e* stand together but are parts of different syllables:

fi ery headi er si esta

Reference: Donald W. Lee, *College English,* 1944, 6:156-159.

either **1.** *Either* means primarily "one or the other of two," as an adjective (either way you look at it) or as a pronoun (bring me either). For emphasis the pronoun is usually supported by *one* (bring me either one). Used of three or more objects (either of the corners), it is loose and rare; "any one of the corners" is the more usual idiom.

Either is usually construed as singular, though its use as a plural is increasing (Fries, p. 56):

> Either is good enough for me.
> Either Grace or Phyllis is [or: are] expected.

2. *Either* with the meaning "each" is rare in present English and definitely Formal: "broil the fish on either side, with one turning"—"on either side of the river." *Each* or *both* would be more common in such expressions.

3. The pronunciation ī′thər or ī′thə has not made so much progress in the United States as in England, and outside some communities in New England and a few families or circles that radiate from New England it is usually an affectation. Say ē′thər, unless your family or social group generally says ī′thə(r). Similarly, *neither* is usually nē′thər, occasionally nī′thə(r). The use of ī′thə(r) and nī′thə(r) by a public speaker affects an audience unfavorably in a large part of the country.

elder, eldest These archaic forms of *old,* which survive in Formal English, are used only for members of the same family—"the elder brother," "our eldest daughter"—and in some phrases like "the elder statesmen."

Ellipsis (. . .) **1.** A punctuation mark of three or sometimes four spaced periods to indicate something not expressed is called an ellipsis (plural *ellipses*). Formerly asterisks (* * *) were used, but they have been generally discontinued because they are too conspicuous. When an ellipsis comes at the end of a statement marked with a period, that period is added, as in the first and third instances in this passage:

> As Beret drank in these words the tenseness all left her; the weapon she had seized dropped from her hand; her body straightened up; she looked about in wide-eyed wonder. . . . Were those church bells she heard? . . . But the voices were beginning again on the other side of the wall. . . . Hush! Hush!—O. E. RÖLVAAG, *Giants in the Earth,* p. 416

2. (a) The ellipsis is an editorial mark showing where a word or more, which is not needed for the purpose of the writer using the quotation, has been left out. The preceding sentence might be quoted with the *which* clause omitted: "The ellipsis is an editorial mark showing where a word or more . . . has been left out." Every such omission in quoted matter should be indicated by an ellipsis.

b) An ellipsis is also used to show that a series or enumeration continues beyond the units named; it is equivalent to *et cetera:*

> the coordinating conjunctions (and, but, for . . .)

3. In narrative an ellipsis is used to mark hesitation in the action, suggesting passage of time, as in the quotation on page 510 from *Giants in the Earth,* and in the quotation below from Conrad Aiken:

> "Well–I can see this much. You *are* in love with her. Or you couldn't possibly be such a fool. But it's precisely when you're in love that you need to keep your wits about you. Or the wits of your friends. . . . You *mustn't* marry her, Harry."
> "Well–I don't know."
> "No! . . . It would be ruinous."–CONRAD AIKEN, "Spider! Spider!"

It is also used to mark a statement that is unfinished or is let die away:

> I go away to a town, a big strange town, and try to hammer out a good book. The days come, the days go, and big ships sail into the harbor. . . . –ALBERT HALPER, "Young Writer Remembering Chicago"

4. An ellipsis is sometimes used in advertising copy or in instructions to separate statements for emphasis: RINSE BY HAND . . . Rinse thoroughly to remove all soap . . . DO NOT WRING . . . as wringing will tend to add wrinkles.

Elliptical constructions *Ellipsis* and *elliptical* refer to a construction in which a word or more that can be supplied from a neighboring construction is omitted:

> I work a good deal harder than you [Supply: *work*].

The notion of ellipsis has often been misused to apply to the shorter way of expressing a notion. A person may write either:

> We went through the same experience that you did. [or]
> We went through the same experience you did.

The second form is not actually elliptical but a shorter idiom; a *that* is not "omitted," it just isn't thought or spoken or written. The choice between the longer and shorter constructions is a matter of style rather than grammar. Formal English uses the longer ones, tends to fill out all constructions. General and Informal English use the shorter constructions freely. (See Ch. 7, "Long and short constructions," p. 188. References: Curme, *Syntax,* p. 2 and index references; Jespersen, *The Philosophy of Grammar,* p. 306 and index references.)

else 1. Because *else* follows the word it modifies (usually a pronoun), it takes the sign of the possessive:

> I hated wearing somebody else's clothes.
> At first he thought the book was his, but finally decided it was somebody else's.

2. *Else* is sometimes used in speech as an *intensive, but in writing, it is *deadwood and should be removed:

> Finally I started talking, just to hear something [else] besides the roar of the motor.

3. *Nothing else but* is sometimes used for emphasis in speech, but the *else* would not ordinarily be used in writing:

Written: There was nothing but wheat as far as you could see.
Spoken: There was nothing else but wheat as far as you could see.

emigrate–immigrate *Emigrate* means to move out of a country or region, *immigrate* to move into a country. An *emigrant* from Norway would be an *immigrant* to the United States.

Emphasis Revision: Strengthen the emphasis of this passage by one or more of the methods suggested below.

Emph 1. *Position.* 2. *Mass or proportion.* 3. *Distinction of expression.* 4. *Separation, distinctness.* 5. *Repetition.* 6. *Intensives.* 7. *Mechanical devices.*

The idea of emphasis is to lead your reader to see your ideas in the same relative importance as you do—the most important as most important, the less important as less important, the incidental as incidental.

Ways in which emphasis can be conveyed are discussed more fully in other sections of the *Guide-Index,* referred to in this summary.

1. *Position.* In most types of writing, except news stories and reference works, the most emphatic position is the end and the second most emphatic position is the beginning. Emphasis by position applies to sentences (pp. 194-196), to paragraphs (pp. 155-159), and to whole papers (pp. 165-170, 286-287, 291-292).

2. *Mass or proportion.* Position is supported by the amount of space given to a particular point. Watch the last topics in a paper, which are likely to be hurried over and so underdeveloped that they do not seem as important as their writer intends.

3. *Distinction of expression.* In general, big words and long *function words and phrases weaken a statement, as do abstract and indefinite words. Fresh, concrete words in direct and economical constructions make for a clear-cut emphasis. (See Ch. 8, pp. 217-241.)

4. *Separation, distinctness.* Marking the stages of thought in a paper by extra spacing or by numbers makes separate ideas stand out more strongly. Careful paragraphing sets off units that help clarify the relationship between topics. Putting ideas in separate sentences keeps them distinct, and putting the important statements in main clauses and the contributing statements in subordinate elements shows their relative importance. (See pp. 193-194.)

5. *Repetition.* Repetition of significant words drives them home, and repetition of statements either in similar words or in different, perhaps figurative expressions, is a useful form of emphasis if it is not overdone. (See pp. 191-193.)

6. *Intensives.* Words added to intensify meaning are generally used in speaking, but they are less useful in writing. (See *very and pp. 190-191.)

Labeling a statement "It is interesting to note," "This is an important phase of the subject" is seldom convincing. Such phrases can be done away with in revision by making the fact or opinion stand out in other ways. (See *Labeling material.)

7. *Mechanical devices.* Writing and printing have various mechanical means—*underlining (italics), *capitals, emphatic punctuation—for stressing words and passages. These devices are often used by amateur writers in an attempt to make up for deficiencies in style or content. (See p. 190.)

Emphasis should be tested in revision, when the writer takes the role of reader and tries to see if his paper really represents his view of the subject.

employee This spelling is much more common than *employé.*

en-, in- *In-* is either a native English prefix or a prefix of Latin origin; *en-* is the same Latin prefix modified in French. (*Em-* and *im-* are variant forms.) For several common words usage is divided, though usually one form is more common. Fowler and other British dictionaries are not safe guides to American usage for this problem because Americans tend to use *in-* more than the English do. The safest way is to consult a recent American dictionary, but even American dictionaries are not consistent, so that the choice is often a matter of style. Formal writers tend to use more *en-* forms, General writers more *in-* forms.

Here are a few samples with the dictionaries' preference first where there seems to be one:

encase–incase
enclose–inclose (gaining)
encumber–incumber
endorse–indorse (gaining)
engulf–ingulf
entrust–intrust
incrust–encrust
infold–enfold
inquire–enquire
insure–ensure (Always *insure* in the financial sense, *insurance,* etc.)

End-stop is a mark of punctuation—usually a period, exclamation mark, or question mark—used at the end of a sentence. The double or two-em dash (—— *Dash §8) is used as an end-stop in conversation when a speech is interrupted. The *ellipsis (. . .) is often used as an end-stop for a sentence that is intentionally left unfinished or that is let die away.

When two end-stops would fall together at the end of a sentence, as when a question stands within a sentence, only one mark, the more emphatic or more necessary for meaning, is used:

> When we say, for example, that Miss A. *plays* well, only an irredeemable outsider would reply "Plays what?" So, too, . . . —C. ALPHONSO SMITH, *Studies in English Syntax,* p. 8.

(For further comment on end-stops see the articles on the individual marks.)

English language 1. *Indo-European.* English belongs to the Indo-European family of languages, which includes most of the languages of Europe, a number of languages of India, the languages of Persia and of certain adjoining regions. The Indo-European family is usually divided into nine branches. English belongs to one of these, Germanic. On page 515 is a diagram showing the relations.

A brief selection of facts about the different periods of our language will show some of the roots of the richness–and complexity–of Modern English.

2. *Old English, 450-1050.* The Angles, Saxons, and Jutes brought to England from their old homes in northeastern Europe somewhat differing Lowland West Germanic dialects. They pushed back the native Celts from the parts of the island they conquered, so that Celtic speech contributed almost nothing to English but survived as Welsh, Cornish, and Highland Scotch. The conquerors' languages developed into several main dialects–Northumbrian, Mercian, Kentish, West Saxon–which together are known as Old English (or Anglo-Saxon). These dialects still leave their marks in the regional speech of various parts of England. Most of these dialects made some contribution to the Standard language, but it was principally from the East Midland dialect, a descendant of Mercian, that Modern English developed.

Somewhat less than a quarter of the total present English vocabulary goes back to the words of Old English. The modern descendants of Old English words are often changed in meaning and almost always in pronunciation, according to regular processes: Old English *stan* (stän) becomes Modern English *stone, ban* (bän) becomes *bone,* etc. Our common verbs (*go, sit, eat, fight, whistle*), many of our most common nouns (*meat, house, breakfast, land, water*), and adjectives like *fast, slow, high* go back to Old English words, so that though less than a fourth of the words in an unabridged dictionary are of this "native" origin, they play a part in our speech out of all proportion to their number.

Furthermore, most of the machinery of our language is from Old English: the articles *a, an, the;* most of the connecting words–*around, at, by, for, from, in, into, out, under . . . as, like, since, when;* most of the pronouns (*I, we, us, . . .*); the inflectional endings of nouns (*house–houses, boy–boys–boy's*) and of adjectives and adverbs: *merry–merrier–merriest* or *more merry–most merry;* harsh*ly*, kind*ly;* the forms of verbs: pass, pass*es,* pass*ed,* pass*ing*. These endings are applied to words taken from other languages (*indict-ed, political -ly*), so that although three quarters of the vocabulary may come from Romance or other languages, the borrowed words are built into an English pattern. And when we consider word order, we see that the texture of English is Germanic too. For all these reasons, English

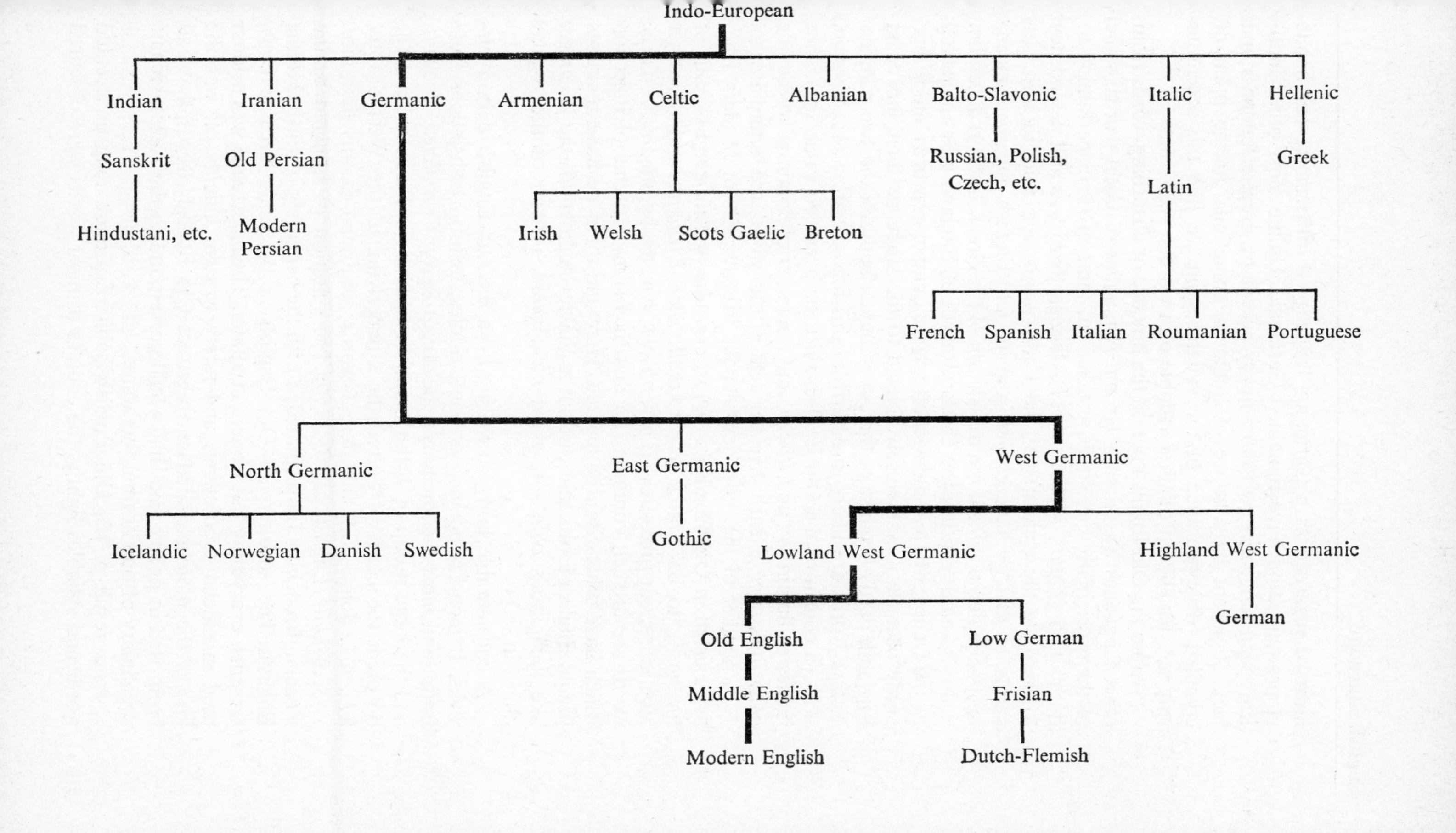
Indo-European
Indian
Sanskrit
Hindustani, etc.
Iranian
Old Persian
Modern Persian
Germanic
Armenian
Celtic
Irish
Welsh
Scots Gaelic
Breton
Albanian
Balto-Slavonic
Russian, Polish, Czech, etc.
Italic
Latin
French
Spanish
Italian
Roumanian
Portuguese
Hellenic
Greek
North Germanic
Icelandic
Norwegian
Danish
Swedish
East Germanic
Gothic
West Germanic
Lowland West Germanic
Old English
Middle English
Modern English
Low German
Frisian
Dutch-Flemish
Highland West Germanic
German

must be regarded as a Germanic language. Furthermore, our habits of pronunciation have remained Germanic. Unlike most other Indo-European languages, we show heavy accent by greater loudness and lack of accent by absence of loudness, sometimes to the point of complete disappearance of the syllable, and we like the accent to stay put, usually on the first syllable of a word.

Within the Old English period the practice of absorbing words from other languages was already strong. A number of Latin words, some of them originally Greek, were taken in, most of them pertaining to the church (*abbot, priest, school*), though there was still a tendency to translate the elements of the Latin words into Old English elements, so that we have *gospel* from the Old English *god spell,* meaning "good news," which is a translation of the Greek-Latin *evangelium.*

In the ninth century the east and north of England was conquered by the Danes, whose language left a large number of words and forms, partly because it was closely related to the language then spoken in England, partly because of the close contact between the two peoples. The *sk* words are likely to date from this mixture–*sky, skin, scream, skirt* (a cousin of the Old English *shirt,* both related to *short*), place names ending in *-by* and *-thorp,* and a number of common words like *odd, anger, egg.* Nearly five per cent of our words are Scandinavian.

A number of the most conspicuous irregularities of Modern English existed in Old English: **be, is, are, was, were, been* as forms of the verb "to be"; *may, might, shall, should, ought,* and the other auxiliaries; our pronouns–*I, my, me, we, our, us, he, she, it. . . .* These words are in such common use that they show patterns of inflection which have otherwise disappeared. Here and there we have remnants of Old English forms that lost out in the development of the language, like the plurals *children, oxen, men, geese,* instead of the regular plural in *-s.*

A considerable body of writing from the Old English period survives. It includes poems, sermons, riddles, history, translations from Latin, and most conspicuously the *Anglo-Saxon Chronicles, Beowulf,* and the large group of writings and translations in West Saxon made by or at the court of Alfred the Great, King of the West Saxons, 871-901. Some 30,000 different words are found in this literature.

3. *Middle English, 1050-1450.* The conquest of England by the Norman French in 1066 coincided with the beginning of Early Middle English. The speakers of Old English in the main became serfs, servants, everything but leaders in affairs. Their language was seldom used in official proceedings and rarely written. One result was the loss of the more elevated and abstract Old English words that had been used in poetry and that would correspond to the rather archaic vocabulary of our Formal literature.

As a result of the Old English habit of pronouncing unaccented words and syllables lightly, the endings of most words were obscured and could no longer be distinguished. A far-reaching development of this period was therefore the decline and in some instances complete loss of the inflectional endings of Old English. The definite article no longer had distinctive form (our *the* is the sole descendant of ten forms in Old English); *-n* disappeared from the infinitive of most verbs; and other unstressed endings also dropped away. This process went far to make English one of the least inflected of Indo-European languages.

On the other hand the language of the invaders made headway. The words for the acts of the ruling class–war, government, law, social activity–were Norman French and they have generally come down to Modern English: *siege, soldier, judge, jury, suit, dinner, servant, obey*. The majority of the Norman French words were ultimately from Latin, though considerably changed in form. For many notions Modern English has two roughly synonymous words, one Latin or French, one Old English: *dress–clothes, aid–help, cottage–hut, solitary–lonely*. Some French spellings made their way into English, like *gu* for hard *g–guest, guess; qu* for *cw–queen* for Old English *cwen.*

In 1362 English was restored as the language of the law courts, an official recognition that it was asserting itself once more in higher circles. The speech of the region around London was now the basis for future development not only of the spoken language but of the literary language. How far English had incorporated French resources can be seen from a few lines by Chaucer, written in the 1380's. The French words are in italics:

> "What folk ben ye, that at myn hoomcominge
> Perturben so my feste with *cryinge?*"
> Quod Theseus, "have ye so greet *envye*
> Of myn *honour,* that thus *compleyne* and *crye?*
> Or who hath yow misboden, or *offended?*
> And telleth me if it may been *amended;*
> And why that ye ben clothed thus in blak?"
>
> –GEOFFREY CHAUCER, "The Knightes Tale"

Except for the Old English *misboden* ("insulted"), all of these words, both native and French, are in use today, though *quod* (quoth) is archaic, and in spite of some differences in spelling, the passage can be read by anyone. Many of the words show inflectional endings that have since been dropped or changed: *ben* (for *are* or *be*), perturb*en,* tell*eth,* and the final *e* of nouns.

4. *Early Modern English, 1450-1700*. In this period we have the beginnings of conscious concern for the language and actual or attempted "improvement" by manipulation of words and constructions –"schoolmastering the speech." The early printers, from 1476 on, felt the need for uniformity, especially in spelling and choice of word forms, and began the domination of these traits that has been exercised by publishers ever since. Translators and writers sometimes considered the language rough, unpolished, incapable of doing what Latin and Greek had done and what Italian could do. They set about enlarging the vocabulary, chiefly by transliterating words from Greek and Latin. More than twenty-five per cent of Modern English words are pretty directly from classical languages, and very often we have two words that go back to the same Latin original, one brought in by the Norman French and one taken in directly later: *paint–picture, certainty–certitude*. Latin was the language of the Church at the beginning of this period, though after the Reformation the Book of Common Prayer, and after 1611 the King James translation of the Bible, became tremendous forces for elevated English. Most books of the learned world were in Latin, and college classes were conducted in Latin, even in America, until less than two centuries ago.

The spoken language was vigorous and was written down in some popular literature, but most literature that has survived was from the hands of educated men and conscious stylists. Shakespeare shows the complete range, from formal, Latinized lines to rough and tumble lines, often combining the elevated and the simple in a single speech:

> No, this my hand will rather
> The multitudinous seas incarnadine
> Making the green one red.

Prose style lagged behind poetic, especially in sentence sense, producing "sentence heaps" running to hundreds of words. In the sixteen hundreds the wealth of experiment of the preceding century was analyzed and many words and phrases were disposed of. The less useful and more ponderous of the Latin importations were dropped, and interest in native words increased the proportion of native words in use. Prose style especially developed in directness and sureness until in Dryden Modern English prose is usually said to be established. In spite of small differences in idiom and word order, this paragraph does not seem nearly 300 years old:

> To begin, then, with Shakespeare. He was the man who of all modern, and perhaps ancient poets, had the largest and most comprehensive soul. All the images of nature were still present to him, and he drew them, not laboriously, but luckily; when he describes anything, you more than see it, you feel it too. Those who accuse him to have wanted learning, give him the greater commendation: he was naturally learned; he needed not the spectacles of books to read nature; he looked inwards, and found her there. I cannot say he is everywhere alike; were he so, I should do him injury to compare him with the greatest of mankind. He is many times flat, insipid; his comic wit degenerating into clenches, his serious swelling into bombast. But he is always great, when some great occasion is presented to him; no man can say he ever had a fit subject for his wit, and did not then raise himself as high above the rest of the poets,
>
> *Quantum lenta solent inter viburna cupressi.*
> [As the cypresses tower among the humbler trees.]

The consideration of this made Mr. Hales of Eaton say, that there was no subject of which any poet ever writ, but he would produce it much better done in Shakespeare; and however others are now generally preferred before him, yet the age wherein he lived, which had contemporaries with him Fletcher and Jonson, never equalled them to him in their esteem: and in the last king's court, when Ben's reputation was at highest, set our Shakespeare far above him.–JOHN DRYDEN, *An Essay of Dramatic Poesy* (1668)

5. *Modern English, 1700-* . This *Index* gives a partial picture of current English, especially as it appears in print, and suggests in some of its specific articles changes that have taken place in the last few generations. Such articles may be taken as continuations of this brief historical sketch, for by 1700 English had become substantially the language we now know and use. The vocabulary has been enlarged in the last two centuries chiefly from two sources: borrowings from India and America and from all peoples touched by British and American traders; and through scientific coinages, chiefly from Greek and Latin roots. There has been, especially in recent years, a tendency toward shorter and more direct sentences. The paragraph has become a more distinct unit in written expression. The most important point for study in this period has probably been the different varieties of usage, and different traditions of style, especially Formal, General, and Informal styles.

Today the language of England and the British Commonwealth and of the United States is spoken by over 250,000,000 people–certainly the largest group of people who can easily understand each other in their native language. In addition English is probably the most important second language in the world today.

The result of this varied history is a language full of anomalies, but of unusual range and flexibility, capable of great subtlety and force of expression.

References: Baugh, Robertson. Otto Jespersen, *Growth and Structure of the English Language* (various editions), describes the accumulation of the English vocabulary, and his *Language* (New York, 1923), Part iv, discusses language change especially apropos of English.

en route Pronounced on ro͞ot′; Formally äɴ ro͞ot′. *On the way* or *going to* often fits a sentence more naturally:

They were en route [on the way] to Philadelphia.

enthuse is a back formation (see *Origin of words § 3d) from *enthusiasm*. Many people object to it, and dictionaries label it "colloquial." But *enthuse* seems to be an improvement over the only locution we have for the idea, the clumsy *be enthusiastic over* or *about*. It is now in General use.

envelop, envelope The verb *envelop* is pronounced in vel′əp or en vel′əp; the noun *envelope*, en′və lōp or, less commonly–reflecting the word's French origin–on′və lōp; en vel′up is Nonstandard.

Epigrams An epigram is a short, pithy statement, in verse or prose, usually with a touch of wit. In prose this means really a detached or detachable and "quotable" sentence. In consecutive prose, epigrams sometimes become too prominent, attract too much attention to themselves, or suggest straining for effect. But they can focus attention or put a fact or opinion so that a reader can remember (and perhaps repeat) it:

> Conscience is the inner voice which warns us that someone may be looking.–H. L. MENCKEN, *The Vinitage Mencken*, p. 231
>
> It's no disgrace to be poor, but it might as well be.
>
> Bees are not as busy as we think they are. They jest can't buzz any slower.–KIN HUBBARD, *The Sayings of Abe Martin*

Closely related to epigrams are *aphorisms*–pithy statements but more likely to be abstract and not necessarily witty. The essays of Francis Bacon are packed with aphorisms, and some modern essayists use them too:

> To spend too much time in studies is sloth; to use them too much for ornament, is affectation; to make judgment wholly by their rules, is the humour of a scholar. . . . Read not to contradict and confute; nor to believe and take for granted; not to find talk and discourse; but to weigh and consider. . . . Reading maketh a full man; conference a ready man; and writing an exact man.–FRANCIS BACON, "Of Studies"

Proverbs are the often quoted, concrete expressions of popular wisdom. They are likely to make observations on character or conduct. As a rule their authors are unknown.

> It never rains but it pours.
> Still waters run deep.
> It's hard for an empty sack to stand upright.
> Alcohol and gasoline don't mix.

A special type of epigram is the *paradox*, which makes a statement that as it stands contradicts fact or common sense or itself and yet suggests a truth or at least a half truth:

> All generalizations are false, including this one.
>
> Dr. Richards is no mystic; he is a behaviourist, a behaviourist being a psychologist who does not believe in psychology.–P. B. BALLARD, *Thought and Language*, p. 265

(Reference: *The Oxford Dictionary of Proverbs* (Oxford, 1936), compiled by William G. Smith.)

-er, -or Names of persons or things performing an act (nouns of agent) and some other nouns are formed in English by adding *-er* to a verb (*doer, killer, painter, thinker*), but many end in *-or,* chiefly nouns taken from Latin or French (*assessor, prevaricator*).

Since the two endings are pronounced the same (ər), it is hard to tell whether *-er* or *-or* should be written. Here are a few as samples; a dictionary will have to settle most questions.

With -er:

advertiser	consumer	peddler (or pedlar)
better (or bettor)	debater	promoter
condenser	manufacturer	propeller

With -or:

accelerator	conductor	motor
administrator	distributor	objector
*advisor (shifted from adviser)	editor	proprietor
	governor	spectator
bachelor	inventor	sponsor
carburetor	(or inventer)	supervisor
competitor	legislator	ventilator

There are a few nouns of agent ending in *-ar: beggar, burglar, liar.*

-er, -re Many words formerly ending in *-re* are now spelled *-er* in American usage. This group includes the following:

caliber	luster	meter	somber
center	maneuver	scepter	specter
fiber	meager	sepulcher	theater

British usage tends to *-re* in most of these words, though Fowler says they are being changed to *-er* one by one, because "we prefer in England to break with our illogicalities slowly."

An American writer who wishes a slightly Formal flavor will tend to use the *-re* forms; most will naturally use the *-er* forms.

Theater is divided in spelling, partly because it is found in a good many proper names of buildings and companies which were set up when *theatre* was the more common spelling, partly because of prestige associations of *theatre*. Keep the form actually used in proper names and ordinarily use *theater* elsewhere.

Acre, lucre, mediocre keep the *-re* to represent a *c* pronounced *k* (contrast *soccer*), and *ogre* is the current form, though some words with *g,* like *meager,* have changed.

err Standard pronunciation of *err* is ûr; but as it occurs infrequently in speech, there is some tendency to pronounce it er, from *analogy with *error* (er′ər).

Esq., Esquire Written following a man's name in the inside and outside address of a letter, *Esq*. or *Esquire* is Formal, with archaic or British suggestion, and in the United States is not often used except occasionally to professional men, chiefly to lawyers. If used, no other title (*Mr., Dr., Hon.*) should precede the word: Harry A. Kinne, Esq.

etc., et cetera *Etc.,* read *et cetera* or *and so forth,* is sometimes a convenient way to end a series that samples rather than completes an enumeration, but it belongs primarily to reference and business usage, where the reader can be assumed capable of supplying the missing items from his own background.

The case is suitable for prints, maps, blueprints, etc.

Its inappropriateness can be seen in a sentence like this:

A student's professors can be of immense aid to him because of their knowledge of boys and their habits, customs, needs, ideals, etc.

Writing out *et cetera* now seems an affectation. In consecutive writing most people prefer the English "and so forth." It is better to avoid these end tags (which really take away from emphasis by putting a catchall at the end of a clause or sentence) by rephrasing the list, preceding it by *such as* or some other warning that the list you are giving is not exhaustive:

The case is suitable for large sheets such as prints, maps, and blueprints.

Using *and etc.* shows the writer doesn't realize that the *et* of *etc.* means *and,* so that he is writing *and and so forth.*

Euphemisms A euphemism is a softened word used in place of one that names more vigorously some suffering, or something unpleasant, or something regarded as not quite nice: *natural son* for *illegitimate son* or *bastard, separate from the college* for *expel* or *fire* or *flunk out.*

Occasionally euphemisms are warranted to avoid hurting someone's feelings. But in general it is safer–and better style–to call things by their right names, even if they are somewhat unpleasant. (For further discussion and examples see Ch. 8, "Euphemisms," p. 227.)

every and its compounds 1. *Every, everybody, everyone* in the early development of the language were treated as singulars and are often so used today.

Every man on the team did his best.
Everybody likes the new minister.
Everyone took his purchases home with him.

Very often these words are treated as collectives in all varieties of English. A verb immediately following *everyone* or *everybody* is usually singular, but a pronoun referring back to it from a little distance is likely to be plural: Everybody is taking off their hats.

This construction, especially common in British printed practice, is reasonable, since the reference is to a number of people. To make these expressions conform to Formal American written usage, it is often better to change the *everybody* to a more accurate plural or collective than to change the later pronoun:

They all did their best. The crowd are taking off their hats.

(Reference: Fries, *AEG,* p. 50.)

2. *Everybody* is always written as one word; *everyone* is usually written as one word, but when the *one* is stressed, as two:

Everybody knew what the end would be.
Everyone knew what the end would be.
Every one of the family knew what the end would be.

3. *Every so often, every bit as* are useful General idioms:

Every so often someone in the crowd would give a terrific shout.
They are every bit as happy as they expected to be.

4. *Every place* is an adverbial phrase, more widely used than *any place* (*any, § 4):

Every place I looked the people said the same thing.

except, accept *Except,* as a verb, means to "leave out, exclude": He excepted those who had done the assignment from the extra reading. It is decidedly Formal, and *excused* would be more natural in the sentence given.

Accept means to "receive" or to "answer affirmatively" and is slightly Formal: I accept with pleasure; He accepted the position.

We confuse these two words in writing partly because they are often pronounced alike but mainly because of carelessness. Remember that we see and write the preposition *except* (Everyone except you) much oftener than we do either of the verbs.

Exclamation mark (!) An exclamation mark (or point) is used after an emphatic interjection, after a phrase, clause, or sentence that is genuinely exclamatory, and after forceful commands. Clear-cut exclamations offer no problem:

Oh! Ouch! No, no, no!
"But," he protested, "it's the chance of a lifetime!"
A number of children playing on the quay saw him, and with a wild cry of "Squirrel! Squirrel!" went after him.– W. H. HUDSON, *The Book of a Naturalist,* p. 61

But many interjections are weak and deserve no more than a comma: Well, well, so you're in college now.

Often sentences cast in exclamatory pattern are really statements put that way for variety (*Exclamations) and the exclamation mark is optional. Its use would depend chiefly on appropriateness and the emphasis intended and on whether the writer tends to close punctuation (which is likely to show a number of exclamation marks) or open (which is more likely to rely on commas).

The country! [Or, a period] Why anybody ever went to the country. [Or, an exclamation mark] . . . He might be in New York with the gang. Playing ball in the streets, dodging the trucks, the cars, the cabs! [Or, a period]

Exclamation marks are more characteristic of imaginative writing, especially of fiction, than of factual writing. In factual writing it is well to remember that in some newspaper offices the exclamation mark is known as a screamer–and that its overuse is a mark of nervousness or of *schoolgirl style.

On a typewriter the mark can be made by typing a period below an apostrophe.

Exclamations are expressions of strong feeling or emphatic statements of fact or opinion. They range from the simple and often involuntary *Oh!* or *Ouch!* to fully developed sentences.

One word exclamations may be regarded as full sentences if they deserve that much emphasis (*Oh! You nearly upset my plate.*), or as parts of sentences if they seem to belong with other sentence elements: *Oh! you're here at last!* (or) *Oh, you're here at last!*

Many exclamations begin with *what* or *how*: *What a view! How could you! How lucky you are!*

An exclamation expressing an emphatic opinion gives not only emphasis but variety in a passage:

> But the methods chosen for the transition must always bear those human values in mind, for a whole new social order must inevitably result from a new kind of economic system, and in the process of slow nurture and growth initial trends may be all-important. Compulsion is a bad way to make men free!—ALFRED M. BINGHAM, *Insurgent America,* p. 6

Used just for variety or to give emphasis to what are really commonplaces, exclamations are ordinarily ineffective and give the effect of a strained or schoolgirl style:

> Think how often you have judged a person by the way in which he speaks! Think of a salesman who is a poor talker! It sounds like the height of unreality, but what a situation in this highly competitive world! Think of a college professor who could not intelligently lecture to his classes because he had not learned the art of elocution!

excuse, pardon Small slips are *excused;* more considerable faults (and crimes) are *pardoned*. "Pardon me" is sometimes considered more elegant than "Excuse me" in upper-class social situations. Either is appropriate for the numerous perfunctory apologies we make in everyday life. *Excuse* also has the special meaning of "giving permission to leave."

expect means "to look forward to" and also "to look for with confidence." In Formal English it is usually kept close to some meaning involving anticipation, but in Informal usage its meaning is extended and weakened to "suppose"—"I expect you'd better be going."

Experiment in written English Language and literary style tend to become stereotyped; as the same kinds of words are used over and over in the same kinds of constructions, their effectiveness in conveying individual impressions decreases. The more skillful writers escape monotony by the force of their message or the individuality of their expression, and most of them more or less consciously either ignore conventions of language or experiment with words or constructions.

Almost anyone with an interest in writing will experiment in his own Informal writing, trying out spelling, unusual words or combinations of words, unorthodox sentence patterns. Some writers in their published work experiment also. We might call any departure from the commonly written and printed English an experiment—if it is not just the result of carelessness or ignorance. Advertisers are active experimenters, using shortened spellings, created words, and free sentence forms. At the other extreme purists may also be regarded as experimenters, trying to limit speaking and writing to the Formal vocabulary and Formal constructions, as it never has been in all its history.

Writers like Damon Runyon and P. G. Wodehouse are really experimenters, since they create a lingo for their stories by taking ordinary traits of speech and pushing them further than natural usage would. This bit from Mr. Wodehouse shows his potpourri of colloquialisms, slang, literary phrases (and allusions), and created words (*bonhomous*):

> From his earliest years the Biscuit had nourished an unwavering conviction that Providence was saving up something particularly juicy in the way of rewards for him and that it was only a question of time before it came across and delivered the goods. He based this belief on the fact that he had always tried to be a reasonably bonhomous sort of bird and was one who, like Abou Ben Adhem, loved his fellow men. Abou had clicked, and Lord Biskerton expected to click. But not in his most sanguine moments, not even after a Bump Supper at Oxford or the celebration of somebody's birthday at the Drones, had he ever expected to click on this colossal scale. It just showed that, when Providence knew it had got hold of a good man, the sky was the limit.—P. G. WODEHOUSE, *Big Money*, p. 286

Writers like James Joyce, Gertrude Stein, and E. E. Cummings have experimented in English prose. One of the chief interests of these writers, aside from freshening the nature of English prose, has been to carry expression closer to thought, especially creating sentence patterns that follow or at least suggest the actual thought of a character or of the writer himself.

Gertrude Stein's explanation of why she did not use commas conventionally both describes and illustrates an experimental approach to these problems of language:

> As I say commas are servile and they have no life of their own, and their use is not a use, it is a way of replacing one's own interest and I do decidedly like to like my own interest my own interest in what I am doing. A comma by helping you along holding your coat for you and putting on your shoes keeps you from living your life as actively as you should lead it and to me for many years and I still do feel that way about it only now I do not pay as much attention to them, the use of them was positively degrading....
>
> ...And what does a comma do, a comma does nothing but make easy a thing that if you like it enough is easy enough without the comma. A long complicated sentence should force itself upon you, make you know yourself knowing it and the comma, well at the most a comma is a poor period that it lets you stop and take a breath but if you want to take a breath you ought to know yourself that you want to take a breath. It is not like stopping altogether which is what a period does stopping altogether has something to do with going on, but taking a breath well you are always taking a breath and why emphasize one breath rather than

another breath. Anyway that is the way I felt about it and I felt that about it very strongly. And so I almost never used a comma. The longer, the more complicated the sentence the greater the number of the same kind of words I had following one after another, the more the very many more I had of them the more I felt the passionate need of their taking care of themselves by themselves and not helping them, and thereby enfeebling them by putting in a comma.—GERTRUDE STEIN, *Lectures in America,* pp. 219-21

In *Finnegans Wake* James Joyce went on to experiment with words, breaking up familiar words, changing sounds slightly, combining elements:

> Yet he made leave to many a door beside of Finglas wold for so witness his chambered cairns silent that are at browse up hill and down coombe and on eolithostroton, at Howth or at Coolock or at Enniskerry. Olivers lambs we do call them and they shall be gathered unto him, their herd and paladin, in that day when he skall wake from earthsleep in his valle of briers and o'er dun and dale the Wulverulverlord (protect us!) his mighty horn skall roll, orland, roll.
>
> Liverpool? Sot a bit of it! His braynes coolt parritch, his pelt nassy, his heart's adrone, his bluidstreams acrawl, his puff but a piff, his extremities extremely so. Humph is in his doge. Words weigh no more to him than raindrops to Rethfernhim. Which we all like. Rain. When we sleep. Drops. But wait until our sleeping. Drain. Sdops.

For most readers this is carrying experiment too far. Certainly it is paying little attention to a reader or to demands of communication. A writer of course can write merely to please himself or for the fun of it (and there is much sheer fun back of most of this experimentation), but he cannot blame readers if they do not feel like bothering to decipher his cryptograms. Joyce was doing this quite voluntarily (or wilfully), for in *The Portrait of the Artist as a Young Man* and in the volume of short stories *Dubliners* he wrote a flexible and effective English. Similarly E. E. Cummings, whose *Eimi* is the story of a visit to Russia written in experimental prose, wrote one of the classics of the First World War—*The Enormous Room*—in a conventional but thoroughly individual prose. These experiments are not the work of writers who can't write English but of talented writers who are trying to make English prose more expressive, to make it come closer to representing their individual view of things.

Imitating the external traits of the style of experimental writers will usually mean failure because the imitator's needs are not the same as those of the pioneers. But reading such writers should give a writer courage to try to find a method of presenting his material as he sees it, even if that means departing from some of the conventions of writing. This is part of the spirit of modern literature.

References: Bonamy Dobrée, "Experiments," *Modern Prose Style,* Part iv, § 2; Gertrude Stein, "Poetry and Grammar," *Lectures in America* (New York, 1935).

Expository writing, exposition Writing that is intended primarily to inform its readers–by presenting facts, giving directions, recording events, interpreting facts, developing opinions–is expository.

The bulk of college writing, probably all except imaginative writing done in advanced composition courses, is expository. Some common types of exposition are discussed in Chapters 10-13. See also *Factual and imaginative writing, *Forms of discourse.

extracurricular means "outside the course of study" (extracurricular activities); it is sometimes hyphened but usually not. *Extracurriculum* is occasionally found as an alternate adjectival form.

F

The sound of *f* occurs spelled *f, ff, ph,* and *gh* (see *-ough). The words with *ph* go back to Greek words with *phi* (Φ): *philosophy, telephone;* a few have been simplified to *f: fantasy, sulfur.*

Nouns ending in *-f* usually have the corresponding voiced sound (v) in the plural: *leaf–leaves, loaf–loaves, wife–wives; beef* has either *beeves* or *beefs.*

Factual and imaginative writing The fundamental distinction underlying types of writing is that in some types the writer's first responsibility is confining himself to facts (in so far as they can be found) or to reasoning based on facts; in others he has the liberty of fabricating any action or picture or idea that may serve his purpose.

The principal types of factual writing are news stories, interviews, characterizations of people, biography, history, informational articles of all kinds; and, involving reasoning upon facts, reviews, editorials, critical articles on all sorts of subjects, personal essays, and discussions of more general ideas such as demonstration of hypotheses, theories, ideals, philosophical concepts. Whatever other qualities these articles may have, whatever their virtues or faults, they are fundamentally good or bad according as they approach the truth and correspond to some strand of human observation or experience. (This book discusses some of the types of factual writing in Chs. 10-13.)

The imaginative types, in which the writer's conception is the controlling factor, are poems, plays, short stories, novels.

falls, woods Though plural in form these words are really singular (or collective) in meaning. We speak of *a falls* or *a woods* but ordinarily use them with plural verbs (The falls *are* almost dry in August). In proper names they are frequently used with a singular verb (Niagara Falls *is* receding). The form *wood* is still common in England but seems Formal or archaic to us.

famed When *famed* is used for *famous* or *well known,* it usually suggests a journalese style, or a staccato one (as in *Time*):

famed eating place   famed Nobel prize winner
At seven-thirty we anchored off the famed yachting center.

It is often a sign of amateur writing to label as *famed* (or as *famous,* for that matter) really well-known people.

farther–further In Informal English no distinction is usually made between *farther* and *further,* and there is a marked tendency for *further* to be used in all senses.

In Formal English most people make a distinction between *farther* and *further,* confining the first to expressions of physical distance and the second to abstract relationships of degree or quantity:

We went on twenty miles *farther*. He went *farther* than I, but neither of us reached the town.

He carries that sort of thing *further* than I would. He went *further* into his family history. He got *further* and *further* into debt.

In General English, *farther* is usually used of distance, *further* for both distance and degree.

faze has worked its way from dialect (*feeze,* to disturb) into General usage. It means "to daunt or disconcert" and is almost always used negatively (The bawling out didn't faze him). Do not confuse this word with *phase,* meaning "aspect."

fellow is General and Informal when used to mean "person" but Formal in sense of "associate." It is most commonly used in writing in the function of an adjective: his fellow sufferers, a fellow feeling ("a similar feeling," or "sympathy").

female Usage now restricts *female* to designations of sex, usually in scientific contexts. This leaves English without a single word for female-human-being-regardless-of-age.

fiancé, fiancée About a century ago the English *betrothed* was replaced by the French word (probably by "society" journalists), and now we are cursed not only with accent marks but with separate forms for the man (fiancé) and the woman (fiancée). Pronunciation for both is fē′ən sā′, with a tendency to fē än′sā. The plurals are fiancés, fiancées. In newspapers and much General writing the accent mark is dropped, and it will probably soon disappear generally.

Fig **Figures of speech** Revision: This figure of speech is inappropriate, inconsistent, or threadbare. Revise the passage.

Words can be used in their usual meaning, or they can be borrowed to apply to other things. We can talk of music in terms of color, or moral problems in terms of a game, and so on. Fresh and appropriate figures can help a reader see and understand what you are talking about, but careless or tasteless figures detract. They may be threadbare, used as often as "a ribbon of concrete" or "old man Winter." This sentence has one trite and one fresh figure:

The strident shriek of a siren [Trite:] split the silence and [Fresh:] two searching fingers of light swung around the corner as if feeling for the scene of the disturbance.

They may be strained and unnatural, as in this description of dawn:

Over yonder hill Apollo thrust the blade of his golden sword, severing the filmy mist that blanketed the paths of old Onondaga.

Or they may be inconsistent ("mixed"), as in this mélange:

But then the molehill of annoyance grew into a mountain of hate and chased love out of the home.

Such figures stamp a person as an immature or careless writer.

The effective use of figures of speech is discussed in Chapter 8, "Figurative use of words," page 232. The most common figures (metaphors, similes, metonymy, irony, exaggeration, and understatement) are described in that chapter. Other figures are discussed in *Index* articles: *Alliteration, *Epigrams (and proverbs, paradoxes), *Imitative words and phrases, *Negatives, *Personification, *Puns.

finance, financier Pronunciation of these words is divided:

Verb: fi nans′, fī′nans

Noun: fi nans′, fī′nans (the latter conforming to the English *noun and verb stress)

Noun: fin′ən sir′, fī′nən sir′; occasionally (British) fi nan′si ər

The i-ī variation also occurs in *finan′cial,* but the accent stays on the second syllable.

fine is widely used as a *counter word of general approval, slightly more vigorous than *nice,* but of little value in writing and better omitted:

Spring football practice has one aim, to weld eleven men into a [fine,] coordinated team.

It may, of course, be used in any of its more restricted senses.

Finite verbs A finite verb form is one that is limited (Latin *finis,* "end, limit")—that is, that can be limited in *person* (by one of the pronouns or by a subject), or in *time* (by a tense form: *goes, went*), or in *number* (singular or plural). These are contrasted with the "infinite" parts—the infinitives (*go, to go, to have gone*), participles (*going, gone*), and verbal nouns (*going*)—which are not limited in person or number. These become "finite" in verb phrases in which the variable characteristics are indicated by an "auxiliary" or function word (he *is* going, he *will* go, he *has* gone).

Finite verbs can be main verbs in clauses and sentences (I *had gone* before he *came*); infinite parts are ordinarily in subordinate constructions (*Verbids): Before *coming; Gone* with the wind. (But see *Infinitives § 5 and *Participles § 4.)

fish The plural is also *fish* (We got only six fish after fishing all day), except in speaking of various species of fish, as in "Most of the income of the island is from these fishes: cod, halibut, and sword."

fix In Formal usage *fix* means to "fasten in place"; in General usage it means to "repair" or to "put in shape." *Fix* as a noun meaning "predicament" (to be in a fix) is Informal, as is its sense of "a bribed arrangement."

flaunt–flout *Flaunt* (flônt) to "wave, display boastfully," and *flout* (flout), to "insult, treat with contempt," are sometimes confused.

folk–folks Formal English and some local speech use *folk* as the plural; General usage has *folks,* especially in the sense of "members of a family."

Folklore and *folkway* are written as one word, *folk dance, folk music, folk tale* usually as two; *folk song* and *folksong* are both used.

for For distinction between *because* and *for,* see *because.

A comma is usually needed between two coordinate clauses joined by *for;* without it the *for* might be read as a preposition:

> He was glad to go, for Mrs. Crane had been especially good to him. (Not: He was glad to go for Mrs. Crane....)

Since *for* almost always comes between the clauses it joins, it is usually classified as a coordinating conjunction, but the clause it introduces is often actually subordinate: He was exhausted, for he had gone two nights without sleep. (Reference: Henry L. Wilson, "The Classification of the Conjunction 'For,'" *American Speech,* 1952, 27:257-260.)

Foreign words in English 1. *Anglicizing foreign words.* English has always borrowed words and roots freely from other languages and is still borrowing, especially from Greek and French. Most borrowed words that have been used for a long time cannot be told from native English words, but those taken in recently often raise questions. They usually cross the threshold of English with their foreign pronunciation and spelling and perhaps with un-English plurals or other forms. The process of anglicizing brings them more or less in line with English usage, but they may keep some of their foreign quality, like the *i* of *machine,* the silent *s* in *debris,* the *t* where English is tempted to put a *d* in *kindergarten.*

Many loan words are in a transition stage, showing two spellings (*maneuver–manoeuvre, role–rôle*); with others we are experimenting with pronunciations, the winner not yet clearly seen (*melee:* mā lā′, mā′lā, mel′ā, and even mē′lē; *zwieback:* tsvē′bäk, tswē′bäk, swī′bak, zwī′bak). Some words that have been in English a considerable time are still changing, especially in stress (*debris:* də brē′–deb′rē) and in consonant sounds (*massage:* mə säzh′–mə säj′). These words show how a rough compromise is worked out between English practice and the original form.

The speed and degree of anglicizing depends on how frequently the word is used, the circumstances in which it is used, and the people who use it. The attitude of linguists is that if a word proves useful it will assume a natural English form. *Hors d'oeuvre* is a useful word, but its looks are conspicuously un-English. If menu makers would spell it *orderve,* we could all be happy with it. (Instead they seem to be adapting the English *starter.*)

Formal writers and conservative editors tend to keep the foreign spellings longer than General writers and editors. If the words come in through the spoken language, like those of the automobile vocabulary, they usually become English or near-English sooner than if they come in by way of literature: we have *chassis* (shas′i or shas′is, sometimes chas′is), *chauffeur* (shō′fər—the spelling lagging), *garage* (gə räzh′ or gə räj′—in England gar′ij), *detour* (dē′toor). Words that come in through and remain in literary, scholarly, or "polite" circles change more slowly, in both spelling and pronunciation: *tête-à-tête, faux pas, nouveau riche.*

2. *Use of borrowed words.* The best reason for using an unnaturalized or partly naturalized word is that it supplies a real lack in English—perhaps says in one word what English would have to use a phrase or sentence to express. *Entrepreneur,* "one who undertakes business, especially assumes commercial risk," is useful since the English *undertaker* has a special meaning of its own. *Beige,* "the color of unbleached wool or cotton," *suede, tableau, protégé* are useful. We have also taken in a number of words and phrases of doubtful usefulness: *entre nous,* when we have *between ourselves,* or *in confidence; affaire du coeur* for *love affair, raison d'être* for *reason for being,* and so on. Most of the words given in the list in § 5 are a definite convenience to users of English, but the general use of foreign words needs to be watched.

Sometimes the gain is in force or tone or suggestion, as *ersatz* is stronger than *substitute,* and *liaison* brings with it either a connotation of social unconventionality or of military activity, depending on the context. *Nouveau riche* brings its suggestion of dispraise, replacing an earlier borrowing, *parvenu,* which in turn displaced the more blunt *upstart.* French words are often used for tone, especially in discussing (and more especially in advertising) women's fashions: *chic, svelte, lapin* (*rabbit* in other places)—and even *sacque,* which doesn't exist in French. A couple of generations ago French was used a good deal for polite social euphemisms, to avoid plain English: *demimonde, fille de joie, femme de chambre, enceinte, accouchement.* Now these have generally gone out of use, their place once more taken by straight English, except with the falsely modest. Parading foreign words, a temptation to some who are learning a language or have just returned from abroad, is usually in bad taste, and their use even by people wholly at home with the languages is likely to be inappropriate. Fitness to material, to readers, and to the writer himself will usually decide whether a foreign word should be used.

3. *Handling borrowed words in copy.*

a) Italics. Words which have not been completely anglicized are printed in italics in magazines and books and should be underlined in copy. Newspapers do not use italics for such purposes, and their practice of course has tended to lessen the use of italics by others. There are always many words on the borderline which will be found sometimes in italics, sometimes not. Formal writers tend to use more italics; General, fewer. Consult a recent dictionary for doubtful words —remembering that it will represent conservative usage.

b) Accent and other marks. Words recently taken in from French are usually written with accent marks if they were so written in French. Newspapers do not use accent marks except sometimes in departments like the editorial, art, music, and fashion pages. After they have been used for a time in English, the accents are usually dropped unless they are necessary to indicate pronunciation. *Matinee, melee, role* do not need marks; *blasé* does. Similarly *cañon* is now usually spelled *canyon,* but: *piñon.* A cedilla shows that a *c* before *a* or *o* is pronounced *s: façade, soupçon.*

In German all nouns are capitalized, and recent or infrequent borrowings from German are capitalized in English, particularly if they are still printed in italics. *Anschluss, Realpolitik, Weltanschauung,* but hinterland, kindergarten, blitzkrieg. The umlaut can be replaced by an *e* after the vowel: *Mädchen* or *Maedchen.*

c) Plurals. English usually brings borrowed words into its own system of conjugation and declension, though some words change slowly, especially words used mainly in Formal writing (**formulae–formulas*). *Beaus* is now more common than *beaux,* and *tableaus* is gaining on *tableaux.* (See *Plurals § 4.)

A few French adjectives may keep both masculine and feminine forms: **blond, blonde; debonair, debonaire.*

4. *Pronunciation.* For pronunciation of borrowed words, see the examples given in § 5 or consult a dictionary. Because the speech sounds of one language are different from those of another, it is almost impossible to say a foreign word the way it is spoken in its original language unless you are thoroughly familiar with that language. If there is an established English pronunciation, you should use it, especially since you are more likely to be understood.

5. *List of borrowed words.* This list contains a small selection of loan words in fairly common use. Those in italics would ordinarily be italicized in print. When two forms are separated by a dash, they are both common. A form in brackets is less common than the other. Pronunciations are indicated for words which might offer difficulty. For words not given here consult a recent dictionary. See *Pronunciation § 1 for key to symbols.

aid-de-camp–aide-de-camp (ād′də kamp′)
*a la
à la carte
alamode
bourgeois (boor′zhwä–boor zhwä′)
brassiere [brassière] (brə zir′)
buffet (bə fā′–boo fā′)

bushido (bo͞o′shē dō′)
café (ka fā′–kə fā′)
chic (shēk–shik; often chik)
cliché (klē shā′)
coiffure (kwä fyoor′)
communiqué (kə mū′nə kā′–kə mū′nə kā)
corps; plu. corps (kōr; plu. kōrz)
coup; plu. coups(ko͞o; plu. ko͞oz)
coup d'état (ko͞o dā tä′)
coupé–coupe (ko͞o pā′–ko͞op)
crèche [creche] (krāsh–kresh)
crepe–crêpe–crape (krāp)
crescendo (krə shen′dō–krə sen′dō)
debut (di bū′–dā′bū–dā bū′)
debutante (deb′yoo tänt–deb′yə tant)
dirndl
Don Juan (don jo͞o′ən–don hwän′)
Don Quixote (don kwik′sət–don kē hō′tē)
dramatis personae (dram′ə tis pər sō′nē)
éclair–eclair (ā klar′)
entree–entrée (än′trā)
fete [fête] (fāt)
hari-kari (hä′ri kä′ri)
lingerie (lan′zhə rē′–län′zhə rā′)
matériel–materiel
matinee (mat ə nā′–mat′ə nā)
mayonnaise
menu (men′ū–mā′nū; French pronunciation not current)
milieu (mē lyû′)
monsieur (mə syû′); plu. messieurs–messrs. (mes′ərz–mə syû′)
muzhik–moujik (mo͞o zhik′–mo͞o′zhik)
negligee [négligé] (neg′lə zhā′–neg′lə zhā′)
obbligato–obligato (ob′li gä′tō)
papier-mâché (pā′pər mə shā′)
passé (pa sā′–pas′ā)
précis (prā′sē–prā sē′)
premiere–première (pri mir′–prə myer′)
protégé (masc.), protégée (fem.) (prō′tə zhā)
quasi (kwa′si–kwa′zi [kwä′si])
questionnaire [questionary] (kwes′chən ãr′)
rendezvous (rän′də vo͞o); plu. rendezvous (rän′də vo͞oz)
repertoire (rep′ər twär [rep′ər twôr])–repertory
résumé (rez′oo mā′)
ricochet (rik ə shā′–rik ə shet′)
salon (sə lon′)–*salon* (sä lôɴ′)
slalom (slä′lōm [slā′ləm])
status quo (stā′təs kwō–stat′əs kwō)
stein (stīn)
suede–suède (swād)
vs.–vs (vûr′səs)
Weltschmertz (velt′shmerts′)

See *English language, *Latin and English, *Origin of words, *Plurals § 4. References: Kenyon and Knott, § 122; Brander Matthews, "The Englishing of French Words," *Society for Pure English Tracts,* 1920, v, 3-20; T. R. Palfrey, "The Contribution of Foreign Language Study to Mastery of the Vernacular," *Modern Language Journal,* 1941, pages 550-557.

Formal English Revision: The word or passage marked is too Formal for the subject or for the style of the rest of the paper. Revise, making it more General. *Form*

Formal English is the usage characteristic of people who work a good deal with books, particularly members of the various professions. It is appropriate for discussions of ideas, for scientific and scholarly writing, for addresses to audiences of considerable education, for literary works that are intended for a somewhat restricted reading public. Formal English is not so appropriate for day to day speaking and writing, for accounts of personal experience, casual comment, and other sorts of writing intended for the general reading public. (For discussion and examples, see Ch. 1, "Formal English," p. 20.)

former–first, latter–last *Former* and *latter* refer only to two units:

> The mountain and the squirrel
> Had a quarrel,
> And the former called the latter, "little prig";
>
> RALPH WALDO EMERSON, *Fable*

First and *last* refer to items in a series, usually of more than two:

> The first president had set up a very informal organization.
> His last act was to advise his family on their future.

Latest refers to a series that is still continuing (the latest fashions). *Last* refers either to the final item of a completed series (their last attempt was successful) or to the most recent item of a continuing series (the last election).

Forms of discourse For the last hundred years or so it has been conventional to divide writing into "four forms of discourse"—narration, description, exposition, and argument. This division allows concentration on certain traits of material, organization, and style peculiar to each type. It is now less used than formerly because the types are rarely found in a pure state—description contributes to all, notably to narration, and so on—and a person does not think of himself as writing one of these forms but rather a particular sort of article or type of literature.

This book divides writing into two broad types, factual writing (biography, history, informational and critical articles and books of all sorts) and imaginative writing (poems, plays, short stories, novels). (See *Factual and imaginative writing and Chs. 9-13.)

formula The plural is *formulas* or *formulae,* the former the more common.

Formulas Every language has some phrases that have become fixed by long usage in certain situations: *Once upon a time, Ladies and gentlemen, Good morning, How are you? How do you do? Best wishes, Yours truly*. Occasionally fresh substitutes can be found for these, but more often the attempt merely calls attention to itself. Such phrases, though stereotyped, are too useful to be called trite, and they are not, as most trite expressions are, substitutes for some simpler locution. They should be used without apology and without embarrassment whenever they are needed.

Fractions Fractions are written in figures when they are attached to other figures (72¾), or are in a series that is being written in figures

(½, ⅔, 1, 2, 4), or are in tables or reference matter. In consecutive writing they are usually written in words (In the local newspaper three fourths of the space was given to advertising, one eighth to news, and one eighth to miscellaneous matters). Hyphens may be used between the numerator and denominator if neither part itself contains a hyphen, but they are less used than formerly and are not used at all when the numerator has the value of an adjective (as in "He sold one half and kept the other").

seven tenths [seven-tenths] eight twenty-sevenths
twenty-nine fortieths–twenty nine fortieths

Decimals are increasingly used in place of fractions in expository writing, since they are more flexible and may be more accurate. They are always written in figures: .7 .42 3.14159

See *Numbers.

Fragmentary sentence Revision: The construction marked is not a complete sentence. Revise by completing its form, by joining to a neighboring sentence, or by rewriting the passage. *Frag*

A fragmentary sentence (sentence fragment) is a sentence part—usually a phrase or subordinate clause—carelessly or ineffectively punctuated as a whole sentence. By its form, it suggests dependence on another construction, and editors usually make sure it does not stand as a sentence. Ordinarily one should be joined to the preceding or following sentence or made into an independent sentence. In college writing fragmentary sentences are usually the result of carelessness; they are one of the most serious errors and should be avoided.

Three common types with suggested revision follow:

Fragmentary sentence	*Revised*
Since 1939 we had been walking slowly in the direction of war. [Phrase:] Step by step until finally there was no other alternative but to declare war.	Since 1939 we had been walking slowly in the direction of war, step by step, until finally there was no other alternative but to declare war.
He talked for fifty minutes without taking his eyes off his notes. [Participial phrase:] Apparently not noticing that half the class was asleep.	He talked for fifty minutes without taking his eyes off his notes. Apparently he did not notice that half the class was asleep.
The first six books I looked for couldn't be taken out of the library. [Subordinate clause:] Because they were on reserve for an advanced history course.	The first six books I looked for couldn't be taken out of the library because they were on reserve for an advanced history course.

(For further discussion and other examples see Ch. 2, "Revising sentence fragments," p. 54. See also *Clauses, *Phrases.)

freshman, freshmen Since these words are pronounced alike (fresh′mən), their spelling is often confused, not so often when they are used as nouns (a freshman, forty freshmen) as when *freshman* is used as a modifier (freshman class, freshman spirit). *Freshmen* should never stand before a noun in this construction.

It is not necessary to capitalize *freshman* (or *sophomore, junior, senior*), but courtesy or emphasis sometimes makes a capital appropriate, and often one is used when speaking of the Freshman Class, the Junior Class, as a definite organization.

-ful, full When the adjective *full* is used as a suffix to nouns of measure (*basketful, spoonful*) or of feeling or quality (*peaceful, sorrowful, soulful*) it has only one *l*.

The plural of nouns ending in *-ful* is usually made with *-s: spoonfuls, basketfuls* (or *basketsful*). See *spoonful, spoonfuls.

Function words **1.** Some words carry relatively little independent meaning in themselves, serving rather to indicate relationships, to point out grammatical functions. Some such words are:

Prepositions, which join nouns to other words in a construction; the *of* in the phrase form of the genitive (of the man) is conspicuously a function word.

Conjunctions, which show the relation between clauses.

Auxiliary verbs when they indicate time, person, number, of a verb (*is* asking, *has* asked, *did* he ask) without otherwise modifying meaning.

Some adverbs and adjectives, most conspicuously *more* and *most* in comparisons of adjectives and adverbs (more handsome, most handsome).

2. *Stylistic qualities of function words.* Different varieties of usage have some characteristic habits in the use of function words. The more elaborate sentences of Formal English tend to make appropriate heavier connectives, such as *conjunctive adverbs (*however, accordingly* . . .); General style tends to rely more on coordinating conjunctions (*but, for, and* . . .) and subordinating conjunctions (*although, because, since* . . .).

Informal English shows a good many compound or group prepositions, for many of which Formal English would use a single preposition: *in back of* (*behind*); *in regard to* (*about*). Too many of these long connectives tend to give a sentence a rather weak movement and a rhythm without many strong stresses. In rapid speech they are passed over easily, but they sometimes become conspicuous in writing.

Linguists vary in their use of the category of function words. The fullest treatment is in Fries, *Structure,* Chapter 6. The subject has not been sufficiently examined to be regarded as a stable part of the description of English. (See *Parts of speech, *Conjunctions, *Prepositions.)

Fundamentals The selection of what can be regarded as fundamentals in estimating a piece of writing depends on judgment, and judgments vary. In this book the fundamentals are taken to be the following, the most important first:

1) *The material presented is the most fundamental factor* and deserves most consideration in the process of writing and most weight in criticizing and evaluating a piece of writing. Nothing can take the place of important and interesting material, though its values can be increased or diminished by the treatment.

2) *The method and attitude of the writer* is of next importance. He may use too few details or too many; he may select them according to an intelligent or an unwise or biased principle; he may have an exaggerated idea of the importance of his subject, or approach it with too much or too little sentiment, reverence, humor, or realism; he may or may not direct his statements to readers.

3) *The plan* of an article is important, since in part through it the writer guides the reader to see his sense of the matter. Too slow a beginning and too trivial an end are serious faults, as is failure to show relation between parts.

4) Finally a piece of writing is affected by the *mechanics and style* of the writer, which may either hinder the reader or increase his satisfaction. Poor material presentably written has no future, but worthwhile material even if poorly written can with sufficient work be made presentable.

We consciously or unconsciously make some such balancing of qualities in deciding what we think of what we read. Realizing the relative worth of these qualities makes it easier for student and teacher to understand each other's judgments.

funny In Formal English *funny* means only "comical," "laughable," but in Informal English it means also "odd": "That's funny. I thought he did."

Fused sentence A *fused sentence* is the name sometimes given to two grammatically complete sentences written with no mark of punctuation between them (The dress shop was sponsoring a style show they asked Jeanine to model since she was a steady customer). It is simply exceptional carelessness in writing, one step worse than the typical comma fault. (See Ch. 2, "Revising comma faults," p. 56 and *Comma faults.)

G

G, like *c,* spells a "hard" and a "soft" sound. The hard sound is more common than the soft.

1. *"Hard g"* (g). *G* is hard before *a, o,* and *u* (except in *margarine* and the British gaol [jail]): *garrulous, gong, gutter;* when doubled: *doggerel, noggin, toboggan;* at the ends of words: *beg, dig, fig;* before another consonant in the same syllable: *togs, glen;* frequently before *i: begin, gill* (of a fish), *gig;* and as an exception in *get.*

Gh spells hard *g,* helpfully in *ghetto* but uselessly in *aghast* and *ghost,* since the *g* would be hard anyway before the *a* and *o.*

Gu, taken from French, spells hard *g: guard, guess, guide, guernsey.*

2. *"Soft g"* (j) is found typically before *e* and *i: gem, gentleman, genus, gill* (the measure), *gibbet, gin.* It is often spelled *ge* or *dge, age* (āj), *edge* (ej), *fudge* (fuj); other spellings of the sound are *j*oy, exa*gg*erate, ver*du*re, gran*de*ur, sol*di*er.

3. *G* is sometimes pronounced *zh,* chiefly in partly anglicized words from French: *garage, massage, mirage.* These words tend to have soft *g* after they have been in English a long time (*carriage, marriage*): *garage* is often gə räj′ (in England, gar′ij); *massage* is tending toward mə säj′.

4. *"Silent g."* Initial *g* is silent in *gnaw, gnat, gnome, gnu . . . ,* and within a word *g* is often silent before *m* or *n: diaphragm, sign.* It is sounded in some derivatives of this latter type of word: *signal.*

5. *"Dropping g's."* In Formal and much General usage the present participle ends in the consonant sound that is spelled *ng;* in Informal speech the *ng* sound is often replaced by *n: singin', laughin'.* Because of the spelling, this is usually referred to as "dropping *g*'s," though actually there is no *g* sound involved but two different nasal consonants. The form ending in *-n* is the older. Originally the present participle ended in *-and* and later in *-en* or *-in,* and this has always been the form for the majority of speakers of English. In the speech of London and vicinity, which became the basis of written English, the present participle was confused with the verbal noun, ending in *-ung.* Now everyone *writes* the participle with *-ing,* but many continue the old pronunciation with *-in.* (See Milton Ellis, *English Journal,* 1937, 26:753. Compare *ng. Reference: Kenyon and Knott, *-ing.*)

Gender Gender as applied to English is the indication of sex or sexlessness. Many languages have special endings for masculine, feminine, and neuter nouns and for articles and adjectives modifying them (and in these languages gender is a strictly grammatical concept), but English abandoned this system several hundred years ago. Now, except in the pronouns *he, she, it* and a few nouns with endings such as *-ess, -us, -a, -or, -ix, -e, -eur, -euse* (*actress, mistress, alumnus, alumna, actor, aviator, aviatrix, administratrix, blonde, comedienne, masseur, masseuse*), gender is indicated only by the meaning of a word: *man—woman, nephew—niece, rooster—hen.* Compounds, partly to show gender, partly for emphasis, are common and expressive: *she-witch, he-bear, boy friend, girl friend.* Nouns referring to inanimate objects are neuter. For most English words gender is identifiable only by the choice of pronoun (*he, she, it*) that would be used to refer to them—and is consequently not a very important grammatical category:

The speaker hesitated, choosing *his* next words deliberately.
The novelist has presented *her* chief character effectively.

In Formal, literary English there is a weak sort of personification (or animation) in which the sun or moon or a ship or almost any object may be referred to as *he* (The sun sent forth his cheering beams) or more often as *she* (The moon has cast her gentle light). In Informal English *she* frequently replaces *it,* especially if intimacy or affection is involved: a car or a college or a country or any object may be a *she.*

We need a pronoun to represent either-he-or-she. Referring to a baby or an animal of unknown sex, *it* is the usual solution; otherwise *he.* (See *he-or-she, *blond, blonde, *naive–naïve.)

Genitive case Revision: Correct the form of the genitive case marked. (Usually this means using an apostrophe.) *Gen*

1. The genitive (or possessive) case in English is shown in four ways:

a) The *s*-genitive. *'s* is the spelling of the genitive case of all singular and a few plural nouns in which the word is pronounced with an added sound (s or z) and of the indefinite pronouns (*anyone, everybody . . .*):

boy's	horse's	one's	King of England's
men's	brother-in-law's	somebody's	

An apostrophe alone may be added to words that already end in an *s, sh,* or *z* sound, as in regularly made plurals in *-s:*

horses'	Moses'	*Jones' (singular) or Jones's
Joneses' (plural)	coaches'	conscience' (for conscience' sake)

Words of one syllable ending in these sounds have either the apostrophe alone or *'s,* pronounced as an added syllable:

Charles' (chärlz)–Charles's (chärl′zəz) coach's (gōch′əz)
fish's (fish′əz) Zeus' (zo͞os)–Zeus's (zo͞os′əz)

The apostrophe is an inaudible mark which can show the genitive only in writing; in speech the genitive is distinguished from the plural by its position before a noun (the doctor's first case) or as a predicate where the context would make a plural impossible (The criticism is Gamble's). In writing, the genitive plural is distinguished from the singular by the position of the apostrophe, but in speech the number is not always clear: I saw the boy's (boys') books.

When two coordinate nouns are in the genitive, the sign of the case is often added only to the last one:

Fred and Bert's first attempt. (Formal: Fred's and Bert's).
He had never thought of his wife and children's future.
But: Mary's and Tom's bicycles. (Separate objects possessed)

b) The *of*-genitive: He had never known the love of a child (= a child's love); the plays of Shakespeare.

The *of*-genitive always stands after the noun it limits: the leaves of the tree (= the tree's leaves).

The *of*-genitive is rather more common with names of inanimate objects than the *s*-genitive is, but both are used; the *s*-genitive is the more common form with names of people, though both are used:

the car's rattles	the rattles of the car
a stone's throw	the flowers of the field
a day's work	the work of a lifetime
Doctor Clark's house	the house of Doctor Clark

(Reference: "Current English Forum," *College English,* 1953, 14:236-239; 1954, 16:55-56.)

In most instances sound–euphony and rhythm–decides whether the *s*- or *of*-genitive is used. Since the *of*-form is longer, it often fits into sonorous and emotional phrases (at the home of Doctor Clark) and allows a more characteristic English rhythm than the compact *s*-genitive.

There is also a possible difference of meaning between the two forms. "Jane's picture" would usually mean a picture belonging to Jane, though it might mean a picture of Jane. "A picture of Jane" can mean only that Jane is represented in the picture.

c) Double genitive. Using both the *s*- and *of*-genitives together is an English idiom of long and respectable standing. It is especially common in locutions beginning with *that* or *this* and usually has an Informal flavor:

that boy of Henry's, friends of my father's, these hobbies of Miss Filene's

It is useful in avoiding the ambiguity mentioned at the end of § b above: "Jane's picture" is resolved either as "the picture of Jane" or "the picture of Jane's."

d) Genitive of the personal pronouns. The personal and relative pronouns have genitive forms without an apostrophe:

my your his her its our their whose

It is as important *not* to put apostrophes in these pronouns (and in the forms used without nouns: *ours, yours, theirs, hers*) as it is to put one in a noun in the genitive. (See *Pronouns § 1, *its, *which, *who.)

2. *Uses of the genitive.* The most common function of the genitive is to indicate possession:

the professor's house   my son   Bert's wife

The genitive also indicates a number of other relationships:

Description: a man's job   children's toys   suit of wool

Doer of an act ("Subjective genitive"): the wind's force   the force of the wind   Sinclair Lewis' second novel   with the dean's permission   with the permission of the dean (The subjective genitive usual with gerunds:) The doctor's coming relieved the strain. (See *Gerund.)

Recipient of an act ("Objective genitive"): the policeman's murderer the murderer of the policeman   the bill's defeat

Adverb: He drops in of an evening.

See Chapter 3, "Using apostrophes," page 82. More details of these and other genitive relations will be found in the large grammars. References: Curme, *Parts of Speech,* pages 133-136, *Syntax,* pages 70-88; Fries, *AEG,* pages 72-88.

Gerund Revision: Make the construction with this gerund idiomatic. *Ger*

1. *Form and use.* 2. *Subject of a gerund.* 3. *Phrases with gerunds.* 4. *Without "the."* 5. *Idioms with gerunds.*

1. *Form and use.* A *gerund*—also called a verbal noun—is the form of the verb ending in *-ing* used in the function of a noun. It has the same form as the present participle but differs in use:

Gerund: *Running* a hotel appealed to him. (*Running* is the subject.)

Participle: *Running* around the corner, he bumped into a cop. (*Running* modifies *he.*)

Broncho Bill Schindler started the ball *rolling* [participle, modifying *ball*] by *crashing* [gerund, object of *by*] into the heavy guardrail.

A gerund may take an object (as in *running a hotel*) or a complement (*being a hero*), and it may serve in any noun function:

Subject: *Looking* for an apartment always fascinated her.

Object: He taught *dancing.*

Predicate noun: Seeing is *believing.*

Used as modifier: a *fishing* boat (a boat for fishing, not a boat that fishes), *boiling* point, a *living* wage.

When not in one of these constructions, a gerund is related to the rest of the sentence by a preposition (§ 3).

Gerunds may show tense:

	Active	*Passive*
Present:	Just *seeing* the fire was enough.	*Being seen* was bad enough.
Perfect:	Just *having seen* the fire was enough.	*Having been seen* was bad enough.

Gerunds may be modified by adjectives when the noun function is uppermost or by adverbs when the verb function is emphasized:

Modified by adjective: *Good boxing* is first-rate entertainment.

Modified by adverb: *Playing well* was his great pride.

2. *Subject of a gerund.* The subject of a gerund sometimes has the genitive and sometimes the accusative (or common) case. In Formal writing the genitive is more usual; in General writing usage is divided.

a) When the subject is a personal pronoun or a word standing for a person, it is usually in the genitive:

His coming was all that she looked forward to.

She looked forward to *Bob's coming.*

b) If the subject is a plural noun, it is likely to be in the common form:

I don't approve of *men drinking.*
I don't approve of *students coming and going* as they like.
With a pronoun: I don't approve of *them drinking.* (Or:) I don't approve of *their drinking.*

c) If the subject is abstract or the name of an inanimate object, it is usually in the common form:

It was a case of *imagination getting* out of control.
The *roof* [or *roof's*] *falling in* was only the first disaster.

d) When the subject is modified by other words, it is in the common form:

In spite of the *plan* of the committee *being voted down* no one could offer a better one.
The principal's *contract running out* gave an excuse for letting him go.

e) When the subject is stressed, it is usually in the accusative, even if it is a pronoun:

Who would have thought of *him* [stressed] *getting* the prize?
Have you heard about *Gertrude* [stressed] *getting* a job?

3. *Phrases with gerunds.* Gerunds are often used in phrases that have the value and function of subordinate clauses (see *Verbids):

In coming to an agreement, they had compromised on all points.
It's the best thing *for coughing at night.*

The relation of the gerund phrase to the word it modifies should be immediately apparent. In the first two examples below, though there is no real ambiguity since only one interpretation is possible, there is likely to be some interruption of the flow of communication as the reader pauses to make sure just what it is that the writer intended:

Dangling: *In coming to an agreement,* a compromise had to be voted. (The compromise did not come to the agreement, but *they* or some other word meaning the voters.)
Dangling: *After reading sixteen books,* the subject is still a blank to me.
Immediately clear: *After reading sixteen books,* I am still blank about the subject.

(See Ch. 2, "Revising dangling modifiers," p. 64.)

4. *Without "the."* In current style there is a tendency to use gerunds without *the* and with a direct object rather than an *of* phrase. This emphasizes the verbal phase of the word and makes for economy and force.

His chief amusement is *telling jokes* on the President. (Rather than: His chief amusement is *the telling of jokes* on the President.)

In *revising the first draft,* a writer can check all the spellings. (Rather than: In *the revising of the first draft* . . . .)

5. *Idioms with gerunds.* Some words are characteristically followed by gerunds, others by infinitives. For example:

Gerunds	*Infinitives*
cannot help *doing*	compelled *to do*
capable *of painting*	able *to paint*
the habit *of giving*	the tendency *to give*
an idea *of selling*	a wish *to sell*
his object *in doing*	obligation *to pay*

With many words, especially common ones, either idiom is used: the way *of doing* something, the way *to do* something.

See Chapter 3, "Infinitive or gerund," page 91. Compare *Participles, *Infinitives. Reference: Curme, *Syntax,* Chapter 24.

get, got **1.** *Forms.* Principal parts: *get, got, got* and *gotten:*

I am getting a new racket. I got six inside an hour.
I had already got [gotten] mine.
Rebel though I was, I had got the religion of scholarship and science. —LINCOLN STEFFENS, *Autobiography,* p. 127

Gotten was brought to America by the colonists of the seventeenth century, when it was the usual English form, and has remained in general American usage ever since, while in England the form has given way to *got*. Today both forms are used by Americans as the past participle (except in "have got," as in § 2 below), the choice between them depending largely on the emphasis and rhythm of the particular sentence and on the user's speech habits. *Gotten* is probably the more common.

He could have [*gotten* or *got*] here by now.
In the past I have [*gotten* or *got*] a good meal here.

2. *Have got. Got* (and not *gotten*) is used as an Informal way of intensifying *have* in the sense of possess or of being obligated (Have you got a pencil?—I've got to study now). The *have* alone could carry the meaning, but it is unemphatic, especially when contracted, because it is so frequently used as a mere auxiliary of tense that we are not accustomed to feeling it as a verb of full meaning. Consequently the *got* has a considerable advantage in speech. Some Formal writers avoid it, but the idiom is in General use and is appropriate in any but the most Formal situation. (Reference: Albert H. Marckwardt, " 'Have Got' in Expressions of Possession and Obligation," *College English,* 1955, 16:309-310.)

3. *"Get" in idioms. Get* is one of the most popular verbs in idiomatic phrases, in most of which it doesn't have its original meaning shown in the sentences under § 1 but is a relatively colorless linking verb. Most of these idioms are Informal:

get cold	get sick	get tired	get scared
get going	get to go	get in touch with	get supper
get left	get on my nerves	get away with	get along with
get me?	get it across	get together	

"But I got to," she cried. "I just have to talk to somebody. I didn't go home. I got worried, awful scared...."—ARTHUR SOMERS ROCHE, *Shadow of Doubt,* p. 93

4. *"Get" as a passive auxiliary. Get* is increasingly used as an Informal emphatic passive auxiliary:

He got thrown out inside of an hour. Our house is getting painted.

(See Adelaide C. Bartlett, *College English,* 1949, 10:280-282; Curme, *Parts of Speech,* p. 218; Pooley, pp. 148-151.)

Given names Ordinarily either spell out or use the initial of given names (also called Christian names) rather than such abbreviations as *Chas., Thos., Wm.:*

F. T. Graves	or	Frederick T. Graves
T. W. Lane	or	Thomas W. Lane

gladiolus is a revealing example of *divided usage. The singular is pronounced glad i ō′ləs or glə dī′ ə ləs, and, especially among florists, *gladiola,* glad i ō′lə; the plural glad i ō′lī, glə dī′o lī, glad i ō′ləs iz, and (of *gladiola*), glad i ō′ləz. Gla dī′o lus is the closest to the word's Latin origin and is usual with botanists for the name of the genus. The clips *glad* or *glads* are a way out of the confusion.

glamor–glamour The first is the normal American spelling (See *-or, -our), but in the fashion and entertainment "worlds" *glamour* is more common (glamour girl). The adjective is generally *glamorous.*

go 1. *Go* is a useful little word, especially as a *linking verb in a number of idioms, most of which are Informal:

go blind	go on! (=I don't believe you!)
go back on	go in for

2. *Go and* is a spoken form of emphasis: Go and try it yourself (no actual movement meant); She went and shot the bear herself. These are primarily oral expressions, but they are appropriate in some Informal and General writing.

Gobbledygook A suggestive label for an abuse of Formal English, characteristic of some government and business communications, marked by overheavy (abstract) words and confusing, pseudo-legal or pseudo-scientific sentences. What relatively simple statement is being made in this sample?

By encouraging and maintaining a reciprocal interest between the prime contractor and his subcontractors in the business matter of fulfilling the obligations of the prime contract, contractual requirements, particularly inspection, can be greatly assisted in furnishing the consignee with the required information that material has received inspection in accordance with the contract.

 (See Ch. 8, "Big words," p. 228.)

good–well *Good* is an adjective; *well* is either an adjective or an adverb: "I feel *good*" and "I feel *well*" (adjectives) are both usual but have different meanings (*good* implying actual bodily sensation, *well* referring merely to a state, "not ill").

In Nonstandard usage *well* is rarely used, *good* taking its place ("He rowed good" for "He rowed well"). Avoid this usage.

good-by–good-bye Both are in use, but the hyphen is dropping out in General use: *goodbye, goodby.*

government Kenyon and Knott say: "No competent observer can doubt the prevalence of [guv′ər mənt, guv′ə mənt] among the leading statesmen of U.S. and England, even in formal public address." This General pronunciation leads us sometimes to omit the *n* in spelling, but *government* is the only Standard written form.

grade school–graded school *Graded school* is the older word but *grade school* is much more common, and always appropriate.

graduate The idiom *to be graduated from* an institution has generally gone out of use except in Formal and somewhat archaic writing and has been replaced by *graduated from:* He graduated from Yale in 1902. Omitting the *from* is Nonstandard: He *graduated* high school in 1957.

Grammar *Grammar* derives from the Greek *gramma,* meaning a written symbol; the first grammarians were teachers of writing and reading. In the Middle Ages, to know grammar meant not only to know how to read and write Latin but to possess the powers of a literate man in a largely illiterate society. In modern English, *grammar* is used in several senses:

1. *The basic structure of a language.* Every language is a complex of patterns developed over a long period of time by the people using it. In the English sentence *You see it,* we know *you* is the subject (here the actor) and *it* is the object (the thing seen), because *you* precedes the verb and *it* follows it. In French, however, the sentence would be written *Tu le vois,* with the subject first, object second, and verb last. The order of the elements, as well as their form, depends on the conventions of the particular language. Every native speaker learns these and a host of other patterns in his language as a child and can understand and use them automatically. These patterns may be called the complete or total grammar of the language; in this sense English grammar is "the English way of saying things."

2. *Descriptive grammar.* This is an attempt to describe as systematically and objectively as possible the total system of a language. The method of the descriptive grammarian is scientific: he observes and describes the language as it is, without attempting to guide the language habits of speakers and writers. Since a language is both extensive and complex, a particular grammar will never be complete but will be a selection of the facts of language that suit the writer's purpose.

When the description of a language covers a considerable period of time, describing the evolution of words and forms and constructions, perhaps explaining present usage in the light of the past, it is called *historical grammar*. When several related languages are compared, as English might be with Latin or German, it is called *comparative grammar*.

3. *Prescriptive grammar*. Besides these types of scientific grammar we also speak of *prescriptive* or *normative grammar*. A prescriptive grammar is a body of rules presented as guides to expression, statements of how, in the belief of the writer, people should speak and write. Many English grammars of this type, represented principally by textbooks prepared for the use of students, are now in disrepute because they are out of touch with scientific grammar and with actual usage. Too many school grammars represent either older usage or traditional rules that are not consistently followed and some that have never been followed by users of English. Typically they present Formal English as though it was the only English and discourage General and Informal usage, which occupy the center stage in the scientific grammars.

One unfortunate result of prescriptive grammar is that the teaching of Formal English has seemed so unreal to students that, unable to separate the useful from the useless advice, they have paid almost no attention at all to it. If they talked as their textbooks said they should, they would be laughed at; consequently they have usually continued their old speech habits.

Although the usage recommended in schools will probably always be a little more Formal than that being practiced by actual writers, school grammar is now gradually getting away from traditional prescriptive grammar and is coming closer in line with the picture of actual usage presented by scientific grammars.

4. *Grammar as remedy*. Many people are occasionally oppressed by a feeling of inadequacy in their use of English. They believe that all their deficiencies, real or imagined, in vocabulary, effective expression, spelling, usage, and punctuation would be removed if they studied "grammar" conscientiously. This is back of the demand for "More grammar!" in the schools. The desire is really for more varied and more acceptable *usage,* "Good English" as discussed in Chapter 1, pages 26-34. The best remedy is wide listening and reading and practice in using language effectively. Grammar plays a useful but subordinate part in summarizing and describing the facts of the current language, but it is not itself the remedy.

5. *Grammatical terms*. When you use *grammar* in speaking or writing, you should be aware of its various meanings and varied uses, and if necessary indicate the sense in which you are using it. In this book the term is restricted to the first two senses described in this article, the exact meaning being shown by the context.

The terms used within grammar deserve a comment also. The analysis of language is a discipline more than two thousand years old, going back in Western culture to the philosophers and rhetoricians of ancient Greece. The terminology devised by the Greeks was used with little modification until the modern scientific study of language made its inadequacy for the description of other languages apparent. Some of the old terms have been kept and given more restricted or more precise definition and new terms have been introduced. Many grammatical and linguistic terms are still not standardized, but by making their reference clear we can and must use them in discussing language.

Many people steadfastly refuse to learn the technical terms of grammar. Students who gaily toss about *schizophrenic, marginal utility, Hanseatic League, dicotyledonous,* or *trinitrotoluene* will not learn the pronunciation and meaning of *predicate adjective, metonymy,* or even *apostrophe* or *agreement,* and some teachers of the subject try to work without naming exactly what they are talking about. Many of the words are a bit difficult–Greek or Latin names that have been taken into the language–but they are not nearly so difficult as the vocabulary of psychology or chemistry. This book uses a good many of these terms, without apology, though when there is a choice of name the simpler and more suggestive has usually been taken. It is only good sense to gain control of the words that name common facts of usage and style.

See *Linguistics; *Latin and English § 3. References: The works in the bibliography at the beginning of this *Guide-Index,* specifically Fries and Pooley, discuss many of the particular rules of prescriptive grammar besides offering their own observation of usage; see especially Fries, *AEG,* Chapters 1, 2, 11, and Robert C. Pooley, *Teaching English Grammar* (New York, 1957).

gray is a much more common spelling than *grey,* but both are used.

Greek alphabet The first college societies, usually organized for both social and intellectual aims, were formed when Greek was a prominent subject in the course of study. Many of them had Greek names or Greek mottoes and referred to themselves by the abbreviations for these words: Phi Beta Kappa (ΦΒΚ) for Φιλοσοφία Βίου Κυβερνήτης ("Philosophy is the guide of life"). Their descendant societies, though very few of their members know any Greek, are still "Greek letter societies."

Scientists frequently use Greek letters to name members of a series, as *alpha, beta, gamma rays.*

Neither the classical nor the English names of these letters are used consistently in fraternity names or other uses of Greek letters in English. Even in the pronunciation of *Phi Beta Kappa* the two systems are mixed: fī (English) bā′tə (classical) kap′ə (English). This worries a few purists, but the prevalent pronunciation should be followed. The accompanying table may be helpful.

THE GREEK ALPHABET

Greek letters Capital	Greek letters Small	English equivalents	English name of letter	Pronunciation of the name: Classical	Pronunciation of the name: English
Α	α	a	alpha	älfa (alfa)	†al′fə
Β	β	b	beta	†bāta[2]	bē′tə
Γ	γ	g	gamma	gäma (gama)	†gam′ə
Δ	δ	d	delta	delta	del′tə
Ε	ϵ	e	epsilon	epsilon	ep′sə lon
Ζ	ζ	z (dz)	zeta	†zāta	zē′tə
Η	η	a (ā)	eta	†āta	ē′tə
Θ	θ	th (thin)	theta	†thāta	thē′tə
Ι	ι	ē	iota	ēōta	†ī ō′tə
Κ	κ	k	kappa	käpa	†kap′ə
Λ	λ	l	lambda	lämda	†lam′də
Μ	μ	m	mu	mōō	†mū
Ν	ν	n	nu	nōō	†nū
Ξ	ξ	x (ks)	xi	ksē	†zī, sī
Ο	ο	o	omicron	ōmikron	om′ə kron
Π	π	p	pi	pē	†pī
Ρ	ρ	r	rho	rō	rō
Σ	σ s[1]	s	sigma	sigma	sig′mə
Τ	τ	t	tau	tou	†tô
Υ	υ	y (u)	upsilon	ōōpsilon	†ūp′sə lon,′ up′sə lon
Φ	φ	f (ph)	phi	fē	†fī
Χ	χ	ch	chi	chē (Ger. ch)	†kī
Ψ	ψ	ps	psi	psē	†sī
Ω	ω	ō	omega	omāga	ō meg′ə, ō mē′gə

[1] *s* is used at the end of a word, elsewhere σ.
[2] † marks pronunciation more frequently used.

Group words In English many groups of two or more words (that is, phrases) function as though they were single words. *High school* is not the noun *school* modified by the adjective *high* so much as a noun in its own right; it might well be spelled as a single word (and sometimes is). Many of our verbs are made up of a verb plus an adverb: *close up, hold off, look into* (see *Verb-adverb combinations); many prepositions are phrases: *according to, in opposition to.*

Other typical group words are:

Nouns: hay fever back door holding company home run safety razor baby blue school year sacrifice hit express train

Verbs: dig in back water back step (military) flare up follow through follow up show up blow up

Prepositions: in spite of in consequence of previous to due to

"In such cases," Professor Krapp says, "it is contrary to the idiom of the language to try to analyze the groups into their constituent parts so as to give every word, standing alone, a clearly defined structural value." Consequently in this book we ignore the superficial difference between a part of speech that is one word and one that is a group of words. "Noun" or "verb" or "preposition" refers both to single words and to *group words* functioning as noun or verb or preposition. (References: Curme, *Syntax,* Ch. 30; George P. Krapp, *The Knowledge of English* (New York, 1927), pp. 313-316 [where he calls such phrases "function groups"].)

gypsy–gipsy Partly because of the odd appearance of the two *y*'s in *gypsy,* the spelling is shifting to *gipsy.* Capitalize as the name of a specific people and use small letter for the sense merely of "wanderer" (the more common use). Compare *pigmy–pygmy.*

H

1. As a distinctive sound, *h* (h) always occurs at the beginning of syllables: *harsh, heel, high, horrible, ahead.*

2. *H* is likely to be silent at the beginning of unstressed syllables: *forehead* (for′id), *behind* (when spoken rapidly in unstressed part of phrase, bi īnd′), *he, his, her,* etc., when lightly spoken (Give it to *him′* versus *Give′* it to [h]im).

H is silent in *rh* words–*rhetoric, rhyme, rhythm.*

In many words from French the *h* was formerly not pronounced: *habit, history, hotel* . . . but now is except in *heir, honest, honor, hour.* So long as the *h* was not pronounced, *an* was used before these words, and it is still by some people in the forms in which the stress is not on the first syllable: *an historical work, an habitual error,* though *a* is now more common. (See *a, an.)

In words like *huge* and *humor* many people drop the *h,* leaving ūj and ū′mər. (Compare *wh.)

Habitual action *Would* is the typical auxiliary for habitual action in the past, especially in Formal English:

> He would always go by the longer way.

Habitual action is also expressed by *used to* or by an adverb:

> He used to go by the longer way.
> He usually went by the longer way.

had better, had rather *Had better* is the usual idiom for giving advice or making an indirect command:

> You had better take care of that cold.   You'd better go.

The assimilation of the *d* of *you'd* by the *b* of *better* has given rise to the Informal construction without *had:*

> If he asks you to do it, you better do it.

Had rather and *would rather* are both used to express preference, the latter the more Formal:

He would rather ski than eat. He had [He'd] rather ski than eat.

Since the *had* or *would* is unstressed in speech (and the contraction *he'd* is frequently used), it is impossible to tell which is being said.

half The more Formal idiom is *a half;* the General, *half a:*

Formal: He ran a half mile; a half hour.
General: He ran half a mile; half an hour.

A half a (a half an hour) is a redundancy sometimes found in Informal and Nonstandard speech. It should not be written.

hanged–hung In Formal English the principal parts of *hang* when referring to the death penalty are *hang, hanged, hanged,* the archaic forms kept alive by legal phrases such as "hanged by the neck until dead"; in other senses they are *hang, hung, hung:* Murderers are *hanged,* pictures are *hung.*

General and Informal usage does not keep this distinction, often using *hang, hung, hung* in all senses:

They hung the Turk that invented work
In the Big Rock Candy Mountain.

have 1. *Auxiliary.* Have occurs most frequently in the perfect tenses, for which it is now the sole auxiliary in English (in earlier English *be* was also used). *Have* plus a past participle makes the perfect tense (They have come); *shall have* or *will have* plus a past participle makes the future perfect tense (They will have gone by then); *had* plus a past participle makes the past perfect (They had gone to the beach before we arrived). In this use it is a *function word–a signal of tense. (See *Tenses of verbs.)

2. *Independent meaning.* As a verb of independent meaning *have* means to "own, possess," in a literal (have a car) or transferred sense (have the measles), or "to be under obligation" (I have to go home early). There are many idioms with *have* such as:

to have a look the book (or gossip) has it that
have it your own way to have it out
to have the ocean in view
Informal: He had his arm broken.
General: He had a broken arm.
Formal: He suffered a broken arm.

Because *have* occurs so frequently as an "empty" auxiliary word, its meaning as an independent word is often reinforced by *got.* (See *get, got, § 2.)

3. *Contractions.* In speech, *he, she, it has* are contracted to *he's, she's, it's* (He's not tried to in years; It's rained for over a week). This contraction is indistinguishable from that of *is; He's gone* may be *He has gone* or *He is gone. I, you, we, they have* are contracted to *I've, you've, we've, they've.*

Would have, wouldn't have are sometimes written *would of, wouldn't of,* an unconventional transcription of what is spoken as *would've, wouldn't've.*

4. *Nonstandard idioms. Had ought* and *hadn't ought* are spoken idioms, common in Nonstandard English and creeping into Informal speech, especially *hadn't ought:*

> Nonstandard: He had ought to take better care of himself.
> Standard: He ought to take better care of himself.
> Nonstandard: He hadn't ought to lie like that.
> Standard: He shouldn't [or: ought not to] lie like that.

5. *Other idioms.* For *have got* see *get, got § 2. Also see *had better, had rather. *Have* plus a *to*-infinitive is the equivalent of *must* in the affirmative and has the advantage that it can be conjugated in all tenses (*have to go, had to go, will have to go,* etc.).

Headword A word modified by another word, especially a noun modified by one or more adjectives (his first long *sleep*) or a verb modified by one or more adverbs (*run* slowly around the rim). The term is used variously by different linguists, but always to mean a word that is regarded as primary in a word group. (See: Harold Whitehall, *Structural Essentials of English* (New York, 1954), Ch. 2; Paul Roberts, *Patterns of English* (New York, 1956), pp. 77-105.)

healthful, healthy *Healthful* means "giving health"; places and food are healthful. *Healthy* means "having good health"; persons and animals are healthy. But *healthy* can also mean "giving health" and is used so much in this sense that *healthful* is falling into disuse.

height–heighth Nonstandard English usually has *heighth,* like *width* and *breadth* (and the original Old English form had *th*), but *height* is the usual form in Standard English. (Contrast *drought–drouth.)

he-or-she Since English has no third person singular pronoun to refer to individuals of either or both sexes, English speakers are faced with a problem unique in Indo-European languages; in all the others the third person singular pronouns have grammatical reference, not sexual (see *Gender). As we must often refer to nouns that name either or both male and female, the language has developed three ways of making up for the lack of an accurate pronoun:

1. The usual way is to use *he* or *his* alone even when some of the persons are female:

> There is considerable discussion whether a man or a woman will be appointed to the vacant cabinet post. Whoever receives the appointment will find *his* task a difficult one.
>
> Mr. Brown and Miss Trevor led the discussion, each giving *his* opinion of the poem.

Sometimes when the typical individuals or the majority of the group referred to would be women, *her* is used in the same way:

> Each one of the teachers in this school is required to submit *her* report to the principal in person.

2. A common way in General usage is to resort to a plural pronoun because it evades the sex issue:

Neither [a man and a woman] tasted what *they* ate.—KATHERINE ANNE PORTER, *Flowering Judas,* p. 26

3. Sometimes both *he* and *she* are used:

A teacher gives *his* or *her* own opinions on matters of politics and religion and often influences a pupil to think as *he* or *she* does. (Either of the two pronouns would be better in this sentence than both of them.)

Every student wishes to participate in some activity authorized by *his* or *her* college. (*His or her* sounds pedantic here; *his* alone would be better.)

The two pronouns are almost always clumsy and really no more accurate, since the meaning is determined by the antecedent.

highbrow After a period of slang overuse, *highbrow* (and *lowbrow* too) has settled down as a useful General word.

The cult of the lowbrow and the technique of showmanship have unquestionably invaded every field of literary and intellectual activity. —*The Saturday Review of Literature*

Middlebrow, a more recent coinage, is making its way.

high school Capitalize only when referring to a particular school (some newspaper styles do not use capitals even then):

I graduated from high school at seventeen.
I graduated from Bismarck High School in 1957.
These two high schools will now play for the championship.
Working on a high school paper is good training. (A hyphen may be used here.)

A few periodicals are now printing the word as a compound: *highschool.*

himself, herself *Himself* and *herself* are used in two ways:

1. As reflexive pronouns, referring to the subject of the sentence:

George has always taken himself pretty seriously.
She looked at herself in the window and gave her hat a little pull.

2. As *intensives for emphasis:

He told me himself.
I looked up and there was Mrs. Goodenow herself.

(Compare *myself.)

home, homely **1.** *Home* is used in the function of a noun, verb, adjective, or adverb—an example of the English habit of making one form serve several functions (see *Parts of speech):

Noun: His home was now in Cleveland.
Verb: The bird homed in an hour and twenty minutes.
Adverbial modifier: He came home unexpectedly. His remark went home.
Adjectival modifier: home duties, home manufactures.

In "They are home," *home* is a General expression for *at home. To home* in these phrases is Nonstandard.

2. *Home–house.* For a realtor a *home* is any house; in sentimental (and some Formal) use a *home* is only the "place of one's domestic affections." But in General use *home* is a lived-in house (or any extension needed for animal, plant, or object).

3. *Homely.* In Formal English *homely* means "informal, unassuming, characteristic of home life." In the United States *homely* usually means "ugly in appearance." In this country it is therefore safer to use the word only in the second sense.

Homonyms Two words of different meanings that are pronounced alike (*bear, bare; plain, plane*) are called *homonyms* (or *homophones*).

English has a great many such pairs of words, most of them in common use. They have developed for different reasons. Some Old English words once different in sound have come to be pronounced alike because of changes in form through the centuries: *bear* (the animal) from *bera, bear* (the verb) from *beran; plain* and *plane* both go back to Latin *planus,* but the spelling of the first was altered in coming through Old French. Many words are from different languages, having fallen into similar forms by accident: *rest* meaning "peace" is from Old English, *rest* meaning "remainder" is from French; and *bark* of a tree is from Scandinavian, *bark* of a dog from Old English, and *bark,* the vessel, a more recent borrowing from French-Italian.

There is very little chance of misunderstanding these words because their context will tell which is which–though their similarity is often capitalized on in *puns. Where real difficulty exists, the conflict has usually been resolved by one or both words going out of use. The verb *halve* hardly exists in speech anymore because of almost certain confusion with have: "We'll halve (have) the pie." But homophones like *plain–plane* make a good deal of trouble in spelling. Much of this confusion is really carelessness, for the words are common. Try to visualize the troublesome ones in phrases that show their meaning, something like these:

priest at the *altar*–Who can *alter* human nature?
Father gave his *assent* to the marriage.–the *ascent* of Mount Everest
bearing pain–*baring* his arm
a lower *berth*–his tenth *birth*day
born in June 1922–*borne* by the wind
the *bridal* party, *bridal* suite–a horse's *bridle,* the *bridle* path
The *capital* of Illinois is Springfield.–The *capitol* has a gilded dome.
A woman despises insincere *compliments.*–the *complement* of the angle
There are five members of the *council.–Counsel* is advice.–*counsel* for the defense
a *dual* personality–a pistol *duel*
A *mantle* covered her.–the trophy cups on the *mantel*
a *piece* of paper–*peace* or war
air*plane, plane* geometry–the Great *Plains,* a *plain* statement

pore over a book–*pour* coffee
He *rode* horseback.–The *road* was macadam.–He *rowed* a dory.
a box of *stationery*–a *stationary* engine–*stationary* desks
tea to drink–*tee* on a golf course

(Reference: Arthur G. Kennedy, *Current English* (Boston, 1935), § 82.)

Honorable As a title of respect, for persons in political office of some prestige, this word is capitalized and is usually preceded by *the;* it may be abbreviated in addresses when initials or first names are used:

the Honorable Lyndon Johnson — the Hon. Lyndon Johnson
the Honorable Member from Texas

hope Both *in hope of* and *in hopes of* are in General usage, with the former perhaps preferred because of sound:

After leaving Montreal we drove on *in hope of* [or, *in hopes of*] reaching Quebec as soon as possible. (Or, *in the hope of* reaching)

The participle *hoping* is probably more usual:

After leaving Montreal we drove on, *hoping* to reach Quebec as soon as possible.

Hours In consecutive writing, especially if it is Formal, hours are written in words: at four o'clock.

In newspapers and in much General writing, figures are used, especially if several times are mentioned:

at 4 p.m. just after 9 a.m. from 10 to 12 (See *a.m. and p.m.)

however As a connective, *however* is more appropriate to the fully developed sentences of Formal style and is especially useful as a connective between sentences:

Occasionally the beat man writes his own story in the press room of the public building in which he is stationed, and sends it to the office by messenger. This, however, is unusual as it involves loss of time.–C. D. MacDougall, *Reporting for Beginners,* p. 65

Amateur writers are likely to overuse *however; but* would usually be more appropriate to the simple directness of their statements:

During the eight weeks I was in the hospital, Al visited me twice, assuring me that as soon as I was able, I could have my old job. But [better than *however*] after four weeks of convalescing at home, it was time for me to go to college.

Clauses in one sentence connected by *however* are usually substantial enough to be separated by a semicolon. (See *Conjunctive adverbs, *but.)

human, once a noun in good standing, fell to the level of humorous and undignified usage but now seems to be coming back into good standing:

With all his heart he wants to come close to some other human, touch someone with his hands, be touched by the hand of another.–Sherwood Anderson, *Winesburg, Ohio,* p. 287

Hyphen (-)

1. *In compound words.* 2. *In modifiers.* 3. *With prefixes.* 4. *Miscellaneous uses.*

The hyphen is a mark of punctuation, rather than of spelling, that is used sometimes to join and sometimes to keep distinct two word elements. Its commonest use is to mark the division of a word at the end of a line of manuscript or type (see *Division of words). Other uses are somewhat variable: dictionaries and publishers' stylebooks do not always agree on specific practices. Consequently they are in part a matter of style, with Formal writers tending to use more hyphens than General writers. The following uses are fairly well standardized and may be taken as a guide for General writing.

1. *In compound words.* Many compound words will be found written in three ways: as two words, or hyphened, or as one word (*super market, super-market, supermarket*). As a rule the form does not affect meaning: *tax payers, tax-payers,* and *taxpayers* all pay taxes. In the past, words that were becoming fused into compounds passed through a probationary period with hyphens before being written as single words. *Baseball,* for instance, was hyphened for a time, and *football* and *basketball* too were once hyphened. There is less tendency now, except in quite Formal writing, to use such hyphens, and compounds are made immediately without hyphens if the words are needed.

Two words of one syllable are most often written solid (*bedroom, kickback, lineman, skylight*), but a hyphen is likely if the first is not a simple modifier of the second: *by-pass, close-up, cure-all, hair-do.* A hyphen is more likely to be used when one of the elements, especially the first, has two or more syllables, though two words is always an option:

> . . . and we have even seen their guilty simulacra in tenement-house and shopfronts.–LEWIS MUMFORD, *Sticks and Stones,* p. 180

Schoolbook is usually written solid; *reference book* is two words.

A hyphen is conventional in three groups of words:

a) In the compound numerals from twenty-one to ninety-nine, and in fractions, though this use is not universal:

forty-seven ninety-ninth one hundred sixty-two
three-sixteenths one thirty-second

b) In names of family relationships:

Hyphened: father-in-law, daughter-in-law
One word: stepson, stepdaughter, stepmother
Two words: half brother, half sister (sometimes hyphened)

c) In compounds with *self-,* which are usually hyphened in dictionaries but are often found in print as two words:

self-contained self-government–self government
self-help–self help self-importance self-pity–self pity

Selfhood and *selfless* are written as one word.

A hyphen or a separation is used if the first member of the compound ends in the same vowel that the second begins with (*fire-eater, fire-escape* or *fire escape*) or if a misleading or awkward combination of consonants would result by joining the words (*mess hall* or *mess-hall, bell-like*).

If a compound word raises a question, look it up in a reliable recent dictionary, and if the word is not given there, use a hyphen or not as your taste dictates.

2. *In modifiers.*

a) A number of adjectives composed of two words are conventionally hyphened when they precede a noun:

clear-cut	easy-going	up-to-date
clear-eyed	first-class	worth-while
clear-headed	narrow-minded	would-be

The more commonly used ones are given in dictionaries. Most of them are an adverb plus a verb; and other phrases formed on this pattern are hyphened when the adverb does not end in *-ly:*

a late-flowering iris   slow-moving goods
a well-marked trail   (but) a plainly marked trail

Usually such modifiers are not hyphened in predicate position:

a worth-while trip   (but) The trip was worth while.

Such phrases should not be hyphened in a verb construction:

a well-matched pair. They were well matched.
They were well suited to each other.

Short, frequently used combinations are generally hyphened:

a two-year term   a small-town sheriff   a no-hit, no-run game

Longer phrase modifiers are usually hyphened:

on a pay-as-you-go basis
a 5-cent-an-hour wage increase
a detailed question-and-answer sheet
two-hundred-pound, six-foot-two halfbacks

b) Usage is divided on hyphening noun phrases when used as modifiers, as in *seventeenth century philosophy.* Formal writers would usually write *seventeenth-century;* General, *seventeenth century.* This division applies to such expressions as the following:

a Seventh Avenue shop   summer vacation freedom

c) Occasionally some pairs of modifiers might be ambiguous without a hyphen: *a light yellow scarf* might be either a light scarf that was yellow or a scarf that was light yellow, so that *light-yellow* is safest for the latter meaning, and *light, yellow scarf* for the first. There is a distinction between a *great-grandfather* (indicating relationship only) and a *great grandfather* (indicating quality of a grandfather), and between a new car-owner and a new-car owner.

d) A numeral as part of a modifier (5-cent, 27 9-inch boards) and a letter linked to a noun (H-bomb, T-square, X-ray) are hyphened.

e) A hyphen may be used to carry the force of a modifier over to a later noun ("suspension hyphen"):

The third-, fourth-, and fifth-grade rooms have been redecorated.
In both thirteenth- and fourteenth-century texts

3. *With prefixes.* In certain types of compounds of a prefix and a root word a hyphen is used to avoid confusion, or for emphasis or for appearance:

a) Between a prefix ending with a vowel and a root word beginning with the same vowel:

re-elected re-enter pre-eminent pre-existent

(See *pre-, re-.)

Usage is divided on words made with *co-*, the more common ones now generally being written solid:

cooperate or co-operate coordinate or co-ordinate

b) To avoid confusion with another word:

re-collect–recollect re-cover–recover

c) Between a prefix and a proper name:

pre-Sputnik ex-President Truman pro-Eisenhower

d) When the prefix is stressed:

ex-husband ex-wife anti-vivisection (or antivivisection)

4. *Miscellaneous uses.*

a) Between the letters showing how a word is spelled:

The loser spelled *receive* r-e-c-i-e-v-e.

b) Often to show syllabication:

hy-pos-ta-ti-za-tion

The fact is that hyphening is more an editor's worry than a writer's. A publisher may wish for uniformity in principle and may struggle to get it in printing particular words, though absolute consistency is impossible. The manual of the Government Printing Office devotes over fifty pages to rules for hyphening, and stylebooks of newspaper and other publications have numerous rules, many of them arbitrary choices of form made simply to insure consistency. In a person's ordinary writing, he does not need to be so particular. For words in common use he can consult a dictionary or do as he finds reputable publications doing.

The conclusion one comes to after a serious consideration of current habits in the use of hyphens is well put by John Benbow in *Manuscript & Proof,* the stylebook of the Oxford University Press of New York: "If you take hyphens seriously you will surely go mad."

References: *GPO Manual,* pages 63-120; Kenyon and Knott, sections 48-53; Summey, Chapter 10.

I

1. *"Long i"* (ī). The sound of long *i* is a diphthong, sliding from *a* or *ä* to short *i* or short *e: ice, wild, find, guide, night, tiny.* It is also spelled as in *aisle, aye, height, eye, by, buy, bye, lie, choir.*

In unstressed syllables ī has the same sound but is somewhat shorter: dī am′ə tər.

2. *"Short i"* (i). As in *bit, city.* This sound is spelled in a number of other ways: s*ie*ve, dut*y*, forf*ei*t, all*ey,* mess*a*ge, Sund*ay*, marr*ia*ge, foreh*ea*d, mount*ai*n, min*u*te, bisc*ui*t.

3. *"Continental i"* (ē). In a few words the Continental (European) value of *i* is preserved: *machine* (mə shēn′), *police* (pə lēs′), *visa* (vē′zə), and in recent unanglicized borrowings.

4. *As a consonant* (y). *I* may represent a *y* sound before a vowel, especially in rapid pronunciation: *opinion* (ə pin′yən). For the plural *-ies* see *Plurals § 1b and *Y. See also *-ile and *J.

5. *Before* r. *I* may spell the sound represented by û: *bird* (bûrd), *third* (thûrd).

I **1.** *Capital.* The pronoun *I* is written with a capital simply because in the old manuscripts a small *i* was likely to be lost or to get attached to a neighboring word, and a capital helped keep it a distinct word. There is no conceit implied.

2. *As first word.* The widely circulated rumor that *I* should not be the first word in a letter (sometimes even that it should not be the first word of a sentence) is unfounded. *I* can be used wherever it is needed. It can start a sentence but it shouldn't open many consecutive sentences. People with only average concern for themselves need not worry; the conceited will give themselves away anyway. Circumlocutions to get around the natural use of *I* are usually awkward and likely to attract attention to themselves:

> There is a feeling in me [I feel] that relief projects are unsound.

The best way to avoid conspicuous use of *I* (or of any other word) is to keep it out of emphatic sentence positions, especially from the stressed beginning of a sentence. A subordinate clause or longish phrase put first will throw the stress off the *I:*

> After a long struggle I decided to go. (Instead of: I decided to go, after a long struggle.)

3. *Omission of I.* In clipped personal writing—diaries, casual and Informal letters—*I* is often appropriately omitted if the style is also clipped in other respects:

A drive to Nahant yesterday afternoon. Stopped at Rice's, and afterwards walked down to the steamboat wharf to see the passengers land.
—NATHANIEL HAWTHORNE, *American Note-Books,* Aug. 31, 1835

(See *It's me, *myself, *we § 2 ("editorial we").)

idea strictly means a "concept," something thought about something. It is frequently used as a substitute for *intention* and similar words in constructions that are usually wordy:

I got the idea that [I thought] every policeman was my enemy.
Wordy: We started out with the idea in mind of going to a dance.
Improved: We started out intending to go to a dance.

Idiolect An *idiolect* is the speech of an individual. A dialect or a language is the speech habits of people with similar idiolects, the similarities being closer in the former.

Idiom and idioms Revision: The expression marked is not the idiomatic English construction. Revise it, referring to an article in this *Index* or to a dictionary if you are not sure what it should be. *Id*

The word *idiom* is used in two different, almost opposed, senses:

1. It may mean *the usual forms of expression of a particular language,* as we may compare German idiom with English idiom, meaning the ways in which words are characteristically put together in the two languages. German has been fond of suspended constructions (*Ich habe den alten Mann schon gesehen*—I have the old man already seen), the separable prefixes, and participial constructions, but English tends to complete its constructions immediately. In French, adjectives usually come after the nouns they modify (*une maison blanche*), in English they usually come before (*a white house*). "Idiomatic English" connotes *natural, meaningful* English. It ordinarily is contrasted with stilted usage and suggests a mastery of the basic constructions of General English.

2. The word *idiom* may also mean an *accepted phrase that differs from the usual construction of the language,* either departing from the typical grammar (like *somebody else's,* in which the sign of the possessive is added to the adjective rather than to the noun) or from normal meaning (like *to center around,* which is ridiculous when analyzed). These idioms are usually particular phrases which we learn as separate items—easily in our own language, with difficulty in another—differing from the idioms discussed in the preceding section, which are patterns for large numbers of locutions.

Collecting English idioms is a good sport and trying to analyze them an even better one. Considering them grammatically and literally, what can you make of these?

to come in handy	be your age
how do you do	strike a bargain
to catch fire	to be taken in (deceived)
catch his eye	takes after her mother

a hot cup of coffee | look up an old friend
to make a date | hard put to it

The point to remember about these expressions is that though they are exceptional in some way, they are thoroughly respectable members of the language. No one needs to apologize for using them, for they are part of the stock in trade of the language and most of them are appropriate in all varieties.

The dictionaries give a great many idioms, usually listed under the most important word in the phrase. The *Oxford English Dictionary* is especially rich in idioms. (See Ch. 3, "Revising unidiomatic expressions," p. 90; *Phrases, *Prepositions.)

if **1.** *Subordinating conjunction. If* is a subordinating conjunction introducing a condition:

If the weather holds good, we shall stay another week.

If they had known the beacon was out, they would have come in before sunset.

(See *Conditions. Reference: Fries, *AEG,* pp. 224-225.)

2. *"If" and "whether."* In Formal and General usage, *if* is used for conditions, and *whether,* usually with *or,* is used, though not consistently, in indirect questions and in expressions of doubt:

Simple condition: If the weather holds, we will come.

Indirect question: He asked whether the mail had come in. He asked whether they were all going or only some of them.

Doubt: They had all been wondering whether the doctor would get there in time.

From the first returns they could not be sure whether the state was Republican or Democratic.

In Formal English *if* is not used with *or:*

No matter whether [Not: *if*] the boy goes to preparatory school or high school, his father has to pay local school taxes.

In Informal English *whether* is rarely used:

He asked if they were all going or only some of them.

He asked if the mail had come in.

He was so old, and so shrunken, that it was difficult to tell, at first, if he was a man or woman.—William March, *The Little Wife,* p. 101

3. *For "although" or "but."* In some idioms *if* is used for *although* or *but:*

She was a good dog, if she did bark at strangers.

(See *when, as, and if.)

-ile Usage is divided on the pronunciation of words ending in *-ile.* Some of the more common are:

agile	aj′il [aj′īl]	infantile	in′fən tīl, in′fən til
fertile	fûr′til	juvenile	jo͞o′və nil, jo͞o′və nīl
futile	fū′til	reptile	rep′til
gentile	jen′tīl	senile	sē′nīl, sē′nil
hostile	hos′til	textile	teks′til, teks′tīl

British pronunciation more commonly has -īl: fûr′tīl, hos′tīl, rep′tīl.

illiterate Strictly, *illiterate* means "not able to read or write"; loosely it means "uncultivated." Usage that is often loosely referred to as *illiterate* is called Nonstandard in this book. See Chapter 1, "Nonstandard English," page 24.

illusion *Illusion*–"a deceptive appearance," as *an optical illusion, an illusion of wealth*–is, because of similarity in pronunciation, sometimes confused with *allusion,* "a reference to something": He opened his talk with an allusion to recent events.

Illustration (Pictorial) Pictorial illustration may greatly help the interest and understandability of an article–though it cannot (in spite of the picture magazines) take the place of text. Illustrations for articles and books are often arranged for by the publisher, but the writer can suggest possibilities or he can submit drawings or photographs. Many feature articles are accepted by newspapers and magazines largely because of their illustrations.

A student can often add considerably to the value of a paper by drawings or by snapshots. These can be inserted by tucking the corners into slits cut in the manuscript pages, so that they can be taken off after they have served their purpose. Travel papers, narratives of experience, and explanations of processes profit especially from illustration. (Compare *Diagrams, graphs, etc.)

Imagery An image is a word or group of words that may make an appeal to one of the "senses": sight (*bright, yellow, thick brown hair*), hearing (*rumble, faraway shouts, three loud booms*), taste (*sweet, sour, a pickled pear*), smell (*jasmine, a blown-out candle*), touch (*smooth, glassy, a tweed coat*), and the muscular tension known as the kinesthetic sense (*squirm, jogging heavily along*). Obviously a word may appeal to more than one sense (*tweed, glassy, jasmine*), though in a specific context one would usually be dominant. Whether a reader's senses are actually "aroused" depends chiefly on his suggestibility. Some people are easily stimulated by words; some are more sensitive to one sense than to another. For the study of imagery in writing, it is enough that words *capable* of suggesting sensory images are present; we cannot be sure of the response of anyone but ourselves. But images–actually sensed or potential–are the foundation of much writing, of all in fact that is not dealing principally with ideas.

Imagery is especially characteristic of poetry, in which ideas, states of mind, and feelings are often represented by images and what they suggest:

> Jack Ellyat felt that turning of the year
> Stir in his blood like drowsy fiddle-music
> And knew he was glad to be Connecticut-born
> And young enough to find Connecticut winter

Was a black pond to cut with silver skates
And not a scalping-knife against the throat.
STEPHEN VINCENT BENÉT, *John Brown's Body*, p. 22

Fiction, too, since it must present pictures of people and places and actions, has much imagery:

> The sun came in warm in long streaks across the floor, and the giant geranium plants made a pattern across its gold. When we touched our glasses, white circles of light would move on the walls and ceiling, and the cut-glass dish with the peaches in it made a rainbow-bar on the cloth.—JOSEPHINE JOHNSON, *Now in November*, p. 83

In expository prose, images are the basis of discussions of people, of experience and situations, of things and processes. Even in expressions of opinion and discussions of ideas, most writers keep in close touch with the visible and touchable world. Current writing is conspicuously concrete and imagerial.

Studying the images in a writer's work will usually show what has impressed him in his experience, what appeals to him—colors, lines, odors, what not—and your writing also should show images drawn from your experience. Images that come from your own experience and that definitely appeal to you will carry over clearly to a reader and are infinitely better than the trite roses and violets of accumulated literature. Don't take out of your writing an image that really appeals to you, unless it would be inappropriate or would mislead a reader. (See Ch. 8, pp. 217-220 and 232-239.)

Imitative words and phrases A number of words imitate, or suggest in their pronunciation, particular sounds: *bang, buzz, clank, swish, splash, whirr, pop, clatter, cuckoo, ping pong.* These words have become definite members of the English vocabulary and will be found in dictionaries. It is possible to make new ones to fit specific sounds, and they are often necessary, especially in fiction. Sometimes it is better to use the conventional forms even when they are not very exact (*humph, uh huh*) rather than make new ones, which may puzzle a reader.

When such words are used for special effect in writing they form a trait of style known as *onomatopoeia* (on′ə mat′ə pē′ə). Imitative words or sounds in a series that suggest the action or idea or tone of the subject matter are a useful form of intensification of meaning, as in Pope's famous lines:

'Tis not enough no harshness gives offense,
The sound must seem an Echo to the sense:
Soft is the strain when Zephyr gently blows,
And the smooth stream in smoother numbers flows;
But when the loud surges lash the sounding shore,
The hoarse, rough verse should like the torrent roar:
When Ajax strives some rock's vast weight to throw,
The line too labours, and the words move slow;
ALEXANDER POPE, *An Essay on Criticism*, lines 364-71

Often a picture or a narrative can be sharpened by using an imitative word instead of a general or colorless word like *said* or *walked: barked, droned, snarled, whined; clattered, stamped, strutted.* Conspicuous striving for such words will make a passage seem melodramatic, but accurate words that come naturally will add to its effectiveness.

In *The Red Badge of Courage* Stephen Crane frequently uses imitative words to good effect:

> The regiment snorted and blew....The song of the bullets was in the air and shells snarled among the tree-tops....Near where they stood shells were flip-flapping and hooting....Occasional bullets buzzed in the air and spanged into tree trunks....

Immediate constituent Linguists use *immediate constituent,* usually abbreviated to IC, to indicate one of the two elements into which a specific expression can be analyzed. The ICs of a typical English sentence are the complete subject and the complete predicate, each of which may be made up of ICs, which in turn may be analyzable into smaller elements. The analysis can be carried down to the elements of words (morphemes) and to the sounds (phonemes) of which they are composed.

This system of analysis has a characteristic form of diagram, which for a very simple sentence might go:

<table>
<tr><td rowspan="3">They</td><td rowspan="2">bought</td><td>gaudy</td><td>trinkets.</td></tr>
<tr><td colspan="2">(ICs of the object)</td></tr>
<tr><td colspan="3">(ICs of the predicate)</td></tr>
<tr><td colspan="4">(ICs of the sentence)</td></tr>
</table>

Like other diagrams, this is a device for analysis and exposition, more useful to a specialist than to a person concerned for his own language. Handling a sentence of average complexity requires a considerable amount of linguistic knowledge, especially if the suprasegmental *phonemes of pitch and juncture are included. The notion of immediate constituents, however, is necessary for any analysis of language, especially for syntax, which looks for the relations between elements in utterances. This approach emphasizes the fact that utterances are not "built up" of sounds and words, as a stone house is built of stones, but that they are continuous bits of behavior that can be (though they ordinarily need not be) analyzed into elements. (References: Fries, *Structure,* pp. 256-273, and most recent books in linguistics.)

imply–infer Strictly a writer or speaker *implies* something in his words or manner; a reader or listener *infers* something from what he reads or hears.

The dean implied, by the way he tilted his head and half closed his eyes, that he doubted my story.

One might infer from his opening words that the speaker was hostile to all social change.

Infer has been used so much with the meaning of "imply" that that is given as a secondary sense of the word in dictionaries.

in 1. *Uses.*

Preposition: in the box   in town   in the rain   in a circle   in training   in words   in bronze

Adverb: mix in   They are not in.   Put in the butter.

Adjective: the in box

Noun: the ins and the outs

Verb: (local) to in the beets, to in the car

2. *In combinations.* In speech *in* is often used in combination with another preposition: *in back of, in behind, in between.*

In most writing these would be simply: *back of, behind, between.* (See *Prepositions § 3b.)

in–into–in to *In* generally shows location (literal or figurative); *into* generally shows direction:

He was in the house.	He came into the house.
He was in a stupor.	He fell into a deep sleep.
He walked in the street.	He walked into the street.

Informally *in* is often used for *into:*

He fell in the brook.

In to is the adverb *in* followed by the preposition *to:*

They went into the dining room. They went in to dinner.

in-, un- *In-* or *un-* (variants *im-, il-*) prefixed to many words gives them a negative meaning: *inconsiderate, incapable, uneven, unlovable, unlovely, unloved.* If you are not sure whether a word takes *in-* or *un-*, you will have to consult a dictionary—an American dictionary, since British usage differs in many words. *Un-* is likely to be used with words from Old English and *in-* with words from Latin, but this is not a safe guide (witness *indigestible, undigested, inequality, unequal, inadvisable, unadvised*). A sample list follows:

inadequate	†indistinguishable	immoral	uncontrollable
inadvisable	inept	impractical	uncontrolled
inartistic	†inescapable	unacceptable	undistinguished
inaudible	inexperienced	unadvised	unessential
incommunicable	infallible	unalterable	unnamed
incompatible	†infrequent	unbelievable	unnatural
incomplete	†insubstantial	uncertain	unnecessary
incomprehensible	†insupportable	uncollected	unrecognizable
inconclusive	illiberal	uncommunicative	unresponsive
inconsequential	illiterate		unsustained
†indecipherable	immoderate	uncompleted	unversed

Those marked † are also found with *un-*.

Not all words beginning with *in-* are negatives (*innate, insure, intoxicate*), and *invaluable* means having a value so great it cannot be determined; *un-* is also tricky—see *unbend, unbending* in a dictionary.

Incoherence Writing is incoherent when it lacks connection within itself or when the relationship between parts (of a sentence, of a paragraph, of a whole paper) is not evident. Various examples of incoherence are discussed in *Dangling modifiers, *Participles, Chapter 2, and Chapter 6, "Continuity in paragraphs," page 159.

incredible–incredulous A story or situation is *incredible* (unbelievable); a person is *incredulous* (unbelieving).

Indention *Indenting* in manuscript or printed copy is beginning a line in from the left-hand margin. In longhand copy, paragraphs are indented about an inch, in typewritten copy from five to eight spaces.

Hanging indention is setting in lines below the first line, as in many newspaper headlines, outlines (see Ch. 9, pp. 255-256), headings, and addresses of *letters. If a line of verse is too long to stand on one line, the part brought over to the second line should be indented:

> Why do they prate of the blessings of Peace? we have
> made them a curse,
> Pickpockets, each hand lusting for all that is not its
> own;
>
> ALFRED TENNYSON, "Maud"

Aside from these uses, indention is mainly a publisher's problem, treated in detail by the stylebooks. (For indenting quotations, see *Quotation marks §1d.)

Indicative mood is the usual form of the verb in sentences and clauses:

> They *sat* on the porch even though it *was* late October.
> *Will* you *come* if you *are invited?*

(See *Verbs; compare *Subjunctives.)

Indirect discourse (Indirect quotation) Quotations that are paraphrased or summarized in the writer's words instead of being quoted exactly as originally spoken or written are in indirect discourse:

> Indirect: He said he wouldn't take it if they gave it to him.
> Direct: He said, "I won't take it if they give it to me."

(See *Quotation marks § 2d, *Tenses of verbs § 3, and *Mood.)

Indirect question An *indirect question* is a question restated at second hand:

> Indirect: He asked if everyone was all right.
> Direct: He asked, "Is everyone all right?"

(See *Questions § 3.)

Infinitives *Infinitive* is a Latin grammatical term for a verb form expressing the general sense of the verb without restriction as to person or number. In English, there is no distinctive infinitive form; instead, the base form of the verb is used in the infinitive function. Usually *to* precedes the base form, but after certain auxiliary verbs *to* does not occur. So-called infinitive constructions cause great difficulty to foreign learners of English, but native speakers generally need be concerned only with the divided usage discussed in the last part of § 5 and in § 6.

1. *Tenses.* What are traditionally called the infinitive forms are:

	Active		*Passive*
	simple	*progressive*	
Present:	(to) ask	(to) be asking	(to) be asked
Perfect:	(to) have asked	(to) have been asking	(to) have been asked

The present infinitive indicates a time the same as or future to that of the main verb: He is here now *to ask* you . . .; They had come *to ask* you . . .; He is coming (future) *to ask* you. . . .

The perfect infinitive primarily indicates action previous to the time of the main verb: I am glad *to have been* one of his boys.

2. *The "to" infinitive. To* is the "sign of the infinitive" used in most infinitive constructions—that is, it connects the infinitive to the finite verb—but it is not part of the infinitive.

They all tried *to get* in first. He set out *to get* Phi Beta Kappa.

3. *The "bare" infinitive.* After a few verbs (*can, may, must, shall, will; do, dare, need,* etc.) *to* is never or seldom used:

I can *see.* He must *carry* it. We might *be seeing* him.
He does *care.* It does me good *to see* him.

With some other verbs usage is divided:

I helped him *to learn* to drive. I helped him *learn* driving.
You had better not *go.* You had *to go.*

In short, clear, unemphatic series of infinitives in parallel constructions, the *to* is not repeated; in more Formal series, when the actions are not part of one general process, or when the separate verbs deserve emphasis, the *to* is repeated (See examples under § 4 [Subject] below).

4. *Other uses of infinitives.*

Subject:

To sit and *smoke* and *think* and *dream* was his idea of pleasure.

To walk around among these exhibits, *to see* the horse races where runners, trotters, and pacers with Kentucky and Tennessee pedigrees compete on a mile track, and then *to listen* to the political speakers discussing "purr-ins-a-pulls" and "the Const-ti-too-shun"—this made a holiday for the farmers and city people who came.—Carl Sandburg, *Abraham Lincoln: The Prairie Years,* 2:6

Object:

He wanted *to go* fishing. He tries *to do* every one at least once.

Adjectival modifier:

wool *to spin,* money *to burn.* They have plenty of fish *to eat.*

Adverbial modifier (to show purpose, result, etc.):

He bought *to sell* again. They came *to play*. Reporters are constantly on the move *to cover* important events.

With auxiliaries:

He will *pass* this time. He didn't *dare* go along.

5. *Subject of infinitive.* Infinitives are increasingly used in subordinate constructions as alternatives to finite verbs:

It would be better *for you and me to discuss the matter* before calling in the others.

as the alternative to

It would be better *if you and I discussed the matter* before calling in the others.

If the subject of the infinitive is a pronoun, it is in the accusative case:

Supposing *them to be new men,* we all shouted, "Get off the grass."

Often these constructions are *absolute phrases:

To judge by the appearances, the party must have been pretty rough.
To make a long story short, they didn't go.

After the infinitive of a linking verb that has no expressed subject, Formal English usually has a nominative complement; General, an accusative:

General: I always wanted to be *him.*
Formal: I always wanted to be *he.*

(Compare *Participles §§ 3, 4; *Gerund.)

6. *Split infinitive.* See *Split infinitive.

References: Curme, *Syntax,* Chapter 23; Jespersen, Chapter 32; Roberts, pages 359-367.

Inflection in grammar refers to the change of form by which some words indicate certain grammatical relationships, as the plural of nouns or the past tense of verbs. For English inflections see *Case, and the articles referred to there; *Plurals; *Pronouns; *Verbs; *Comparison of adjectives and adverbs. (Reference: Curme, *Parts of Speech.*)

Informal English Revision: The word or passage marked is too Informal for the subject or for the style of the rest of the paper. Revise, making it more appropriate. *Inf*

Informal English, as described on pages 22-24, is appropriate to some personal narratives and light topics, but its words and constructions in General or Formal papers, except for an occasional intended effect, violate the tone. A conspicuously Informal expression marked on a paper should be changed to one more characteristic of General English.

inquiry Pronunciation is divided: in kwīr′i, in′kwə ri.

institutions of higher learning is a clumsy phrase, and more abstract than *colleges and universities*. It would be convenient if we had one word for the notion, or a group word as economical even as *secondary schools* for "high and preparatory schools." Either *colleges* or *universities* is often used to apply to both.

Intensives Adverbs like *very, too, much,* and some constructions, like the superlative of adjectives and adverbs, are used to emphasize meaning. (See Ch. 7, "Intensives," p. 190, for discussion, and *very, *Comparison of adjectives and adverbs § 5, *himself, *myself. References: Fries, *AEG,* pp. 200-206; Curme, *Parts of Speech,* pp. 48-50.)

Intonation *Intonation* is a general term for the "melody" of a language, used by linguists to include somewhat varying groups of sound qualities, usually those of juncture, pitch, and stress described in *phonemes § 2. We acquire the intonation of our own language by unconscious imitation and rarely make a mistake in it, but it is usually the last quality attained in learning a second language–witness the French and German of most Americans or the melody of someone who has learned English in his later years. Intonation is one of the most conspicuous differences between British and American English, especially obvious in questions. An easy way to observe the differences between the intonations of two languages is in many bilingual radio broadcasts, in which the commercial may be given first, say, in Italian, and then repeated in English with perhaps the words and the individual consonant and vowel sounds quite accurate but with the intonation or melody of the Italian.

intramural has no hyphen. It means etymologically "within the walls," specifically college activities carried on by groups of the same college; the opposite of *intercollegiate*.

Inversion means placing the verb before its subject–a rather uncommon order in English, largely restricted to a few established constructions: "What a fool is he!" "Long may it wave." "Out gushed the water." "Among the callers was Mrs. Brown." There is a sort of compromise inversion, which is used grammatically in questions, with the auxiliary before the subject and the infinitive or participle after it (Is he coming? Will she go? Did he like it?). See Chapter 7, "Inverted movement," page 182.

invite is ordinarily a verb. Its use as a noun (in′vīt) is Informal or would-be humorous: Did you get an invite?

Irony Irony is implying something markedly different, sometimes even the opposite, from what is actually said. (See Ch. 8, "Degree of statement," p. 234.)

irregardless is careless duplication of meaning (negative prefix *ir* [*in-*] and negative suffix *-less*); not used in reputable writing and better avoided in speech.

isolate Pronunciation is divided: ī′sə lāt, is′ə lāt, with the first more common; also ī′sə lā′shən, is′ə lā′shən.

it is the neuter third person singular pronoun, used to refer to an object, a situation, or an idea. *It* is also used to refer to a baby or an animal whose sex is unknown or unimportant for the statement (The dog wagged *its* tail) and in certain impersonal statements about the weather, events in general (impersonal *it*):

It rained all night. It's the way things go.

It is also used to refer to the idea of a preceding statement:

We changed two tires in record time. It is not easy to do on a dark and rainy night.

Sentences beginning "It is . . ." or "It was . . ." (anticipatory subject) are often wordy and weakening, since they have put a colorless locution in the emphatic beginning of the sentence:

[It was] then [that] his wife had taken to going with other men.

But this *preparatory it* may be useful when what it represents could not conveniently be placed in the usual position:

It is no use trying to evade the question asked you.

It may also stand in the object position:

He always made it a rule to check every one of his quotations.

It is also used in a number of idiomatic constructions:

There would have been no party if it hadn't been for your help.
You'll catch it if you don't hurry home.
We'll make a night of it.

(See *there is, there are, *its, *it's, *It's me. Reference: Emerson Beauchamp, Jr., "A Study of 'It': Handbook Treatment and Magazine Use," *American Speech,* 1951, 26:173-180.)

Italics In manuscript, both longhand and typewritten, italics are shown by underlining. Specific uses of italics are listed in *Underlining. (See also Ch. 5, "Underlining for italics," p. 131, *Foreign words in English, *Titles of articles, books, etc.)

its The possessive pronoun does not have an apostrophe:

The dog wagged *its* tail. A car is judged by *its* performance.
But we were deceived about *its* real value.

Associate *its* with *his* and *hers*.

it's is the contraction of *it is* or *it has:*

It's going to rain. *It's* rained for over a week now.

It's me The argument over "It's me" is a case of narrow theory versus established practice. The theory is that after the verb *be* the subject form should always be used, but this theory is consistently contradicted by the actual usage of good speakers.

We tend to use the nominative form of a pronoun when it is the subject and stands before a verb and to use the accusative in most other positions, especially when it comes after the verb—"object territory," as Professor Fries calls it. (Compare *who, whom.)

All the large grammars of English regard *it's me* as acceptable colloquial usage—and since the expression is not likely to occur except in speech, that gives it full standing. Fowler approves it, and one of the "judges" in *Current English Usage* (p. 108) wrote:

> *I* sounds quite mad in certain cases; e.g., pointing to a photo: "Which is I?"!!! "Oh, I see, that's I"!!! Absolutely non-English, hang all the grammarians on earth.

Us and *him* after *be* are less common, but usage is divided. *Current English Usage* found "If it had been *us,* we would admit it" uncertainly established and "I'll swear that was *him*" and "I suppose that's *him*" disputable. Very often speakers who try to be correct resort to some circumlocution, saying instead of "It was *she* (or *her*)" "That's who it was."

The upshot of the discussion is that in their natural settings "It's me," "It was him all right," "Something was wrong—was it him or the crowd?" are appropriate. (References: Marckwardt and Walcott, pp. 77-78; Wallace Rice, "Who's there? Me," *American Speech,* 1933, No. 3, 58-63; Robertson, pp. 492-503; Fries, *AEG,* p. 91. See *Case.)

-ize, -ise English has many verbs ending in the sound of īz, some of which are spelled *-ise* and some *-ize;* on many usage is divided. American usage, differing somewhat from British, prefers *-ize,* as in the following common verbs of this class:

anesthetize	dramatize	revolutionize	sympathize
apologize	memorize	sensitize	visualize
characterize	realize	standardize	

In the following *-ise* is the usual spelling:

advise	despise	exercise	surmise
arise	devise	revise	surprise
chastise	disguise	supervise	

Both *-ize* and *-ise* are commonly found in:

advertise–advertize analyze–analyse criticize–criticise

In general, follow American usage, and when that is divided, use whichever you are accustomed to. When in doubt, consult a good dictionary.

Some readers object to recent extension of the verbs in *-ize,* such as *concertize, picturize,* but aside from the fact that any new word is a bit disconcerting, there seems little reason for the objection except when one duplicates in meaning a verb already in common use.

J

J is a common spelling for the "soft *g*" sound at the beginning of syllables: *jam, jet, jibe, journey, jury.* At the end of a syllable the sound is variously spelled, often by *-dge: edge* (ej), *judge* (juj). For other spellings of the sound see *G § 2.

Some foreign sounds of *j* are kept in particular words: Latin (y), *Hallelujah;* French (zh), *bijou* (bē′zhōō), *jabot* (zha bō′); Spanish (h), *marijuana* (mä′ri hwä′nə).

No distinction in form was made between *i* and *j* by the Romans, though the letter had both a vowel and a consonant function in Latin. Only in recent times has it gained a separate place in our alphabet.

Jabberwocky Linguists have borrowed from *Through the Looking-Glass* the device of the verses of "Jabberwocky" ('Twas brillig, and the slithy toves/ Did gyre and gimble in the wabe) to show that it is possible to recognize the forms and grammatical functions of English words without reference to meaning. For instance, you have no difficulty in identifying four parts of speech and four inflectional forms in: The harbiger ligs' sollips drave brustrily in the stroks.

Jargon 1. *Applied to style.* Sir Arthur Quiller-Couch popularized *jargon* as the name for verbal fuzziness of various sorts–wordiness, abstract for concrete words, big words, and the use of words that add nothing to the meaning of a statement. (See Ch. 7, "Removing deadwood," p. 186; Ch. 8, "Choice of appropriate words," p. 224; "Concrete words," p. 217; "Abstract words," p. 219; *Legal language. Reference: Sir Arthur Quiller-Couch, *On the Art of Writing* (New York, 1916), pp. 100-126.)

2. *Linguistic sense. Jargon* is a word used among linguists to mean a dialect composed of the mixture of two or more languages. Jargons involving English are used by non-English-speaking peoples in doing business with the English. The best known of these are the Chinook jargon of the Pacific Northwest, beach-la-Mar (or bêche-de-mer) of the Pacific islands, and the Chinese-English jargon, pidgin English. (References: Otto Jespersen, *Language* (New York, 1922), pp. 216-236; and the sources referred to there.)

job is General for the Formal *position:* He got a job at an oil refinery. The word *position* has more dignity and what it refers to is usually thought of as better paid. *Job* is Informal for something made, such as an automobile or refrigerator ("a nice little job there").

Jones–plural and possessive forms The plural of *Jones* and of most nouns ending in an *s* or *z* sound is formed by adding *-es,* pronounced as a separate syllable: *Joneses* (jōn′zəz), *consciences* (kon′shən səz), *Jameses.* When two syllables ending in an *s* or *z* sound are in the root word, usage is divided: *the Moses* or *the Moseses.*

In the possessive, usage is divided. We may write (and, less frequently, say) *Dr. Jones'* (jōnz) *office;* or write and say *Dr. Jones's* (jōn′zəz) *office.* Probably the first form is the more common in writing. Also: For *goodness'* sake, *Charles'* collection, though *Charles's* (chärl′zəz) is equally reputable.

The possessive plural is pronounced the same as the plural and is written by adding (') to the plural form: *Joneses', Moses'* or *Moseses'*.

judgment–judgement *Judgment* is the more common American spelling.

K

The *k* sound, as in *keep,* is spelled *c* in many words (*call, actual, cute*), *cc* (*accord*), *ck* (*back, track*), and also with other letters, as in *queen, chord, ox, strength, cheque. K* before *n* is silent in a number of Germanic words (*knave, kneel, knife*).

Business changes many words spelled with *c* to *k* (*Kwick Kleaners*), either to make the alliteration more obvious or to make a trademark. (See Louise Pound, "The Kraze for 'K,'" *American Speech,* 1925, 1:43-44.) Such substitution is not acceptable in ordinary writing.

kid *Kid* is Informal for *child, youngster; kids* is the plural.

kind, sort *Kind* and *sort* are both singular nouns in form:

> This kind of person is a menace at any party.
> This sort of thing shouldn't be allowed.

As singular nouns, they are expected to take singular demonstrative adjectives in General and Formal writing:

> That kind of story doesn't interest me.
> Problems of this sort bother him.

But *kind* and *sort* are so closely associated with the noun they stand before that they seem like modifiers and in speech and Informal writing the demonstrative adjectives used with them agree with the principal noun of the construction:

> Those sort of ideas in his head and that sort of life with his wife. . . . –A. S. M. HUTCHINSON, *If Winter Comes,* p. 324
>
> You next reach the conclusion that, as these kind of marks have not been left by any other animal than man. . . .–T. H. HUXLEY, "The Method of Scientific Investigation"

The *Oxford English Dictionary* has examples of *these kind of* and *these sort of* from the fourteenth century to the present, many of them from the "best authors." Fries found the plural regularly used with *kind* and *sort* by his Group I (Standard English) writers (*AEG,* p. 58). Only the vigilance of editorial copy readers keeps the construction from being as common in writing as in speech. (Jespersen, p. 202, even suggests that *kind* and *sort* be regarded as unchanged plurals and therefore correct.) But the construction is still felt by many to be Nonstandard. (Reference: Curme, *Syntax,* pp. 544-546.)

kind of, sort of *Kind of* and *sort of* are used as Informal adverbs, equivalent to *rather* or *somewhat* in more Formal usage:

I feel kind of logy today. It was sort of dull, but he said a lot.

Especially in writing, these would be:

I was rather [somewhat, a little, very, pretty] tired.
It was pretty [very, rather] dull, but he said a good deal.

kind of [a], sort of [a] Strictly you have a *kind* or *sort* of a class of objects, not of one object: *a kind of story,* not *a kind of a story.* But in General English *kind of a* and *sort of a* are very common, and they are fairly common among respected writers:

I want to find someone on the earth so intelligent that he welcomes opinions which he condemns–I want to be this kind of a man and I want to have known this kind of a man.–JOHN JAY CHAPMAN, *Letters,* p. 124

Now, suppose the battle of Salamis had been fought, not in the full light of Greek history, but in the misty dawn of the Epos, what sort of a story should we have had?–GILBERT MURRAY, *The Rise of the Greek Epic,* p. 200

These two sentences from the same short story show the two idioms in differing degrees of Formality, in different tempos:

...he had never once brought her a comical, stuffed animal or any sort of an object with a picture of a Scottie on it.

Bob McEwen wasn't the sort of man to do a sentimental thing like that unless he meant it.–SALLY BENSON, *People Are Fascinating,* pp. 30, 31

In Formal writing *kind of a* and *sort of a* should be avoided, but it is an accepted General idiom.

L

L is a "liquid" consonant that varies considerably in quality in the speech of individuals and groups and with its position in a word: *land, leaf, almost, silly, fill. L* is silent in a few common words: *almond* (usually), *folk, half, salmon, talk, walk, would, yolk.* It is often not sounded in other words as in *golf course* (gôf′kors′). Despite its frequency in spelling, the doubled *l* sounds just like the single one; compare *collar, color; llama, lamb; fell, fail.*

In many syllables no specific vowel is sounded before an *l,* and the pronunciation can be indicated by "syllabic *l*" (l̩): *marble* (mär′bl̩), *tickle* (tik′l̩).

Labeling material It should usually be unnecessary to label a statement as *interesting, amusing,* or *important,* or to point out a joke or a dig by (?) or (!). A good storyteller doesn't need to begin "You'll laugh at this," and a good writer can usually *show* that what he is saying is interesting or important without labeling it. Instead of beginning "Let me relate an amusing incident," just tell it well and the reader will see that it is amusing.

Labeling an emotion that is clearly suggested in a narrative weakens the effect:

> "What was it, conductor, did we blow a fuse?"
>
> "No," he said, "we just killed three people back at a crossing."
>
> [The label:] The effect of this sentence was electrifying. "We just killed three people. . . ." Maybe they were college boys going home for Christmas.

laissez faire, laisser faire The spelling is still French, and the pronunciation (les′ā far′) still an attempt at French, but the word is not italicized except in conspicuously Formal writing.

last (at long last) A recently revived archaic idiom, *at long last* is slightly more emphatic than *at last*, at least when it is spoken, but usually the phrase has a British or Formal connotation, as in this:

> An economic power born of the travail of men at long last asserts its title to political dominance.—HAROLD J. LASKI, *The Rise of Liberalism*

last, latest In Formal usage *last* refers to the final item of a series; *latest,* the most recent in time of a series which may or may not be continued:

> His latest (we hope it won't be his last) biography is of Peter Cooper.

This distinction is not strictly kept, so that both words are used as superlatives of *late*.

Latin and English **1.** *Latin words.* Many Latin words came into English in early periods of the language, either direct or through French, and cannot now be told from other English words: *patience, candle, receive, wine* (see *English language). Most borrowings from Latin are subject to the same process of anglicizing as other *foreign words in English, and in general they are pronounced as English words —*agenda* (ə jen′də), *erratum* (i rā′təm or i rä′təm)—instead of according to the system of sounds now taught in Latin classes.

Since Latin is dead as a first language and no considerable people speaks it as a second language, new borrowings come in through written rather than spoken use and belong to the Formal dialects, used chiefly in science, law, religion, medicine, and academic work. Since practically all college work was carried on in Latin until about 1750, and a good deal of it later than that, considerable Latin is preserved in college use. Many diplomas are in Latin, and at some institutions the commencement formulas are in Latin. At a more routine level, several Latin words and abbreviations are used in the footnotes of academic research (*ibid., passim, supra, infra, loc. cit.*), though there is a tendency to use English words for many of these.

Prefixes of Latin origin (*ante-, ex-, in-, pre-, re-, sub-*) and other compounding elements, such as *uni-* (*unilateral*), *bi-* (*biweekly*), are active in forming new English words. At present scientific words are being formed more from Greek than from Latin elements.

2. *Latin forms.* English continues to use the Latin forms for some words that are used principally in the Formal dialects (**alumnus*—

alumna, bacillus–bacilli), but those commonly used have either English plurals or both (*formula, formulas* or *formulae; focus, focuses* or *foci; stadium, stadiums* or *stadia*). See *Plurals § 4, *data.

3. *Latin and English grammar.* The first and a number of other English grammars were composed by men thoroughly familiar with Latin, many of whom believed that English should be a language like Latin. As a result, English, which was a Germanic language in structure, was described in terms of Latin grammar, and rules were devised for making the language fit the picture. This may be one reason for the old taboo of the *split infinitive (which would be impossible in Latin because the infinitive is one word, as in *laborare,* where English has *to work*) and of putting a preposition at the end of a sentence (*Prepositions § 3d), which almost never occurs in Latin but is a characteristic English idiom.

Only recently has English grammar begun to be based squarely on a study of the English language and freed from some of the categories and rules of Latin grammar. See *Linguistics.

latter, later *Latter* (lat′ər) and *later* (lā′tər) are often carelessly confused in spelling. The habit of reading your copy aloud to yourself should catch this type of error. (See *former–first, latter–last.)

lay–lie In much spoken English the work of these two verbs is done by one (*lay; lay* or *laid; laid*). In writing they should be kept distinct:

> lie ("to recline," intransitive), lay, lain
> lay ("to place," transitive), laid, laid

You *lie* down for a rest or *lie* down on the job; a farm *lies* in a valley. You *lay* a floor, *lay* a book on the table, *lay* a bet, *lay* out clothes. Yesterday you *lay* down to rest (in speech often indistinguishable from *laid*); you *laid* a book on the table. Egg laying is *lay, laid, laid.*

-le words A large and interesting group of English verbs ends in *-le*—*fiddle, giggle, meddle, tickle, waddle, whistle, whittle*—in which the ending usually suggests an action continued or habitually repeated.

In spelling, lab*el,* mant*el* (the shelf), mod*el,* and nick*el* give some trouble because they are exceptions to the usual English spelling of this final syllable.

lead, led *Lead* and *led* show the confusion we suffer because English spelling represents one sound by different symbols. *Lead* (lēd), the present tense of the verb, gives no trouble; but *led,* the past tense, is often incorrectly spelled with *ea* by analogy with *read* (rēd), *read* (red), and the noun *lead.*

> Please *lead* the horse away.
> The culprit was *led* into the office.

Leaders Leaders, or "period leaders," are a line of spaced periods used to guide the reader's eye across a page. They are often used in statistical tables and the table of contents of a book:

In typed copy, hyphens are often used instead of periods.

learn–teach Nonstandard English often uses *learn* in the sense of *teach* (He *learned* me how to tie six kinds of knots). Educated usage makes the distinction: He *taught* me how to tie six kinds of knots; I *learned* how to tie knots from him.

-ledge, -lege Two common words are spelled with the ending *-ledge: acknowledge* (*acknowledging, acknowledgment*), *knowledge.*

Words spelled with *-lege* should not be confused with them: *allege* (*alleged, alleging*), *college, sacrilege* (*sacrilegious*).

Legal language Most legal matters are carried on in a style bristling with long series of synonyms ("do hereby give, grant, bargain, sell and convey"), archaic or foreign (French, Latin) words for everyday things and situations, abbreviations and stereotyped phrases that puzzle laymen and sometimes lawyers themselves. The need for certain technical words is great, but the reason for much of the jargon is unconsidered tradition. Perhaps it must be tolerated in legal business, but lawyers and others who have much to do with law should realize that it is a trade dialect (shoptalk).

Many lawyers and judges write with distinction, using only the technical terms demanded by the subject. Although they use an appropriately Formal style and must allude to cases that give precedents, they still find room for allusion to general experience, without any loss of exactness.

A brief dissenting opinion of Mr. Justice Holmes illustrates a compact but readable judicial style. A majority of the Supreme Court had decided that the State of Ohio could tax a membership in the New York Stock Exchange owned by a resident of Ohio, on the ground that it was personal property, not like real estate, which would be taxed by the state in which it lay.

> The question whether a seat in the New York Stock Exchange is taxable in Ohio consistently with the principles established by this Court seems to me more difficult than it does to my brethren. All rights are intangible personal relations between the subject and the object of them created by law. But it is established that it is not enough that the subject, the owner of the right, is within the power of the taxing State. He cannot be taxed for land situated elsewhere, and the same is true of personal property permanently out of the jurisdiction. It does not matter, I take it, whether the interest is legal or equitable, or what the machinery by which it is reached, but the question is whether the object of the right is so local in its foundation and prime meaning that it should stand like an interest in land. If left to myself I should have thought that the foundation and substance of the plaintiff's right was the

right of himself and his associates personally to enter the New York Stock Exchange building and to do business there. I should have thought that all the rest was incidental to that and that that on its face was localized in New York. If so, it does not matter whether it is real or personal property or that it adds to the owner's credit and facilities in Ohio. The same would be true of a great estate in New York land.—*Representative Opinions of Mr. Justice Holmes,* edited by Alfred Lief, pp. 265-6

References: Benjamin N. Cardozo, "Law and Literature" (pp. 3-40 in the volume of the same title—New York, 1931); F. A. Philbrick, *Language and the Law* (New York, 1949).

leisure The usual American pronunciation is lē′zhər, sometimes lezh′ər.

less, fewer *Fewer* refers only to number and things that are *counted:*

Fewer cars were on the road. There were fewer than sixty present.

In Formal usage *less* refers only to amount or quantity and things measured:

There was a good deal less tardiness in the second term [amount].
There was even less hay than the summer before.

Fewer seems to be declining in use and *less* often takes its place:

Less hands were required for this work....—KENNETH BURKE, *Attitudes Toward History,* p. 175

...but polled only a sliver of additional votes and won three less seats.—*Foreign Policy Bulletin,* Mar. 3, 1950, p. 2

Many readers find this usage stylistically objectionable.

less, lesser Both are used as comparatives (of *little*)—*less* more usually referring to size or quantity (less time, less food); *lesser,* a Formal word, referring to value or importance (the lesser of two evils, a lesser writer).

let (leave) A common Nonstandard idiom is the use of *leave* where Standard English has *let*. Both idioms are shown in this sentence by a student who was obviously making a transition between the two varieties:

In high school I was cured of the practice of leaving [Nonstandard] notebooks go, but I fell into the habit of letting [Standard] homework slide.

Use *let—let it go, let it lie where it is.*

let's, the contraction of *let us,* needs an apostrophe. *Let's us go, let's you and me go,* though common in speech, have no place in writing.

Letters 1. *General observations on correspondence.*

a) Materials. The stationery stores are full of novelties, which may appeal to one's taste, but the standard sizes and styles of paper are never outmoded and are usually cheaper and of better quality:

Note paper—A four-page sheet to be folded once across the middle for the envelope.

Club paper–A sheet about 7¼ by 11 inches, with two folds fitting an envelope 3¾ by 7½.

Business letter paper–8½ by 11 inches, to be folded twice across for a long envelope or folded across the middle and then twice more for the ordinary envelope about six inches long.

A fairly good quality of stationery is worth its cost in the good impression it helps make on the reader.

Typewritten copy is of course the norm in business correspondence. In personal letters there is some question, though in the United States so many people do their own typing that among acquaintances typewritten copy is quite good form–and usually welcome. In the earlier stages of a friendship longhand is perhaps preferable, and it should almost always be used for invitations and acknowledgments and in any letters conveying unusual sentiment or feeling. (See *Typewritten copy.)

b) Styles. The pages should appeal to the reader's eye. This means leaving good margins, centering the body of the letter on the page so that the whole presents a neatly proportioned appearance, spacing the parts of the letter so that they are distinct but still form a unit, and so on. The paragraphs are usually short, three or four sentences or less, and spaced distinctly.

Ingenuity can usually find a way of subduing even long addresses that must sometimes be used in headings. Find an arrangement of the lines that looks well in your typing or longhand.

Style in indenting at the end of display lines is divided. In typed letters a straight lining at the left of the heading and inside address is more usual now than *indention:

Straight form–more common	*Indented form–less common*

Graham, Sutton and Company
1007 E. Newgate Street
Chicago 3, Illinois
	Graham, Sutton and Company
	  1007 E. Newgate Street
	    Chicago 3, Illinois

In longhand letters the indented form is perhaps more common.

The form used for the address on the envelope should be consistent with that used for the heading and the address on the first page of the letter; that is, either the straight or the indented form should be used throughout. Punctuation marks are not now used at the ends of the lines of address or heading:

Old-fashioned style	*Current style*

Graham, Sutton and Company,
  1007 E. Newgate Street,
    Chicago 3, Illinois.
	Graham, Sutton and Company
	1007 E. Newgate Street
	Chicago 3, Illinois

c) Envelopes. The first requirements of the address on the envelope are completeness and clearness, for the sake of the post office. Address your mail to street and number, and in cities include the postal zone.

2. *Business letters.* Since business letters usually pass between people who are not acquainted or who at least are not writing for reasons of friendship at the moment, certain matters of form are important in handling routine information.

The writer's complete address is necessary, either in a printed letterhead or in a written heading, to serve as an address for the reply. An inside address is conventional (and useful when the letter is dictated or when several are being written at the same time or when a carbon is to be filed). In addressing a firm, *Messrs.* is not often used in the United States. The salutations are:

Dear Sir: Gentlemen: Dear Sirs:
Dear Madam: Ladies: (Formal or showy, Mesdames:)

When a letter is intended for a particular member of a firm, this form is sometimes used:

Graham, Sutton and Company
1007 E. Newgate Street
Chicago 3, Illinois
Attention Mr. Stephen Lange
Gentlemen:

A less Formal and more direct form of address is perhaps more commonly used:

Mr. Stephen Lange
Graham, Sutton and Company
1007 E. Newgate Street
Chicago 3, Illinois
Dear Mr. Lange:

When a man's position is made part of the inside address, arrange it so that no one line becomes conspicuously longer than the others. In general the title should be joined to the individual's rather than to the firm's name:

Mr. Leonard T. Hosic
Personnel Director
Allen, Swift and Company
4826 Commercial Street
Allentown, Ohio

The body of a business letter should be clear, direct, and as brief as is consistent with clearness. A separate paragraph is used for each item or for each subdivision of the message. The tone may be curt in routine matters—amateurs are apt to indulge in unnecessary explanation—or it may be full and persuasive. In all letters, especially those asking questions or outlining plans, all relevant information should be given.

The desire for brevity should not lead to a telegraphic style or short-cuts in expression. The old tags like "Yours received and contents noted," "In reply to your favor of the 12th inst.," and "Would say" have disappeared entirely from the correspondence of careful business houses.

TAYLOR BOOKSHOP
80 WINCHESTER STREET
NEW YORK CITY

June 16, 1958

Mr. James T. Foster
2645 Grantham Terrace
Kew Gardens, L.I., N.Y.

Dear Mr. Foster:

Several weeks ago you asked us to let you know when the new Fischer edition of Shakespeare would be on sale. It is obtainable now, and we think you will like it very much. The volumes are three by four inches in size, bound in red and gold.

There are 25 books in the complete set, which costs $15.75, but separate volumes may be bought for 65¢ each. We are enclosing a list of the works included in the Fischer edition.

If you wish to place an order, we shall be glad to take care of it for you.

Yours truly,

Elizabeth Reagan

Elizabeth Reagan

Form for Business Letter

The best way to become informed on business letters is to study the practice of reputable companies. If you are specially interested in business correspondence, start a collection of the best examples that come your way.

The close of a business letter is:

Yours truly, Sincerely yours, Very truly yours,

or some such formula. Only the first word is capitalized and the phrase is followed by a comma (though some writers are dropping the comma, since it is as unnecessary as those once standing after the display lines).

Although in Formal correspondence a woman does not use *Mrs.* or *Miss* with her name in a signature, in Informal and business correspondence it is frequently used and is a courtesy to the receiver of the letter, who may otherwise not know whether to reply to *Mrs.* or *Miss.* The title should be restricted to the typed signature.

(Mrs.) Dorothy Olson   (Miss) Dorothy Olson   Dorothy Olson
(Mrs. Henry Olson)

See *Business English. Recent manuals of business writing will give further details of form and suggestions for content.

3. *Personal letters.*

a) Form. The form of personal letters varies with the intimacy between the writer and recipient. No heading except the date is needed between regular correspondents, but the writer's address in the heading is often a convenience and a necessity in letters to occasional correspondents. They may not keep address books and aren't likely to remember exact addresses.

The salutation varies:

Dear Bob,   Dear Miss Breckenridge,
Dear Miss Breckenridge: (The colon is more Formal.)
Formal: My dear Miss Breckenridge:

Formal personal letters, especially between professional men who are not intimate, may have the salutation "Dear Sir:" and the recipient's name and address at the bottom, flush with the left margin.

The complimentary close ranges from "Yours" or any other expression of sentiment to "Yours sincerely," "Cordially yours," "Yours very truly," between people little acquainted. When there is any doubt, rely on one of the regular formulas for the close, "Yours truly," "Yours very truly." Sentence conclusions ("Assuring you of our continued interest, I beg to remain, Yours very truly") are now out of fashion.

b) Tone and style. It would be useless to lay down rules to govern letters to relatives and friends. They should represent your own sense of what the reader will like and what will sound like yourself. They are like conversation, and the style will ordinarily be Informal or whatever you would use when face to face with the recipient. But, as in so much conversation, we often sink to our laziest in letters to the people we write the oftenest. It is worth while occasionally to read over a letter to see if *we* would enjoy receiving it, to see if we have told enough to make the incidents interesting, to see if we have written with reasonable care, if we are paying our readers the courtesy they deserve in neatness and appropriate expression. Revising an occasional letter will perhaps raise the average of them all.

It is conventional to say that the art of letter writing is dead. Perhaps not so many Contributor's Club essays are sent through the mail as formerly, but an occasional letter we receive and an occasional published volume show that letter writers can still describe events racily, can still hit off the people they meet in apt characterizations, and can occasionally discuss ideas with some insight and gusto. These letters are a challenge to us when we have material that deserves special attention.

For Formal invitations and so on, see *Social correspondence.

Levels of usage In previous editions of this book the *varieties* of usage in English were called *levels*. But since *levels* suggests a value judgment, *varieties* (a more accurate term) is now used in this book. (See Ch. 1, pp. 15-26.)

lever Both lev′ər and lē′vər are in good use.

lighted–lit Both forms are in good use as the past tense and past participle of *light*. *Lighted* is more common as the adjective and past participle:

a lighted lamp He had lighted a fire.

Lit is perhaps more common as the past tense:

He lit a cigaret. (or) He lighted a cigaret.

lightning, lightening The flash is *lightning;* making lighter (a load) is *lightening*. There is also a verb *lighten,* which means "to flash, to make brighter": Before the thunder it was lightening.

like–as 1. *As prepositions*. In all varieties of English *like* is used as a preposition introducing a comparison:

The description fits him like a glove.
Habit grips a person like an octopus.
She took to selling like a duck to water.

As seems to be increasing in use in this position:

He was built as a sword fish. . . .–ERNEST HEMINGWAY, *The Old Man and the Sea*

Dr. James, as any other rational man, foresees a not distant future when. . . .–*Times Literary Supplement*, July 20, 1951, p. 456

2. *As conjunctions*.

a) In all varieties of English *as, as if,* and *as though* are used as conjunctions introducing clauses of comparison:

People try to get to college *as* they used to try to get to heaven.
Habit grips a person *as* an octopus does.
It looked *as if* he would land flat, but he entered the water perfectly.
He walked *as though* he was hurt.

b) *Like* appears regionally in both educated and uneducated usage, more in the West and South than in the East, as a conjunction introducing clauses of comparison. Consequently it is appropriately used in representing conversation, as in the first example below, and in narrative, as in the second example, from a story with a Southern setting:

They're laying bets, just like it was a dog fight. . . . Now let's don't go at it like it was our last New Year's on earth.–BILL GULICK, "The Marriage of Moon Wind," *Saturday Evening Post*, Dec. 31, 1955, p. 43

And with the grandsons and Isaac's wife and Miss Sarah, all sitting there at their plates like she had done something to make them ashamed of her.–P. H. LOWREY, "A Country Life," *Accent*, 1951, 11:179

c) In the last few years the use of *like* as a conjunction has greatly increased, and it is certainly now within the range of Standard English:

She looked now like she had looked the last times he had seen her.—MORLEY CALLAGHAN, *Now That April's Here*, p. 22

More and more we are treating children like a rich man incapable of love might treat his wife—trying to fob off on them material things in place of the vital things that they have a right to.—HENRY STEELE COMMAGER, *Saturday Review*, May 10, 1952, p. 46

She plays on the audience like she plays on the zither in the "Tra-la-la-lay" number of her current show at the Booth Theatre.—MILTON BRACKER, "An Evening with Bea Lillie," *New York Times*, Oct. 19, 1952, Drama section, p. 3

Historically both forms are good, since both are parts of the older *like as* ("Like as a father pitieth his children . . ."). The speakers of some regions have taken *as*, of others *like*. *Like* is preferable from the standpoint of meaning, because *as* has several different meanings and several functions in the language and so is relatively weak. *Like* is more exact and more emphatic in a comparison than *as* can be. But many people are prejudiced against the use of *like* as a conjunction, perhaps because they associate it with advertising and radio comedy programs, and consequently young writers should avoid it except in distinctly Informal papers. It is a good instance of change in usage, and of resistance to it. (References: Curme, *Syntax*, pp. 281-282; Pooley, pp. 153-155; "Current English Forum," *College English*, May 1952, 13:463-464.)

likely—apt—liable The principal meanings of these words are:

likely: expected, probably
apt: tending toward, naturally fit
liable: possible (of an unpleasant event); responsible (as for damages)

Likely is the most commonly needed of the three. *Apt* is widely used in the sense of *likely*, as well as in its own narrower meaning, and is so recorded in dictionaries. The use of *liable* in the sense of *likely* is local and should be confined to Informal speech.

It's *likely* [or, *apt;* or, locally, *liable*] to rain when the wind is southwest.

line is business English (What's your line?—a line of goods) or Informal (He handed her a line). As a *counter word it is usually deadwood and could better be left out:

My own experience along business lines [that is, *in business*] has been slight.

Another book along the same lines as *Microbe Hunters* [similar to *Microbe Hunters*], but with a fine story, is *Arrowsmith*.

Linguistics The scientific study of language is called *linguistics*, and a scientific student of language is a *linguist*. The principal divisions of contemporary linguistics are:

1) *Phonology,* including *Phonetics,* the making of speech sounds and their characteristic qualities, and *Phonemics,* the use and perception of sounds in a particular language. (See *Phonemes.)

2) *Morphology,* the study of the meaningful elements of a language–for example, words, parts of words, inflections ("endings"), certain patterns of stress and pitch. (See *Morpheme.)

3) *Syntax,* the study of the arrangements and relationships of morphemes in sentences.

These divisions are interdependent, morphemes being described in terms of phonemes and syntax largely in terms of morphemes.

Other systematic studies of language involve nonlinguistic fields as well, such as dialectology, linguistic geography, historical and comparative studies, and semantics or meaning. Strict linguists regard such fields as belonging in *metalinguistics,* since they involve "more than" linguistic material. Linguists are helped by other scientists–biologists and physicists (in phonetics), psychologists, anthropologists, and sociologists, and in turn give materials to them. In addition linguists contribute to such practical activities as *lexicography,* the making of dictionaries, *orthography,* the study of spelling, and *paleography,* the study of ancient texts.

1. *The analysis of languages.* In the last few decades linguists have developed a rigorous technique for the analysis of languages, in part in reaction against previous methods of study, particularly of philology, which was concerned chiefly with the Indo-European languages and based largely on the study of literature, especially of written literature. A basic principle of linguistics is that language is primarily speech; the methods of analyzing speech (such as establishing categories by comparing "minimal pairs," two locutions alike in all but one linguistic feature) have become relatively standardized and have been applied to other aspects of language. Perhaps the most difficult aspect of linguistics has been the separating (for the purposes of analysis) of linguistic activities from the current of life in which they appear. The words *structure* and *structural,* often applied to linguistic study (sometimes almost with a mystical or magical overtone), emphasize this separation. Structural linguistics isolates the linguistic activity and stresses that despite the variety in a language there is a system or a series of patterns which can be discovered and described by linguistic methods and which alone are the proper subject of linguistics.

Because of the tremendous importance of language in life, there have been numerous pressures for practical applications of the methods and findings of the new science. To date the notable successes have been in recording languages not previously written, rescuing many that were on the point of extinction, and in teaching the spoken form of a second language through more detailed and accurate phonemic analysis.

2. *The reanalysis of English.* Considerable progress has been made in describing English in scientific linguistic terms. Formerly neglected features like word order and intonation patterns have been explored. Real advances have been made in abandoning or at least minimizing some categories inherited from Latin grammar but not significant for English, such as case in nouns and mood in verbs; in defining various categories more precisely, such as the parts of speech (or form classes)–defining them by reference to form and function rather than to meaning; in giving more definite recognition to the phrase patterns basic to syntax; and in providing the beginnings of a syntax grounded in observation of speech.

At least four books by experienced linguists primarily describing English are announced and will presumably appear between the writing of this paragraph and its appearance in print. These will certainly advance the description of our language notably. But it is safe to prophesy that together they will not form a complete or consistent description of the current language. They will probably differ somewhat in their phonemic analysis, especially in the suprasegmental phonemes; in discriminating the parts of speech; in identifying some types of morphemes; in indicating the relation of linguistic analysis to meaning and the relation between the spoken and written forms of the language; and, almost certainly, because of lack of previous discussion, in describing syntactical categories. This is a healthy situation in a relatively new and rapidly developing science, since discussion will bring added insights and increased agreement, even though a single comprehensive system may not come for a long time, if ever.

In the meantime the lack of agreement among linguists raises problems for anyone attempting to present some account of English for nonspecialists. At the present time any coherent linguistic description practically has to be a simplification of the work of a single linguist and consequently must be incomplete and possibly idiosyncratic. The immediate future will be a period of transition in the description of English, for which some such policy as the following seems reasonable:

To accept, certainly not to contradict, and to use where feasible the generally agreed upon principles of linguistic science;

To use some of the simpler and better established particular items of the linguistic description, incorporating them into the traditional system;

To become familiar with some terms and methods and categories (even though their exact definition at the present time varies among reputable linguists) in order to see where the points of growth are, in the hope that they will with further study and discussion become stabilized.

3. *Linguistics in a composition course.* The purpose of a composition or communication course is to further the communicative skills of the students. Its organization and general direction should be to this end, based on the methods of composition (rhetoric). The current language is the medium, and consequently should be presented from this point of view. (In the last few generations "grammar" has often triumphed over "rhetoric," partly because of the unquestioned deficiencies of many students and partly because the elementary facts of language have seemed more definite and consequently easier to present and test.)

The description of English should be as accurate as possible, and eventually linguistics will furnish a sufficiently complete and consistent description. Even now there may be gains in using some of the terms and categories of linguistics: new terms break with the years of past instruction and may make an impression on students who have developed resistance to the repetition of traditional matter; a few topics such as sentence boundaries and restrictive punctuation can be more accurately presented than formerly, even though the precise definitions of the terminals involved are uncertain; and the instructor works with enthusiasm because he is learning or has recently learned something new. But a composition course is not an introduction to linguistics and can hardly spare time for a very secure grounding in such a technical field.

The language part of a composition course, beyond a few pretty elementary topics, is certainly in the area of metalinguistics, involving social habits and attitudes. Most of the questions are of the order of "Shall I say or write this in this situation?" Linguistic generalizations, whether in traditional or more scientific form, can help in presenting general patterns, in summarizing general practices, but they do not go far in guiding choices between similar expressions when both are in the range of Standard English. To make these decisions students need not only the paradigms but a wide knowledge of the varieties of current usage, what educated people say and write. Since this knowledge by itself will not answer the questions, principles are also needed, especially principles of appropriateness. These involve value judgments, the cultivation of taste and some sensitiveness to styles, and these lie somewhat outside the range of science. The better his scientific training, the more modest a person should feel in the face of his robust and rangy language. Furthermore, the integrity of the methods of scientific linguistics will be safeguarded by not pressing for too immediate application, by regarding style and usage as complementary emphases in the study of language.

See *Style, *Usage; Chapter 1, The varieties of English. References: The linguistic works listed in the general bibliography: Bloomfield, Carroll, Fries *Structure,* Gleason; and, in confident expectation, the impending books by Archibald A. Hill, Charles F. Hockett, Sumner Ives, and James Sledd.

Linking verbs A verb may be used so that it has little meaning of its own but functions chiefly in connecting a subject with a modifier. In such a construction it is called a *linking verb* or *copula.*

Be is most commonly used as a linking verb, followed by modifiers which function as adjectives or nouns (single words, phrases, or clauses), traditionally known as *predicate adjectives* and *predicate nominatives,* respectively.

This bottle *was* full. The man *is* a carpenter.

Many other verbs are used as linking verbs–Curme counts about sixty in current English. Instead of having a verb of full meaning like *colden,* English uses the nearly meaningless verb *turn* or *get* and the adjective *cold* (which carries the chief part of the meaning) in such a sentence as "The weather *turned* cold." Many verbs are used both with full meaning of their own (as *fell* in "The tree *fell* into the water") and as linking verbs (*fell* in "She *fell* silent" or "He *fell* ill"). Some typical linking verbs are:

He *became* a doctor. The butter *tastes* rancid. She *felt* sad. He *acts* old. The ground *sounds* hollow. He *grew* more and more aloof. He *appeared* to be gaining ground. This *looks* first rate. His story *seemed* credible.

It is perhaps because many speakers are unaware that the same verb may function either as a linking verb or as a transitive verb that the modifier is sometimes treated as adverbial when it is in fact adjectival: "He felt *sadly*" for "He felt *sad.*"

See *be § 2, *Predicate adjective, Predicate noun. References: Curme, *Parts of Speech,* pages 66-69, *Syntax,* pages 26-28 (list on page 27).

literary *Literary,* as applied to style, usually means possessing traits that are characteristic of the more conservative tradition of English literature. Its connotation may be "distinguished" or it may be "bookish." (See Ch. 1, "Formal English," p. 20.)

little *Little* is overused by sentimentalists ("little dear" and so on).

loan as a verb In spite of attempts to keep *loan* only as a noun and to make *lend* the corresponding verb, *loan* is regularly a verb, at least in American usage:

Verb: I loaned [or lent] him $2. Noun: He got a loan of two dollars.

Localisms Revision: The expression marked is in local use only. Replace it by a word or construction in General American use. *Local*

A *localism,* or *provincialism,* is a word or other expression in regular use in a certain region but not in others in which the same language is used. The southern, western, and northeastern sections of the United States differ somewhat in sounds, in words, and in constructions. Localisms are appropriate to conversation and to much Informal writing but are often out of place in impersonal and Formal writing. (For discussion see Ch. 1, "Variations due to place," p. 8.)

locate is used for *settle* (The family located near the present town of Nashua) and for *find* (I can't locate the letter now). It is *deadwood in defining the location of specific places or people:

> He is now [located] with the Ford Motor Company in Detroit.

Locution is a handy term for referring to a word or a unified group of words; that is, it may be applied to a single word or to a phrase or clause considered as a meaning group. *Phrase, a meaning group, that is* are three locutions.

Logic 1. *Logic and language.* Sometimes items of usage are objected to as being "illogical," as *he don't, the *reason is because.* The former is a matter of history and of language variety, *he doesn't* being Standard English and *he don't* now generally Nonstandard. When the objection to the second is elaborated, it is usually "that an adverbial clause (because . . .) is equated with a noun (reason)"; these terms are from grammar rather than from logic. Logic proper is not involved in either objection.

A great many *idioms are not the cumulation of the meaning of their separate words: *get sick, hard to come by, a little water, many is the time, out of order.* These show, more clearly than the equally arbitrary general habits of the language, that language is a human development, the result of millions of speech situations, not a preplanned system; it is not illogical but simply nonlogical. The wonder is that it is as systematic as it is.

Probably arguments from logic had an influence in establishing the *double negative as Nonstandard English, since in language ordinarily the more negatives there are, the more definitely negative the statement is. But arguments from logic have had few such successes, and the term *logical* cannot be applied to language in its technical sense but only in its most general popular sense of "more or less systematic."

2. *Logic and composition.* Formal or classical logic furnishes a technique for testing the validity (rather than the accuracy or "truth") of reasoning by means of syllogisms. For example, the pattern of "Kangaroos are marsupials, and wallabies are kangaroos; therefore wallabies are marsupials" is that of a *syllogism.* In this kind of syllogism, there are three statements: the *major premise* makes a statement about all the members of a class, the *minor premise* relates the subject of the argument to the previously mentioned class, and the *conclusion* states what necessarily follows:

> Major premise: All *kangaroos* are *marsupials.*
> Minor premise: *Wallabies* are *kangaroos.*
> Conclusion: Therefore *wallabies* are *marsupials.*

Each statement has two terms connected by a verb, and the entire syllogism consists of three terms, each used twice.

Here are some common patterns, represented by letters, with their counterparts in argument:

1)	"Of course this tap water is safe to drink. It's city water."
All A is B.	All *city drinking water* is *pure.*
C is A.	*This tap water* is *city drinking water.*
C is B.	*This tap water* is *pure.*
2)	"We should give this plan serious consideration because it offers a possible solution to the East-West deadlock."
Any AB is AC.	Any *plan which offers a possible solution to the East-West deadlock* is *a plan which should be given serious consideration.*
D is AB.	*This plan* is *a plan which offers a possible solution to the East-West deadlock.*
D is AC.	*This plan* is *a plan which should be given serious consideration.*
3)	"I know some of my friends are good swimmers; they wouldn't be in the water show if they weren't."
All A's are B's.	All *participants in the water show* are *good swimmers.*
Some C's are A's.	*Some of my friends* are *participants in the water show.*
Some C's are B's.	*Some of my friends* are *good swimmers.*
4)	"It's unreasonable to suppose that Mr. Laux, a staunch Republican, voted for a Democratic governor."
No A is B.	No *staunch Republican* is *a person who votes for a Democratic governor.*
C is A.	*Mr. Laux* is *a staunch Republican.*
C is not B.	*Mr. Laux* is not *a person who votes for a Democratic governor.*

Because full syllogisms are not found in most discourse, you will have to reconstruct them to use this method. Most often the minor premise and the conclusion are given, and looking for the omitted or implied major premise is a good way to bring into the open assumptions you may be taking for granted or may not realize that you are making. Here are several ways the first statement might be written. Notice that in each, one premise has been omitted:

(Minor premise:) A wallaby is a kangaroo, (Conclusion:) so it must be a marsupial.

(Minor premise:) Since a wallaby is a kind of kangaroo, (Conclusion:) it is a marsupial.

(Conclusion:) Wallabies must be marsupials; (Minor premise:) they are kangaroos.

(Major premise:) Kangaroos are marsupials, (Conclusion:) and so wallabies must be.

To reconstruct the syllogism, first find the conclusion. *So, therefore,* and *must be* are sometimes indicators. If the first term of the conclusion is also the first term of the other statement, you have a minor premise. In the statement "Whales must be fish because they live in water," we find the conclusion *whales must be fish* and the minor premise *whales live in water.* What is the major premise? Remembering that the second term of the minor premise is the first term of the major premise, and changing the minor premise to get the necessary two terms and a verb, we complete the syllogism:

All *creatures that live in water* are *fish.*
Whales are *creatures that live in water.*
Whales are *fish.*

The major premise is not true, and so the conclusion is unreliable. On the other hand, in the argument "All fish have gills, and whales are fish; therefore whales have gills" we have a false minor premise; and again the conclusion is unreliable. One test, then, of a syllogism is this: *Are both the premises true?* If either or both are false, the syllogism is unsound, even though the reasoning may be "valid."

But in addition to determining the truth of the premises, you need to check the logical relationship: *Is the syllogism valid?* Does the conclusion inevitably follow from the premises? Are there only three terms, and is each one used twice? Are the terms in the right positions? For example, from the statements (both true) that "American flags are red, white, and blue; this flag is red, white, and blue," can we conclude that "this flag" is an American flag? Such a conclusion is not justified, even though both premises are true. Flags other than American flags may have these colors, so that the conclusion does not *necessarily* follow from the premises.

Another invalid syllogism takes this form: some A's are B's, and all C's are A's, and so some C's are B's. "Some human beings are two feet tall; all college students are human beings; therefore, some college students are two feet tall." There is no certain conclusion possible when the major premise uses "some" or "a few" or even "most."

A third test of a syllogism is: *Are the terms used in the same sense both times?* "Americans have the highest standard of living in the world, and Peruvians are Americans; therefore Peruvians have the highest standard of living in the world." In this argument "Americans" has two different meanings. If its terms are ambiguous, a syllogism is unsound.

Logic also has terms for a number of fallacies—errors in reasoning. Our common sense helps us with obviously unreasonable statements, but some unreasonable statements appear plausible enough to deceive us. Some of the commoner fallacies are these:

Begging the question, when you assume what needs to be proved. "Should the antiquated electoral system be continued?" takes for granted that the system *is* obsolete. "Should a dangerous man like

James Doe be paroled?" assumes that he is dangerous, but the conclusion partially depends on proving that point. Examine your proposition (the statement upon which your paper is built, the taking-off point of your argument) to be sure it contains no assumptions which need to be proved.

Arguing in a circle, when you expect readers to assume that the conclusion is true in order to prove it. Reduced to its simplest form, the circular argument asserts *X is true because X is true:* "In our society it is necessary to keep up with the latest styles because it is essential to be fashionably dressed." This fallacy is often hard to recognize when it is buried in a long chain of argument. To correct it, you need to find satisfactory proof for the conclusion.

Non sequitur ("It doesn't follow"), when you skip so many steps in your argument that your readers fail to see the connection between your statements. For example, "I read a fascinating book last week, and so I'm saving my money to go to Europe." A fuller statement of this example might be: "Before last week I had never been much interested in traveling abroad, but after reading Herbert Kubly's *American in Italy,* I changed my mind. I'm saving my money to go to Europe." To correct a non sequitur, supply the missing links in your reasoning so that the conclusion follows logically. Sometimes you may find that there are no missing steps but a real gap, and so you will have to abandon the idea.

Argumentum ad hominem, when rather than arguing the question under discussion you attack those who hold it or resort to direct emotional appeals. This may be, at its lowest, name-calling: "People who believe this are stupid." More legitimately, but still not a very serious argument, you may use as ammunition for your side something your opponent has said, or something that he does: "How can you say it's wrong to cram for tests when you do it yourself?" From here the devices go to various emotional appeals, usually in words heavy with connotations, and with verbal devices of repetition, alliteration, catchwords, and slogans.

Such fallacies, and other more rhetorical checks on reasoning, are discussed in Chapter 12, "Some special considerations," page 328.

Although there are some obvious advantages in these approaches from logic, especially in getting names for some characteristics of our thinking, there are two limitations to the use of logic in a composition course:

1) A writer needs to work directly from his material and learn to develop its potentialities, and to become sensitive to the accuracy and legitimacy of his statements as they will stand in his paper, without, for example, translating them into syllogisms. Few "straight thinkers" actually make use of them.

2) Logic is a field by itself, in most modern treatments covering a considerable range of topics, from vagueness and ambiguity to

criteria of scientific method. Merely sampled, as it has to be in a college composition course, its actual values are incompletely and unfairly represented, and a brief exposure may actually do harm by giving a false sense of security, or even of superiority. A full course in logic can be a valuable experience.

References: Some good introductory logics are: Max Black, *Critical Thinking* (New York, 1946 and revisions); Morris R. Cohen and Ernest Nagel, *An Introduction to Logic and Scientific Method* (New York, 1934); Ralph Monroe Eaton, *General Logic* (New York, 1931).

Long variants Some amateur writers are tempted to add an extra prefix or suffix to a word that already carries the meaning they intend. They write *ir*regardless, though *regardless* already means "without regard to." Some like to add sonorous suffixes that are quite useless, like the *-ation* in *origination,* which means no more than *origin*. Some other long variants to be avoided are:

analyzation for *analysis*
certificated for *certified*
confliction for *conflict*
emotionality when only *emotion* is meant
commercialistic for *commercial*
ruination for *ruin* (*ruination* is a local emphatic form of *ruin*)
hotness for *heat*
intermingle for *mingle*
orientate for *orient*
repay when simple *pay* is meant, as in paying dividends
subsidization for *subsidizing*
Unnecessary *-al* endings, as *transportation* [al] system, *government*[al] policy
utilize when only *use* is meant

Some of these words are not in good use at all (*analyzation*) and show lack of observation of language by anyone who uses them. Others are in use but show poor judgment in the writer who chooses them when more compact forms exist. (Occasionally the longer form acquires a special sense: A *certificated* teacher is one who has a certificate from the state licensing him to teach.) If a number of long variants are used they will weigh down a piece of writing and make it flabby. (See *Origin of words § 3 and compare Ch. 8, "Big words," p. 228. Reference: Fowler, "Long variants.")

look When used as a verb of complete meaning (to use the eyes, gaze), *look* is modified by an adverb: *look searchingly, look longingly*.

As a linking verb, equivalent to *appear, look* is followed by an adjective which modifies the subject: *He looks well, or healthy, or tired. . . .* (See *Linking verbs.)

lose, loose Associate the spelling of these words with the pronunciation and meaning:

lose (lo͞oz)—lose a bet, lose sleep, lose money
loose (lo͞os)—loose a knot, a loose screw
loosed (lo͞ost)—He loosed the boat from its moorings
lost (lôst)—a lost road, a lost soul, lost his way, have lost

lot, lots of Both *a lot of* and *lots of* are in General use, though they, particularly *lots,* tend to be avoided in Formal writing: We tried a lot of different kinds. He has lots of friends . . . a lot of money. (Formal: He has many friends . . . a good deal of money.)

Do not spell the article and the noun as one word: *a lot,* not *alot.*

lousy Except when meaning "infested with lice" (a sense in which it is rarely needed any more), *lousy* is a strong Informal word of abuse, now weakened to a *counter word of disapproval, expressive if not used too often, but offensive to most ears.

lovely is a *counter word of approval, popular perhaps because its pronunciation can (by some people) be drawn out indefinitely and practically sung (a lovely time).

Lower case Revision: Use a lower case ("small") letter instead of a capital in this word. *lc*

See *Capital letters and Chapter 5, "Using capital letters," page 130.

M

The sound represented by the letter *m* is a nasal consonant made with lips closed: *man, music, diamond, drummer, sum, lamp; m* is the only regular spelling for this sound, but it often occurs with other letters which are not sounded, so*me,* sole*mn,* co*mb.*

M may represent a syllable by itself ("syllabic *m*"): *spasm* (spaz'm̩ or spaz'əm), *tell 'em* (tel'm̩ or tel'əm). Some people tend to make *m* syllabic in words like *elm, film* (el'm̩, fil'm̩) instead of using the more standard pronunciations: elm, film.

madam As a formula of address *Madam* or *Dear Madam* is used for both married and unmarried women. The French spelling *madame* (better pronounced mad'əm) is used as the title for a foreign married woman, often for a woman musician, and sometimes in social and commercial contexts. In speech *madam* is usually *ma'am:* "Yes Ma'am," pronounced mam or mäm. As a word of address or in social use (journalistic or Formal) the plural of *madam* is *mesdames* (mā däm').

majority, plurality Strictly *majority* means "more than half of" a certain number; *plurality* means "more than the next highest." *Plurality* is not much used now in the United States, the meaning of *majority* being extended to "an excess of votes over all others cast"—and even often used in the exact sense of *plurality,* simply the excess of votes over the next highest. In an election with three candidates and 12,000 votes cast, one received 7000, one 3000, and one 2000; the winner would have a *plurality* of 4000 (in common usage, a majority of 4000); strictly speaking, he would have a *majority* of 1000.

Informally *majority* is often used of amounts or quantities as well as of numbers:

Informal: We spent the majority of the day there.
General: We spent most [or: the greater part] of the day there.
Wordy: The majority of students are interested in football.
Better: Most students are interested in football.

Malapropism A malapropism is a confusion of two words somewhat similar in sound but different in meaning, with a consequent ludicrous kind of sense, as *arduous* love for *ardent* love. Malapropisms are the cause of many *boners but are often intentionally used for humorous effect, as they were by Sheridan in creating the part of Mrs. Malaprop in *The Rivals,* whose speeches gave the name to these confusions in language:

"I would by no means wish a daughter of mine to be a progeny of learning. . . . Then, sir, she should have a supercilious knowledge in accounts;–and as she grew up, I would have her instructed in geometry, that she might know something of the contagious countries. . . ."–RICHARD BRINSLEY SHERIDAN, *The Rivals,* Act I, Scene ii

man, woman These are preferred to the more pretentious *gentleman* or *lady,* except when *man* or *woman* would sound conspicuously blunt.

In business English the original social distinctions between *woman–lady,* and *man–gentleman* have been almost reversed. A salesman faced with a customer who wanted to exchange a purchase, turned to his fellow salesmen and said, "Did any of you gentlemen wait on this man?" And a woman looking for work asked, "Are you the woman who wanted a lady to wash for her?"

Ladies and gentlemen is a *formula in addressing an audience.

The singular forms alone are used as modifiers:

manpower   manholes   woman hater   woman suffrage

(Compare *freshman, freshmen.)

Manner Adverbs of manner answer the question *How? Barely, brightly, gracefully, nicely, quick* or *quickly, swimmingly* are adverbs of manner. They are formed now by adding *-ly* to adjectives and participles, though a number of older adverbs of manner do not have the *-ly: sharp* or *sharply, slow* or *slowly,* etc. (See *Adverbs, types and forms § 1.)

As, as if, as though (Formal) and **like* are conjunctions introducing adverbial clauses of manner:

He looked as if he'd seen a ghost.   They left as noisily as they came.

MS **Manuscript form** Revision: Your manuscript does not have the proper form. Revise or rewrite as directed.

See Chapter 9, "Preparing the manuscript," page 262, for details of good manuscript practice. See also *Typewritten copy.

matinee is spelled without an accent mark. It is usually pronounced mat′ə nā′ (mat′n̥ ā′) but tends toward mat′ə nā′ (as in England).

may be, maybe *Maybe* is an adverb meaning "perhaps," a reduction of *it may be; may be* is a verb form:

Maybe you'll have better luck next time.   He may be the next mayor.

In speech *maybe* often becomes me′bi, with the ā sound becoming e as it has in the *break* of *breakfast*.

medieval Some years ago the American Historical Association decided to change the spelling from *mediaeval* to *medieval,* now the usual form. Pronunciation is mē′di ē′vl̥, or med′i ē′vl̥, not mid ē′vl̥.

medium The plural of *medium* is usually *mediums*–always in the spiritualistic sense, practically always in the general sense. *Media* is most used in scientific contexts and in the phrase *mass media* (of communication) and usually now as applied to the different advertising *media* (newspapers, magazines, television, billboards, etc.).

messrs. is the abbreviation of French *messieurs* but in English is pronounced mes′ərz. It is used as the plural of *Mr.* (Messrs. Ives and Johnson) and sometimes, though rarely now in American usage, used in addressing firms (Messrs. Brown, Hubbell and Company). The occasions for its use are Formal.

meter is now a more common spelling than *metre*. The second *e* drops out in derivatives: *metrical, metrics, metric system.*

For a description of English meters see *Verse form.

mix, mixer *Mix* is Informal for *associate with; mixer* for *sociable person* or for the person who develops new acquaintances readily. Though slang in their origin, they seem excusable because of the colorlessness of the more reputable words.

Mixed usage Many errors in writing spring from the unintentional mixture of different varieties of usage. Conspicuously Informal words or idioms may stray into Formal writing; Nonstandard locutions or words usually confined to law or business may appear in General writing. Distinctly Formal words and idioms are equally inappropriate in General writing though they often appear because the writer is trying to avoid some natural expression. The principal way to develop in language is to cultivate feeling for different styles and their fitness for a given job. (See Ch. 1.)

Modal auxiliaries **can, could, may, might; must; ought; *shall, should; will, would* are called modal auxiliaries (though they have nothing to do with grammatical "mood"). They differ from other verbs in having no *s* in the third person singular, no participles, and therefore no compound forms, and they always occur as part of verb phrases. *Dare* and **need* are also sometimes used as modal auxiliaries.

Modifiers are words or word groups that stand in a sentence in a secondary relationship to other words or word groups (*Headwords). Typically they limit and make more exact the meaning of the headword. In these examples the words in italics modify the words in small capitals:

a *cold, windy* DAY He FAILED *miserably*. a *truly* GREAT–a *truly great* MAN. *Coming around the corner,* WE met him head on. *As we came around the corner,* WE SAW HIM BOARDING A TROLLEY.

(See Ch. 3, "Revising modifiers," p. 88; *Adjectives in use; *Adverbs in use; *Clauses; *Dangling modifiers; *Participles; *Phrases; *Restrictive and nonrestrictive.)

Money 1. Exact sums of money are usually written in figures:

72¢ $4.98 $5 $168.75 $42,810

Round sums are more likely to be written in words: two hundred dollars, a million and a half dollars.

In factual books or articles involving frequent references to sums of money, however, figures are often used throughout.

2. In consecutive writing, amounts are usually written out when they are used as modifiers: *a million dollar* project. Informally, figures are often used: an 85¢ seat.

3. Commas and periods, $ and ¢ signs are used as in the examples in § 1 above. (For an example of writing sums of money in text, see the paragraphs of illustration in *Numbers § 2.)

Monosyllables A monosyllable is a word of one syllable:

asked bright feel fill longed word

Monosyllables should not be divided at the end of lines, not even words like *asked, longed*. (See *Division of words.)

A *polysyllable* strictly has three or more syllables, but since we use *dissyllable* (having two syllables) rather rarely, *polysyllable* usually means a word having two or more syllables.

Months In reference matter and Informal writing, the names of months with more than four letters are often abbreviated in dates:

Jan. 21, 1958 16 Aug., 1958 Dec. 25, 1957
But: May 1, 1956 June 30, 1955 4 July, 1958

When only the month or month and year are given, abbreviation would be rare:

January 1959 Every January he tries again

In Formal writing, the names of the months would not be abbreviated at all. (See *Numbers § 1a; *Dates.)

Mood By the forms of mood (occasionally, mode), verbs in many languages may distinguish the way in which a statement is regarded by the writer. It is doubtful if modern English verbs actually have moods, but they are still conventionally described:

Indicative: as a fact, a statement I am

Subjunctive:	as a wish, possibility, doubt	If I were
Imperative:	as a command	Stop!

(See the articles *Indicative mood, *Subjunctives, *Commands and requests, *Verbs.)

moral, morale Although the *e* is not in the French noun we borrowed as mə ral′ ("a confident mental state"), it is a convenient and natural English way of showing there is something peculiar in the pronunciation. It also distinguishes this *morale* from *moral* ("concerning right conduct").

Morpheme is a term in linguistics most briefly described as the smallest meaningful unit in a language. It may be a word (*boy, tall, Massachusetts*) or a part of a word that can combine with other elements (*-s, -ing, anti-, -ness*). Some elements of intonation may be morphemes, as stress is in con′duct and con duct′. In the sentence *The boys unloaded the boxes,* the morphemes are the elements spelled *the, boy, s, un, load, ed, the, box,* and *es.* (See *Linguistics, *Parts of speech, *Origin of words. Reference: Gleason, Chs. 5-11.)

most (almost) In speech *almost* is often reduced to *most* "A drop in prices will appeal to *most* anybody." *Most,* used thus, is Informal and ordinarily out of place in written English. If you can substitute *almost* for *most* in a sentence (*almost* always, *almost* anywhere), *almost* is the word you need. (Reference: Pooley, p. 156.)

Mr. is written out only when it represents spoken usage and when it is used without a name:

"They're only two for five, mister." (But:) Mr. Schlesser Mr. John T. Flynn

Mrs. is usually written out only to represent Nonstandard usage and is then spelled *missis* (or *missus*):

Mrs. Dorothy M. Adams Mrs. Adams "Where's the missis?"

Mrs. is not combined with a husband's title except in small town journalese. Write *Mrs. Dodd,* not *Mrs. Prof. Dodd.*

A man and wife register at hotels as *Mr. and Mrs. Alex T. Schofield* rather than as *Alex T. Schofield and wife.*

MS. *MS.,* usually in caps, is the conventional abbreviation for *manuscript;* plural MSS. The shoptalk word for manuscript intended for publication is *copy.*

must has recently become an adjective modifier in General use:

the President's must legislation
This is a must article for every intelligent American.

It has long been a noun in newspaper shoptalk, a B.O.M. being a *Business Office Must,* a story that has to be run because of some advertising tieup. (See *Auxiliary verb.)

myself is a reflexive or intensive pronoun, referring back to *I* when used as an object or as an intensive:

Object: I shave myself.
Intensive: I saw the whole thing myself.

Myself and the other *-self* pronouns are used as subjects or objects commonly in speech but rarely in writing. They are seldom appropriate in good written style:

Informal: Another fellow and myself saw the whole thing.
General: Another fellow and I saw the whole thing.
Informal: Sam invited John and *myself* to dinner.
General: Sam invited John and me to dinner.

(See *Pronouns § 4, *self, *himself, herself. Reference: Josephine M. Burnham, "The -Self Forms as Personal Pronouns," *American Speech,* 1950, 25:264-267.)

N

N (n), as in *now, gnaw, inning, been. N* may be a syllable by itself ("syllabic *n*"), as in *often, listen, garden* (ôf′n̩, lis′n̩, gär′dn̩); *n* is the only regular spelling for this sound, but it often occurs with other letters which are not sounded: *kn*ife, *pn*eumonia, *gn*aw.

N is generally silent in *kiln* and in a number of words after *m: autumn, damn, hymn, solemn.* In derivatives of such words usage is divided on sounding the *n.* It is not sounded in *hymned* (himd) and in *damned* only in archaic or ultra poetic contexts (dam′ned). It is sounded in *autumnal, damnation, hymnal, solemnity,* and in general before a suffix when the suffix begins with a vowel.

An *ñ* (the wavy line is called a *tilde*) is found in some words from Spanish. If the word is commonly used, the spelling is usually changed to *ny* (*canyon* instead of cañon). See *ng.

naive–naïve The form without the dieresis (*naive*) is slowly gaining over naïve. It is unnecessary to keep the French masculine form *naif* in English because we do not have the grammatical gender which requires it. *Naive* can do all the work. Pronounced nä ēv′.

namely and other introductory words 1. The beginning of wisdom in handling "introductory words" like *namely, that is, for example, such as* is to use them as seldom as possible. *Namely, viz., i.e., e.g.,* and some others are often found in Formal scholarly prose, but *for example, for instance, such as* are more appropriate to most writing. Very often such words can be omitted altogether in compact, General writing:

He instructed us in the mysteries of punctuation: [such as] semicolons between clauses of a compound sentence, position of quotation marks with other marks, commas with nonrestrictive clauses.

2. In Formal style or in a long, rather complicated sentence, an introductory word would usually be preceded by a semicolon:

The interview is of value, then, because it aids in discovering certain traits; e.g., emotional and temperamental attitudes—which do not submit so readily to other modes of attack.—G. D. HIGGINSON, *Fields of Psychology*, p. 395

When one of these words introduces a series of short items, it is more often followed by a comma than by a colon:

The boys in training are thoroughly grounded in the fundamental processes of the work, for example, planning, building, and launching.

No comma should follow *such as:*

Large animals, such as bears, moose, and elk, are often found here.

Names In factual writing all names used should be complete and accurate. In current writing, made-up names and other dodges are not used much except in humor. In the following they stamp the paper as amateur:

Across the table sat Cornelius Van Stuck-up between two feminine admirers whose names I will not mention but will call Miss X and Miss Y. Miss X said to Miss Y. . . .

Use the real names of people and places unless there are serious reasons for avoiding them, and if there are, invent convincing names or use pronouns or "a man" or some inconspicuous device. This use of actual names is one trait of the specificness and immediacy of current style.

In imaginative writing judgment and ingenuity are needed to choose satisfactory names for characters. They should suggest real names of people of the right social stratum but not intentionally be the names of actual people. They should not be the commonest names nor should they be eccentric ones either; ordinarily they should be somewhere between *John* and *Mary* and *Ichabod* and *Jacquinetta.* Studying names, collecting them, and noting those used in stories will furnish raw materials for naming your own creations. (See *Proper names.)

necessary is spelled with one *c* and two *s*'s. Very often a verb is more direct and emphatic but less polite than a construction with *necessary:*

You *must* [or *have to,* rather than *It is necessary that you*] pay your tuition before receiving your class cards.

necessity The idiom is *necessity of* or *for* doing something (not *to* do something):

I don't see *the necessity of* [or: *for*] *reading* so many pages to get so few facts. (Or, more concise: I don't see *the need of reading* so many pages. . . .)

need—needs Both are third person singular of the verb *need,* but used in different idioms. *Needs* is the form in affirmative statements, *need* or *does not need* in negative statements, *need* or *does . . . need* in questions:

He needs a haircut.
He needs to have a haircut. (Infinitive with *to*)
Does he need a haircut?

Formal: He need not come. (Infinitive without *to*)
General: He doesn't need to come. (Also:) He needn't come.
Formal: Need she come?
General: Does she need to come?

Need followed by the past participle rather than the present infinitive is a localism:

General: It needs to be covered.
Local: It needs covered.

Negatives The meaning of a negative in language is not always equivalent to its meaning in mathematics, where —3 is as much less than 0 as +3 is more than 0 and — (—3) = +3 because the only mathematical alternative of — is +. In language a contrary is likely to be stated by another positive (good–evil, white–black); the negative usually means "less than" or "different from": *not good* is less than good but not necessarily evil, and *not white* is different from white but not necessarily black. This quality of negation provides the weakened positive which results from a negated negative: in *not uncommon,* we get a reduced reduction; *uncommon* is less than common, *not uncommon* is less than less than common or not quite common.

On the other hand, when two (or more) negatives in a sentence affect different words (In "He can't never do no work," *n't* affects *can* and *never,* and *no* affects *do* and *work*), they actually reinforce the negation. But this cumulative effect is no longer used in Standard English. (See *Double negative.)

Sometimes the negative form shows unexpected variation from the affirmative: *must go* and *have to go* are nearly synonymous; *mustn't go* and *don't have to go* are not. (Reference: Otto Jespersen, *Philosophy of Grammar* (New York, 1924), Ch. 24.)

1. *Emphasis.* A statement may sometimes be made more emphatic or striking by being put negatively (in a figure of speech known as *litotes* or *understatement*):

He was . . . extremely the antithesis of coarse which "refined" somehow does not imply. . . .–E. E. CUMMINGS, *The Enormous Room*

The assimilating power of the English language is not less remarkable than the complexity of its sources.–J. B. GREENOUGH and G. L. KITTREDGE, *Words and Their Ways in English Speech,* p. 147

2. *Separation from positive.* In a specific construction words of positive and negative meaning usually need to be separated:

I have learned through this practice to overcome stage fright, and I have gained in vividness of speech. (Not: I have learned . . . to overcome stage fright and vividness of speech.)

3. *Double negative.* See *Double negative.

Negro Capitalize, like *Caucasian, Indian.* Plural, *Negroes.*

Neutral vowel A good many words give spelling trouble because they contain various spellings for the vowel sound represented in this book by ə (*schwa): ə kad′ə mi (*a*cademy). This is Standard pronunciation, so that no drill in sounding the syllable can help. A number of these words are related to others in which this syllable has a stress, so that the vowel stands out. Such pairs as the following may help you to spell accurately the vowel italicized in the first word:

acad*e*my–acad*em*ic	d*e*spair–*des*peration, *des*perado
affirm*a*tive–affir*ma*tion	extravag*a*nce, extravag*a*nt–extrava*ganza*
ang*e*l–an*gel*ic	hypocr*i*sy–hypo*crit*ical
comp*a*rable–com*pare*	med*i*cine–me*dic*inal
comp*e*tition–com*pete*	prep*a*ration–pre*pare*
defin*i*tely–defi*ni*tion	rep*e*tition–re*peat*
degr*a*dation–de*grade*	rid*i*cule–ri*dic*ulous
democr*a*cy–demo*crat*ic	

But for the great majority of words with the neutral vowel either a good memory or a good dictionary is essential.

Newspaper English **1.** *Its virtues.* Joseph Pulitzer's famous motto for workers on the old *New York World* still stands as the ideal for the material and style of newswriting–*Accuracy, Terseness, Accuracy.* Complete accuracy is not easy for a reporter who has perhaps only a few minutes to get the facts of a complicated event, and terseness is not easy either for a man who writes habitually, often of very similar happenings, with little personal interest in his material. The result is that newspapers contain some of the worst writing that gets into print and some of the best.

There is no special dialect for newswriting, though the organization of a newspaper story is, of course, likely to be different from a historical account of the same event. Papers have some conventions for giving ages, names, places of residence, and other routine matters, but good newspaper English is simply General English applied to the daily recording of affairs. It is a style written to be read rapidly and grasped by the eye–except in headlines, tricks of sound are out of place. The sentences are typically short (except in leads) and direct; the words are concrete and from the General vocabulary.

2. *Journalese.* The two most common sins of newswriting are inflation (*big words) and *triteness, which we can lump as symptoms of *journalese.* Granting that "our fair city," "ample outlet for her histrionic ability," and scores of such trite phrases belonging to paleojournalism are not found now outside small town papers, there is still a vast amount of wordy and lazy writing in newspapers. Every *stylebook contains a list of journalese expressions to be avoided. Here are a few collected (and translated) by George Olds, of the Springfield, Missouri, *News:*

According to the report issued this morning by City Auditor Ernest Jared	City Auditor Ernest Jared reported today

Shields denied he made a statement he was alleged to have made to police officers admitting he knew	Shields denied admitting to police he knew
Affirming the assumption that he was resentful of the meeting	Admitting he resented
But Judge Holly dismissed the charges against her. Although he dismissed the charges against Mrs. Coates, Judge Holly commented that her conduct had been "suspicious."	But Judge Holly dismissed the charges against her, although he termed her conduct "suspicious."

Editor and Publisher, Feb. 2, 1935

Triteness is the next worst offense in journalese. In *The New Yorker,* Frank Sullivan had his cliché expert, Mr. Arbuthnot, testify to journalistic triteness, including such special topics as these:

> Q–Mr. Arbuthnot, what happens at railroad stations on holidays?
> A–Well, there is what our Society of Cliché Experts likes to refer to as a holiday exodus. I mean to say, fully 1,500,000 pleasure-seekers leave the city, railroad officials estimate. Every means of transportation is taxed to its utmost capacity. . . .
> Q–Mr. Arbuthnot, what kind of hopes do you have?
> A–High hopes, and I don't have them; I entertain them. I express concern. I discard precedent. When I am in earnest, I am in deadly earnest. When I am devoted, I am devoted solely. When a task comes along, it confronts me. When I stop, I stop short. I take but one kind of steps–those in the right direction. I am a force to be reckoned with.
> –FRANK SULLIVAN, "The Cliché Expert Tells All," *The New Yorker,* June 20, 1936

3. *Headlines and headlinese.* While writers of news stories have to write with an eye on inches of space, headline writers have to watch every letter. A given style of head has a "count" of so many letters, and, as the compositor says, "there ain't no rubber type." This necessity for compression and a desire to "sell the papers" gives rise to the punch of headlines. As the Waterbury, Conn., *Republican* style sheet puts it:

PUT PUNCH IN HEADS
SAYS OLD SLOT MAN

Wants Accurate, Terse, Positive
and Pungent Guides to
News

BEGS FOR ACTIVE VERBS

Bald-Domed Editor Wants Blue
Pencil Novices to Lay Off
Fuzzy Words

This leads to the omission of *function words (*a, an, the,* connectives) and to the use of short words and clipped forms:

> Fly ocean; tell fight with gale 3 miles in air—12 Navy planes battered

To save space, short words are used, nouns are used as verbs, verbs as nouns, and any words or even long phrases as adjectives:

> Senate Set for Votes on Trade Bill Curbs
> Superintendent and Supervisor Refute
> Charge of Spying on *Traction Company*
> *Bus Drivers' Union Enrollment* Meeting

Worrying that headline style will ruin our language is silly; nobody ever talks headlinese—it's too concentrated. The feeble circumlocution of the stories that often stand below the heads is a greater menace to our language than the clipped, emphatic heads.

References: There are many textbooks on newspaper writing. Two of the most useful are: Curtis D. MacDougall, *Interpretative Reporting* (New York, 1948) and George C. Bastian and Leland D. Case, *Editing the Day's News* (New York, 1943). The stylebooks of newspapers are important. Some, like those of *The Detroit News* and *The New York Times* (1950), are for sale. The magazine *Editor and Publisher* is the best source on current American journalism.

Nexus Jespersen introduced *junction* and *nexus* as names for what he considered two radically different relations of noun and modifier. He called the relationship in which two or more words are joined to form a single name (*a warm day, a first-class speech*) *junction.* The relationship in which the two terms are joined by a verb but are kept distinct (*The day is warm. The speech sounded first rate*) he called *nexus.* Under nexus he included locutions that were similar in pattern but did not have a verb, such as He left *the window open* (which obviously is quite different from the junction *the open window*) and *Happy the man* (which is different from *the happy man*), and various others. The value of the terms can be illustrated in such sentences as:

> They found the man dead.
> They found the dead man.

The relation between *man* and *dead* in the first sentence is nexus; in the second, junction. The doctrine of nexus is elaborated in Jespersen's *The Philosophy of Grammar,* Chapters 8 and 9, and in *Essentials of English Grammar,* Chapter 9.

ng is the pronunciation symbol for the sound produced with the back of the tongue against the soft palate and the air coming through the nose with the vocal cords vibrating, most frequently spelled *ng* (*long, bringing*) but also spelled *n: anchor* (ang′kər), *angry* (ang′gri), *sink* (singk), *uncle* (ung′kəl).

Pronunciation is divided when a syllable ending in *-n* is followed by one beginning with *g* or *k: congress* (kong′gris) but *congressional* (kən gresh′ən ḷ or kong gresh′ən ḷ). See *G § 5.

nice is a *counter word indicating mild approval, useful in speech but so general in meaning that it is of little use in writing. The word's former meaning of "exact, precise," as in *a nice distinction,* is confined to Formal writing. (See Charles C. Fries, *The English Journal,* 1927, 16:602-604.)

Nicknames Nicknames are rarely appropriate in Formal writing. In other writing they are often appropriate and should be used naturally, without apology. Some writers will put a nickname in quotes the first time it is used but not when it is repeated.

No. The abbreviation *No.* for *number* (from the Latin *numero,* "by number") is written with a capital. It is appropriate chiefly in business and technical English. In the United States *No.* is not written with street numbers.

nobody, nothing, nowhere are written as single words. *Nobody* and *nothing* are singular in form and are usually treated grammatically as such, though *nobody* is Informally treated as a collective (see *every and its compounds):

Nobody thinks that his own dog is a nuisance.
Informal: Nobody thinks their own dog is a nuisance.
Nothing is further from the truth.
The dog could be found nowhere.

nohow Nonstandard: *We couldn't get there nohow;* Standard: . . . *by any means* (or) . . . *any way we tried.*

Nominative case A noun or pronoun that is the subject of a finite verb is sometimes said to be in the nominative (or subjective) case. The form of the nominative singular is the common form of the noun, the form to which, typically, the endings for the genitive and for the plural are added. *I, you, he, she, it, we, you, they* are the nominative forms of the personal pronouns; *who, which,* and *that* are the nominative forms of the relative pronouns. These forms are the usual ones for the nominative function; but see *It's me and *Pronouns. See also *Subject and verb.

Nonce word Strictly, a word used but once so far as existing writing shows; a word coined for the occasion and not attaining general use, as *thrillier* in a theater sign: "Thrillier than *Diabolique.*"

none, no one *None* is a single word, but *no one* is often used instead of *none,* for emphasis. *None* may be either singular or plural but is now more common with the plural:

As only ten jurors have been chosen so far, none of the witnesses were called [or: was called].
She tried on ten hats, but none of them were attractive.
I read three books on the subject, no one of which was helpful.

(Reference: Fries, *AEG,* pp. 50, 56.)

NS **Nonstandard English** Revision: Change the Nonstandard word, form, or idiom to one appropriate to Standard usage. See Chapter 1, pages 15-26.

not to exceed is a business and legal locution; in other contexts *not more than* is usual:

The undersigned will be liable for property damages, not to exceed $500 for one accident.

The enrollment in the course was to be not more than fifty.

Not more than two people could live on that pay.

notorious means well known for unsavory reasons—"a notorious cheat"; *famous* is well known for accomplishment or excellence—"a famous writer, aviator"; *infamous* means odious or detestable—"an infamous deed." *Noted* is journalistic for *famous* or *well known.*

Noun and verb stress A number of nouns and verbs are differentiated in speaking by stressing the first syllable in the noun and the last in the verb, though the spelling is identical. When this shift occurs, the verb often has an altered vowel sound. Some of these are listed below:

Noun	*Verb*
com′press	com press′
con′duct	con duct′
con′flict	con flict′ (often con′flict)
con′trast	con trast′ (often con′trast)
con′vict	con vict′
de′crease (and de crease′)	de crease′
di′gest	di gest′
es′cort	es cort′
ex′tract	ex tract′
in′cline	in cline′
in′crease	in crease′ (often in′crease)
in′sult	in sult′
ob′ject	ob ject′
prod′uce, pro′duce	pro duce′
rec′ord	re cord′

Several of these verbs in common use show the natural English tendency to shift the stress back to the first syllable. The following words are both nouns and verbs with the same stress:

ac′cent cos′tume dis′count im′port

Noun clauses A noun clause is a construction having a subject and *finite verb and functioning typically in a sentence as a subject or object. Many noun clauses are introduced by *that,* some by *what, who, whoever, whatever, why, when,* and other connectives.

Subject: *That anyone could raise his grade by studying* had never occurred to him. *Whether or not he should go* had bothered him for days.

Object: He assured me *that it would never happen again.* (Or:) He assured me *it would never happen again.*

Predicate noun: His guests were *whomever he met on the way home.*

Object of preposition: Sam is always sure of *what he does.*

Appositive: The doctrine *that we must avoid entangling alliances* was first stated by Washington.

That and *whether* clauses as subjects are, as the examples above show, distinctly Formal constructions. (See *Clauses, *reason is because.)

Nouns **1.** *Forms.* In English we identify nouns basically by their forms:

Most nouns have a plural form in an s or z sound, spelled *s: hats, kindnesses, manufacturers.* (Minor types are described in *Plurals.)

They add the same sound for a singular genitive case, written with an apostrophe: *boy's, boys'* (the plural). (See *Genitive case.)

There are a few distinctive endings found in groups of nouns, such as *-*er* or *-or, -ness, -th, -tion.*

A very few nouns in English have different forms for masculine and feminine: *actor–actress, confidant–confidante, executor–executrix.* (See *Gender.)

Nouns may be single words or compound words written solid, as two words, or hyphened: *bathroom, bookcase, high school, hub cap, go-getter, stick-up, log-rolling.* (See *Group words, *Hyphen.)

2. *Position and functions.* Nouns can be identified by their typical positions in sentences: standing before a verb as subject or after it as object, being preceded by an article (*a/an, the*) or demonstrative (*this, that,* and so on), or being the headword in a prepositional phrase.

The principal functions of nouns in sentences are:

Subject of a sentence: The *wind* blew for three days. (See *Subject and verb.)

Object of a verb: The wind blew the *silo* over. (See *Objects.)

Object of a preposition: in the *night,* behind the *house,* after *breakfast,* of the *president* (See *Prepositions.)

Predicate noun: He became *president* of the firm. (See *Predicate adjective, Predicate noun.)

Possession: the *woman's* first dress for two years (See *Genitive case § 2.)

Apposition: The first settler, *Thomas Sanborn,* came in 1780. (See *Apposition, appositives.)

Modifier of other nouns: a *baby* hippopotamus; the best *high school basketball* team in years (See *Genitive case, *Parts of speech, *Adjectives, types and forms § 5.)

Modifier of verbs or statements: He came two *months* ago. *Mornings* he would work a little. (See *Adverbs, types and forms § 4.)

3. *Classes of nouns.* Nouns are conventionally classified as follows:

a) Proper nouns, names of particular people and places, written with capitals and usually without *the* or *a: Anne, George W. Loomis, London, Georgia, France, the Bay of Naples.* (See *Proper names.)

In contrast with these proper nouns, all the other groups are *common nouns.*

b) Concrete nouns, names of objects: *leaf, leaves, road, panda, manufacturer.* (See Ch. 8, "Concrete words," p. 217.)

c) Mass nouns, names of materials in general rather than materials in particular forms: *water, coffee, cement, steel, corn.*

d) Collective nouns, names of a group of things regarded as a unit: *fleet, army, company, committee, trio, bevy.* (See *Collective nouns.)

e) Abstract nouns, names of qualities, actions, ideas: *kindness, hate, manufacture, idealism, fantasy, concept.* Many of these are *gerunds: *fishing, drinking, manufacturing.* (See Ch. 8, "Abstract words," p. 219.)

References: Curme, *Parts of Speech,* Chapters 1, 9, *Syntax,* Chapters 2, 4, 26, and other references; Fries, *Structure,* pages 65-79.

nowhere near is an Informal usage: It was a good score but *nowhere near* as large as we'd hoped for. (General: "not so large as" or "not nearly so large as.")

nowheres Nonstandard for *nowhere.*

Number *Number* in English is the singular and plural aspect of nouns and pronouns and verbs. The indication of number is of great importance in nouns and pronouns (though *you* is ambiguous), of little importance in verbs, which in most forms cannot show number. (See *Plurals, *Subject and verb, *Reference of pronouns.)

number is a collective noun, taking a singular or plural verb according as the total or the individual units are meant:

A number of tickets have already been sold.
The number of tickets sold is astonishing.
A number of the pages were torn.
The number of pages assigned for translation was gradually increased to eight.

(See also *amount, number.)

Numbers Revision: Revise the figure or figures in this passage in the light of the suggestions below. *Num*

1. *Uses.* 2. *Figures or words.* 3. *Arabic and Roman numerals.* 4. *Plural of figures.* 5. *Cardinal and ordinal numbers.*

1. *Uses.* Figures are used for:

a) Dates. Only in Formal *social correspondence are dates written out in words. *1st, 2nd (2d),* and so on may be used when a date is given without the year, but not ordinarily with the year:

Oct. 4, 1960 October 4, 1960 October 4 October 4th

Years are always written in figures.

b) Hours when *a.m. or p.m. is used:

5 p.m. But: five o'clock

c) Street numbers (with no comma between thousands):

2841 Washington Avenue Apartment 3C, 781 Grand Street

d) Pages and other references:

page 642 pp. 431-482 Chapter 14 (or: Chapter XIV)
Act III, scene iv, line 28

e) Sums of money, except sums in round numbers or, in Formal style, sums that can be written in two or three words:

$4.98 75¢ a million dollars (or: $1,000,000)

f) Statistics and series of more than one or two numbers:

In the political science class mock election the Republicans gained 50 seats in the House, 6 seats in the Senate, and 13 new governorships.

2. *Figures or words.* Usage varies in writing numbers that are parts of consecutive sentences. In general, newspapers and Informal writing have figures for numbers over ten, words for smaller numbers; magazine and book styles (most General writing) have figures for numbers over 100 except when the numbers can be written in two words:

Informal (newspaper): four, ten, 15, 92, 114
General (book): four, ten, fifteen, ninety-two, 114. (But practice is not uniform.)

This passage illustrates a typical book style in use of figures and sums of money:

With a well-integrated, rapidly growing organization, Swedish coöperators were ready to go forward to new triumphs—over galoshes this time. It sounds funny but it is not at all; the victory over the galosh cartel—really the rubber cartel—was a very tangible achievement. Galoshes are a necessity in the Swedish winter, to say nothing of the Swedish spring and the Swedish fall. And four manufacturing firms, formed into an air-tight trust, exploited this necessity for years. Annual profits of 60 per cent, 62 per cent and even, in one exceptional year, 77 per cent were recorded. On a capital of less than a million dollars the four factories realized in fourteen years more than twelve and a half million dollars and voted many stock dividends besides. As in the case of the milling cartel, the public yelled long and loud but with no visible results.

. . . Within a few weeks, merely on the basis of this announcement, the cartel reduced the price of a pair of men's galoshes more than fifty cents, with corresponding reductions all down the line. . . . The result, within a year, was another seventy cents sliced off the price of a pair of galoshes. Having achieved this, K. F. began the manufacture of automobile tires at the Gislaved plant and by 1932 was producing 50,000 tires a year.—Marquis W. Childs, *Sweden—The Middle Way*, pp. 12-13

When most writing was longhand it was conventional to express numbers in words and then repeat them in figures in parenthesis. In clear copy, especially in typewritten copy, this is not done except in legal or important business documents.

Except in dates and street numbers, a comma is used to separate thousands, millions, etc., though it may be omitted in four-digit numbers:

1952 (the year) 1,952 (or 1952) bushels 4,682,921 $14,672.

Numbers in two words between 21 and 99 are usually hyphened, though the practice is declining: *forty-two* or *forty two.*

In consecutive writing a number at the very beginning of a sentence is written in words rather than in figures:

Two to 3% of loading and up to 10% is common and 20 to 30% in specially surfaced papers. . . . —"Paper Manufacture," *Encyclopaedia Britannica,* p. 234

(Reference: *GPO Manual,* pp. 155-159.)

3. *Arabic and Roman numerals.* Arabic numerals (*1, 2, 88* . . .) are used in almost all places where numbers are not expressed in words. Roman numerals, either lower case or capitals (i, ii, cxlvi . . .; I, II, CXLVI . . .), are occasionally used to number units in rather short series, as in outlines, chapters of a book, acts of a play, though now less often than formerly. The preliminary pages of books are almost always numbered with Roman numerals, because a new pagination is begun with the body of the book. Sometimes they are used on title pages for the date and on formal inscriptions.

In Roman numerals a small number preceding a larger is to be subtracted from the larger (ix = 9, xc = 90). The following table shows the common Roman numerals (lower case):

1	i	12	xii	40	xl	101	ci
2	ii	13	xiii	41	xli	110	cx
3	iii	14	xiv	49	xlix	199	cxcix
4	iv	15	xv	50	l	200	cc
5	v	19	xix	51	li	400	cd
6	vi	20	xx	60	lx	500	d
7	vii	21	xxi	70	lxx	600	dc
8	viii	25	xxv	80	lxxx	900	cm
9	ix	27	xxvii	90	xc	1000	m
10	x	29	xxix	99	xcix	1500	md
11	xi	30	xxx	100	c	1958	mcmlviii

4. *Plurals of figures.* The plural of a figure is written either with *s* or *'s:*

Six fives: six 5s, six 5's By tens: by 10s, by 10's

5. *Cardinal and ordinal numbers.* The numbers in simple counting, indicating number only, are *cardinal numbers: 1, 2, 3, 68, 129. . . .* The numbers indicating order, *first, second, third* . . . are *ordinal numbers.* Except in numbering items in a rather routine enumeration, ordinals should be spelled out rather than abbreviated to *1st, 2nd, 3rd. . . .*

Since the simple forms *first, second,* and so on can be either adjective or adverb, the forms in *-ly* (*firstly*) are unnecessary and now are rarely used.

See also *Fractions, *Money.

O

Speakers of English vary in their pronunciation of the *o* sounds as they do of the *a* sounds. Pronunciation of particular words, especially with short *o,* can be indicated only roughly because of this widespread variation. Three general types of *o* can be distinguished:

1. *"Long o"* (ō), the sound in *go, hoe, oh, oats, note, shoulder, soldier, sew, slow, beau.*

Before spelled *r* the sound of long *o* is somewhat modified, as in *door* (dōr), and may approach "open *o*" (ô), as in some pronunciations of *horse, born,* and so on. (See *R.)

In unstressed and rapidly spoken words the sound of long *o* is shorter and many differ in quality: *obey* (ō bā′ or ə bā′), *hotel* (hō tel′).

2. *"Short o"* (o). A rounded short *o* is not very frequent and is more characteristic of New England than of other parts of the country. The more common American sound is the unrounded or "open *o*" (ô) or especially in Western English, broad *a* (ä): *soft* (sôft, säft, soft), *pond* (pônd, pänd, pond). Since there is no single pronunciation of these words throughout the United States, the symbol o is used for them without indicating the regional variants.

3. *"Open o"* (ô), most clearly identified in its spelling *aw* (*law, lawn, spawn*) but also the vowel sound in *lord, all, fault, fought, taught, cloth, broad, talk* (lôrd, ôl, fôlt, fôt, tôt, klôth, brôd, tôk).

In unstressed syllables *o* may spell the neutral vowel ə: *actor* (ak′tər), *nation* (nā′shən), *button* (but′ən), or it may entirely disappear as in most people's pronunciation of *chocolate* (chôk′lit) or *sophomore* (sof′mōr or at most sof′ə̣mōr).

O represents several other vowel sounds: o͞o as in *move,* oo as in *wolf,* and u as in *son, money;* û as in *work.* (See also *ou.)

O, oh *O* is always capitalized, and usually it is so closely related to some other word, often a name in direct address, that it is not followed by a mark of punctuation:

> O dear, I suppose so. O yes. O God, unseen, but ever near.

Oh is an exclamation, followed by a comma if the force is weak, by an exclamation mark if the stress is strong. It is capitalized at the beginning of a sentence but not in the middle of a sentence: Oh! Don't do that! Oh, I wish he would.

In Informal writing the distinction between *O* and *oh* is not always kept, and *O* is often found where traditional usage would have *oh.*

Objects 1. *Direct objects*

a) An *object of a verb* is the noun element (noun, pronoun, noun clause) *following* a verb and intimately related to it, though less so than is the *subject. In meaning it ordinarily names what is affected or effected by the action of the verb. In certain pronouns the accusative case form (*me, him, her, us, them, whom*) in addition to position helps identify the object.

> They made the *boat* themselves. Terry chased the *cat* up a tree.
> He took *her* to the three formals of the year.
> I didn't believe *that he told the truth.*

Occasionally, for emphasis, the object precedes both the subject and the verb:

This boat [object] the boys [subject] built themselves.

b) It has been conventional to call the object in certain passive constructions a "retained object" and even to proscribe the construction on the ground that a passive verb by definition is incapable of taking an object. But since the position and the relation to the verb are not different from the typical object's, it is simpler to say that a passive verb may take an object:

He was given a *subscription* to a book club.

2. *Indirect objects.* With verbs of asking, telling, giving, and so on there is often a second or "indirect" object that names the receiver of the message, gift, etc.:

He gave the *church* a memorial window.
In desperation she showed *him* the snapshot album.

In American usage the indirect object usually comes before the direct object, as in the sentences just given. A prepositional phrase is common for the indirect object when it follows the direct object:

He gave a memorial window *to the church.*
In desperation she showed the snapshot album *to him.*

3. *Objects of prepositions.* The object of a preposition is the noun element whose relation to some other part of the sentence is shown by the preposition, as *some other part of the sentence* is the object of *to* and *the preposition* is the object of *by* in this sentence. The *what* clause in "Your grade will depend chiefly on *what you do on the examination*" is the object of *on.* (See *Prepositions.)

4. *Objects of adjectives.* A few adjectives take objects:

It was worth *a fortune.*
Are you sure *that she will come?*
He is like *his father.*

occasion, occasional, occasionally are spelled with two *c*'s and one *s.*

of, off Besides its use as a preposition of numerous meanings, *of* is used to make the phrasal genitive: *of a man=man's,* and so on.

Of is frequently used in speech in the doubling of prepositions—*inside of, off of, outside of. Inside of* and *outside of* are sometimes used in Informal writing, *off of* less so and should be reduced to *off:* He stepped off (of) the sidewalk.

Of is sometimes used by fiction writers (Ring Lardner, Erle Stanley Gardner, for example) to spell the contraction of *have,* but this spelling should not be used in General writing: He *should have* (possible but awkward: *should've;* not *should of*) known better.

often The Standard prounciation is of′ən. The *t* is sometimes sounded (occasionally even by Standard speakers), but the pronunciation of′tən is regarded as an affectation by most people.

OK, O.K. is Business and Informal English for "correct, all right, approved" (The foreman put his OK on the shipment). Occasionally it is spelled okay. As a verb the forms are OK, OK'ed; or OK'd, OK'ing; *Oke* and *okeydoke* are slang.

one **1.** The use of the impersonal pronoun *one* is characteristically Formal, especially if it must be repeated:

Formal: One can't be too careful, can one?

General: You can't be too careful, can you? (Where *you* is really impersonal.)

Repetition of *one,* to avoid *I* or when *you* would be more natural, is deadly.

American usage stands firmly by older English usage in referring back to *one* by pronouns of the third person—*he, his, him* (or *she, her*):

One is warned to be cautious if he would avoid offending his friends and bringing their displeasure down upon his head.

(See *they, *you.)

2. *One* may be used to avoid repeating a noun in the second of two compound elements:

Fred took the new copy and I took the old one.

The plural *ones* is often used; there is nothing illogical about this use, because *one* is not only a number but an indefinite pronoun.

She has two velvet dresses and three silk ones.

3. *One* is very often *deadwood, taking emphasis from the adjective which carries the real meaning:

The plan was certainly [an] original [one].

(Reference: Fries, *AEG,* pp. 245-246.)

-one *One* is written solid with *any-, every-, some-* in making an indefinite pronoun; but when the *one* is stressed it is written as a separate word:

Anyone can do that. Any one of the four will be all right.
Everyone may study late. Every one of us was surprised.
Someone ought to tell her. Some one of the plans will work.

(See *any § 2, *every and its compounds, *some.)

one of those who In written English the clause following *one of those who* and similar locutions is usually plural:

He is one of those people who believe in the perfectibility of man. (*Who* refers to *people.*)

That's one of the books that make you change your ideas. (*That* refers to *books.*)

In Informal speech and writing and sometimes in General writing the second verb is attracted to the singular by the emphatic main subject:

He is one of those people who believes in the perfectibility of man.

(Reference: John S. Kenyon, "'One of Those Who Is,'" *American Speech,* 1951, 26:161-165.)

only 1. The importance of the position of *only* has been greatly exaggerated. "Logically," perhaps, it should stand immediately before the element modified:

I need only six more to have a full hundred.

But usage in this construction is conspicuously in favor of placing the *only* before the verb of the statement. There is no possible misunderstanding in the meaning of:

I only need six more to have a full hundred.

There are instances in which the placing of *only* can make a foolish or a funny statement (with only a face that a mother could love). But placing *only* with the verb is a characteristic and reputable English idiom:

In reality we only have succession and coexistence, and the "force" is something that we imagine.—HAVELOCK ELLIS, *The Dance of Life,* p. 91

They only opened one bag and took the passports in and looked at them.—ERNEST HEMINGWAY, *The Sun Also Rises,* p. 94

(References: Gladys Haase, "Current English Forum," *College English,* 1950, 12:400-402; J. S. Kenyon, "Current English Forum," *College English,* 1951, 13:116-117.)

2. In this respect *even, ever, nearly, just, exactly,* and other such limiting adverbs are similar to *only*. But since they are used much less than *only,* and some of them only in Formal English, the idiom is not so common. Like *only* they can be placed so that they spoil the emphasis:

The way I can stand in front of a store window and persuade myself that I need some novel article even surprises me [surprises even me].

onto—on to When *on* is an adverb and *to* a preposition in a separate locution, they should be written as two words:

The rest of us drove on to the city.

When the words together make a preposition, they are written solid:

The team trotted onto the floor. They looked out onto the park.

Onto is frequently used as a double preposition in speech when *on* or *to* by itself would be used in writing:

They finally got on [Spoken: onto] the bus.
The crowd got to [Spoken: onto] James Street.

or is a coordinating conjunction and, like *and, but,* and *for,* should connect words, phrases, or clauses of equal value. (See *Coordinating conjunctions, *Compound sentences.)

Words: He must be drunk or crazy.
Phrases: We could go by car or by train.
Clauses: We could go by car or we could go by train.

Two subjects joined by *or* take a singular verb if each is singular, a plural verb if both are plural or if the one nearer the verb is plural:

Cod liver oil or halibut oil is often prescribed.
Cod liver oil or cod liver oil capsules have the same effect.
Cod liver oil capsules or cod liver oil has the same effect.

The second construction would usually be used instead of the third.

Or correlates with *either* and sometimes with *neither:*

General: Either ē′thər or ī′thər is correct.
Less common: Neither ā′thər or ī′thər is widely used in America.
General: Neither ā′thər nor ī′thər is widely used in America.

(See *Correlative conjunctions.)

-or, (-our) American spelling prefers *-or* in such words as *color, governor, honor.* When referring to Jesus Christ, *Saviour* is frequently spelled with the *u* but in other senses without it. *Glamour* is used in advertising and social contexts.

British usage is divided on this point, though of course to an American reader the words in *-our* are conspicuous. Fowler said that the American change to *-or* has actually hindered the simplification that was going on in England:

> Those who are willing to put national prejudice aside & examine the facts quickly realize, first, that the British *-our* words are much fewer in proportion to the *-or* words than they supposed, &, secondly, that there seems to be no discoverable line between the two sets so based on principle as to serve any useful purpose. By the side of *favour* there is *horror,* beside *ardour pallor,* beside *odour tremor,* & so forth. Of agent-nouns *saviour* (with its echo *paviour*) is perhaps the only one that now retains *-our, governor* being the latest to shed its *-u-*.—FOWLER, p. 415

In quoting directly from British writings and in referring to British institutions, like the Labour party, their spelling should be exactly followed; otherwise use *-or.* (References: Fowler, "-our & -or"; *Oxford English Dictionary,* "-or"; John Benbow, *Manuscript & Proof* (New York, 1937), pp. 75-77, discusses spelling in American books that are to be circulated in England.)

oral, verbal Etymologically, *oral* means "spoken," and *verbal* means "in words"; but *verbal* has been so long used in the sense of *oral* that the sense is recognized in dictionaries:

He delivered an oral message. He had only a verbal agreement.

Org **Organization** Revision: Improve the organization of your paper and/or correct the form of your outline. General methods of organizing papers are discussed in Chapter 9, pages 250-259. Pointers on organizing particular types of papers will be found in Chapter 10, Personal experience papers, page 274; Chapter 11, Information papers, page 299; Chapter 12, Opinion papers, page 324; and Chapter 13, Reference papers, pages 370-372. Methods for organizing paragraphs are discussed in Chapter 6, pages 139-165.

Outline form is illustrated in Chapter 9, pages 254-259.

Origin of words 1. *The study of word origins.* Every word has a history. Some, like *chauffeur, mores, television, parapsychology,* are relatively new in English; some have been in the language for centuries, like *home, candle, go, kitchen;* others have recently added new meanings, like *antenna,* a biological term for the "feelers" of insects, which probably now means for most people a piece of radio or television equipment. *Etymology,* the study of word origins, traces the changes of forms and combinations of word elements(as in *dis/service, wild/ness, bath/room, room/mate*) and pursues the word or its component parts to Old English and beyond or to a foreign language from which it came into English, and so on back to the earliest discoverable forms. Of some words, especially Informal words like *dude, stooge, rumpus,* earlier forms are unknown; for others, like *OK* or *blizzard,* the sources are debated. But the efforts of generations of scholars have discovered pretty full histories for most words. These are given briefly in most dictionaries and more fully in the *Oxford English Dictionary* and in special works.

Most people working with words have some curiosity about where they come from and about how new ones can be made. They find that many of our everyday words come down directly from Old English (*brother, go, house, tell*) or, if they are of foreign origin, that they were borrowed many centuries ago (*candle, debt, pay, travel*). The vocabulary of high society has many French words, of both early and recent borrowing (*debutante, gallant, fiancée*). The vocabulary of philosophy and abstract thought has a large Latin element (*concept, fallacy, rational, idealism*), and the vocabulary of science has many Greek elements (*atom, hemoglobin, seismograph*).

The sources of words will often reveal something about our history, as the many Norman French and Latin words in law (*fine, tort, certiorari, subpoena*) remind us of the time, following 1066, when the government of England was in the hands of the Norman French. But it is more interesting to discover what meanings the words have had in their earlier career in English and in the foreign languages from which they have come. *Supercilium* in Latin meant "eyebrow"; *rehearse* is from a French word meaning to "harrow again"; *sarcophagus* is, according to its Greek originals, " a flesh eater," referring to the limestone coffins that hastened the disintegration of bodies; *profane* (Latin) meant "outside the temple" and gathered the meaning of "against religion, the opposite of sacred"; *alcohol* goes back to an Arabic word for a finely ground powder, used for painting eyelids, and from its fineness the word became applied, in Spanish, to specially distilled spirits, and so to our alcohol.

Following up the biographies of words makes a good hobby—and it may sharpen a writer's sense for the exact meaning and for the suggestion carried by a given word, even though he must use it in its present sense. This article chiefly presents the various ways in which words have arrived and are still arriving in English. There are two general processes–making new words, either created or borrowed, and compounding or clipping words and parts of words that are already in the language. Then this stock of words is increased in usefulness by changes in the meanings of the forms which are already established.

2. *New words.*

a) Creation of words. Outright creation, "coinage," of words is rare. Even *gas,* first used by Van Helmont (1578-1644), a Belgian scientist, may have had the Greek *chaos* or some Dutch or Flemish word behind it. *Kodak* is probably an actual creation, as are some other trade names. Informal words like *dud, burble* were also creations, good sounding words someone made up. *Imitative words like *buzz, honk, swish, whiz* are attempts to translate the sounds of nature into the sounds of language. Various exclamations of surprise, pain, scorn started unconsciously–*ow, ouch, fie, phooey*–and then became regular words, used by anyone. Of course at the beginning of a language the words were created somehow, but just how is guesswork.

Occasionally a person coins a word for a particular statement, known as a *nonce word (used but once). One might write that a certain person "was the acme of hasbeenivity" and *hasbeenivity* would be a nonce word, and would probably remain one. As a rule arbitrary coinages do not stick. Of the large group suggested by Gelett Burgess (in *Burgess Unabridged*) not many are used, and only two have made the serious dictionaries (*blurp, goop*). Many similar words used in localities or in particular families, perhaps originated by children, never become part of the language.

b) Borrowed words. English has always borrowed words freely, from Latin, German, French, and from other languages with which English-speaking people have come in contact. It has assimilated words of quite un-English form: *khaki* (Hindustani), *seersucker* (Persian, Hindustani), *tycoon* (Japanese), *ski* (Norwegian), *hors d'oeuvres* (French), *intelligentsia* (Russian). The various words for *porch,* itself Norman French but the oldest and the most English-seeming of the group, come from various languages: *piazza* (Italian), *portico* (Italian), *stoop* (Dutch), *veranda* (Anglo-Indian).

Borrowing is still going on, though perhaps more slowly than at some periods. Some words come into Formal English and remain Formal words: *intelligentsia, bourgeois, chef-d'oeuvre, objet d'art, Zeitgeist, Anschluss,* and many others of political, philosophical, scientific, or literary bearing. *Sphygmograph* and many other scientific words are recent compoundings of Latin and especially of Greek words which are not otherwise in English usage, so that they may be regarded as borrowings as well as compounds. Others come in as General words, especially when large numbers of people go abroad, as during a war (*blitzkrieg, camouflage, ersatz*) or when a foreign invention becomes suddenly popular, as in *chauffeur, garage, chassis* of the automobile vocabulary. Some words brought by immigrants have stuck: *sauerkraut, kohlrabi, pronto, piñon, kosher, goulash.*

Many are dropped before they gain any general currency. The useful words are more or less adapted to English spelling and pronunciation and become true English words. See *English language, and for suggestions about the use of recently borrowed words, *Foreign words in English.

3. *Changes in form of words.*

a) Word composition. Most new words are made by putting together two or more word elements to make a new word of different meaning or function, as *un-* added to *interesting* gives a word of the opposite meaning, *uninteresting,* or *-ize* added to the noun *canal* gives a verb, *canalize.* The fact that dictionaries separate words formed with prefixes into two groups, those to be defined and those which are self-explanatory, shows how deceptive affixes can be. The elements may be a prefix placed before the root word (*mis-related*), or a suffix added (*foolish-ness*), or a combining element like *mono-* (*monosyllable, mono-rail*), or two independent words built together (*bookcase, basket-ball, gentle-man*). *Group words like *high school, out of town,* though not written as single words, could be included as a type of word composition.

A list of prefixes and suffixes that are still active in English would take several pages. A few of the more common prefixes are:

*a- (not): asymmetrical, amoral, atypical
ante- (before): anteprohibition era
anti- (against): antiprohibition
bi- (two): bivalve, biplane, bicycle
dis- (not): disinterested, dispraise
in- (in): income, impart, instill
in- (not): inelegant, impractical
mis- (wrong): mistake, misnomer
*pre- (before): preview, prenatal, pre-empt
*re- (again): revise, redecorate
up- (up): upend (verb), upswirl (noun)

A few suffixes are:

-en (to form a verb): heighten, lighten, weaken
-ful (full): playful, spoonful
-fy (to make): electrify, horrify
-ish (to form an adjective): dryish, foolish, smallish
-ize (to form a verb): circularize

Combining elements include a number of words or roots, many of them Greek:

-graph- (writing): biography, photograph
micro- (small): microcosm, micrometer, microphone
mono- (one) monotone, monorail
-phil- (loving): philanthropy, philately, Anglophile
-side-: sidewall, sideswipe, ringside

-smith: locksmith, silversmith, gunsmith
tele- (distant): television, telemeter
-trop (turning): geotropic, heliotropic

At first a compound has no more than the meaning to be expected by putting its elements together: unable = not able. But often a compound will develop an independent sense which can hardly be guessed at from the meanings of its elements: *cupboard, loudspeaker.*

Sometimes unnecessary elements are added to words, as in *(ir)regardless, origin(ation).* See *Long variants.

Several pairs of prefixes and suffixes have the same meaning, so that often two words of the same meaning but somewhat different in form exist side by side, especially words with *in-* (not) and *un-* and nouns with *-ness, -ity,* or *-tion:*

aridness, aridity
completeness, completion
corruption, corruptness
ferociousness, ferocity
indistinguishable, undistinguishable
torridness, torridity
unobliging, disobliging
unrobe, disrobe

When such a pair exists, take the one that is more familiar to you or that fits best in the rhythm of the sentence. But try not to make your style conspicuous by coining a form when there is already a similar word in good use. The only sure way to know is to consult a good dictionary.

b) Blends. Informal English has a number of words that show the liberties that the users of language have always taken with their words and always will take. Some of their experiments have proved useful and have become a part of the main English vocabulary.

One common type is *blends,* or portmanteau words, made by telescoping two words into one, often making a letter or syllable do double duty. *Squish* is probably a blend of *squirt* and *swish; electrocute* of *electro-* and *execute; avigation* of *aviation* and *navigation.* They are common in business: *servicenter, corrasable* (a paper—*correct* plus *erasable*), the names of many firms and products. In humor they abound: *posilutely, absotively, solemncholy, absogoshdarnlutely,* and also in more serious conversation, often presenting two ideas at once: *snoopervize (snoop—supervise), politricks, happenstance, anecdotage, slanguage.* They may be useful in a humorous context or in one of suggested dispraise.

c) Clipped words. One of the commonest types of word change is clipping, dropping one or more syllables to make a shorter and more speakable form: *ad* from *advertisement, bus* from *omnibus, taxi* from *taxicab* (earlier from *taximeter cab*), *quote* from *quotation, mob* (an eighteenth-century clip from *mobile vulgus*), *auto, movie, plane, phone,* and so on. *Shoptalk has many clips—*mike* for *microphone* or *micrometer.* The speech of any closely related group is full of clips; campus vocabulary shows a full line: *ec, home ec, poly sci, grad, prom, dorm, ad building, varsity, lab, exam, gym, prof, pre-med,* and scores more. Clipped words are written (when they are appropriate to the context) without apostrophe or period.

d) Back formations. A back formation differs from clips like *exam* and *auto* chiefly in that it is formed on *analogy with other words and is usually needed to serve as a different part of speech. *Beg* was formed from *beggar,* corresponding to *hunt, hunter.* A number of back formations have made their way, like *diagnose* from *diagnosis, edit* from *editor;* some, like **enthuse,* are slowly making their way; but most are formed in fun, like *burgle,* and are used either in humor or in a derogatory sense, like *orate. Donate* seems unnecessary, since we have *give,* but *enthuse* is more justifiable, since it takes the place of the clumsy *be enthusiastic over.*

e) Common nouns from proper names. A number of words have come into general use because of some association with a person or place: *boycott,* from the name of an Irish land agent who was "boycotted"; *macadam,* from the name of the inventor of the road surface, John L. MacAdam; *sandwich,* from an Earl of Sandwich; *jersey,* from the island of Jersey; *madras* from Madras, India.

f) Playful formations. Blends and back formations are likely to have a playful note and so do some other word shifts that can't be classified, except that they often represent a popular pronunciation, like *colyumist. Colyum* and *colyumist* are making their way, since they make it possible to point out a particular kind of *column.* Some, like *hire education,* are convenient puns. Some become quite generally used: *dingus, doodad, beanery. Jalopy* seems a perfect word for its meaning.

Watching these recent and familiar formations may lead to a study of the earlier and less obvious origins of words in the General English vocabulary.

References: The great authority on the origin of English words is the *Oxford English Dictionary,* and now the *Dictionary of American English* and the *Dictionary of Americanisms* are supplementing it for words peculiar to the United States.

Besides general books on English, the following pay special attention to origin of words: Otto Jespersen, *Growth and Structure of the English Language* (various editions); George H. McKnight, *English Words and Their Backgrounds* (New York, 1923).

Originality is applied to writing in two somewhat different senses:

1. The first sense refers to material. Material is "original" when it is gathered by the writer from his experience, from his observation of people, events, or places, or from documents like letters and newspapers. Secondary or second-hand material has been worked over by someone else, as in textbooks, encyclopedias, most magazine articles and books. This material has been organized and given form in words. Original material has to be sorted, selected, and laid out by the writer. Obviously one can learn more and find more profitable practice in handling significant original material than in handling most secondary material.

Most student papers should contain some original material. The content may come entirely from the writer's experience. At least the central idea, the purpose can come from his present desires, some of the examples, details, or applications can come from his observation, and the opinions and the point of view can represent the way he thinks. Merely rewriting a magazine article is not a very profitable exercise in composition. Putting together material from several such secondary sources is more useful, since it requires selection and comparison of material. But the most useful work for growth in writing is composing papers in which a good deal of the material is original. The writing is a little harder, but it is more fun, and the gain is much greater than in simply working over what others have done. (Compare *Plagiarism.)

2. Originality in expression, in style, is a different matter. The English language has been used a long time, and absolutely new words and phrases are rare. The most threadbare figures and phrases can be avoided, and an honest attempt to tell exactly what the writer sees and believes will ordinarily result in straightforward, readable writing, which is more valuable than mere novelty. The one sure fact is that striving too hard for originality is almost certain to result in strained writing, uncomfortable to writer and reader alike. When a style deserving the label "original" appears, it is usually the by-product of an active and independent mind, not the result of trying to be different.

ou In the *Pronunciation key (§ 1) *ou* represents the sound of ou in *bout, out, house;* the sound is also spelled *ow* in *cow* (kou), *ough* in *bough* (bou).

Words spelled with *ou* are variously pronounced: trouble (trub'l̩), soul (sōl), soup (sōōp), trousseau (trōō'sō).

-ough (-augh) A handful of words containing *-ough* and *-augh* are one of the minor scandals of English spelling. They are common words, so that we learn most of them well enough—but it is hard to believe we should be asked to do so.

The objection to these forms is not so much that they are cumbersome, as that they "spell" such different sounds—*although, bough, cough, thorough, through, bought, taught, laugh*. This can be explained by the history of the pronunciation of the individual words, chiefly by the fact that the pronunciations now generally current have come from different localities of early English speech—but that does not justify them.

At present *altho* and *tho* and to a less extent *thru* and *thoro* are widely used in personal writing and in business writing, especially in advertising. They are used in a few periodicals and in some books, though most publishers still go by traditional stylebooks. They are given as alternative spellings in the recent dictionaries. In a questionnaire answered by over a hundred college and university English teachers, nearly one half allowed or encouraged the use of these forms in themes. They are still out of place in Formal writing, and their use in General writing should depend chiefly on their appropriateness to other traits of style and to the expectations of readers.

-ous, -us *-ous* is an adjective ending: *fictitious, ominous; -us* is a noun ending: *cactus, campus, impetus.*

out of date *Out of date, out of doors, out of town* are usually hyphened when they stand before a noun but not when they are in the predicate: He has an out-of-date model; His model is out of date.

over- Compounds with *over-* are not usually hyphened:

overanxious overalls overdraft overseas

P

spells the sound as in *purr, tip, puppy*. It is silent in a few common words (*corps, cupboard, raspberry, receipt*) and in a number of words from Greek—*pneumonia, psalm, pseudo-, psychology*.

After *m, p* is often silent in such words as *empty* (em′ti), and a *p* is generally sounded after *m* in words such as *dreamt* (drempt) and *warmth* (wômpth). In *pumpkin,* two pronunciations are recognized, pump′kin and pung′kən.

paid (payed) *Paid* is the spelling of the past tense and past participle of *pay* (He *paid* his bills) in all senses except *payed out a line, rope, etc.,* and occasionally in that sense also.

pair In General usage the plural of *pair* is ordinarily *pair* when it comes after a number: six pair of socks. In other positions *pairs* is the usual plural.

pants–trousers The Formal word is always *trousers;* the General and Informal, *pants* (clipped from *pantaloons*) or *trousers*—but always *ski pants.*

Paragraph indention, No paragraph indention Revision: Indent here for new paragraph; or join this paragraph to the preceding one. ¶ *No* ¶

For a discussion of paragraph division, see Chapter 6, "Adequate development," page 147.

Paragraphs Revision: This paragraph is unsatisfactory. Revise or rewrite it. *Par*

The most common faults in paragraphs are:

1. *Underdevelopment*—Lack of details to establish the picture or idea intended.

2. *Lack of connection*—Either actually unrelated statements put together or the existing relation between statements not made clear to a reader.

Paragraphs are fully discussed in Chapter 6, "Paragraphs," page 138.

Parallel constructions Revision: Make the two or more elements in this series parallel in form.

Paral

Typical shifted (unparallel) constructions are these:

Shifted:	*Made parallel:*
To me orientation week seems both [noun:] a necessity and [adjective:] worth while.	To me orientation week seems both [two adjectives:] necessary and worth while.
Jack has received offers from Hollywood not only [phrase:] for his fishing experiences but [clause:] because he resembles the late Will Rogers.	Jack has received offers from Hollywood not only [two phrases:] for his fishing experiences but for his resemblance to the late Will Rogers.

For other examples and suggested remedies see *Shifted constructions; Chapter 2, "Making constructions consistent," page 65, and Chapter 7, "Parallelism and balance," page 185.

Paraphrase A paraphrase is a restatement of a writer's ideas in different words. It is now usually applied to digesting the contents of a passage in one's own words, as in note-taking. (See Ch. 13, "Suggestions for the summarizing note," p. 368.)

Parentheses ( )

1. *For additions.* 2. *For apologetic asides.* 3. *To inclose numbers in an enumeration.* 4. *For action on different planes.* 5. *With other marks.*

1. *For additions.* Parentheses (often called *curves* and by printers called *parens*) are sometimes used in writing, chiefly to inclose words, phrases, or whole sentences that add to the clearness of a statement without altering its meaning and that are allowed to stand outside the construction of the sentence. These additions are likely to be (1) illustrations, (2) definitions, or (3) added information thrown in for good measure, as in the first sentence of this paragraph.

He has a scholarship at Cornell (Iowa).

This bill, commonly called the Lockport plan, has been the basis of all later city-manager charters (there are now 438).

Of all such emotions religious earnestness is the most fatal to pure biography. Not only does it carry with it all the vices of hagiography (the desire to prove a case, to depict an example—the sheer perversion, for such purposes, of fact), but it disinterests the biographer in his subject.—HAROLD NICOLSON, *The Development of English Biography,* p. 111

Sondelius even brought in the negro doctor, Oliver Marchand, not on the ground he was the most intelligent person in the island (which happened to be Sondelius's reason) but because he "represented the plantation hands."—SINCLAIR LEWIS, *Arrowsmith,* p. 376

His concerts were well received in most cities (in Chicago the reviews were so enthusiastic that he was given a return engagement), but he was still dissatisfied with his performance.

These uses are slightly stiff, belonging most appropriately to rather Formal exposition, and should be used sparingly.

2. *For apologetic asides.* Sometimes parentheses are used to mark an apologetic aside, as much as to say "You know this, but let me remind you"–though this use is less common today than formerly.

James Madison (the fifth President) enunciated the doctrine in 1823.

3. *To inclose numbers in an enumeration.* Parentheses are often used to inclose the letters or figures used to mark items in an enumeration, as in § 1 of this article, though this tends to make the numbers or letters more conspicuous than they deserve to be.

4. *For action on different planes.* Recent fiction has developed another use of parentheses. When the action is carried on in two different planes–one in the present, another in the past; one in a character's mind, the other in the action–the one which receives less space, is less emphatic, may be put in parentheses:

> . . . ears are still in outside world, peeping Toms sticking out on both sides of my head, why can't I take them in like snails, but you can't, you can close your eyes but you can't make your ears stop thinking. ("Thirty love! Net ball!" float in from that other world.) Voices outside losing their separateness, merging, sweet distant song, like shell held to ear, going round and round in Natalie's brain, ears going to sleep at last. . . .–TESS SLESINGER, *Time: The Present,* p. 341

5. *With other marks.* When the parenthetical unit is a complete sentence, the period comes *inside* the curves, but it is usually omitted if the expression falls within a sentence. Punctuation marks belonging to the sentence including the parenthesis come *after* the second curve:

> Some words have various meanings with different prepositions, as agree *with* (a person), agree *to* (a suggestion), agree *in* (principles, qualities).

Do not confuse parentheses and brackets; see *Brackets; see also *Dashes § 4.

part (on the part of) is often a rather clumsy way of saying *by, among, for,* and the like:

> In the past ten years there has been a definite move on the part of [*by* or *among*] our religious leaders to unite all Protestants in one church.
>
> It resulted in less wild driving on the part of [by] young people.

Participles 1. *Forms of participles.*

	Active	*Passive*
Present:	asking; singing	being asked; being sung
Past:	having asked; having sung	asked, having been asked; sung, having been sung

The simple participle forms (*asking, asked*) are used in various verb phrases:

I am asking   I am being asked   I have asked   I have been asked

Although the participles are usually referred to as present and past, they do not indicate definite time themselves but time in relation to the context in which they are used.

2. *As modifiers.* When not a part of a phrasal verb form, the participles are most commonly used like adjectives. They have qualities of adjectives in that they modify nouns and pronouns (the pen *used* in signing the treaty; a *coming* era; the leaves *falling* in the street). They have qualities of verbs in that they may take an object (*Following these clues,* he soon found her) and be modified by adverbs (The car, *rolling crazily . . .*).

Sometimes in analyzing a sentence it is difficult to tell a participle used like an adjective from a participle which is a part of a passive verb form. The decision rests on whether the participle modifies the subject, as a predicate adjective with a linking verb, or whether it describes an action.

Passive voice: The candidate of the Republican party *was defeated.*
Predicate adjective: The candidate was *defeated* but happy.

When used as a modifier, a participle should refer clearly to some particular noun or pronoun:

Opening his shirt at the neck, he went back to his chopping. (*Opening* modifies *he.*)

A college education, looked at from this point of view, may be a liability. (*Looked* modifies *college education.*)

There should be no reasonable doubt of what is modified. A modifying participle "dangles" or is "misrelated" when it seems to refer to a word the writer does not mean it to refer to:

Dangling: Walking on the campus, several of my class pass by.
Clearer: Walking on the campus, I usually meet . . . .
Dangling: Combined with his scientific understanding, Dr. Hertzler is a man who would have made his name for wisdom in any profession.
Clearer: Dr. Hertzler's scientific understanding would have made him a name in any profession.

Because the reader expects these participles to refer to the subject of the following clause, he is disappointed. It is not so much a matter of meaning, for the sentence with a dangling participle is rarely ambiguous (though it may be amusing). It is rather a matter of accurate expression: Participles used adjectivally should modify definite words. (See *Dangling modifiers and Ch. 2, "Revising dangling modifiers," p. 64.)

3. *In absolute constructions.* The participle-as-adjective should not be confused with the participle in a phrase which relates to the whole sentence (to the situation) rather than to a particular word. Some such phrases are very common, even *formulas.

Judging from her looks, she isn't under fifty.
Beginning with the class of 1958, the tuition was raised $50.

(See *Verbid.)

4. *Stylistically objectionable participles.* The use of participles and verbal nouns in English seems to be increasing, but there is a tendency for amateur writers to use participles in constructions in which a subordinate clause would sound better:

Uncle Joe was prompt, *necessitating our hurrying* [so that we had to hurry].

The sea was running heavily, *being boosted* by a strong southeast wind. (Omit the *being.*)

Especially conspicuous are clumsy "nominative absolutes," made like Latin ablative absolutes:

He being right there, I let him do the work. (Since he was right there. . . .)

Then, *the feature being ended,* everyone began to file out of the theater. (Then, after the feature was over . . .; *or, perhaps:* The feature over, everyone. . . .)

For *very* with participles see *very § 2. Compare *Gerunds. References: Curme, *Syntax,* pages 158-160; C. A. Smith, *Interpretative Syntax* (Boston, 1906), pages 55-59; Reuben Steinbach, "The Misrelated Constructions," *American Speech,* 1930, 5:181-197; H. C. Wyld, *A Short History of English,* pages 237-258.

Parts of speech To describe the enormous number of words in a language it is necessary to have some ways of grouping them. The "parts of speech" is one such traditional grouping. In some languages, *form* (declensions, conjugations, derivational endings) is a reliable basis for allocating words to the parts of speech, though there is always a residue of "particles" with only one form. In English, change of form works moderately well for identifying nouns, verbs, adjectives, and adverbs, which are consequently often referred to as *form classes.* Even in these classes, however, there are exceptions and minor variations, like our nouns with plural in *-en* instead of the usual *-s,* or with a foreign language plural, or with only a singular or a plural form; and there are adverbs that are not compared (like *almost, quite, very*) and verbs with only one form (like *may* and *shall*). These differences must be provided for, either by treating such words as separate parts of speech or as subtypes of a group. Many languages have derivational endings that indicate the part of speech; English has a few, like *-ize* to make a verb from a noun (*dramatize*) and *-ed* to make an adjective from a noun (*fair-minded*), but such endings indicate the part of speech of a very small number of words.

Since form is not always a reliable way of classifying words in English, their *typical function in sentences* is used as supporting data or as the main data. It is, in fact, a characteristic of English to use the same word form in the function of more than one part of speech. Sometimes a word develops the forms characteristic of more than one part, as *radio* has the forms of a verb (*radios, radioing, radioed*) and of a noun (*radios* as the plural and the same form spelled *radio's* or *radios'* as a genitive), or *yellow* has the forms of an adjective (*yellower, yellowest*), of a noun (*yellows, yellow's*), and of a verb (*yellows, yellowing, yellowed*). In a dictionary or other general discussion of words, such words have to be given as "belonging to" (that is, having the basic characteristics of) more than one part of

PARTS OF SPEECH IN ENGLISH:

Formal characteristics (as spelled)	Some derivational endings	Central syntactical functions	Common secondary functions
Nouns: Plural *-s, -es* or alternatives; Genitive *'s, s'*	*-ance, -ee, -er (-or), -ism, -ment, -th*	Subject or object of verb; object of preposition	Modifier of another noun; apposition; adverbial modifier
Pronouns: See *Pronouns, types and forms	———	Subject or object of verb; object of preposition	Modifier of noun; apposition
Verbs: *-s, -ing, -ed,* or vowel change; phrases with auxiliaries	*-ate, -ize, -en, -fy*	Predicate	As a gerund or infinitive, a subject or object; as an infinitive or participle, a modifier of noun
Adjectives: Comparison with *-er, -est* or *more, most*	*-able, -al, -ant, -ary, -ic, -ish, -ous*	Modifier of noun	Subject or object when preceded by *a/an, the*
Adverbs: Comparison with *-er, -est* or *more, most* (Except *almost, very,* etc.)	*-ly, -wise*	Modifier of verb, adverb, adjective, clause, or sentence	Connective; occasional modifier of noun
Prepositions: ———	———	Forming phrase with noun or noun equivalent as headword	Joining phrase to a word or sentence
Conjunctions: ———	———	Coordinating: joining words, phrases, clauses Subordinating: introducing, forming a clause and joining it to another clause or to some other sentence element	
Interjections, or exclamations, may be regarded as a subtype of Adverbs			

SUMMARY OF CHARACTERISTICS

Typical position in sentences	Principal subtypes	Word groups with same function	Traditional definition
Before and after verb; after *a/an*, *the*, *our*, *this*, *some*, etc.; followed by *of*-phrase	Common, proper; abstract, concrete; mass, collective, etc.	Clauses with *that*, *whoever*, etc.	The name of a person, place, thing, relationship, etc.
Before and after verb; after preposition	See *Pronouns, types and forms	—	A word used in place of a noun
Following subject in statements; often first in commands and questions	Linking verbs; auxiliaries	Verb-adverb combination	A word indicating action, state, or being
Between *a/an*, *the*, etc., and noun; after linking verb	Descriptive, limiting, proper	Clauses with *who*, *that*, etc.; wide variety of phrases	A word qualifying, making more exact, the meaning of a noun
Variable; after verb plus object	See *Adverbs, types and forms	Clauses with *when*, *since*, *although*, etc.; wide variety of prepositional phrases	A word modifying a verb, adjective, or another adverb
Before a noun or noun and its modifiers	—	—	A word relating a noun to another word
At beginning of clause or sentence	Coordinating, subordinating, correlative, conjunctive adverbs	—	A word joining two words, phrases, clauses, or sentences

speech. In a specific sentence, the syntactical function, the way the word is used, is the final clue, as *walk* is a noun in "Let's go for a walk" and a verb in "They would rather walk than ride."

Often, however, a word is used in the function of another part of speech without acquiring the characteristic changes of form; *bomb* has the forms and functions of a noun as well as those of a verb but is used as a modifier (as in bomb shelter) without acquiring the comparative forms of an adjective. In the past there has been much loose description of this trait. *Stone* in *stone cabin,* for instance, has been called "an adjective" or, somewhat more accurately, has been said to be "used *as* an adjective." Actually it is used *like* an adjective, in the function of an adjective–that is, as the modifier of a noun. Some linguists use separate terms for the parts of speech and for these functional shifts or for phrases and clauses used in the function of a part of speech. Most commonly they add the suffix *-al* to the name of the corresponding part of speech: an adjective used in the function of a noun (*The poor* we have always with us) or a clause used in a typical function of a noun (*What she said* didn't matter to him) is called a *nounal;* nouns used like adjectives (the *house* mother) are sometimes called *adjectivals;* nouns used like adverbs (Then we went *home*) are sometimes called *adverbials;* and so on. These distinctions do not seem necessary, since from the point of view of syntax such words are subjects, objects, modifiers, and so on, regardless of what part of speech may be their home base or of what their form is. (The need for the distinction, if one is felt, is probably a hangover from the old parsing, which gave both the part of speech and the function of each word, or, at a more sophisticated level, it is a blurring of morphology and syntax.) In this book, words used in such functional shifts are labeled by their function in a sentence, as subject or verb or modifier (adj.) or modifier (adv.): *the light headed* might be a subject or object; in "*Whoever was in that car* saw it," the clause is the subject. Referring to clauses as noun, adjective, or adverb clauses or to phrases as adjective or adverb phrases is a convenient way of saying that they are used *like* the part of speech indicated.

In spite of a number of good tries, linguists have not yet agreed upon a system for describing the parts of speech in English. (It is fortunate that the category is not actually so important for our language as it is for many languages.) This book therefore uses basically the traditional categories with somewhat more precise criteria in their definitions. The table on pages 626-627 lists the principal points regarding the parts of speech; some further details will be found in the *Index* entry on each.

References: Sumner Ives, "Defining Parts of Speech in English," *College English,* 1957, 18:341-348, is a good introduction to the problem. All books on English treat the parts of speech. Any one may have important points, but no single one can be whole-heartedly recommended at the moment.

passed, past The past tense and the past participle of *pass* are *passed* (He *passed* the first post; He had *passed*), though *past* is fairly common as the participle. *Past* is the adjective (*past* favors), preposition (*past* the crisis), and adverb (*past* due, They went *past*). Pronunciation: past or (Eastern) päst. (See *A § 3.)

passer-by Usually hyphened; plural *passers-by.*

Passive verbs Revision: Change the passive verb or verbs to active. *Pass*

Amateur writers tend to use passive statements when active verbs would sound more natural ("The music *was enjoyed* by us" instead of "We *enjoyed* the music"). Awkward passives are sometimes used to avoid *I:*

> Passive: The situation *was taken in* by me with great amusement.
> Active: I took in the situation with great amusement.

This passage shows both effective and ineffective passives:

> 1959 is here. With it comes a host of '59 model automobiles. Most of these cars *were heralded in* during the closing months of 1958. They *were awaited* in anxious curiosity by the buying public. In many instances, they *were looked forward to* with too much anticipation.

Although an awkward phrase, *were heralded in* is a legitimate passive, because the "heralders" need not be named; the passive *were awaited* places *the buying public* at the end of the sentence for emphasis and would not be noticeable if it was not followed by *were looked forward to,* which clearly shows that the writer was not paying attention to his work. Those two sentences might better stand:

> The buyers awaited them in anxious curiosity, often with too much anticipation.

The use of passive verbs is often objectionable because it involves a thoughtless shift from the active voice and adds to the wordiness of what is usually already wordy and fuzzy writing. (For the formation of the passive voice and its profitable use see *Voice § 3.)

patriot, patriotic Pā'tri ət and pā'tri ot'ik are the dominant American pronunciations. Of the two variant pronunciations, pat'ri ot'ik is more common than pat'ri ət.

peeve Informal for *annoy* and *annoyance. Peeve* is a back formation from *peevish* (*Origin of words § 3d). It is used most commonly as a modifier: *peeved.*

per *Per* (Latin, "through, by, by the, among," etc.) is most appropriate when used in phrases that are still close to their Latin originals–*per capita, per cent,* or in a definitely commercial setting–*$18 per week, $2.60 per yard, forty-four hours per week,* or in certain standardized technical phrases–*revolutions per minute.*

Because of its commercial and technical connotation, *per* is less appropriate in General English, where the English equivalent phrase usually fits more naturally: *$18 a week, 20¢ a quart, four times a year.*

per-, pre- Do not spell the *per-* words with *pre-:* write *per*form, *per*spire, *per*fect, and so on. Remember that *pre-* means "before" (*pre*war, *pre*school, *pre*-eminent).

percent is not followed by a period, and it may be written as two words. In Informal and General writing it is often used instead of *percentage* or even of *proportion:* Only a small percent of the class was [or, *were*–collective agreement] there.

With figures the percent sign (%) is ordinarily used: 97.6%.

Period (.) 1. *At the end of statements.* The principal function of the period is to mark the end of a statement–that is, the end of every completed sentence not definitely a question or exclamation.

Sometimes sentences in the form of exclamations or questions are really to be regarded as statements. After such a sentence a writer may use the exclamation mark or question mark, but he will usually have a period if the tone is lacking in emphasis or if he wishes to minimize the emphasis of the sentence form he has chosen. (See *Rhetorical questions.)

2. *Miscellaneous conventional uses.*

a) After *abbreviations: Oct. n.b. Mr. Wm. Fraser

b) In sums of money, between dollars and cents: $5.66. The period is not used unless the dollar sign is used: 66 cents or 66¢; $0.66.

c) Before decimals, or between the whole number and the decimal: .6, 3.14159, 44.6%

d) A period is sometimes used between hours and minutes represented in figures (2.36 p.m.), though a colon is usual in the United States (2:36 p.m.).

e) Three space periods (. . .) are used as *ellipses, to mark the omission of words; several are often used to guide a reader's eye across the page. (See *Leaders.)

3. *Period with quotation marks.* Most American publishers place a period coming at the end of a quotation inside the quotation marks: "The longer you put it off," he said, "the harder it's going to be." (See *Quotation marks § 4b.)

Person Pronouns are classified according to *person* (first, second, and third) and *number* (singular and plural):

First person, the one speaking: (Singular) *I, my, me;* (Plural) *we, our, us*

Second person, the one spoken to: (Singular and plural) *you, your*

Third person, the one spoken of: (This singular also shows masculine, feminine, and neuter) *he, him, his; she, her; it, its;* (Plural) *they, them, their*

Nouns are regarded as third person.

Except in the verb *be* (*I am, you are, he is* . . .) English verbs have only one form to distinguish person and number, the third singular of the present tense: I have, you have, he *has;* we, you, they have; and the *auxiliary verbs don't even have that.

person is the ordinary word for referring to a human being. *Individual* has the same meaning (though it is applied also to single objects and animals as well) but emphasizes the person's singleness, aloneness, and is slightly heavy or pretentious unless that emphasis is needed. *Party* is legal or light. In British usage *person* sometimes has an unfavorable connotation.

Personally is sometimes used as a conversational intensive (I personally think) but is usually inappropriate in writing.

Personification is a *figure of speech in which an object or animal or quality or ideal is given some attributes of a human being:

> Deal gently, *Love,* with him and her
> who live together now!
>
> REX WARNER, *Poems,* p. 71

It is less common today than formerly, and less common in prose than in verse. Flat and unessential personification is likely to have an amateur sound: No steam engine can brag of such efficiency.

ph is a *digraph for the *f* sound in words of Greek origin: *phlox, photography, photograph. . . .* In *Stephen* (and formerly in *nephew*), *ph* represents *v.*

Most words with *ph* belong to the Formal vocabulary, so that the natural and expected simplification to *f* is very slow. A few, like *fantasy* and *sulfur* are already changed. Advertisers and humorists are experimenting with *telegraf, foto,* and so on.

The first syllable of *diphtheria* is often pronounced dip- and of *naphtha* usually nap-.

phenomenon, phenomena *Phenomenon* is the singular and *phenomena* the plural (phenomena of the mind).

Originally *phenomenon* meant "any observable event," but now it also means "something remarkable," and *phenomenal* is almost always used in this sense. Often a shorter or more exact word is preferable.

phone is a clip for *telephone,* in General use as noun, verb, and modifier (on the phone; phone me later; the phone book). It is written without an apostrophe.

Phonemes In linguistics a *phoneme* is the term for what the speakers of a variety of a language hear as "the same speech sound." "The same sound" actually is a range of similar sounds. We make the *p* at the beginning of *pit* by cutting off the flow of air from our lungs and by closing our lips, then opening the lips suddenly with a consequent audible explosion. The *p* at the end of *stop,* on the other hand, can be clearly recognized merely from the abrupt cutting off of the vowel sound caused by closing our lips; we don't have to open them and make the explosion. In these words spelled with *p,* the actual initial and final *p* sounds are evidently quite different. Yet we call them "the same sound" because we interpret what we hear as the same thing. The phonetically slightly different sounds that are interpreted by listeners as "the same sound" are *allophones;* a phoneme then is a group of allophones.

Phonemes are classified into two categories, those which the letters of conventional alphabets more or less accurately represent–*segmental* phonemes–and those that are not represented by letters–*suprasegmental* phonemes.

1. *Segmental phonemes.* Linguists record the sounds of English with more precision than our alphabet can represent them (or than most of us can hear them). They are described phonetically, according to the way they are made by the speech organs (as *u* is a high back round vowel and *s* a voiced apico-alveolar sibilant) and are written in a phonetic alphabet. To record a language, linguists select from this phonetic alphabet the symbols that are phonemes in the particular language. For example, English does not need the *ch* sound of German (except perhaps for the dialect of English spoken in Scotland) or the French or German *u* sound; nor do those languages need the symbols for the sounds we spell *th.* In English, consonants are fairly well represented by the conventional alphabet, but for accurate recording, the vowels need more symbols than our conventional five. For phonemic transcriptions linguists use various adaptations of the International Phonetic Alphabet, which can be found in any book on linguistics and in most dictionaries.

2. *Suprasegmental phonemes.* The study of these sound features is relatively recent, and the symbols for them, in fact even their actual number, are not well agreed on, but all current books on linguistics treat *stress, pitch,* and *juncture.*

a) Stress. The greater loudness of the last syllable of *today* is evident to anyone; and the fact that the third syllable of *dictionary* is not so loud as the first but louder than the second and last is apparent to any speaker of English. Every dictionary therefore marks these distinctions as primary, secondary, and no accent. But when two or more words are involved there may be a fourth degree of loudness. In *biological dictionary* we may wish to emphasize that the book is a dictionary, *not* a textbook, or that the dictionary is for biology, *not* for chemistry. The relative loudness of the syllables within each word will remain the same; but for the first distinction the loudest syllable of *dictionary* will be louder than the loudest in *biological* (bì o lôg i cal díc tion àr y); for the second distinction the reverse will be true (bì o lóg i cal dîc tion àr y). There are, then, at least four degrees of distinctive stress in English. In transcribing consecutive utterances, therefore, four degrees of stress can be marked:

primary ′ secondary ^ tertiary ` neutral ˘

The neutral degree is usually not indicated by a symbol.

b) Pitch. Linguists usually identify four distinctions in relative pitch, marked by superior figures from 1 to 4; 1 now usually indicating low pitch and 4 high, with 2 representing the common pitch of the utterance. Frequently, especially in terminal syllables, the pitch glides within the syllable, as *here* in "Look here" might start on 3 and end on 1. In "He's never late, oh no" if the emphasis is on *he,* the pitches might go ^{3}he's ^{2}never late, oh ^{3}no^{1}. Pitch is closely associated with stress, and it takes a good deal of training to be able to distinguish it with accuracy.

c) Juncture. Ordinarily in speech we do not separate individual words by pauses as they are separated by space in print–the stream of speech seems to be continuous. After larger elements–phrases, for example–the continuous flow of sound may be briefly interrupted. These interruptions vary in length and are usually combined with variations in pitch. Although linguists are not entirely agreed on the description of these junctures or transitions, and are even less uniform in applying them, there is an obvious and important fact of language here. Ordinarily five distinctions are made. (Besides their descriptive names–close, open, level, rising, falling–they are often called by the symbol used to mark them–plus +; single bar |; double bar ||; and double cross #. The last three are known as terminals.)

1) Close or normal transition is the uninterrupted utterance: *anoldhouse*.

2) Open, or plus, juncture, is a brief interruption coming within a phrase and often indicating a word break, as the floating mass of ice might be *an+iceberg* and a little town might be *a+niceburg.*

3) Level, or single bar, juncture is slightly more distinct and may occur between words (Summer+school where summer's|cool) or between constructions (The man | who was older than we thought | sat down beside us). The pitch after the construction is the same as the pitch before it.

4) Rising, or double bar, juncture follows a rise in pitch and can be heard in many questions: Are you scared ||

5) Falling, or double cross, juncture is also a terminal and is characteristic of the ends of statements: Not at all #

This brief and incomplete account of the suprasegmental phonemes does not give an adequate idea of their importance. They obviously convey a good deal of the meaning of speech. A native speaker learns them unconsciously and rarely "makes a mistake" in them, except perhaps from nervousness or inattention, as when a radio announcer reads a commercial mechanically, without sensing what he is reading. Neglect or misuse of them reveals the speaker as a foreigner or as one who is speaking artificially. The proper formation of the segmental phonemes is essential to intelligibility, and of the suprasegmental phonemes for effective oral communication. But suprasegmental phonemes are not essential to intelligibility, as is evident from their virtual elimination in song and their general omission in writing.

An understanding of the suprasegmental phonemes is helpful in learning a second language (see *Intonation); in describing scientifically the sounds of English, especially in finding the boundaries of constructions; and in correcting some momentary ambiguities in silent reading, as in occasional newspaper headlines and sentences like "It will never do for a mind merely to live through its passions or perceptions," which has to be read with a level juncture between *live* and *through* rather than after *through*. Understanding of these phonemes–with or without a knowledge of the term–is also helpful in revising one's writing where they have some bearing on punctuation; but since the written language has had a somewhat independent development they cannot be accepted as infallible guides.

References: Gleason, Chapters 12-18, and other recent books on linguistics.

Phrasal verb A verb formed by an auxiliary and an infinitive or past participle is called a *phrasal verb: will go, must go, has gone, had gone*. Even in the tenses which have simple forms (*goes, went*), we get slightly different shades of meaning by using phrasal forms (*am going, did go, was going,* etc.). Phrasal verbs are also called *periphrastic* verbs. (See *Verbs.)

Phrases 1. *Forms and functions.* A phrase is a group of two or more words without a subject and finite verb that functions as a grammatical unit in a clause or sentence. Phrases are conventionally classified according to one of the words of which they are composed:

Prepositional: in the morning   before the war   in the room
Participial: coming into the room   pasted on the wall
Gerund: his learning French
Infinitive: to live peacefully   to catch fish

The term *phrase* is somewhat confusing because it covers these various and actually quite different patterns of expression. It would be clearer to apply the term phrase only to expressions centered on nouns (up the steep hill) and use another, as *verbid* is used in this book, for those centered on participles, gerunds, and infinitives.

Other word groups that function as syntactical units may be referred to as phrases (*have gone, a large house*), but the term is better limited to those listed in the first paragraph of this article.

Phrases function like single sentence elements:

Nouns: (Subject) *The first four games* were lost. (Object) He lost *the first four games.* (Genitive) the works *of the masters*

Adjectives: a heart *of gold* *Crossing the street,* he nearly was hit by a car.

Adverbs: beyond the town in the morning He did it *in the Dutch manner.*

Prepositions: in regard to in order to alongside of

2. *A unit of expression.* Most words by themselves, as they stand in a dictionary, cannot fit into sentences until they are set in phrases.

They need modifiers to make their meaning more exact; they need connectives to tie them to other words. Out of such phrases, clauses and sentences are built. A good case could be made for regarding phrases as the central feature of writing and speaking, more fundamental than sentences, rivaled only by paragraphs in importance for study and practice.

Phrases are not only units of meaning; they are the physical units of reading, since we read by meaningful groups of words rather than by single words. Most phrases fall within the limits of the typical eye span (what an eye grasps at one fixation)–six words or thirty letters. Phrases that are easy to grasp with the eye and easy to comprehend with the mind are fundamental to good writing.

For the use of phrases see *Idiom and idioms, *Participles, *Prepositions, and Chapter 2, "Revising dangling modifiers," page 64.

pianist, piano Pronunciation is divided: pi an′ist, pē′ə nist, the first much the more common. The word applies to both men and women players, so that *pianiste* is unnecessary as a feminine form.

Piano is pronounced pi an′o; rarely pi ä′no. The plural is *pianos*.

picnic Before endings beginning with a vowel, *k* is added to the second *c* to make sure the *k* is sounded: *picnicker, picnicked, picnicking;* also *trafficked, panicked.*

Plagiarism *Plagiarism* means taking material written by another and offering it as one's own. The copied matter may range from a few sentences to a whole paper copied from another student or from a book or magazine. (We are not considering here the more complicated problem of plots taken from stories or movies, and so on.) There are various reasons for copied papers in a composition course. A very few students are dishonest, trying to get credit without any mental effort. Once in a while one is playing the ancient game of putting-something-over-on-the-instructor, in part at least to see if it can be done. More often, at least in beginning courses, the motives are more complex. A student who plagiarizes may be so scared or so befogged in what is for him a difficult or puzzling course that he resorts to the only way he sees of getting a desired grade. And sometimes a student doesn't clearly understand what rights he has in using the materials of others or in receiving help.

Compositions should obviously be prepared independently, not in "collaboration" with another student.

If he copies from dishonest motives, the student must take the consequences if the source of his paper is recognized, or even if the instructor is sure by comparing it with his other papers that it is not his own work. If he copies from fear or ignorance of proper practices, he deserves consideration and help. Whatever the motive, the penalty–failing the paper or perhaps, if it is an important one, failing the course–does not represent the vengeance of the instructor but the failure of the student, failure in the fundamental purpose of a composition course, which is to increase students' skill in communicating their information, ideas, and fictions to others. Copying others' work is the most complete failure possible.

The student who is scared or puzzled should go at once to his instructor and discuss his situation frankly, the reasons for his difficulties, the present faults in his work, and ways to overcome them. Serious effort intelligently directed will always bring improvement. And a student who feels he is moving in the right direction, even if he is moving slowly, is doing something important, and in the long run work is more satisfying and less wearing than worry.

The student who has not learned how to handle material obtained from reading and study needs guidance in the fundamentals of study and scholarship. A writer expects that what he has published will be read and will be used; but he has a right to expect that his exact words will not be used without his receiving credit and that his facts and ideas will not be used in print without his permission.

Anyone using published material, then, has a twofold responsibility: first, of absorbing the ideas into his own thought and, second, of giving credit to important sources. A student—or anyone else—is not *composing* when he is merely copying. He should read and digest the material, get it into his own words (except for brief, important quotations that are shown to be quotations). He should be able to *talk* about the subject before he *writes* about it. Then he should refer to any sources he has used. This is not only courtesy but a sign of good workmanship, part of the morality of writing. In an informal paper the credit can be given informally, perhaps a note on the cover saying "This paper is based on . . ."; or it may be in the body of the paper: "Professor Keane said in a lecture . . . ," "Walter Lippmann wrote recently . . . ," or "So-and-so said . . . ." Or credit may be given more formally in footnotes at the bottom of the page (as described in Ch. 13, "Footnotes: crediting sources," p. 374). Footnotes must be used in a research paper, but one or two would be in order in any paper for which a student has found material in print. The greatest temptation to plagiarize is in a research paper, in which the material is expected to be based on reading various sources. But a research paper offers also the best opportunity for learning how to gather, digest, and give credit for material from published sources. At any rate it is necessary for college students to learn how to use such material accurately and honestly—by getting it into their own words and giving appropriate credit to sources used.

plenty *Plenty* as an adverb (I was plenty worried—The car is plenty large) is marked colloquial by the dictionaries. It is in good Informal use but would rarely be found in Formal writing.

The omission of *of* after *plenty* in speech (plenty [ ] time) results in an adjectival use. This idiom is rarely found in print:

Out into darkness, out to night,
My flaming heart gave plenty light, . . .
JOHN MASEFIELD, *The Everlasting Mercy*

Pleonasm Pleonasm is using two words for the same grammatical function (My Uncle Fred, *he* said he would give me twenty-five cents for every bird I could find and name). It is quite common in speech and is used occasionally in writing for emphasis, but it should not be written without good reason.

Plurals of nouns

1. *Special groups in "-s" or "-es."* 2. *Same form for both singular and plural.* 3. *Survivals of older English plural forms.* 4. *Foreign language plurals.* 5. *Compound and group words.* 6. *Plurals of figures, words, letters.* 7. *Plural substitutes.*

The plural of the great majority of English nouns is made by adding an s or z sound, spelled *-s,* to the singular form of the noun. This *-s* is pronounced as part of the syllable to which it is added.

buckets rats days rooms trees
There are five *Romes* in the United States.

Since this is the usual way of forming the plural, dictionaries list only the exceptional plurals. But several groups of words form their plurals in other ways:

1. *Special groups in "-s" or "-es,"* chiefly a matter of spelling:

a) Nouns ending in the *sound* of ch, j (*edge*), s, sh, or z, in which the *-s* could not be pronounced as part of the final syllable, add the sound iz, spelled *es:*

birches churches bridges ledges *buses (or busses)
kisses bushes *Joneses axes fixes buzzes quizzes

b) Common nouns ending in *-y* preceded by a consonant change the *y* to *i* and add *-es:*

beauties bodies caddies cherries cities cries enemies

Exceptions to this rule are proper nouns (Henrys) and a few common nouns: *stand-bys, drys* (prohibitionists), *emptys* (bottles).

Words ending in *-y* preceded by a vowel merely add *-s:*

bays boys moneys [sometimes *monies*] monkeys toys

These plural forms should not be confused in writing with the genitive singular in *'s: beauty's, body's, caddy's,* and so on.

c) Words ending in *-o* preceded by a vowel make a regular plural with *-s: cameos, folios, radios, studios.*

Words ending in *-o* preceded by a consonant vary and have to be remembered or looked up in a dictionary. Some of the commoner of these are:

With *-s* only: banjos cantos dynamos Eskimos Filipinos pianos silos solos sopranos

With *-es:* echoes heroes Negroes noes potatoes tomatoes torpedoes vetoes

Several words ending in *-o* are used with either *-s* or *-es*. The *-es* form is usually the more common, but the increasing number of *-os* forms suggests that English is gradually reducing these irregular words to the regular plural form:

cargoes, cargos   desperadoes, desperados
zeros, zeroes   hoboes, hobos

d) Some common nouns ending in an *f* sound have their plural in *-ves:*

calf, calves	half, halves	knife, knives	leaf, leaves	wife, wives
self, selves	shelf, shelves	thief, thieves	loaf, loaves	wolf, wolves

But proper nouns do not: *Wolf, Wolfs.*

Many words ending in *f* sounds are regular:

beliefs   chiefs   dwarfs   fifes   gulfs   proofs   roofs

Some have two forms:

elf, elves–elfs   hoof, hoofs–hooves   scarf, scarfs–scarves
staff, staffs–staves   wharf, wharfs–wharves

2. *Same form for both singular and plural:*

Names of some animals: fowl, sheep, fish [*fishes* for varieties of fish]
All words in *-ics:* athletics, civics, mathematics, politics
Common measurements: foot, pair, ton
A number of words rarely, if ever, used in the singular:

barracks	headquarters	odds [in betting]	smallpox
bellows	means	pants	species
billiards	measles	pincers	tactics
gallows	morals	scissors	trousers
goods	mumps	slacks	

3. *Survivals of older English plural forms:*

In *-en:* child, children   ox, oxen   brother, brethren [Church use]
Change of vowel: foot, feet   goose, geese   louse, lice   man, men
mouse, mice   tooth, teeth   woman, women

4. *Foreign language plurals.* English keeps the foreign form of many words that have been borrowed from other languages. As they become more commonly used, the plural is usually formed regularly in *-s;* words used chiefly in scientific or Formal writing tend to keep the foreign form longer. *Antenna,* for instance, makes *antennae* in biology but *antennas* for the more common radio and television use. When the word is in transition, both forms will be found.

A few borrowed words that now regularly have plurals in *-s* or *-es* will suggest the extent of the change to English forms:

area	campus	encyclopedia	museum
arena	circus	era	panacea
asylum	dilemma	ignoramus	panorama
bonus	diploma	metropolis	plateau
bureau	dogma	minus	quota

Some common words that still have the foreign form or sometimes are found with the foreign plural (as in Formal, academic, or scientific writing) are:

addendum -da
alumna -nae
*alumnus -ni
ameba -bae, -bas
analysis -ses
apparatus -tus, -tuses
appendix -dixes, -dices
automaton -ta, -tons
axis axes
bacillus -li
basis bases
*beau beaus [beaux]
cactus -ti, -tuses
chateau -teaus, -teaux
cherub cherubs, cherubim (scriptural)
crisis crises
criterion -teria
curriculum -lums, -la
datum *data
diagnosis -ses
erratum -ta
focus -ci (scientific), -cuses (General)
*formula -las, -lae
fungus -gi, -guses
*gladiolus -luses, -li
hiatus -tuses, hiatus
hypothesis -ses
index indexes, indices
larva -vae
libretto -tos, -ti
locus loci
madame mesdames
matrix -trixes, -trices
*medium -dia, -diums
memorandum -da, -dums
momentum -tums, -ta
monsieur messieurs
moratorium -iums, -ia
nebula -las, -lae
neurosis -ses
nucleus -clei, -cleuses
oasis oases
opus opera
ovum ova
parenthesis -ses
psychosis -ses
radius radii, radiuses
rostrum -trums, -tra
species species
stadium -diums, -dia
stimulus -li
stratum -ta, -tums
syllabus -bi, buses
synopsis -ses
synthesis -ses
tableau -bleaus, -bleaux
terminus -nuses, -ni
thesis -ses
trousseau -seaus, -seaux
vertebra -brae, -bras
vortex -tices, -texes

5. *Compound and group words.* Most compound words and group words add *-s* to the end of the group, whether written as one word or several:

attorney generals (or attorneys general) bookcases high schools
cross examinations postmaster generals (or postmasters general)

In a few the plural sign is added to the first element:

daughters-in-law kings of England mothers-in-law passers-by
poets laureate (also, poet laureates) sons-in-law

6. *Plurals of figures, words, letters.* Usually the plural of a letter of the alphabet, of a word discussed as a word, or of a figure is written with *-'s:*

There are two *c*'s and two *m*'s in *accommodate.*
Three 2's six 8's
Don't use several *that*'s in a row.

But usage is divided and the plural of figures and capital letters especially is increasingly made with *-s* alone:

three 2s six 8s two Cs and two Fs

And there are few more useful practical suggestions in composition than this: Use no more *ands* or *buts* than you can help.—BARRETT WENDELL, *English Composition,* p. 145

7. *Plural substitutes.* A plural notion is expressed often by a phrase that remains grammatically singular:

College after college has gone in for intramural sports.

The coach, with the captain and manager, makes up the schedule

The coach, together with the captain and manager, makes [often *make*] up the schedule.

Singular and plural constructions are treated in *Subject and verb, *Reference of pronouns.

References: Curme, *Parts of Speech,* pages 112-127, *Syntax,* pages 539-548; Fries, *AEG,* page 40 ff.

Poetry When verse is quoted, it should be lined off as written. If possible, the quoted lines should be approximately centered on the page, indented according to the scheme of the original. When so spaced, quotation marks are not needed around lines of verse quoted in prose. The first word of each line should be capitalized if it was capitalized in the original. (See *Verse form for English meters.)

politics is construed as either a singular or plural word but should not be both in the same passage.

In almost any group, politics is a subject which will arouse controversy.

Republican politics were offensive to the Federalists.

Positive degree of adjectives and adverbs is the simple adjective form (*poor, high, golden*) or adverb form (*slow, slowly, bitterly*). See *Comparison of adjectives and adverbs.

Possessive adjective *My, your, his, her, its, our, your, their* (the genitive case forms of the personal pronouns) are often called possessive adjectives when they modify a noun:

my car   his first lecture   their experiences

practical *Practical* and its derivatives give some trouble in spelling:

practical, adjective: a practical scheme, He has a practical mind.

practically, adverb: They were practically inclined. (Informal in phrases like "practically all there")

practicable, adjective: a practicable method.

practicability, noun: They questioned the practicability of the idea.

pre- The prefix *pre-,* meaning *before* in time (*pre-exist, pre-Victorian*), or in place (*precerebral*), or rank (*pre-eminent*), is separated by a hyphen from the root to which it is joined: (1) when the root begins with *e: pre-election, pre-eminent, pre-empt, pre-engaged, pre-existence;* and (2) when the root is a proper name: *pre-American, pre-Elizabethan, pre-Raphaelite.* To other words it is joined directly: *prearrange, preoccupied, preheat, preprint, preview, prewar, predate, prevision, presuppose.*

Précis A *précis* (prā′sē) is a concise summary of facts or, more often, of an article or other written document, giving in a brief space the essential content, the attitudes, and the emphasis of the original.

Precious, preciosity Applied to style, *precious* and *preciosity* (or *preciousness*) mean "excessive attention to, fastidiousness in the use of words." The terms were borrowed from French and, though sometimes useful, have limited currency.

Predicate The predicate of a clause or sentence is the verb with its modifiers, object, complement, etc., and predication is the function of a full verb in a clause or sentence. The subject and predicate are the two main elements of a sentence. The predicate may be a simple verb of complete meaning (The big bell *tolled*), a verb and adverbial modifier (The sun *went behind the cloud*), a transitive verb and its object (He *finally landed the big fish*), a *linking verb and complement (The oldest member of a family *is usually the first to go*).

Two verbs depending upon one subject are known as a *compound predicate:

The three of them *washed* and *wiped* the whole lot in fifteen minutes.

(See *Subject and verb, *Compound sentences, Ch. 2, "Complex Sentences," p. 50, and Ch. 7, "Reducing predication," p. 189.)

Predicate adjective, Predicate noun Revision: Use an adjective here, since the verb is a linking verb. *P Adj*

Adjectives and nouns that follow linking verbs are called predicate adjectives and predicate nouns (or nominatives):

Predicate adjective: The horse is *fast*. I feel *bad*. It is going to turn *warm*. It got *colder*. That one is *best*.

Predicate noun: Gibbon was a *historian*. Jackson became a *doctor*.

(See *Linking verbs and Ch. 3, "Predicate adjectives," p. 90.)

predominant is the adjective: "a predominant sentiment," "a sentiment predominant in the village." *Predominate* is the verb: "This sentiment predominated in the village." The present participle *predominating* is often used adjectivally. These words are heavy for *prevailing, prevail,* or some such word.

prefer *To* is ordinarily used with *prefer:*

I prefer *Babbitt* to *Main Street.*
He preferred going by train to going in their car.

**Had* (or *would*) *rather . . . than* is less Formal and more used:

He *had* [or *would* or *He'd*] rather go by train than in their car.

Prefix A prefix is an element that can be placed before a word or root to make another word with a different meaning or function: *anti-* (*antiprohibition*), *bi-* (*biweekly*), *mis-* (*misfit*). See *Origin of words § 3a.

Prepositional phrase A phrase made up of a preposition and its object: *without hope, in a hurry, toward a more abundant life.*

Prepositional phrases are modifiers, used in the functions of adverbs or adjectives:

They came *at just the right time.* (Adverbial modifier)
He lives *in the white house.* (Adverbial modifier)
The woman *in the black dress* has left. (Adjective modifier)

To suggest the importance of prepositional phrases in English, here is a sentence of forty-two words in which twenty-seven stand in prepositional phrases (in italics), fifteen in other constructions:

The settings *of the novels* ranged *from the fiords of Norway to the coasts of Tasmania,* and every page betrayed that intimate knowledge *of a foreign country* which can only be acquired *by a thorough study of the chattier sort of guide-books.*—STEPHEN VINCENT BENÉT, *Thirteen O'Clock,* p. 71

Prepositions Revision: Change the preposition, making it more exact or idiomatic (§ 3a), less conspicuous (§ 3b), or making the construction less Informal (§ 3, d).

Prep

1. *Definitions.* 2. *List of prepositions.* 3. *Uses of prepositions.*

1. *Definitions.* The principal function of a preposition is to signal the unity of the phrase it introduces: *in turn, after the first try, for a long time.* The phrase then takes its place in a sentence as a unit, and the preposition, partly through its meaning, helps relate it to some other sentence element: to a verb (He showed her *to* her room), to a noun (the click *of* flying wheels), or to an adjective (old *in* experience). A noun following a preposition is called its object (*room, wheels, experience* in the examples just given). Prepositions may be word groups as well as single words: *in regard to, according to.* Many words used as prepositions are also used as adverbs or conjunctions, and some, like *after, but, since,* serve in the functions of all three parts of speech:

Preposition: The wettest summer *since* the Flood.
Conjunction: *Since* the price was so low, we took three.
Adverb: He hasn't been around *since.*

For this reason some grammarians group these three types of words as *particles* with varying functions. In this article and the ones on conjunctions and adverbs we shall not draw the lines very closely.

There has lately been a tendency to minimize the meaning of prepositions. In concrete senses they carry as much meaning as other words: being *under* a bed is quite different from being *on* a bed. Even in more abstract contexts, prepositions have meaning, though it may seem more arbitrary: *beneath* contempt, *for* love, *in* or *with* haste, agree *to* a proposal or *with* a person. These meanings, like those of abstract nouns, are learned in a context of language rather than of physical experience, but none the less learned.

2. *List of prepositions.* The following list shows characteristic uses of the commoner prepositions. Many of them show both a concrete and an abstract meaning (*at* home, *at* odds). Fries estimates that nine of them (*at, by, for, from, in, of, on, to, with*) account for over 92% of prepositions used.

aboard aboard the airliner (Formal: on board)
about about the town, about her, about his work
**above* above the clouds, above the average, above suspicion
according to according to the reports, according to Hoyle
across across the bow, across the street
after after dark, we all ran after him (Technical: of a drawing based on another's drawing–after Newcourt)
against against the door, against the grain
ahead of ahead of his generation, ahead of time
along along the shore, along the route
alongside alongside the dock (Informal: alongside of)
amid (*amidst*) Formal: amid the smoke, amidst the ruins
among among the lucky ones (used of three or more)
apart from apart from the others, apart from his own earnings (rather Formal)
apropos Formal: apropos our discussion; or, apropos of our discussion
around around the edge, around the town
as far as as far as the door, as far as New Orleans
**as to* as to the objection, as to your interest
at at home, at Johnstown, at his suggestion, at midnight
back of back of the screen, back of the house, back of the proposal
because of because of the war, because of his need
before before the flood, before an audience, before replying
behind behind the door, behind the pretense
below below the surface, below our level
beneath beneath the surface, beneath contempt (more Formal than *below*)
**beside* beside the sea, beside the point, beside oneself
besides besides those named, no other besides this
**between* between New York and Philadelphia, between life and death
beyond beyond the river, beyond reach, beyond my understanding
by by the house, by an inch, by force, by himself, by night
concerning concerning my friend, concerning our interests
contrary to contrary to orders, contrary to our expectation
despite Formal: despite hostile criticism
down down the chute, down the slope, down the list
**due to* due to an error, due to carelessness
during during the last ten years, during the services
for for you, for profit, for the community
from from the attic, from the Far East, from fear
in in the country, in the house, in the Bible, in trouble
in place of in place of the old regulations
inside inside the house, inside ten minutes (Often, somewhat Informally, *inside of:* inside of ten minutes)
in spite of in spite of the law, in spite of his prejudices
in view of in view of these concessions
into into the mountains, into the subject (*in–into–in to)

like like a horse, like a tornado
near near the window, near the top, near exhaustion
**of* of Wisconsin, of the same color, of my opinion, of the king
**off* off the path, off the platform (Redundant: off of the path)
on account of on account of the weather, on account of his belief
**onto* onto the train, onto the beach
out of out of the auditorium, out of sight
over over the fence, over the plains, over her head
owing to owing to the emergency, owing to our inability
past past the stores, past the mark, past the hour
**per* per day, per pound
round round the Maypole, round the town
since since his election, since Victorian days
through through the first barrier, through accident
throughout throughout the day, throughout his speech
**till* till morning, till the intermission
to to Los Angeles, to the ocean, to Governor Smith, to the point
**toward* toward Fort Worth, toward dinner time, toward the truth
under under the awning, under cover, under the arch
until until dusk, until two o'clock (*till, until, 'til)
unto Archaic: unto death, unto the last drop
up up the slope, up the scale
upon upon a sure foundation, upon further investigation
up to up to this point
via via the Nickel Plate
with with his fellows, with caution, with the affirmative
within within bounds, within the city, within a year

3. *Use of prepositions.*

a) Exact or idiomatic prepositions. A number of words are accompanied by certain prepositions, as contented *with* conditions, *in* my estimation. Some words have various meanings with different prepositions: agree *with* (a person), agree *to* (a suggestion), agree *in* (principles, qualities).

You can add indefinitely to the following list:

deprive *of* pleasure
eligible *for* membership
fascinated *by* this glamor
This glamor had fascination *for* him
fear *of* fire, fear *for* his safety
hindrance *to* advancement
impressed *by* (or *with*) his ability
means *of* winning
pride *in* his college
unconscious *of* their stares

The right preposition does not give much trouble with words that we use commonly, because we learn the words by hearing or seeing them in their usual constructions. Obviously it is safer to learn words as they are actually used, to learn *acquiesce in* (acquiesce in a decision) rather than just *acquiesce*. If a person uses an unidiomatic preposition, it is probably because he is not at home with the word or is confused because usage is divided on that particular locution (as *different *from* or *than* or *to*). Dictionaries give the appropriate preposition used with particular words. This book treats a few idioms that are likely to raise questions: *ability (to); *agree to, agree with; *all (of); *compare–contrast; *different.

A special reminder is needed that when two words are used which are completed by different prepositions *both* prepositions should be used, though in Informal speech the omission of the second preposition often passes unnoticed:

> The first lesson learned by the sturdy Italian boy just over from the "old country" was *obedience to* and *respect for* others besides his parents. (Not: obedience and respect *for* others)
>
> Some people cannot reconcile their *interest in* and their *fear of* snakes.
>
> The committee acknowledged its *interest in,* but denied its *responsibility for,* housing conditions.

When both words call for the same preposition, it need not be repeated:

> The box office refused to make any *allowance* or *refund for* tickets purchased from an agent.

b) Prepositions bulking too large. English has a number of group prepositions (*according to, in regard to, by means of*) that sometimes become conspicuous because they bulk too large for their purely functional work of showing relationship. They are not grammatically wrong, but used in any noticeable numbers they tend to make a flat-footed style. For many of them a simple preposition can be substituted with real gain.

In these examples, sometimes one or more of the italicized words (in brackets) can be omitted or a simple preposition (in brackets) can be substituted:

> We made supper [*out*] *of* beans, fried potatoes, and steak.
>
> Consumers Union attempts to furnish reliable information *in regard to* [about] all sorts of goods and services.
>
> For politeness' sake the pronoun of the first person stands last when used [*in connection*] *with* other pronouns: "He, you, and I had better do it."
>
> It has been said that in six months after graduation from college a man can pick up as much practical knowledge *connected with* [of] business administration as a nongraduate can in ten years.
>
> . . . recent demonstrations *on the part of* [by] certain students . . . .

Prepositions sometimes bulk too large in writing because we carry over to paper our tendency in speech to use double prepositions when single ones would do the work: *in back of* for *back of, outside of* for *outside, off of* for *off*. . . . These are not appropriate in Formal English, which at its best makes one word do its exact duty, but may be in order in Informal English if they help give an easy tone and if they do not become too noticeable. The writer should decide whether these idioms are appropriate to other traits of his style. (For further examples and discussion see the articles *as to, *of, off, *onto, and so on.)

c) Omission of prepositions. Spoken English shows not only a frequent piling up of prepositions but the opposite tendency too–dropping a preposition that would ordinarily be used in writing. Prepositions, especially *of,* receive so little stress that they naturally drop out entirely in rapid speech, and this same trait is now increasingly found in writers whose style is conspicuously Informal. A few examples (with the preposition usual in General English in brackets) will suggest the tendency:

The color [of] cloth she preferred was out of stock.

The most notable piece of equipment was an apparatus which made it possible to run the presses [at] almost twice their former speed.

A *couple [of] days later....

d) Preposition at end of sentence. It was once fashionable for textbooks to put a stigma upon prepositions standing at the end of their constructions (What did you do it *for?*). But postponing the preposition is a characteristic English idiom, even though it runs contrary to our usual tendency to keep words of a construction close together. In fact it is so generally the normal word order that the real danger is in clumsiness from trying to avoid a preposition at the end of a clause or sentence:

Tell me what it is to which you object [Natural: what you object to].

To whatever authority we may appeal, he will quibble over the method to be adopted [Natural: Whatever authority we may appeal to . . .].

Extreme cases are possible (like the boy's "What did you bring that book for me to be read to out of for?"), but there is no reason for hesitating to let a preposition fall at the end if natural idiom and rhythm place it there. (Often the final word is not a preposition but an adverb, as in the old saw "A preposition is a bad word to end a sentence with." Compare *Verb-adverb combinations.)

Placing the preposition at the end is such a firmly fixed habit that sometimes we use one at the beginning and at the end:

. . . in the lives of individuals *with* whom he had come in contact *with.*

Obviously such a sentence shows lack of revision.

References: Curme, *Syntax,* pages 566-569; Fowler, pages 457-459 and other index entries; Fries, *AEG,* Chapter 7; Hall, pages 213-217; M. Bertens Charnley, "The Syntax of Deferred Prepositions," *American Speech,* 1949, 24:268-277.

principal–principle Associate *principal* as an adjective (the *principal* reason–the *principal* man of the town–the *principal* force involved) with other adjectives ending in *-al:* historic*al,* politic*al,* music*al.*

Principal as a noun is probably an abbreviation of a phrase in which it was originally an adjective: the *principal* that draws interest was once *the principal sum;* the *principal* of a school, *the principal teacher;* the *principal* in a legal action, *the principal party;* the *principals* in the cast of a play or movie, *the principal actors*. These are the only common uses of *principal* as a noun.

The noun meaning a general truth (the *principles* of science) or a rule of conduct (a man of high *principles*) is *principle*.

Principal parts of verbs Revision: Change the verb form to the one in good use, as given in the list below or in a dictionary. *Prin*

The principal parts of a verb are the base form or infinitive (*ask*), the past tense form (*asked*), and the past participle (*asked*). Most English verbs are "regular"–that is, their past tense and past participle are formed by adding *-ed* to the base form. A number, most of them descended from Old English strong verbs (compare the strong verbs in modern German), make these parts by a change in vowel (*ride, rode, ridden*). Some of these are becoming regular (*shined, weaved*), and many are made regular in speech and Nonstandard usage (*blowed, growed*).

The following list includes a number of verbs with these irregular parts or with some other question of form. A form in parentheses is decidedly less common in writing, and those labeled NS (Nonstandard) would not ordinarily occur in current writing. A recent dictionary should be consulted for other verbs. But usage is by no means uniform, even among speakers and writers of Standard English, and dictionaries do not record all variations.

Infinitive	*Past tense*	*Past participle*
arise	arose	arisen
bear	bore	borne *born (given birth to)
begin	began (NS, begun)	begun (NS, began)
bid (to offer)	bid	bid
bid (order)	bade	bidden, bid
bite	bit	bitten, bit
blow	blew (NS, blowed)	blown (NS, blowed)
break	broke	broken (Inf. or NS, broke)
bring	brought (NS, brung)	brought (NS, brung)
*burst	burst	burst
catch	caught	caught
choose (chōōz)	chose (chōz)	chosen
come	came (NS, come)	come
dig	dug (archaic: digged)	dug
dive	*dove, dived	dived, dove
*do	did	done
draw	drew	drawn (NS, drawed)
dream	dreamed, dreamt	dreamed, dreamt

drink	drank (archaic and NS, drunk)	*drunk (drank–drunken)
*eat	ate (local and British: eat [et])	eaten (eat)
fall	fell	fallen
find	found	found
fit	fit, fitted	fit, fitted
flee	fled	fled
fly	flew	flown
forget	forgot	forgotten, forgot
freeze	froze	frozen (NS, froze)
*get	got	got, gotten
give	gave (NS, give)	given
go	went	gone (NS, went)
grow	grew (NS, growed)	grown
hang	hung	hung
hang (to execute)	hung, *hanged	hung, hanged
hear	heard	heard
knit	knitted, knit	knitted, knit
know	knew (NS, knowed)	known
*lay	laid	laid
lead	led	led
lend (*loan)	lent	lent
let	let	let
lie (see *lay)	*lay	lain
light	*lighted, lit	lighted, lit
lose	lost	lost
pay	*paid (of ropes: payed)	paid (payed)
plead	pleaded, plead, pled	pleaded, plead, pled (the second and third forms pronounced pled)
prove	proved	*proved, proven
ride	rode	ridden
ring	rang, rung	rung
rise	rose	risen
run	ran (NS, run)	run
say	said	said
see	saw	seen
set	set	set
shine	shone, shined	shone, shined
show	showed	showed, shown
shrink	shrunk, shrank	shrunk
sing	sang, sung	sung
sink	sank, sunk	sunk
sit	sat (NS, set)	sat (NS, set)
slide	slid	slid (slidden)
sow	sowed	sown, sowed
speak	spoke	spoken
spit	spit, spat	spit, spat
spring	sprang, sprung	sprung
stand	stood	stood

steal	stole	stolen
stink	stunk, stank	stunk
sweat	sweated, sweat	sweated, sweat
swim	swam, swum	swum
take	took	taken
tear	tore	torn
throw	threw (NS, throwed)	thrown
tread	trod	trodden, trod
wake	waked, woke	waked, woke (woken)
wear	wore	worn
weave	wove (weaved)	woven, wove
win	won	won
wind (wīnd)	wound (nautical: winded)	wound
wring	wrung	wrung
write	wrote (archaic, writ)	written (NS, wrote; archaic: writ)

The evidence of the *Linguistic Atlas of the United States* is already providing for revision of some of these descriptions. The past participle *drank* is much more prevalent in Standard English, especially in New England, than dictionaries suggest (Walter S. Avis, "The Past Participle of *Drank:* Standard American English?" *American Speech,* 1953, 28:106-111); and *shrunk* seems to be more common than *shrank* (H. B. Allen, "Current English Forum," *College English,* 1957, 18:283); both popular and Standard usage favor *knit, laid, pled, fit,* and *sweat* as the past tense forms of *knit, lie, plead, fit,* and *sweat* (E. Bagby Atwood, *A Survey of Verb Forms in the Eastern United States,* Ann Arbor, 1953).

References: Fries, *AEG,* pages 59-71; Mencken, page 430 ff.

prior to Heavy for *before:* Prior to (Before) coming here he had been at Stanford.

process, procedure, proceed *Process* and *procedure,* the nouns, are spelled with one *e* after the *c; proceed,* the verb, has two *e*'s. (The spelling situation is further confused by the verb *precede.*) The pronunciation prō′ses is British rather than American; say pros′es. Pros′ə sēz is usually an affectation for the plural, say pros′es əz.

Proceed means "to go," strictly in a rather formal fashion, and is best kept for movement (We proceeded at a decent rate of speed). "We proceeded to unpack" usually means no more than "We unpacked" or "Then we unpacked."

Profanity Styles change in the handling of cuss words and profanity. At present most writers, most editors, and most publishers are liberal, much more liberal than formerly. In fiction, where the words represent a character, simply be sure they are fitting and called for. Both cussing and cursing are primarily oral, matters of muscular release more than of meaning, and in print they often attract more attention to themselves than they deserve. You can't put on paper all the vulgarity proper to a vulgar person's speech; the effect will be suggested by an occasional sample. In biography, criticism, and miscellaneous informational articles you have less freedom. There double dashes and euphemistic blankety-blanks are more likely to be found. Such devices ordinarily give the impression of a writer who is playing at being tough or who hasn't the courage to use language he believes is really appropriate. Use the expressions the subject seriously calls for, compromising as little or as much as your temperament and circumstance demand. In matter submitted to magazines, editors will make whatever alterations their policies demand.

Professor Write:

Professor Tewksbury [or] Prof. E. W. Tewksbury
[or] E. W. Tewksbury, a professor of electrical engineering
[or, as a formal title] E. W. Tewksbury, Professor of Electrical Engineering

The colloquial *prof* is a clipped word, not an abbreviation, and if it is written should not have a period:

He said all profs were a little crazy anyway.

Strictly speaking *professor* should be confined to names of assistant professors, associate professors, and professors. When the title comes before the name (without the *of* phrase), Professor is used for all three ranks; when it follows the name and has the *of* phrase, the exact rank is usually indicated: *Professor A. B. Plant; A. B. Plant, Assistant Professor of English.* Applying it to instructors is sometimes a well meant courtesy but more often carelessness. In official and business usage an *instructor* who has a doctor's degree is often addressed as *doctor,* though now that so many teachers have the degree, the title has lost its distinction. It would be better to address all teachers as *Mr.* or *Miss* or *Mrs.*–as many professors would prefer; but students should follow the conventions of their own campus.

Progressive verb forms is a grammatical term applied to the verb phrases made with *to be* and the present participle: I am asking, he was asking, they have been asking. (See *Tenses of verbs, *Verbs.)

Pronominal adjectives Several types of pronouns, used also like adjectives, are called pronominal adjectives:

Interrogative:	*Which* way did he go?			
Demonstrative:	*that* way	*this* book	*those* boys	
Possessive:	*my* hat	*his* idea	*your* dog	*their* seats
Indefinite:	*some* people	*each* person	*all* men	

Pronouns, types and forms Revision: Change the form of the pronoun marked to the one expected in the grammatical construction in which it stands.

Pron

1. *The personal pronouns.* 2. *Relative pronouns.* 3. *Interrogative pronouns.* 4. *Reflexive pronouns.* 5. *Reciprocal pronouns.* 6. *Numeral*

pronouns. 7. *Demonstrative pronouns.* 8. *Indefinite pronouns.* 9. *Impersonal pronouns.*

Pronouns in the English language are hard to define because traditionally this part of speech includes several groups of quite different words. They all are used in the principal syntactical functions of nouns, serving as subjects and objects, and a number have genitives. Perhaps it is enough to say that a pronoun is a word that can be replaced by a noun in a specific context. Many, like nouns, have an *s* genitive and also a plural.

The uses of pronouns are described in *Reference of pronouns. This article lists the various types of pronouns and their forms.

1. *The personal pronouns.* Some of the most common grammatical problems come from the fact that separate nominative and accusative case forms survive for personal and relative pronouns though not for nouns (*between you and me, *It's me, *who, whom §§ 2, 3).

		Nominative	*Genitive*	*Accusative*
1st person	Singular:	*I	my, mine	me
	Plural:	we	our, ours	us
2d person	Singular:	you	your, yours	you
	Plural:	you	your, yours	you
3d person	Singular:			
	masculine:	he	his	him
	feminine:	she	her, hers	her
	neuter:	*it	its (of it)	it
	either gender:	*one	one's	one
	Plural:	they	their, theirs	them

Archaic forms of the second person singular, *thou, thy* or *thine, thee,* are used only in religious services, by the Society of Friends (*thee* only), and occasionally in poetry.

Mine, formerly used before words beginning with a vowel or *h* (*mine eyes, mine help*), is no longer so used: *my eyes, my help.* The emphatic form of the genitive is used without a noun, rarely directly after a noun:

The money is *mine* [*ours, yours, hers, theirs*].
Yours came a whole week before *mine.*
Baby *mine.*

2. *Relative pronouns.*

Nominative	*Genitive*	*Accusative*
*who	whose	whom
*that	of that	that
*which	of which, whose	which, whom

Whoever, whichever, whatever (and archaic: *whosoever, whichsoever, whatsoever*) are less definite than the simple relatives and may have an accent of surprise, emphasis, or playfulness.

3. *Interrogative pronouns.* *who, *which, what; occasionally whoever, whatever

4. *Reflexive pronouns.* Reflexive or intensive pronouns are made of the personal pronouns plus the suffix *-self* or *-selves.* The formations are irregular; the suffix is added to *my, our, your* (genitive); *him, them* (accusative); *her, it* [*s*]. They are called reflexive because the action of the verb is directed toward the subject of the construction: He shaves *himself;* She bought *herself* two hats. (See *himself, herself, *myself.)

When used as intensives, these words are usually construed as pronouns in apposition:

The mayor himself delivered the address.
I can finish the job myself.

5. *Reciprocal pronouns.* See *each other; one another (Formal).

6. *Numeral pronouns.* The cardinal numbers (one, two, three ...) and the ordinals (first, second, third ...) are used as pronouns: *Three* were there; The *eighth* won.

7. *Demonstrative pronouns.*

*this, these   *that, those   (Compare *kind, sort)
the *former, the latter, the first, the second ...
*such, *so (I told you so)   *same

8. *Indefinite pronouns.* A large number of words, of greater or less indefiniteness, often function as pronouns:

all	everybody (*every § 2)	nothing
another	everyone	*one, oneself
*any	everything	other
anybody	few	several
anyone	many	*some
anything	much	somebody
*both	neither	someone
*each	*nobody	something
each one	*none	*such
either	no one	

9. *Impersonal pronouns.* See *it.

Questions on the uses of pronouns are discussed in *Reference of pronouns. References: Curme, *Parts of Speech,* Chapter 10; *Syntax,* index references; Fries, *AEG,* index references.

Pronunciation 1. *Pronunciation key.* The pronunciation of words is indicated in this *Guide and Index* by respelling them with the letters and diacritic marks (with some few exceptions) used in the Thorndike-Barnhart Dictionaries, as follows:

a	apple (ap′əl), fact (fakt)
ā	age (āj), say (sā), inflate (in flāt′)
ä	far (fär), father (fä′ŧħər)
b	back (bak), robber (rob′ər)
ch	child (chīld), church (chûrch)

d	do (do͞o), did (did)
e	bet (bet), effect (i fekt′)
ē	equal (ē′kwəl), see (sē), police (pə lēs′)
f	fat (fat), stuff (stuf)
g	go (gō), baggage (bag′ij)
h	hotel (hō tel′), boyhood (boi′hood)
hw	wheel (hwēl), whether (hwet̶h̶′ər)
i	if (if), pithy (pith′i)
ī	ice (īs), buy (bī)
j	jam (jam), edge (ej), age (āj)
k	king (king), back (bak), cocoa (kō′kō)
l	life (līf), silly (sil′i), fill (fil)
m	am (am), meet (mēt), sample (sam′pəl)
n	note (nōt), inner (in′ər)
ng	sing (sing), song (sông)
o	rock (rok), stop (stop)
ō	open (ō′pən), hope (hōp), go (gō)
ô	bought (bôt), ball (bôl), caught (kôt), four (fôr)
oi	voice (vois), boil (boil)
oo	book (book), put (poot)
o͞o	tool (to͞ol), rule (ro͞ol), move (mo͞ov)
ou	house (hous), out (out), cow (kou)
p	paper (pā′pər), cap (kap)
r	reach (rēch), try (trī), tired (tīrd), door (dōr)
s	say (sā), listen (lis′ən), yes (yes)
sh	she (shē), rush (rush), cushion (koosh′ən)
t	tie (tī), sit (sit), kitten (kit′ən)
th	thin (thin), both (bōth), bath (bath)
t̶h̶	that (t̶h̶at), bother (bot̶h̶′ər), bathe (bāt̶h̶)
u	cup (kup), butter (but′ər)
ū	useful (ūs′fəl), music (mū′zik) [begins with a *y* sound]
û	urge (ûrge), bird (bûrd), term (tûrm)
v	very (ver′i), salve (sav or säv), save (sāv)
w	will (wil), with (wit̶h̶ or with), won't (wōnt)
y	young (yung), yellow (yel′ō)
z	zero (zir′ō), breeze (brēz), trees (trēz)
zh	measure (mezh′ər), rouge (ro͞ozh)
ə	Called schwa (shwä), represents the indefinite vowel sound of many unstressed syllables. It is variously spelled: *a* in *sofa* (sō′fə), *e* in *secretary* (sek′rə ter′i), and by the other vowels and combinations of vowels.
ḷ, ṃ, ṇ, ṛ	Syllabic consonants, used in unstressed syllables when no vowel sound can be distinguished: little (lit′ḷ), wooden (wood′ṇ). When spoken slowly these syllables have ə, and are sometimes so respelled.

The stress of syllables is represented by a ′ for a main stress and a ′ for a lighter stress, placed after the stressed syllable; ag′ri kul′chər.

A vowel sound in a stressed syllable will be more fully sounded than in one without stress (contrast the *o* of *below* [bi lō′] and of *obey* [which ranges from ō bā′ to ə bā′]. In unstressed syllables they tend to become the "neutral vowel" (ə) as in the italicized vowels in *a*gain, acad*e*my, dorm*i*tory, curs*o*ry, circ*u*s. (For suggestions on spelling such words see *Neutral vowel.)

An *r* following a vowel changes the vowel's sound, as in *care, sere, core, sure,* but a separate symbol is not used to represent the change: kar, sēr, kōr, sho͞or.

Further details of the sounds represented by each letter of the alphabet, with examples, will be found in the articles on the separate letters, *A, *B, *C, and so on, in this *Index.*

2. *Special points in pronunciation.*

a) Stress. In general, English is a rather strongly stressed (accented) language. The force of the stress varies a good deal among individual speakers. The stress of particular words (*detail, *address) varies with their meaning and with their position in sentences. (See also *Noun and verb stress.)

b) Secondary stress. A word of three or especially of four syllables is likely to have a main and a secondary stress: *secondary* sek′ən der′i, *incidental* in′sə den′tel. One of the differences between British and American pronunciation is that we tend to keep secondary stresses in many words in which the British have but one:

necessary: American nes′ə ser′i; British nes′əs ri
dictionary: American dik′shə ner′i; British dik′shn̩ ri

A few Americans foolishly attempt to follow the British shortening of such words, in the belief that the shorter pronunciation is the more genteel.

c) Pronunciation and spelling. Words really live in their oral forms, and any guide to pronunciation must start with the spoken words, not the written. But our spelling represents, roughly at least, the sounds of words, or often it represents the sounds they once had.

When words are acquired from reading rather than from hearing, they are very often overpronounced, in what are known as "spelling pronunciations." *Sophomore* on most campuses is two syllables, sof′mōr, but people who see it more than they hear it are likely to sound the middle *o* slightly (sof′ə mōr); *yearling* is yûr′ling where it is regularly used, yēr′ling as a spelling pronunciation. Spelling pronunciation may introduce sounds that are not in the Standard pronunciation of the word (*soften* as sof′tən). Sometimes these pronunciations become acceptable, usually as a minor pronunciation (*often* as of′tən), occasionally even forcing out the older established pronunciation (*Indian,* formerly in′jən). Genuine familiarity with words is shown by using the oral rather than the spelling pronunciation.

3. *Standards of pronunciation.* Standard written English is the same in all parts of the United States. But standard speech varies somewhat in different parts of our country and is basically that of the educated people of the region. It shows some regional qualities, though less than the speech of uneducated people. (See Ch. 1, "Variations due to place," p. 8.)

A person's pronunciation should be appropriate as far as possible to the situation in which he is speaking. The elaborateness of "stage" pronunciation is out of place in conversation, even in "cultivated" conversation. Too conscious attention to pronunciation will handicap the speaker and irritate the listener. Pronunciation in speaking to groups must necessarily be somewhat slower, more distinct, but fundamentally it is a refinement of the speaker's better conversational style.

The problem of a person going to live in a different part of the country is more complex. Should he drop his native speech and do as the Romans do? If he makes a specific and hasty effort to pick up the new speech, he will be almost sure to make mistakes–that is, he will confuse the two. If he can stand off the first attacks on his speech-ways, he will soon find that he will attract less attention. Then he will naturally acquire, bit by bit and without forcing, many of the new ways. He need not be ashamed of honest traces remaining of his native speech.

The words to worry about are not those in everyday use so much as the new ones acquired in taking up new work or a new social status or new ideas or, in college, new subjects of study. Care should be taken to get a conventional pronunciation of these new words (*acclimate, desultory, schizophrenic* . . .) as they are learned, to be at home with them from the beginning.

As Fowler puts it (p. 466), "The broad principles are: Pronounce as your neighbours do, not better." For the majority of words, your neighbors are the general public. For words in more restricted use, your neighbors are the group that uses them. Consequently there will be more local flavor in General and Informal speech, less in speaking to limited and special audiences. It is more important to avoid Nonstandard pronunciations than the regional pronunciations of educated people.

4. *Pronunciation list.* The following list is in part to raise questions of pronunciation. The pronunciations suggested should be tested by comparing them with those you hear. For most words that raise questions of pronunciation, consult a good recent dictionary.

Pronunciations of other words will be found in the articles on each letter of the alphabet, *Foreign words in English, *Spelling, *Proper names, and in various articles on particular words.

When two forms are given, no choice is implied; a distinctly less common form stands in brackets. A large number of words are spoken in two or more ways in good usage.

An * means that there is a separate entry on that word.

abdomen ab′də mən, ab dō′mən
absorb ab sôrb′, ab zôrb′
absurd ab sûrd′ [ab zûrd′]
acclimate ə klī′mit, ak′lə māt
adult ə dult′, ad′ult
advertisement ad vûr′tiz mənt, ad vûr′tis mənt, ad′vər tīz′mənt
ally (noun) al′ī, ə lī′; plural more often ə līz′; verb ə lī′

*alma mater al′mə mā′ter,
  al′mə mä′tər [äl′mə mä′tər]
alternate (verb) ôl′tər nāt,
  al′tər nāt;
  (adjective) ôl′tər nit, al′tər nit
amateur am′ə choor, am′ə chər,
  am′ə tyoor, am′ə tûr′
apparatus ap′ə rā′təs, ap′ə rat′əs
applicable ap′lə kə bəl,
  ə plik′ə bəl
Aryan ar yən, ar i ən
atypical ə tip′ə kəl, ā tip′ə kəl
  (See *a-)
aviation ā′vi ā′shn̩,
  av′i ā′shn̩
aye (yes) ī
bade bad
*biography bī og′rə fi, bi og′rə fi
bureaucracy bū rok′rə si
business biz′nis
chauffeur shō′fər, shō fûr′
chic shēk, shik [chik]
combatant kəm bat′ənt,
  kom′bə tənt
*contents kon′tents [kən tents′]
coup ko͞o [ko͞op]
coupon ko͞o′pon, kū′pon
coyote kī ō′tē, kī′ōt
*data dā′tə, dat′ə, dä′tə
debut di bū′, dā′bū, deb′ū
decade dek′ād, de kād′, dek′əd
desperado des′pər ā′dō,
  des′pər ä′dō
diphtheria dif thir′i ə, dip thir′i ə
diphthong dif′thông, dif′thong,
  dip′thong
disputable dis pūt′ə bl̩,
  dis′pū tə bl̩
drama drä′mə, dram′ə [drā′mə]
*economics ē′kə nom′iks,
  ek′ə nom′iks
*either ē′t͟hər [ī′t͟hər]
electricity i lek′tris′ə ti,
  ē′lek tris′ə ti
Elizabethan i liz′ə bē′thn̩,
  i liz′ə beth′ n̩
err ûr [er]
exquisite eks′kwi zit, iks kwiz′it
finance fə nans′, fī′nans, fi nans′
formidable fôr′mə də bəl
fortnight fôrt′nīt, fôrt′nit
gibbous gib′əs
*gladiolus glad′i ō′ləs,
  glə dī′ə ləs
gunwale gun′əl
harass har′əs, hə ras′
heinous hā′nəs
*human hū′mən [ū′mən]
idea ī dē′ə [ī′di ə]
impious im′pi əs
indict in dīt′
isolate ī′sə lāt, is′ə lāt
juvenile jo͞o′və nəl, jo͞o′və nīl
kimono kə mō′nə [kə mō′nō]
laugh laf, läf (*A § 4)
launch lônch, länch
*leisure lē′zhər, lezh′ər
lever lev′ər, lē′vər
lilacs lī′ləks, lī′laks
matrix mat′riks, mā′triks
menu men′ū, mā′nū
mischievous mis′chə vəs
news no͞oz, nūz
oasis ō ā′sis, ō′ə sis
orgy ôr′ji
parliament pär′lə mənt
patriot pā′tri ət, pā′tri ot
  [pat′ri ət]
penalize pē′nəl īz, pen′əl īz
percolator pûr′kə lā′tər
*pianist pi an′ist, pē′ə nist
pleasure plezh′ər, plā′zhər
premier pri mir′, prē′mi ər
presentation prez′n̩ tā′shn̩,
  prē′zn̩ tā′shn̩
process pros′es, prō′ses
pronunciation prə nun′si ā′shn̩
quay kē
ratio rā′shi ō, rā′shō
real rē′əl, rēl
reel rēl
research ri sûrch′, rē′sûrch
rodeo rō′di ō, rō dā′ō
rotogravure rō′tə grə vyoor′,
  rō′tə grā′vyoor
*route ro͞ot, rout
sociology sō′si ol′ə ji,
  sō′shi ol′ə ji
strictly strikt′li, strik′li
sumac so͞o′mak, sho͞o′mak

the thə, thi [thē]
tomato tə mā′tō, tə mä′tō, [tə mat′ō]
usage ūs′ij, ūz′ij
vaudeville vôd′ə vil, vōd′vil, vôd′vil
white hwīt, [wīt]
worsted (yarn) woos′tid

References: Kenyon and Knott; J. S. Kenyon, *American Pronunciation* (Ann Arbor, 1957); C. K. Thomas, *Phonetics of American English* (New York, 1947); *Webster's New International Dictionary,* second edition, especially the "Guide to Pronunciation."

Proofreading A check of copy is the last act before giving a manuscript to anyone for serious consideration. Proofreading the final copy

Proofreader's Marks

℘	Delete
℘̑	Delete and close up
𝔬	Reverse
⌒	Close up
#	Insert space
⌒/#	Close up and insert space
¶	Paragraph
□	Indent 1 em
⊏	Move to left
⊐	Move to right
⊔	Lower
⊓	Raise
∧	Insert marginal addition
V∧	Space evenly
✗	Broken letter—used in margin
⊥	Push down space
=	Straighten line
‖	Align type
∧,	Insert comma
∨'	Insert apostrophe
∨"	Insert quotation mark
=/	Insert hyphen
em/	Insert em dash
en/	Insert en dash
∧;	Insert semicolon
⊙:	Insert colon and en quad
⊙	Insert period and en quad
?/	Insert interrogation point
ⓠ	Query to author
⌒	Use ligature
Ⓢⓟ	Spell out
tr	Transpose
wf	Wrong font
bf	Set in **bold face** type
rom	Set in roman type
ital	Set in *italic* type
caps	Set in CAPITALS
sc	Set in SMALL CAPITALS
lc	Set in lower case
X	Lower-case letter
stet	Let it stand; restore words crossed out
no ¶	Run in same paragraph
ld in	Insert lead between lines
hr #	Hair space between letters

From *A Manual of Style,* The University of Chicago Press.

of a theme for mechanical mistakes that may have slipped in while copying it is an important part of the work in a composition course—and one that pays dividends.

After copy has been set in type it must be checked for typographical and other mistakes before it is ready to be printed. A tentative print is made on long sheets known as *galley proof*. After the type has been corrected and made up into the pages which are to be finally printed, *page proofs* are taken and read for a last check.

Corrections are indicated in proof by abbreviations and symbols placed at one side of the line to be changed, with a *caret (∧) inserted at the exact point in the line where the change is to be made. Proofreader's marks are illustrated on page 657. See publishers' stylebooks for further details.

Proper adjectives Proper nouns used like adjectives and adjectives directly derived from proper names and still referring to the place or person are capitalized. After proper adjectives lose the reference to their origins, they become simple adjectives and are no longer capitalized:

the French language American interests
the Indian service, but india ink
a Paris (or Parisian) café, but paris green
the Roman Forum, but roman type

Languages differ in their practices of capitalizing, so that students learning foreign languages should be careful to keep the English and foreign practices separated.

Proper names Considerable care needs to be taken to spell and pronounce the names of people, places, companies, institutions as the people most concerned with them wish to have them spelled and pronounced. Many are rare or in some way unusual—*Thames* (temz), *Worcester* (woos′tər), *San Joaquin* (san′wô kēn′). Analogy cannot be relied on: it is Waco (wā′kō), Texas, but Saco (saw′kō), Maine. *Cairo* is kī′rō for Egypt, kā′rō for Illinois.

In place names the recommendation to use the pronunciation current in the place is complicated because the inhabitants often do not agree. *Chicago* is pronounced shə kô′gō and shə kä′gō, as well as with minor variants. English has tended to anglicize many foreign place names and even to prefer an alternative name for some: *Paris* (pa′ris instead of pä rē′); *Munich* for *München* and *Finland* for *Suomi*.

Many fairly common names occur in various forms: *Burns–Byrnes, Harvey–Hervey, Cohen–Cohn–Kohen, Mac–Mc–M',* and so on. Special care is needed with names having silent letters or some peculiarity of spelling or phrasing: Pittsburg*h* (but Gettysburg), the John*s* Hopkins University, the State University of Iowa, the Ohio State University.

Dictionaries and encyclopedias give the pronunciation and spelling of the names of the best known people and places. For foreign names in current news, we can try to follow the national newscasters. They will show some variation, but they have made an effort to find a reasonable pronunciation.

Getting proper names in the right form is courtesy as well as accuracy. This is especially important in all published work.

References: Allen W. Read, "The Basis of Correctness in the Pronunciation of Place-Names," *American Speech,* 1933, 8:42-46; *Webster's Biographical Dictionary, Webster's Geographical Dictionary,* W. Cabell Greet, *World Words* (New York, 1948); Kenyon and Knott, and recent dictionaries. *Course names.

proposition Its use as a business word for *offer, plan, proposal* has made it inappropriate in General usage. "I have a proposition for you" = "I have a plan. . . ."

proved–proven As the past participle of *prove, proved* is much more common than *proven* and is always acceptable (He had proved . . .). But *proven* is often used (It had proven quite satisfactory), especially where the rhythm is more comfortable with two syllables.

provided–providing Both are used as conjunctions: He should be home soon provided (or: providing) the buses haven't been held up. There is some prejudice against *providing* in this use. (See *Divided usage.)

psychology, psychiatry Watch the spelling of these words:

psychiatry (sī kī′ə tri), psychiatrist (sī kī′ə trist), and psychiatric (sī′ki at′rik)
psychology, psychologist, psychoanalyze, and psychoanalysis

The pronunciation of *psychiatry, psychiatrist* with short i in the first syllable is increasing.

public is a *collective noun and takes either a singular or plural construction depending on whether the writer wishes to stress the whole group or the individuals:

The *public is* invited. The *public are* invited.
His *public is made up* of the very young and the fairly old.
Consult the libraries and you will find that the ordinary public do not read poetry.—P. B. BALLARD, *Thought and Language,* p. 250

Punctuation, No punctuation Revision: Correct the obvious error in punctuation by either inserting appropriate punctuation or deleting confusing punctuation. If the change to be made is not clear to you, consult the *Index* article on the particular mark. *Pn* *NoPn*

A discussion of the function and general uses of the punctuation marks, and of differing styles of punctuation ("open" and "close") will be found in Chapter 5, page 114.

Details of the uses of the individual marks will be found in the *Index* articles on each:

'	*Apostrophe	{ }	*Brace
*	*Asterisk	[ ]	*Brackets

^	*Caret	. . . .	*Leaders
:	*Colon	( )	*Parentheses
,	*Comma	.	*Period
–	*Dash (including the long dash ——)	?	*Question mark
. . .	*Ellipsis	" "	*Quotation marks
!	*Exclamation mark	;	*Semicolon
-	*Hyphen	———	*Underlining (for italic type)

See also: *Division of words; *Letters; *Restrictive and nonrestrictive; *Series.

Puns A *pun* is a *figure of speech in which a word is used in two senses at once (the nut that holds the wheel=automobile driver) or in which a word is substituted for another of similar sound but different meaning (hire education). Reasonable punning, funny or serious, is a healthy use of language. Objection is often made to puns because of their overuse or because they involve sound and not meaning. Good puns are appropriate to Informal usage, usually giving an accent of ironic humor (as in Dorothy Parker's "a girl's best friend is her mutter") or of mild satire:

> The taking of the census makes it clear that America is still a land of opportunity. Every person, however humble, has a chance to become a national figure.–HOWARD BRUBAKER, *The New Yorker*, Apr. 8, 1950

(Compare *Homonyms and see Ch. 8, "Word play," p. 235.)

purist A purist is a person who is overcareful in the use of language, especially one who wishes everyone to follow the rules of prescriptive grammar (*Grammar § 3) and who tries to hold words to their strictest meanings. Dictionaries and scientific grammars are descriptive and consequently reflect the actual situation more accurately.

Purpose Adverbial clauses of purpose are most commonly introduced by *so that:*

> He is packing tonight *so that* he can start early in the morning.

That used alone is more Formal, almost archaic; and *in order that* is wordy. Informally **so* is used alone:

> He is packing tonight *so* he can start early in the morning.

put in–put across *Put in* is good Informal usage for *spend* (put in time). *Put over* (a plan, a sale), *put across* (a scheme, an idea) are also Informal but are often objected to because they are too frequently used.

Q

Q is an unnecessary letter in the English alphabet. It was brought into English spelling in words borrowed from French, originally derived from Latin (*question, quarter, quit*), and later borrowings directly from Latin added to the number (*quorum, quota*). Some Old English words with *kw* sound (spelled *cw*) were respelled with *qu: quick* (from *cwic*), *queen* (from *cwen*), *quench* (from *cwencan*).

Q is always followed by *u* in English except in a few foreign place names (Gulf of Aqaba). *Qu* is ordinarily pronounced *kw* (*quite, quill, quadrilateral*), though in a few words the French value, *k*, is kept: *coquette* (kō ket′), *quatorze* (kə tôrz′). Final *-que* is *k: antique* (an tēk′), *unique* (ū nēk′). The French pronunciation should not be attempted in words that have been anglicized: *Quebec* (kwi bek′), **questionnaire.*

Question mark (?) Revision: Punctuate this sentence as a question. *Ques*

1. The principal use of the question mark is as the end stop of a question: What was the real reason?

2. A question mark may or may not be used after a request that is phrased as a question, depending on the Formality of the style:

> Formal: Will you please return this at your earliest convenience?
> General: Will you please return this at your earliest convenience.

3. A question mark is not used after an indirect question: He wanted to know what the real reason was.

4. A question mark is used to show that a statement is approximate or questionable, as with uncertain dates:

> Geoffrey Chaucer 1340?–1400 [or] Geoffrey Chaucer 1340(?)–1400

5. A question mark in parentheses as a mildly sarcastic comment or as a label for would-be witticisms is now out of fashion and is better omitted:

> No fashionable woman would think of going to a football game unless she looked like a giant squirrel or some other innocent(?) [Better omitted] fur-bearing animal.

6. When a question mark and quotation marks fall together, the question mark is outside if the quoting sentence is the question, inside if the quotation is the question:

> He asked, "Did you really say that?"
> Did you really say "I thought you were older than that"?

After a double question only one question mark is used.

> Did she ask, "How many are coming?"

(See *Quotation marks § 4.)

questionnaire keeps the French spelling, with two *n*'s, but is pronounced as an English word: kwes′chən ar′. The British form *questionary* has not made much progress.

Questions 1. In speech, questions are identified by word order, interrogative words, and intonation. The intonation patterns for questions are complex; some questions end with the voice rising, some with it falling. Since in writing, these patterns must all be summed up by the question mark—which does not appear until the end of the sentence—a written question is most easily identified by interrogative words and word order. It may be introduced by an interrogative word:

Pronoun: *Who* was that? *What* would you do in his place?
Adjective: *Which* way did he go? *What* book shall I read next?
Adverb: *Where* shall we eat? *When* will you be coming back? *How much* is that one? *Why* didn't you say so in the first place?

A question may be indicated by inverted word order, the verb coming before its subject. In older English any verb could stand first (*Came* he yesterday?), but now this order is found only with *be, have, shall, will, can, may, must, need,* and *ought* (*Was* he there?) and in Informal, usually spoken, subjectless sentences (*Want* this one?). Ordinarily a phrasal verb is used, with the auxiliary coming before the subject as a sort of compromise inversion (*Do you think* he would go if he was asked?). A statement may be turned into a question by an inverted clause at the end (He didn't try, did he?).

A direct question that is parenthetically part of another sentence sometimes begins with a capital and sometimes not:

He felt a strong urge—as indeed who doesn't?—to write a really good modern novel.—NOEL COWARD, *To Step Aside*, p. 9

2. An indirect question is a question that is not quoted directly but is made a subordinate member of another sentence. An indirect question is not marked either with a question mark or with quotation marks; the tense of the verb is changed, if necessary, to fit the sentence in which it stands, and often a subordinating conjunction is introduced (*if, whether*):

Direct: "What are our plans for tomorrow?"
Indirect: He asked what our plans for tomorrow were.
Direct: He asked, "Do you really understand what you have read?"
Indirect: He asked us if we really understood what we had read.
He always asks us whether we understand what we have read.

3. A "leading question" is one phrased to suggest the answer desired, as "You wouldn't do that, would you?" (contrasted with "Would you do that?").

4. For the stylistic use of questions, see Chapter 7, "Questions," page 183, and *Rhetorical questions.

Quotation marks (" ") Revision: Make the quotation marks conform to conventional usage.

Quot

1. *Methods of indicating quotations.* 2. *Principal uses.* 3. *Miscellaneous uses.* 4. *With other marks.* 5. *Indicating quotations in foreign languages.*

1. *Methods of indicating quotations.*

a) Double quotes (" ") are the usual marks. The mark before the quoted matter is the *open-quote;* the one after is the *close-quote.*

b) The use of single quotes (‘ ’) is common in England and is increasing in the United States. The single quotes are as accurate as the double and are much less spotty on the page.

c) For quotations within quotations, double and single quotes are alternated. If you begin with the double marks: “ ‘ . . . ’ ”; if you begin with the single: ‘ “ . . . ” ’. If there are quotations within two such quotations, continue to alternate the double and single quotes.

d) Indenting is used to indicate quotations, especially in factual writing involving numerous quotations of some length, as in this book. No quotation marks are used, and in print the size of type is usually reduced. Publishing houses have rules about how long a quotation must be to be reduced and indented–that it should run to at least five lines, for example, or consist of more than one complete sentence. In double spaced typewritten copy, such quotations are usually indented and single spaced; in longhand copy they are indented.

e) When a long quotation which is not indented includes more than one paragraph, the marks are placed at the beginning of each paragraph of the quotation but at the end of only the last paragraph.

2. *Principal uses of quotation marks.*

a) Quotation marks are used to indicate all passages taken from another writer, whether a phrase or a page or more (except when the quotation is indented). The quoted matter may be worked into the constructions of the quoter's sentence, or it may stand by itself:

> From the enormous mass of material put at his disposal, Mr. Garnett chose those letters that would make “a book in which Lawrence's career, his intellectual development and the details of his life should be recorded, traced and documented almost entirely in his own words.”–CHARLES POORE, *The New York Times,* Mar. 10, 1939

When speeches or a short conversation are not given for their own sake but to illustrate a point, they are usually put in the body of the paragraph:

> Do these instances of the beginnings of new words give us any hints in the search for those new words for which every passing month shows the urgent need? I think they do. First, simplicity and euphony–though not simplicity at all costs. Many years ago, I was chaffing an old friend about the deficiency of his native Welsh. “It's very lacking in the most ordinary scientific terms,” I remarked. “For example?” “Well, what's the Welsh for *galvanometer?*” I asked. “And if it comes to that, what's the English for it?” A very proper rejoinder which, correctly interpreted, means that *gas* is preferable to *aeriform fluid,* and *drop-counter* to *stalagmometer.* All within reason, of course: does it follow, for example, that *foreword* is better than *preface?*–ALLAN FERGUSON, “The Scientist's Need for New Words,” *The Listener,* Apr. 21, 1937

b) There are no half quotes. A sentence is either an exact quotation in quotation marks, or else it isn't and so is not quoted. A speech summarized or quoted “indirectly” is not marked:

Direct quotation: The manager told me, "I work harder in one day keeping the girls busy than they work all week."

Indirect quotation: The manager told me that he worked harder in one day keeping the girls busy than they worked all week. (Not: The manager told me "that he worked harder in one day keeping the girls busy than they worked all week.")

c) Some writers of fiction—William Saroyan, William Carlos Williams (in *Life Along the Passaic River*), and others—do not use quotation marks in the dialog of their stories, but the practice is not common, and dropping them is somewhat confusing. (See Ch. 10, "Conversation," p. 289 for their use in dialog.)

3. *Miscellaneous uses of quotation marks.*

a) Many magazines use quotes around titles of books and periodicals, for which Formal writing uses italics:

Down on Boston's historic waterfront, a yachting-supply firm has in its window a display of books intended for the practical use of mariners. Standing between Bowditch's "New American Practical Navigator" and Dutton's "Navigation and Nautical Astronomy" is Mitchell's "Gone with the Wind."—*The New Yorker,* Dec. 4, 1937

In academic style, which uses italics for titles of books and the names of periodicals, quotes are used for titles of written works shorter than volume length, for single poems, short stories, magazine articles, but not ordinarily for chapter titles. (See Ch. 13, "Form of bibliographical entries," p. 363, and *Titles of articles, books, etc.)

b) In Formal writing words that are used as words rather than for their meaning are put in italics (underlined in manuscript); in General writing they would often be put in quotes:

"Capitalism" is thus a shape, a form, which speaks, commands, fights, runs away. Asked to define it, the debater on the left introduces more abstractions: "Absentee ownership," "surplus value," "class struggle," "private ownership of the means of production," "exploitation of the masses," "imperialism," "vested interests," "proletariat," "bourgeoisie," the "profit system," and many more. The great words roll.—STUART CHASE, *The Tyranny of Words,* p. 275

c) In Formal writing a word from a conspicuously different variety of speech may be put in quotation marks, but this practice is less common than formerly. In General writing there is less need for these apologetic quotes, because there is greater latitude in choice of words. If the word is appropriate, use it without apology, and if it isn't appropriate, ordinarily don't use it.

Everybody told Bib what a sucker [not "sucker"] he was, but he still had confidence in the designer of the plane.

After the Yale man had said his piece, the Dartmouth frosh started to blow his horn again. (The question here is whether the *said his piece, frosh,* and *blow his horn* are appropriate; if they are not, quotes will not make the sentence any better.)

Common figures of speech do not need to be quoted:

A dirt path would be easier to walk on and at the same time wouldn't wear out so much cowhide. (Not "cowhide")

d) Practice differs in writing single words that are spoken or thought:

Stephen said "Yes," so we went to work at once.
Stephen said *Yes,* so we went to work at once.
Stephen said Yes, so we went to work at once.

Probably the first form is the most common.

4. *Quotation marks and other marks.*

a) When a question mark or an exclamation mark ends a quotation, it is placed inside the quotes:

"Don't go near that wire!" he shouted.
Then in a calm voice she asked, "Why didn't you say so before?"

When a question mark or exclamation mark belongs to a sentence that includes a quotation, it is placed after the quotes:

What kind of work can a man put into "the cheapest building that will last fifteen years"?–LEWIS MUMFORD, *Sticks and Stones,* p. 172

b) Most American publishers put commas and periods inside the close-quotes, whether they belong with the quotation or not. The reason for this is that the quotes help fill the small spot of white that would be left if the comma or period came outside. Some writers follow the conventions that apply to the exclamation and question marks, putting comma or period inside the quotes if it belongs with the quotation, outside if it belongs with the quoting sentence, but this usage is much less common.

Semicolons usually stand after the quotation mark.

c) Introductory words and stage directions are set off by a comma, or by two commas if they interrupt the quotation:

Robert said, "I should think that by now you would have learned that."
"History," it has been said, "does not repeat itself. The historians repeat one another."–MAX BEERBOHM, *Works,* p. 43

(Note that *does* is not capitalized after the interruption because it does not begin a sentence.)

The comma with a short introductory phrase is really unnecessary, since the quotes keep the two elements distinct, and there is a noticeable tendency to do without it:

The OED says 'The stress conte′nt is historical, & still common among the educated.'–H. W. FOWLER, p. 93
"Poetry gives most pleasure" said Coleridge "when only generally and not perfectly understood"; . . .–A. E. HOUSMAN, *The Name and Nature of Poetry,* p. 36

When quoted phrases are closely built into the construction of a sentence, they are not set off by commas:

I hurried past the zero case with its cream molds, just barely saying "Hi!" to Danny and the girls behind it.

"I give him the book" has two equally correct passives: "He is given the book" and "The book is given to him."—E. H. STURTEVANT, *Linguistic Change*, p. 138

A Formal introduction to a quotation is usually followed by a colon, as in the statements introducing the examples in this article.

5. *Indicating quotations in foreign languages.* The methods of indicating quotations are different for other languages. If you have occasion to quote a passage in another language which includes a quotation, you should consult a stylebook.

R

(r) as in *ready, arch, arrears, car.*

The *r* sound shows wide variation, more than that of any other consonant. It varies in different English-speaking regions, from Scotch and North of England "burrs" to replacement by ə (as in dōə for *door*) or even to complete omission.

The *r* sound also varies according to its position in a word. It is strongest, in all regions, before a vowel: *real, rob, cheering, fairy.* Before a consonant sound it varies, as from bäk to bärk for *bark.* Final *r* is most apparent in Western pronunciation, less conspicuous in the pronunciations of New England, the South, and metropolitan New York.

In Eastern and Southern speech *r* after a vowel often becomes ə or disappears entirely (*farther,* fä′thə), except when the *r* is final and comes before a word starting with a vowel (*far away,* fär′ə wā′). Some speakers may even intrude an *r* between a word ending with a vowel and one beginning with a vowel (the idea-r is good). In the rest of the country *r* after a vowel is altered to a special vowel which is, however, heard as *r.*

In this *Guide and Index* the *r* symbol as an indication of pronunciation is to be interpreted to mean the sort of *r* sound the speaker is used to making. (For further details of *r* in American pronunciation see Kenyon and Knott, §§ 26, 82-85.)

racket The spelling *racquet* is British. Write *tennis racket.*

Racket in the sense of an illegitimate way of making money, usually involving threats of violence, has made its way from slang into the General language. Used to mean any business or particular way of making money (the baseball racket, the lumber racket), it is Informal unless used to imply illegitimate means.

radio takes the regular verb and noun endings: *radioed, radioing, radios, radio's.* The pronunciation rad′i ō is Nonstandard.

raise–rear *Rear* is now Formal in the sense of *rearing* a child or of being *reared*. *Bring up* in this sense is current in all varieties of usage. *Raised* is General usage: I was born and raised in Kentucky.

rarely means "seldom" (or in archaic and Formal English, "with rare skill," as "a rarely carved panel").

Rarely ever (I rarely ever go), probably a telescoping of *rarely if ever,* is an established idiom.

ration (rations) Pronunciation is about evenly divided: rā′shən or rash′ən.

re- The prefix *re-*, meaning "again," is hyphened: (1) when the word to which it is joined begins with *e: re-enact, re-enlist, re-enter, re-examine,* and (2) when the form with hyphen can have a different meaning from the form without:

> *reform,* to change, improve–*re-form,* to shape again
> *recover,* to regain–*re-cover,* to cover again

and (3) (rarely) for emphasis, as in "now *re-seated* in fair comfort," or in Informal or humorous compounds, *re-re-married.*

Otherwise there is no hyphen: *rearrange, refine, remit.*

reaction has escaped from chemistry and the biological sciences to become a General word for any response of feeling or idea:

> Let me have your reaction to [often *on*] this.
> She reacted violently when he appeared.
> My reaction to this poem was on the whole favorable.

It is used too freely and has tended to crowd out more appropriate or more exact words–*opinion, attitude, feeling, response, impression,* and any number of words for exact feelings and opinions.

Reading and writing We read for entertainment and for instruction; inclination leads us to the first and either inclination or necessity to the second. Besides these fundamental motives for reading, anyone interested in writing has another–reading to set a goal for his own writing. This does not mean conscious imitation of *Time* or *The New Yorker* or Walter Lippmann, Ernest Hemingway, or E. B. White. Rather it means reading with attention and occasional analysis the writers who genuinely appeal to us and allowing their work to influence ours casually and naturally.

This sort of reading influence is especially necessary in college because a student must read so much in textbooks and reference books and in the literature of earlier periods. Textbooks and reference books provide information and the earlier literature furnishes material for thought and feeling; but the former, unfortunately, are seldom appealing, and the latter often causes the reader to lose touch with the idiom of his own time. If you are interested in writing well you should complement this college reading by reading as widely as you can in the better current magazines and books, fiction and nonfiction, especially of the type that you hope to write. The material you read is likely to be better than what you write, and a good background for judging your own work can come from a sensitive and critical reading of the somewhat similar work of the more important writers of your own time.

In college you also have a chance to hear a great variety of spoken English, some of it well worth listening to. Although it would be a mistake to assume that good written styles are mere transcriptions of good speech, a written English which has an echo of the spoken in it is likely to be lively and interesting. Among your classmates there will be a few who talk especially well. And among your teachers there will be some who use language with conspicuous skill. You will soon learn who the good talkers are; make a practice of listening to them as receptively as you can. Attentive listening is necessary in the college classroom, and if the teacher is a good talker, you will unconsciously absorb a good deal that will improve your written English. (See *Spoken and written English.)

real–really *Real* is always an adjective in Standard English: a *real* experience, a *real* chore. *Really* is the adverb: a *really* successful party. It *really* went off well.

In Nonstandard English and Informal conversation, *real* is often used adverbially: Write *real* soon; It's *real* pretty; It went off *real* well. This use should not be written except in reporting conversation. (Reference: Pooley, pp. 161-163.)

realtor This business coinage has an advantage not possessed by most of its class, since it is much more economical than *real estate agent.* Pronounced rē′əl tər, rē′əl tôr.

reason is because In Formal English the construction beginning "The reason is . . ." is completed by a noun or a noun clause, to balance the noun *reason:*

> The reason for my poor work in French was [noun:] my intense dislike of the subject.
>
> The reason for my poor work in French was [noun clause:] that I disliked the subject intensely.

Since in speech not many noun clauses are introduced by *that,* and *because* is the connective that most obviously stresses the notion of reason, in spoken English we usually find:

> The reason for my poor work in French was because I didn't like the subject.

"The reason is because . . ." is also frequently found in writing:

> In general it may be said that the reason why scholasticism was held to be an obstacle to truth was because it seemed to discourage further enquiry along experimental lines.–Basil Willey, *The Seventeenth Century Background,* p. 7

Marckwardt and Walcott call this construction "Acceptable colloquially" (pp. 31, 112). In such use the *because* clause, in spite of its form, is a noun clause, not adverbial.

Because of widespread prejudice against the construction students should usually follow Formal usage. (References: Pooley, pp. 134-135, and *College English,* 18:110-111; F. N. Cherry, "Some Evidence in the Case of 'is because.' "–*American Speech,* 1933, 8:55-60.)

recipe–receipt (res′ə pi–ri sēt′) Both words mean "a formula, directions for making something." *Recipe* is now the more common in General English, though locally one or the other may be preferred by cooks, and they are interchangeable in meaning. *Receipt* also means "a written acknowledgment for something received."

Reciprocal pronouns *Each other, one another* are called reciprocal pronouns. They are used only as objects of verbs or prepositions. In Formal usage some writers keep *each other* to refer to two, *one another* for more than two. General usage has *each other* in all senses.

> They had hated each other for years.
> Formal: For the first time all the members really saw one another.
> General: For the first time all the members really saw each other.

Reference of pronouns Revision: Change the pronoun marked (or revise the sentence) so that its reference will be exact and obvious and the pronoun itself will be in the conventional form. *Ref*

1. *Clear reference.* 2. *Agreement.* 3. *Indefinite reference.* 4. *Avoiding pronouns.* 5. *Omissions.*

The syntax of a personal, relative, or demonstrative pronoun, as well as its complete meaning, often depends in part on its relation (or reference) to a previous noun in a passage, called its *antecedent.* This fact makes the accurate use of pronouns more complicated than the use of other words. The personal pronouns and one of the relative pronouns–*who*–are further complicated by having a separate accusative case form, as English nouns no longer do. And in writing, the form and reference of pronouns can be seen clearly, so that their casual use, which does not attract attention in speech, should be made more exact and the conventions of published usage should be followed. For these reasons a writer needs to watch his pronouns especially, and in revising a paper he should make sure that they are accurate in form and in reference. Since a college student almost always knows the form that is appropriate in a given sentence, an exact use of pronouns is simply a matter of care. This article runs over the main points in the use of pronouns in Standard written English.

1. *Exact and clear reference.*

a) If the meaning of a pronoun is completed by reference to a particular noun, the reference to this antecedent should be exact and obvious, as in the following examples:

The first hundred miles, *which* we covered before lunch, were rough, but *they* seemed to go faster than the sixty we did in the afternoon. (The noun *miles* is the antecedent of *which* and of *they*.)

All purchases for the University pass through a central purchasing office. *These* include books, trucks, building materials, food, and hundreds of other items. (*These* refers to *purchases*.)

Swimming may be more fun than calisthenics, but *it* can't give such a general development. (*It* refers to *swimming*.)

On July 3 Mr. Havermeyer asked Mr. Paige to come to *his* house. (*His* refers to *Mr. Havermeyer*. Although another name has been mentioned, only a perverse reader would fail to understand the statement. *The former's* instead of *his* would be pedantic here.)

Professor Frank thought that McKinly was grateful to *him* for allowing *him* to graduate. (The first *him* refers to *Professor Frank,* the second to *McKinly*. Actually no ambiguity is possible here and the sentence would be all right in speech and General writing.)

Confusion may arise when the pronoun seems to refer to a nearby noun to which it cannot sensibly refer or when there is no noun nearby; when it refers to a noun used subordinately in the preceding construction, perhaps to one used as a possessive or as an adjective; and when two or more pronouns are crossed so that the exact reference isn't readily clear. Usually to improve such a reference the sentence must be revised, as in the following examples:

He isn't married and doesn't plan on *it*. (. . . and doesn't *plan to marry*.)

The next year he had an attack of acute appendicitis. *It* broke before the doctors had a chance to operate. (*It* cannot refer to *appendicitis* in the statement made. The second sentence should begin *His appendix broke*. Slips in reference are common when the pronoun refers back to a noun in the preceding sentence.)

A legislator should be a man who knows a little about law and government and he should know how to apply *them* to the best interests of his people. (For *them* put *his knowledge*.)

Bill provided more excitement one afternoon when he was skipping rocks across the swimming hole and cut open *a young girl's head who* was swimming under water. (. . . and cut open *the head of a young girl who* was swimming under water.)

To many of us the word *geology* means little in our everyday lives. Yet *it* deals with materials in use for making our homes and factories, metals of which our cars are made, and the fuel which enables us to drive them. (*It* should refer to *geology* [the science] not to *the word*. To revise, drop *the word* in the first line.)

Businessmen without regard for anyone else have exploited the mass of workers at every point, not caring whether *they* were earning a decent living wage, but only whether *they* were getting a lot of money. (The first *they* refers to *workers,* the second to *businessmen*. The sentence needs complete rewriting, but the second part could be improved somewhat by saying: . . . not caring whether they paid a decent living wage, but only whether they were getting a lot of money.)

Remember that clear reference is a matter of *meaning,* not just of the presence or position of certain words.

b) General English uses *which, that, this,* and sometimes *it* to refer to the idea of a previous clause. Formal usage tends to avoid this type of reference or to limit it to *this.*

General: Her friend was jealous of her clothes and money and had taken this way of showing it. (*It* refers to the idea in *was jealous.*)

Formal: Her friend was jealous of her clothes and money and had taken this way of showing her feeling.

General: He never seemed to realize when academic tempests were brewing, which was probably a good thing.–J. R. PARKER, *Academic Procession,* p. 86 (*Which* refers to the idea of the first clause.)

Formal: He never seemed to realize when academic tempests were brewing. This was probably a good thing.

General: From his firm grip, piercing eyes, and stern mouth I could see that he was not to be trifled with, which was well proved later. (*Which* refers to the *that*-clause.)

Formal: From his firm grip, piercing eyes, and stern mouth I could see that he was not to be trifled with. This was well proved later.

c) In conversation the reference of pronouns is freer than in writing. The following examples, which would probably pass unnoticed in a conversation, show one reason why, in written work, we sometimes find pronouns that seem inexact or that do not conform to editorial standards.

Spoken	*Written*
Gordon's mother asked me to take him fishing because he was so interested in *it* but had never caught *one.*	Gordon's mother asked me to take him fishing because he was so interested in *it* but had never caught a *fish.*
Everyone likes to dance and knew he would get plenty of *it* during the party weekend.	Everyone likes to dance and knew he would get plenty of *dancing* during the party weekend.
In aquaplaning the ropes should never be wound around the wrists, because if thrown *he* would be dragged along and injured.	The ropes should never be wound around *the planer's* wrists, because if thrown *he* would be dragged along and injured.

2. *Agreement of pronoun with antecedent.* Pronouns referring to specific antecedents generally agree with the antecedents in number, gender, and person.

a) Agreement in number. A pronoun agrees with its antecedent in number: singular antecedent, singular pronoun; plural antecedent, plural pronoun.

Singular: *Jimmy* tried to go quietly, but *he* couldn't keep from whistling.

Plural: *The boys* had tried to go quietly, but *they* couldn't keep from whistling.

In Formal American English, *each, every, everyone* are generally referred to by singular pronouns (*every and its compounds § 1):

Almost everyone has some little superstitions which *he* would not violate for love or money.

In spoken English these words are treated as collectives and are found usually with a plural pronoun:

Almost everyone has some little superstitions which *they* would not violate for love or money.

Maugham takes anyone from a gigolo to a lord and develops them [Formal: him] with equal ease and finesse.

This colloquial agreement is sometimes found in print, but editors usually bring it in line with Formal usage before publication. (Reference: Russell Thomas, "Concord Based on *Meaning* versus Concord Based on *Form:* The Indefinites," *College English,* 1939, 1:38-45.)

A collective noun is referred to by either a singular or a plural pronoun, depending upon its meaning in the sentence (*Collective nouns):

Singular: When a *gang* of rabbit hunters spreads out over a field, *it* doesn't lose any time.

Plural: When a *gang* of rabbit hunters spread out over a field, *they* don't lose any time.

Often when a pronoun does not agree with its antecedent, the antecedent should be changed rather than the pronoun:

Putting himself in the shoes of the slave owner, Lincoln realized that they had a right to feel as they did toward emancipation. (This could be made consistent by making *slave owner* plural better than by changing *they* to *he.*)

Labor's third and major contention is that they do not receive an adequate return for the services they render. (Here changing *Labor's* to *The workers'* would be more accurate than changing the pronouns to the singular.)

b) Agreement in person. Except in indefinite pronouns (§ 3 of this article), there is little difficulty with agreement:

First person: I wish Mr. Patterson had told *me* before.
Second person: You should have thought of that *yourself.*
Third person: The woman had said *she* was over twenty-one.

A relative pronoun agrees with its antecedent:

I, *who am* your nearest relative, would help you. (Because of the unusualness of the *who am,* it would not ordinarily be said or written: I, your nearest relative. . . .)

He is one of those people who do just what they want to. (*They* refers to *who,* which refers to *people.*)

c) Case of pronouns. The case of a pronoun depends upon the construction in which it stands, not upon its antecedent. (See *Case and the articles there referred to; *be § 2, *between you and me, *It's me, *who, whom.)

3. *Indefinite reference.* Often pronouns are used to refer to the readers or to people in general instead of to specifically mentioned people. English has no such convenient indefinite pronoun as the German *man* or the French *on.* Our *one* has a definitely Formal and stiffish connotation. *We* and *you* seem to be slightly more personal, more expressive, and are very generally used, as in various articles in this book. This is a question of style rather than of grammar, and whether *you* or *they* ("They say . . . ") or *we* or *one* or *people* or some other noun is used depends on its fitness in the passage.

Care should be taken to keep indefinite pronouns consistent, not shifting from *one* to *you,* for example:

When *you* have worked a day here *you* have really earned your money.

Or: When *one* has worked a day here *he* has really earned his money.

Not: When *one* has worked a day here *you* have really earned your money.

An indefinite pronoun should not be substituted for a definite personal pronoun:

For *me* there is no fun in reading unless *I* can put myself in the position of the characters and feel that *I* am really in the scene. (Not: For *me* there is no fun in reading unless *you* can put yourself in the position of the characters and feel that *you* are really in the scene.)

The indefinite pronouns (*all, any, each, everybody, few, nobody,* and so on.—*Pronouns § 8) have no expressed antecedent, so that their use involves consistency but not agreement with an antecedent.

Since English has no single pronoun to mean he-or-she, the masculine *he* is conventionally used (*he-or-she):

The time comes to every senior when *he* [Not: *he or she*] anxiously looks forward to that eventful day.

The best way out of the difficulty is to use the plural:

The time comes to all seniors when *they*. . . .

4. *Avoiding pronouns.* Pronouns are necessary and convenient, but since they sometimes lead to inconsistent uses (that are marked by teachers and editors), some writers tend to avoid them, using a noun instead. The result is usually unidiomatic or clumsy English:

That's the reason I hesitate to picture the owner of *a grip* from the appearance of *the bag.* (Better: That's the reason I hesitate to picture the owner of *the bag* from *its* appearance.)

Arrest of *the woman* yesterday followed several days of observation of *the woman's* [Better: *her*] activities by agents of the Stores Mutual Protective Association.

Pronouns are especially useful to bind together clauses and sentences. In the following paragraph each sentence seems to be a new beginning, but with pronouns instead of *Mr. Frothingham,* the paragraph would be closely connected:

Roland W. Frothingham died at his home on Commonwealth avenue on Tuesday. Mr. Frothingham [He] was born in Boston in 1868 and had lived here ever since. Mr. Frothingham's [His] ancestors came from Ipswich. Mr. Frothingham [He] was educated at Harvard College.

5. *Omission of pronouns.* In Informal writing and in conversation, pronouns, especially *I*, are often omitted (*I § 3; Ch. 2, "Subjectless sentences," p. 52), and in all varieties of English the relative pronoun is often not used in relative clauses (*Relative clauses): The first man (that) I met had never heard of such a street.

For the classes and forms of pronouns, see *Pronouns; for further instances of their use, see the articles on particular pronouns, *I, *we, *who, whom, *himself, herself, *myself. See also Chapter 3, "Checking pronouns," page 84. References: All grammars treat the use of pronouns. The discussion in the large grammars (Curme, Jespersen . . .) are extended and discuss many special uses.

References in scientific papers Research papers in the sciences use a system of reference to sources quite different from the system of the humanities and social sciences described in Chapter 13. The references have the same purpose–giving the author, title, and facts of publication of articles and books used, to acknowledge the source of material and to make it possible for a reader to go directly to a source if he wishes further information. The details of form vary considerably among the different scientific and technical fields and often among the books and journals within a field. If you are writing a paper on a scientific or technical subject, you will have to select among the systems given in this article (or follow your instructor's specification of which to use) or study the form of a particular journal and follow its practice.

1. *General points.*

a) A few scientific journals give references to sources in footnotes at the bottom of a page, but most of them, and most scientific books, use footnotes only for explanatory comments or for additional facts, as in this one:

```
3Some attempt has also been made to extend its coverage to
perceptual problems involved in social judgments and social change
(Helson, 1948).
```

Such footnotes are kept few and brief.

b) The reference to a source is usually given in parentheses in the text, immediately following the writer's name or following the relevant statement, as illustrated in sections 2 and 3.

c) The references and the bibliographical entries are made as economical as possible:

Arabic numerals rather than roman are used for volumes: 24:62-63. Sometimes the volume number is printed in boldface type (**24**:62-63), indicated in manuscript by a wavy line under the figures, or in italic type (*24*:62-63), indicated by one line under the figures; but most often they are in ordinary type.

Sometimes authors' names in a bibliography are printed in capitals and small capitals: BROWNE, C. A. (Small capitals are indicated by two lines under the letters in manuscript.) But most often they are in ordinary type.

In titles usually only the first word and proper names are capitalized, and the titles of articles are not put in quotation marks. Usually the titles of periodicals or other series (bulletins, monographs) are in italics (underlined in manuscript).

Prepositions are often omitted in the titles of periodicals: *J. Nutrition, Jour. Forestry* (for *Journal of Nutrition, Journal of Forestry*).

The names of journals and other series of publications are usually abbreviated. Some common abbreviations are:

Bull.	Bulletin	Pub.	Publication(s)
J. (Jour.)	Journal	Rev.	Review
Mon.	Monograph(s)	Sci.	Science
Proc.	Proceedings	ser.	series

Abbreviations are given for commonly used words, like Am. (American), Assoc. (Association), Soc. (Society), and the names of fields (Biol., Geol.), and of well-known organizations, like IRE (Institute of Radio Engineers). The Latin abbreviation *et al.* (*et alii,* and others) is used when a work has more than two authors, and *op. cit.* (*opere citato,* in the work cited) occasionally for later references to a work.

d) In some systems the title of a periodical article is not given:

A. S. Newton, *Anal. Chem.,* **28,** 1214 (1956).
T. J. Tompson, *Phys. Rev.,* **85,** 765 (1952).

e) When the reference is to the general method described in a relatively short article or to the general conclusion of a work, specific pages are not given.

f) Little direct quotation is used, but when it is, the source is given between the closing quotation marks and the period ending the sentence:

> . . . although it might be added that "the oldest unit of the Detroit River group, the Sylvania sandstone, is succeeded respectively by the Amherstburg dolomite, the Lucas dolomite, and the Anderson Limestone" (Ehlers, 1950, p. 1455).

g) Since dates are especially important in scientific work—a scientist presumably is familiar with previous work on his subject and builds upon it—they are usually given prominence by being given first or last in the facts of publication of the bibliography and are used as a key item in the reference system described in section 3.

h) Acknowledgment of special assistance of individuals is made either in a footnote early in the article or under a heading *Acknowledgments* just before the bibliography.

i) The bibliography at the end of an article may be headed *References* or *Literature cited,* but most often *Bibliography.*

j) In general, then, the source of material used in a scientific paper is indicated by the combined reference in parentheses in the text and an entry in the bibliography. The two most common systems are given in sections 2 and 3. Use one of these unless you have reason to use some of the variations indicated.

2. *References by bibliography numbers.* In this system the items of the bibliography are arranged alphabetically by author (the rare unsigned item usually under *Anonymous*) and then numbered from 1 up. The parenthetical references in the text are to these numbers in the bibliography.

Here are some sentences from an article (Robert A. Gardner and John L. Retzer, "Interpretive Soil Classification: Timber, Range, and Watersheds," *Soil Science,* 1949, 67:151-157), with the reference numbers in parentheses. The sentences occurred in the order in which they stand here, though not consecutively.

> Kittredge (9) pointed out the advantages that natural forest areas offer to the study of soils, long undisturbed, in relation to forest type—advantages that cultivated soil areas cannot offer.
>
> Veatch (15) has made extensive use of soil-forest relations in approximating areas and kinds of original forest cover in Michigan, and Roe (12) has grouped soil types of the originally forested part of the lake states. . . .
>
> The more important relatively permanent criteria of use in the natural classification of forest soils listed by Lutz and Chandler (10) are also of importance in crop production.
>
> The nutritive value of pasture forage as related to soils has received considerable study (1, 11), but in the main the nutritive value of range forage as related to soils is an almost untouched field (3).

The bibliography entries referred to in these sentences are given at the end of the article as follows:

(1) Browne, C. A. 1938 Some relationships of soil to plant and animal nutrition—the major elements. *U.S. Dept. Agr. Yearbook* 1938: 777-806.

(3) Cardon, P. V., *et al.* 1939 Pasture and range in livestock feeding. *U.S. Dept. Agr. Yearbook* 1939: 925-955.

(9) Kittredge, J., Jr. 1928 The use of soil surveys in forestry. *First Internatl. Cong. Soil Sci. Proc. and Papers* (1927) 4 (Comn. V): 562-565.

(10) Lutz, H. J., and Chandler, R. F., Jr. 1946 *Forest Soils.* John Wiley and Sons, Inc., New York.

(11) McMurtrey, J. E., Jr., and Robinson, W. O. 1938 Neglected soil constituents that affect plant and animal development. *U.S. Dept. Agr. Yearbook* 1938: 807-829.

(12) Roe, E. I. 1935 Forest soils—the basis of forest management. Lake States Forest Exp. Sta., Processed Rpt.

(15) Veatch, J. O. 1932 Soil maps as a basis for mapping original forest cover. *Papers Mich. Acad. Sci., Arts, and Letters* (1931) 15: 267-273.

This bibliography does not use capitals or quotation marks in article titles. The year is given before the title. Only inclusive pages (for the whole item referred to) are given. This would handicap a reader who wanted to refer to the source, especially for entry 10, which is a whole book. Usually in references of this type the pages directly involved in the statement are given in the parenthetical references:

> . . . in the natural classification of forest soils listed by Lutz and Chandler (10, pp. 262-266). . . .

A variation of the numbered bibliography system is listing the sources in the bibliography in the order in which they are referred to in the text–1 for the first mentioned source, 2 for the second, and so on. This works well for quite short bibliographies but becomes a nuisance if there are many items and especially if the same source is referred to several times. In this system the specific pages referred to are usually made part of the bibliography entry rather than put in the parentheses.

3. *Reference by author and date.* Perhaps the most widely used system is giving author and date of publication. The items of the bibliography are arranged alphabetically by author. The reference is in parentheses in the text and includes author, date of the publication, and pages when the source to be indicated is only a part of the item.

These examples are from Floyd H. Allport, *Theories of Perception and the Concept of Structure,* New York, John Wiley & Sons, 1955:

In this first example, the full data (in parentheses) stands at the end of a paragraph:

> The term meaning has been further extended to apply to the experience of *insight* into one's behavior; for behavior with insight is an evidence of the existence of some manifest ego-field organization. (Koffka, 1935, pp. 175-176, 382.)

If the author's name is given in the sentence, as it frequently is, only the date and page (or chapter of a book) are given in the parentheses. If the reference is to the whole work, only the date is needed.

> Hebb has presented his own account of insight and the "meaning of meaning" (1949, pp. 126-134).
>
> The case for perceptual and cognitive learning has also been well stated by Hilgard (1948, Chapter 12).
>
> We recall the experiment performed by Stratton (1897) and Ewert (1930).

If there is more than one item by the same writer, they are identified by the years of publication, and if there is more than one by the same writer in the same year, each is given a letter in addition to the date:

> The first type, the associationistic, or S-R, theories are best represented by Hull's objective theory of behavior (1943*b*, 1951, 1952).

If the item specifically referred to is included in another work, the reference is to the latter (in the bibliography McCleary and Lazarus is not listed):

> This proposition, the most challenging of all the directive-state hypotheses, was tested in its various parts by McGinnies (1949) and by McCleary and Lazarus (see Bruner and Krech, eds., 1950, pp. 171-179).

The bibliography of Allport's book is very extensive. The works referred to in the quotations just given are entered as follows:

Bruner, J. S., and D. Krech. 1950. *Perception and personality: a symposium.* Durham: Duke Univ. Press.

Ewert, P. H. 1930. A study of the effect of inverted retinal stimulation upon spatially coordinated behavior. *Genet. Psychol. Monogr., 7,* Nos. 3 and 4.

Hebb, D. O. 1949. *The organization of behavior.* New York: Wiley.

Hilgard, E. R. 1948. *Theories of learning.* New York: Appleton-Century-Crofts.

Hull, C. L. 1943*a*. The problem of intervening variables in molar behavior theory. *Psychol. Rev., 50,* 273-291.

Hull, C. L. 1943*b*. *Principles of behavior: an introduction to behavior theory.* New York: Appleton-Century-Crofts.

Hull, C. L. 1951. *Essentials of behavior.* New Haven: Yale Univ. Press.

Hull, C. L. 1952. *A behavior system: an introduction to behavior theory concerning the individual organism.* New Haven: Yale Univ. Press.

Koffka, W. 1935. *Principles of gestalt psychology.* New York: Harcourt.

McGinnies, E. 1949. Emotionality and perceptual defense. *Psychol. Rev., 56,* 244-251.

Stratton, G. M. 1897. Vision without inversion of the retinal image. *Psychol. Rev., 4,* 341-360; 463-481.

This bibliography shows one of the standard systems of capitalizing and of punctuating entries, with the period the usual mark between elements except that commas are used within the parts of a periodical reference.

Familiarity with the practices of their scientific field is useful for majors in the scientific and technical departments, both for reading material in the field and for writing papers in advanced courses.

Referent (ref′ər ənt) is the object, class of objects, act, situation, quality, or fancy which a word is the verbal symbol for. The referent of *book* is either a particular book being discussed or a generalized notion based on our observation of various books. (For discussion see Ch. 8, "The nature of meaning," p. 216.)

regard (regards) Good English uses the prepositional phrase *in regard to;* Nonstandard often uses *in regards to.*

regardless *-less* is a negative ending and makes the word mean "without regard to"; prefixing an *ir-* (*irregardless*) doubles the negative and makes a word so far regarded as unacceptable in writing though in frequent colloquial use.

Relative clauses A relative clause is an adjective clause, introduced by a relative pronoun (*that, which,* or *who*), or a relative adverb (*where, when, why*), or without a connective:

The rain *that began in the morning* kept on all night.

The coach was now abused by the alumni *who two years before had worshiped him.*

The road to the left, *which looked almost impassable,* was ours.

The first place *where they camped* turned out to be impossible.

The man *I met that afternoon* has been my friend ever since. (Formal: The man *whom* I met . . . .)

The ideas *we held in common* were few indeed. (Formal: The ideas *that* we held . . . .)

A relative clause stands after the noun it modifies. In the first sentence above, the clause modifies *rain,* in the second *alumni,* in the third *road,* the fourth *place,* the fifth *man,* and the sixth *ideas.* (See *that, *who, whom, *which, *Restrictive and nonrestrictive.)

Several relative clauses in succession make for an awkward, or at least conspicuous, house-that-Jack-built sentence that should be avoided:

People *who* buy houses *that* have been built in times *which* had conspicuous traits of architecture *which* have been since abandoned often have to remodel their purchases completely.

Relative pronouns The relative pronouns are *who* (*whose, whom*), *which* (*of which, whose*), *that, what, whoever* (*whomever*), *whatever,* and occasionally *as.*

Somebody, *who* [or *whom*] I don't know, shouted, "Put 'em out."

The Senator, *whose* term expires next year, is already worrying.

I haven't read the same book *that* [*as*] you have.

That refers to persons or things, *who* to persons. *Which* in Standard English now refers only to animals or objects or situations, and also to collective nouns even if they refer to persons:

The army which mobilizes first has the advantage.

The Board of Directors, which met on Saturday . . . .

The Board of Directors, who are all bankers, . . .

In older English–and still in Nonstandard–*which* applies also to persons: "Our Father which art in heaven . . . ."–The Bible (King James), Matt. 6:9. (Particular points in the use of these relatives will be found in separate entries on each, especially those on *that, *which, *who, whom. See also *Restrictive and nonrestrictive.)

remember In Nonstandard English *remember* is supported by *of:* I don't remember of doing that. In most written English the unsupported verb is used: I don't remember doing it; I don't remember that at all.

Renaissance–Renascence *Renaissance* is the more common spelling. It is pronounced ren′ə säns′ or ren′ə zäns′, or, less commonly, ri nā′-

sǝns; *Renascence* is usually pronounced ri nas′ǝns. The word is capitalized when it refers to the period of history, but not when it refers to a revival, as "the prewar renaissance (renascence) in poetry."

Rep **Repetition** Revision: Revise so as to remove the ineffective repetition of word, thought, or sound.

Repetition of word, thought, or sound may be an effective trait of style, contributing especially to emphasis. Unhappy repetition is discussed in Chapter 7, "Repetition," page 191; successful repetition is discussed in the same section, page 193. This article reviews only some unsuccessful sorts of repetition that ordinarily require revision.

1. *Of words and phrases.* A word that is the name of the subject of a paper or of one of its important parts must occur frequently, though pronouns and economical sentences can keep down the repetition. Unnecessary, ineffective repetition is usually a mark of carelessness or insensitiveness. An attentive reading of the following sentences would have led the writers to revise them, removing the obvious repetitions and other *deadwood too:

> The administration of the Incan government was [based] on a decimal basis.
>
> The Indian's culture was so different from the white man's [culture] that he has done very well to change as much as he has in such a short [period of] time.
>
> From here on there was no trail, and if there had been it would have been snowed under [by the snow of] the night before.

Especially conspicuous is repetition of a word used in a different sense:

> Our club is as much a fraternity as any house along the row. Our unity and fraternity [Substitute: *brotherhood*] have brought us real satisfaction and much success.

2. *Of meaning.* Meaning of single words or of longer groups is often repeated in near synonyms:

> . . . where he did very successful work [there].
>
> In *many* books the setting [very often] is in some foreign country.
>
> At eight-thirty [in the morning] you punch the time clock for the start of the day.
>
> Here comes an elderly woman whose feet and legs are harnessed into a pair of [antiquated and] almost obsolete high-button shoes.
>
> New leg kicks are shown him, new arm stretches are demonstrated, and different ways of breathing illustrated. (Rewritten: He is shown new leg kicks, new arm stretches, and different ways of breathing.)

3. *Of sound.* Jingles and rhyming words are out of place in prose and do not occur as often as repetitions of unstressed syllables, especially the *-ly* of adverbs and the endings of some abstract nouns, like *-tion,* which are unpleasant when noticeable.

Reports A report is essentially *an orderly presentation of data arranged for a specific purpose.* In business or technical reports that purpose may be to present the results of laboratory or field research; to give a routine account of some activity, process, or advance; or to recommend some action or decision, after going over the evidence upon which the recommendation is based.

Reports vary in form, including memorandums, form reports, letter reports, and the "full" technical report. Since in some fields the exact form of the report is rigidly specified, it is wise in preparing such reports to follow the procedures outlined in one of the texts below.

A report needs to be clear and compact, quickly understandable to the readers for whom it is intended. Since its sole aim is presentation of data gathered for a specific purpose, it does not lend itself to amateur practice, but a student would do well to familiarize himself with the type of report likely to be used in the field he expects to work in, and if possible make a collection of reports for future guidance.

Detailed discussions of report writing will be found in books devoted to the subject, such as the following: John Ball and Cecil B. Williams, *Report Writing* (New York, 1955); Frank Kerekes and Robley Winfrey, *Report Preparation. . . .* (Ames, Iowa, 1951); James W. Souther, *Technical Report Writing* (New York, 1957); W. O. Sypherd, Alvin M. Fountain, and V. E. Gibbens, *Manual of Technical Writing* (Chicago, 1957); B. H. Weil, ed., *The Technical Report, Its Preparation, Processing, and Use in Industry and Government* (New York, 1954).

researcher has been added to the English vocabulary as a needed shortening for *research worker* and now appears in dictionaries.

Resolutions A resolution is a formal record of action taken by an organization. It is used typically in expression of sympathy or in recording of sentiment or in recommendation of action. The style is Formal and the expression arranged in a standardized formula:

> WHEREAS, The experiences of the past few weeks have shown . . .; and
> WHEREAS, Our expectations of a more favorable attitude on the part of . . .; therefore be it
> *Resolved,* That this body feels it its duty to inform . . .; and be it further
> *Resolved,* That a copy of these resolutions be sent . . . .
> John W. Appel, Secretary

rest There are two *rest*'s in English, both in good standing. *Rest,* repose, is from Old English *rest; rest,* remainder, is from French *reste.*

Restrictive and nonrestrictive Revision: If the modifier marked is restrictive, it should not be separated from the word it modifies by a comma; if it is nonrestrictive, it should be set off by a comma or by two commas. *Rest*

1. *Restrictive, or close, modifiers.* A restrictive modifier defines, limits, identifies the word it refers to; that is, it provides information essential to the meaning of the sentence. In speaking or reading aloud, there is little pause before the restrictive modifier and the voice is usually sustained, kept level. Actually the modifier becomes closely attached to, practically a part of, the element modified. If the modifier is omitted, the statement either becomes meaningless, as in the first sentence below, or else it has a quite different meaning, as in the second:

It was a quite different looking person *who walked out into the cold, frosty air a few minutes later.*

The right of the dictatorships *to decide how long this wholesale killing goes on* is unquestioned.

The italicized elements in the following sentences are restrictive and should stand as they are here, without commas:

His opponent appeared at one of the really important rallies *with a drink too much in him.*

Reform should be an application *to wider fields* of methods *with which people are already familiar* and *of which they approve.*

In many states parole boards still persist in turning loose prisoners *who should remain behind bars.*

Mr. Colman proves his versatility as an actor *when he philosophizes one minute and punches his brother on the nose the next.* He portrays a man of action *if the occasion requires* and at the same time a mild-mannered, soft-spoken individual *who gives the impression of being able to think.* He has to make important decisions *when his brother and Margo tell him that this Utopia is a lot of hooey.* Mr. Colman is the only actor I have ever seen *who can show that he is thinking.*

2. *Nonrestrictive, or loose, modifiers.* Modifiers which do not limit the meaning of a noun but add a descriptive detail are nonrestrictive and are set off by a comma or commas. In speaking or reading aloud, there is usually a slight pause and change in level of voice, a drop in tone, before and after a loose modifier. As a rule a nonrestrictive modifier can be omitted without altering the fundamental meaning of the statement.

The new road, *for which appropriations have been made,* will pass just north of here.

The building program includes a new building for the English department, *which now has classes all over the campus.*

Sophomores, *who were freshmen just last year,* have an exaggerated sense of their maturity.

A modifier that follows a proper noun is usually nonrestrictive, since the name itself identifies exactly the person or place mentioned:

Josie, *aged 16,* told Ma and Pa Pansky a thing or two.

Just below Poughkeepsie, *which we reached in a little over two hours,* we had another breakfast in a roadside lunch wagon.

3. *Optional punctuation.* Not all modifiers are clearly restrictive or nonrestrictive: there are degrees of closeness. Use of commas emphasizes a slight relationship, lack of commas suggests a closer relation. Some modifiers can be spoken or read with pause and drop in tone, or not, with some slight change in emphasis. The difference in such sentences is more of tone, of movement than of meaning. The italicized modifiers in these sentences might or might not be set off by commas:

These physicians *who so vigorously oppose state medicine* have definite bases for their opinions.

They had *of course* more experience by then.

The sound of swing music reached my ears from a room down the hall *even before I heard the tramping feet that seemed to go with it.*

In open punctuation fewer commas are used, tending to bind the parts of a sentence closer together. As a rule the safest test is reading the sentence aloud, using commas if you pause slightly and change your tone of voice before the modifier.

See Chapter 5, "Before subordinate elements," page 122. Reference: W. Paul Jones, "Punctuating Nonrestrictives," *College English,* 1948, 10:158-162.

Result Adverbial clauses of result are introduced typically by *so that, so, so . . . that, such . . . that,* and *that. So* is rather Informal, *such . . . that* and *that* likely to be Formal. The most common is *so that.*

He had been taught always to expect the worst, so that [so] he wasn't surprised.

He was so used to suffering that one more disaster made little difference.

The house was such an expense that they were giving it up.

Reverend It is better form to use *Reverend* as a title only when the full name or the initials and the last name of the person to whom it refers follow; the abbreviation is used in newspaper and more or less Informal writing:

Reverend James Shaw	Rev. James Shaw
Reverend J. T. Shaw	Rev. J. T. Shaw

But *Reverend* before the surname alone, corresponding to *Doctor* or *Professor,* is increasingly found: Reverend Shaw, Rev. Shaw.

The Reverend before a name is rather more Formal: the Reverend James T. Shaw, the Reverend Mr. Shaw.

The reverend used instead of a clergyman's name (The reverend wasn't there) is distinctly Informal.

In the salutation of a letter, after an inside address, write *Dear Sir:* or *Dear Mr. Shaw:*

Rhetoric is the study of the theory and practice of composition, both oral and written.

The principles of rhetoric are so liable to abuse that the terms *rhetoric* and *rhetorical* are often used in a derogatory sense to imply excessive elaborateness in style, a show of words rather than a show of meaning. Partly because of this degradation of the word *rhetoric, composition* is often used in its place.

See Chapters 9-13, which treat various points of rhetoric.

Rhetorical questions are really statements in the form of questions, since no direct answer is expected and the writer does not intend to give one. In conversation they often carry some special accent, of accusation, for example: "Could you have done any better?"

> . . . Why out of the first forty-six names in the Hall of Fame, have twenty-six of them from one to three relatives of national renown? Does it not argue that they probably belong to great breeds, truly noble strains of blood? Why is it, that if you are born from certain strains of blood you have one chance in five of having a celebrated relative, and if from other strains your chance in this respect is hardly one in a thousand? Why has the Edwards family, living in thirty-three different countries, under differing environments, out of one thousand four hundred members given us one thousand four hundred social servants, many of world distinction, while the Ishmael family, studied by Eastbrook, out of approximately fifteen thousand members has given us nearly fifteen thousand social scourges?—ALBERT EDWARD WIGGAM, *The New Decalogue of Science,* p. 46

right *Right along, right away, right off* are Informal idioms.

In the sense of "very," *right* is a localism, in good standing in the South: We'll be right glad to see you.

rise In referring to people, *arise* is Formal and poetic; *rise* is rather Formal; *get up* is General.

role In Formal usage role (a role in a play) is still sometimes spelled with the circumflex (rôle), but the accent ordinarily is dropped:

> Any role that seemed heroic attracted me.—CLARENCE DAY, *Life With Father,* p. 82

round—around In General usage *round* and *around* are used interchangeably.

In Formal English there is some tendency to keep *around* to mean "here and there" or "in every direction" and *round* for "in a circular motion" or "in a reverse motion":

I have looked all around.	There aren't any around here.
He is going round the world.	Everyone turned round.

Around is Informal in the sense of "about, near":

> He had around $200 in bills. Is anybody around [that is, around here]?

All-round is a General adjective (an all-round flour, an all-round athlete); all-around is often used in the same sense.

Round has no apostrophe.

run *Run* is in good General use in the sense of "manage, operate": He runs a hotel in Florida.

S

S represents principally two sounds, *s* and *z: s* as in *so, sorry, biscuit, crops; z* as in *easy, was, Jones.* In a few words *s* spells *sh:*

tension, sure, sugar; and in some *zh: leisure, pleasure, measure.* The sound is also spelled *c,* as in *city.*

S is silent in several words, most of them from French: *aisle, debris, rendezvous, island, Arkansas, Louisville,* often in *St. Louis,* and usually in *Illinois.* (See *sh; for plurals in *-s* *Plurals § 1, *Jones; for the genitive of words ending in *-s,* *Genitive case § 1a.)

said As a modifier *said* (the said person, the said idea) is legal usage; it is not used in ordinary writing.

saint The abbreviation *St.* is commonly used with names of places (*St. Albans, St. Louis*); *Saint* is more often written out with the name of a canonized saint (*Saint John, Saint Anthony of Padua*). The plural of the abbreviation is *SS.* (*SS. Peter and Paul*). Occasionally the French feminine form, *Sainte,* is used (*Sault Sainte Marie*). The abbreviation of the feminine form is *Ste.*

same *Same* is used as an adjective (the same color) and as a pronoun in such expressions as "The same happened to me once" and popularly in "I'll take the same," "more of the same."

Same as a pronoun is also characteristic of legal and outmoded business use: "and enclose check for same" where better style would have *it* or *them* instead.

Sarcasm Sarcasm is a quality of bitterness or reproach in a statement—ironical (that is, to be interpreted differently from the actual statement) or direct. (See Ch. 8 "Irony," p. 235.)

say *Say* is the usual word for speaking. *Talk* implies a continued "saying." *State* implies a formal "saying" and is better kept for this meaning (Not: "Mr. Owen stated that he was ready if we were").

Unless there is a reason for using a more specific word, *said* is the best word to use in labeling the speeches of characters in a story, since it attracts least attention. (See Ch. 10 "Conversation," p. 289.)

Say in the sense of "suppose," "perhaps," "for instance" is Informal: Say they went sixteen miles.

Schoolgirl style The "schoolgirl style" is characterized by sentimental *counter words (*lovely, cute*), by exaggeration, and by reliance on all sorts of mechanical forms of emphasis–exclamation marks, dashes, capitals, one, two, and even three underlinings. These serve as satisfying muscular release to the writer and may add a sort of glow to a letter, but they should not be transferred to the printed page, and any suggestion of the style should be avoided, except to help portray a character.

schwa (ə) Schwa (shwä) is the name for the neutral vowel sound frequently occurring in unstressed syllables: *a*head, ang*e*l, def*i*nite, *o*ccur, s*u*ggest; the symbol for it is ə. (See *Neutral vowel.)

Scientific and technical writing The ideal of scientific writing was expressed very early in the modern scientific movement in Thomas

Sprat's *History of the Royal Society* (1667). The members of the Society, he said, tried

> to return back to the primitive purity, and shortness, when men delivered so many things, almost in an equal number of words. They have exacted from all their members a close, naked, natural way of speaking; positive expressions; clear senses; a native easiness: bringing all things as near the mathematical plainness as they can; and preferring the language of artizans, countrymen, and merchants, before that of wits or scholars.

Exactness rather than grace or variety, or even emphasis, is the goal of most scientific and scholarly writing, of most writing that is done by members of a profession to be read by other members. Occasionally it attains the ideal of "delivering so many things, almost in an equal number of words":

> A stable, stainless, organic mercury compound solution of high germicidal value, particularly in serum and other protein media.

But today Thomas Sprat would find that much scientific writing has departed far from "the language of artizans, countrymen, and merchants."

The chief reason for the "big words" that seem to a layman the most conspicuous trait of scientific writing is that scientists have discovered and named qualities and things of which the average person is quite unaware. Their descriptions are more detailed than people in general need. On page 13 of *Webster's New Collegiate Dictionary,* for instance, is a scientific description of the *n* sound:

> § 66. *n* as in *none, knit, canny, inn,* etc., is the voiced tongue-point alveolar nasal continuant corresponding to the voiced tongue-point stop *d* and the voiceless tongue-point stop *t*. All three sounds are made with the tongue point on the alveolar ridge (teethridge), and are hence sometimes called alveolar consonants, or, less accurately, dentals.—By permission. From *Webster's New Collegiate Dictionary,* copyright, 1949, by G. & C. Merriam Co.

In contrast to the rather loose meanings of words in general usage, scientific writers try to confine their words to a single specific meaning. Ordinary people speak of *biliousness* and *eyestrain,* though those words have no definite meaning for doctors or oculists. Some scientific words are taken from the General vocabulary and given special meanings, like *magnitude* in astronomy, *force* in physics, *complex* in psychoanalysis, *dip* and *incline* in geology. But the tendency now is to build words from Latin or more often from Greek roots that are self-explanatory (to anyone who knows their elements): *photomicrography, beta-methyl-amido-croton-anilide*.

The sentence structure and other traits of style in scientific writing are Formal, appropriately so because its audience is specialized. The style is impersonal—completely impersonal in monographs, textbooks, and articles in the scientific journals, less impersonal in popular treatments of scientific subjects. Three levels of scientific writing are illustrated in the following quotations. The first paragraph is a simple statement of fact:

> The nature of the force exerted by a wave upon any obstacle, such as a cliff or beach, depends in part upon the type of wave and its condition at the moment of collision with the obstacle. If an unbroken oscillatory wave strikes a vertical wall or cliff the base of which reaches down to deep water, the wave is reflected back. At the instant of contact the crest of the wave rises to twice its normal height and the cliff is subjected to the hydrostatic pressure of this unusually high water column. The absence of any forward thrust of the water mass under these conditions is shown by the behavior of boats which have been observed to rise and fall with successive waves without touching the vertical wall only a few feet distant. Hagen concludes that under such circumstances débris must accumulate at the base of the wall and that therefore the prejudice against vertical sea walls and harbor walls, based on the fear of undermining by wave action, is ill-founded.—DOUGLAS W. JOHNSON, *Shore Processes and Shoreline Development,* p. 57

This is part of an informative treatment of wave action, accurate and compact. It would be read, however, only by someone who was consciously looking for knowledge of the subject. The following passage is intended for a more general audience, though one limited to people with a definite interest in more than the superficial appearance of their world. The facts are presented with a minimum of technical language and made more vivid by the use of familiar comparisons ("rather like relays of messengers . . .").

> These molecules move with very high speeds; in the ordinary air of an ordinary room, the average molecular speed is about 500 yards a second. This is roughly the speed of a rifle-bullet, and is rather more than the ordinary speed of sound. As we are familiar with this latter speed from everyday experience, it is easy to form some conception of molecular speeds in a gas. It is not a mere accident that molecular speeds are comparable with the speed of sound. Sound is a disturbance which one molecule passes on to another when it collides with it, rather like relays of messengers passing a message on to one another, or Greek torch-bearers handing on their lights. Between collisions the message is carried forward at exactly the speed at which the molecules travel. If these all traveled with precisely the same speed and in precisely the same direction, the sound would of course travel with just the speed of molecules. But many of them travel on oblique courses, so that although the average speed of individual molecules in ordinary air is about 500 yards a second, the net forward velocity of the sound is only about 370 yards a second.—SIR JAMES JEANS, *The Universe Around Us,* p. 101

For a still more popular audience the subject matter must be further simplified and the facts made dramatic, if possible, by being presented in action. Some technical words are used, but they seem to be incidental, even decorative, rather than fundamental as in

Formal scientific writing. The beginning of a discussion of coal-tar dyes illustrates this popular approach to scientific discussion:

> If you put a bit of soft coal into a test tube (or, if you haven't a test tube, into a clay tobacco pipe and lute it over with clay) and heat it you will find a gas coming out of the end of the tube that will burn with a yellow smoky flame. After all the gas comes off you will find in the bottom of the test tube a chunk of dry, porous coke. These, then, are the two main products of the destructive distillation of coal. But if you are an unusually observant person, that is, if you are a born chemist with an eye to by-products, you will notice along in the middle of the tube where it is neither too hot nor too cold some dirty drops of water and some black sticky stuff. If you are just an ordinary person you won't pay any attention to this because there is only a little of it and because what you are after is the coke and gas. You regard the nasty, smelly mess that comes in between as merely a nuisance because it clogs up and spoils your nice, clean tube.
>
> Now that is the way the gas-makers and coke-makers–being for the most part ordinary persons and not born chemists–used to regard the water and tar that got into their pipes. They washed it out so as to have the gas clean and then ran it into the creek. But the neighbors–especially those who fished in the stream below the gas-works–made a fuss about spoiling the water, so the gas-men gave away the tar to the boys for use in celebrating the Fourth of July and election night or sold it for roofing.–EDWIN E. SLOSSON, *Creative Chemistry,* copyright 1930, D. Appleton-Century Company.

Beyond such popularizations are the sensational treatments of scientific subjects which we associate with the magazine sections of some Sunday papers. Because of the cheapness and the inaccuracy of many of these articles, scientists and scholars have tended to scorn all popularizing of their materials. But in recent years there has been an increase of reliable and interesting scientific writing for general readers as more specialists have found a challenge in seeing how much of their subject matter they can find a way of conveying to them. They are now leaving less of the work of popularizing to writers not sufficiently trained to do it accurately. Some of the publishers of inexpensive paper-bound books have made outstanding contributions in this area.

Until a person can write with authority about a specialized subject, he will most likely be doing popular or semipopular papers. Students in college can try their hand at preparing material for a somewhat limited but nonprofessional group of readers. The style of such papers would be rather Formal, and it has one real danger. The necessity for using genuine scientific words often leads to using *unnecessary* *big words. Writers in the social sciences especially have substituted unfamiliar words or *long variants for words of the General English vocabulary, as in "It is necessary to structure into a complex culture like ours a congruent hospitality to change in all institutional areas." If such writers visualized their readers, they would make more use of the General English vocabulary. Professor P. B. Ballard puts the general principle from the reader's point of view: "and when the common language fails in clearness, in dignity, or in freedom from ambiguity, it should be eked out by the language of the laboratory and of the study. Technical jargon is an evil, but a necessary evil. And necessary evils should be kept to a minimum." It is worth trying to see how much of your specialized information you can make available to an intelligent general reader.

An increasing number of jobs now depend on some competence in writing scientific or technical letters, reports, or articles. The director of research in a large corporation says:

> If you can't tell in written or oral English what your results are, it is impossible to get along in any industry. For instance, the laboratory worker must submit a condensed report of his experiments to his laboratory head. This man must in turn condense the reports of many workers and send a new report on to his superior. And so on, all the way up the line. If you can't put your thoughts and figures on paper in concise readable language, you're sunk.

See *Reports. References: Meta Emberger and Marion Hall, *Scientific Writing* (New York, 1955); W. O. Sypherd, Alvin M. Fountain, and V. E. Gibbens, *Manual of Technical Writing* (Chicago, 1957) —with useful bibliography, pages 545-553; Sam F. Trelease, *The Scientific Paper* (2nd ed., Baltimore, 1952).

Seasons *Spring, summer, fall, autumn, midsummer,* and so on are not capitalized except for stylistic emphasis, as sometimes in poetry or nature essays.

seem *Seem* is often used as a counter verb, making a statement needlessly qualified or distant:

> The letters of Flaubert [seem to] bring us as near to the writing of *Madame Bovary* as we can come.

In such a use *seem* is *deadwood.

Can't seem may be "illogical," but it is a useful Informal idiom for "be unable": I can't seem to learn physics.

self *Self* as a suffix forms the reflexive and intensive pronouns: *myself, yourself, himself, herself, itself, oneself, ourselves, yourselves, themselves.* These are used chiefly for emphasis (I can do that myself) or as a reflexive object (I couldn't help myself). See *himself, herself, *myself.

As a prefix, *self* is joined to the root word by a hyphen: *self-control, self-explanatory, self-made, self-respect.*

When *self* is the root word there is no hyphen: *selfhood, selfish, selfless, selfsame.*

semi- *Semi-* is a prefix meaning "half or approximately half" (*semicylindrical*), "twice within a certain period" (*semiweekly, semiannual*) or "partially, imperfectly" (*semicivilized, semiprofessional*).

It is not usually hyphened except before proper names (*semi-Christian*) or words beginning with *i* (*semi-invalid*). Pronounced sem′i and often sem′ī.

Semi **Semicolon (;)** **Revision: Use a semicolon as the mark of separation between these sentence elements.**

1. *To separate elements containing commas.* 2. *To separate coordinate clauses.* 3. *Semicolon and colon.* 4. *Semicolons and other traits of style.*

A semicolon is used to mark a degree of separation between sentence elements considerably greater than that marked by a comma, nearly as great as that marked by a period. (Professor Bonner's suggestion that we call it *semiperiod* has much to recommend it.) Although the chief question regarding its use is of appropriateness to traits of style (§ 4), there are a few situations in which a semicolon is usually found.

1. *To separate units that contain smaller elements separated by commas.* These may be items in a series, enumerations, figures, scores, or clauses with commas within them:

> Other periodicals not entirely dissimilar were John Harris's *The English Lucian,* 1698; Ward's *Weekly Comedy,* 1699; "Sylvester Partridge's" *The Infallible Astrologer,* 1700; and the *Merry Mercury,* 1700. –GEORGE CARVER, *Periodical Essays of the Eighteenth Century,* p. xviii

> Three things which a social system can provide or withhold are helpful to mental creation: first, technical training; second, liberty to follow the creative impulse; third, at least the possibility of ultimate appreciation by some public, whether large or small.–BERTRAND RUSSELL, *Proposed Roads to Freedom,* p. 169

2. *To separate coordinate clauses not closely related.*

a) Between contact clauses. A semicolon is used, especially in somewhat Formal writing, between two *contact clauses (clauses with no expressed connective) if the separation in thought and structure is conspicuous. Usually the two statements could stand as separate sentences, but the writer wishes to have them considered part of one idea. Contrasting statements are often punctuated with semicolons, as in these examples:

> Words and sentences are subjects of revision; paragraphs and whole compositions are subjects of prevision.–BARRETT WENDELL, *English Composition,* p. 117

> Your religion does not promise you a perfect life on earth, nor freedom from suffering; it does guarantee you the strength to bear suffering. Your religion does not expect you to be free from sin or mistakes in judgment; it does promise you forgiveness for your mistakes. Your religion expects you to continue making the best efforts you can on behalf of others; it does not guarantee that you or anyone can arrange the lives of people as he pleases.–HENRY C. LINK, *The Return to Religion,* pp. 68-9

 (See Ch. 2, "Revising comma faults," p. 56.)

b) With heavy connectives. A semicolon is used between clauses connected by the weightier conjunctive adverbs (*however, moreover, nevertheless, consequently* . . .). These are heavy connectives and usually link rather long clauses in a Formal style.

> This program implies better orientation of individuals to the manifold problems of adjustment; therefore, certain character traits, as well as specific abilities, should show positive change.—*The English Journal,* June 1937

A comma is now usually more common between clauses connected by the lighter conjunctive adverbs (*so, then* . . .). See *Conjunctive adverbs.

c) With coordinating conjunctions. A semicolon is used between clauses connected by coordinating conjunctions (*and, but, for, or* . . .) if the clauses are long or if the connection is not close, if they contain commas, or if for some reason (often for contrast) the writer wishes to show an emphatic separation between them.

> History as actuality includes all that has been said, felt, done, and thought by human beings on this planet since humanity began its long career; and, if Darwin is right, since the evolution of the human organism began in the primeval dawn.—C. A. BEARD, *The Discussion of Human Affairs,* p. 69

> She already had some furniture of her own, including what she could take from Truda; and Louis could let her have some of his—yes?—G. B. STERN, *The Matriarch,* p. 199

> Therefore those teachers who cannot admit that they may be wrong should not teach English composition; nor should those who never suspect that their pupils may be abler than they.—L. R. BRIGGS, *To College Teachers of English Composition,* p. 19

> The semicolon is used to separate parts of the sentence which are of more importance, or which show a division more distinct, than those separated by commas; or to separate sections already separated by commas.—JOHN BENBOW, *Manuscript & Proof,* p. 89

3. *Semicolon and colon.* Do not use a semicolon, which is a mark of *separation* as the examples in this article show, in place of a colon (:), which is a mark of *anticipation:*

> There are two principal considerations in the use of semicolons: the degree of separation to be indicated between statements and the formality of the style of the passage.

(See *Colon. § 4.)

4. *Semicolons and other traits of style.* Except for the specific situations described in § 1, the use of semicolons is in part a stylistic matter. They are more appropriate, more necessary, in rather Formal styles and in long, aggregating sentences. They tend to slow up the reading and are consequently fewer in narrative than in exposition. In General styles commas would be used in preference, or if the distinction between the clauses is considerable, two sentences would be written. In the following paragraph Mr. Cowley has chosen to rely on semicolons. Commas and periods that might have been used in a more Informal writing of the same passage are put in brackets.

> College students inhabit an easy world of their own; [.] except for very rich people and certain types of childless wives they form the only American class that takes leisure for granted. Many, of course, earn their board and tuition tending furnaces, waiting on table or running back kick-offs for a touchdown; what I am about to say does not apply to them. The others–almost always the ruling clique of a big university, the students who set the tone for the rest–are supported practically without efforts of their own. They write a few begging letters; [,] perhaps they study a little harder in order to win a scholarship; [,] but usually they don't stop to think where the money comes from. Above them, the president knows the source of the hard cash that runs this great educational factory; [.] he knows that the stream of donations can be stopped by a crash in the stock market or reduced in volume by newspaper reports of a professor gone bolshevik; [.] he knows what he has to tell his trustees or the state legislators when he goes to them begging for funds. The scrubwomen in the library, the chambermaids and janitors, know how they earn their food; but the students themselves, and many of their professors, are blind to economic forces; [.] society, as the source of food and football fields and professors' salaries, is a remote abstraction.–MALCOLM COWLEY, *Exile's Return*, pp. 36-7

Students tend to use more semicolons than would be used by professional writers today in General writing. They should consider the weight of the mark in view of the general movement of their writing and make sure that the movement of the particular sentence needs the degree of separation marked by the semicolon. (Compare *Comma, *Colon. Reference: Summey, pp. 97-101.)

S **Sentences** Revision: Eliminate the fault in the sentence marked.

The characteristics and problems of sentences are discussed in Chapters 2 and 7 and in the following *Index* entries that treat the most commonly needed points:

*Agreement
*Comma fault
*Conjunctions, use
*Dangling modifiers
*Emphasis
*Fragmentary sentence
*Idiom and idioms
*Parallel constructions
*Reference of pronouns
*Shifted constructions
*Subject and verb
*Wordiness
*Word order

Series Commas are used between the items of a series of three or more short items:

> The supposed contents of the physical world are *prima facie* very different from these: [four short clauses:] *molecules have no colour, atoms make no noise, electrons have no taste, and corpuscles do not even smell.*–BERTRAND RUSSELL, *Mysticism and Logic*, p. 145

> There are two or three large chests, a bedstead, the inevitable cradle occupied by the latest addition to the family. The small windows are seldom curtained. There are shelves for pots and pans, spoons and forks (often wooden), jars of gherkins, bottles of this and that, loaves of

bread, sacks of flour, baskets of dried fruit.—LOUIS ADAMIC, *The Native's Return,* p. 271

Usage is divided over the use of a comma before the last item of such a series. Using a comma helps to prevent ambiguity, especially if one member is compound. But many writers, especially in General and Informal styles, do not use one:

> Ministers, teachers [,] and editorial writers all united against the proposal.

If the members of the series are long, or not closely connected, or if the members have commas within them, they are separated by semicolons:

> "Quite a few people get credit lines in this big, handsome and heavy book: Dr. Albert Sirmay, who did the arrangements; Frederick E. Banbery, who painted the pictures; Newman Levy, who wrote an introduction to each show."—HERBERT KUPPERBERG, review of *The Rogers and Hammerstein Song Book, New York Herald Tribune Book Review,* Dec. 7, 1958, Vol. 35, No. 18.

(For further examples and details see Ch. 5 "In lists and series," p. 126; *Comma § 5, *Semicolon § 1. Reference: R. J. McCutcheon, "The Serial Comma Before 'and' and 'or,'" *American Speech,* 1940, 15:250-254.)

service The verb *service* (to service a car, a refrigerator) is needed and appropriate in all varieties of English. It means more than *repair* and has a different connotation from *maintain* or *keep up.*

set, sit People and things *sit* (past, *sat*) or they are *set* (past *set*)—that is, are "placed":

> I like to sit in a hotel lobby.
> I have sat in this same seat for three semesters.
> She set the soup down with a flourish.
> The post was set three feet in the ground.

A hen, however, *sets* (on her eggs) and the sun *sets.* In speech *set* is increasingly used for both verbs.

sh *Sh* is a digraph for a sound which is not a combination of the sounds usually represented by *s* or *h: shall, shove, ash.* The *sh* sound is represented by various other spellings: *machine* (mə shēn′), *tissue* (tish′ōō), *conscientious* (kon′shi en′shəs), *ocean* (ō′shən). Compare *zh.

shall–will

1. *General usage.* 2. *Formal usage.* 3. *Overuse of "shall."*

Future time is expressed by a number of locutions in English:

I am going to ask for a raise.
I am asking for a raise tomorrow.
There is to be a dance Friday.
He may go next week.
He comes next week.
Come again.
It's time he left.
He is sure to come tomorrow.
If he had the money tomorrow he would pay it.
I'll try to be on time.
I shall try to be on time.
I will try to be on time.

Expressions like the first nine are probably more common than the last three, so that it is hardly accurate to say that the future is expressed only with *shall* and *will*. But since distinctions between these auxiliaries have been regarded as an important item of reputable usage, it is necessary to discuss them in more detail than they deserve. Their use has never been uniform in English, though some grammarians have attempted to insist on uniformity. The general practices in the common situations needing these words are as follows:

1. *General usage.*

a) Simple future. In speech and writing the prevailing use in the United States, and in many other parts of the English-speaking world, is *will* in all persons (*I will ask, you will ask, he will ask . . .*).

b) Emphatic future. In expressing determination in the future or for some special emphasis, General usage is divided. In speech the determination is expressed by stress, which may be used on either word: I shall′ go, I will′ go. There is some tendency to use *shall* in all persons as the emphatic form, because *shall* is so rare that it makes a more emphatic word than *will:* I, you, he, she, we, you, they *shall* ask. Other constructions (I have to go . . .) are also used.

c) Contractions. In speaking and Informal writing in which contractions are used, the future becomes *I'll, you'll, he'll,* and so on, which do not discriminate between *shall* and *will. Won't* is used for *will not* (formed from an obsolete *woll* and *not*) and *shan't* for *shall not,* the latter even more rare than the uncontracted form.

d) In questions. In asking questions *shall* is likely to be used in the first and third persons and *will* in the second, but practice is not consistent. Even here *shall* is likely to be avoided, replaced where possible by *'ll*:

Shall I go?	Will you go?
What shall [What'll] we do now?	What will [What'll] you do now?
What shall [What'll] he do?	What will [What'll] he do with it?

In the negative, *won't* is much the more common:

Won't I look funny in that? What won't he think of next?

e) Shall is usual in laws, resolutions, etc.:

A permanent organization shall be set up within a year.
No singer shall receive more than $700 a performance.

The Biblical *thou shalt not* would now be expressed by *you must not.*

2. *Formal usage.* Some writers and editors use *shall* in the first person and *will* in the second and third persons in making the future tense, following handbook "rules" rather than actual usage.

First person:	I shall ask	we shall ask
Second person:	you will ask	you will ask
Third person:	he, she will ask	they will ask

In the emphatic future, expressing determination of the speaker, Formal English theoretically reverses this use of *shall* and *will:*

First person:	I will ask	we will ask
Second person:	you shall ask	you shall ask
Third person:	he, she shall ask	they shall ask

In asking questions a few people even use the form of *shall* or *will* in a question that the answerer would use in his reply. This usage is distinctly Formal and usually sounds unnatural.

Shall you go? Answer: I shall (shall not) go.

The efforts of purists to establish this Formal usage as General is now declining, and few editors today change copy to conform to it.

3. *Overuse of "shall."* The stress that schools have put on *shall* sometimes leads to an unidiomatic use:

Whether or not Congress will [not: shall] favor or pass laws against lynching is not for me to guess.

(See *should–would.)

References: Much has been written about the use of these words. As a beginning: Curme, *Syntax,* pages 362-371; Fries, *AEG,* pages 150-168 (a good short summary of actual usage); C. C. Fries, "The Expression of the Future," *Language,* 3:87-95; Jespersen, Chapters 25, 26 for British practice, though also illuminating for American usage; Amos L. Herold, *The English Journal,* 1936, 25:670-676; Robertson, pages 516-520.

shan't There is only one apostrophe in the contraction of *shall not.*

shape is Informal in the sense of "manner, condition": They were in good shape for the trip.

Shifted constructions Revision: Make the constructions marked consistent (parallel) in form.

Shift

Two or more sentence elements that have the same relationship to another element in the sentence should be expressed by words in the same grammatical construction; that is, the constructions should be parallel. Adjectives should be paralleled by adjectives, nouns by nouns; a specific verb form should be continued in a similar construction; active or passive voice should be kept consistently in a sentence or passage; and so on. (The three *should be* constructions in the preceding sentence are parallel.) Shifting from one form to another may confuse or disturb a reader because it is a failure to follow established patterns of writing. Shifts can be removed in revision.

Some commonly shifted constructions are:

Shifted	*Consistent*
1) Shift in subject	
Once *the car* is started, *you* will get along all right.	Once *you* get the car started, *you* will get along all right.
2) Adjective–Noun	
This book seems *interesting* and *an informative piece of work.*	This book seems *interesting* and *informative.*

3) Personal–Impersonal

In fact going to summer school is worse than no vacation at all, for when *you* have no vacation *you* do not think about all the things *a person* could do if *he* had one.	. . . for when *you* have no vacation *you* do not think about all the things you could do if *you* had one.

4) Adverb–Adjective

Along these walks are the cottages, many of which have stood *since the founding* [adverbial phrase], and others *more recent* [adjective].	. . . many of which have stood *since the founding,* and others of which have been built *more recently.*

5) Noun–Adverb

Associating [noun] with these fellows and *how to adapt myself to live with them* [adverbial phrase] will be helpful to me when I am through college.	*Associating* with these fellows and *adapting* myself to live with them will be helpful to me when I am through college.

6) Noun–Adjective

Anyone who has *persistence* [noun] or is *desperate* [adjective] enough can get a job on a ship.	Anyone who is *persistent* or who is *desperate* enough . . . .

7) Noun–Clause

The most important factors are *time* and *temperature,* careful *control* at every point, and *the mechanical equipment must be in perfect operating condition at any time of the day or night.*	. . . and *mechanical equipment in perfect operating condition at any time of the day or night.*

8) Participle–Clause

How many times have you seen a fisherman *trying* to get to his favorite fishing spot without scaring all the fish away but instead *he sends out* messages with his rhythmical squeak-splash, squeak-splash.	. . . but instead *sending out* messages . . . .

9) Phrase–Clause

I have heard complaints *about the plot being weak* and *that the setting was played up too much.*	. . . and *the setting being played up too much.*

For other examples see Chapter 2, "Making constructions consistent," page 65.

Ships' names The names of ships are indicated in three ways:

1) In most books and generally in Formal writing they are italicized (underlined in the manuscript):

The *Caryatid,* in ballast, was steaming down the river at half-speed . . . .—WILLIAM MCFEE, *Casuals of the Sea,* p. 317

2) In newspapers and personal writing there is a growing tendency to regard the names of ships simply as proper names, capitalizing them but not otherwise setting them off:

The Magellan weighed anchor at 9:20 A.M. and moved slowly to her berth at Pier H, Weehawken, N.J.—*The New York Times,* Feb. 3, 1950

3) Occasionally ships' names are found in quotation marks:

The summer of 1926 David spent as a junior member of the American Museum Greenland Expedition, . . . on the stout little schooner "Morrissey." [Jacket of *David Goes to Greenland.* In the book *Morrissey* is italicized.]

Shoptalk *Shoptalk* is the offhand talk of people in various occupations, from medicine and law to ditchdigging and panhandling. It varies with the social class and personal taste of its users, from the talk of a garage hand to that of an automotive engineer or professor of physics. Its distinguishing feature is vocabulary. Many of the words are the necessary names for materials and processes and tools and for the people—for everything that is commonly referred to in a line of work—like *em, en, pica, pi, spreaders, platen, rule, chase,* from a printing shop. Such words are usually given in dictionaries with the name of the occupation to which they belong. Shoptalk may also include technical and scientific words, as in the conversation of internes and nurses, but it is set off from Formal technical and professional writing by the conversational tone and by the presence of the slang of the field, sometimes called *cant,* which would not be found at the Formal level.

Shoptalk has a vigorous and often figurative vocabulary, in which words are formed with great freedom. Especially convenient are short substitutes for long technical words. A *mike* may be a microphone in a radio studio, a microscope in a laboratory, a micrometer in a shop; *hypo* is a fixing bath to a photographer and a hypodermic injection in a medical context; *soup* is the name of a pourable mixture in scores of manufacturing processes. Racing has *place, show, on the nose, tipster, bookie;* unlisted securities are *cats and dogs;* football players have *skull practice;* a student pilot must *dual* for many hours before he is allowed to *solo;* a *gagman* makes up the comedian's lines; and so on.

Some of these words, like *fade-out* from the movies, are useful in discussing other subjects, and they may become a part of the General vocabulary, like *third degree.* Shoptalk is appropriate and necessary in speaking or writing about the particular occupation in which it is used, usually with some explanations required for readers who are not acquainted with it. It is often appropriate in Informal writing, but it is usually out of place in General writing and almost always out of place in Formal writing.

References: *American Speech* has many articles dealing with the vocabularies of particular occupations.

should–would 1. *Should* and *would* are used in statements that carry some doubt or uncertainty about the statement that is being made. They are also used in polite or unemphatic requests:

They should be there by Monday. (Contrast: They will be there by Monday.)

Would you please shut the door on your way out? (Contrast: Will you please. . . .)

In the first person both *should* and *would* are used:

I would be much obliged if you could do this.
I should be much obliged if you could do this.

Usage is so much divided on the choice between these forms that one's feeling is probably the safest guide. Be sure, though, that you follow one or the other usage consistently in a piece of writing.

2. *Should* as an auxiliary used with all persons expresses a mild sense of obligation, weaker than *ought:*

I should pay this bill. (Contrast: I ought to pay this bill.)

In indirect discourse *should* and *would* represent the future tense of the direct speech, following the "sequence of tenses." (See *Tenses of verbs § 3.)

Direct: "I will be ready at three," Mildred said.
Indirect: Mildred said that she would be ready at three.

Would has some currency in Informal or half-humorous idiom "that would be her picture," meaning "That is her picture, isn't it?"

show is Informal, or theatrical *shoptalk, in the sense of "a play"; is usually humorous or Nonstandard for a dignified public performance, as of a concert; General when applied to the movies (short for *picture show*). It is Informal for "chance" (They didn't have a show of winning).

show up is Informal for *appear* (He didn't show up for two hours) and for *expose* (I showed him up, all right).

sic *Sic* (Latin for *thus, so;* pronounced sik) in brackets is sometimes used to mark an error in quoted matter. It shows the reader that the deviant spelling or grammar was in the quoted material, not made by the quoter: The letter was headed "Danbury, Conneticut [*sic*], Jan. 2."

sick *Ill* is the more Formal word. The two words mean the same, except that Informally and in British usage *sick* is often specialized to mean "nauseated." In the United States *sick* in the sense of *nauseated* is made clear by adding a phrase: It made me *sick to my stomach.*

Silent letters English spells a great many words with silent letters–that is, letters which do not represent any speech sound. A few of them are the result of mistaken analogies, like the *s* of *island,* which is there from confusion with the French *isle,* though it comes from Old English *igland* and has never had the *s* sounded. Renaissance scholars inserted a number of letters that had been in the Greek and Latin words from which the English ones derived but that had never been sounded in English: Chaucer could write *det,* but we must write *debt* because the scholars recognized the word's descent from *debitum;* and the addition of the *h* to Middle English *trone* has established the spelling pronunciation *throne.* (See *Pronunciation § 3c.)

But most of our silent letters act, as Professor Lounsbury put it, "as a sort of tombstone to mark the place where lie the unsightly remains of a dead and forgotten pronunciation": the pronunciation has changed but the spelling hasn't, or hasn't changed enough. There they stand, those final *b*'s in *bomb, comb, climb,* the initial *g*'s and *k*'s in *gnarl, gnash, knack, knave, knee, knife, knuckle,* the *p*'s in Greekish words like *pneumonia* and *psychology,* the *gh*'s in *through* and *night* and *caught* that mark former pronounced gutterals.

Silent letters are sometimes defended because they tend to remind us of a word's ancestry, but that fact is of use only to scholars, and there are not enough scholars to pay to spell the language for them. Besides, it's not always true: *delight* is from French *delite,* the *gh* being by analogy with *light.* Some people think these spellings have an esthetic value, that *night* has a beauty not in *nite* or that the superfluous *h* gives *ghost* a special weirdness. But this reason doesn't seem very substantial, since we learn these words from hearing them, and whatever quality *ghost* has as a word comes more likely from the tone in which we have heard it spoken.

These silent letters are gradually being dropped, quietly, almost surreptitiously. *Apophthegm* has recently lost its *ph*–it may sometime lose its *g* too. In familiar writing *altho* is quite common; business and familiar English use *nite* and other shortened forms. But most of the silent letters hold firm, making spelling difficult.

Sometimes people who are not familiar with the sound of a word are led to pronounce a silent letter, giving a "spelling pronunciation," as pronouncing *indict* in dikt′ instead of in dīt′. (See Ch. 4, "Reasons for difficulties in spelling," p. 103, Pronunciation § 1c. Reference: For groupings of silent letter words see W. A. Craigie, *English Spelling,* pp. 36-39, 67-73.)

similar The last syllable is *-lar.* Contrast *familiar.* Note the pronunciations: sim′ə lər, fə mil′yər.

similar to is a wordy way of saying *like:* It was my first wreck and I hope I may never have another similar to that one (like it).

situated is often *deadwood:

> I was staying with friends in a little town in Canada called Picton, [situated] in the Province of Ontario.
>
> It was a biplane and the front cockpit was [situated] right over the lower wing.

size As a modifier, *size* (a small size hat, king size) is in General usage. *Sized* is more Formal and is still probably the more common form in writing. But it is often better omitted altogether (a small hat). See *-ed § 3.

ski The plural is *skis,* sometimes *ski.* The verb is *ski, skied, skiing.* The pronunciation is skē (or sometimes, following the Scandinavian, shē).

Slang It is hard to draw a line between slang and other sorts of Informal English. Many people use the term too broadly–for almost any word not in the General vocabulary–and dictionaries are too generous with the label, marking as "Slang" many words that perhaps suggest spoken rather than written style. (Actually dictionaries include very few genuine slang expressions, because by the time they appear in their collection of quotations they have almost necessarily achieved considerable currency in print.)

The central characteristic of slang comes from the motive for its use: a desire for novelty, for vivid emphasis, for being in the know, up with the times or a little ahead. These are essentially qualities of style, and the tone and the connotation are as important as the central meaning of the words. Other varieties of the language have ways of expressing the ideas of slang words, but they are often roundabout and their tone is quieter, more conventional. Young people like novelty, as do fashionable and sporty grown-ups, and comedians need it in their trade. Slang is especially common in talking about sports and amusements and all sorts of everyday activities–eating, drinking, use of money, the relations between people–for which the ordinary terms seem to have worn thin.

Slang words are made by natural linguistic processes. Their slang quality may lie in the intonation of a phrase (*or what have you, you and who else*). Slang abounds in clipped words (*razz, natch, hood*), and in compounds and derivatives of ordinary words (*screwball, sourpuss, cockeyed*). Many are borrowed from the *shoptalk of sports and the popular arts, especially jazz (*square, cool, real gone*). And a great many are figurative extensions of General words (*fierce* as a term of approval, *hack around, rock* for a hard guy, and the words for human stupidity, like *numb, feeble*). To *park* a car is General English; to *park* a hat or a piece of gum is probably still slang. In the desire for novelty and emphasis one word simply leads to another, as *square* went to *cube*. Sound is often an important factor, as in *goof off, booboo, barf.*

Many slang words have short lives–*skiddoo, twenty-three, vamoose, beat it, scram, hit the trail, take a powder, drag out, shag out* have succeeded each other almost within a generation. Words for being drunk (*soused, plastered, blotto*), for girls (*baby, doll, dream boat*), and words of approval (*tops, a wow, neat, the most*) and disapproval (*all wet, screwy, square*) change almost from year to year. Many slang words prove more permanently useful and become a part at least of the Informal vocabulary (*blind date, boy friend, go steady, copesetic*). Others have in time become General English (*ballyhoo, highbrow, lowbrow*).

Slang belongs primarily to familiar and rather flashy speech and comedy, to which it can give a note of freshness. This freshness wears off after some hundreds of repetitions so that the prime virtue of the words is lost. In writing, slang is less often appropriate, partly because of triteness and partly because many of the words name general impressions instead of specific ones, so that they rank with *nice* and *good*. Slang is out of place in Formal writing, and if used for some special purpose would ordinarily be put in quotation marks. It should not be used in General writing unless it would add a quality that is appropriate and that the writer wishes. In Informal writing it is often appropriate, especially in recounting personal experiences and for discussions of sports and campus affairs, though even with such subjects the taste of expected readers should be considered. If slang expressions are appropriate, they should be used without apology (that is, without quotation marks), and if they are not appropriate, they should not be used. The chief objections to slang, aside from its possible conspicuousness, are to its overuse and to its use in place of more exact expressions.

slow, slowly Both *slow* and *slowly* are adverbs, each going back to an old English adverb form (*slawe* and *slawlice* respectively). Use whichever sounds better in the sentence. *Slow* is rather more vigorous: *Go slow*. There are, however, some people with a strong prejudice against adverbial *slow*. (See *Adverbs, types and forms § 1 and *Divided usage.)

so Informally, especially in speech, *so* is used as a subordinating conjunction to introduce clauses of purpose:

> Informal: He started early so he could get good seats.
> General: He started early so that he could get good seats; . . . in order to get good seats; . . . to get good seats.

So is similarly used in clauses of result, in which General English would usually have *so that* or change to a *since* construction:

> Informal: I wondered what they would do with the logs, so I followed them through the woods.
> General: Since [Because] I wondered what they would do with the logs, I followed them through the woods.
> Informal: He is a fast reader, so he got through before I did.
> General: Since he is a fast reader, he got through before I did.

Formal English would also use *so that* or the more exact *because* or *since* in these two constructions.

As an intensive *so* is common in speech and is often stressed (He's *so* handsome! I was *so* excited.) and has been called the "feminine *so*." But it is sometimes also used as an intensive in General writing: This confinement was hard for him–he had been so active all his life. (References: Fries, *AEG*, pp. 226-227); Russell

Thomas, "The Use of *So* as an Intensifier," *College English,* 1951, 12:453-454.)

so-called If you have to use *so-called,* don't duplicate the idea by putting the name of the so-called object in quotes: Not *the so-called "champion,"* but *the so-called champion.* The word is rather stiff and in General writing quotation marks would often be used instead (the "champion").

So-called is usually hyphened when it precedes its principal word but not when it follows:

> Their so-called liberal views were merely an echo of the conservative attitude. (Their "liberal" views were . . . .)
>
> Their justice, so called, smacked of partiality.

so . . . that Even when several words come between *so* and *that* no comma should precede *that:*

> All strands of the story are so artfully and inextricably interwoven [ ] that anything but the author's desired effect is impossible.

Social correspondence 1. *Informal notes.* The form and tone of Informal social notes–invitations, answers to invitations, thank you letters –are those of personal letters. (See *Letters §§ 1 and 2.) Giving all the necessary information of time, place, and so on, being prompt in answering notes, and maintaining a tone of courtesy are more important than mechanical form. If the correspondents are not intimately acquainted, a more Formal style and more details of address may be needed than if they are intimates. The first note below is written to an intimate acquaintance; the other two passed between teacher and student.

> Dear Helen,
>
> My sister will be home this weekend, and I'm planning a little tea for her on Saturday afternoon at four. I hope you can join us and help celebrate the homecoming. Please let me know if you can come.
>
> Affectionately yours,
> Dorothy

> Dear Helen,
>
> I am having a little supper-party for my voice students next Sunday evening, and I hope that you will be able to come. We shall eat at six o'clock and later listen to a special broadcast of fine voices that should give us some helpful pointers. The program won't be long; so if you have an engagement later in the evening this should not interfere.
>
> Cordially yours,
> Marion Hall

> Dear Miss Hall,
>
> Thank you for your invitation for Sunday evening. As luck would have it, though, our sorority is giving a Pledge Banquet that same evening and it is obligatory that I attend. Consequently I am afraid I cannot be at your home then. I am sorry to have to miss it, for home cooking is a treat and I would very much like to hear the broadcast.
>
> Very sincerely yours,
> Helen James

2. *Formal notes.* Formal social correspondence—announcements, invitations, answers to invitations—is impersonal and standardized. It is used for social events indicating, usually, formal dress or a gathering with distinguished guests. The illustration below shows the characteristic form of a printed or engraved invitation. Names are given in full, dates and other numbers are written in words, no punctuation is used at the ends of lines. Usually a reply is requested, either by *R.S.V.P.* ("répondez, s'il vous plaît" = "please answer") or by *The favor of a reply is requested.* The engraver or printer will help with the style of the note.

Delta Kappa Epsilon

requests the pleasure of your company

at a reception

in honor of

John Hughes Hunter

on Friday, the twenty-sixth of May

at eight o'clock in the evening

The favor of a reply
is requested

Even though the note is in longhand, the form of engraved notes is still followed:

Miss Jeanette Ames
Miss Eva Loy
request the pleasure of
Mrs. Henry Jackson's
company at a breakfast bridge
on June twenty-eighth
at the Kingston Club. Ten o'clock

In answering an invitation the form of the invitation is adopted, and the exact words are followed so far as possible. The names, dates, and place are repeated.

Mrs. Henry Jackson
accepts with pleasure
the kind invitation of
Miss Jeanette Ames and Miss Eva Loy
to a breakfast bridge
on June twenty-eighth
at the Kingston Club. Ten o'clock

Solecism A solecism (sol′ə siz′əm) is an error in the use of words or constructions. The term is now distinctly Formal.

some, and compounds with some **1.** In written English, *some* is usually an indefinite pronoun (Some travel and some don't) or an adjective (some people, some ideas).

2. As an adverb, *some* is Informally used with comparatives (It was some better than I expected), instead of the more Formal *somewhat.* It is also Informal when used with verbs (We traded some that afternoon).

3. The compounds *somebody, someway, somewhat, somewhere* are written as one word. Someone is usually one word (Someone is coming) but may be two if the *one* is stressed (Some one of them). *Someday* is written as one word or as two.

4. *Some place* is Informal for *somewhere* (I lost it some place). *Someway* and *someways* are also Informal, and *somewheres* is Nonstandard. (Compare *any, and compounds with any.)

sooner . . . than After *no sooner* the preferable connective is *than,* not *when:*

> The fly had no sooner hit the water than [not *when*] a huge trout snapped at it.

sophomore In spite of the dictionaries, *sophomore* is usually pronounced as two syllables, sof′ mōr. The word is both noun and adjective. The adjective *sophomoric* (sof′ [ə] môr′ ik) refers to supposed undesirable traits of sophomores, as in *a sophomoric style* or *sophomoric conduct.*

species *Species* has the same form in both singular and plural, though some distinguish in pronunciation: singular, spē′shiz; plural, spē′shiz or spē′shēz.

Specie (spē′shi), meaning money in coin, is a different word, a collective noun without plural form.

Sp **Spelling** Revision: Correct the spelling of the word marked, referring to a dictionary if necessary.

Chapter 4, page 102, describes some of the general characteristics of English spelling and makes some specific suggestions for improving spelling habits. It is useful also to study groups of words that have some trait in common. The following *Index* articles treat such groups. Those marked † give the most useful rules or suggestions for mastering large groups of words.

-able, -ible (desirable, legible)
-ae-, -oe- (ameba, esthetic)
† -al ly (fatal, politically)
-ance, -ence (-ant, -ent) (attendance, existence)
Apostrophe (Bob's picture, the companies' charter)
Capital letters
† -ce, -ge (peaceable, courageous)
Contractions (didn't, he'll)
† Doubling final consonants (refer–referred)
† E § 5, silent or mute *e* (changeable, likeness)
-ed (exceptions to rule)
† -ei-, -ie- (feign, receive, achieve)
en-, in- (encourage, inquire)
-er, -or (debater, objector)
-er, -re (luster, scepter)
Foreign words in English (chauffeur, ersatz; accent marks)
† Homonyms (words pronounced alike but usually spelled differently: plain, plane; altar, alter)
Hyphen (re-enter, father-in-law)
in-, un- (incapable, unedited)
-ize, -ise (apologize, advertise)
-le words (meddle, nickel)
† Neutral vowel (comparable, repetition)
-or (-our) (honor, Saviour)
-ough (-augh) (although, laugh)
Plurals (beauties, birches, heroes, knives)
Principal parts of verbs
Pronunciation § 4
re- (reform, re-form)
Silent letters (debt, night)

The following list contains many words that give difficulty in spelling. It is not exhaustive and is by no means a substitute for a dictionary, but it can be used as the basis for a discussion of spelling. Perhaps it can be most useful if you check the particular words in it that you are not sure of and occasionally study those to fix them better in mind. In the margins add others that have troubled you–in every way possible make it *your* list.

*means that there is an *Index* article discussing that word.

A dash separating two words (*adviser–advisor*) means that the two forms are about equally common.

A second form in brackets (*encyclopedia* [*encyclopaedia*]) means that the form in brackets is now less common than the other.

A few words are identified by pronunciation or definition in parentheses.

The words are divided into syllables so that they can be visualized in relation to their pronunciation.

ab sence
ac cept, -ance, -able
ac cess, ac ces si ble
ac ci den tal ly

ac com mo date
ac com pa ny ing,
ac com pa nied,
ac com pa ni ment
ac cus tom
ache
a chieve
ac quaint, -ed, -ance
ac quired
a cross
ac tu al, -ly
ad ap ta tion
*ad dress
ad o les cence
ad vice (noun)
ad vise (verb)
*ad vis er—ad vis or
*af fect (to influence)
a gainst
ag gra vate
ag gres sion, ag gres sor
*air plane [aeroplane]
aisle (of a theater)
al co hol
al lege
all read y
*all right
al lu sion
*al ma ma ter
al read y
al tar (of a church)
al ter (to change)
*al though—al tho
al to geth er
*a lum nus, a lum ni,
a lum na, a lum nae
am a teur
a nal o gous, a nal o gy
a nal y sis
an a lyze [analyse]
an es thet ic [anaesthetic]
an gel (ān′jəl)
an gle (ang′gəl)
an nounc er
an nu al
an swer
anx i e ty
a pol o gy
ap pa ra tus
ap par ent
ap pear, -ance, ap pear anc es
ap pre ci ate
ap prox i mate
arc tic
ar gue, ar gu ing, ar gu ment
a roused
as cent (going up)
as sas sin
as sent (agreement)
as so ci a tion
*ath lete, ath let ics
at tacked
at tend, -ance, -ant
at ti tude
at tor ney
at trac tive
au di ence
au to bi og ra phy
aux il ia ry
bach e lor
bal ance
ba sis, bas i cal ly
bat tal ion
be lieve
ben e fit ed, ben e fi cial
berth (a bed)
bib li og ra phy
birth (being born)
breath (breth)
breathe (brēth)
brid al (of a bride)
bri dle (of a horse)
bril liant
Brit ain (Great Britain)
bu reau
bu reauc ra cy
*bus, bus es—bus ses
ca fe te ri a
cal en dar (of days)
cal i ber [calibre]
can't
can vas (sailcloth)
can vass (to go about)
cap i tal (city), -ism
cap i tol (building)
cap tain
car bu re tor [carburettor]
care, -ful, -less
car goes
cas u al ties

cat e go ries
ceil ing
cen ter [centre]
cer tain ly
chal leng er
cham pagne
change a ble
*chap er on [chaperone]
char ac ter is tic, char ac ter ized
chauf feur
chief, -tain
choose, choos ing (present)
chose, cho sen (past)
cig a ret—cig a rette
col lar
col le gi ate
colo nel
col or
co los sal
*col umn
com e dy
com ing
com mit
com mit tee
com par a tive
com par i son
com pel, com pelled
com pet i tor
com plaint
com ple ment (to fill out)
com pli ment (to praise)
con cede
con ceive
con cer to (kən cher′tō)
con demn
con nois seur (kon′ə sûr′)
con quer or
con science
con sci en tious
con scious, -ness
con sen sus
con sist ent
con tempt i ble
con tin u ous
con trol, con trolled, con trol ling
con tro ver sy, con tro ver sial
con ven ient, con ven ience
con vert i ble
co op er a tive—co-op er a tive
[coöperative]
corps (kôr)

corpse (kôrps)
coun cil (a group)
coun ci lor—coun cil lor
coun sel (advice)
coun sel or—coun sel lor
cour te ous, cour te sy
crept
crit i cism, crit i cize
cu ri ous, cu ri os i ty
cur ric u lar (adjective)
*cur ric u lum (noun)
cur tain
cus tom
cy lin dri cal

dair y (dār′i)
damned
dealt
de bat er
de ceased (də sēst′)
de ceive
de cent (dē′sənt)
de fend ants
def i nite, def i ni tion
de pend ent (adj. or noun)
de scend ant
de scent (də sent′)
de scribe, de scrip tion
de sert (də zert′, leave)
des ert (dez′ərt, waste)
de sire, de sir a bil i ty
de spair, des per ate
des sert (də zert′, of a meal)
de vel op [develope]
dex ter ous—dex trous
di a gram mat ic
di a phragm
di a ry (dī′ə ri)
die, dies, dy ing
die sel
di e ti tian [dietician]
dif fer ent
di lap i dat ed
din ing room
din ning (noise)
diph ther i a
dis ap pear ance
dis ap point ment
dis as trous
dis cre tion
dis eased (di zēzd′)

dis gust ed
dis patch [despatch]
dis si pate
dis trib u tor
dis turb ance
di vide
di vine
dom i nant
don't
dor mi to ry
dry, dri er, dri est
du al (two)
du el (fight)
dye, dyed, dye ing

ech o, ech oes
ec sta sies
ef fect (*affect)
ef fi cient, ef fi cien cy
el i gi ble, el i gi bil i ty
em bar rass
em pha size, em phat ic,
em phat ic al ly
em ploy ee, em ploy ees
[employe, employé]
en cy clo pe di a [encyclopaedia]
en er get ic
en force
en vi ron ment
e quip ment, e quipped
es pe cial ly
es thet ic–aesthetic
ex ag ger ate
ex am ine, ex am in ing,
ex am i na tion
ex ceed, ex ces sive
ex cel, -lence, -lent
*ex cept (to omit)
ex cit a ble
ex er cise
ex haust ed
ex hil a rat ing
ex ist, -ence
ex pe di tion ar y
ex pense
ex pe ri ence
ex per i ment
*ex tra cur ric u lar
ex trav a gant
ex treme ly
ex u ber ance

fac ile, fa cil i ty
fair way (golf)
fal la cy
fa mil iar
fan ta sy, fan ta sies
fas ci na tion
fa vor ite
Feb ru ar y
*fi an cé, fiancée
fic ti tious
fier y
fi nal ly
fi nan cial ly
fin an cier
fli er–fly er
fore head (for'id)
for eign
for feit
for mal ly
for mer ly
for ty-four–for ty four
fourth
frame house
fran ti cal ly [franticly]
fra ter ni ties
*fresh man
friend, -li ness
ful fill–ful fil
fun da men tal, -ly
fur ni ture
fur ther

gage–gauge
gel a tine–gel a tin
ghost
gov ern ment
gov er nor
*grade school–graded school
gram mar, gram mat i cal, -ly
*gray [grey]
grief
grue some [grewsome]
guar an tee, guar an teed
guard i an
guer ril la–gue ril la (fighting)
guid ance

hand i cap, hand i capped
hand ker chief
hand some
hang ar

hap pi ness
hear
here
*height
he ro, he roes, her o ine
hid e ous
hin drance
hoard
hoarse (in throat)
horde
hor i zon tal
hors d'oeu vre (ôr dû′vr)
huge
hu man (hū′mən)
hu mane (hū mān′)
hun gri ly
hur ried ly
hy giene
hyp no sis, hyp not ic, hyp no tize
[hypnotise]
hy poc ri sy, hyp o crite
hys ter i cal

ig no rance, ig no rant
il log i cal
im ag ine, im ag i na tion,
im ag i nar y
im me di ate ly
im ple ment
im promp tu, im promp tus
in ad e quate
in ces sant ly
in ci den tal ly
*in cred i ble
in de pend ence
in dict ment (in dīt′mənt)
in dis pen sa ble
in flu ence, in flu en tial
in gen ious
in gen u ous
in i ti a tion
in nu en do, in nu en does
in oc u late
in tel lec tu al
in tel li gent
in ter est
in tern [interne]
in ter pre tive [interpretative]
in ter rupt
in tol er ance
in ven tor–in ven ter

ir rel e vant
ir re li gious
ir re sist i ble
ir rev er ent
*its, it's
it self

ja lop y
john ny cake
jol li ty
*judg ment [judgement]

kha ki
kid nap, kid naped [kidnapped]
ki mo no, ki mo nos
kin der gar ten
kitch en ette
knowl edge

la bor, -er, -ious ly
lab o ra to ry
lat er (lā′tər)
*lat ter (lat′ər)
lau rel
lax a tive
*lead, led
leg a cy
le git i mate
lei sure ly
length, -en ing
li a ble
li ar
li brar i an
li cense
light en ing (making lighter)
*light ning (a flash)
lik a ble [likeable]
like, -ness, -ly, -li hood
li queur
liq uor
liv a ble [liveable]
live li hood
lone, -ly, -li ness
loose (lo͞os)
*lose (lo͞oz), los ing
lux u ry

mack er el
mag a zine
mag nif i cent, mag nif i cence
main tain, main te nance

man tel (the shelf)
man tle (the cloak)
man u al
man u fac tur er
mar riage
math e mat ics
mean, meant
med i cine
*me di e val [mediaeval]
me di o cre
Me di ter ra ne an
met al
met tle
mil lion aire
min i a ture
min ute
mis chief, mis chie vous
mis spelled
mold [mould]
*mor al (môr′əl), -ly
mo rale (mə ral′)
mort gage
moun tain ous
mur mur
mus cle
mus tache
mys te ri ous

*na ive–na ïve
nat u ral ly
nec es sar y, nec es sar i ly
*Ne gro, Ne groes
nei ther
nick el
niece
nine ty-ninth–nine ty ninth
no tice a ble, no tic ing
no to ri e ty

o bey, o be di ence
o bliged
ob sta cle
*oc ca sion, -al ly
oc cur, -ring, -rence, oc curred
of fi cial
oil y
o mit, -ted, o mis sion
one self
op er ate
op po nent
op por tu ni ty

op ti mism
or gan i za tion [organisation]
or gan ize [organise]
or i gin, -al
out ra geous

*paid
pa ja ma [pyjama]
pam phlet
pan to mime
par al lel, par al leled
par lia ment
pa roled
par tic i pate
par tic u lar ly
*passed, past
pas time
ped es tal
per ceive
per form
per ma nent
per mit, per mis si ble
per se ver ance
per sist ent
per son al
per son nel
per spi ra tion
per suade, per sua sion
phase
Phil ip pines
phi los o phy
phys i cal
phy si cian
pi an o, pi an os
pick le
*pic nic, pic nicked
piece
pique (pēk)
pi qué (pi kā′)
plain
plane
planned
play wright
pleas ant
pneu mat ic
pneu mo nia
*pol i tics, pol i ti cian
pos si bil i ty
po ta to, po ta toes
prac ti ca bil i ty
*prac ti cal

prac tice [practise]
pre cede, pre ced ing
pref er ence, pre ferred
prej u dice
prep a ra tion
pres ence
prev a lent
prim i tive
*prin ci pal
prin ci ple
priv i lege
prob a ble, prob a bly
pro ce dure
pro ceed
pro fes sion
pro fes sor
pro gram [programme]
prom i nent
pro nounce, pro nun ci a tion
prop a gan da
pro pel ler
pro te in
psy cho a nal y sis,
psy cho an a lyze
*psy chol o gy
psy cho path ic
psy cho so mat ic
pub lic ly
pump kin
pur sue, pur suit

quan ti ty
quan tum
quar an tine
quay [quai] (kē)
qui et
quite
quix ot ic
quiz, quiz zes

re al ly
re ceive
*rec i pe, re ceipt
re cip i ent
rec la ma tion
rec og ni tion
rec om mend
re-en ter
re fer, -ence, re ferred
re for est a tion
rel a tive
rel e vant
re lieve
re li gion, re li gious
re mem ber
rem i nisce
*Ren ais sance [Re nas cence]
ren dez vous
re pel lent
rep e ti tion, rep e ti tious
res er voir
re sist ance
re spect ful ly
re spec tive ly
res tau rant
rev er ent
rhet o ric
rhyme [rime]
rhythm, rhyth mi cal
ri dic u lous
room mate

sac ri fice
sac ri le gious
safe ty
sal a ry
sand wich
sax o phone
scan dal ous
scar (skär)
scare (skar)
sce nar i o
scene, sce nic
sched ule
sec re tar i al
seize
se mes ter
sen a tor
sense, sen si ble
sen tence
sep a rate, sep a ra tion
ser geant (sär′jənt)
sev er al
se vere ly, se ver i ty
shear (verb)
sheer (adj.)
shin ing
sieve
sig nif i cance
*sim i lar
sin cere ly, sin cer i ty
site (of a city)

skep ti cal [sceptical]
*ski, skis, skied, ski ing
slim y
slug gish
soc cer
sol u ble
so phis ti ca tion
*soph o more
source
speak, speech
spe cif i cal ly
spec i men, spec i mens
spec ter [spectre]
spic y, spic i ness
spon sor
stac ca to
sta tion ar y (fixed)
sta tion er y (paper)
stat ue
stat ure
stat ute
stom ach ache
sto ry [storey] (of a building)
straight
strength
stretched
stud y ing
sub stan tial
sub tle [subtile]
suc ceed, suc cess
suc cess ful, suc ces sion
*suit (sōōt)
suite (swēt–sōōt)
sul fa
sul fur–sul phur
sum ma ry, summed
su per in tend ent
su per sede
sup pose
sup press
sur prise
sus cep ti ble
sus pense
syl la ble
sym bol
sym me try, sym met ri cal
syn on y mous
syph i lis
syr up–sir up

*ta boo [tabu]
tar iff
tech nique [technic]
tem per a ment, tem per a men tal
tend en cy
than
*the a ter [theatre]
their
the o ry, the o ries
then
there
there fore
they're
thor ough [thoro]
though–tho
thought
thou sandths
through–thru
to, too, two
to day [to-day]
to geth er
traf fic, traf fick ing
trag e dy, trag ic
tries, tried
tru ly
Tues day
typ i cal
tyr an ny

un doubt ed ly
un nec es sar y
un prec e dent ed
un til (*till)
un u su al
use, -ful, -less, us ing
u su al ly
u ten sil

vac u um
var ies
var i ous
veg e ta bles
venge ance
ven ti late, ven ti la tion
ver ti cal
vice (evil)
view
vig i lance
vig i lan tes
vil i fy
vil lain
vise [vice] (the tool)

vis i bil i ty
vi ta min [vitamine]
vol ume

war rant
war ring
weath er
weight, -y
weird
wheth er
whis key [whisky]
whole

whoop
who's (who is)
whose
wool en [woollen]
wool ly–wool y
write, writ ing, writ er, writ ten

yacht
yield
you're (you are)

zo ol o gy [zoölogy], zo o log i cal

For references on English spelling, see page 104.

Split infinitive The word order in which an adverb comes between the *to* and the infinitive (The receptionist asked them *to kindly sit down*) is called a split infinitive.

Since the adverb modifies the verb, its natural position is next to the actual verb form, and writers of General English have never taken the puristic efforts to prohibit the construction very seriously. Changing the position of *eventually* in this sentence would result in awkwardness:

> He requested the Ministry of Forests to reforest the barren mountains in Macedonia in order to eventually eliminate the mosquito-breeding swamps.–LOUIS ADAMIC, *The Native's Return,* p. 321

There is no point in rearranging a sentence just to avoid splitting an infinitive unless it is an awkard one. But awkward split infinitives are to be avoided:

> Awkward: After a while I was able to, although not very accurately, distinguish the good customers from the sulky ones.
>
> Improved: After a while I was able to distinguish–though not very accurately–the good customers from the sulky ones.

(References: Curme, *Syntax,* pp. 458-465; Fowler, "Split Infinitive" (for overprecise distinctions); Fries, *AEG,* pp. 132, 144.)

Spoken and written English **1.** *Speech and writing.* Language originated in speech; the writing of it came very late in its history, some 6000 years ago. The number of significant differentiations in sound which a speaker uses is considerably larger than the number of symbols available in any traditional system of writing. In English we have about forty speech sounds, four levels of pitch, four degrees of stress, and varying durations of sound and silence. (See *Phonemes.) To represent these elements of our speech, we have twenty-six letters, nine marks of punctuation, and a few devices like capitals and italics. As an exact representation of speech, our system of writing is obviously unsatisfactory.

The inventors of systems of writing were no doubt less concerned with transcribing every significant detail of the spoken language than with providing a reliable system of verbal communication which had permanence and could be understood visually. The fact that the heavy accent falls on the first syllable of *daily* but on the second of *today* need not be shown because the five symbols arranged in their familiar order tell the reader what word is intended; as soon as he recognizes the word, he knows where to accent it. Even with *desert,* the context will tell him whether the noun or the verb is intended and therefore whether the accent falls on the first or second syllable. Sometimes, in fact, the written forms provide more information than we really need, as a stenographer can testify from the fact that *bread* and *bred, two* and *too,* and all other homophones will look the same in shorthand and yet most will be intelligible. Although writing is never a complete transcription of speech–is no more than a hint at what might be spoken–it is a satisfactory system of communication.

Even with its limitations, writing can be a very powerful and effective medium. It is therefore legitimate to speak of the written language (or at least of the *written styles* of a language) as an entity in itself. Although *writing,* to some, suggests a weak reflection of speech, the enormous and vital prose literature of the last two or three centuries proves that such a connotation is incorrect. Most prose literature was written to be communicated through the eye, not the ear; and though oral reading often increases its effectiveness, its survival depends mainly on its capacity for communicating without the direct use of sound. What the printed material would sound like if read aloud is still important to its effect, but the actual hearing is not crucial. Many native speakers of English whose pronunciation of French is atrocious can read French prose with delight–Voltaire, for example–though they may find that even the greatest French verse–Racine or Victor Hugo–is unrewarding.

There are some instances in which the written language does better than the spoken; sometimes it makes clear what is almost impossible to communicate in speech, such as detailed instructions, which must be read repeatedly; extensive use of brief quotations, especially quotations within quotations, which can be efficiently indicated by the punctuation; some homophones which would be ambiguous in speech: *We'll halve it,* which could be mistaken for *we'll have it.*

The written language must retain a relationship to the spoken, but it should be an immediately understandable one that does not require the reader to puzzle out from inadequate transcription what would be obvious in speech. Sometimes this means the spoken language must be rephrased for writing. For instance, in *more competent men, more* might modify either *competent* or *competent men.* In speech the distinction would be shown by greater stress on *more* if it modified *competent men.* In writing, the distinction might be shown by *more men who are competent,* or if *more* modified *competent* only, by adding a modifier as in *more really competent men.*

2. *"Colloquial" English.* Dictionaries mark words *Colloq.* to suggest that in the editors' judgment they are more common in speech than in writing. Many people take this label to mean that the dictionary frowns upon the use of these words, but the Webster definition of *colloquial* shows that this is not true:

> acceptable and appropriate in ordinary conversational context, as in intimate speech among cultivated people, in familiar letters, in informal speeches or writings but not in formal written discourse (*flabbergast; go slow; harum-scarum*). Colloquial speech may be as correct as formal speech.—By permission. From *Webster's New International Dictionary,* Second Edition, copyright 1934, 1939, 1945, 1950, by G. & C. Merriam Co.

The three expressions given as examples show that *colloquial* is not being used as a word of dispraise or even of suspicion, for though *flabbergast, go slow,* and *harum-scarum* may be more appropriate in speech than in Formal writing, they are accurate, expressive words that could be used in most General as well as Informal writing. But since a good many people continue to interpret *colloquial* as condemnatory, the label is used in this book only infrequently and cautiously. If a usage is more common in speech than in writing, that fact is stated; if the word or expression is in good use but would rarely be found in General or Formal writing, it is labeled Informal.

Of course there are different varieties of spoken English, from Nonstandard and even Slovenly to distinctly Formal. Many educated people, especially in the professions, get most of their information from periodicals and books, so that their speech reflects the written language. Sometimes the written language may determine the spoken. Topics important in certain limited areas—especially the upper levels of scientific, scholarly, and professional fields, and in some literature —may be much more frequently written than spoken about and may almost never be discussed in ordinary speech. Here the written forms may become the norms, imitated in speech. But for the greater part of the written language, speech, somewhat condensed and made more precise, is the basis.

The closeness of the written literary English to the spoken English of the time has varied from period to period. In the nineteenth century the two were rather far apart—consider Arnold and Ruskin, and even more the rank and file of lesser writers, such as Sir Arthur Helps. Since 1880 or so in England and since 1910 in the United States there has been a closer approach of written to spoken style. Today, how closely one's written style should approximate his spoken style depends upon appropriateness; he should feel free to use words and constructions characteristic of speech when they fit naturally with other traits of his style.

See Chapter 1, "Difference between speaking and writing," page 12, Chapter 10, "Conversation," page 289.

Spoonerism A spoonerism is an unintentional (except for humorous effect) exchange of the initial sounds of two words, as in "a half-warmed fish" for "a half-formed wish."

spoonful, spoonfuls The Standard plurals of *spoonful, tablespoonful, teaspoonful* are *spoonfuls, tablespoonfuls, teaspoonfuls* (similarly, *basketfuls, carfuls, cupfuls, shovelfuls, tubfuls*).

Cupsful, carsful, shovelsful, and so on are often heard, though they rarely appear in written English.

Staccato style A staccato style has—as its principal characteristic—short, emphatic sentences, often exclamations or questions, usually without expressed connectives between the statements. The words, especially verbs, are likely to be vigorous. It is effective in short passages that deserve sharp stressing but is likely to be tiresome and to lose its emphasis if it is long continued.

> Hindenburg was shortening his lines. He was quitting northern France and Belgium. But he was holding the Argonne. Day by day the representatives of our G. H. Q. had shown us the map with every enemy division and reserve force marked. Hindenburg had thirty-two reserve divisions at the beginning of our Argonne drive. When November began two or three remained. What had become of an army of German reserves?—GEORGE SELDES, *You Can't Print That!* p. 35

Compare *Telegraphic style.

still *Still* is an adverb in the sentence "It's still raining" and a conjunction (*Conjunctive adverbs) in "I can see your point of view; still I don't agree with you."

story A *story* is a narrative of either real or imaginary happenings. Typically we think of a story as an imaginary tale, a short story or novel, though a newspaper account of actual events is a news story.

A discussion of ideas may be an editorial, an article, a critical article, a review, a treatise, but it is not a story. A poem might be referred to as a story only if it was a narrative, and though plays are stories, their special form calls for reference to them by their proper name. Try to keep *story* for its established meaning.

strata is the plural of the singular *stratum*. It is pronounced strā′tə or strat′ə.

street In many newspapers and in some Informal writing, *street* is not capitalized as part of an address. In Formal and most General writing it would be capitalized (41 High Street).

The abbreviation *St.* or *st.* is not much used except to save space in newspapers, lists, or reference works.

Style Style has been the subject of a number of well-known aphorisms: "Proper words in proper places make the true definition of a style" (Jonathan Swift); "Style is the dress of thoughts" (Lord Chesterfield); "Style is this: to add to a given thought all the circumstances fitted to produce the whole effect that the thought ought to produce"

(Stendhal); "Style is the ultimate morality of mind" (A. N. Whitehead); and, most often quoted of all, "The style is the man" (Comte de Buffon).

These are all provocative statements, and properly idealistic, but they tend to defeat profitable discussion; a student of literature or a writer needs something more explicit. Although *style* may be defined variously, it is basically the characteristics, the qualities of the language in a particular piece of discourse. (There are oral styles as well as written, but in this brief treatment only the written will be discussed.) A writer has a wide range to choose from for words, constructions, sentence patterns, and arrangement and emphasis of his material. The style is the choices he makes, consciously or unconsciously, among the options offered by the language. The formation of most noun plurals and the past tense of most verbs, the agreement of subjects and verbs, the standard word order of English are part of the structure of the language and not distinctive traits of style. But the relative length and complexity of sentences, the variations in the order of sentence elements, the use of long or short constructions, the choice and especially the connotation of words may be. The study of style is an effort to discover what qualities of the language used in a particular story, essay, or article give rise to certain of the reader's impressions of it, especially to his response to the tones that are aside from its denotation, the part of the meaning that would be largely lost in a summary or paraphrase of the passage.

1. *The study of style.* The study of style is, then, one emphasis in the study of language. It is closely related to linguistics (some books in linguistics have a term for it, usually "stylistics") and will increasingly use the methods and data of the science. But the study of style is interpretive as well as descriptive; it is concerned primarily with the study of specific items of discourse rather than with the general system of the language, and it takes account of meaning and effect, matters at least currently not much explored in linguistics. The aim of the study of style is increased awareness of the qualities of language in use, viewed especially as the source of a reader's impressions.

The first step in studying a style is a natural, attentive reading, usually more than one reading. It is a good idea to make notes of the traits of language that you believe will repay further investigation and of your early impressions, perhaps describing the style as compact or diffuse, literal or allusive or figurative, flat or emphatic, direct or involved, and so on—however it strikes you as a whole.

The next step is a detailed, analytic reading of the passage. Some counting (of kinds of words, types of phrases, length and type of sentences. . .) is in order, not to accumulate figures but to gather evidence for the rightness of your first impressions (this reading may of course prove to you that your first impressions were mistaken) and to enable you to demonstrate the validity of your judgment of the style to others. (It is surprising what previously unnoticed traits will force themselves on your attention while you are concentrating almost mechanically on, perhaps, adjectives or metaphors.)

Finally, read the piece again "for its own sake" and to see the individual traits as a part of the whole. This reading should be more perceptive and more rewarding than the first. Such occasional careful studies of particular pieces should increase the fullness of your first response to others.

2. *Elements of style.* There are no standard categories for the study of style, but some are needed to guide observation. The headings given in this section will serve to organize most of the elements of language usually considered as traits of style. Many of the topics are discussed in chapters of the *Guide* from the point of view of a writer, but the same points can be used to begin the observation and discussion of something already written. The three short passages on page 719 will be referred to for illustrating some of the points.

a) Thought movement. It is hard to substantiate objectively impressions such as thin, diffuse, pithy, meaty, dense, but they can be pretty well demonstrated by looking at the contribution made by individual sentences. The rapidity or slowness of movement, the kind of statement (simple, complex, or compound; periodic or loose...), the marks of continuity, the interrelations of details and generalizations vary widely among writers and contribute to the stylistic impression. The Orwell passage is closely packed with visual detail; the Thurber is more relaxed, a series of individual impressions bearing on the generalization of the first two sentences; the Conrad passage, though organized as narrative, is chiefly visual detail elaborating the narrative movement.

Chapter 6, pages 138-171, discusses thought movement in some detail.

b) Qualities of sound. There is a question how big a part sound plays in a literature that is written primarily for silent reading. It is obviously important in verse, but it has some importance in prose literature as well. Inattention to sound is responsible for some of the shortcomings of much journalistic and "bureaucratic" prose–it is obviously not "heard" by the writer. We have to be especially cautious in discussing the intonation: for example, an American would read aloud a passage by a British writer rather differently from the way its author would read it, and a Northerner's reading of a story by a Southern writer would be different from the writer's in some respects.

Even in reading "silently" we are somewhat conscious of the possible sounds, and in reading slowly we may almost form them–certainly part of our impression of a passage comes from its "sound." The important sounds are those in stressed syllables. There may be a conspicuous series of the same sound, or more often of sounds similar in some phonetic respect: voiced consonants (b, g, v, z, and so on) or

Passages Illustrating Points of Style

The canal path was a mixture of cinders and frozen mud, criss-crossed by the imprints of innumerable clogs, and all round, as far as the slag-heaps in the distance, stretched the "flashes"—pools of stagnant water that had seeped into the hollows caused by the subsidence of the ancient pits. It was horribly cold. The "flashes" were covered with ice the colour of raw umber, the bargemen were muffled to the eyes in sacks, the lock gates wore beards of ice. It seemed a world from which vegetation had been banished; nothing existed except smoke, shale, ice, mud, ashes and foul water.—GEORGE ORWELL, "North and South," *The Road to Wigan Pier,* p. 138

The notion that such persons ["writers of light pieces running from a thousand to two thousand words"] are gay of heart and carefree is curiously untrue. They lead, as a matter of fact, an existence of jumpiness and apprehension. They sit on the edge of the chair of Literature. In the house of Life they have the feeling that they have never taken off their overcoats. Afraid of losing themselves in the larger flight of the two-volume novel, or even of the one-volume novel, they stick to short accounts of their misadventures because they never get so deep into them but that they feel they can get out. This type of writing is not a joyous form of self-expression but the manifestation of a twitchiness at once cosmic and mundane. Authors of such pieces have, nobody knows why, a genius for getting into minor difficulties: they walk into the wrong apartments, they drink furniture polish for stomach bitters, they drive their cars into the prize tulip beds of haughty neighbors, they playfully slap gangsters, mistaking them for old school friends. To call such persons humorous, a loose-fitting and ugly word, is to miss the nature of their dilemma and the dilemma of their nature. The little wheels of their invention are set in motion by the damp hand of melancholy.—JAMES THURBER, *My Life and Hard Times,* Preface

In the stillness of the air every tree, every leaf, every bough, every tendril of creeper and every petal of minute blossoms seemed to have been bewitched into an immobility perfect and final. Nothing moved on the river but the eight paddles that rose flashing regularly, dipped together with a single splash; while the steersman swept right and left with a periodic and sudden flourish of his blade describing a glinting semi-circle above his head. The churned-up water frothed alongside with a confused murmur. And the white man's canoe, advancing upstream in the short-lived disturbance of its own making, seemed to enter the portals of a land from which the very memory of motion had forever departed.—JOSEPH CONRAD, "The Lagoon," *Tales of Unrest,* p. 187

unvoiced (p, k, f, s) or "stop" consonants (b, d, g, k, p, t); back vowels (ō, o͞o, ô), or front vowels (ā, ē, a); nasals or sibilants. Or there may be a marked variety (as the vowels in the last Orwell phrase are all different: ō, ā, ī, u a, ou, ô), or marked contrasts in individual sounds or groups of sounds, as in the last part of the last Conrad sentence (". . . a land from which the very memory of motion had forever departed").

Three sequences of sounds are named: *alliteration, the same initial sounds (*m*emory of *m*otion), helps bind phrases together; *assonance, syllables with the same vowel but different consonants (m*i*xture of c*i*nders), and consonance, syllables with the same consonants combined with different vowel and consonant sounds (Rou*nd* ma*ny* wester*n* isla*nd*s have I bee*n*).

There has been a good deal of study of prose rhythm. The older method was to scan the units of prose as verse is scanned, by dividing them into feet (iambic, dactylic, etc.). But the units of prose, actually sense units, are usually longer than a metric foot, so that dividing into feet means even less in prose than it does in verse. The sound movement in prose is essentially the intonation patterns, and the methods of linguistics–the stresses (´ ˆ ` ˘) and junctures (the pauses and rising or falling terminals)–can probably be developed into a workable scheme for describing it. (See *Phonemes § 2.)

Any discussion of the rhythm of prose would have to be very detailed to be accurate or helpful. Reading aloud the passages on page 719 will give some idea of the variety in length of rhythmical units, in intensity of stresses, in position of stresses (especially at the ends of sentences and of important constructions within them), and of the general contribution of sound to the impression of styles.

c) Visual traits. Although the appearance to the eye is not so important for prose as for verse, there is some slight contribution to the effect of prose from such matters as length of paragraphs, use of italic type, stylistic use of capitals (*Capital letters, § 10), and even from punctuation marks–close punctuation usually suggesting a slower movement than open (see Ch. 5). There is just enough effect from these matters to warrant including them in a discussion of style.

d) Minor points of syntax. In contemporary style the smaller elements of syntax are perhaps more important than the frame of sentences. There are some options in word forms: adverbs ending with *-ly* or without (*Adverbs, types and forms); choice between two plurals of nouns from other languages (*Plurals of nouns, § 4); *comparison of adjectives and adverbs with *-er, -est* or with *more, most;* choice between two past forms of a few verbs (*Principal parts of verbs); the use or nonuse of active or *passive verbs and of *subjunctive forms. There is some variation possible in the position of adjectives (an immobility *perfect* and *final*) and more in the position of adverbial modifiers (frothed *alongside with a confused murmur*).

There are distinctly different impressions from constructions with nouns as headwords (by the *subsidence* of the ancient *pits,* the *stillness* of the *air*) and those centered on verbs (as in Thurber's series of mishaps–*they walk . . . drink . . . drive . . . slap . . .*) and the *verbid constructions that often have the syntax of nouns or adjectives with some of the action qualities of verbs (*mistaking* them for old school friends, *describing* a *glinting* semi-circle). A good deal has been written about the stylistic impact of the various parts of speech. People probably differ in their sensitiveness to this trait, but there are differences between styles with nouns especially prominent and those with verbs, and also differences that depend on the number and quality of modifiers (*Adjectives in use, *Adverbs in use). The Orwell passage has very few adjectives, the Conrad several emphatic ones. Pronouns and other personal words are associated with narrative, but they give ease and rapidity to exposition, as in the Thurber passage.

There are numerous devices that make for compactness: two or more verbs with one subject; noun modifiers rather than prepositional phrases ("the *stone* house" instead of "the house of stone") adjective clauses without the introductory pronoun or still further reduced ("ice the colour of raw umber" instead of "ice which was the colour of raw umber"). These qualities are discussed in Chapter 7, "Economy in sentences," page 186.

Taken together these syntactical traits contribute to impressions of diffuseness or compactness and emphasis; to pace, a sense of slowness or rapidity; and often to the degree of Formality or Informality.

e) Sentences. A writer has wide latitude in how much he will put in a single sentence, of which the physical length is the external symptom. Our three passages are too short for any generalizations, but they show some range. The Orwell sentences run from 4 to 50 words, averaging 25.5; Thurber's 9 to 50, averaging 23.2; and Conrad's 9 to 42, averaging 29. Often there is contrast in arrangement, as Orwell's 4-word sentence follows one of 50, and Conrad's 9-word sentence comes between one of 42 and one of 33 words.

Sentence length and some of the other more important variations in sentence patterns are discussed in Chapter 7.

f) Words. English offers a wide range in the choice of words. They differ in the variety of English they come from, in their familiarity, in their degree of concreteness or abstractness, in their precision of meaning, and in their connotations–their tone, the associations from experience or from literature they bring to mind. The three passages show considerable range in words, from the precise words from experience of Orwell to the literary ones of Conrad.

Words are the most familiar element of style, and the easiest to study. Chapters 1 and 8 will furnish the basic points to consider.

g) Imagery. Imagery (picture-forming) is a quality of words, but its importance is sufficient to warrant a separate heading. We have to be liberal in interpreting imagery, making it almost equivalent to concreteness. There is always a possibility that someone will get a sense impression from the words, whether a specific reader does or not. Much depends on the experience of the reader and on his habits of thinking.

Verbal images differ in the senses they represent (sight, sound, taste, smell, touch); sight so predominates in imagery that the use of the other senses often has unusual force. The verbal images may be simple, as in the Orwell passage, or complex, involving movement, as in the Conrad. They may be the substance of the piece, as in the Orwell and Conrad passages, or secondary, supporting an idea, as in Thurber. They differ greatly in precision, sometimes forcing an exact picture on a reader, more often allowing him considerable leeway in what image he will produce from his memory. They may be sampled, highly selective, or massed—as in a detailed description. Their connotations are usually more from the objects named than from the words, so that they may seem to be actually symbols, and often the feeling or mood associated with the objects are aroused in the reader.

h) Figures of speech. Figures of speech, which contribute a great deal to imagery, have always been a part of the treatment of style. The term is rather vague and certainly flexible (some of the old lists of figures of speech ran to over 280), but basically figures of speech include words and phrases that come from a context, an area of meaning, other than the subject being presented; expressions that are intensified or altered in some way; and also turns of phrase that are in some way out of the ordinary. The idea of figures of speech was originally based on the supposition that people used language basically in a literal, referential sense and that other uses were a substitution for this ordinary language—for ornament or impressiveness. We now know that all people use figures of speech freely in their everyday talk and writing—children use many figures—and that the point about metaphor and the figures is not so much their departure from literal meaning as what they contribute to the meaning. This contribution is often to the tone and the connotation, bringing into one context some quality or attitude associated with another—with a resulting freshness and emphasis.

Figures may be relatively pale—the metaphor in Orwell's "beards of ice" seems a familiar and almost literal expression, and the personification implied in the verb *wore* is so slight that it seems chiefly grammatical, allowing a more active verb than a flat *had*. Conrad's "bewitched into an immobility" and "a land from which the very memory of motion had forever departed" are more literary and allusive. The naturalness of figures is shown by Thurber's metaphors, exaggerations, allusions, and the extended metaphor or analogy of the last sentence, and even the relatively rare *chiasmus,* two constructions in which the order of keywords is reversed (the nature of their dilemma and the dilemma of their nature).

It is not necessary to be able to name all of the departures from a precise, literal use of words (most of the figures have Greek names that seem strange to us), though we should be able to identify more than metaphors and similes. The important thing is to see what they add, what associations, connotations, attitudes (many are used just for fun), and emphases the figures bring to bear on the subject being presented.

Several groups of figures are discussed in Chapter 8, "Figurative use of words," page 232, and others in *Index* entries such as *Epigrams, *Imitative words and phrases, *Negatives, *Personification, *Puns.

3. *Generalizations about style.* The impetus to the study of style is to understand and appreciate particular items of discourse, but naturally such studies lead to generalizations, if for no other reason than to help in summarizing observations.

There are many terms for general impressions of a style (some have been mentioned earlier in this article): flexible, varied–rigid or monotonous or mannered; conventional, traditional–individual, original, fresh; tense–relaxed; simple–complex; and so on; as well as terms that emphasize separate qualities: literal–figurative; direct–involved; abstract–concrete, imagistic.

Since the earliest rhetoricians there have been efforts to classify styles in general, and in spite of various experiments in terms they come back to the polarities of the *plain,* the more literal and direct, and *heightened,* the more elaborate, using more of the devices of language, especially with emotional suggestion. In between these is a gradation, often called simply *middle* or *mixed* styles with a conversational base but showing some of the devices of more elaborate styles. The three passages on page 719 illustrate this range: Orwell, the plain; Conrad, the heightened; and Thurber, the middle.

Since it is difficult to talk in detail about style by itself, it is natural to go to its relationships, Style and ——. There are obvious relationships between the individuality of the writer and his style, though asserting specific relationships is risky. There are some traits of style characteristic of various types of writing (fiction, science, advertising, polemic), of various subject matters (politics, religion, law), and of the literary perspectives of humor, satire, tragedy, and so on.

And finally there is the theoretical question of style and meaning, which is easier to sense than to state. Traits of language certainly affect the precision, intensity, emphasis, tone, and suggestiveness of the central message. Neglecting the style in discussing meaning may lead to misinterpretation, as neglecting the intonation of a "yes" or a "no" in conversation may. A full and accurate understanding of the meaning of a passage depends in part on a sensitive response to the style.

4. *Style and an individual's writing.* For a practiced writer, style is not a conscious concern but a by-product of his effort to make the language carry out his purpose. It is best not to be aware of style while actually writing.

But in one's first attempts at writing, an occasional period of concern for style may be profitable. Becoming aware of the traits of Informal, General, and Formal English may lead to a direction of development. Many of the elementary points of style are choices among items of usage. Most writers start under the influence of some other writer and may even intentionally imitate him for a time. But better is a good deal of varied reading that will show the possibilities of the language. You will unconsciously pick up traits that suit your material, your purposes, and your temperament. Occasional rereading and reading aloud from a writer whose work you would like yours to resemble in some way may help. But nothing can take the place of your own experiments and your own purposeful writing. Your style will develop as you improve in effective completion of your own writing projects.

The following references will provide a guide to a fairly full study of style: Paul F. Baum, *The Other Harmony of Prose* (Durham, 1952)–the best starting point for a consideration of prose rhythm; Bonamy Dobrée, *Modern Prose Style* (Oxford, 1934)–discussion of passages of prose grouped by subject matter; Edith Rickert, *New Methods for the Study of Literature* (Chicago, 1927)–a program of detailed analysis; George Saintsbury, *A History of English Prose Rhythm* (London, 1922)–comments on various aspects of the style of past periods; R. A. Sayce, *Style in French Prose* (Oxford, 1953)–a topical discussion with various suggested devices; Norton R. Tempest, *The Rhythm of English Prose* (Cambridge, 1930)–the analysis of rhythm by metrical feet; Stephen Ullmann, *Style in the French Novel* (Cambridge, 1957)–an application of linguistics to style; Richard M. Weaver, *The Ethics of Rhetoric* (Chicago, 1953)–stylistic qualities of the parts of speech; W. K. Wimsatt, Jr., *The Prose Style of Samuel Johnson* (New Haven, 1941)–one of the more detailed studies of the style of an individual writer.

Stylebooks For editors and printers *style* means the method of handling various mechanical matters such as capital letters, punctuation, forms of plurals, division of words, details of typography. Since usage is divided on many of these points, a publisher chooses what form will be used in his publications. Most newspapers, magazines, and publishing houses have stylebooks–documents ranging from a single page to an elaborate volume containing the particular rules to be followed in preparing copy for specific publications. They often show arbitrary choices, to attain a consistency that most publishers feel is desirable. One factor in recent changes in practices in writing and printing has been the decision of some of the book publishers to let authors' copy stand nearly as written, so long as it is consistent.

Most newspaper stylebooks are not generally available, though that of *The New York Times,* revised 1950, is for sale. The University of Chicago Press *A Manual of Style,* eleventh edition (Chicago, 1949), is the most influential stylebook among book publishers. The *United States Government Printing Office Style Manual* (Washington, D. C., 1953) is one of the best stylebooks.

Subject and verb 1. *As sentence elements.* The backbone of the typical English sentence is a subject and a verb. The subject names the starting point of the statement, and the verb advances the statement. The subject is the noun or substantive in most intimate relation to the verb. Except in inverted sentence order the subject stands before the verb, and its position there is the main grammatical device we have to identify it as the subject, just as the position of the object after the verb identifies it. In the sentence "The submarine sank the cruiser" we know that the submarine and not the cruiser did the sinking because *submarine* is in the subject position in the sentence.

2. *Agreement of subject and verb.* When the verb form permits it, a verb shows agreement with its subject in number and person. This usually means with the grammatical number of the subject. But since, except for the verb *be,* our verbs have only one form for both numbers and for all persons except an *-s* in the third singular present, relatively few problems in agreement can arise. Users of English can rely very little on formal indications of relation between subject and verb; therefore lack of agreement in form seldom causes ambiguity, though it may be felt by the hearer or reader to be a serious mistake: I *is,* for example, is entirely intelligible but it is also certainly Nonstandard.

Singular: *I am* more tired than usual. *A chair was placed* in the corner. *This job takes* four weeks. *The job took* four weeks.

Plural: *We are* more tired than usual. *Three chairs were placed* along the wall. *These jobs take* four weeks. *The jobs took* four weeks.

The problems that arise in agreement of the subject and verb are either from a sentence form in which the grammatical number of the subject is uncertain or is blurred by the presence of other words, or from agreement with the meaning of the subject rather than with its grammatical form.

a) Collective nouns. Agreement according to meaning is seen most clearly in collective nouns, which take either a singular or plural verb, depending upon whether the speaker or writer is emphasizing the group as a whole or the individuals of which it is composed. In writing, the verbs and pronouns of a given sentence should be all plural or all singular in referring back to a collective subject.

Emphasizing the unit: The class *is* the largest in six years.

Emphasizing the individuals: The class *are* by no means all intellectual giants, but *they* have done very well. (More likely: The students in this class . . . .)

(For further examples and discussion see *Collective nouns.)

b) Compound subjects. Ordinarily a compound subject has a plural verb:

Alice and Francis *were* the first to arrive.

The text of the poem and the commentary *make* quite a sizable volume.

When the two elements of a compound subject refer to the same person or thing, the verb is singular:

The best teacher and the best scholar here *is* Professor Babcock.

The spirit and accomplishment of these men *speaks* for itself.

The verb is often singular when a compound subject follows:

There *is* both health and wealth in this way of life.

For the winner there *was* a large cash prize and weeks of glory.

When a second part of the subject is connected with the first by *with, together with, as well as,* the agreement varies. In Formal English such a construction is kept singular. In General English a plural is often found if the expression is equivalent to a compound subject:

The rudder is the only essential control in taxiing, and this together with a regulative speed *keeps* the plane going in a relatively straight line.

The winner with the four runners-up *were* given a reception. (To make this more Formal, the *with* should be changed to *and,* rather than the *were* to *was.*)

He is not a good speaker, since his hesitating manner with long "uh's" interspersed in the address *make* [Formal: *makes*] him hard to listen to.

Subjects connected by *or* take a singular verb if both are singular, a plural verb if both are plural or if the one nearer the verb is plural:

A novel or a biography *is* to be read outside of class.

Novels or biographies *were* the same to him.

A novel or five short stories *were* to be read.

In questions the plural is common:

Are [or: *Is*] Fred or Harry in?

c) Plural modifier of singular subject. When a rather long plural modifier of a singular subject comes between it and the verb, Formal and General English usually have a singular verb, but Informal often has a plural verb:

This *group* of essays *is* [not *are*] concerned with problems in sociology and philosophy as they are related to biology.

The *form* of your bibliography and footnotes *is* not standard.

To a beginner on the organ the array of stops and pistons, manuals, couplers, and pedals *seems* [Informal: *seem*] at first quite bewildering.

Two thousand dollars' *worth* of pictures *were* [Formal: *was*] destroyed.

d) Relative pronouns. A relative pronoun referring to a singular noun has a singular verb (The person *who takes* enough pains can do it) and one referring to a plural noun has a plural verb (The people *who take* pains win in the long run). In idioms like "This is one of the most discouraging things that has come out of the situation," Formal usage requires *that have come,* since the antecedent of *that* is *things;* Informal often and General occasionally have *that has come,* because the central idea (of *one*) is singular.

Formal: Jeffrey is one of those moderns *who are* making *their* money talk.

Informal and, less often, General: Jeffrey is one of those moderns *who is* making *his* money talk.

(See *one of those who.)

e) Subject and complement of different number. The verb agrees with the subject:

A day's work is four trips. Four trips make a day's work.

f) Plural subject with singular meaning. When the idea conveyed by a plural subject is singular in intent, the verb is usually singular:

Five years is a long time.

(References: Curme, *Syntax,* Ch. 4; Fries, *AEG,* pp. 188-190, 249-250, and index references; Pooley, pp. 78-88.)

3. *Punctuation between subject and verb.* Since the subject and verb are part of one construction, they should not normally be separated by a comma:

Another example of what can happen [ ] is furnished by the experience of two young women who were staying at the hotel.

See *Comma § 8. Discussion and other examples of subject and verb relations will be found in Chapter 2, "The favorite English sentence," "Minor sentence types," and "Agreement of subject and verb," pages 43, 52, 60; Chapter 5, "Between subjects, verbs, objects," page 120.

Subjunctives It is not necessary to use the category of the subjunctive mood in describing English verbs; it is probably inaccurate to do so for two reasons: very few forms can be surely identified as "subjunctives," hardly enough to furnish a paradigm; and the use of the few identifiable forms is so irregular that no definite syntactical criteria can be stated to define it.

This article presents some facts about the nontypical subject-verb agreement traditionally called the subjunctive.

1. *Form of subjunctives.*

a) Simple subjunctive. In current English the subjunctive form of a verb is identifiable only in certain forms of the verb *be* (I, you, he . . . *be;* I, he . . . *were*), and in forms made with *be* (he *were asking*), and in the third person singular of other verbs ("he *ask*" instead of "he *asks*"; "he *have*" instead of "he *has*").

b) Subjunctive with auxiliaries. Some grammarians include as subjunctives all the locutions that can be used in expressing ideas that may also be, or have at some time been, expressed by the subjunctive, or the forms that could be used in translating subjunctives found in other languages. Under this system several auxiliaries–*may, might, should, would, let, have to,* and others–become subjunctives. This broad interpretation makes consideration of the subjunctive more complicated than is necessary, since the meaning and connotation of such constructions come from the meaning of the auxiliary or from adverbs. For that reason, in the following discussion only the simple subjunctive–that is, a verb form differing from the one ordinarily expected–is considered.

2. *Uses of the subjunctive.* English makes much less use of the mood than most of the modern European languages do. There are a number of idioms in which the subjunctive may be used in English, especially in Formal English, though it is almost always possible to use other verb forms. It is fairly common in wishes, conditions, qualified or doubtful statements, and in *that*-clauses and after expressions like *It is necessary.* The following examples illustrate typical uses of the subjunctive and give alternative idioms that would be more common in speech and most writing.

a) Formulas. The subjunctive is found in numerous formulas, locutions surviving from a time when the subjunctive was used freely. Most of these are no longer common idioms; that is, we do not make other sentences on the pattern of *Far be it from me. . . .*

Suffice it to say	Heaven forbid	Heaven help us	Be it said
If I were you	God bless you	Be that as it may	As it were

Many petty oaths have this form: *Confound it;* Psychology *be hanged.*

Some of these formulas are used in all levels of the language; some, like *Come what may,* are rather Formal, and the oaths are chiefly Informal.

b) In that-clauses. The subjunctive is most idiomatic in idioms for recommendations, resolutions, demands, and so on. These idioms are usually in a Formal context. Note the following examples:

Formal: We recommend that the Commissioner *designate* for this use the land formerly belonging to Mr. Brewster.

Formal: I ask that the interested citizen *watch* closely the movements of these troops.

General: I ask the interested citizen to watch the movements of these troops closely.

Formal: . . . the order that he *be* dropped

General: . . . the order to drop him

Formal: It is necessary that every member *inform* himself of these rules.

General: It is necessary for every member to inform himself of these rules–It is necessary that every member should inform himself of these rules–Every member must [should] inform himself of these rules.

c) In conditions. The subjunctive may be used in *if*-clauses when there is doubt of fulfillment of the condition, or when the condition is "contrary-to-fact"–impossible or not believed by the writer:

> If one good *were* really as good as another, no good would be any good.–IRWIN EDMAN, *Four Ways of Philosophy*, p. 80

The nontypical verb form is not necessary for the meaning, since the contrary-to-factness is conveyed by the use of the past tense (either *was* or *were*) with a present or future meaning. Professor Edman's idea would be as definite if he had written "If one good was as good as another, no good would be any good."

In fact few writers make such a distinction and a large proportion of the "subjunctives" found are in "simple" conditions:

> Formal: If the subject of a verb *be* [More usual: *is*] impersonal, the verb itself may be called impersonal.–ARTHUR G. KENNEDY, *Current English*, p. 296

> The fellow who worked next to him in the plant had been turned off, and Jim could not help wondering if that *were* [More usual: *was*] a sign that some of the rest of them would be discharged, too.–ERSKINE CALDWELL, *Kneel to the Rising Sun*, p. 129

In all of these constructions a speaker or writer has a choice between the "subjunctive" and a regular form of the verb (which may be an "auxiliary") or an infinitive. Professor Fries found that in both Standard and Nonstandard English the subjunctive was used rather seldom, in considerably less than one fifth of the locutions in which it might be. Actually "subjunctives" are a trait of style rather than of grammar and are used by writers, consciously or unconsciously, to set their language a little apart from everyday usage rather than for specific meaning.

Students in foreign language courses should remember that very few French, Latin, and German subjunctives can be satisfactorily translated by an English subjunctive. They should try to find the natural idiomatic way of expressing the idea that is idiomatically expressed by the subjunctive in the language they are translating.

References: The point of view presented in this article will be found in general in Fowler, article "Subjunctives"; Fries, *AEG*, pages 103-107; Hall, pages 311-314; Jespersen, Chapter 27; Marckwardt and Walcott, pages 30, 37, 88, 89; Pooley, pages 55-59; Thyra J. Bevier, "American Use of the Subjunctive," *American Speech*, 1931, 6:207-215. A different point of view will be found in Curme, *Syntax*, Chapter 20; C. A. Lloyd, "Is the Subjunctive Dying?" *The English Journal*, 1937, 26:369-373.

Submitting manuscript The conventions of submitting manuscript for publication are simple:

The manuscript should be carefully typed, double spaced, on good paper (*Typewritten copy). Generous margins should be left for editorial operations. Plenty of space, half a page or so, should be left around the title. Keep a carbon copy for reference.

The writer's name and address should appear in the upper left-hand corner of the first page. The approximate length in words may be put in the upper right-hand corner.

Additional facts, such as an account of sources of material or suggestions for illustrations, may be given in an accompanying letter.

Mail in a comfortable-sized envelope. Short manuscripts can go in 9 inch envelopes, folded twice; those from 4 to 12 pages can go in envelopes about 6x9 inches, folded once; and longer ones in large envelopes, flat. Photographs or drawings should be clearly labeled and carefully packed between stiff cardboard.

Inclose an envelope large enough to hold the manuscript as it is folded, addressed to yourself, and carrying sufficient postage for its return. The editor will probably want to use it.

Subordinating conjunctions The most common subordinating conjunctions–words that connect subordinate clauses with the main clauses of sentences–are:

after	*because	since	unless
*although	before	*so	*when
*as	how	*so that	*where
*as if	*if	though	*while
as long as	in order that	*till	why

The relative pronouns (*who, which, that, what*) function also as subordinating conjunctions. See also *for.

Sub **Subordination** Revision: Make the less important of these statements grammatically subordinate to the more important.

Subordinate sentence elements modify the sentence as a whole, the subject, verb, object, or some other important element. They may be single words, phrases, or clauses; but usually in discussing subordinate constructions an important phrase (like a *verbid phrase) or a subordinate clause is meant. Subordinate clauses are introduced by the connectives listed in *subordinating conjunctions or by relative pronouns. The clauses are used in the grammatical functions of nouns, adjectives, and adverbs.

In general, grammatical subordination should represent or correspond to the relative importance of the ideas: the more important ideas should be in main clauses or principal words, the less important in subordinate constructions. Elementary violations of this principle can be easily detected:

Inaccurate subordination	*More accurate*
The road was blocked, *causing us to make a twenty-mile detour.*	We had to make a twenty-mile detour *because the road was blocked.*
Once in Denver he bought a pack of cigarets with a twenty-dollar bill, *getting back nineteen silver dollars in change.*	*Once when he bought a pack of cigarets in Denver with a twenty-dollar bill,* he got back nineteen silver dollars in change.

Some special types of obviously faulty subordination are illustrated in *Tandem subordination, *Thwarted subordination, *Upside-down subordination.

But the relative importance of "ideas" is not an objective or logical matter. Much depends on the style, on rhythm and other factors of sentence movement. And much depends on the context, the relation of the whole sentence to the passage. From the point of view of historical importance "I was at the movies when the bombing of Pearl Harbor was announced" is obviously "upside-down subordination." In "The bombing of Pearl Harbor was announced while I was at the movies" the idea of the bombing is in the main clause, but the sentence seems unlikely and actually a little amusing. Because the two "ideas" would hardly be put together except in a narrative in which the "I" was the central subject or, at least at the moment, the center of interest, the first sentence might very well represent the right relative importance of the two ideas.

In considering a sentence that raises a question of subordination, it is best to think not only of the relative importance of the two parts of the statement but also of the context of the sentence–if the sentence as a whole represents the emphasis you want at that particular spot.

See Chapter 2, "Complex sentences," page 50.

Substantive is a term that includes nouns and pronouns and other words or groups of words used in the functions of a noun.

such As an intensive, *such* is somewhat Informal (It was such a hot day; such energetic people). In Formal and most General writing the construction would usually be completed by a *that* or an *as* clause (It was *such* a hot day *that* the tar melted; I have never seen *such* energetic people *as* they are). (Reference: Russell Thomas, "*Such* as an Intensive," *College English,* 1954, 15:236-238.)

Idiomatic constructions with *such* are:

There was such a crowd that [not: so that] we couldn't even get to the door.

The invitation is extended to such nonmembers as are interested. (*As* here is a relative pronoun. A more General construction would be: The invitation is extended to all nonmembers who are interested.)

A good lecturer? There's no such thing. (*No such a thing* is Informal.)

The following constructions with *such* are possible but not very common and seem somewhat stiff:

His condition was such that he could not be moved. (More usual: His condition would not allow him to be moved.)

Psychologists could probably find various reasons why it is regarded as such. (. . . why it is so regarded.)

such as As a coordinating conjunction, introducing examples, *such as* has a comma before but not after:

He was interested in all sorts of outlandish subjects, such as palmistry, numerology, and phrenology.

Suffix An element that can be placed after a word or root to make a new word of different meaning or function: *-ize* (*criticize*), *-ish* (*foolish*), *-ful* (*playful*), *-th* (*warmth*) is called a suffix. See *Origin of words § 3a.

Suggestion Making use of the associations, the connotations of words, is called *suggestion*. The words *liberty, immemorial, mystical, butcher, homey,* and thousands of others have acquired associations from their past use that may call to a listener's or reader's mind some feeling or attitude that goes beyond their original core of meaning. Relying on suggestion may be misleading or at least may be a substitute for exactness, but a responsible use of suggestive words adds color and often pleasure and keeps writing from flatness. (For discussion see Ch. 8, "The suggestion of words," p. 220.)

suit, suite *Suit* is pronounced so͞ot; *suite* (a group of attendants, a series of rooms, and so on) is swēt or so͞ot. The latter pronunciation is more usual in commercial talk about a set of furniture.

Sunday school Capitalize only the *Sunday* except in names of particular Sunday schools:

Sunday school   the Methodist Sunday School

sure *Sure* is primarily an adjective (sure footing; as sure as fate; Are you sure?). As an adverb, *sure* instead of *surely*–equivalent to *certainly* or *yes*–is Informal (Sure, I'm coming; That's sure fine of you) and would not ordinarily be written.

swim The principal parts are *swim, swam* or *swum, swum*. "He *swam* half a mile" is more common in writing than "He *swum* half a mile."

Syntax *Syntax* means the relationship between the words or word groups in a sentence. Many articles in this *Index* discuss points of syntax, as, for example, *Adjectives in use, *Subject and verb, *Word order.

T

(t) as in *type, quote, attach, Thomas.*

-Ed is pronounced as t after the sound of *f, k, p,* or *s* in the same syllable: *laughed, fixed, confessed, tipped, picked. T* is silent in *Christmas, listen, thistle, mortgage, mustn't,* and many other words, and in ordinary speech it is absorbed by the *d* in word groups like *sit down* (si doun′). *Ti* is pronounced ch in such words as *question,* and *sh* in such words as *nation, notion.*

The *t* sound is produced exactly like the *d* sound except that the vocal cords do not sound; it is called a voiceless consonant. (See *D.) Double *t* usually is pronounced like single *t:* lat*t*er, la*t*er. In much of the United States *t* (and *tt*) between vowels is voiced and often indistinguishable from *d:* compare the pronunciation of *writer* and *rider.*

taboo–tabu *Taboo* (pronounced tə bo͞o′) is more generally used than *tabu,* except in anthropology. The plural is *taboos;* the past tense of the verb, *tabooed.*

Taboo in language A number of words not used in certain circles–many of them not even appearing in dictionaries–are said to be *tabooed.* Communication in the subjects to which they belong is carried on by accepted substitutes. (Compare Ch. 8, "Euphemisms," p. 227. References: Jespersen, *Language,* p. 239; Edwin R. Hunter and Bernice E. Gaines, "Verbal Taboo in a College Community," *American Speech,* 1938, 13:97-107.)

Tabulations Series of facts can often be more clearly presented in a table systematically arranged in convenient and meaningful columns. See examples of tabulations on page 734 (in *Tenses of verbs).

Occasionally in the body of a paper it is convenient to arrange a series of parallel statements in a numbered tabulated form. The device should not be overworked, but it is a good way of securing emphasis by display:

> The English textbook of the future, to sum up, must recognize the social nature of language, and English in particular, by
>
> 1. acknowledging that language is the tool of the social group,
> 2. granting that utility is the only valid basis for the creation or perpetuity of a language form,
> 3. pointing out the part each individual speaker plays in the retardation or acceleration of change,
> 4. regarding the written language in its proper light as the secondary and partial representation of the real language.–ROBERT C. POOLEY, *Grammar and Usage in Textbooks on English,* p. 151

(Reference: University of Chicago Press *Manual of Style,* pp. 158-172.)

Tandem subordination is an unhappy series of subordinate clauses, each of which depends on an element in the preceding:

> Tandem: He had carefully selected teachers who taught classes that had a slant that was specifically directed toward students who intended to go into business.
>
> Improved: He had carefully selected teachers who slanted their courses toward students intending to go into business [or: toward future businessmen].

taxi The plural of the noun *taxi* is *taxis;* as a verb, the principal parts are *taxi, taxied, taxiing* or *taxying.*

technic *Technic* (tek′nik) is a variant form of *technique.* It is also used, especially in the plural (*technics*), for *technology.*

Telegraphic style "Telegraphic style" refers to writing in which many *function words (especially articles and connectives) are omitted. It suggests also compact constructions and vigorous words. It is not appropriate in ordinary writing but is used in some reference works to save space, in newspaper headlines for vigor (Gang Flees Cops; Find Loot–Ditch Guns, Stolen Cash Near River), and to a certain extent in such styled writing as occurs in *Time.*

Tenses of verbs Revision: Make the tense of this verb conventional in form

Tense (§ 1) or consistent with others in the passage (§§ 3, 4).

1. *Tense forms.* 2. *Tense and time.* 3. *Sequence of tenses.* 4. *Consistent use of tenses.*

1. *Tense forms.* Except for the simple present and past tense forms, English verbs show distinctions of time by various phrase combinations, often supported by adverbs ("he is *about* to go" as a future). The following table presents the verb phrases most commonly associated with time distinctions:

		ACTIVE	PASSIVE
PRESENT TENSE		he asks he is asking he does ask	he is asked he is being asked
PAST TENSES	*Past perfect* (Past of some time in the past)	he had asked he had been asking	he had been asked
	Past (A time in the past not extending to the present)	he asked he was asking he did ask	he was asked he was being asked
	Perfect (Past, extending to the present)	he has asked he has been asking	he has been asked
FUTURE TENSES	*Future* (Future, extending from the present)	he will ask he will be asking he is going to ask	he will be asked
	Future perfect (Past from some future time)	he will have asked he will have been asking	he will have been asked

"Strong verbs" show a change of vowel in the past tense instead of the *-ed* ending (he begins, he began; he rides, he rode) and also in the past participle, often with the ending *-en* (he has begun; he has ridden). (See *Principal parts of verbs. References: Curme, *Parts* *of Speech,* pp. 241-333; Fries, *AEG,* pp. 59-71, 128-198; Mencken, pp. 427-447; Jespersen, Chs. 23-26; Leah Dennis, "The Progressive Tense: Frequency of Its Use in English," *PMLA,* 1940, 55:855-865.)

2. *Tense and time.* In grammar a tense is a distinctive form or phrase of a verb (*ask, asked, have asked*). The traditional names of the tenses are mainly words indicating time (*past, present, future*); it is therefore assumed that the function of tense is to show time and that the time shown is that suggested by the name of the tense. Both assumptions are only partly true. In *He was here, He is here,* and *He will be here,* the tenses of *be* are respectively past, present, future; the times indicated are also past, present, and future; and the function of the verb is primarily to show time. But in *When did you say you were going home?* only one tense, the past, is used; but two times, past and future, are indicated. And in *Art is long but time is fleeting,* though the tense is present, the time is of little consequence. (In the Latin form of the aphorism no verb is used–*Ars longa, vita brevis.*)

In English most sentences require a *finite verb, and the verb necessarily occurs in a tense form. But the indication of time in the sentence may be supplied by an adverb, or the adverb may modify the time suggested by the verb. In *He plays well,* the verb, despite its present tense form, does not declare that his playing is good only at the present moment; we infer, rather, that it is good at all times. But in *He plays tomorrow* the adverb restricts the time to the future, though the tense is still present. In *I've got two letters from him already, I've got time now,* and *I've got two exams tomorrow,* the tense is the same–perfect–but the times are respectively past, present, and future.

The tense names in English should be considered, then, as convenient but rather arbitrary terms used to identify verb forms and phrases, the actual function of the verb in each sentence being finally determined by other elements in the construction. Some unusual functions of the tense forms themselves are:

a) The "progressive phrases" (*is asking, was asking, has been asking . . .*) tend to emphasize the actual activity and are increasingly being used in English.

b) The present tense is used to make a statement that is generally true, without reference to time:

> Oil *floats* on water.
>
> The Captain reminded the ladies that the equator *is* an imaginary line.

c) Participles and infinitives express time in relation to that of the main verb. The present infinitive expresses the same time as the main verb or, often with an adverb, a time in the future:

> Our team is playing *to win.*   I hope *to go abroad* next summer.

A perfect infinitive expresses action prior to that of the main verb:

I am sorry *to have disappointed* you.

A present participle generally refers to the time of the main verb:

Rounding a turn in the road, he came suddenly in full view of the lake.

3. *Sequence of tenses.* When the verb of a main clause is in the past or past perfect tense, the verb in a subordinate clause is also past:

Frank knew that the Statlers were visiting us.
Frank knew that the Statlers would visit us the following week.
The old man wondered whether the train had arrived.
I have never seen Slim when he hadn't [or: *didn't have;* not *hasn't*] a wad of tobacco in his mouth.

A present infinitive is, however, usual after a past verb:

I thought you would have liked to ride [not: to have ridden] in their car.
They intended to stop [not: to have stopped] only an hour in the village.

The perfect infinitive is used chiefly to indicate action previous to the time of the main verb: She is sorry to have started the gossip.

4. *Consistent use of tenses.* It confuses a reader to find tenses shifted without definite reason, as in this paragraph:

I *sit* down at my desk early with intentions of spending the next four hours studying. Before many minutes *passed,* I *hear* a great deal of noise down on the floor below me; a water fight *is* in progress. Study *was forgotten* for half an hour, for it *was* quite impossible to concentrate on Spanish in the midst of all this commotion. After things *quiet* down I *begin* studying again, but I *have* hardly *started* when a magazine salesman *comes* into the room, hoping to snare a large sale. After arguing with him for several minutes I finally *got* rid of him.

Shifts of this sort should be carefully avoided.

In single sentences the inconsistency usually comes from carelessness, especially from forgetting the form of the first of two parallel verbs:

Last fall in the Brown game I saw Bill Geyer hit so hard that he was knocked five feet in the air and then land [for: landed] on his head. (The writer forgot the tense of *was knocked.*)

Reference: Curme, *Syntax,* Chapter 18.

textbook Now usually written as one word and often shortened simply to *text.*

th *Th* spells a single voiceless sound (th) as in *path* (path), *think* (thingk), and a single voiced sound (t̶h̶) as in *paths* (pat̶h̶z), *the* (t̶h̶ə, t̶h̶i, t̶h̶ē), *bathe* (bāt̶h̶). *Th* is silent in *isthmus* and pronounced *t* in *Thomas, Thames,* and *thyme.* (See *ye=the.) In some proper names the older *t* sound has been partly or completely replaced by *th* on the basis of the spelling: *Theodore* and *Arthur*–always th (but *Ted* and *Art*); *Anthony*–th and t (but *Tony*).

than **1.** *Conjunction. Than* as a conjunction introduces the second member of a comparison in which one thing or situation is greater than the other:

Their house was bigger than ours.
Nobody was more aware of the need for action than he was.

Than is the idiom after *no sooner:*

He had no sooner opened the door than the flames flared up.

(For other idioms, see *Comparison of adjectives and adverbs.)

2. *Preposition. Than* is often a preposition. Since the clause with *than* is usually verbless (*than he, than I*), *than* here seems to be a preposition rather than a conjunction and frequently in Informal usage, especially in speech, is followed by an accusative:

Formal and General: You are certainly faster than I.
Informal: You are certainly faster than him.

In the Formal *than whom,* it is a preposition:

We admire the power of Jack Kramer, than whom there is no greater tennis player.

(References: Jespersen, p. 133; Pooley, pp. 166-170.)

3. *Confusion with "then." Then* is often carelessly written for *than.* (See *then–than.)

See *different. Reference: Dwight L. Bolinger, "Analogical Correlatives of 'Than,'" *American Speech,* 1946, 21:199-202.

that **1.** *Conjunction.*

a) *That* should usually be repeated with each of a series of parallel subordinate clauses:

But he also sees *that* Lafayette was a rigorously honest and honorable man, *that* he had many of the essential talents of the political compromiser, the moderate, and *that* these very talents help explain his failure in the French Revolution.—CRANE BRINTON, *The Saturday Review of Literature,* Dec. 3, 1938

b) *That* should not be repeated within a single clause:

Many people think that if an article is advertised by a good joker or a good band [not: that] it is a good product to buy.

That is usually needed in the second of two parallel clauses:

I had hoped the book would be finished by June and that it would be published by January.

2. *Relative pronoun. That* refers to persons or things, *who* usually to persons, *which* usually to things:

The number of men *that* [or *who*] fell within the age limits of the draft was 3,500,000.
He solved in five minutes a problem *that* [or *which*] I had struggled with for five hours.

Which usually introduces clauses that are nonrestrictive; *that* more often introduces clauses that are restrictive but may also introduce nonrestrictive clauses:

The book *that she selected for her report* [restrictive] was the longest on the list.

The privilege of free speech, *which we hold so dear* [nonrestrictive], is now endangered. (*That* is also possible here.)

3. *Clauses without "that."* Clauses are often made without the introductory *that*. These constructions are not elliptical (for *that* is not "omitted" or to be "understood") but are a commonly used shorter idiom. They are Standard usage in both speech and writing:

He said he would go. (Or: He said that he would go.)

I remembered my mother's birthday fell on March 10. (Or: I remembered that my mother's birthday fell on March 10.)

The first man he met turned out to be Alexander. (Or: The first man that he met turned out to be Alexander.)

The *that* is necessary when the clause comes first (That one could be punished for such a thing had not occurred to him); in appositive clauses after such nouns as *wish, belief, desire* (My hope that he would finish today was not fulfilled); and with anticipatory *it* (It is not true that I promised to pay the whole sum at once), though in short constructions, especially in speech, it is not needed (It isn't true he likes me better than he does you). References: Curme, *Syntax*, index references; Jespersen, pages 350-351.

4. *That which. That which* is Formal and rather archaic for *what:*

He had no clear idea of *what* [not: *that which*] he was trying to say.

5. *Referring to an idea. That* (or *this*) is used to refer to the whole idea of a preceding statement when the reference is clear:

While I was studying, he sometimes turned on the radio. That was annoying, but I didn't object.

If the *that* refers to an idea suggested but not contained in a particular word, the sentence should be revised to make the reference clear:

Vague reference: My uncle is a doctor, and that is the profession I intend to enter.

Exact: My uncle's profession is medicine and that is going to be mine too.

6. *"That" as an adverb.* Adverbial *that* is General English in such constructions as "I didn't go that far." It is sometimes used in constructions like "I'm that hungry I could eat shoe leather," but *so* would be more common.

that is *That is* introduces a statement the equivalent of, or the explanation of, what precedes. It is a Formal connective and is best kept to introduce series or complete statements. In such a use it is usually preceded by a semicolon and followed by a comma:

The men worked continuously for three whole weeks to complete the dam on time; that is, they worked twenty-four hours a day in three shifts, seven days a week.

In briefer constructions a comma would be more usual, and the *that is* would not be used:

Formal: They used the safest explosive for the purpose, that is, dynamite.

General: They used the safest explosive for the purpose, dynamite.

(Compare *namely and other introductory words.)

the **1.** Repetition of the article before the various nouns of a series emphasizes their distinctness:

The color, *the* fragrance, and *the* beautiful patterns of these flowers make them universal favorites.

The color, fragrance, and pattern of these flowers are distinctive.

2. In the idiom *the . . . the,* the second *the* is a survival of the Old English instrumental case form of *the* and functions adverbially. Usage is divided over the punctuation. In Formal writing a comma is frequently used between the phrases, in General usage not:

General: The greater one's economic insecurity the greater the tendency to sacrifice spiritual independence.–STUART CHASE, "The Luxury of Integrity," *The Nemesis of American Business*

Formal: The greater one's economic insecurity, the greater the tendency to sacrifice spiritual independence.

3. Sometimes a possessive pronoun is used where *the* would be more idiomatic:

We stopped to see *the* [rather than *our*] first unusual sight.

4. Keep *the* with the name of our country: *the* United States.

5. *The* is given minimum stress in speech, with the pronunciation thə before consonants, thi before vowels. In rare instances where *the* has demonstrative force and is emphasized, it is pronounced thē.

theater, theatre *Theater* is now the usual spelling except in names established some time ago. (See *-er, -re.)

their *Their* is the genitive of they. *Theirs* is the emphatic or absolute form: This table is exactly like theirs.

Informally *their* is often used to refer to the collective indefinite pronouns (*anybody, anyone, everybody, everyone*), though these are singular in form:

Informal and sometimes General: Everybody finally found their hats and coats.

General and Formal: Everybody finally found his hat and coat.

(See *every and its compounds.)

then *Then* is an adverb of time, frequently used as a connective (conjunctive adverb). Often the connection between clauses is made closer by using *and* with the *then:*

The next three hours we spent in sightseeing; *then* we settled down to the business of being delegates to a convention.

He ate a good meal, *and then* he took a nap before starting home again.

then–than These words are often carelessly confused in writing. *Then* is an adverb of time, *than* a conjunction in clauses of comparison:

Then the whole crowd went to Louie's.

I think *The Big Sky* was better *than* any other novel I read last year.

Although etymologically *then* and *than* come from the same source, they must now be carefully distinguished in writing.

then too is overused as a connective in amateur writing:

A reader enjoys a fast moving story; then too he may enjoy something that will set him thinking.

Better: A reader enjoys a fast moving story, but he may also enjoy something that will set him thinking.

Then too is an especially mechanical connective when used between paragraphs.

there is, there are 1. *There* and *it* are used as "anticipatory subjects," with the real subject following the verb. *There is* is usually followed by a singular subject (though often, especially in speech, by a plural), *there are* by a plural:

There is a size for every need.

There are several ways in which this can be done.

A singular verb (there *is,* there *was*) followed by a plural subject is common, and the choice between a singular or plural verb is pretty much a matter of taste when the first element of the compound subject is singular:

There is too much starch and fat in the food we eat.

There was both affection and pride in her message.

(References: Fries, *AEG,* p. 56; David S. Berkeley, "Agreement of Subject and Verb in Anticipatory Clauses," *American Speech,* 1953, 28:92-96; Robert J. Geist, "Current English Forum," *College English,* 1952, 14:115-116; 1954, 16:188-189.)

2. Frequent use of these impersonal constructions tends to give a lack of emphasis:

There was a vague feeling of discontent evident in everyone's manner.

Direct: A vague feeling of discontent was evident in everyone's manner.

There are a good many college students who are easily discouraged.

Direct: A good many college students are easily discouraged.

(See *it.)

therefore The conjunctive adverb *therefore* is a rather heavy connective seldom needed in ordinary writing:

Formal: My experiences in preparatory school had been very unpleasant; therefore I was surprised to find college students and college teachers so agreeable.

General: My experiences in preparatory school had been so unpleasant that I was surprised to find college students and college teachers so agreeable.

 therein is archaic or Formal for *in it, in that respect.*

they *They* is often used as an indefinite pronoun (They say . . .), when another construction would seem more compact:

They have had no serious accidents at that crossing for over two years. (More compact: There have been no serious accidents. . . .)

They made the great reflector at Corning. (More compact: The great reflector was made at Corning.)

thing *Thing* is often *deadwood in writing:

The other thing that I have in mind is going to France.
Improved: I am also thinking of going to France.
The first thing you do is to get a few small twigs burning.
Improved: First you get a few small twigs burning.

this 1. *This,* like *that,* is regularly used to refer to the idea of a preceding clause or sentence:

He had always had his own way at home, and this made him a poor roommate.

The company train their salesmen in their own school. This [More Formally: This practice] assures them a group of men with the same sales methods.

(Reference: Paul Roberts, "Pronominal 'This': A Quantitative Analysis," *American Speech,* 1952, 27:171-178.)

2. *This* is used Informally as a sort of intensified definite article: "This old man went into this restaurant." Such a use is ordinarily out of place in writing.

thou *Thou, thy, thine, thee* are archaic pronouns for the second person, now used in Standard English only in the Formal language of church services. Amateur poets should avoid them except in archaic contexts. Although they correspond grammatically to the second person pronouns of various European languages, they preserve none of the connotative force that they have in those languages and should not ordinarily be used in making translations.

though For use as a conjunction see *although.

Colloquially *though* is used as a word of qualification or hesitation: "I didn't think he would do it, though." This use is less common in writing. If used, *though* would normally be set off by a comma or commas.

Thwarted subordination Sometimes amateur writers add an *and* or *but* to a construction already sufficiently connected with the rest of the sentence by a subordinating conjunction or a relative pronoun. This has been called "thwarted subordination." It is most commonly found as *and which* and *but which* constructions (*which § 4):

The first semester of the course had used three textbooks, [not: and] which had been continued for the second semester.

Tilde The *tilde* is a mark (~) placed over a letter, as in the Spanish *cañon,* represented in English by *ny* (*canyon*).

till, until, ['til] These three words are not distinguishable in meaning. Since *'til* in speech sounds the same as *till* and looks slightly odd on paper, it is rarely used now. Use *till* or *until* according to the stress or the feel of the phrase you want. *Until* is most often used at the beginning of sentences or clauses:

> Until he went to college, he never had thought of his speech.
> He had never thought of his speech till [or: until] he went to college.

Time In subordinate clauses the various time relationships are indicated by the conjunctions *after, *as, as long as, as often as, as soon as, before, since, *till, until, when, whenever, *while.* (See also *Tenses of verbs; *Centuries, *Dates, *Hours.)

Titles of articles, books, etc. **1.** *Formal usage.* In most college writing, in most books, and in some periodicals, the titles of books and the names of magazines and newspapers are put in italics (indicated in manuscript by underlining). Capitals are used for the first word, for all nouns, pronouns, verbs, adjectives, and adverbs, and for prepositions that stand last or that contain more than five letters:

No Place to Hide
Wit and Its Relation to the Unconscious
The Atlantic Monthly
You Can't Take It with You
Parts of Speech and Accidence
The Kansas City Star

Often the *the* of magazine and newspaper titles is not regarded as a part of the title and so is not capitalized. In some periodicals the name of the city in a newspaper name is not italicized (the Milwaukee *Sentinel*). Usage is divided on this point. If the name of the city is not part of the name of the newspaper, it would not, of course, be italicized: the London *Times.*

If the official title of a work does not follow these conventions, references to it may use the exact title or standardize it (as, *The Story of a Novel,* which was printed as *the story of a NOVEL*). Library catalogs and some long bibliographies do not use italics and capitalize only first words and proper nouns or adjectives.

Titles of short stories and magazine articles are put in quotation marks when they are used with or near titles of books or names of periodicals. They are often italicized when used without reference to their means of publication, especially in discussion of them as works of literature. Usage is divided on the titles of poems, but academic writing tends to use italics, though the titles of short poems are often in quotation marks.

The words *Preface* and *Introduction* and the titles of chapters in books are capitalized but not italicized or quoted. (Reference: University of Chicago Press *Manual of Style,* index references.)

2. *Informal usage.* In many magazines (*The New Republic, The Saturday Evening Post,* for example) and in most newspapers, titles of books and names of periodicals are treated as proper names, capitalized but not quoted or italicized.

In Formal papers for college courses and in theses Formal usage should be followed; in other college papers either style may be used, as the instructor prefers.

3. *Typed copy.* In typed copy that is not going to be printed it is simpler to write titles all in capitals (to save backing up and underlining). This is the common form in publishers' letters. (See Ch. 13, "Form of bibliographical entries," p. 363.)

Titles of themes Since titles help interest a reader in a paper, a striking and easily remembered title is an advantage. But strained titles are often ludicrous, and if no good title comes to mind, it is better just to name the subject of the paper as exactly as possible in a few words and let it go at that. As a rule titles that give no clue to the subject, such as *The Moving Finger Writes* or *The Greeks Had a Name for It,* are better avoided. Don't postpone writing a paper (or handing one in) to hunt for a clever title. In published work the title is more often made by the editor than by the writer.

The title is not a part of the paper, and the first sentence should not refer to it by a pronoun. Leave a blank line between the title and the beginning of the text.

to 1. The confusion of *to* and *too* in writing is conspicuously careless and one of the small matters to be watched in revision of papers.

2. It is generally understood that in expressions like "pages 56 to 89" the last numbered unit is included. Hours are an exception, as in 1 to 3 p.m. *Up to* or *till* excludes the last unit.

today 1. *Today* (like *tonight* and *tomorrow*) is rarely hyphened except by people who learned to spell when hyphen was generally used.

2. *Today, of today* are often *deadwood, adding nothing to the meaning of a statement already placed in the present:

> Economic conditions [of today] are more unsettled than they have been for two generations.

too When *too* in the sense of *also* comes within a construction, it is usually set off by commas, but in Informal writing it usually is not when it comes at the end:

> "I, too, have become a philosopher," she said sadly.–IRWIN EDMAN, *Philosopher's Holiday,* p. 74
>
> I'm going too. (More Formal: I'm going, too.)

toward–towards These words are identical in meaning.

Transitive and intransitive verbs A verb is transitive when it is used with an object to complete its meaning (They fought the whole gang; He was given a book). A verb is intransitive when it does not have an object (The choir will sing; The hymn was sung by the choir; They hid in the tall grass). Many verbs are used in both constructions, often with different meanings (He wrote two books [transitive]; She cannot write [intransitive]). Dictionaries note whether a verb is typically used transitively or intransitively, and in what senses. *Lie* and *sit* are intransitive, *lay and *set are transitive. *Linking verbs (*be, become, taste* . . .) are regarded as intransitive. (Reference: Curme, *Parts of Speech,* Ch. 4.)

Tr **Transpose** Revision: Transpose, that is, reverse the order of the elements marked, for greater clearness or a more emphatic order.

A change in the order of sentences or paragraphs in copy can be shown by using numbers in the margin opposite the elements to be changed, or by circling and drawing arrows.

The transposition of letters is shown by a curved line:

Connetcicut   reciehve

Triads Parallel series of three units are so common in writing, especially in Formal writing, that they form a definite trait of style. Such a series is called a triad:

> To delight in war is a merit in the soldier, a dangerous quality in the captain, and a positive crime in the statesman.—GEORGE SANTAYANA, *Reason in Society,* p. 84

Trite **Trite** Revision: Replace the trite expression with one that is simpler and fresher.

Trite words are usually worn out figures of speech or phrases: *the picture of health, the order of the day, reign supreme, from the face of the earth, crack of dawn.* Such expressions weigh down a style and are a mark of amateur writing or of insensitiveness to words.

For fuller discussion and examples see Chapter 8, "Trite words," page 225.

try and–try to The Formal idiom is *try to* (Try to get your work done before five o'clock). The General idiom is *try and* (Try and do it; Try and get your work done before five o'clock). The General idiom is old and its users include such careful stylists as Thackeray and Matthew Arnold. Parallel idioms are: *Go and* find one; *Come and* get it. (See Hall, p. 309.)

Type Typography is a complex technical field, but many people make a hobby of it, and most writers have some curiosity about it. A few of the fundamental facts about type are given here:

1. *Type faces.* There are many different type faces, each with its characteristic appearance. They may differ in thickness of line in the letters, in length of ascenders and descenders (as in *h* or *y*), in wideness of letters, in serifs (thin or smaller lines used to finish off a main stroke of a letter, as at the top and bottom of *M*), and in other features. Every type face is made in many standard sizes and style variations. Some popular faces for book and periodical use are set here in ten point size:

This type face is Caslon

This type face is Bodoni

This type face is Garamond

This type face is Baskerville

This type face is Granjon

This *Guide-Index* is set in the following type faces and sizes:

The text is set in 10 point Times Roman.

The quotations are set in 9 point Times Roman.

The footnotes are set in 6 point Times Roman.

The entry words are set in 10 point Times Roman bold.

The subheads are set in 10 point Times Roman italic.

2. *Type style variations.* A given face and size of type is available in several standard variations of style. The most common are:

Name and example	*Abbreviation*	*Indicated in manuscript by:*
ROMAN CAPITALS	Caps.	Three lines underneath
roman lower case	l. c.	Unmarked manuscript
ROMAN SMALL CAPITALS	s. c.	Two lines underneath
ITALIC CAPITALS	Ital. Caps.	One line underneath and labeled "all caps"
italic lower case	ital.	One line underneath
BOLD FACE CAPITALS	b. f. caps.	Wavy line underneath and labeled "all caps"
bold face lower case	b. f.	Wavy line underneath

There are, of course, combinations of the above styles: Caps and lower case, CAPS AND SMALL CAPS, *Italic Caps and lower case,* **Bold Face Caps and lower case.**

3. *Type measurement.* Type is measured in *points,* a point equaling 1/72 of an inch. A square unit of type of any size is an *em.* Space is usually measured in *pica* (12 point) *ems* (1/6 of an inch).

This line is set in six point type.

This line is set in ten point type.

This line is set in fourteen point type.

(See *Proofreading. References: The University of Chicago Press *Manual of Style* contains much information about type, as do other stylebooks and books on journalism, advertising, and typography.)

-type is an overused suffix: *handsome-type man.* (Compare *-wise.)

type of The idiom *type of* is being shortened colloquially by omitting the *of:* this type letter. Although the construction is beginning to appear in print, General usage should still be followed: this type of letter (and not: this type of *a* letter).

Typewritten copy Manuscript for a printer, business letters and reports, and impersonal writing should be typed. In the United States we are so accustomed to typescript (and our handwriting is on the whole so illegible) that it can be used in a good deal of personal correspondence. There is felt to be an added courtesy in longhand, and "social correspondence" should usually be handwritten. Students believe they receive better grades on course papers that are typed. The ease of reading typescript may have this result when the instructor is reading principally for content, but in English compositions that advantage may be offset in part by the clearness with which the errors stand out.

In general, typewritten copy follows the customs of good manuscript, but some points need special emphasis. Use only one side of the sheet, leave wide margins (especially at the right side, since letters cannot be compressed as in longhand), keep type clean, and change ribbons regularly. Ordinarily use a black ribbon.

Regular manuscript should be double spaced. Personal writing may be single spaced, and for economy single space is generally used in business writing. If single spaced, the lines should be kept fairly short to make the reading easier. Full, crowded pages are forbidding reading. In typing first drafts, leave plenty of space for revision, perhaps using triple space between lines and extra space between paragraphs.

In single spaced typing, use double space between paragraphs. For double spaced typing, make a triple space between paragraphs only if you wish an open appearance or special emphasis on the paragraphs. Indent paragraph first lines from five to eight spaces.

Long quotations may be indicated in double spaced copy by indenting the number of spaces used for paragraphs and single spacing the quoted matter. No quotation marks are used with this style.

The standard typewriter keyboard has no symbol for the figure 1. Use the small l (not I). For a dash use two hyphens not spaced away from the words on each side. Use space after all other punctuation marks.

Transposed letters should be erased and retyped or corrected by the proofreader's symbol. (See *Proofreading.) Strikeovers are often hard to read. A few mistakes can be corrected in ink, but if there are so many that the page will look messy it should be retyped.

For directions on how to type ç, !, and [ ], see *Cedilla, *Exclamation mark, and *Brackets. (See Ch. 9, "Preparing the manuscript," p. 262.)

U

1. There are two "long *u*" sounds: (o͞o) as in *rule* (ro͞ol), *blew* (blo͞o), *shoe* (sho͞o), *true* (tro͞o), *juice* (jo͞os), *move* (mo͞ov), *lose* (lo͞oz), *booby* (bo͞o′bi), *hoodoo* (ho͞o′do͞o); and (ū), a diphthong beginning with a *y* sound and ending with o͞o, as in *use* (ūs or ūz), also spelled as in *few, cute, beauty, you, hue, nuisance, neuter, view, yew, yule, ewe.*

After *t, d, n, s, st* usage is divided between these two sounds: *tune* (tūn, to͞on), *duty* (dū′ti, do͞o′ti), *news* (nūz, no͞oz), *stew* (stū, sto͞o). In such words the o͞o sound is frequent and is increasingly used by educated speakers in spite of widespread prejudice against it. (See Knott and Kenyon, § 109 and their entries on particular words of this type.)

2. There are two "short *u*" sounds: (u) as in *cup* (kup), *fun* (fun), *under* (un′dər), *son* (sun), *love* (luv), *come* (kum), *trouble* (trub′əl), *does* (duz), *other* (uth′ər), *blood* (blud); and (oo) as in *full* (fool), *pull* (pool), *wood* (wood), *woman* (woom′ən), *wolf* (woolf), *should* (shood).

3. *U* as in *burn* and *curl* is represented by û (bûrn, kûrl).

An unpronounced *u* is sometimes spelled after *g,* as in *guest,* usually in words from French to show the "hard" value of g.

The letter *u* is one form of a Latin letter of which the other form is *v;* only within the last few hundred years have the two been consistently differentiated in English.

Underlining Revision: In longhand and typewritten copy underline words and passages to correspond to the conventions of using italic type. *Und*

These conventions are of great importance in Formal manuscript and in material to be printed. Newspapers have generally abandoned italic type, but most magazines and books use it, and in academic writing–course papers, articles in the learned journals, monographs, dissertations, reference books–rather strict conventions are still followed. (See Ch. 5, "Underlining for italics," p. 131.)

Underlining is used:

1. *To indicate titles of books and periodicals.* The complete title should be underlined:

I like Babbitt and Arrowsmith the best.

He took Time and The Reader's Digest.

For details of this use see *Titles of articles, books, etc., and Chapter 13, "Form of bibliographical entries," page 363. Compare *Ships' names. (Reference: University of Chicago Press *Manual of Style,* pp. 43-50.)

2. *For emphasis.* Words that would be heavily stressed if spoken may be underlined:

He was the man that night.

Any word a writer wishes to emphasize may be underlined (italicized in print), but this is a rather mechanical form of emphasis and loses its force if overused. Whole sentences, except in textbooks and manuals, are better not underlined, since there are more intelligent ways of securing emphasis. As Fowler (p. 305) put it: "To italicize whole sentences or large parts of them as a guarantee that some portion of what one has written is really worth attending to is a miserable confession that the rest is negligible." (See *Emphasis § 7, *Schoolgirl style.)

3. *To mark words and locutions considered not for their meaning but as words.* This is a common use of underlining in this and all books on language:

> If we take such a sentence as *I am hungry,* neither a grammarian nor a logician would have any difficulty in pointing out the predicate, though one would say that it was *am hungry* and the other that it was simply *hungry.*–P. B. BALLARD, *Thought and Language,* p. 88

4. *To mark foreign words.*

> But good clothes were a *sine qua non.*

(See *Foreign words in English.)

unique In strict Formal usage *unique* means "single, sole, unequaled," and consequently cannot be compared. In General usage, like so many other words of absolute meaning, it has become somewhat extended, and as an emphatic *rare,* it is sometimes found compared with *more* or *most:*

> . . . the more unique his nature, the more peculiarly his own will be the colouring of his language.–OTTO JESPERSEN, *Mankind, Nation and Individual from a Linguistic Point of View,* p. 204

(See *Comparison of adjectives and adverbs § 4.)

United States We live in *the* United States. The temptation to drop *the* is greatest when *United States* is forced to do duty as an adjective: Europe needs the money from United States imports. In such a case it is better to use *American* or *of the United States.* (See *American.)

Unity Unity in writing is a by-product of clear thinking. It is a relative quality. Gross disregard of unity, including material that is quite unrelated to a paragraph or to a paper or that distracts from its main point, can be easily discovered by a reader. But genuine unity is to be judged in the light of the writer's purpose. Any statement that he can build into his discussion and relate to his subject will be appropriate. The test of unity is found not in any general principles that can be applied in every situation but in appropriateness to the writer's view of his material and his consistent carrying out of his purpose.

Various matters related to unity are discussed in Chapter 6, Paragraphs, and Chapter 7, Sentences.

unquote is used orally to indicate the end of a quotation.

up *Up* is a member of many typical *verb-adverb combinations in general use (give up, grow up, sit up, use up). It is also an intensive in a number of others to which it contributes no new element of meaning (divide up, fill up, raise up, join up). The latter usage is appropriate in General writing but is usually avoided in Formal.

Upside-down subordination Putting the main idea in a phrase or subordinate clause instead of in the main clause is sometimes called "upside-down subordination."

Upside-down: When the lightning struck the barn with a blinding flash, she had just finished dusting the hall table.

Accurate: Just as she had finished dusting the hall table, lightning struck the barn with a blinding flash.

(See Ch. 2, "Compound sentences," "Complex sentences," pp. 49, 50.)

Usage The view presented in this book is that there are three emphases in the study of current English–on linguistics, on style, and on usage. The same materials are studied and the methods have much in common, but there are characteristic differences in the three emphases, particularly in purposes. *Linguists* are chiefly concerned with the objective observation and analysis of the language–primarily of the spoken language–in order to discover and describe its system or "structure." Students of *style* examine specific examples of language–in our culture especially of written literature–primarily to find the qualities of language that are the source of a listener's or reader's impressions. Students of *usage* observe specific items in the language–both spoken and written–primarily to ascertain their currency and appropriateness in speech and writing of various sorts.

Some would regard style and usage simply as divisions of linguistics, but while linguistics furnishes much of the data and methods of the other two, and will do so increasingly, style and usage involve some consideration of social attitudes and responses usually not the concern of linguistics. An analysis made by a linguist will usually be more detailed than a student of usage requires, and often more detailed even than a student of style needs. Many linguists are sensitive to qualities of style and are excellent judges of the appropriateness of usage, but they seldom consider these their primary concern and probably feel that too much preoccupation with such questions may interfere with their scientific purpose. Although all people working with current English need a good deal of the same basic training, some division of labor, based on a recognition of the different purposes of the three emphases, will work not only for simplicity but for efficiency.

1. *The varying emphases of usage, style, and linguistics.* The data of usage can be grouped under six headings. Comparing under these six headings the concerns of usage with those of style and linguistics will illustrate some of the differences among the three studies.

a) Pronunciation. *Usage*–the pronunciation of words and phrases, and, where pronunciations vary, the relative currency and standing of differing pronunciations. *Style*–the qualities of the sounds, their harmony or contrast, and features such as alliteration, assonance, and rhythm. *Linguistics*–phonetic and especially phonemic analysis (developed in detail and perhaps the foundation of the science).

b) Word forms. *Usage*–the parts of speech and their forms, the modifications for plurals, past tenses, and so on, with special attention to differences between Standard and Nonstandard forms and to differences within Standard English. *Style*–choices among forms is a minor concern; more important is predominance of one of the parts of speech in number or in qualitative emphasis. *Linguistics*–the form classes and their affixes and other modifications.

c) Word groups. *Usage*–the typical patterns of phrases and clauses, specific idioms, such as fixed prepositions with certain nouns, adjectives, or verbs, and *idioms that do not conform to the general system of the language. *Style*–the dominance of noun-headed or verb-centered constructions, long or short constructions, and so on. *Linguistics*–the basic combinations of morphemes into syntactical units, usually determined by and described in terms of intonation.

d) Sentences. *Usage*–the favorite and minor types of sentence, with special attention to the patterns and variety of written sentences, in general from the point of view of clarity and effective communication. *Style*–variations in length and in arrangement of sentence elements, qualities of emphasis. *Linguistics*–the basic sentence patterns, with relatively little attention to the combination of these in the elaborated sentences of discourse.

e) Vocabulary. *Usage*–the meanings and qualities of words, especially their conventional uses and their range in the varieties of English. *Style*–the qualities of the words, especially their associations and connotations, imagery, and figurative use. *Linguistics*–not so much attention to individual words; semantics, the contribution of linguistics to the study of meaning, not yet very fully elaborated.

f) Conventions of writing. *Usage*–the conventions of spelling, punctuation, capitalization bulk rather large. *Style*–they are of minor importance. *Linguistics*–they are of very little importance except as the means by which the spoken language is represented in writing.

Beyond these primarily observational categories, usage is concerned with questions of "standards," style with literary effects and effectiveness, and linguistics with the understanding of language as an aspect of human behavior and other theoretical questions.

2. *The study of usage.* The study of usage helps to answer the question: Should I say or write this in this situation? Such a question comes usually either from lack of knowledge of what people say or write in a particular variety of English or from uncertainty because of differing practices. Since people are usually less at home in writing than in speaking, their questions often relate to written usage.

The study of usage has the general structure of the language as its frame, but it involves even more an accumulation of specific instances. It depends on wide observation of what people say and write in various situations as a basis for judgment of the standing of particular words, forms, and constructions. No one person can cover thoroughly this vast field, though he can amass a considerable body of data. However, since many people make special studies of individual points and present them in articles–in *American Speech,* the "Current English Forum" of *College English, Word Study,* and other periodicals–considerable reliable information accumulates. Three important books on usage are worth studying for their method, data, and conclusions:

C. C. Fries in *American English Grammar* (1940) discusses the usage found in a large group of letters and considers it in relation to the education and social position of the writers. Mr. Fries' study made clear that educated writers of Standard English show more variation in usage than was commonly thought.

George Summey, Jr., in *American Punctuation* (revised 1949) discusses the practices in punctuation he discovered from studying a large body of printed material. Although Mr. Summey discovered considerable range, he found prevailing practices that could be safely followed by individual writers.

Albert H. Marckwardt and Fred G. Walcott in *Facts About Current English Usage* (1938) present not so much a record of actual usage as of attitudes toward it. They include the results of the Leonard questionnaire to editors, teachers, and businessmen asking their judgment of a number of debatable items and add the record of dictionaries on individual words. They give recommendations representing this data.

As a result of these and other usage studies we now have a more accurate picture of what educated users of English say and, more especially, write. Such studies, presenting not a "liberal" but simply a more accurate picture of the language in use, have done a good deal to limit the puristic tendencies of textbooks on grammar and usage.

But recording usage by itself is not enough, partly because there is so much variety, especially in the very matters that are likely to raise questions. Relative frequency of occurrence is an important fact, but it gives only the range of usage. Reasoning on the data and further study are needed. Dictionaries record what their files show on particular words and phrases and give "usage labels" for many, designating them as colloquial or slang or restricted to some occupation. Such books are useful but are likely to be rather traditional. The *stylebooks of publishers, such as the *United States Government Printing Office Style Manual* or the Associated Press *Stylebook,* give the choices their publishers have made for printed matter and should be taken into account. The history of a word or construction, in the *Oxford English Dictionary* or a history of the language, is often instructive (*shall–will, *don't), because such histories reveal that a good many of the more puristic strictures on usage are of relatively recent origin. Another source of information is the explicit or incidental comments by writers, defending their own preferences or lamenting others'.

It must be remembered that people's attitudes toward usages as well as actual usage are important. **Disinterested* is widely used in the sense of "uninterested" and is so recorded in dictionaries, but many people object to it; the same is true of *like as a conjunction, the construction "the *reason is because," and many others. Actual use of *shall* and *will* has not materially changed in recent years, but the attitudes toward the usage have changed. In fact, most questions are concerned not with differences between Standard and Nonstandard English (**ain't,* the *double negative) but with matters of *divided usage within Standard English. A student of usage, then, has not only to observe widely what is said and written but also to note the attitudes of people toward particular items.

And finally he has to use his judgment, based on his accumulated data. Judgments will vary somewhat, depending on the range of the individual's information and to a certain extent on his preferences in language. The best safeguard against avoidable bias is awareness of some principles of selection. Details of the principles of appropriateness used in this book are presented on pages 27-35.

3. *Amateur students of usage.* In a sense any speaker of a language is an amateur student of usage. Unconsciously or perhaps consciously he notes and imitates things he hears. Children amass their stock of language in this way. Later most people's attention seems not to focus on the details of language–they become so accustomed to the steady flow of speech around them that they don't notice the details. Even though their circumstances may change and call for different or at least new elements of language, they often keep on speaking and writing as they did before.

Although we should not be too conscious of our language, it would be well to cultivate our observation occasionally and to become students of usage at least on a small scale. And anyone professionally concerned with English or anyone who wants to make it a hobby, should make some systematic study, to sharpen his observation, so that he won't have to be dependent on dictionaries or handbooks. He might concentrate on a few topics, such as sentence patterns, or idioms, or constructions like the prepositions used with *different.*

The easiest way to keep track of usage items is to have a file of 3x5 or 4x6 cards. The slips should be labeled at the top with the name of the particular point dealt with. Exact reference should be

1. Example of Usage

Sub-class of the topic

```
①  Verbless sentence--Answers to questions

②      When an editor does the work and you still have to make
       corrections on the proof because his work was not
       perfect, can you make him pay for them?  Not likely.  If
       the printer does the preparation and you have to make the
       corrections in the type to get a satisfactory result,
       will the printer make the corrections gratis?  Hardly,
       unless you have a very clear agreement with him in
       writing.

③                          John Benbow, Manuscript & Proof
                           N.Y.  Oxford 1937 p. 22
```

1. Label–the topic illustrated. 2. The example. 3. Exact source–If from speech put down time, place, and identify speaker.

2. Topic with Record of Investigation

```
      drought--drouth

①  Web.New Coll.Dict.:  drought.  Also drouth
   Am.Coll.Dict.:  drought. Also drouth
   Kenyon and Knott:  Separate entries for each, apparently, linking
   pronunciation and spelling.
   Not in Fowler

②  Sylvanus Kingsley, editorial writer Portland Oregonian. in Words
   Sept. 1936: prefers drouth as 'the more practical and popular
   etymology'--but 6 of 1 and half dozen of the other

③  OE drugath. th puts it in group with abstracts width, breadth.
   See height-heighth.  Shows influence of events on language, since
   notable dryness of recent years has given the word currency and
   brought into prominence the colloquial form

④  Usage divided.  Drought probably more common in formal use, but
   drouth also Standard and apparently gaining esp. in newspapers.
```

1. Label "Authorities." 2. Special source. 3. History and reasoning. 4. Conclusion.

made to the source of the quotation, or to the speaker and place and circumstances of speaking. Even a small collection will allow you to make accurate judgments about some items of usage and will provide you with good evidence to back them up. And your collection may not only give you confidence in the particular item studied but show something of the way the language in general goes.

The first slip reproduced on page 753 shows a quotation taken to illustrate the use of verbless sentences. The second contains data that stands back of the entry *drought–drouth in this *Index.*

used to The spelling *use to* comes closer than *used to* in representing what we say, but the *d* is expected in writing: *used to.* (See *-ed.)

utilize is frequently put for the simpler *use.* It means specifically "put to use."

V

(v) as in *very* (ver′i), *vivid* (viv′id), *save* (sāv); also spelled *ph* in *Stephen* (stē′vən); and *f* in *of* (ov). The letter is a variant of *u* (see *U).

varsity, a shortened form of an older pronunciation of *university,* as the name of the first team of a college or university is in the dictionaries and needs no apostrophe or apologetic quotation marks.

vase Pronounced vās, or much less often vāz. Väz is more common in British English.

Verb-adverb combinations In "I looked up at the top of the tree," the verb *look* is used in its ordinary sense and is modified by the adverb *up.* In "I looked up the word in the dictionary," *looked up* is a verb meaning "investigated," a meaning not explained by a literal use of the two words. Similarly a man may *break out* (literally) of jail, or *break out* with measles; he can *look after* a departing car, or *look after* the children. In each of these pairs of expressions, the first has a verb modified by an adverb in its ordinary meaning, and the second is really a different verb, with a meaning of its own, composed of two elements. These have become a single word, the parts of which can sometimes be manipulated in a sentence. Compare "I *looked up* the word in a dictionary" and "I *looked* the word *up* in a dictionary."

There are hundreds of such verb-adverb combinations in use, most of them one-syllabled verbs with adverbs like *about, around, at, by, down, for, in, out, through, to, up, with.* They are widely used in General English and often give an emphatic rhythm differing from the more Formal *investigate, sacrifice* (*give up*), *surrender* (*give up*). This pattern is now the most active way of forming new verbs in English. (See *Prepositions § 3b.)

Verbals The parts of a verb that function as nouns or adjectives are grouped as *verbals*. *Gerunds* (or verbal nouns) are used in the function of nouns (though they may, like verbs, have a subject or object), *participles* are used in the function of adjectives, and *infinitives* in the functions of adjectives or nouns:

Gerunds: *Swimming* is better exercise than *rowing*. *Having been invited* pleased him enormously.

Infinitives: His only ambition was *to pass*. It was too good *to last*. *To have asked* for more would have wrecked the whole conference. He had plenty of money *to spend*.

Participles: He reached the float, *swimming* as easily as he had before he had been hurt. *Asked* to take a part, he refused at first but finally accepted. *Having been invited*, he began to make plans.

For the various uses of verbals see *Gerunds, *Infinitives, and *Participles.

Verbid In this book we are keeping the term *verbal* for gerunds, infinitives, and participles when they are used simply in the functions of nouns or adjectives and are calling them *verbids* when they are used with some verbal characteristics, such as taking an object:

They had tried four times *to get him up*.
This policy, *covering your household goods*, expires September 18.
Running a motel wasn't as simple as they had expected.

These verbid constructions are usually called phrases but in several respects behave more like clauses and raise some questions of grammar. (See *Gerunds, *Infinitives, *Participles.)

Verbs 1. *Verbs as a part of speech.* Verbs can be identified by their capacity of adding to the base form (*ask, sing, tear*) the suffix *-ing*, and the suffix *-s* (when the verb has as its subject a singular noun or the pronouns *he, she, it*). The great majority of verbs also can add *-ed*. *Ask*, for example, has the forms *ask, asks, asking, asked*. Some verbs use other formal devices instead of the *-ed*. *Sing*, for example, has the forms *sing, sings, singing, sang, sung; tear* has *tear, tears, tearing, tore, torn*. A few verbs do not fit these patterns and must be learned separately: *be* has eight forms (*be, am, is, are, was, were, being, been*); *can, may, must*, and other *auxiliaries have only one form. We recognize verbs by their form and sentence position even when we don't know their meaning. In "I am sure that his words will coruscate," we know that *am, will*, and *coruscate* are verbs—*am* and *will* because we have already learned their forms, functions, and meanings, and *coruscate* because it depends on *will*, even if we have no notion of its meaning.

The syntactical function of verbs is typically to form the predicate of a clause or sentence—that is, to join with a subject, and perhaps an object, to form a single construction. For convenience we are using *verb* instead of some more specific word like *predicator* to indicate this function as well as to indicate the part of speech.

2. *Details of verb forms.* The following *Index* entries give details of the principal characteristics of verbs:

*Auxiliary verb
*Commands and requests
*Gerund
*Infinitives
*Linking verbs
*Participles
*Principal parts of verbs
*Subjunctives
*Tenses of verbs
*Transitive and intransitive verbs
*Verbals
*Voice

3. *Syntax of verbs.* Besides entries on numerous particular verbs (such as *ain't, *be, *do, *can–may, *get, *need, *shall–will), the following entries are especially concerned with the use of verbs in speaking and writing:

*Absolute phrases
*Clauses
*Collective nouns
*Commands and requests
*Conditions
*Dangling modifiers
*Finite verbs
*Fragmentary sentence
*Gerund
*Infinitives
*Objects
*Participles
*Passive verbs
*Predicate adjective, Predicate noun
*Split infinitive
*Subject and verb
*Subjunctives
*Tenses of verbs
*Verb-adverb combinations
*Voice

References: Fries, Curme, Jespersen, and all grammars treat verbs; see especially Fries, *AEG,* Chapter 8, and Fries, *Structure,* Chapters 5-7.

Vernacular English vernacular formerly referred to the native, spoken language—as opposed to the literary languages of Latin or Norman French. It now usually means Nonstandard and perhaps Informal English, the native homely, spoken language as contrasted with Formal or literary English, usually with the implication that the vernacular has more vitality and force.

Verse form The form of a line of verse is described by telling the arrangement of the stressed syllables (the kind of "foot"), the length of the line (the number of feet), and any other qualities of movement or variation from the typical movement that it shows. This article presents the vocabulary and an outline of the facts necessary for describing verse form.

The feet:

Iambic x / (An iamb)
Trochaic / x (A trochee)
Anapestic x x / (An anapest)
Dactylic / x x (A dactyl)
Spondaic / / (A spondee)

The length of lines:

Dimeter: Two feet
Trimeter: Three feet
Tetrameter: Four feet
Pentameter: Five feet
Hexameter: Six feet

Other facts:

A line is *end-stopped* if its end corresponds with a distinct sense pause, either the end of a sentence or of a major sentence element; it is *run-on* when the construction is carried over the end of the line.

Alexandrine: A line containing six iambic feet
Anacrusis: An extra unstressed syllable at the beginning of a line
Catalexis: The dropping of the final unstressed syllable
Feminine ending: An extra unstressed syllable at the end
Refrain: A line repeated, typically at the end of each stanza of a poem

A *cesura* (*caesura*) is a rhythmic pause within a line.

Two successive lines rhyming are a *couplet.*

A four-line stanza is a *quatrain,* which may have any rhyme scheme: abab, abba; an iambic tetrameter quatrain rhyming abcb is the *ballad stanza.*

More complex stanza forms (sonnet, ode, ballade, and so on) are described in books on literature and poetry.

Blank verse is unrhymed iambic pentameter. *Free verse* is verse of varied length lines with a flexible movement, usually unrhymed.

Examples of scansion:

Iambic pentameter (feminine ending):

x / x / x / x / x / x
A thing of beauty is a joy forever

Anapestic tetrameter:

x x / x x / x x / x x /
There are brains, though they moulder, that dream in the tomb

Trochaic tetrameter (catalectic), a couplet:

/ x / x / x /
Souls of poets dead and gone,

/ x / x x / x /
What Elysium have ye known,

These examples show that scansion tells the typical physical characteristic of verse but does not define the rhythm, which is far more important. (Reference: For the more important qualities of poetry, such as imagery, tone, color, rhythm (not to mention meaning), see books on poetry and literature.)

vertebra The plural is either *vertebrae* (vûr′tə brē) or *vertebras,* with *vertebrae* still the more common.

very 1. *"Very" as an intensive. Very* has been so overused that it is of doubtful value as an intensive. A writer should make sure that it really adds to the meaning of his phrase.

The *Emporia Gazette* once described its war upon *very* this way:

> "If you feel you must write 'very,' write 'damn.' " So when the urge for emphasis is on him, the reporter writes "It was a damn fine victory.

I am damn tired but damn well–and damn excited." Then, because it is the Emporia (Kan.) Gazette, the copy desk deletes the profanity and the quotation reads: "It was a fine victory. I am tired but well–and excited." That's how the Gazette attains its restrained, simple, and forceful style. Very simple.

2. *"Very" and past participles.* In Formal English many people will not use *very* with a past participle (He was very excited), because *very,* now used primarily as an intensive, supposedly marks only a high degree of a *quality,* as in *very happy,* and the verb function of the participle denotes an action rather than a quality. The Formal locution would be: He was *very much* excited.

This distinction, since it is based purely on grammatical reasoning, is too insubstantial for users of General English, who use *very* to modify such participles without any qualms (I shall be very pleased to come; We shall be very delighted to have you).

When the President and the trustees finally decided to allow the Psychology Department to sponsor a clinic, Dr. Bonham was very elated.–JAMES REID PARKER, *Academic Procession,* p. 13

viewpoint is a natural and economical substitute for *point of view.* It is not stigmatized in the dictionaries.

Before we condemn him for affectation and distortion we must realize his viewpoint.–E. M. FORSTER, *Aspects of the Novel,* p. 182

viz. *Viz.* is the abbreviation of the Latin *videlicet* (vi del′ə sit), which means "to wit, namely." *Viz.* exists only in the language of rather Formal documents or reference works. It is usually read "namely."

Voice 1. *Definition and forms.* Voice is the category in which English verb forms are classified as active or passive. The passive voice is made with the *past* participle and some form of the verb *be* (*was killed*); all other forms are active.

	Active	*Passive*
Present:	he (is asking) asks	he is asked (is being asked)
Future:	he will ask	he will be asked
Perfect:	he has asked	he has been asked
Infinitives:	to ask, to have asked	to be asked, to have been asked
Participles:	asking, having asked	being asked, asked

Get and *become* are used especially in Informal English:

If he should get elected, we'd be lost.
Our house is getting painted.
They had become separated from their guide.

The traditional definition in terms of meaning is a useful guide in identifying active and passive verbs. When the subject of a verb is the doer of the action or is in the condition named by its verb, the verb is said to be in the active voice:

The congregation *sang* "Abide with Me."
They *will go* swimming.
Jimmy's father *gave* him a car.
Our side *had been winning.*
We *rested* an hour.

When the subject of a verb receives the action, the verb is said to be in the passive voice:

"Abide with Me" *was sung* by the congregation.
Jimmy *was given* a car by his father.
The pit *was dug* fully eight feet deep.
They *had been caught.*

These different expressions of the verb give considerable flexibility in sentence word order. They allow the speaker or writer to emphasize by position the thing that is most important to him:

The *house* was finished by the crew in record time.
The *crew* finished the house in record time.

Or, more often, they merely allow the speaker to approach the statement from the viewpoint of his thinking about it (the house or the crew, for example, in the sentences above). The construction in English is more important as a matter of style than of grammar and is one of the devices that make it possible for one's expression to come close to his process of thought.

2. *Use of active verbs.* Active verbs are more common than passive because we are accustomed to the actor-action-goal pattern of expression. In the text of the preceding paragraph, for example, the seven finite verbs (*give, allow, is, allow, is, is, make*) and the three infinitives (*to emphasize, to approach, to come*) are active.

3. *Use of passive verbs.* Passive verbs may be less frequent, but they have several important uses.

The object, the goal, may be more important, in the writer's mind, than the doer:

The bill *was passed* without opposition.
The well *was drilled* in solid rock.
Our house *was painted* last year.

In indefinite statements the passive is often used when the actors may not be known or are not to be named in the statement:

Much *has been written* on both sides.
Many records *have been set* in past Olympics.

The passive allows various degrees of emphasis by placing the name of the act or of the doer at the end:

Our house *is being painted.* (Active: They *are painting* our house.)

Our house *was painted* by Joe Mead and his brother. (Active: Joe Mead and his brother *painted* our house.)

"Abide with Me" was sung by the choir [that is, not by the congregation].

Sometimes the passive shows a change in the relation between subject and verb (though the shift should not be made within a sentence unless the action is continuous):

We *drove* [active] there and *were taken out* [passive] in a dory.

(For discussion of the object of a passive verb, see *Objects § 1b.)

4. *Overuse of the passive.* For the objectionable use of passive verbs when active would be more effective, see *Passive verbs.

References: Curme, *Syntax,* pages 102-103; Fries, *AEG,* pages 188-193; Jespersen, Chapter 12.

Voiced, voiceless sounds In voiced sounds the vocal cords vibrate, as in the vowels and *b, d, g, v, z, zh,* and *th* (t͟h). *P, t, k, f, s, sh,* and *th* (th) are the voiceless sounds corresponding to these voiced consonants. In addition there are the voiced consonants *m, n, ng, w, y, r* and the voiceless *h;* some phoneticians would add *j* (voiced) and *ch* (voiceless), though others consider these as combinations of *d* plus *zh* and *t* plus *sh.*

Some nouns and verbs are distinguished by voicing of the consonant in the verb: *use* (noun, ūs—verb, ūz), *proof—prove* (noun, prōōf—verb, prōōv), *grief—grieve* (grēf—grēv).

A few spelling errors seem to be caused by a confusion between voicing and non-voicing, as *significance* (-kəns) often appears as *signifigance* (-gəns).

W

W (w) as in *wild* (wīld), *twinkle* (twing′kəl); also spelled as in *quick* (kwik), *choir* (kwīr). *W* is silent in *write* (rīt), *two* (tōō), *sword* (sōrd), and other words, and spoken though not spelled in *one* (wun), *once* (wuns).

The letter, as the name indicates, is two *u*'s—formerly written vv —together.

wake English is oversupplied with verbs for waking from sleep (intransitive) and waking someone else from sleep (transitive): Each is used in both senses:

awake (*awaked, awaked* or *awoke, awoke*). Rather Formal; more commonly used intransitively (I awoke).

awaken (*awakened, awakened*). Formal.

wake (*waked* or *woke, waked* or *woke* [*woken*]). More widely used than the preceding.

waken (*wakened, wakened*). Less common than *wake.*

The usual solution is the *verb-adverb combination *wake up* (*waked* or *woke up*):

She waked up [woke up] at eleven. She waked [woke] me up at six.

want The General idiom with *want* has an infinitive:

General: I want you to get all you can from the year's work.
Local: I want for you to get all you can from the year's work.
Local: I want that you should get all you can from the year's work.

Want is Informal for *ought, had better:* You want to review all the notes if you're going to pass his exam.

In the sense of *lack* or *need, want* is Formal and suggests British usage: The letter, though clear, wants correcting.

Want in, want out without a complementary verb (The dog wants out) seems to be of Scotch rather than German origin and is widely used in the United States. (See Albert H. Marckwardt, "*Want* with Ellipsis of Verbs of Action," *American Speech,* 1948, 23:3-9.)

way, ways *Way* is Informally used for *away* (way over across the valley). *Way* is used in a number of General and Informal idioms (*in a bad way, out our way,* I don't see how she can act *the way* she does).

Ways is locally used for *way* in expressions like *a little ways* down the road.

we **1.** *Indefinite we. We* is frequently used as an indefinite pronoun in expressions like *We find, We sometimes feel,* to avoid passive and impersonal constructions. (See *Reference of pronouns § 3.)

2. *Editorial we.* In editorial columns and in some other regular departments of periodicals, like "The Talk of the Town" in *The New Yorker,* the writer refers to himself as *we,* which leads to the curious form *ourself.* In some instances the *we* refers to an editorial board that determines the opinions expressed but more often it is a convention. It is less used than formerly.

The usage has passed into Informal writing, especially of a light tone. Used merely to avoid *I, we* is usually conspicuous and to be avoided. (See *I § 2.)

3. *Parental we. We* is used Informally in softened requests, especially to children (We won't lose our mittens, will we?). This is a more effective use than the nurse's "How are we feeling this morning?"–sometimes called the "medical we."

wh is the English spelling for the sound of *hw: what* (hwot or hwut), *when* (hwen), *wheel* (hwēl), *whether* (hweth'ər), *why* (hwī). In *who* (hōō), *whole* (hōl), *whoop* (hōōp), *wholly* (hōl'i) and so on, *wh* represents h.

Other words spelled with *wh* are frequently pronounced with w: *white* (wīt), *whether* (weth'ər), *why* (wī). The practice seems to be increasing in the United States and is recognized in Knott and Kenyon. See that book, page xliv; *Oxford English Dictionary, wh;* Raven I. McDavid, Jr., "Our Initial Consonant 'H,' " *College English,* 1950, 11:459-460.

when Most handbooks warn against statements like "Welding is when two pieces of metal are heated and made into one." The reason given is that it is illogical or ungrammatical to equate an "adverbial clause" with a noun. This reasoning is fallacious because a clause cannot be classified solely by its introductory word. *When* (and *where*) clauses are frequently used (1) in noun constructions, as in "Do you have any way of knowing *when she will come*?" in which the *when* clause is the object of *knowing,* and (2) as adjective modifiers, as in "There comes a time *when a man has to be careful of his diet,*" in which the clause modifies *time.*

The objection to the construction is stylistic rather than grammatical and comes from the overuse of *when* clauses in amateurish definitions (Communism is when all property is owned by all the people together or by the state). The more Formal pattern would be: Communism is a system in which all property is owned by all the people together or by the state.

The construction, then, is to be discouraged rather than forbidden. (References: Fries, *AEG,* pp. 233-234; Marckwardt and Walcott, p. 115; Russell Thomas, *College English,* 1949, 10:406-408. Compare *reason is because.)

when, as, and if Securities are advertised "when, as, and if issued," and the phrase *when and if* or *if and when* is used in talking about goods whose future is uncertain. It should not be used when the matter is certain, or in nonbusiness contexts except when appropriate to the tone.

where *Where* clauses frequently are used as adjective modifiers, most commonly when some notion of place is involved:

General: This is the place where the trucks stop.
General: He wants a job where he will be with people.
More Formal: He wants a job in which he will be with people.

Where clauses in definitions are subject to the same objections that *when* clauses (see *when) are—that is, they frequently sound amateurish:

Amateurish: Etching is where you cut lines in a copper plate and then print from them.

General: Etching is the process of cutting lines in a copper plate and then printing from it.

English once had *whither,* place to which; *whence,* place from which. They are now rarely used, and *where* has taken their place with help from other words: always with *from* to replace *whence;* often with *to* for *whither.*

"Where is your room *at*?" smacks of Nonstandard English. (References: Fries, *AEG,* pp. 234-235; Marckwardt and Walcott, p. 115.)

whether *Whether* is used in indirect questions: He asked whether you could come.

In statements *whether* is used with *or* to indicate two alternatives: They have never decided whether he committed suicide or was murdered.

In Formal usage *or not* is frequently used with *whether* to indicate a second alternative when it is simply the negative of the one stated (They have never decided whether or not he was murdered). But in General usage *or not* is frequently omitted (They have never decided whether he was murdered), and should not be used if it will make an awkward statement:

General: Whether or not this was the best plan, they went ahead. *Or:* Whether this was the best plan or not, they went ahead.

General: It is a sorry state when pupils don't know whether or not to believe their teachers.

Clumsy: It is a sorry state when pupils don't know whether to believe their teachers or not [Omit the *or not*].

(Reference: Fries, *AEG,* pp. 207, 217. See *if § 2, *Conditions.)

which **1.** *Which* refers to things and to groups of people regarded impersonally (The legislature which passed the act...). It is no longer used in Standard English to refer to a person or persons.

2. *Which* (like *that* and *this*) frequently has as its antecedent the idea of a phrase or clause:

Relative pronouns are as troublesome to the inexpert but conscientious writer as they are useful to everyone, *which* is saying much.—H. W. Fowler, *A Dictionary of Modern English Usage,* p. 709

As with other uses of pronouns, the reference should be clear. (See *which* in Webster's New International Dictionary. Compare *this.)

3. *Whose* is often used as the genitive of *which,* instead of the more cumbersome *of which:*

This story of the life of General Custer is *Boots and Saddles,* whose author is the General's wife.

4. *And* and *but* are carelessly used to join a *which* clause, which is subordinate, to a main statement.

Inaccurate: He got the contract to install new copper work on the Post Office, and which will require 4500 pounds of lead-coated copper.

Accurate: He got the contract to install new copper work on the Post Office, which will require 4500 pounds of lead-coated copper.

while *While* most exactly is a connective of time:

While the rest were studying, he was playing cards.

While also means *though* or *but,* but rather weakly:

Magazines, newspapers, and scientific books became my chief interest, while [More exact: *but*] plays and poems were still a torture to me.

While is occasionally used for *and:*

The second number was an acrobatic exhibition, while [Better: *and*] the third was a lady trapeze artist.

Awhile is an adverb, written as one word: *Awhile ago.* In phrases in which *while* is a noun, the *a* should be written separate: *In a while; After a while.* (Reference: Fries, *AEG,* pp. 236-237.)

Whitespace Whitespace has the function of a punctuation mark in display matter. It has now taken the place of commas and periods at the ends of lines in envelope addresses, in letter headings, in titles of books and articles, in outlines, in lines that are spaced off in advertisements, posters, etc., in matter set in tables or columns. No punctuation marks are used at the ends of lines in Formal social notes. In indented quotations whitespace has displaced the quote marks. These various uses have helped relieve the spottiness of correspondence and many printed pages.

who, whom **1.** *Antecedent of "who." Who* refers to people, to personified objects (a ship, a country), and occasionally to animals:

> Diogenes Checkpoints says what is needed is a list of horses who should be out of training.—AUDAX MINOR, *The New Yorker,* Aug. 27, 1938

Whose is commonly used as the genitive of *which.* (Reference: Hall, pp. 320-327. See *which § 3.)

2. *"Who" versus "whom."* In 1928 the *Oxford English Dictionary* said *whom* was "no longer current in natural colloquial speech." The struggle to make writing conform to grammatical rules of case is consequently difficult and full of problems. *Whom* consistently occurs only when it immediately follows a preposition as object (I don't know to whom I should go). But since the preposition often comes last in the expression, in General usage we find *who* (I don't know who I should go to). The most important reason for the development of this usage is that we no longer expect to have the form indicate the case function (except genitive). None of the other relative pronouns show case function by form, nor do the nouns (again except genitives); and the personal pronouns are too few to keep us sensitive to case forms. Three other factors combine to make this *who* construction usual: (1) the position before the verb—the "subject-territory," (2) the infrequent use of *whom* in speech, and (3) our habit of not using relative pronouns to introduce clauses (I know the man [whom] you mean).

Formal usage, no doubt largely enforced by copy editors, generally keeps the objective form when the pronoun is used as an object:

> Formal: Whom [object of *introduce*] do you introduce to whom [object of the immediately preceding *to*]?
>
> General: Who do you introduce to whom?
>
> Formal: No matter whom [object of *meets*] one meets, the first thing one mentions is the weather.
>
> General: No matter who you meet, the first thing you mention is the weather.

Which you use, then, depends on the variety and tone of the particular piece of writing. In Formal and academic writing and in much General writing you should use *whom;* in Informal narratives and personal writing *who* is usually appropriate when the pronoun is used as an object. (References: Fries, *AEG,* pp. 88-96, 237; Pooley, pp. 72-77, 221; all other competent grammarians.)

3. *"Who" separated from verb.* When *who* is the subject of a verb separated from it by other words, care should be taken to keep the subject form:

He made a list of all the writers who [subject of *were*] he thought were important in the period.

4. *The number of the verb.* A verb with *who* as its subject has the number of the antecedent of the *who:*

I'm one of the few people who don't [antecedent *people*] like to read many books.

I'm one who doesn't [antecedent *one*] like to read books.

Informally there is a strong tendency to make the verb of the *who* clause agree with the principal subject, which would give *doesn't* in the first sentence above. This is avoided in careful writing. (See *one of those who.)

wire *Wire* is General and Informal for *telegram, telegraph.*

-wise This suffix has long had a limited currency in forming adverbs from nouns (*edgewise, lengthwise, slantwise*). Recently it has greatly increased in use, especially in an abstract rather than spatial sense: *average-wise, budget-wise, legislation-wise, tax-wise.* (It is usually hyphened in these new formations.)

This use of *-wise* occurs chiefly in commercial, journalistic, and political contexts; it carries the connotation of jargon as well as of faddish overuse and should not be used in General writing. It does have some advantages in economy (economy-wise), taking the place of a prepositional phrase.

with There seems to be a temptation to use *with* when another preposition or a different construction would be more accurate:

Our outfit was composed of two platoons with [Better: of] 43 men each.

I'll never forget the farmer who, not seeing the wave, tried to get his few cows to safety and was washed away with [Better: by] the water.

Americans believe in freedom, but with Germans it is different [Perhaps: but Germans are different].

Wordiness Revision: Compress this passage by replacing the wordy expressions with more compact and exact ones.

Wdy

1. *Circumlocution.* 2. *Long function words.* 3. *Deadwood.* 4. *Formless, fuzzy writing.*

The use of unnecessary words in conveying one's ideas results in flabby writing. Unprofitable words can be removed or replaced by more economical ones in revision. The commonest types of wordiness are:

1. *Circumlocution*–the use of several words instead of one exact word:

destroyed by fire means *burned*
come in contact with usually means *meet* or *know*
the necessary funds usually means no more than *the money*
in this day and age means *today*
the sort of metal they use for plating the shiny parts of automobiles might mean *chromium*

2. *Long function words*–function phrases that might be replaced by one or by fewer words:

During the time that [*while*] she was in Los Angeles she had at least six different jobs.

(See *Function words § 2.)

3. *Deadwood*–words which add nothing to the meaning:

The cars are neat and graceful [in appearance].
In the majority of cases they do not. (*For:* The majority do not.)
The home of my boyfriend was in a town called Hillsdale. (*For: My* boyfriend's home was in Hillsdale.)

(See Ch. 7, "Economy in sentences," p. 186.)

4. *Formless, fuzzy writing:*

Wordy	*Revised*
It has some of the best ski trails in the country and as far as the other cold weather sports are concerned, they have them too, along with one of the most fashionable hotels in the country.	They have a very fashionable hotel, all the cold weather sports, and some of the best ski trails in the country.

(See also Ch. 7, "Long and short constructions," "Repetition," pp. 188, 191, and specific articles like *case, *Passive verbs, *seem, *there is, there are.)

Word order Revision: Change the order of words or other elements so that the meaning is more clear, or the sentence is more natural, or more effective.

WO

1. *Position changed for emphasis.* 2. *Interrupted constructions.* 3. *Misleading word order.*

The order of words and of other locutions in a sentence is the most important device of English grammar to show the relations of words in sentences. It plays a large part in style, especially emphasis. The work done in many languages by inflections (endings) is in English performed largely by *function words (prepositions, auxiliary verbs, and so on–whose function is made clear by their position) and by the word order. Since we pick up the standard word order as we learn to talk, it offers little difficulty. We use naturally the subject-verb-object order of clauses and sentences; we put adjectives before their nouns and relative clauses after their nouns and in general put modifiers near the words modified.

This article is intended to bring the fact of word order to your attention rather than to cover its large number of details. It emphasizes three instances in which the order is variable.

1. *Position changed for emphasis.* As a rule an element taken out of its usual position receives increased emphasis, as when the object is put before both subject and verb:

Object first: That book I read when I was sixteen. (Instead of: I read that book when I was sixteen.)

Predicate adjective first: Lucky are the ones who register early. (Instead of: The ones who register early are lucky.)

(See Ch. 7, "Position," p. 194.)

2. *Interrupted constructions.* When a word or words interrupt a construction, the effect is usually unhappy unless the interrupting word deserves special emphasis:

Between subject and verb: Newspaper headlines in these trying and confused times are continually intensifying the fears of the American people. (More natural: In these trying and confused times newspaper headlines are. . . .)

Between verb and adverb: He played quietly, efficiently on. He took a pack from his pocket and she took one thoughtfully out. (More natural: He played on, quietly, efficiently. He took a pack from his pocket and she took one out thoughtfully [or: and she thoughtfully took one out].)

(See Ch. 7, "Interrupted movement, p. 193, *Split infinitive.)

3. *Misleading word order.* English usually has a modifier close to the word modified and care must be taken that modifiers separated from their main words are not misleading.

Misleading	*Improved*
I wish to order one of the machines which I saw advertised in *The Saturday Evening Post* sent to the above address.	I wish to order sent to the above address one of the machines which I saw advertised in *The Saturday Evening Post.*
Her uncle, King Leopold, was even unable to influence her.	Even her uncle, King Leopold, was unable to influence her.
This success in villages will probably be duplicated in the cities as time goes on at an accelerated rate.	As time goes on, this success in villages will probably be duplicated at an accelerated rate in cities.
Until recently the chains have been able to get special prices on the goods they buy from producers with little opposition.	Until recently the chains have been able to get with little opposition special prices on the goods they buy from manufacturers.

(See *Ambiguity § 2. References: Margaret M. Bryant, *College English,* 1944, 5:434-438: Fries, *AEG.* Ch. 10; Curme, *Syntax,* Ch. 17;

C. Alphonso Smith, *Studies in English Syntax* (Boston, 1906), Ch. 2.)

Words Revision: Replace the word marked by one that is more exact, more effective, or more appropriate.

WW

General questions of the use of words are treated in Chapter 8, "Words." Many specific words that are likely to raise questions have articles of their own (*contact, *drunk, *hope, *however, *notorious, *try and–try to, *ye=the . . .). Very often the solution to a question of diction can be found in a good dictionary.

Some of the more general topics about words or their uses will be found under the following heads, in the *Index* articles marked * or in the chapters at the pages given.

worth while is written as two words, or hyphened (especially when preceding its noun: a worth-while book), or (occasionally) as one word.

X

X is an unnecessary letter in English. It spells several sounds represented by different phonetic symbols (ks) as in *fox* (foks), *exclusive* (iks klōō′siv), *exceed* (ik sēd′); (gz) as in *exist* (ig zist′), *exhibit* (ig zib′it); (ksh) as in *luxury* (luk′shə ri); (gzh) as in *luxurious* (lug zhoor′i əs or luk shoor′i əs); (z) in *xylophone, Xantippe, Xavier* (not eksz ā viar). In British usage *ct* is sometimes spelled *x* as in *inflexion.*

Xmas is an Informal word used chiefly in advertising; it is pronounced like *Christmas,* for which it stands. The *X* is from the initial letter of the Greek spelling of *Christ.*

 X-ray is hyphened; it may be spelled with or without a capital.

Y (y) as in *yes* (yes), *beyond* (bi yond′). *Y* also spells ī and i, as in *sky* (skī), *bloody* (blud′i).

A final *y* following a consonant is changed to *i* before a suffix beginning with a vowel except *i: duty–dutiable, try–tries, body–bodies, bodied;* but *play–played, playing, playable, fly–flying.*

ye = the In Old English the sound of *th* in *thin* was represented by the letter thorn, þ. In early printing the letter *y,* which looked most like the thorn, was used to represent it. Consequently we find *ye* (*the*), *yat* (*that*), *yem* (*them*) in early books and even oftener find the forms in manuscript down to about 1800.

This *y* then represents *th* and is pronounced *th.* Its use in recent faking of antiquity has not changed this fact: Ye Olde Coffee Shoppe is just The Old Coffee Shop and should be so pronounced.

ye = you *Ye,* originally the nominative plural and then also the nominative singular of the second person pronoun (now *you*), survived for a long time in poetry and other literature with a tendency to be archaic (sermons, florid oratory). It is now obsolete in writing, though the unstressed pronunciation of *you* is probably much like what *ye* used to represent.

yes *Yes* and *no* are adverbs. They may modify a sentence (Yes, you're right) or may have the value of a coordinate clause (No; but you should have told me) or may stand as complete sentences. ("Do you really intend to go with him?" "Yes.")

Yes often has variants in speech, where there are innumerable substitutes, from *ye-us* to *yop* and the "colloquial nasals," not to mention the current slang affirmatives and the longer lived ones like *OK.*

yet *Yet* is an adverb (The books haven't come yet); and in rather Formal English it is also used as a *coordinating conjunction, equivalent to *but:* His speech was almost unintelligible, yet for some unknown reason I enjoyed it.

you *You* is used as an indefinite pronoun (It's a good book, if you like detective stories) in General writing. Formal English would more often use *one* or a different construction, though the prejudice against *you* is declining. (See *one, *they.)

When *you* is used in an Informal approach to readers or to an audience, it sometimes may be unintentionally personal (or even insulting) or seem to indicate an invidious distinction between writer and reader (Take, for instance, *your* [better: *our* or *one's*] family problems). In speech the indefinite *you* is distinguished from the personal *you* by the reduced stress on it.

You was and *you is* are Nonstandard constructions.

you all In Southern American *you all,* contracted to *y'all,* is frequently used as the plural of *you,* as in some other regions *you folks* is used. It is also used when addressing one person regarded as one of a group, usually a family, as in Benbow's speech to Popeye, "If it's whiskey, I don't care how much you all make or sell or buy" (William Faulkner, *Sanctuary,* p. 4), in which the *you all* refers to Popeye and his household.

It is sometimes asserted that *you all* is also used as a singular, addressing one. (See almost any volume of *American Speech,* especially ii and iv.) It apparently is occasionally used as a singular but this use is regarded by educated Southerners as an error.

There are at least three current locutions that attempt to remedy the lack of distinction between second person singular and plural in English: *youse, you'uns,* and *you all.* Only *you all* has achieved respectability. (Reference: Mencken, pp. 449-450.)

your–you're In revision check for careless confusion of these words. *Your* is a possessive pronoun (your books); *you're* is a subject and verb (you're all right).

youth is overused in the sense of "young people" and suggests a ministerial style.

Z

(z) as in *Zion* (zī′ən), *buzz* (buz), *busy* (biz′i), *shoes* (sho͞oz). The sound is also spelled *s* (*desire*), *x* (*anxiety*), *ss* (*scissors*).

zh The phonetic symbol representing the sound in *rouge* (ro͞ozh), *measure* (mezh′ər) and so on. (See *G § 3.)

zoology In spite of several dictionaries, zoology is prevailingly spelled without a dieresis or hyphen. It is well to resist the temptation to pronounce it zo͞o ol′i ji and keep it zō ol′i ji.

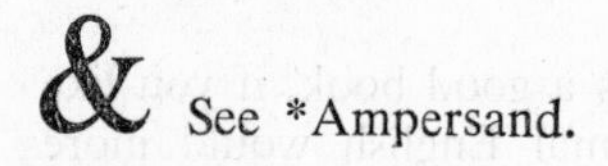

See *Ampersand.

ACKNOWLEDGMENTS

The author gratefully acknowledges the kindness of authors and publishers in giving permission to reproduce their materials in *Writer's Guide and Index to English.* Where the territory rights are divided among various publishers, the acknowledgment states what permission was granted. An unqualified acknowledgment indicates that world permission was granted.

George Allen & Unwin Ltd.: British Empire for selections from *Mysticism and Logic* by Bertrand Russell, and *Prejudices: Fifth Series* by H. L. Mencken.

American Association of University Professors Bulletin: selection from "The Functional Bases of Appraising Academic Performance" by Logan Wilson; used by permission of the American Association of University Professors and Logan Wilson.

American Speech: selections from "Soap Opera Grammar" by Theodore Williams, *American Speech,* May 1957, copyright Columbia University Press.

Appleton-Century-Crofts, Inc.: selections from *American English Grammar,* by Charles Carpenter Fries. Copyright, 1940, The National Council of Teachers of English and Charles C. Fries. Reprinted by permission of Appleton-Century-Crofts, Inc. From *Text into Type* by Marjorie E. Skillin and Robert M. Gay, copyright 1948, Appleton-Century-Crofts, Inc.

Edward Arnold & Co.: World exclusive of the United States for selections from *Aspects of the Novel* by E. M. Forster.

The Atlantic Monthly: from selections in *The Atlantic Monthly:* "News and the Whole Truth" by Elmer Davis, August 1952; "Star Light, Star Bright" by Anitra Freeman, November 1956; and "Cotton Picker" by Dorothy Otis Wyre, August 1957.

Arthur Barker Ltd.: British Empire for selection from *Time: The Present* by Tess Slesinger.

The Bobbs-Merrill Company Inc.: selection from *The New Decalogue of Science* by Albert Edward Wiggam. Copyright 1923. Used by special permission of the publishers, The Bobbs-Merrill Company Inc.

Brandt & Brandt: selection from "The Blood of the Martyrs" in *Thirteen O'Clock* by Stephen Vincent Benét, published by Farrar and Rinehart, Inc. Copyright, 1932, by the Butterick Company. Copyright, 1925, 1928, 1930, 1932, 1935, 1936, 1937, by Stephen Vincent Benét. Selections from *John Brown's Body* by Stephen Vincent Benét, published by Farrar & Rinehart, Inc. Copyright, 1927, 1928, by Stephen Vincent Benét. World exclusive of the United States and Canada for selection from *The Yearling* by Marjorie Kinnan Rawlings.

Bulletin of the Atomic Scientists: selection from "National Security with the Arms Race Limited" by David Inglis, June 1956.

Cambridge University Press: selection from *The Universe Around Us* by Sir James Jeans.

H. S. Canby: selections from *Saturday Papers,* edited by H. S. Canby and others; and "War or Peace in Literature" in *Designed for Reading* by H. S. Canby, W. R. Benét and A. Loveman, published by The Macmillan Company.

Jonathan Cape Limited: British Empire except Canada for selections from *Green Hills of Africa* by Ernest Hemingway.

Chicago Sun-Times: selection from "If You Die Without a Will," June 25, 1957.

The Clarendon Press: selection from *Modern Prose Style* by Bonamy Dobrée.

Constable & Company Limited: World exclusive of the United States for selection from *Persons and Places* by George Santayana.

Malcolm Cowley: selection from *Exile's Return* by Malcolm Cowley.

Cresset Press Ltd.: selection from *The American People* by Geoffrey Gorer.

F. S. Crofts and Co.: selection from "Scientific Method in Economics" by Frank H. Knight from *The Trend of Economics* edited by R. G. Tugwell, copyright 1924, F. S. Crofts and Co.

Thomas Y. Crowell: selection from *Of Whales and Women* by Frank B. Gilbreth, Jr.

Curtis Brown Ltd.: selections from *Now in November* by Josephine Johnson. World exclusive of the United States and Canada for selection from *Hard Lines* by Ogden Nash. Copyright 1931 by Ogden Nash. Reprinted by permission of Little, Brown & Company and the author.

Curtis Publishing Company: selection from *My Scotland Yard Adventures* by Sir Ronald Howe, © 1947 Curtis Publishing Company, permission granted by Willis Kingsley Wing.

J. M. Dent & Sons Ltd.: selection from "The Lagoon" in *Tales of Unrest* by Joseph Conrad, copyright, 1898, 1920, by Doubleday, Doran & Company, Inc.

Dodd, Mead & Company: selection reprinted by permission of Dodd, Mead & Company from *The New World*—Volume II of *A History of the English-Speaking Peoples* by Winston S. Churchill. © 1956 by Winston S. Churchill. Also by permission of Cassell and Company Ltd. Selection from *Modern American Painting* by Peyton Boswell, Jr. Reprinted by permission of the publishers, Dodd, Mead & Company, Inc. Selection reprinted by permission of Dodd, Mead & Company from *Autumn Across America* by Edwin Way Teale. Copyright 1950, 1951, by Edwin Way Teale. © 1956 by Edwin Way Teale.

Doubleday & Company, Inc.: selection from *For Authors Only* by Kenneth Roberts; used by permission of Doubleday & Company, Inc., and Kenneth Roberts.

Duell, Sloan & Pearce, Inc.: selection from *Virgin Spain* by Waldo Frank. Copyright, 1926, 1942, by Waldo Frank.

Editor & Publisher: selection from "Shoptalk" by George Olds in *Editor & Publisher,* February 5, 1935. Copyright, *Editor & Publisher.*

Eyre & Spottiswoode Limited: selections from *A Time for Greatness* by Herbert Agar. World permission granted by Eyre & Spottiswoode Limited; Little, Brown & Company; and Herbert Agar.

Faber and Faber Limited: World exclusive of the United States for selections from *After Strange Gods* and "Gerontion" by T. S. Eliot.

Farrar, Straus and Cudahy, Inc.: selection from *The Lottery* by Shirley Jackson, copyright 1949 by Shirley Jackson. Used by permission of the publishers, Farrar, Straus and Cudahy, Inc. Selection from *Life Among the Savages* by Shirley Jackson, copyright 1948, 1949, 1950, 1951, 1952, 1953 by Shirley Jackson. Used by permission of the publishers, Farrar, Straus and Cudahy, Inc.

Allan Ferguson: selection from "The Scientist's Need for New Words" by Allan Ferguson in *The Listener,* April 21, 1937.

C. C. Fries: selection from *What Is Good English?* by C. C. Fries.

Garrett Publications, Inc.: selections from "Confessions of a Playwright" by William Saroyan in *Tomorrow,* February 1949; used by permission of Garrett Publications, Inc., New York, and William Saroyan.

Good Housekeeping: selection from *Good Housekeeping,* July 1947, reprinted by permission of *Good Housekeeping.*

Harcourt, Brace and Company, Inc.: selection from *You Can't Print That* by George Seldes. World exclusive of the British Empire for selection from *Language in Thought and Action* by S. I. Hayakawa. United States and Canada for selection from *The Tyranny of Words* by Stuart Chase, copyright 1938 by Stuart Chase. United States for selections from *Aspects of the Novel* by E. M. Forster, copyright, 1927, by E. M. Forster. Selection from *Coming Up for Air* by George Orwell. Copyright © 1950 by Harcourt, Brace and Company, Inc. Also reprinted by permission of Secker & Warburg, Ltd. Selection from *The Road to Wigan Pier* by George Orwell.

Harper & Brothers: selections from *Insurgent America* by Alfred M. Bingham, copyright, 1935, by Harper & Brothers; from an article by Carl Landauer in *The American Way* by D. C. Coyle and others, copyright, 1938, by Harper & Brothers; from *The Horse and Buggy Doctor* by Arthur E. Hertzler, copyright, 1938, by Paul B. Hoeber, Inc.; from *Proper Studies* by Aldous Huxley, copyright, 1927, by George H. Doran Co.; *Personality* by Gardner Murphy, copyright, 1947; "Bubbles" in *Best Stories of Wilbur Daniel Steele,* copyright, 1946, by Wilbur Daniel Steele; *My Life and Hard Times* by James Thurber, copyright, 1933, by James Thurber; *Forty Plus and Fancy Free* by Emily Kimbrough; *Pagan Spain* by Richard Wright; "The Changing Past" by Lynn White, Jr. in *Frontiers of Knowledge in the Study of Man; A Tramp Abroad* by Mark Twain; *Only Yesterday* by Frederick Lewis Allen; *Call to Greatness* by Adlai E. Stevenson.

Harper's Magazine: from selections in *Harper's Magazine:* "Families on Wheels" by Alvin L. Schorr, January 1958; "South Carolina's Incurable Aristocrats" by William Francis Guess, "Inside Russia's Treasure House" by Sterling A. Callisen, "Unnoticed Changes in America" by D. W. Brogan, "Philadelphia Does It: The Battle for Penn Center" by James Reichley, "The Gourmets Get Out of Hand" by Marilyn Mercer, "How Safe Are the New Cars?" by Paul W.

Kearney, and "Foreign Aid: Is It Still Necessary?" by Dan Lacy, February 1957; "The Polar Path: Where Every Direction Is South" by Wolfgang Langewiesche, November 1956; "The Mass Mind: Our Favorite Folly" by Joyce Cary, March 1952; and from articles by Duncan Aikman, April 1925, and Paul Pickrel, January 1958.

Harvard University Press: *Three Philosophical Poets* by George Santayana, published by Harvard University Press.

Holiday Magazine: selection from "The Incredible Battles of Bull Run" by Bruce Catton, *Holiday Magazine,* July 1956.

Henry Holt and Company, Inc.: selections from *Jungle Peace* by William Beebe, *Four Ways of Philosophy* by Irwin Edman, and *English Prose Style* by Herbert Read.

Houghton Mifflin Company: selections from *Books and Battles* by Irene and Allen Cleaton, and *The Pleasures of an Absentee Landlord* by Samuel McChord Crothers. World exclusive of the British Empire for selections from *Dance of Life* by Havelock Ellis.

Bruce Humphries, Inc.: selection from "Dawn" in *Al Que Quiere!* by William Carlos Williams, copyright 1917 by The Four Seas Company; used by permission of Bruce Humphries, Inc.

Alfred A. Knopf Incorporated: selections from *Life With Father* by Clarence Day, *Poems* by Rex Warner, and "Golden Bough" in *Collected Poems* by Elinor Wylie. World exclusive of the British Empire for selections from *Prejudices: Fifth Series* by H. L. Mencken. United States and Canada for "A Queer Heart" from *Look at All Those Roses* by Elizabeth Bowen.

Life Magazine: selection from *Life,* December 9, 1957, courtesy *Life* Magazine. Copyright 1957 Time, Inc.

Linguistic Atlas of the United States and Canada: earthworm chart from *Handbook of the Linguistic Geography of New England;* used by permission of Hans Kurath, Chairman, *Linguistic Atlas of the United States and Canada.*

Little, Brown & Company: selection from *Teacher in America* by Jacques Barzun. United States and Canada for selections from *No Place to Hide* by David Bradley, reprinted by permission of Little, Brown & Company and the author; and "The Cliché Expert Testifies on Politics" by Frank Sullivan in *A Rock in Every Snowball.* Selections from *A Time for Greatness* by Herbert Agar; permission granted by Little, Brown & Company; Eyre & Spottiswoode Limited; and Herbert Agar. United States and Canada for selection from *Hard Lines* by Ogden Nash. Copyright 1931 by Ogden Nash. Reprinted by permission of Little, Brown & Company and the author.

Longmans, Green & Co., Inc.: selections from *Writing and Speaking* by Charles Sears Baldwin, copyright 1911.

Louisiana State University Press: selection from "The Autobiography of an Uneducated Man" by Robert M. Hutchins in *Education for Freedom.*

The Macmillan Company: selections from *The Discussion of Human Affairs* by C. A. Beard, *The Return to Religion* by Henry C. Link, and *A Preface to Morals* and *The Phantom Public* by Walter Lippmann. *Small Town* by Granville Hicks, copyright 1946 by Granville Hicks and used with the permission of The Macmillan Company.

United States and Canada for selection from *The Everlasting Mercy* by John Masefield. Selection from "Universities and Their Function" in *The Aims of Education* by Alfred North Whitehead, copyright 1929. Reprinted by permission of The Macmillan Company.

Macrae Smith: selections from *It Happens Every Thursday* by Jane S. McIlyaine, reprinted by permission of Macrae Smith and the author.

McGraw-Hill Company, Inc.: selection from *Propaganda and the News* by Will Irwin. Copyright 1936. Courtesy of McGraw-Hill Book Company, New York. United States and Canada for *Bears in My Kitchen* by Margaret Merrill, and "Pleasant Agony" by John Mason Brown in *Still Seeing Things.*

Scott Meredith: World exclusive of the British Empire for selection from *Big Money* by P. G. Wodehouse, copyright, 1930, 1931. By permission of the author and his agent, Scott Meredith.

G. and C. Merriam Company: selections by permission from *Webster's New Collegiate Dictionary,* copyright, 1949, by G. and C. Merriam Company.

New York Herald Tribune: selections from an article in the *New York Herald Tribune,* January 12, 1958, used by permission of the *New York Herald Tribune* and the author, John Crosby.

The New Yorker: from selections in *The New Yorker:* "Uncle Russell's Weekends" by Joyce Warren, May 25, 1957; "The Bromley Touch" by Edward Newhouse, May 18, 1957; "The Easygoing Method" by E. J. Kahn, Jr., May 18, 1957; "Return to the Randolph" by Montgomery Newman, May 11, 1957; "The Surprise of the Century" by Janet Flanner, March 9, 1957; "A Pageant in Sack Suits" by Christopher Rand, January 19, 1957; "The Talk of the Town," February 19, 1949; "Millions for Mausoleums" by Lewis Mumford, February 30, 1939; and "The Cliché Expert Tells All" by Frank Sullivan, June 20, 1936. Selections from articles by Meyer Berger, November 26, 1938; and *The New Yorker* of January 17, 1948.

W. W. Norton & Company, Inc.: World exclusive of the British Empire for selection from *Mysticism and Logic* by Bertrand Russell. United States and the Philippines for selection from *The American People* by Geoffrey Gorer. Reprinted by permission of W. W. Norton & Company, Cresset Press Ltd., and Ann Watkins.

Ohio Wesleyan University: chart from *Newspaper Organization* by D. J. Hornberger and Douglass W. Miller; used by permission of Ohio Wesleyan University and D. J. Hornberger.

Oxford University Press, Inc. (New York): selection from *The Philosophy of Rhetoric*. United States and Canada for *Under the Sea Wind* by Rachel L. Carson; and *The Uses of the Past* by Herbert J. Muller.

The Pacific Spectator: selection from "The Beleaguered Wagon Train" by Arthur Ames in *The Pacific Spectator,* 1950, Volume IV.

Penguin Books Ltd.: selections from *The Pyramids of Egypt* by I. E. S. Edwards, reprinted by permission of Penguin Books Ltd.

The Phi Delta Kappan: selection from "Poor People Have Brains, Too" by Allison Davis in *The Phi Delta Kappan,* April 1949.

Robert C. Pooley: selection from *Grammar and Usage in Textbooks on English* by Robert C. Pooley.

Prentice-Hall, Inc.: selection reprinted with permission of Prentice-Hall,

Inc. from *The Open Self* by Charles Morris. © 1958 by Prentice-Hall, Inc., Englewood Cliffs, New Jersey. Published by Prentice-Hall, Inc. From *Conserving American Resources* by Ruben L. Parson.

G. P. Putnam's Sons: selection from *Jungle Days* by William Beebe.

Random House, Inc.: selections from *Home Is Where You Hang Your Childhood* by Leane Zugsmith. From *The Daring Young Man on the Flying Trapeze* by William Saroyan, copyright, 1934, 1941, by The Modern Library, Inc.; *Jurgen* by James Branch Cabell. United States and Canada for selections from *Lectures in America* by Gertrude Stein; from *The American College Dictionary,* edited by Clarence L. Barnhart. Reprinted by permission of Random House, Inc. From "Spotted Horses" from *The Hamlet,* by William Faulkner. Copyright 1931 by William Faulkner. Reprinted by permission of Random House, Inc.

The Reporter: selection from "Adman's Nightmare: Is the Prune a Witch?" by Robert Graham, *The Reporter,* October 13, 1953. Copyright © 1953 by The Reporter Magazine Company. Reprinted by permission of Harold Ober Associates Incorporated.

The Saturday Review: selections from "Steichen: Dissatisfied Genius" by Lenore Cisney and John Reddy, *The Saturday Review,* December 14, 1957. By permission of *The Saturday Review, The Reader's Digest,* and the authors. From SR Research Section: Science and Humanity by John Lear, Science Editor, July 6, 1957.

School and Society: selection from "Higher Education for the Days Ahead" by Ordway Tead, July 12, 1952.

School Arts Magazine: selection from "Time to Get Tough with Busywork Art" by John C. Bigham, November 1957.

Science: selection from "Amino Acids in Human Bone" by Harriett C. Ezra and S. F. Cook, July 12, 1957.

Science and Mechanics: Diagram "Construction of Skis" in *Science and Mechanics,* February 1939.

Scientific American: selection from "The Wonderful Net" by P. F. Scholander, April 1957.

Charles Scribner's Sons: selections from "Haircut" in *Roundup* by Ring Lardner, and *English Composition* by Barrett Wendell. From "An Escapade" in *A Native Agony* by Morley Callaghan; used by permission of Charles Scribner's Sons and Morley Callaghan. World exclusive of the British Empire for selections from *Green Hills of Africa* by Ernest Hemingway. United States and Canada for selections from *The Man of Property* by John Galsworthy, and from *Persons and Places* by George Santayana. Selection from *The Art of Letters* by Robert Lynd; permission granted by Charles Scribner's Sons and Gerald Duckworth and Co. Ltd. United States and Canada for selection from *The Yearling* by Marjorie Kinnan Rawlings.

Simon and Schuster, Inc.: selections from *Reading I've Liked* by Clifton Fadiman; and *Winter Orchard* by Josephine Johnson, copyright, 1935. World exclusive of the British Empire for selections reprinted from *With Malice Toward Some* by Margaret Halsey by permission of Simon and Schuster, Publishers. Copyright, 1938, by Margaret Halsey. From *Time: The Present* by Tess Slesinger, copyright 1935. United States and Canada for selections from *Now in November* by Josephine Johnson, copyright, 1934; used by permission of Simon and Schuster, Inc., Victor Gollancz, Ltd., and Curtis Brown Ltd.; *The Organization Man* by William H. Whyte, Jr., used by permission of Simon and Schuster and the author; *Arts of the South Seas* by Ralph Linton and Paul S. Wingert, used by permission of Simon and Schuster and the authors; *The Public Arts* by Gilbert Seldes, used by permission of Simon and Schuster and the author; *An Irwin Edman Reader* by Irwin Edman, edited by Charles Frankel, used by permission of Simon and Schuster and the author.

William Sloane Associates, Inc.: selections from *Listen for a Lonesome Drum* by Carl Carmer. Copyright 1936, 1950, by Carl Carmer. From *The Big Sky* by A. B. Guthrie. Copyright, 1947, by A. B. Guthrie, Jr.

Social Science Research Council: selection from *Local History–How to Gather It, Write It, and Publish It* by Donald D. Parker, published by Social Science Research Council.

The Society of Authors: World exclusive of the United States and Canada for selection from *The Everlasting Mercy* by John Masefield; used by permission of The Society of Authors and John Masefield. From *The Dance of Life* by Havelock Ellis; British Empire permission granted by The Society of Authors, literary representatives of the estate of Havelock Ellis.

Soil Science: selection from "Interpretive Soil Classification: Timber, Range, and Watershed" by Robert A. Gardner and John L. Retzer, 1949. Published by Williams and Wilkins Company.

Joseph Tiefebrun: selections from *People Are Fascinating* by Sally Benson. Copyright, Sally Benson, 1936.

The Times Literary Supplement: selection from "Evolutionary Principles," August 31, 1951, *The Times Literary Supplement, The Times,* London.

United Feature Syndicate: selection from "Candle Is Remarkable Invention" by Inez Robb. Printed in Seattle *Post-Intelligencer,* February 6, 1954.

University of California Press: selection from *Art and Visual Perception* by Rudolph Arnheim.

The University of Chicago Press: selection from *No Friendly Voice* by Robert Maynard Hutchins; and "Proofreader's Marks" from *A Manual of Style,* Eleventh Edition.

University of London Press Limited: selection from *Thought and Language* by P. B. Ballard.

University of Oklahoma Press: selection from *Cow Country* by Edward Everett Dale.

University of Washington Press: selection from *Garden Design* by John A. and Carol L. Grant.

U. S. News & World Report: selection from "Jobs Aren't Where They Used To Be," a copyrighted article in *U.S. News & World Report,* July 12, 1957.

Vanguard Press, Inc.: selection from *Representative Opinions of Mr. Justice Holmes,* edited by Alfred Lief.

D. Van Nostrand Company, Inc.: selection from *High Fidelity Music Systems* by William R. Wellman. Copyright 1955, D. Van Nostrand Company, Inc., Princeton, N. J.

The Viking Press Inc.: selections from *Finnegans Wake* by James Joyce, copyright 1939; *Sea of Cortez* by John Steinbeck and Edward F. Ricketts; *Philosopher's Holiday* by Irwin Edman; and *Sea and Sardinia* by D. H. Lawrence. From *The Literary Situation* by Malcolm Cowley, reprinted by permission of The Viking Press. From *The Walls Came Tumbling Down* by Henrietta Roosenburg. Copyright © 1956, 1957 by Henrietta Roosenburg. Originally published in *The New Yorker*. Reprinted by permission of The Viking Press, Inc., New York.

Warwick & York, Incorporated: selection from *How Much English Grammar?* by M. J. Stormzand and M. V. O'Shea.

Ives Washburn, Inc.: selection from *Once More the Thunderer* by Henry Beetle Hough.

Ann Watkins, Inc.: selection from *The American People* by Geoffrey Gorer; World permission exclusive of the United States and the Philippines granted by Ann Watkins, Inc., and Cresset Press, Ltd. From *The Tyranny of Words* by Stuart Chase; World permission exclusive of the United States and Canada granted by Ann Watkins, Inc., and Methuen & Co. Ltd.

A. P. Watt & Son: British Empire for selection from *Big Money* by P. G. Wodehouse, copyright, 1930, 1931.

John Wiley & Sons, Inc.: selections reprinted by permission from *Shore Processes and Shoreline Development* by Douglas W. Johnson, and from *Theories of Perception and the Concept of Structure* by Floyd H. Allport, published by John Wiley & Sons, Inc.

The H. W. Wilson Company: excerpt from *The Readers' Guide to Periodical Literature,* July 1958.

Woman's Day: selection from "Homily for a Troubled Time" by Bernard DeVoto, January 1951.

Yale University Press: selections from *The Heavenly City of the Eighteenth-Century Philosophers* by Carl Becker, *The Gentleman from New York: A Life of Roscoe Conkling* by Donald B. Chidsey, and *Sweden: The Middle Way* by Marquis Childs.

LIST OF WRITERS AND SOURCES QUOTED

List of writers and sources from whom the longer quotations in the *Writer's Guide and Index to English* were taken.

General Index

A

D

F

G

H

I

J

K

L

M

N

O

P

Q

R

S

T

U

V

W

Z

4 5 6 7 8 9 10 11 12 13 14 15 68 67 66 65 64 63 62 61

Abbreviations for marking themes

To the student: These theme revision abbreviations cover the common errors in composition. When one is marked on your paper, look up the page where the error is discussed and make the suggested revision. A ring around words or phrases indicates that there are *Index* articles for them which you should consult.

Ab Mistake in *abbreviation,* 404

Abst Use concrete word instead of *abstract,* 407

Adv Make the adjective marked an *adverb* by adding *ly,* 414

Agr Mistake in *agreement* between **1** subject and verb, 418; **2** pronoun and antecedent, 419; **3** demonstrative adjective and noun modified, 419

Amb Statement *ambiguous* because of **1** inexact reference of pronoun, 423; **2** loose modifier, 423; **3** incomplete idiom, 423

Apos Mistake in use of *apostrophe* in **1** genitives, 431; **2** contractions, 432; **3** plurals, 432; **4** representing speech, 432; **5** personal pronouns, 432; **6** simplified spellings, 432

Awk(K) Revise *awkward* passage, 436

Beg Revise *beginning* paragraph, 165, 286, 305

BigW Use simpler word instead of *big word* marked, 228

Cap Mistake in use of *capital* letter, 447

CF Revise *comma fault* to make an effective sentence, 469

Coh Revise sentence, sentences, or paragraphs so that they are *coherent,* 458

Coll Make verb and/or pronoun agree with *collective* noun, 459

Colon Use a *colon* here, 460

Comma (C) Insert or remove a *comma* at the place marked: **1** between coordinate clauses, 463; **2** with subordinate clauses, 463; **3** with nonrestrictive modifiers, 465; **4** with interrupting and parenthetical words and phrases, 466; **5** in lists and series, 466; **6** for emphasis and contrast, 467; **7** for clearness, 467; **8** with main sentence elements, 468; **9** in conventional uses, 468; **10** combined with other marks, 469

Comp Mistake in *comparison* of adjective or adverb: **1** faulty comparative, 472; **2** faulty superlative, 472; **3** wrong idiom with comparative, 473; **4** comparison of absolutes, 473

Concl Revise *concluding* paragraph, 168, 291

Concr Use *concrete* word instead of abstract, 476

Conj Use a *conjunction* that is **1** more accurate, 478; **2** more appropriate to the style of the passage, 478

D (*Diction*) Replace word marked with one that is more exact, more effective, or more appropriate, 497

Dead (*Deadwood*) Remove meaningless word or words, 491

Det Develop topic more fully by giving pertinent *details,* 493

Div Mistake in *division of words,* 500

DM Revise sentence so that the *dangling modifier* is clearly related to the word it is intended to modify, 487

Emph Strengthen *emphasis* of this passage by **1** position, 512; **2** mass or proportion, 512; **3** distinction of expression, 512; **4** separation, distinctness, 512; **5** repetition, 512

Fig *Figure of speech* is inappropriate, inconsistent, or threadbare, 528